The Spice & Herb Bible

THIRD EDITION

The Spice & Herb Bible

THIRD EDITION

Ian Hemphill

with recipes by
Kate Hemphill

Robert ROSE

The Spice & Herb Bible, Third Edition
Text copyright © 2000, 2002, 2006, 2014 Ian Hemphill
Photographs copyright © 2002, 2006, 2014 Robert Rose Inc. (unless otherwise stated, see details page 785)
Cover and text design copyright © 2014 Robert Rose Inc.

This is a revised and expanded edition of *The Spice and Herb Bible, Second Edition*, originally published by Robert Rose Inc. in 2006, and *Spice Notes*, originally published by Pan Macmillan Australia Pty Limited in 2002.

The recipe on page 240 is based on 'Stir-Fried Beef with Spices' from *Thai Food* by David Thompson, 2nd edition, Lantern (Penguin), 2010. Used with permission of the author and the publisher.

For complete cataloguing information, see page 785.

Disclaimer
The recipes in this book have been carefully tested by our kitchen and our tasters. To the best of our knowledge, they are safe and nutritious for ordinary use and users. For those people with food or other allergies, or who have special food requirements or health issues, please read the suggested contents of each recipe carefully and determine whether or not they may create a problem for you. All recipes are used at the risk of the consumer.

We cannot be responsible for any hazards, loss or damage that may occur as a result of any recipe use.

For those with special needs, allergies, requirements or health problems, in the event of any doubt, please contact your medical adviser prior to the use of any recipe.

Design and Production: Kevin Cockburn/PageWave Graphics Inc.
Senior Editor: Judith Finlayson
Editors: Tracy Bordian and Sue Sumeraj
Copy Editor: Gillian Watts
Proofreader: Gillian Watts
Indexer: Gillian Watts

Cover image: Assorted spices © istockphoto.com/Jasmina007

We acknowledge the financial support of the Government of Canada through the Book Publishing Industry Development Program (BPIDP) for our publishing activities.

Published by Robert Rose Inc.
120 Eglinton Avenue East, Suite 800, Toronto, Ontario, Canada M4P 1E2
Tel: (416) 322-6552 Fax: (416) 322-6936
www.robertrose.ca

Printed and bound in China

2 3 4 5 6 7 8 9 PPLS 22 21 20 19 18 17 16 15 14

Contents

PART THREE

The Art of Combining Spices

The Spice Blends

Preface

WHEN ONE GROWS up on a herb farm and then proceeds to spend the next 50 years working in the herb and spice industry, it is easy to assume that everyone feels comfortable using herbs and spices when cooking. Of course this is far from the reality, and over the years I have been asked many questions, from basic to bizarre. What people want most is an insight into the world of spices from someone who works with these miracles of nature every day. In this book I have set out to give you the "inside story," based on the learning and experiences I have assimilated in this ancient and stimulating industry.

It seems appropriate to begin in Part One by explaining some of the basics and sharing interesting facts that apply to all herbs and spices. Because spices play such an important role in the signature dishes of foods from different countries, I have provided some background information on how we use spices on a daily basis, as well as some basic information on the history of the spice trade. I have also included some technical information on the various uses and descriptions of spices and herbs, along with some fundamental information on growing, drying and storing spices and herbs.

Part Two looks at individual herbs and spices, in alphabetical order by common English name (to assist in looking up a reference quickly), as well as proper botanical name. I also include basic culinary information, including usage, as well as information on buying and storage. Where appropriate, "local color" is added with anecdotal information gleaned from personal experience and travels.

Part Three deals with the art of combining spices by making your own spice blends. Both Parts Two and Three include recipes utilizing individual spices or spice blends.

Once you have an understanding of the individual herb and spice characteristics, it is a logical next step to bring surprisingly diverse flavors together to create completely unimaginable and satisfying results. I hope you will find this interesting and stimulating and, most important, will feel that with the help of this book, the art of using spices successfully in everyday cooking has been demystified and made more enjoyable.

— *Ian Hemphill*

Acknowledgments

WHILE THIS BOOK is the culmination of a lifetime's experiences in the spice industry, there are certain individuals who have been particularly generous in sharing their knowledge over the years and who have provided me with specific information and support during the course of writing the original book and this new edition. Foremost, my deep appreciation must go to my wife, Elizabeth, who has always supported my obsession with spices and has been prepared to endure "holidays" in obscure hot, tropical and often far from comfortable destinations in the pursuit of another rare spice. Elizabeth's enthusiasm, common sense and natural editorial talents were invaluable while this book was being written. Our three daughters, Kate, Margaret and Sophie, have provided the love and moral support needed when completely preoccupied with writing a book such as this. To have had the opportunity to work with our eldest daughter, Kate, who developed, tested and refined all the recipes, has been a great pleasure that makes this father very proud. My parents, John and Rosemary, who imbued me with this passion and helped check and recheck the original manuscript, provided the encouragement and guidance that only parents can give.

The spice industry is akin to a brotherhood, and while my friends and associates in the spice trade are too numerous to mention, no one could write a book on spices without the generosity of Dr. P. S. S. Thampi, Director of Publicity at the Spices Board of India. Dr. Thampi has become a dear friend over the many years and shares our enthusiasm for this ancient and intoxicating trade. He has helped us find organic spice growers in Mangalore, view cardamom auctions in Kerala and visit spice research facilities in Gujarat. Special thanks also go to the late Neil Stewart, who gave our family invaluable advice when we first began marketing packaged herbs and spices in the 1960s. We are indebted to Craig Semple, an Australian spice trader residing in Turkey, who arranged for us to visit farms in the southeast of Turkey; Pepe Sanchez of El Clarin in Spain, who smuggled us into the saffron festival in Consuegra; Mark Barnett from Hanoi, who helped us find the cassia forests in North Vietnam; the Aboriginal women and Janet and Roy Chisholm of Napperby Station in the Northern Territory of Australia; Yuden Dorji and Kadola from the Ministry of Agriculture in Bhutan;

Stelios Damala and his daughter Maria from the Gum Mastic Producers Association in Chios; the Skracic family in Croatia, who took us to the wild sage growing on the island of Kornati; and numerous other farmers, spice traders and merchants who have shared their knowledge and treated us with warmth and hospitality. In Australia, Rolf Hulscher has always been a supporter of Herbie's Spices and our spice tours. Lawrence Lonergan and Hugh Talbot have always been prepared to share their knowledge and provide advice when we are faced with a difficult sourcing or technical issue.

Finally, the original *Spice and Herb Bible* would never have happened had it not been for the persistence and support of my agent, Philippa Sandall, the patience and attention to detail of editors Elspeth Menzies and Catherine Proctor, and the enthusiasm and commitment of publisher Jane Curry. This new edition, in which I am able to include even more useful information, contains details of 97 herbs and spices, 66 spice blends and more than 170 new easy-to-use, mouthwatering recipes, thanks to the recipe-developing skills and creativity of my wife, Elizabeth, and the professionalism of our classically trained daughter Kate. And all this has been made possible by the support of publisher Bob Dees of Robert Rose Inc. and the amazing quality of advice and attention to detail by editors Judith Finlayson, Sue Sumeraj and Tracy Bordian. Kevin Cockburn of PageWave Graphics has performed an amazing feat in bringing 800 pages of information together in such an accessible and appealing design.

Part One

The World of Spices

The Spices in Our Lives

CAN YOU IMAGINE a world without herbs and spices? What if there were no such thing as vanilla ice cream, cinnamon buns or the aromatic flavor of juniper in gin? Imagine life without basil pesto, Worcestershire sauce, mustard, pickles, chili sauce, seeded breads or tacos topped with zesty salsa. Most of us eat spices every day. Contrary to popular belief, spicy food is not necessarily hot. Perhaps we should refer to it as "*spiced* food" from now on! And let's not forget that panoply of medicinal herbs and spices that nurtured and sustained our health for thousands of years. In fact, many contemporary pharmaceuticals were developed from the active constituents in herbs and spices.

The expression "to spice food" is used loosely to describe the act of adding almost any type of flavor-enhancing substance in small proportions to impart a particular taste to an overall dish. The word *spice* carries connotations of power and efficacy, which is understandable when you consider how small a quantity is often required to create a potent effect on a substantial amount of food. Just to give two examples, a tiny amount of vanilla flavors a whole tub of ice cream, and a small quantity of chile and cumin can transform pounds of beans and ground beef into delicious chili con carne.

For thousands of years human beings have been adding spice to food to make it more appetizing, to aid with preservation and, in extreme cases, to mask its identity because it tasted quite awful on its own. More than 2,000 years ago, when the use of spices began to be documented, most were a luxury only the wealthy could afford. As new spices were discovered, their origins remained surrounded in mystery because spice traders were keen to maintain exclusive access to these products. The spice trade was extremely lucrative: single voyages were likely to yield profits of ten times the initial investment.

A Short History of the Spice Trade

THE FOLLOWING HISTORY of the spice trade is brief. Its aim is to provide some insight into how much this ancient and traditional trade has affected the development of the human race, and what an important part spice played—and still does—in our lives.

Folklore from many cultures supports the notion that herbs and spices have been a part of human evolution for more than 5,000 years. However, the first authentic, if fragmented, records of the use of herbs and spices date from the age of the pyramids in Egypt, around 2600 to 2100 BCE. Onions and garlic were fed to the 100,000 laborers who reputedly toiled on construction of the Great Pyramid of Cheops. Since then, garlic and onions have been used not only for sustenance but also for their medicinal properties and to preserve health.

▶ 2000 BCE

Around 2000 BCE, cinnamon and cassia became essential ingredients in the Egyptian embalming process and were imported from China and Southeast Asia. In ancient civilizations, unpleasant odors were associated with evil, and sweet, clean scents were linked with purity and goodness. Thus a demand was created for pleasant-smelling fragrances.

At this time no clear distinction was made among plants used for flavoring food, those used as medicines and those used as sacrificial plants in religious rituals. When certain leaves, seeds, roots and gums were identified as having pleasant tastes and agreeable odors, interest in them gradually developed. This culminated in a demand for their use as condiments. Medicinal herbs and spices may have tasted quite unpleasant, but their efficacy was subsequently appreciated and embraced by health practitioners. Religious overtones were applied to spices that "smelled of Paradise," and the burning of resins from plants as incense was believed to transport—via the smoke—one's devotions up to the gods.

▶ 1700 BCE

An archaeological dig in Syria (ancient Mesopotamia) discovered the remains of cloves in a domestic kitchen dating from about 1700 BCE. At that time cloves were grown only on a handful of islands in the Indonesian archipelago. One can only begin to imagine the extraordinary journey those cloves must have travelled to reach this destination, halfway around the world!

One of the First Oils

At a very early date, the Assyrians used sesame as a vegetable oil.

▶ 1500 BCE

In 1874 a German Egyptologist, Georg Ebers, discovered a document dated about 1550 BCE, which is now known as the Ebers Papyrus. This document contained extensive information about surgery and internal medicine, as well as a list of some 800 medicinal drugs, all based on natural plant materials. The Egyptians employed these aromatic herbs and spices in medicine, cosmetic ointments, perfumes, fumigation and embalming, as well as cooking.

▶ 1000 BCE

Excavations in the Indus Valley, in what is now Pakistan and northwestern India, reveal that herbs and spices were used there before 1000 BCE.

During the second and first millennia BCE, Arabia's monopoly on transporting goods from the East to the West created great prosperity. The Arabian traders who supplied spices to what are now parts of Europe protected their business interests by deliberately shrouding the sources of their products in mystery. Many unlikely tales still prevail about the origins of some spices. For many centuries these merchants maintained a strict monopoly on spices from Asia by pretending that cassia and cinnamon came from Africa and deliberately discouraging Mediterranean importers from establishing connections to the appropriate sources. It was not until the first century CE that the Roman scholar Pliny the Elder pointed out that many tall stories had been fabricated by these traders to inflate the prices of their exotic wares.

▶ 600 BCE

A scroll of cuneiform writing from the great library in Nineveh, established by King Ashurbanipal of Assyria (668 to 633 BCE), records a long list of aromatic plants, among them thyme, sesame, cardamom, turmeric, saffron, poppy, garlic, cumin, anise, coriander and dill.

▶ 300 BCE

The use of spices increased in Greece and Rome from 331 BCE to 641 CE. Alexander the Great extended Greek influence throughout lands that had previously been part of the Persian Empire, including Egypt. Starting in 331 BCE, his conquests established Greek settlements and commercial posts between the Mediterranean and India. These colonies were situated along the western section of the trade route that would become known as the Silk Road. After his conquest of Egypt, Alexander founded the port of Alexandria, which became the gateway to the East and the most important trading center between the Mediterranean and the Indian Ocean.

▶ 100 CE

Recognition of the role that the monsoons played in propelling sailing ships forward, or hampering their progress when blowing in the opposite direction, paved the way for establishment of a direct sea route from ports in Roman Egypt to the pepper markets on the Malabar Coast of India.

▶ 641 CE

The fall of the Roman Empire in 641 brought major changes that affected the spice trade. The well-organized trading in commodities between India and Rome was brought to an end by the spread of Islam. Traditional trade routes were interrupted as the Arab conquest shattered Mediterranean unity and brought confusion and stagnation to commerce.

▶ 800 CE

By the middle of the eighth century, the great empire founded by Mohammed extended from Spain in the west to the borders of China in the east. Muslim influence also extended to Ceylon and Java, mostly through the activities of roving Arab traders. Having won religious victories in India by force, Muslim missionaries settled on the Malabar Coast and became spice traders.

Charlemagne (742 to 814 CE), King of the Franks and Emperor of the West, was an important figure in the development of herb production in Europe. A patron of literature, art and science, he was the first to organize large, orderly plantings of herbs in his realm. In 812 Charlemagne ordered a number of useful plants—among them anise, fennel and fenugreek—to be grown on the imperial farms in Germany.

▶ 900 CE

The period between 641 (the fall of Alexandria) and 1096 (the First Crusade) is known as the Dark Ages. Information concerning spices in Europe during this period is rather scarce. North of the Italian Alps, the use of Asian spices was rare in a normal diet. Only small amounts could be obtained, and their use was limited to religious groups

More Than a Prophet

Mohammed (570 to 632 CE), who established the principles of Islam in the Koran, was not only a great prophet, legislator and founder of one of the world's major religions, he was also an experienced spice merchant who married the daughter of his employer.

A Very Dark Time

In Europe throughout the Dark Ages, cultivation of herbs and spices was primarily the role of the Church, and most were grown in Benedictine monastery gardens. During this period, society was bombarded with dubious herbal remedies peddled by the early medieval equivalent of snake-oil salesmen. The concoctions prepared by these self-styled apothecaries mixed fantasy with tidbits of common sense, the results ranging from harmless though sometimes effective folk remedies to dangerous abortives, nauseating love potions and absolute poisons.

and a few well-connected merchants. In England at the end of the 10th century, the Statutes of Ethelred required Easterlings (Germans from the Baltic and Hanseatic towns) to pay a tribute for the privilege of trading with London merchants. It included 10 pounds (5 kg) of pepper.

▶ 1096

The First Crusade took place in 1096. Before then reports from occasional travelers constituted information about the Near East. Now thousands of pilgrims were exposed to the lifestyles of Syria and Palestine. One result was a new taste for delights such as spiced food.

▶ 1180

In 1180, during the reign of Henry II, a guild of wholesale pepper merchants was established in London. In 1429 it became the Grocers' Company. It was granted a charter by Henry VI to sell wholesale—*vendre en gros*, from which the word *grocer* derives.

▶ 1200

In the 13th century in England, 2 pounds (1 kg) of pepper cost one pound sterling, which is more than US$1,000 in today's money. Peppercorns, counted out one by one, were used as currency. In relative terms, in those days spices were much more expensive than they are today. It's easy to understand how essential they must have been to make the available fare—such as very bland foods or strongly flavored, gamey meats—more palatable.

By the end of the 13th century Marco Polo had returned from his voyages. He recounted astonishing tales of the fabulous wealth of China and the fertility of what is now known as Tamil Nadu, in South India. He reported, with remarkable accuracy, stories of vast plantations in Java and other islands in the South China Sea that grew pepper, nutmegs, cloves and other valuable spices.

▶ 1453

Following the fall of Constantinople to the Turks in 1453, the need for a safe sea route to Asia became more urgent. Because the spread of the Ottoman Empire had made the old land routes unsafe, Prince Henry of Portugal equipped expeditions to find a sea route to India. In 1486 Bartolomeu Dias rounded the Cape of Good Hope, confirming that the Indian Ocean could be reached by sea. Christopher

Columbus acquired much of his seafaring knowledge in the service of the Portuguese, although he "discovered" the New World on behalf of Spain. Columbus identified vanilla beans and allspice as well as chile peppers, which are members of the capsicum family rather than the *Piper nigrum* variety for which he was searching.

▶ 1498

Vasco da Gama arrived at Calicut, on the west coast of India, in 1498, completing the first sea voyage from western Europe around Africa to the East. This was the most significant feat in the history of the spice trade, as it opened up faster and safer routes between the most important spice trading ports.

▶ 1520

Ferdinand Magellan sailed through the Straits of Patagonia in 1520. A year later, after a difficult voyage during which many of his crew died, he reached the Philippines. Magellan himself was killed, but the survivors returned home with 29 tons of cloves and many sacks filled with nutmegs and cinnamon. Despite the enormous losses of life, the expedition was a financial success.

▶ 1600

The British founded their East India Company in 1600, and two years later the United Dutch East India Company, known as the VOC (Vereenigde Oost-Indische Compagnie), was formed. This highly successful business venture marked the establishment of a Dutch empire in Asia.

▶ 1629

The Dutch retour ship *Batavia* was built in Amsterdam in 1628 specifically to carry spices to the Netherlands from the Indonesian Spice Islands. Its features included special holds that allowed ventilation, to ensure the precious cargo wouldn't spoil on the long journey through the tropics. Sadly, there was significant unrest among the crew, a portion of whom mutinied, and in June 1629 the ship was wrecked off the west coast of Western Australia. A horrible scene unfolded among the survivors and mutineers, and many people were slaughtered. *Batavia* never carried the bounty of spices it was built to transport, but partly because of the gruesome outcome, the story has lived on. It is an early part of the continent's history that took place more than a century before Australia was officially "discovered" by the English.

A Great Explorer's Resting Place

In 1524 Vasco da Gama died in Cochin, which is on India's Malabar Coast. He was initially interred in the city's St. Francis Church, where the burial site can still be observed. However, his body was repatriated to Portugal in 1539, where his remains are entombed at Vidigueira in a jewel-encrusted casket.

A Dutch Monopoly

Between 1605 and 1621 the Dutch managed to drive the Portuguese out of the Spice Islands, which gave the Netherlands a monopoly over the clove and nutmeg trade.

▶ 1770

Pierre Poivre (the original Peter Piper) was the French administrator of the island of Mauritius, off the east coast of Africa, then known as Île-de-France. At the risk of being executed, he smuggled clove, nutmeg and cassia plants out of the Dutch-controlled Spice Islands. After several attempts he showed that these plants could be grown outside of their country of origin. His success provided a model for other tropical countries, which followed suit. This broke the Dutch monopoly on the clove and nutmeg trade once and for all.

▶ 1800

Toward the end of the 18th century, the United States plunged into the world spice trade. For most of the early 19th century, thanks to its aggressive shippers, swift vessels and experienced mariners, the New England port of Salem enjoyed a virtual monopoly on the Sumatra pepper trade. During that period the Salem pepper trade flourished, except for three years during the War of 1812, when the British blockaded American ports. Its demise followed the outbreak of the Civil War in 1861.

▶ 1900 to the Present Day

Although herbs and spices are still produced in many traditional areas, during the 20th century their cultivation became far more decentralized. Today virtually no country holds a monopoly on any one major commodity. India, Indonesia, Vietnam and Malaysia are all major pepper producers. Substantial spice and herb plantations have been established in China and the Americas. As well, modern technology has created new and more convenient ways to process, store and use spices. We should not forget, though, that the vast majority of spices traded around the world are still grown by the methods that have prevailed for countless generations. I have tried to capture some of these timeless practices in the sections titled "Spice Notes" and "Travels in the Spice Trade," which are scattered throughout the listings in this book.

Herbs and spices have played an important role in the discovery and evolution of the commercial world as we know it. Although the quest for spices no longer drives exploration and commerce, these natural commodities are still precious and will continue to give culinary pleasure, as well as medicinal benefits, to the human race for many centuries to come.

You Can Never Have Enough

Although Indonesia is one of the world's largest producers of cloves, it is also a net importer of this spice, because such enormous quantities are used in the manufacture of their unique *kretek* cigarettes.

What Is the Difference Between a Spice and a Herb?

One of the questions I am most often asked is "What is the difference between a herb and a spice?" Generally we refer to the leaf of a plant used in cooking as a culinary herb; any other part of the plant, often dried, is called a spice. Spices can be buds (cloves), bark (cinnamon), roots (ginger), berries (peppercorns), aromatic seeds (cumin) or even the stigma of a flower (saffron). Many of the aromatic seeds we call spices are actually gathered from what we call herb plants after they have finished flowering. A familiar example would be coriander: we refer to the leaves as a herb (cilantro) but the dried seeds are always called a spice.

So where does that leave the stems and roots of coriander, which are also used in cooking, as well as garlic and that delicious bulb of fennel? These sections of vegetable material tend to be classified as herbs because they are often used fresh and cooked in a similar way to herbs.

An important characteristic of most spices is that many are used in their dried form. In fact, many spices gain their key flavor attributes only after drying. During drying their naturally occurring enzymes are activated, which creates their unique flavors. Spices in which this process is particularly evident include cloves, pepper and allspice.

A Spoonful of Coriander

It is worth noting that an extract of the seed spice coriander was often added to herbal medicines to reduce their bitter notes.

Because the majority of spices come from equatorial regions of the world (seed spices from temperate regions are available only after flowering), we are fortunate that most do not need to be used in their fresh form. Spices can be harvested at exactly the right time, dried to achieve optimum flavor and then shipped to all corners of the world. This has had a powerful influence on the ability to ship, trade and store spices—prerequisites for the enduring success of any commodity.

Culinary and Medicinal Herbs and Spices

Culinary herbs and spices are those that are used primarily to flavor food. They may be included during cooking or added as a condiment after the food is cooked. Many culinary herbs and spices are also used medicinally; garlic, thyme, cloves, cinnamon and turmeric are just a few examples of herbs and spices with crossover applications.

Medicinal herbs and spices are used exclusively for their medicinal properties and often have strong, disagreeable flavors. I haven't included the medicinal uses of culinary herbs and spices in this book because I'm not a medical expert, so I don't feel comfortable treading in that territory. That said, it is widely acknowledged that the high levels of antioxidants and phytochemicals that naturally occur in herbs and spices can contribute to one's overall well-being, and the medicinal value of these foods is being actively explored by scientists. By weight, few foods are as high in these health-giving properties.

Essential Oils, Oleoresins, Essences and Extracts

People often ask for definitions of the terms *essential oil*, *oleoresin*, *essence* and *extract*, which are often used with respect to herbs and spices. The following explanations are by no means exhaustive, but they will help you to understand these terms when you come across them.

Essential oils are the fragrant products obtained from natural raw materials such as leaves, stems, roots or seeds, by steam distillation or by a mechanical crushing and pressing process. These potent distillations are the basic raw materials used by perfumers and flavorists for centuries. (Sadly, most perfumes and many flavors are now the products of a clever alchemy of chemicals.)

Spice Oils

Some companies have produced diluted spice oils intended for convenient domestic use. However, in my opinion, nothing beats the real thing in most recipes. It seems as though these products are already being relegated to the gimmick category, having fallen out of favor with serious cooks.

These days we most commonly hear about essential oils in reference to aromatherapy. A large proportion of aromatherapy oils are obtained from herbs and spices. However, cooks should be warned against the temptation to use aromatherapy oils in culinary applications—these oils have not been manufactured for human consumption. Some may contain toxins or be in concentrations so strong that they could be harmful if ingested. My father used to buy a very expensive rose geranium essential oil to blend with orris root powder and ground cinnamon to add to potpourri, a fragrant blend of herbs and flowers enjoyed for its perfume, but it was certainly never eaten.

Oleoresins are produced by an extraction process that uses a particular volatile solvent. After extraction, the solvent is removed by evaporation in a vacuum at low temperature. A more recent development has been the production of oleoresins by carbon dioxide extraction; this process creates an end product entirely free of solvent residues. Oleoresins contain all the flavoring that was in the original herb or spice and deliver a broader spectrum of the flavor profile than an essential oil, which contains only the volatile notes. For this reason oleoresins are popular with food manufacturers: the spice flavoring can be added without any concerns about flavor strength, which may vary from crop to crop. Oleoresins are not available for domestic use, as their correct dilution and use with food is not practical in the home kitchen.

Essence is the term used to describe the essential flavor of something; it may be natural or artificial. Thus vanilla essence may be either a natural vanilla-bean extract or something completely different that does not contain any true vanilla at all. Nonetheless, because it tastes something like vanilla (this is a point that could be debated at length), it represents the essence of the flavor of vanilla.

An **extract**, however, is by definition natural because the only way to make an extract of something is to begin with the real thing. For instance, vanilla extract is made by soaking vanilla beans in alcohol; the alcohol extracts the flavor of vanilla, which is then held in suspension. This extract, which contains only vanilla, alcohol and water, is also known as an essence, because it too represents the essence of the flavor of vanilla. Totally confused? I hope not. Most food laws stipulate that artificial essences be labeled as such, so always check the label (a good habit in any case) to see if the word *artificial* appears.

Growing Your Own Herbs

IN THIS BOOK I have endeavored to include nearly every culinary spice and herb you are likely to come across. Some may be difficult to source, but I hope you'll find that part of the enjoyment of spice discovery lies in hunting them down.

Although spice production can be quite complex and depends on very specific climatic and soil conditions, you may want to grow some herbs that are difficult to locate in their fresh form. Growing your own can be very satisfying.

Herbs grow as well in tubs and pots as they do in the garden; they can occupy as much or as little space as you like. A basic understanding of their requirements is all you need to grow them successfully. Because the main objective when growing herbs is to have them fresh for everyday use in the kitchen, it is advisable to grow them in a convenient spot. The ultimate "kitchen garden," wherever it is located, is one that is accessible and enjoyed.

Herbs are generally robust and have simple needs. After all, they have been around for millennia and have demonstrated their ability to survive and prosper with or without our intervention. However, there are a few basic guidelines you'll need to follow. Herbs, like us, need sunshine and fresh air. I have rarely seen herbs grow well indoors; they need to be outside where they will get plenty of fresh air.

A number of herbs live for only one season and then die as part of their natural life cycle. This is the distinction between annuals and perennials. *Annuals*, such as basil, coriander, fennel and dill, live for one season; a few that prosper for two years, such as alexanders, caraway, celery and chervil, are called *biennials*. Herbs that do not die off after a season or two, such as thyme, rosemary, oregano and bay trees, are called *perennials*; the majority of perennials are reasonably robust shrubs.

Some annuals, such as coriander and basil, grow very quickly in warm climates, blossom early, flower prolifically, go to seed and then die. This seemingly inevitable fate can be arrested, although not postponed indefinitely. I suggest picking off the flower buds as soon as they appear, literally nipping them in the bud. This will prevent the herbs from flowering and then going to seed and finishing their life cycle too early.

Perennials are much less work but they also need some care. Herbs such as thyme, sage, oregano and rosemary may become straggly and woody if they are not regularly harvested or pruned. At the end of summer, up to half its foliage can be pruned from a perennial herb—this is the time to shape the plant. Rather than throwing away the prunings, dry them for use through the winter, when new growth will be slower to emerge or will cease altogether.

When it comes to soil and growing conditions, herbs are relatively undemanding. This is an endearing quality when you consider how much they give back to us in flavor, aroma and efficacy. Nearly all herbs like friable, well-drained soil that has been conditioned with good compost. It is not necessary to give herbs lots of fertilizers and expensive nutrients—they won't appreciate them. Many herbs grown in relatively poor soil have a stronger flavor than their lush overfed and overwatered counterparts.

Growing Herbs in Pots

Herbs will grow equally well in pots, tubs or hanging baskets. There are just a few details you need to know for success.

It is important to make sure the container is big enough for the plant's root system. A basic rule of thumb for shrubs is that the depth of the pot should equal the height of the plant. So if you are planting common garden thyme, which grows to about 8 inches (20 cm) tall, make sure the container is at least that deep. For shrubs such as bay trees, the depth of the pot can be approximately one-third the height of the mature tree.

Always use a good-quality potting mix; commercial potting mixes have been blended to deliver the optimum balance between water retention and suitable drainage. Put some flat rocks or pieces of broken pottery in the bottom of the pot to ensure that it drains effectively and that the soil is not washed out through the holes in the base. Where you place the pot depends on what is recommended for the particular herb. Although nearly all herbs should be outdoors, their preferences range from semi-shade and well sheltered to full sun and exposure to the elements.

Most important, don't forget to water your pots. If you neglect it, a herb growing in the garden can send out roots looking for moisture and it may survive your inattentiveness. However, a herb growing in a pot is entirely dependent upon you to keep it watered. If the pot dries out completely, the roots have nowhere to go for moisture and the plant will die. So think of your potted herb as being like a canary in a cage: it must be cared for daily!

Purchasing Plants

You can buy herbs—and a limited range of spice plants such as coriander, dill and fennel (for their seeds) and ginger, turmeric and galangal (for their rhizomes)—from a variety of retailers. Nurseries and garden centers tend to stock the most complete range of herbs, but supermarkets and grocery stores often sell them as well. Ask the salesperson if they have been "hardened off." Some mass producers put plants on sale that have come straight from a greenhouse; they may suffer from shock when exposed to natural conditions, which could cause them to die off.

Propagating Your Own Plants

There are four main types of propagation suitable for herbs and spices: root division, cuttings, layering and sowing seeds.

Root Division

Root division is most suitable for herbs such as mint, which will spread and grow into sizeable clumps. One way to keep them healthy and to propagate more plants is to divide them. This is easily achieved by digging up the clump. Carefully separate an 8-inch (20 cm) root system into five smaller clumps of $1^1/_2$ to 2 inches (4 to 5 cm) each and replant.

Cuttings

Growing from cuttings is an ancient form of propagation. This involves taking a piece of the plant and cultivating it to produce roots. The cuttings method is most appropriate for woody herbs such as rosemary and thyme and trees such as bay, cinnamon, allspice, clove and nutmeg.

To take a cutting, use a sharp knife or pruning shears. Take tip (end-of-branch) cuttings of reasonably firm growth about 4 inches (10 cm) long, cutting the stem just below a leaf node. Remove the leaves from the lower $1^1/_2$ inches (4 cm) of the cut stem (this portion will be buried in the sand), leaving at least a third of the foliage on the top. When preparing cuttings, always pull off leaves upward or use pruning shears, to avoid tearing the bark.

After taking cuttings (the technical term is *striking*) from a parent plant, keep the cuttings in water or wrapped in a damp cloth until you're ready to plant them in sand. Be sure they do not wilt. Use coarse river sand, available from nurseries, firmly packed into a pot; never use beach sand, as it is too fine and may contain salt residues. Never push cuttings into the sand, as this will damage the end and hinder the chances of making a successful strike. First, make a hole in the sand with a skewer or pencil that is slightly thicker than the cutting. Moisten the end of the cutting and dip the bottom $1/_2$ inch (1 cm) into a suitable rooting powder (available from nurseries). Shake off excess powder and insert the lower third of the cutting into the hole in the sand. Try to cover at least two leaf nodes (the parts where you pulled off the leaves) and press the sand firmly around the cutting. Flood with water and be sure to keep the cutting moist at all times.

Planting Cuttings

You may plant several cuttings in a single pot as long as they are about 1 inch (2.5 cm) apart. Place the pot in a semi-shady spot so the sun's rays won't dry out the sand too quickly or burn the cuttings. After several weeks, depending on the weather, the cuttings will have formed roots. At that point they can be separated and placed in potting mix in their own pots to become established before they are replanted into larger pots or the garden.

Layering

Propagation by layering works on the same principle as taking cuttings, except that you don't cut the stem off the host plant until it has formed roots. Layering works best for plants that send out horizontal stems or ones that can be easily bent down to ground level, such as French lavender (*Lavandula dentata*).

Select a length of stem and bend it toward the ground. Carefully trim the leaves from the last 2 inches (5 cm) of the stem (starting from the part touching the ground) in exactly the same way as you would for a cutting. Moisten a couple of leaf nodes, dust them with rooting powder and bury them up to 1 inch (2.5 cm) below the surface. It is a good idea to push a little hoop of wire over the stem and into the ground to stop the stem from springing back up. Keep the area well watered. After several weeks you can pull up the layered stem, which will have developed roots, and cut it from the parent plant. It can then be grown from its own newly developed root system as a separate plant.

Sowing Seeds

Herbs can also be grown from seed. They should be planted in a fifty-fifty mix of river sand and soil in a pot about 8 inches (20 cm) in diameter or a shallow trough. Tamp down the sand-and-soil mix with a small piece of wood and make furrows in the surface about $1/4$ inch (5 mm) deep. Sprinkle the seeds into the furrow; ideally there should be a slight space between each seed. Cover the seeds with more sand-and-soil mix, making sure there are no lumps. Tamp down the surface again and give the whole surface a good soaking—but do it gently so the seeds are not disturbed or washed away.

Keep the seedbed moist at all times; if it dries out for even a short period, germination may cease. Place the container on a level surface (this helps prevent accidental overwatering or a heavy rain from washing all the seeds to one end). When the seedlings are about 2 inches (5 cm) tall, carefully remove them from the seedbed and repot in individual pots so they can grow larger. When they have reached the appropriate size, plant them in large pots or out in the garden.

Drying Your Own Herbs

WHEN YOU GROW your own herbs, it is practical and satisfying to dry them yourself. Some herbs most appropriate for home-drying are thyme, sage, marjoram, oregano, rosemary and the seeds of coriander and fennel. The following relates primarily to herbs, as most home gardeners don't grow spices. Drying details for some spices (for example, chile, pepper and vanilla) are contained in the spice listings.

Air Drying in Bunches

The traditional method of drying, still used in many countries, is to tie the stems into bunches about the size of a small broom. Hang the bunches in a dark, warm, dry and well-aired place for up to a week. The time herbs need to dry is determined by the relative humidity. In climates where the humidity is low, drying may take only a few days. Greece, Turkey and Egypt are large producers of dried herbs, and their climate allows growers to dry herbs without expensive, energy-consuming dehydrators.

When the leaves feel perfectly crisp and dry, strip them off the stems and store them in an airtight container. If the leaves feel at all soft or leathery, they are not dry enough and will develop mold when stored.

Air Drying on Frames

For enthusiasts, it is not difficult to make square drying frames out of wood. A convenient-sized frame is about $1^1/_2$ feet (45 cm) square and 4 inches (10 cm) deep. Stretch insect screening across the base and secure with cable ties or nails. The herbs will dry more quickly if the leaves are removed and the stems discarded. That way you are not trying to remove moisture from the thicker stems at the same time as the thinner leaves. Spread out the leaves loosely on the frames to an approximate depth of 1 inch (2.5 cm). Place the frames in a dark, well-aired place where air can circulate freely.

A particular challenge for commercial growers is that because every herb has its own structural characteristics, each variety will dry a little differently. Leaf size, density, moisture content and a host of other physical attributes will cause individual herbs to yield up their water content in different ways. This means that when drying your own, you always need to feel for the telltale crunchy texture of a properly dried herb.

Fresh Is Best

Herbs will always dry best when you pick your own. Fresh herbs bought from the store may have been kept in cold storage or transported for long distances after harvesting. Herbs that are not freshly picked will often develop spots of discoloration on the leaves, caused by oxidization or partial fermenting; as a result, when dried they produce an inferior product, with poor color and flavor. Gather your herbs in the morning, just after the dew has dried and before the heat of the day has reduced their pungency.

Drying in an Oven or Microwave

Herbs may also be dried in conventional and microwave ovens. To dry herbs in a conventional oven, preheat it to about 250°F (120°C). Remove the leaves from their stems and arrange in a single layer on a parchment-lined baking sheet. Slide the sheet into the oven, turn off the heat and leave the door open a crack. After half an hour, remove the herbs, preheat the oven again and repeat the process. Repeat until the leaves are crisp and dry. (This may take three to five sessions.)

To dry herbs in a microwave, remove the leaves from their stems and arrange in a single layer on a paper towel. Place a cup half-filled with water alongside and microwave on High for 20 seconds. Remove any dry, crisp leaves. Continue microwaving in 10-second bursts, removing the dried leaves each time, until all the leaves are dry. You won't damage your microwave because even when all but a few leaves have been taken out, the water in the cup will still absorb the microwaves.

An Easy Alternative

An easy alternative to making a frame is to use the method on page 29 with the leaves spread out in a single layer on paper. Turn the leaves every day or two, as on paper you don't get the air circulation a screen provides.

Buying and Storing Spices and Herbs

Storing Fresh Herbs

Most fresh soft-leaf herbs—such as basil, chervil, cilantro, dill, parsley and tarragon—may be kept for up to a week in a glass of water in the refrigerator. After washing the herbs in clean, cold water, immerse the bottom inch (2.5 cm) of the stems in water and cover the foliage with a clean plastic bag. Fresh herbs with harder stems and more robust foliage—such as thyme, sage, marjoram and rosemary—may be kept for up to a week in a glass of water at room temperature, exposed to the air. In either case, change the water every couple of days.

When a longer storage period is desired, many herbs may be frozen. Hard-stemmed herbs freeze well when the sprigs are wrapped in foil, then placed in a resealable bag. A convenient method for freezing softer herbs uses ice-cube trays. Chop the herb finely (with a herb such as cilantro the entire plant can be used, so chop the leaves, stems and roots). Fill each section of the tray two-thirds full with the chopped herb, add water just to cover, and freeze. When frozen, turn out the cubes into a resealable bag (to prevent them from picking up unwanted aromas from other foods) and store in the freezer.

What to Look for When Buying

When buying dried herbs and spices, never purchase them in cardboard or low-barrier plastic packages, even though they're often cheaper than the alternatives. Poor packaging allows the volatile oils to escape and oxygen to enter, which means the product is already deteriorating by the time you take it home.

Spices scooped from bulk bins look fantastic and have emotional appeal. However, they may have been exposed to insects, bacteria and a considerable amount of air. They may also have been cross-contaminated by other produce. Jars with secure lids are preferable but still not ideal, unless the seal is properly airtight. As a jar empties, the surface area of the spice or herb is exposed to air and the effectiveness of the container diminishes. The latest packaging technology—multi-laminate high-barrier resealable packages—is quite effective. You can squeeze the air out of these packages before resealing, so the contents will last longer.

Don't Use Directly from the Package

Avoid shaking or pouring packages of herbs over a steaming saucepan. The steam will condense around the inside of the opening of the package, and the moisture will make the spice go hard or oxidize more rapidly—or worse still, mold may form.

Testing Dried Herbs for Freshness

To test dried herbs for freshness, put a few leaves in the palm of your hand and rub them back and forth with your thumb. As they turn to powder, smell the aroma that is generated by the rubbing action and the warmth of your hand. If the aroma is noticeable and pleasant, the herbs should be okay to use. If the smell is either musty or straw-like, like old grass clippings, you might as well throw the herb away.

Storing Dried Herbs and Spices

If you like to keep dried herbs and spices on display in a spice rack, place the rack out of direct sunlight and use it only for whole spices or those you use frequently. Any dried herb with a delicate cell structure, such as chives or parsley, and any that is used infrequently are better kept in the pantry, away from light, heat and humidity.

Storing dried herbs or spices in the refrigerator or freezer is not generally recommended. When the package is taken out of the cold environment, condensation forms, which introduces unwanted moisture. However, if you live in a very hot climate or have a spice that will not be used again for many months, freezer storage may be best. Before opening the package, let it warm to room temperature and make sure that all signs of condensation have disappeared.

Shelf Life and Storage

Herbs and spices—even those that have been dried—get their aroma and flavor from the volatile oils and oleoresins held in their cell structure. All herbs and spices will deteriorate over time; as the oils gradually evaporate, the flavor and aroma dissipate. Therefore, when stocking your pantry with dried herbs and spices, try not to buy quantities that are too large. Finish up a herb or spice by the use-by or best-before date. When you spring-clean, don't hesitate to throw away any herbs and spices that are past their use-by date. It's not worth adding something with hardly any flavor to a meal. And don't be tempted to simply use more of an old spice. It will have lost its fragrant volatile top notes, but the deeper base notes, contained in the oleoresins, will be less deteriorated. Using too much will introduce sharp, potentially bitter flavor notes.

If you're wondering whether your ground spices are still good to use, simply smell them. If you can detect some aroma and pungency, they should be all right. To check the freshness of whole spices you need to either break a piece (for cinnamon sticks or cloves) or scrape it with a knife or grater (for a spice such as nutmeg). Have a little sniff of any spice you are adding (except chile flakes or ground chile!) every time you cook with it. You will become familiar with the aroma, which will help you gain an understanding of good versus poor quality. In addition, you will get a feel for what flavors work best in your recipes.

Buyer Beware

A word of caution about buying spices from unknown traders or in colorful exotic markets. Spices and herbs are agricultural commodities with many variations. How these affect individual spices and herbs is discussed in their own sections. There are some broad-brush factors it's worth being aware of:

- Be very careful when buying saffron. It is the world's most expensive and most misrepresented spice.
- Look for insect infestation in spices stored in open sacks.
- Make sure the spice is packed in a sealed bag with its name; customs and quarantine officials in many countries take a dim view of travelers carrying unidentified substances!

Quality Control and Best Practices

Although the spice industry has achieved new heights of sophistication in terms of quality control, shipping, packing, storage, marketing and usage, at the farm level the majority of spices and herbs are harvested and dried much as they have been for centuries. Nearly every peppercorn you buy has been hand-picked; every true cinnamon stick has been hand-stripped and -rolled by traditional cinnamon peelers in Sri Lanka; every vanilla orchid has been hand-pollinated and every vanilla pod has been handled dozens of times during the arduous curing process. It is not surprising, therefore, that many spices can carry abnormally high levels of bacteria transmitted by soil, manure and human contact.

When I attended a World Spice Congress in India in 1986, the Indian delegates were at a loss to understand the West's apparent obsession with cleanliness. From their perspective, most of the bacteria on a spice would be sterilized by the heat of cooking. At that point the issue became obvious: in the West we often use spices in ways that do not necessarily sterilize them. For instance, cracked pepper crusted on cheese and paprika sprinkled over eggs kept warm under a heat lamp, are high-risk bacteria-growing situations.

The spice industry then took measures to sterilize spices using ethylene oxide (ETO); however, it was identified as carcinogenic in high concentrations. The use of ETO is now banned in most countries. Aside from improving cleanliness standards at the farm level, only two viable alternatives remain: irradiation and various forms of heat sterilization.

Irradiation involves exposing food to a low dose of ionizing radiation, which kills most bacteria and insect larvae. This method is widely used to sterilize medical products and is permitted for food sterilization in many countries. Consumers, however, are not generally comfortable with the idea of eating irradiated food, and as any irradiated product has to be labeled as such, to date no major spice seller has adopted the practice. The debate about the safety of irradiation continues; to many people, the jury is still out.

Heat sterilization is the most popular method of reducing the bacteria in spices. Essentially the whole spice is subjected to enough instant heat from superheated steam to kill most microorganisms without damaging the flavor. The spice is then ground in a very clean environment.

Is Organic Better?

What about buying organic spices? Some years ago Liz and I visited a cooperative of organic spice farms in Mangalore, India. We were interested to learn why the farmers had returned to organic farming. We were told that some years earlier, a number of pepper shipments to developed countries had been rejected because the pepper contained high levels of pesticide residues (interestingly, the pesticides had been sold to the Indians by those same developed countries). As a result, a group of farmers decided to return to the farming methods that had served their fathers, grandfathers and earlier generations quite well for centuries.

Organic spices and herbs are becoming more readily available. However, as much as we may want to believe it is so, organic certification is not a guarantee of quality; it relates only to the standards set for chemical use by the certification body. In my opinion they are worth their higher cost only if the flavor is as good as or better than material not certified organic, or if you are particularly sensitive to chemicals. Often overlooked is the fact that most developed countries have strict standards with respect to chemical residues in imported foods. This narrows the gap between standard and organic.

Organically Grown

Spices are consumed in relatively small amounts—⅓ ounce (10 g) or less in a meal—so their organic status is far less significant than that of physically larger foods such as vegetables, chicken or steak.

Using Fresh and Dried Spices and Herbs

The Correct Quantity: Dried versus Fresh

When a herb is dried, the water content is removed. This leaves a dry, shriveled leaf that is much reduced in size but still contains the same amount of essential flavor-producing oils. In other words, the dried herb is like a concentrated form of its fresh version. As a result, a general rule of thumb when using dried herbs is to use one-quarter to one-third of the quantity you would use of the fresh herb. However, most dried herbs do lose what we refer to as their "fresh volatile top notes." These fresh notes are particularly noticeable in herbs such as coriander leaves (cilantro), basil, lemongrass, chives and parsley. Even fresh chiles taste quite different from dried chiles.

FRESH IS A MUCH ABUSED and misused term these days in the world of herbs and spices. When a retailer says "fresh" herbs and spices, the term means products that have not been dried, frozen or processed in any way. In some cases a fresh item is clearly preferable. In Thai cooking, for instance, fresh coriander leaf (cilantro), ginger, garlic, lemongrass, lime leaf and chile are essential to achieving a classic flavor. However, there are some dishes—for instance, Mexican moles—in which the fruity caramelized notes of dried chiles are definitely preferable. An Italian salad with fresh tomatoes tastes best with fresh basil, but Bolognese sauce is invariably made with dried herbs such as basil, oregano, thyme and bay leaf.

Dried herbs have more robust, concentrated flavors that amalgamate and infuse more readily into a dish. Because they are dried, the essential oils can migrate easily out of the leaf structure, adding welcome flavor. Should you particularly want the flavor of fresh herbs as well, add them about 10 to 20 minutes before the end of the cooking time. That way the heat of cooking will not destroy the delicate fresh top notes. In other words, when deciding whether to use a fresh or a dried herb, you need to consider what is most appropriate for the application (although there may be times when it's necessary to compromise to allow for the season or availability).

Why Is Drying So Popular?

For centuries people have been drying herbs and spices for varying reasons. The most common is to preserve them in a storable form for later use. However, there is a second important reason why some herbs and spices are dried. The drying or curing process creates enzymatic reactions that produce the distinctive flavor we prefer. For example, when peppercorns are dried in the sun, they turn black and form the volatile oil piperine, which gives pepper its unique taste. Before curing, the vanilla bean is green, odorless and tasteless. Over many months, the kiln-drying and curing process creates the vanilla flavor we know and love, and that flavor comes from a substance formed by enzymes during drying and curing. The enzyme reaction that results from drying pepper and vanilla also works to fully develop

Home Grinding

Grinding spices yourself can be extremely rewarding, especially if you use a mortar and pestle, because their enticing aromas waft up as you crush the contents. Spices vary so much in size, hardness, texture and oil content that it is almost impossible to find a domestic grinder other than a mortar and pestle that will handle them all. Seed spices such as pepper can be ground in a pepper mill. You can also use a clean coffee grinder, but electric grinders may generate excessive heat, which can destroy some of the lighter volatile oils. If using an electric grinder, it's important not to over-grind. Most electric spice grinders are adapted coffee grinders, so any spice that is harder than a coffee bean will damage the mechanism over time. When it comes to the really hard spices, use the trusty mortar and pestle, which has been one of the cook's most useful implements for thousands of years.

the flavors of spices such as cloves, allspice, nutmeg and cardamom, to mention just a few. The third main reason for drying, especially herbs, is to create a form that readily and effectively imparts flavor. Think of trying to make a cup of peppermint tea with fresh peppermint leaves. The result would be an infusion with very little flavor and a low level of the therapeutic volatile oils. However, dried peppermint leaves infuse readily with hot water, producing the characteristic flavor we know so well.

Whole or Ground?

When should you use whole spices and when the ground version? It depends on the cooking method and the most effective way to impart flavor. For example, you might add a whole piece of cinnamon stick to fruit when stewing. This technique infuses the fruit with cinnamon flavor while leaving the liquid clear, while ground cinnamon would make the liquid muddy-looking. However, when making a curry, mixing spices with flour for cakes and cookies, or rubbing spices onto meats before cooking, it's important to use ground spices. Ground spices mix readily with other ingredients, imparting their flavor more rapidly than the whole versions because they have been crushed to a powder.

Some cooks say you should always buy spices whole and then grind them yourself. This is not a bad idea if you're unsure of the quality and freshness of the available ground spices. And if you don't use spices often, whole spices have a longer shelf life than those that are ground. On average, whole spices, when stored as suggested (see page 33), will last for 3 years, while ground spices start losing flavor after 12 to 18 months. Good-quality purchased ground spices are as flavorful as those you have ground yourself, so if you use a lot of spice, go for the convenience of ready-ground.

Does Roasting Improve Flavor?

Some cooks may tell you that roasting spices brings out their flavor, but this is not correct. Roasting spices *changes* their flavor. In the same way that a slice of toast tastes different from a slice of bread, a roasted spice tastes different from an unroasted one. Spices are roasted to create greater depth of flavor and robustness. The majority of Indian curries are enhanced when roasted spices are used, but one would never roast cinnamon, allspice, nutmeg or ginger before adding them to a cake. I also prefer to use unroasted spices in fish and vegetable dishes, as the more delicate, fresh-tasting top notes are still recognizable and complement those foods better than robust, deep, roasted flavors, which are preferable with, for instance, red meats.

Both whole and ground spices may be dry-roasted. Many cooks like to roast spices whole, for the same reason they buy whole spices. But good-quality freshly ground spices will also roast perfectly well. To roast either whole or ground spices, heat a heavy-bottomed pan on the stovetop until it is almost too hot to touch (if it is too hot, the spices may burn, making them bitter). Add your spices to the hot pan and shake it constantly so they don't stick or burn. When they become fragrant and start to darken, they are sufficiently roasted and should be tipped out of the pan to cool completely before storing in an airtight container, ready for use within a day or two. (After roasting, the volatile oils oxidize more rapidly and flavor deteriorates quickly, so don't store roasted spices for more than a few days.)

Part Two

Spice Notes

THIS SECTION OF THE BOOK is designed to be a quick source of information on 97 herbs and spices, selected because they are the ones most used in cooking or have a particularly interesting history and culinary applications. The details included in each entry were selected based on my sense of relevance to the consumer. I have worked in most aspects of the herb and spice business, from growing herbs in my childhood to managing a spice company in Singapore and starting my own artisan herb and spice business in the mid 1990s. Fifty years of giving lectures and classes and talking to a wide variety of consumers, including chefs and food manufacturers, have given me insight into the information people want to know.

For the past eighteen years my wife, Elizabeth, and I have traveled widely on buying trips for our business, Herbie's Spices, which is based in Sydney, Australia. We have also led regular Spice Discovery tours to India. Thanks to our work and our travels, we have been fortunate to experience many fascinating aspects of the spice trade that I feel may be of relevance to readers. I have included some of these useful (I hope) facts and anecdotes in the listings. I trust you will find them interesting.

How to Use the Spice and Herb Listings

THE SPICES AND HERBS are listed in alphabetical order by common name; the botanical name is cited below it. Here is a guide to the various subheadings used.

Common Name

This is the single name for the herb and/or spice that is most commonly used and recognized.

Botanical Name

Many plants, including those from which we harvest spices and herbs, go by a variety of common names. These variations in nomenclature can be extremely confusing, especially to consumers. With a nod toward ensuring clarity, I have included the botanical (scientific) name of every plant with each entry. Although scientists may still argue about some family affiliations among plants, botanical names do provide a system of plant classification that is universally accepted.

The first attempt at classifying plants was made by the Greek philosopher Theophrastus in the fourth century BCE. Theophrastus classified plants as either herbs, shrubs or trees. At the time, the word *herb* was used merely as a reference to plant size; it was not an indication of any culinary or medicinal attributes. The next significant step was made in 1753 by Carl Linnaeus. In his groundbreaking *Species Plantarum* he noted differences in the forms of flowers. This method of classification groups plants according to one particular characteristic; however, it does not necessarily indicate their genetic commonality with other, similar plants. Linnaeus gave a two-part name to each plant, one for its genus, or generic name, and the other for its species. This practice has endured because the use of Latin makes the system universal. The full botanical name is often followed by the name (or its abbreviation) of the botanist who first described the species. So in the case of cardamom, the botanical name for green cardamom is *Elettaria cardamomum* Maton. *Elettaria* is the genus, *cardamomum* is the species and Maton is the name of the botanist who first described it.

Family

The next degree of commonality is the family to which the plant belongs. Many plants have characteristics that are sufficiently similar that we can place them in the same family. Green cardamom has the family name Zingiberaceae. It belongs to the same family as ginger and galangal; all grow similarly from a rhizome. Some family names have been changed to more accurately reflect their commonality. For example, Umbelliferae includes plants with an umbrella-shaped flower (a description I've always liked). The name was changed to Apiaceae, a more accurate description of plants with a hollow stem—the name is derived from the Latin word *apium*, used by the Romans to describe a plant similar to celery. (In botanical circles, both names still tend to be recognized.) When a family name has been updated, such as Umbelliferae to Apiaceae, the former family name is listed following the current one.

Varieties

Some plants have different varieties; for example, within "Basil" we have sweet basil, bush basil, purple basil, camphor basil and holy basil (to mention just a few). Some varieties have occurred naturally through cross-pollination and others have been developed by plant breeders. When a new variety is deliberately created, it is called a cultivar. (As most herbs and spices are not broad-acre, high-volume monoculture crops like rice and wheat, I am not aware of any GMO cultivars having being developed so far.) When appropriate, other varieties of the same plant are listed, along with their botanical names, as for basil.

Other Names

As noted, the common names for plants can vary dramatically, depending on where they are grown or purchased. For example, nigella seeds are often referred to incorrectly as "black cumin" and "black onion" seeds. Ajowan seeds are also called "bishop's weed," "carum" and "white carum" seeds. These "other" names are often used instead of the common name, which can make things very confusing for consumers; for example, coriander leaf is often referred to as cilantro.

As the names of herbs and spices have often been translated from other languages, the spelling of their common names in English may vary considerably. However, they should sound similar—many English spellings are best attempts at phonetic rendition of a name that was not originally written in the Roman alphabet. For example, the English spelling of the Middle Eastern spice sumac might be *sumak*, *sumach* or *summak*. In practice it cannot be said that one version is more correct than another. However, to establish a consistent standard, I have used the most common spelling of the name whenever possible.

Flavor Group

Spices fall into five key flavor groups: sweet, pungent, tangy, hot and amalgamating. Herbs belong to the savory group and can be further classified as mild, medium, strong or pungent. Their flavor group is a useful guide to the relative quantities of these ingredients to use in cooking. If you know it is pungent, be careful how much you use! These groupings are particularly useful when making spice blends. In Part Three, "The Art of Combining Spices," I discuss the effects of combining these different flavor groups to achieve balanced mixes of herbs and spices.

Parts Used

In this section we have listed the various parts of the plant that are used, whether they are commonly dried or used fresh, and whether they are termed a herb or a spice.

Names in Different Languages

Whenever possible, I have provided the names of herbs and spices in languages other than English. When a particular language is not listed, it may indicate that the product is seldom used in countries where that language is spoken. In many countries, different dialects or regional languages may assign different names to a herb or spice, which creates variations within the country. For instance, in India ajowan is called *ajwain*, *omum*, *ajvini*, *javanee*, *yamani*, *carom* and *lovage*, depending upon the region. When writing any of these variations in English, I have used phonetic spellings; names from non-Roman scripts such as Arabic and Chinese have also been indicated phonetically. Chinese names are given in both Cantonese (C) and Mandarin (M).

Background

Some of the most interesting aspects of herbs and spices are their unusual origins and colorful histories, so we have included a brief historical sketch for each plant.

Spice Notes/Travels in the Spice Trade

I have had many interesting experiences during my lifetime of working with herbs and spices. I felt some were worthy of sharing, and so have included a number within the relevant entries. I hope you'll enjoy these stories, but perhaps even more important, I hope you will find that the information heightens your enjoyment of spices and herbs.

The Plant

In this section I have included a non-technical description of the plant using easily understood terms. Relevant information about propagation and growing conditions is sometimes included; however, this book focuses on the culinary use of these plants, so horticultural information definitely comes in second place. If you are interested in knowing more, there is a general section on growing your own spices and herbs (pages 24 to 28). The flavor profiles within this section are included to help you identify and enhance your understanding of the herb and/or spice.

The "Other Varieties" section provides more details on the varieties listed at the beginning of the main entry. It includes information about related plants, as well as plants with similar qualities that aren't related but may be confused with the main listing. In some instances I have mentioned plants that are not edible but have similar common names, to help avoid potential confusion.

Processing

I have included information on how the plants are processed because in many cases the processing method is an essential factor that determines unique flavor characteristics.

Buying and Storage

Whether you are shopping in your neighborhood supermarket, visiting a specialist spice merchant or haggling over saffron in the markets of Istanbul, a basic understanding of what to look for when buying herbs and spices will help you purchase the best available product. And once it arrives home, proper storage is essential for best results.

Use

This section expands on the notes that accompany the recipes, with a view to helping you cook confidently with any of these herbs and spices without necessarily using a specific recipe.

Culinary Information

Combines With

Like a horse and carriage, some herbs and spices go together naturally. This feature lists other herbs and spices with flavors that complement the item under discussion.

Traditional Uses

This section lists the types of foods—both classic and innovative—that the herb or spice is best used with.

Spice Blends

This section lists blends that the herb or spice is most likely to be used in.

Weight per Teaspoon (5 mL)

The weight per teaspoon (5 mL) is the relationship between volume and weight. For example, 1 teaspoon (5 mL) of a whole spice may weigh 3 grams, but 1 teaspoon of the same spice in its ground form may weigh 5 grams. It is important to know this if you are converting a recipe from volumetric measures to weight, or vice versa. I supply these weights in grams only—the equivalent weights in ounces are simply too small to measure accurately at home.

Suggested Quantity per Pound (500 g)

Because the flavor strength of herbs and spices varies, I have provided a suggested quantity to use with 1 pound (500 g) of red meats, white meats (including chicken and fish), vegetables, grains and pulses (legumes), or baked goods.

Recipes

We have included recipes with the entries (as well as with some of the spice blends) because when it comes to using herbs and spices, one of the best starting points is making a recipe that uses the ingredient you have just read about. Sometimes the herb or spice will be the hero; other times it will play an important supporting role. Our daughter Kate has developed recipes that demonstrate both classic and innovative uses for these flavors. Kate's recipes are designed to give you an idea of how these herbs and spices are best used. Having made the recipe, you will be able to think about the flavors and how they enhanced the final dish. From then on, you should feel comfortable including the herb or spice in other recipes.

> **Tip**
>
> The weight per teaspoon (5 mL) is based on premium-grade herbs and spices that have not been adulterated with starches or fillers. It can vary from season to season, but you can use the amounts quoted as a reasonably accurate guide.

Ajowan

Trachyspermum ammi (also known as *Carum ajowan*)

Names in Other Languages

- **Arabic:** kamme muluki, talib-el koubs
- **Chinese (C):** yan douh johng wuih heung
- **Chinese (M):** yin du zang hui xiang
- **Dutch:** ajowan
- **French:** ajowan
- **German:** Adiowan, indischer Kummel
- **Indian:** ajwain, omum, ajvini, javanee, yamani carom, lovage
- **Italian:** ajowan
- **Russian:** ajova, azhgon
- **Spanish:** ajowan
- **Turkish:** misir anason, emmus

Family: Apiaceae (formerly Umbelliferae)

Other Names: ajwain, bishop's weed, carum, white carum seeds (bleached ajowan)

Flavor Group: Pungent

Parts Used: seeds (as a spice)

Background

Ajowan is native to the Indian subcontinent. It is grown in Afghanistan, Egypt, Iran and Pakistan. In the late 19th and early 20th centuries, ajowan was the world's main source of thymol, a volatile oil used in the manufacture of mouthwash, toothpaste, cough syrup, lozenges and some herbal medicines (it is also found in the herb thyme). Until 1914 almost all exports of ajowan seeds were to Germany, for extraction of thymol for medicinal use. Ajowan seeds contain 2.5–5% volatile oil, over 35% of which is thymol.

Culinary Information

Combines with

- chile
- coriander seed
- cumin
- fenugreek seed
- ginger
- mustard
- nutmeg
- paprika
- most herbs

Traditional Uses

- breads
- Moroccan tagines
- pakoras, parathas and samosas
- savory biscuits
- vegetable and fish curries
- vegetable dishes
- whole-grain mustard

Spice Blends

- berbere
- curry powders

The Plant

Ajowan is a close relative of parsley and the plants look similar; however, ajowan leaves are not used in cooking. The seeds are small, tear-shaped and light brown. Resembling celery seeds, they form in umbrella-shaped clusters. Ajowan seeds taste like thyme because of their high levels of the volatile oil thymol—an unusually herby flavor for a seed spice. It is well complemented by slightly sharp, peppery notes and a lingering warm aftertaste. Bleached ajowan seeds, although rarely seen, are milder in flavor and are referred to as white carum seeds.

Processing

Ajowan seeds are ready to harvest in midsummer, when the flower heads turn brown. The plants are uprooted and dried on mats in the sun, then the flowers are rubbed by hand to separate the seeds. The volatile oil thymol is extracted by steam distillation.

Buying and Storage

Ajowan seeds should be uniform in color and free from extraneous pieces of stem material. Always buy whole seeds; if grinding is required, do this yourself using a mortar and pestle or a clean pepper mill. Recently harvested seeds will have a distinct herbal aroma and a somewhat sharp, peppery taste. Should these attributes be missing, the seeds are too old to use in cooking. Store in an airtight container away

Spice Notes

When we travel, my wife, Liz, always carries a packet of ajowan-spiced berbere (see page 697) to liven up bland airline meals. On one flight we were served a hot meal covered with a creamy sauce of indeterminate flavor. When Liz sprinkled the berbere blend over the food, it released a tantalizing aroma. When the flight attendant swooned over the fragrance, Liz had to pass around the berbere to nearby passengers. Since it is now known that high altitudes diminish our sense of taste, people in charge of airline food would be well advised to consider serving a few more dishes containing robust spice blends.

WEIGHT PER TEASPOON (5 mL)
- **whole seeds:** 3.3 g

SUGGESTED QUANTITY PER POUND (500 g)
- **red meats:** 1 tbsp (15 mL)
- **white meats:** 2 tsp (10 mL)
- **vegetables:** 1 tsp (5 mL)
- **grains and pulses:** 1 tsp (5 mL)
- **baked goods:** 1 tsp (5 mL)

from extremes of heat, light and humidity. The optimum storage time under these conditions is 2 to 3 years.

Use

As with many of the seed spices, ajowan complements the flavors of vegetables, grains and pulses. These tiny yet powerful, highly fragrant seeds add a deliciously aromatic taste to savory biscuits and a piquancy to pastry for meat, seafood and vegetable pies. Half a teaspoon (2 mL) of ajowan added to 1 cup (250 mL) steamed cabbage during cooking makes this much-maligned vegetable a delicious accompaniment to grilled meats. Remember to use small amounts when experimenting with ajowan, as the flavor is quite strong. When adding ajowan to pickles and chutneys, you can be a little more liberal, as long cooking times mellow the flavor. Because ajowan is so small and chewable when cooked, you rarely need to grind it.

Potato and Pea Samosas

Samosas are a staple Indian appetizer and are most commonly vegetarian. These potato and pea samosas are gently spiced, allowing the ajowan to shine through in the filling as well as in the pastry. They are a guilty pleasure for takeout, but making them isn't hard at all. I won't allow myself to deep-fry them at home—baking is a perfectly good way to cook them—but if you have a deep-fryer, by all means go ahead. Serve with raita (minted yogurt).

Makes 12 samosas

Preparation time:
20 minutes, plus
30 minutes resting
Cooking time: 1 hour

Tip

Ghee is a type of clarified butter used in Indian cooking. If you don't have any, you can substitute an equal amount of butter or clarified butter.

• **Baking sheet, lined with parchment paper**

PASTRY

2 cups	all-purpose flour	500 mL
1 tsp	fine sea salt	5 mL
½ tsp	ajowan seeds	2 mL
4 tbsp	ghee (see Tip, left)	60 mL
6 to 8 tbsp	water	90 to 120 mL

FILLING

1½ lbs	potatoes, peeled and cut into 1-inch (2.5 cm) cubes (roughly 2 large)	750 g
1 tbsp	oil	15 mL
½	onion, finely diced	½
1 tbsp	freshly grated gingerroot	15 mL
1	green finger chile, seeded and finely diced	1
½ tsp	whole cumin seeds	2 mL
½ tsp	ajowan seeds	2 mL
1 tsp	chaat masala (page 704)	5 mL
½ tsp	fine sea salt	2 mL
¼ tsp	freshly ground black pepper	1 mL
2 tbsp	roughly chopped fresh cilantro leaves	30 mL
½ cup	peas	125 mL
2 tbsp	water	30 mL
2 tbsp	butter, melted	30 mL

1. *Pastry:* In a large bowl, combine flour, salt and ajowan. Using your fingers, rub in ghee until mixture resembles bread crumbs. Add water 1 tbsp (15 mL) at a time, until a firm dough forms. Turn out onto a clean surface and knead for 5 minutes, until smooth. Pat into a ball, wrap in plastic wrap, and set aside at room temperature for at least 30 minutes.

Tip

You can make the samosas ahead and freeze them uncooked, wrapped tightly in plastic wrap or in a resealable bag, for up to one month. When ready to enjoy, bring to room temperature before brushing with butter and baking as outlined in Step 6.

2. *Filling:* Meanwhile, in a saucepan of boiling salted water, cook potatoes until fork-tender, 20 to 30 minutes. Drain and set aside.

3. In a saucepan over medium-high heat, heat oil. Add onion and ginger and sauté for 3 minutes, until soft. Add chile, cumin, ajowan, chaat masala, salt and pepper and cook, stirring often, for about 2 minutes, until fragrant. Add cooked potato, cilantro and peas and cook, stirring often, for about 5 minutes, until potato is well coated with spice mixture and begins to break down. Turn off heat and, using a potato masher or large fork, mash gently. Set aside to cool (transferring the mixture to a bowl will speed up the process).

4. Preheat oven to 400°F (200°C).

5. Divide prepared dough into 12 equal pieces; keep covered with plastic wrap until ready to use. On a lightly floured work surface, using a rolling pin, roll each piece into a square about $1/16$ inch (2 mm) thick. Place a generous tablespoon (15 mL) of potato mixture in the center of each square. Dip your finger in water and run it around the edge of the pastry, then gently fold it over the filling to make a triangle. Press edges tightly to seal. If desired, use a fork to press a pattern into the sealed edges (see Tip, left).

6. Transfer samosas to prepared baking sheet. Brush both sides of each samosa with melted butter. Bake in preheated oven for 20 to 30 minutes, turning once, until pastry is golden and crisp. Serve immediately.

Akudjura

Solanum centrale

Family: Solanaceae

Varieties: bush tomato (*S. chippendalei*), wild tomato (*S. quadriloculatum*)

Other Names: bush raisin, bush sultana, desert raisin, kutjera

Flavor Group: Pungent

Parts Used: berries (as a spice)

Firepower

Like many native Australian plants, akudjura thrives after bushfires. Its initial prolific fruiting steadily declines over a few years until the plant is rejuvenated by the next fire.

Background

Akudjura may be among the oldest spices known to the human race, as the Australian Aborigines have reportedly been using it for thousands of years. Native to Central and Western Australia, akudjura has a strong connection with the mythology of the Warlpiri and Anmatyerr peoples.

Regarded as a staple by the Central Australian native people, akudjura fruits that had dried on the shrub were gathered and ground with water to produce a thick paste. The Aborigines formed this paste into large balls and left them to dry in the blazing sun. Akudjura's high acidity, characterized by its tangy flavor and rich vitamin C content, acted as a preservative, making storage for long periods of time possible. The balls were often wedged into the forks of trees for later use. Although the Australian Aborigines used akudjura primarily for sustenance, our current inquisitiveness and desire for diverse taste experiences has led us to appreciate akudjura as a spice, used in small quantities to enhance the flavor of a wide range of foods in everyday meals.

The Plant

The akudjura shrub, a relative of both potatoes and tomatoes, is a hardy-looking perennial with woody stems bearing long, sharp spikes at 2- to $3^1/_4$-inch (5 to 8 cm) intervals. Soft, down-covered grayish green leaves and young rust-colored leaves set off attractive violet flowers shaped like five-pointed stars, somewhat similar to borage flowers. The fruits are about $3/_4$ inch (2 cm) in diameter, purplish green when young and pale yellow when ripe. As the sticky fruits

Culinary Information

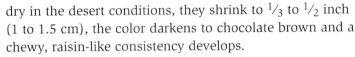

Combines with
- coriander seed
- lemon myrtle
- mustard
- pepper
- thyme
- wattleseed

Traditional Uses
- grilled meats
- slow-cooked soups and casseroles
- baked goods
- pickles and chutneys

Spice Blends
- native Australian spice rubs
- seafood and game seasonings

The Usual Name

Powdered and whole bush tomatoes are referred to generally as akudjura or *kutjera*, their Aboriginal name.

dry in the desert conditions, they shrink to $1/3$ to $1/2$ inch (1 to 1.5 cm), the color darkens to chocolate brown and a chewy, raisin-like consistency develops.

Bush tomatoes have a distinct, pleasant aroma like caramel mingled with sun-dried tomato, with comforting "baked" background notes reminiscent of a whole-grain cookie, or what we refer to in Australia as an Anzac biscuit. The flavor is initially caramel-like, but after about 30 seconds it develops a somewhat bitter lingering aftertaste that leaves the palate unexpectedly refreshed. The color varies from light sandy orange-brown to dark brown, depending on the amount of rainfall the plants received while the fruits were developing.

Other Varieties

Plants other than akudjura are commonly refered to as bush tomatoes. For instance, *Solanum chippendalei*, which is a similar plant. The berries have an insipid taste when compared to the most used culinary variety, *S. centrale*. **Wild tomato** (*S. quadriloculatum*) looks similar to *S. centrale* and *S. chippendalei* but contains levels of toxins that make it unsuitable for eating.

Processing

Akudjura ripens in the wild in Australia's Central Desert; the fruits are allowed to dry naturally on the plant before picking. In the middle of Australia the humidity is so low you can almost feel your eyeballs drying out. The drying process is essential if akudjura is to be eaten with no harmful side effects, because it drives down the level of alkaloids. It also concentrates the flavors, creating more full-bodied and complex flavor notes in the same way that drying in the sun modifies the flavors of many more familiar spices.

Travels in the Spice Trade

If you stick a pin in the center of a map of Australia, you're pretty sure to land on Alice Springs, and that's where I went to harvest wild akudjura with a group of Aboriginal women. One, named Kitty, drew my attention to another variety of the plant, *Solanum chippendalei*. It was almost identical to *S. centrale*, but it bore shiny round green fruits 1¼ inches (3 cm) in diameter suspended from a large, spiky, elf's cap–shaped calyx. Kitty cut one in half and scraped out the seeds (they looked like shiny black sesame seeds) and inner skin, then invited me to taste the flesh, which looked like honeydew melon. It was bland and vaguely reminiscent of cantaloupe; one would never use it to flavor food.

I wouldn't recommend picking your own akudjura without an experienced gatherer to help identify the edible varieties. At one point Kitty pointed out another related plant, *S. quadriloculatum*. This has seemingly identical flowers, large, sage-like leaves and green fruits with a spongy texture; however, they are not edible and contain toxic amounts of the alkaloid solanine. As Kitty said, "Cheeky [poisonous]! Only emu and kangaroo eat."

WEIGHT PER TEASPOON (5 mL)

- **average whole dry berry:** 0.8 g
- **ground:** 2.7 g

SUGGESTED QUANTITY PER POUND (500 g)

- **red meats:** 1 tsp (5 mL)
- **white meats:** ½ tsp (2 mL)
- **vegetables:** ½ tsp (2 mL)
- **grains and pulses:** ½ tsp (2 mL)
- **baked goods:** ½ tsp (2 mL)

Buying and Storage

When buying whole akudjura, you will notice that the color can vary considerably. This is generally not an indication of quality but simply an effect of the amount of rain during the growing season. Most important, the consistency of the fruit should be similar to that of a chewy raisin; any softer is a sign that they have not been dried sufficiently. The powder will sometimes form clumps because of the high levels of oils present. As long as the powder does not feel moist to the touch, some lumps do not affect the quality for culinary applications. Both whole and powdered akudjura are best stored in an airtight container away from extremes of heat, light and humidity. Optimum storage time under these conditions is 2 to 3 years.

Use

The unique flavor of akudjura is best appreciated in small quantities. Like many pungent spices, too much will cause the bitter, sharp notes to dominate and mask the fruity, sweet, caramel flavors. Whole akudjura can be added at the outset to dishes with a long, slow cooking time, such as soups, pickles and chutneys, and casseroles. The powder gives a nostalgic "country-baked" taste to cookies and apple crumble. I have found that it combines particularly well with a mixture of ground coriander seed, wattleseed, lemon myrtle and a little salt as a barbecue rub.

Aussie Damper

Damper is a traditional Australian bread that was made by traveling swagmen and drovers, who carried limited rations. It is similar to a scone and was cooked in the coals of a campfire. As children we used to press the dough around the end of a stick and cook it near the dying flames, then ease it off and fill the center with golden syrup for a decadent after-dinner treat. Indigenous Australians had their own version of this bread, using grains and nuts and including akudjura. Serve with fresh hummus (page 596) for a quick, easy lunch.

Makes 4 servings

Preparation time:
10 minutes

Cooking time: 30 to
40 minutes

Tips

If you can't find self-rising flour in stores, you can make your own. To equal 1 cup (250 mL) self-rising flour, combine 1 cup (250 mL) all-purpose flour, 1½ tsp (7 mL) baking powder and ½ tsp (2 mL) salt.

If you don't have buttermilk, you can make your own. Combine 1½ tsp (7 mL) lemon juice and 1¼ cups (300 mL) milk and set aside for 20 minutes, until it begins to curdle.

- **Baking sheet, lined with parchment paper**
- **Preheat oven to 350°F (180°C)**

1¾ cups	self-rising flour (see Tips, left)	425 mL
1 tbsp	ground akudjura	15 mL
¼ tsp	sweet smoked paprika	1 mL
½ cup	grated Cheddar cheese	125 mL
	Generous pinch fine sea salt	
1¼ cups	buttermilk (see Tips, left)	300 mL

1. In a large bowl, combine flour, akudjura, paprika, Cheddar and salt. Stir in buttermilk, then use your hands to combine into a shaggy dough. Turn onto a lightly floured work surface and knead gently for 1 to 2 minutes, until smooth. Shape into a round loaf about 7 inches (18 cm) in diameter and place on prepared baking sheet. Bake in preheated oven for 30 to 40 minutes, until top is golden and base is firm.

Variation

For added flavor, roughly chop 2 slices of cooked bacon and add to the batter.

Akudjura Risotto

Although this may not be a traditional dish from the Australian outback, tart yet caramelly akudjura tastes wonderful in risotto. For a heartier meal, serve with grilled chicken or shrimp.

Makes
6 servings

Preparation time:
20 minutes

Cooking time:
30 minutes

Tip

If preparing ahead, stop after adding half of the broth in Step 2 and refrigerate. To finish, simply continue cooking, adding the akudjura and remaining broth.

2 tbsp	ground akudjura	30 mL
1 tbsp	boiling water	15 mL
1 tbsp	tomato paste	15 mL
1 tsp	ground wattleseed	5 mL
1 tbsp	extra virgin olive oil	15 mL
1	small onion, chopped	1
2	cloves garlic, crushed	2
1¾ cups	Arborio rice	425 mL
½ cup	dry white wine	125 mL
5 to 6 cups	vegetable or chicken broth	1.25 to 1.5 L
2 tbsp	heavy or whipping (35%) cream	30 mL
	Sea salt and freshly ground black pepper	
2 tbsp	shredded fresh basil leaves	30 mL
	Freshly grated Parmesan cheese	

1. In a small bowl, cover akudjura with boiling water and set aside for 10 to 15 minutes. Drain, discarding soaking liquid. Add tomato paste and wattleseed to soaked akudjura and stir well. Set aside.

2. In a deep skillet or saucepan, heat oil over medium heat. Add onion and cook until soft, about 3 minutes. Add garlic and cook, stirring, for 2 minutes. Add rice, stirring to coat grains with oil. Add wine and cook, stirring constantly, until evaporated, 1 to 2 minutes. Reduce heat to low and add half the broth, 1 cup (250 mL) at a time, stirring after each addition until all the liquid is absorbed (see Tip, left). When half of the broth has been incorporated, add akudjura mixture and stir to combine. Continue adding broth and stirring until the rice is creamy and slightly firm to the bite. Remove from heat, add cream, and season with salt and pepper to taste. Serve garnished with basil and Parmesan.

Alexanders

Smyrnium olusatrum

Family: Apiaceae (formerly Umbelliferae)

Other Names: black lovage, horse parsley, potherb, smyrnium, wild celery

Flavor Group: Mild

Parts Used: leaves (as a herb), stems and flower buds (as a vegetable)

Background

Alexanders is native to the Mediterranean region; it was introduced to England about 2,000 years ago by the Romans. It has thrived there ever since, in sunny locales with moist, rich soils and on rock cliffs close to the sea. Prior to the

Culinary Information

Combines with

*Most herbs, and has a
special affinity with*

- basil
- lovage
- oregano
- parsley
- salad burnet
- savory

Traditional Uses

- beans and peas
- carrots
- potatoes
- salads
- vegetable soups

Spice Blends

- not commonly used in spice blends

A Historical Note

Alexanders is said to be named after Alexander the Great. It also bears a close resemblance to the "rock parsley" (*Petroselinum crispum*) of Alexandria. Despite its early popularity, by the mid 18th century alexanders as a herb had been largely replaced by celery.

widespread use of onions, carrots and turnips to add bulk and flavor to soups and stews, alexanders was cultivated as a potherb, and the young shoots and leafstalks were cooked as a vegetable.

The Plant

Alexanders is a robust-looking biennial herb that grows up to 60 inches (1.5 m) tall on thick, furrowed stalks bearing roundish glossy dark green leaves in groups of three. The old family name was Umbelliferae because the yellow-green flowers are borne in numerous umbels. The small black seeds have been used as a substitute for pepper; it is believed this association is responsible for the alternative name "black lovage." The flavor of the young leaves and stems resembles a cross between celery and parsley, hence the common names "horse parsley" and "wild celery."

Other Varieties

Golden alexanders (*Zizia aurea*) grows in eastern North America and the flowers are sometimes added to salads. The leaves and stems are rarely used because of their bitterness, and it is best to avoid eating the roots, as it has been reported that they may be toxic.

Processing

Alexanders is mainly used fresh and only occasionally in its dried form. To dry the leaves for later use, apply the same techniques you would use to dry parsley and other delicate herbs. Cut the long, leafy stems in the morning and spread

A

out on either paper or wire mesh. Set aside in a dark, warm, well-aired place. Do not hang them in bunches, as touching leaves will tend to turn black at the edges. When the leaves have shriveled to about one-fifth of their size and are quite crisp to the touch, rub them off the stems and store in an airtight container.

Buying and Storage

Alexanders is not commercially available as a dried herb. If you dry this herb yourself, store it in an airtight container in a cool, dark place. Optimum storage time is 1 year.

Use

The young leaves and stems can be finely chopped and added to salads, mild-flavored stir-fries, soups and stews. They can also be used as a garnish for cooked vegetables, when tossed in a little olive oil. The large stems are delicious as a vegetable when steamed and served with olive oil, salt and freshly ground black pepper. A salad can be made from the flower buds by steaming them for about 5 minutes to remove the bitterness. Allow to cool and serve with vinaigrette, or mix into lettuce salads to add contrast.

SUGGESTED QUANTITY PER POUND (500 g)
- **red meats:** 1/2 cup (125 mL)
- **white meats:** 1/2 cup (125 mL)
- **vegetables:** 1 cup (250 mL)
- **grains and pulses:** 1 cup (250 mL)
- **baked goods:** 1 cup (250 mL)

Alexanders Ragtime Salad

My grandfather was a huge fan of jazz music (accompanied by some rather good dancing) and in the 1940s was a fan of the Andrews Sisters. They sang a number called "Alexander's Ragtime Band," which was the inspiration for this salad's name. This is an attractive salad enhanced by the addition of various fresh ragged salad leaves.

Makes 6 side salads

Preparation time:
10 minutes

Cooking time: none

- - - - - - - - - - - - - - - - - -

Tips

If you can't find alexanders, you can substitute ¾ cup (175 mL) roughly chopped fresh parsley leaves and ¼ cup (60 mL) roughly chopped tender young celery leaves.

Choose a soft lettuce such as butter or Bibb for this salad.

The best way to shave fennel is using a mandoline. If you don't have one, use the slicer on a box grater.

1 tbsp	extra virgin olive oil	15 mL
2 tsp	freshly squeezed lemon juice	10 mL
1 cup	lightly packed torn fresh alexanders, leaves and stems (see Tips, left)	250 mL
1 cup	lightly packed torn soft lettuce (see Tips, left)	250 mL
1	bulb fennel, shaved or very thinly sliced (see Tips, left)	1
1 tbsp	fresh oregano leaves	15 mL
2 tsp	capers, drained and rinsed	10 mL
	Freshly ground black pepper	

1. In a small bowl, whisk together oil and lemon juice.
2. In a large serving bowl, combine alexanders, lettuce, fennel, oregano and capers. Toss with prepared dressing and season with pepper (no salt is needed, as the capers are very salty).

Allspice

Pimenta dioica

Names in Other Languages

- **Arabic:** bahar halu, tawabil halua
- **Chinese (C):** do heung gwo
- **Chinese (M):** duo xiang guo
- **Danish:** allehande
- **Dutch:** piment
- **French:** piment de Jamaïque, poivre giroflée
- **German:** Piment
- **Greek:** bahari, aromatopeperi
- **Indian:** kabab cheene, seetful
- **Italian:** pepe de Giamaica
- **Japanese:** hyakumikosho
- **Portuguese:** pimenta da Jamaica
- **Russian:** yamayski pyerets
- **Spanish:** pimenta gorda
- **Swedish:** kryddpeppar
- **Turkish:** yenibahar, Jamaika biberi

Interesting Uses

The Aztecs added allspice, along with vanilla, to a chocolate drink, and the Mayan people included allspice in the embalming process.

Family: Myrtaceae

Varieties: bayberry tree (*P. racemosa*), Carolina allspice (*Calycanthus floridus*), Californian allspice (*Calycanthus occidentalis*)

Other Names: bay rum berry, clove pepper, Jamaica pepper, pimento

Flavor Group: Sweet

Parts Used: berries (as a spice)

Background

The first record of what was probably allspice occurs in the journal of Columbus's first voyage to the Americas in 1492. He showed the natives of Cuba some peppercorns from the *Piper nigrum* vine, which they thought they recognized. Using sign language, they indicated there was an abundance of the berries in the neighborhood. The natives were actually referring to the berries of the allspice tree, and thus the confusion with naming began. These pepper-like berries were given the botanical name *Pimenta*, the Spanish word for "pepper."

Culinary Information

Combines with
- bay leaf
- cardamom
- cinnamon
- cloves
- coriander seed
- cumin
- fennel seed
- ginger
- juniper
- mustard seed
- nutmeg
- paprika
- turmeric

Traditional Uses
- cooked root vegetables
- cooked spinach
- tomato-based sauces
- pâtés and terrines
- meat and vegetable soups
- roast meats
- gravies
- marinades and sauces
- seafood, especially shellfish
- pickles, relishes and preserves (as whole spice)
- cakes, pies and cookies

Spice Blends
- mixed spice/pumpkin pie spice/apple pie spice
- curry powders
- meat seasonings
- jerk seasoning
- tsire powder
- pickling spices
- mulling spices
- pepper-mill blends
- sweet *quatre épices*
- tagine blends
- Chinese master stocks

Fragrant Flowers

When allspice trees are in bloom with their clusters of tiny white flowers, the warm, clove-like perfume in the air is one of the most beautiful aromas imaginable.

In 1532, Felipe IV of Spain was advised that pepper grew wild on trees in Jamaica. Thinking an abundant supply of this precious spice would boost the royal coffers, he instructed his minions to investigate *la pimenta de Jamaica*. There must have been some long faces when the ship returned loaded with allspice and investors realized the cargo was far less valuable than true pepper (*Piper nigrum*). One can only imagine the amount of effort that went into finding uses for this "new" spice. Allspice didn't arrive in England until 1601, where (it is believed) it was first used as a substitute for cardamom. During the 17th century allspice was valued as a preservative, particularly for meat and fish on long sea voyages. It is interesting to note that, even after widespread adoption of modern food-processing and refrigeration practices, allspice continued to be used for its flavor in many manufactured products.

The Plant

Allspice (pimento) is the dried and cured unripe berry of a tropical evergreen tree that is native to Jamaica, Cuba, Guatemala, Honduras and southern Mexico. Pimento trees grow 23 to 33 feet (7 to 10 m) tall, with some reaching a height of 49 feet (15 m). The bark is silvery gray and aromatic, enclosing a hard, durable, close-grained wood

Confusion Still Reigns

The botanical name for allspice was destined to confuse, from the day it was discovered by Columbus, throughout history and right up to today. *Pimenta* is Spanish for "pepper." It can mean pepper from the vine, all members of the capsicum family (which includes sweet bell peppers and chile peppers), and allspice as well. Also, many consumers confuse allspice with "mixed spice," which is a blend of sweet spices. To add to the confusion, the French name for allspice is *toute épice*, and there are some who insist on calling it *quatre épices* (see page 418), despite the fact that this term actually refers to two spice blends, only one of which contains allspice. The name "Jamaica pepper" still comes up in some recipes, as does its other lesser-known incorrect name, "bay rum berry."

that was used for making walking sticks in the 19th century. However, this practice was stopped by legislation for fear that the valuable trees would be destroyed. The leaves are dark green, glossy, leathery and fragrant, grouped in clusters at the end of the slender secondary branches.

Traditionally, allspice trees are not cultivated in orderly plantations; the trees grow where the seeds have been dropped by birds, shooting up along fences and in thickets, where they are protected from livestock. It was once believed that in order to germinate, the seeds had to pass through the intestines of birds; however, it is now known that they will germinate if sown immediately after being removed from fresh ripe fruits. Both male and female trees are required to produce seedlings. Pimento farmers clear away unwanted trees in order to gain ready access for harvesting, creating what the locals call a "walk" rather than a plantation.

The allspice berry, when correctly cured and dried, is dark reddish brown in color, spherical in shape and $1/8$ to $1/4$ inch (3 to 5 mm) in diameter. A small handful shaken vigorously next to your ear will rattle distinctly, thanks to the tiny seeds gyrating inside. While the whole allspice berry emits only a faint perfume, ground allspice releases distinctive aromatic notes reminiscent of cloves, cinnamon and nutmeg.

Other Varieties

The **bayberry tree** (*Pimenta racemosa*) is an allied species. Its leaves are distilled to yield bay oil, which is used in perfumery and to produce the fragrant toiletry known as bay rum. Two other plants with *allspice* in their names are **Carolina allspice** (*Calycanthus floridus*) and **Californian allspice** (*C. occidentalis*), which are both deciduous shrubs with scented leaves. These plants are rarely used in cooking, as they are mildly toxic, although the leaves are sometimes added to potpourri.

Processing

Allspice is another fine example of how the enzymes in spices react when dried to produce pungent characteristic flavors. Allspice is harvested by using clippers to remove the twigs that bear small clusters of unripe berries. These berries are threshed from the stems, then dried and cured; this takes the moisture content down from about 60% to 10–12%. It is interesting to note that, even in its native land, there is no culinary application for the fresh berries.

Travels in the Spice Trade

Seeing the allspice trees on the hillsides above St. Anne's Bay in Jamaica was a truly memorable experience. It's also where we learned how seriously Jamaicans take the allspice industry. Their Ministry of Agriculture has written "the proper procedures for the reaping and curing of pimento" into the Agricultural Practices Act: "Any breach of these regulations constitutes an offence against the law which is punishable by fines or imprisonment."

Although allspice is cultivated in a number of tropical countries, it supposedly never thrives as well as it does in its native habitat. One can certainly understand why the Jamaicans are so protective of this industry. Measures include actively discouraging the traditional practice of breaking the tree's limbs to harvest unripe berries (pickers are paid by weight, and it is much faster for them to break the fruit-laden branches than to cut them properly). Not only does this practice injure the tree, it is one of the main causes of dieback disease and what the Ministry of Agriculture calls "inconsistent bearing." Harvested trees may lose as much as 80–90% of their foliage as a result of this practice and may take as long as four years to recover sufficiently to produce another crop. Moreover, breaking the limbs frequently creates shock in the tree and leaves large open wounds that provide easy access for rot.

Determining Dryness

Most spices are dried to a level of 10–12% moisture—above that mold will grow. The traditional way to determine when the berries are dry is the "hand-shake" method. It's a simple technique—a handful of berries is shaken to see if they rattle. If they do, the moisture level should be around 12%. It isn't very scientific, but it works. Some farmers claim to be able to estimate the moisture content to within 0.5%!

The curing process begins by spreading out the berries over a large concrete area that looks like a tennis court, called a "barbecue," which is painted black to absorb the heat of the sun. The berries are spread evenly over the barbecue to a depth of about 2 inches (5 cm). They are raked a few times during the day to help create even drying. In the past, at night the berries were raked into piles and covered with tarpaulins. However, this practice was changed because robbers often stole the berries. Now the curing berries are raked up and locked in sheds overnight, covered with a tarpaulin to keep in the heat. This "sweating" process encourages the enzyme reaction. It also protects the pimentos from getting wet if they happen to be drying outside.

Buying and Storage

Whole allspice berries should be a consistent dark reddish brown color and spherical. They should have a rough surface, which is caused by the presence of volatile oil glands. The aroma should be pleasant, mildly clove-like and devoid of any mustiness. Variations in the size of berries do not affect quality; however, when using berries whole in foods, it is advisable to select the larger ones for better visual appeal. Whole allspice, when stored in airtight packaging away from extremes of heat, light and humidity, will retain its flavor for up to 3 years.

Ground allspice should be a rich dark brown, have a distinct warm aroma of cloves mildly tempered with cinnamon notes, and be somewhat oily, never dry and dusty, when rubbed between thumb and forefinger. Because a ground spice gives off its volatile elements more readily than a whole spice, ground allspice stored in the same manner as whole allspice has a useful storage life of 12 to 18 months.

Use

Allspice is found in many recipes for cakes and cookies. It is one of the ingredients in "mixed spice," a British baking blend similar to North America's pumpkin pie spice. Some cooks use allspice as a substitute for cloves in sweet dishes, as the clove flavor is imparted more subtly. Allspice contains the same volatile oil, eugenol, that is found in cloves and, surprisingly, in the herb basil. The next time you have a fresh basil leaf, crush it and smell the clove-like aroma. No wonder, then, that allspice also complements the flavor of tomatoes and is widely used in the manufacture of tomato-based barbecue and pasta sauces. The Scandinavians include allspice in their famous marinated raw herring, and it often features in pickles, pâtés and smoked meats.

Use whole allspice berries when you want the flavor without the dark brown powder coloring the dish. For example, add a few allspice berries to stewed fruits along with a cinnamon stick, a whole star anise and a vanilla bean to make a deliciously sweet-spiced dessert. While it is no relation to pepper, a common practice is to add about a teaspoon (5 mL) of small allspice berries to the peppercorns in a pepper mill. When ground, the aromatic sweet spiciness complements traditional freshly ground pepper very well. Allspice is found in many curry blends and commercial spice blends designed for seasoning seafood and red meats. A small amount of allspice can be used to flavor root vegetables and spinach during cooking, and it also complements vegetable soups, especially tomato.

WEIGHT PER TEASPOON (5 mL)

- about 10 whole berries: 2 g
- ground: 2.8 g

SUGGESTED QUANTITY PER POUND (500 g)

- red meats: 1/2 tsp (2 mL)
- white meats: 1/2 tsp (2 mL)
- vegetables: 1/8 tsp (0.5 mL)
- grains and pulses: 1/4 tsp (1 mL)
- baked goods: 1/4 tsp (1 mL)

Jerk Chicken

In the 17th century, the Maroons, Jamaican slaves who had escaped from the British, preserved the wild boar they hunted by marinating it in spices and slow-cooking it over a fire. The technique became known as "jerking," and the seasoning they used remains a Jamaican tradition. This dish has some of the heat and spiciness associated with Cajun blackened fish or chicken, but the allspice gives it a unique, mouth-watering flavor. Serve with rice and salad or in a bun topped with coleslaw.

**Makes
6 servings**

Preparation time:
1 hour, 15 minutes

Cooking time:
15 minutes

Tip

For deeper flavor, marinate the chicken overnight in the refrigerator.

• **Food processor**

MARINADE

1 tbsp	olive oil	15 mL
1	onion, roughly chopped	1
1	clove garlic, chopped	1
2 tbsp	rum	30 mL
1 tsp	packed light brown sugar	5 mL
1 tbsp	freshly squeezed lime juice	15 mL
2 tsp	ground allspice	10 mL
1 tsp	hot pepper flakes	5 mL
1 tsp	ground ginger	5 mL
1 tsp	dried thyme	5 mL
½ tsp	freshly ground black pepper	2 mL
½ tsp	fine sea salt	2 mL
6	chicken thighs	6

1. *Marinade:* In a skillet over medium heat, heat oil. Add onion and garlic and sauté for 2 minutes, until soft.

2. Transfer onion mixture to food processor fitted with the metal blade. Add rum, brown sugar, lime juice, allspice, hot pepper flakes, ginger, thyme, pepper and salt and blitz to a paste. Transfer paste to a resealable bag, add chicken and seal. Turn bag to evenly coat chicken and refrigerate for at least 1 hour (see Tip, left).

3. Broil or grill chicken on medium-high heat for 5 minutes per side, or until juices run clear.

Amchur

Mangifera indica

Names in Other Languages

- **French:** mangue
- **German:** Mango
- **Indian:** aamchoor, amchur
- **Italian:** mango
- **Spanish:** manguey

The name *amchur* comes from the Hindi for "mango" (*am*) and "powder" (*choor*).

Family: Anacardiaceae

Other Names: aamchur, amchoor, green mango powder

Flavor Group: Tangy

Parts Used: fruits (as a spice)

Background

Mango trees are native to India, Burma and the Malaysian peninsula; they have been cultivated in India for more than 4,000 years. The 16th-century Mogul emperor Akbar initiated the planting of 100,000 mango trees during his rule of India. Around the same time, 16th- and 17th-century Europeans spread their cultivation of mango trees to most tropical and subtropical regions of the world, where they thrived.

Culinary Information

Combines with
- cardamom
- chile
- cinnamon
- coriander (leaf and seed)
- cumin
- curry leaf
- ginger
- paprika
- pepper
- star anise
- turmeric

Traditional Uses
- curries
- pickles and chutneys
- meat and seafood
- vegetables

Spice Blends
- curry blends
- chaat masala
- seafood masalas
- seasoning blends
- rubs (as alternative to citric acid)

All parts of the mango tree are used, but the bark, leaves, flowers and seeds are used mostly for medicinal purposes. In times of famine the seeds have been ground into flour. Green mango is used predominantly in Indian and Southeast Asian food.

The Plant

Amchur is made from dried unripe fruit of the mango tree, a tropical evergreen. The tree can reach up to 130 feet (40 m) tall and has a lifespan of 100 years.

For many of us who have enjoyed the abundance of mangoes in northern Australia or have become addicted to the delicious fruit when it is in season, the notion that this tree provides a useful and effective souring agent comes as something of a surprise.

There are two forms of amchur: dried in slices and ground. The dried green mango slices are light brown in color, with a rough texture; when they are ground, the resulting powder is fine and varies in color from a pale gray to yellowish beige, depending on whether and how much tumeric powder has been added (see Processing). The aroma of ground amchur is warm, fruity and slightly resinous; it creates a tingling, almost fizzy sensation at the back of the nose. The flavor is fruit-like and pleasantly acidic from the high proportion of naturally occurring citric acid (around 15%).

Processing

Green unripe mangoes about 2 to 4 inches (5 to 10 cm) long are picked, peeled, sliced and sun-dried. After drying, the slices are ground to a fine gray powder, which is sometimes blended with up to 10% turmeric powder to create a more attractive color. The earthy notes of turmeric also pleasantly balance some of the acidity and resinous character.

Buying and Storage

It is advisable to buy amchur powder, as the slices are not easy to powder at home. Buy fairly small amounts, because the subtle flavor characteristics will diminish within 12 months, even when correctly stored. Store in an airtight container, avoiding extremes of heat, light and humidity.

Use

Amchur powder is used for its souring abilities. It is a good substitute for lemon juice—1 tsp (5 mL) amchur powder can replace 3 tbsp (45 mL) lemon juice. Its pleasing acidic taste also makes amchur a convenient alternative to tamarind in curries and vegetable dishes and with chickpeas. In spice blends it adds a more agreeable tang than citric acid, which is somewhat harsh by comparison. Amchur is often an ingredient in marinades because of its tenderizing effect on meat and its compatibility with other marinating spices, such as ginger, pepper, coriander, cumin and star anise.

WEIGHT PER TEASPOON (5 mL)
- ground: 2.6 g

SUGGESTED QUANTITY PER POUND (500 g)
- red meats: 1 tsp (5 mL)
- white meats: ½ tsp (2 mL)
- vegetables: ½ tsp (2 mL)
- grains and pulses: ½ tsp (2 mL)
- baked goods: ¼ tsp (1 mL)

Amchur and Herb Marinade

This marinade is perfect for salmon or tuna but can also be used on chicken or lamb. The fruity acidity of the amchur complements the fresh herbs in the marinade.

**Makes about
½ cup/125 mL
(enough marinade
for 4 to 6 pieces
of meat or fish)**

Preparation time:
 10 minutes

Cooking time: none

- **Food processor or blender**

1	mild green finger chile, seeded and chopped	1
1 cup	lightly packed fresh cilantro leaves	250 mL
½ cup	lightly packed fresh mint leaves	125 mL
2 tbsp	olive oil	30 mL
1 tsp	amchur powder	5 mL
1 tsp	garam masala	5 mL
1 tsp	ground turmeric	5 mL
3 tbsp	plain Balkan-style yogurt	45 mL
	Sea salt and freshly ground black pepper	

1. In food processor fitted with the metal blade or blender at high speed, combine chile, cilantro, mint, oil, amchur, garam masala and turmeric and blitz into a paste. Add yogurt and pulse to combine. Season with salt and pepper to taste. The marinade will keep in an airtight container in the refrigerator for up to 3 days.

Tangy Chickpea Curry

I love the tartness of this quick and easy curry. The amchur gives it a distinct zing that works so well with the earthy cumin and turmeric. Serve with Basmati Pilaf (page 164) and alongside Shrimp Moilee (page 248).

Makes 4 side servings

Preparation time:
5 minutes

Cooking time:
20 minutes

Tips

Ghee is a type of clarified butter used in Indian cooking. If you don't have any, you can substitute an equal amount of butter or clarified butter.

Kashmiri chiles do not necessarily come from Kashmir. They are a popular Indian chile with a very high color content, turning the food they are used in strikingly red. If not available, a medium-hot ground chile such as a long red chile can be used.

To prepare chickpeas: Soak overnight in a large bowl of water, covering the chickpeas by at least 1 inch (2.5 cm). Drain and rinse well, then place in a large saucepan of salted water, covering the chickpeas by at least 5 inches (12.5 cm). Simmer for 1½ hours or until tender, then drain. Refrigerate for up to 1 week and freeze for up to 3 months.

1 tbsp	ghee (see Tips, left)	15 mL
1	onion, minced	1
3	cloves garlic, minced	3
1½ tsp	ground coriander	7 mL
1 tsp	ground cumin	5 mL
½ tsp	ground turmeric	2 mL
1½ tsp	amchur powder	7 mL
½ tsp	garam masala	2 mL
¼ tsp	fine sea salt	1 mL
¼ tsp	ground Kashmiri chile (see Tips, left)	1 mL
1 cup	crushed tomatoes, with juice	250 mL
2 cups	cooked chickpeas (see Tips, left)	500 mL
1 cup	water	250 mL
	Sea salt and freshly ground black pepper	

1. In a large saucepan over medium heat, melt ghee. Add onion and garlic and sauté for 3 minutes, until soft. Add coriander, cumin, turmeric, amchur, garam masala, salt and ground chile and cook, stirring, for another 2 minutes, until well combined. Add tomatoes, chickpeas and water and mix well. Reduce heat and simmer, stirring occasionally, for 15 minutes, until thickened. Season with salt and pepper to taste.

Angelica

Angelica archangelica (also known as *Archangelica officinalis*)

Family: Apiaceae (formerly Umbelliferae)

Other Names: garden angelica, great angelica, holy ghost, masterwort, wild celery

Flavor Group: Medium

Parts Used: roots, stems, stalks and leaves (as a herb)

Background

The folklore supporting angelica's naming as a "guardian angel" is, to my knowledge, undisputed. It is said that an angel appeared in a monk's dream and revealed the efficacy of angelica as a cure for the plague. Angelica was widely used in pagan and Christian festivals; it is believed to have originated in the far north of Europe, particularly Lapland, Iceland and Russia, although some botanical historians believe it may have its origins in Syria.

Most of us are familiar with angelica as a sugary preserved confection for flavoring and decorating cakes, cookies and ice cream. However, unprocessed angelica has savory applications. In Lapland, for instance, stalks of angelica are gathered before flowering and the leaves are stripped off and dried for later use. The stem is peeled and the fresh, succulent pieces are regarded as a delicacy to be eaten raw. These days the most popular commercial use of angelica root is in liqueurs such as vermouth and chartreuse; it is also a "secret ingredient" in some brands of gin.

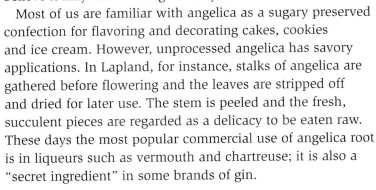

Culinary Information

Combines with
- juniper
- lavender
- lemon balm
- nutmeg
- pepper

Traditional Uses
- **fresh leaves:** with rhubarb and spinach
- **dried leaves:** tea
- **seeds:** extracts in liqueurs
- **crystallized stems:** cakes and cookies

Spice Blends
- not commonly used in herb and spice blends

The Plant

Angelica is one of the most flamboyant-looking herbs. Its long, thick, hollow, celery-like stems groggily support huge umbels of greenish white flower heads above foliage of bright green serrated, flat leaves. Angelica plants grow to around 5 to 8 feet (1.5 to 2.5 m) tall; they don't bear their delicately fragrant flowers until the second year of growth, after which the plants die. All parts of the angelica plant are used. The roots, stems, leaves and seeds contain tannins and acids that convey nuances of an earthy, bittersweet and warm flavor reminiscent of juniper. The stems and leaves appeal to the cook; an essential oil extracted from the roots and seeds by steam distillation is used primarily in food and beverage manufacturing.

Processing

The most popular way to preserve angelica is to crystallize the thick, grooved stems with sugar and green food coloring. This makes an attractive bright green decoration and flavoring for sweets.

Angelica leaves may be dried and infused as a tea. To dry angelica leaves, pick the darker, more mature leaves and spread them out on a sheet of clean paper in a dark, well-ventilated place for a few days. When the leaves feel quite crisp to the touch, crumble them and store in an airtight container.

Angelica seeds may be dried by hanging the dead seed-bearing flower heads upside down in a warm, dark place. When dry, thresh and collect the seeds.

A

Buying and Storage

The availability of fresh angelica is limited, so if you want to use the fresh leaves or stems you will probably need to grow it yourself. Angelica seeds or seedlings are best planted in spring in moist, well-drained, rich soil, with filtered sunlight.

Dried angelica leaves should always be stored away from humidity, preferably in an airtight container. Under these conditions they will keep their color and flavor for up to 3 years. Angelica seeds should be stored in an airtight container away from extremes of heat, light and humidity. Under these conditions, the seeds will keep for up to 2 years.

When buying crystallized or candied angelica, seek some assurance from the merchant that it is actually angelica. Many imitations are passed off as the real thing, the most common being pieces of stiff green jelly.

Use

A few tender young angelica leaves can be added to salads. The stems and stalks impart a complementary sweet flavor to stewed fruits, jams and jellies, especially those made with highly acidic ingredients such as rhubarb and plums. The roots can be cooked and eaten as a vegetable in much the same way as the bulbous root of fennel. A tea, not unlike Chinese green tea, can be made by infusing the dried leaves of angelica in hot water and drinking it without milk or sugar. Crystallized angelica (made from the stems) makes an attractive decoration when cut into small pieces and blended into the batter for cakes, muffins and shortbread cookies or placed on top after baking.

SUGGESTED QUANTITY PER POUND (500 g)
- **vegetables:** ½ cup (125 mL) dried leaves
- **baked goods:** 1 tbsp (15 mL) chopped crystallized stems

Crystallized Angelica

One of my grandmother's friends used to crystallize orange and lemon peel, which was quite a common practice, and it's sad to think that it's not a popular thing anymore. Granny had this recipe for crystallizing angelica, which requires patience. However, the process is time-consuming rather than complicated, and the end result is very rewarding when you use it to decorate your own cakes.

Makes about 1 cup (250 mL)

Preparation time: 1 day

Cooking and drying time: 8 days

- - - - - - - - - - - - - - - -

Tip

For best results, make crystallized angelica when the weather is dry, not humid.

6 to 8	young stems angelica, cut into 4-inch (10 cm) lengths	6 to 8
½ cup	fine sea salt	125 mL
2 cups	boiling water	500 mL
3½ cups	granulated sugar	875 mL
2¾ cups	water	675 mL
	Additional granulated sugar	

1. Place angelica in a large, heat-resistant bowl. In a measuring cup, mix salt with boiling water until completely dissolved. Pour over angelica (it should be fully immersed). Cover and set aside at room temperature for 24 hours.

2. Using a colander, drain angelica. Using your fingers, peel off and discard the outer, celery-like fibers. Wash peeled angelica under cold running water. Set aside.

3. In a medium saucepan over medium-high heat, bring sugar and water to a boil. Add prepared angelica and boil for 20 minutes, until just starting to soften. Using a slotted spoon, transfer to a wire rack to drain (reserve syrup in an airtight container in the refrigerator). Set aside at room temperature, uncovered, for 4 days, until dry and glossy.

4. In a medium saucepan over medium heat, boil prepared angelica in reserved syrup for 20 to 30 minutes, until syrup is absorbed. Remove from heat and set pan aside to cool. Transfer cooled angelica to a wire rack to drain (discard remaining syrup) and set aside, uncovered, for 4 days, until dry and glossy. Dust thoroughly with additional sugar and store in an airtight container for up to 1 year.

Granny's Glazed Pears

Dinner was always a treat at Somerset Cottage, where my grandparents lived. Granny had an amazing herb garden at her disposal and was often testing recipes for her books. Bright green angelica was the best candy we could expect to see on our dessert plate, which made this dish a favorite.

Makes 4 servings

Preparation time:
10 minutes

Cooking time:
30 minutes

Tips

Superfine (caster) sugar is a very fine granulated sugar typically used in recipes that require a faster-dissolving granule. If you can't find it in stores, you can make your own by using a food processor fitted with the metal blade to process granulated sugar into a very fine, sand-like consistency.

If you don't have an abundance of passionfruits on hand, canned passionfruit pulp can be bought in most supermarkets.

PEARS

4	whole Bosc pears, peeled and core removed	4
1 tsp	ground cinnamon	5 mL
1 tsp	superfine (caster) sugar (see Tips, left)	5 mL
2 tbsp	butter, softened	30 mL
1 cup	passionfruit pulp (see Tips, left)	250 mL
4	stems crystallized angelica (see page 76)	4

SYRUP

1 cup	water	250 mL
½ cup	superfine (caster) sugar	125 mL
	Whipped cream or ice cream, to serve	

1. *Pears:* In a small bowl, combine cinnamon and sugar. Place a knob of butter and a quarter of the cinnamon sugar in each pear hollow. Arrange pears, standing upright, in a medium saucepan and set pan aside.

2. *Syrup:* In a small saucepan over medium heat, combine water and sugar and bring to a boil; boil for 10 minutes, stirring constantly, until sugar is completely dissolved.

3. Pour sugar syrup over pears, cover and simmer gently over medium heat until just tender, about 10 minutes (depending on ripeness of pears). Remove from heat and ladle syrup continuously over pears for a few minutes, until nicely glazed.

4. Using a slotted spoon, carefully transfer pears to a serving dish. Add passionfruit pulp to the remaining syrup and whisk to combine. Pour syrup over pears. Decorate each pear with an angelica stem and chill for 1 to 2 hours. Serve with whipped cream or ice cream alongside.

Anise Seed

Pimpenella anisum

Names in Other Languages

- **Arabic:** yanisun, habbet hilwa
- **Chinese (C):** daai wuih heong
- **Chinese (M):** da hui xiang, yang hui xiang
- **Dutch:** anijs
- **French:** anis vert, boucage
- **German:** Anis
- **Greek:** glikaniso, anison
- **Indian:** saunf, sompf, sonf, souf, suara
- **Indonesian:** jintan manis
- **Italian:** anice
- **Japanese:** anisu
- **Portuguese:** erva-doce
- **Russian:** anis
- **Spanish:** anis
- **Swedish:** anis
- **Turkish:** anason, mesir out, nanahan

Family: Apiaceae (formerly Umbelliferae)
Other Names: aniseed, anise, sweet cumin
Flavor Group: Sweet
Parts Used: seeds (as a spice), leaves (as a herb)

Background

Anise is native to the Middle East and is widely cultivated in temperate climates, notably North Africa, Greece, Turkey, southern Russia, Malta, Spain, Italy, Mexico and Central America. It is claimed that anise was found in Egypt as early as 1500 BCE. Certainly it was highly regarded in first century Rome for its digestive properties, which are attributed to the volatile oil compound anethole, a substance also found in fennel seeds and star anise. At the conclusion of indulgent feasts, the ancient Romans (lacking modern antacids) would consume cakes made with anise seeds and other aromatic spices to aid digestion and freshen the breath.

During the Middle Ages its cultivation spread to Europe, which is interesting, since the plant flowers and produces seeds only in warmer climatic conditions. Anise seed was often used to flavor horse and cattle feed. Dogs like its taste too, and it is often included in prepared pet food. It is also thought to attract mice to mousetraps!

Anise oil, extracted by steam distillation, often provides the licorice flavoring in sweets, and it is now widely used in the manufacture of confectionery. Anise also appears in cough drops, a French cordial called anisette, and a number of anise-flavored alcoholic drinks such as ouzo, Pernod, pastis and aguardiente, a Latin American favorite. Anise seed should not be confused with star anise, which is predominantly a Chinese spice. However, the essential oil of star anise is often used as a substitute for anise seed.

Culinary Information

Combines with

- allspice
- cinnamon
- cloves
- coriander seed
- cumin
- dill seed
- fennel seed
- nutmeg
- pepper
- star anise

Traditional Uses

- vegetable and seafood dishes
- pasta sauces with cheese
- cakes and cookies
- chicken and shellfish pies
- liqueurs (extract from seeds)

Spice Blends

- not commonly used in spice blends

The Plant

One of the most delicate of herb plants, anise grows to a spindly 20 inches (50 cm) tall. It has feathery flat, serrated leaves reminiscent of Italian parsley, and in late summer it bears creamy white flowers on fine, wispy stems. Anise seed, which is gathered after flowering and used as a spice, consists of two tiny seeds, oval and crescent-shaped, about $\frac{1}{8}$ inch (3 mm) long. When split, many of these seeds retain the fine stalk that passes through the center of the fruit, giving the seed the appearance, upon close inspection, of a tiny mouse. The pale brown seeds with their fine, lighter-colored ribs have a distinct licorice flavor that is not overly pungent or lingering.

Processing

Anise will flower and fruit only after a long, hot summer; these climatic conditions are also excellent for drying the seeds. The seed heads are harvested and hung or laid out to dry in a warm, well-ventilated area with some direct sunlight. Once dry and crisp, the flower heads are rubbed to separate the seeds from the flowers and pieces of stem, then sieved, which makes them ready for storage. This process will often remove the fine stalk that is attached to some of the seeds, making them look cleaner and more uniform.

Buying and Storage

Confusion often arises when markets incorrectly label fresh fennel bulb as anise or aniseed, which it is not. Anise seed is best purchased in its whole form; when correctly stored, it will retain its flavor for up to 3 years.

Because of their small size, anise seeds are most often used whole in cooking rather than in ground form. The seeds should be greenish brown to light brown in color and contain a minimum amount of husks and fine, hairlike stalks. Store in an airtight container and keep away from extremes of heat, light and humidity, as this will accelerate deterioration and loss of the fresh anise notes.

Use

The fresh, distinctively licorice and fennel flavor notes in anise seed make it an ideal spice for Indian vegetable and seafood dishes, although Indians more often use its close cousin fennel seed. The mild licorice flavor of anise seed complements cookies and cakes, and it is used in traditional baking in both Germany and Italy. Scandinavian rye bread contains anise seed, as does a wide range of processed meats. A small amount of whole or ground anise seed can be added to vegetable soups, white sauces and chicken and shellfish pies. The fresh flavor of the seeds has a balancing effect on rich cheese dishes; it is employed to cut the greasiness of some ingredients in Moroccan cuisine and Turkish and Greek dolmades.

Fresh anise leaves can be included in green salads and added to egg dishes for a subtle tarragon-like flavor.

WEIGHT PER TEASPOON (5 mL)
- **whole:** 2.1 g
- **ground:** 2.7 g

SUGGESTED QUANTITY PER POUND (500 g)
- **red meats:** 2 tsp (10 mL)
- **white meats:** 1 tsp (5 mL)
- **vegetables:** 1 tsp (5 mL)
- **grains and pulses:** 1 tsp (5 mL)
- **baked goods:** 1 tsp (5 mL)

Date Compote

This simple compote is a delicious accompaniment to a cheese board. It also makes a lovely alternative to mayonnaise on a baguette topped with sharp Cheddar and baby spinach leaves.

Makes 2 cups (500 mL)

Preparation time:
10 minutes, plus up to 1 hour for cooling

Cooking time:
15 minutes

Tip

I recommend using Medjool dates for their superior softness.

1 cup	pitted dried dates, quartered (see Tip, left)	250 mL
1 cup	soft dried figs, cut into ½-inch (1 cm) pieces	250 mL
1 cup	port	250 mL
1 tsp	whole anise seed	5 mL

1. In a small saucepan over medium heat, combine dates, figs, port and anise seed and bring to a boil. As soon as mixture begins to boil, remove from heat and cover with a tight-fitting lid. Set aside, covered, until cooled completely. Transfer to an airtight container and refrigerate for up to 2 weeks.

Torcetti

Torcetti ("little twists") are yeast-raised Italian cookies from Piemonte—sort of sweet grissini (breadsticks), if you like. The flavoring varies, but anise seed is a commonly included spice.

Makes 16 large cookies

Preparation time:
10 minutes

Cooking time:
15 minutes

Tips

To activate the yeast, make sure the milk is warmed to blood temperature (about 98°F/37°C) or "hand hot"—if you put your fingers in the liquid, you should not feel a discernible change in temperature.

For smaller cookies, divide each of the 4 large pieces of dough into 6 or 8 equal pieces.

- **Electric mixer**
- **2 baking sheets, lined with parchment paper**

½ cup	warm (not boiling) milk (see Tips, left)	125 mL
2 tsp	granulated sugar	10 mL
1 tsp	instant active dry yeast	5 mL
8 oz	butter, softened	250 g
2	eggs, beaten	2
3 cups	all-purpose flour	750 mL
2 tsp	whole anise seed	10 mL
	Additional ¼ cup (60 mL) sugar, for coating	

1. In a bowl, combine milk, sugar and yeast; stir until dissolved. Set aside for 5 to 10 minutes to activate (the mixture will turn frothy, which means it's ready for use).

2. Using mixer at low speed, cream butter for 1 minute, until pale. Add eggs and beat until incorporated, then add activated yeast mixture. Beat well, then add half of the flour. Mix until incorporated, then add the remaining flour and anise seed and mix until a stiff dough forms. Cover bowl with a kitchen towel and set aside for about 1 hour (it will rise a little, but not like a regular dough).

3. Preheat oven to 375°F (190°C). Place ¼ cup (60 mL) sugar on a plate or in a shallow bowl.

4. Turn dough out onto a lightly floured work surface. Divide into 4 equal pieces, then divide each piece again into 4 pieces (you should have 16 equal pieces). Using the flat of your palm, roll each piece into a thin strip about ½ inch (1 cm) thick and 6 inches (15 cm) long. Keeping each strip lying flat, take the ends and cross them over each other a third of the way up. Firmly pressing down join with your finger to seal (it will look a bit like a ribbon loop or crossed legs). Dredge in additional sugar and transfer to prepared baking sheets. Bake in preheated oven for 10 to 12 minutes, until golden brown. Using a spatula or palette knife, carefully transfer cookies to a wire rack to cool. Store in an airtight container at room temperature for up to for 3 days.

Annatto Seed

Bixa orellana

Names in Other Languages

- **Chinese (C):** yin ju syuh
- **Chinese (M):** yan zhi shu
- **Dutch:** achiote, roucou
- **Filipino:** achuete, atsuete
- **French:** rocou, roucou
- **German:** Annatto
- **Indian:** latkhan, sendri
- **Indonesian:** kesumba
- **Italian:** anotto
- **Russian:** biksa, pomadnoe derevo
- **Spanish:** achiote, achote
- **Turkish:** arnatto
- **Vietnamese:** hot dieu mau

Family: Bixaceae

Other Names: achiote, achuete, bija, latkhan, lipstick tree, natural color E1606, roucou, urucu

Flavor Group: Pungent

Parts Used: seeds (as a spice)

Background

Annatto is native to the Caribbean, Mexico and Central and South America. It is now cultivated in many tropical countries. Spanish colonists from Central America and the West Indies took annatto to the Philippines in the 17th century. The shiny foliage and dramatically beautiful rose-like flowers made annatto a popular hedge shrub in colonial gardens. Annatto's history has been most strongly connected to its use as a coloring for foods and also as "oxblood," which is a dye made from the pulp surrounding annatto seeds, used in textile manufacturing. Annatto was applied as a war paint and sun protection by the Caribs. It is believed that early European settlers in the Americas were referring to this annatto coloring when they coined the term "redskins" to describe the Native Americans. Annatto was also valued by the ancient Mayan peoples of Guatemala.

It's easy to see why annatto is called "lipstick tree"—just a smear of the bright red pulp surrounding the seeds is as effective as many commercial lipsticks. Annatto has been used as a substitute for saffron; although it replicates the color to some degree, it certainly doesn't capture its flavor.

Culinary Information

Combines with

- allspice
- chile
- coriander
- cumin
- garlic
- oregano
- paprika
- pepper

Traditional Uses

- natural yellow coloring (with many foods)
- pastes to season chicken and pork
- Asian roasts and preserved meats

Spice Blends

- achiote paste

A natural color, E1606, is made from annatto. In food manufacturing this has become a popular alternative to the potentially allergenic artificial colors tartrazine (E102) and Sunset Yellow (E110). However, recent studies have indicated that some individuals may also be allergic to annatto.

The Plant

Annatto seeds are collected from a relatively small tropical evergreen tree that grows 16 to 33 feet (5 to 10 m) tall. The leaves are heart-shaped and glossy and provide an attractive background to the large, bright pink flowers, which have the appearance of wild roses. Prickly heart-shaped seed-bearing pods form after flowering; when ripe, they split open to reveal a reddish yellow pulp surrounding about 50 pyramid-shaped, indented red seeds.

Dried annatto seeds are about $1/4$ inch (5 mm) long, look like little stones, and are a dark red oxide (rusty) color. When cut in half, they reveal a white center inside the dusty, finger-staining red skin. The aroma is pleasant, sweetish and peppery and has faint overtones of old dry peppermint. The flavor is dry, mild and earthy.

Processing

The prickly, predator-deterring fruits are harvested when ripe and then macerated in water to allow the dye to settle. This sediment is collected, dried and pressed into cakes for further processing into dyes, cosmetics and food coloring. For culinary use the seeds are simply dried and packed for shipment.

Buying and Storage

Annatto seeds should be a uniform dark red-brick color and free from flaky pieces of dried pulp. Purchase whole seeds and store them in an airtight container away from extremes of heat, light and humidity. When properly stored, good-quality annatto seeds will last up to 3 years.

Use

Annatto is used primarily as a coloring in fish, rice and vegetable dishes. In Jamaica it goes into a traditional sauce for salt cod and ackee, a famous Jamaican dish (ackee is a fruit from West Africa used in Jamaican dishes). In the Philippines annatto is a key element in pipian, a dish made with cubes of chicken and pork. Mexicans use annatto to color their stews, sauces and tacos. When you see fresh chicken on sale in supermarkets in Mexico, you will notice how yellow the flesh looks. This is an indication of quality to consumers; more often than not the coloring has come from annatto. In Yucatán, annatto is an ingredient in pastes such as recado colorado and adobo. In Asian cooking, the Chinese use annatto to color many meats, from roast meats to boiled pigs' snouts, ears and tails. In the West, annatto is an effective colorant in many cheeses, including Red Cheshire and Leicester. The rind of Edam cheese is colored by annatto, as is smoked fish.

There are two ways to effectively extract the color from annatto seeds:

- To color 1 cup (250 mL) rice or vegetable dishes, achieving a result similar to saffron, lightly simmer $1/2$ tsp (2 mL) annatto seeds in 2 tbsp (30 mL) water for a few minutes. Allow the liquid to cool.
- To color curries and meats, make an oil (*aceite*) by heating $1/2$ tsp (2 mL) annatto seeds and 2 tbsp (30 mL) oil in a saucepan over low heat for a few minutes—being careful not to burn the seeds—until the oil turns golden. (When lard is used in place of olive oil, this is called *manteca de achiote*.) Remove from heat and set aside to cool. Using a fine-mesh sieve, strain (discarding seeds) and store in an airtight jar for up to 12 months.

Achiote paste (an important ingredient in Mexican cooking) is arguably the most traditional way to use annatto seeds.

WEIGHT PER TEASPOON (5 mL)
- **whole:** 4.3 g

SUGGESTED QUANTITY PER POUND (500 g)
- **red meats:** 1 tsp (5 mL)
- **white meats:** 1 tsp (5 mL)
- **vegetables:** $1/2$ tsp (2 mL)
- **grains and pulses:** $1/2$ tsp (2 mL)
- **baked goods:** $1/2$ tsp (2 mL)

Achiote Paste

Achiote paste is probably the most traditional way to use annatto seeds, which are renowned for their distinctive earthy flavor and deep coloring. Achiote originated in Mexico's Yucatán Peninsula and is now used in a variety of Mexican dishes, my favorite being Pork Pibil (page 88).

About 3 tbsp (45 mL)

Preparation time:
5 minutes

• **Mortar and pestle or spice grinder**

½ tsp	annatto seeds	2 mL
½ tsp	dried oregano	2 mL
½ tsp	cumin seeds	2 mL
½ tsp	whole black peppercorns	2 mL
½ tsp	whole allspice	2 mL
2	large cloves garlic, crushed	2
1 tbsp	water	15 mL
½ tsp	white vinegar	2 mL
¼ tsp	fine sea salt	1 mL

1. In spice grinder or mortar, combine annatto, oregano, cumin, peppercorns and allspice and grind until mixture becomes a fine powder. Add garlic, water, vinegar and salt and combine thoroughly. Transfer to a sterilized jar and store in the refrigerator for up to 1 week.

Pork Pibil

This recipe from the Yucatán region of Mexico uses a traditional achiote paste (see page 87) made with annatto seeds, which gives it its characteristic red color. The slow-cooked pork is rich with flavor and perfect eaten with rice or used as a filling for tacos.

Makes
6 servings

Preparation time:
20 minutes,
plus 2 hours (or
up to 24 hours)
for marinating

Cooking time: 3 to
4 hours

1	recipe achiote paste (page 87)	1
2 lbs	pork butt (shoulder), cut into roughly 5-inch (12.5 cm) pieces	1 kg
1 cup	freshly squeezed orange juice	250 mL
1	large red onion, halved and sliced	1
3	sprigs fresh oregano	3
1 tbsp	butter	15 mL
2	large tomatoes, roughly chopped	2
1 tsp	fine sea salt	5 mL
½ cup	water	125 mL

1. In a resealable bag or non-reactive bowl, combine prepared achiote paste, pork, orange juice, onion and oregano. Cover and refrigerate for at least 2 hours or overnight.

2. Preheat oven to 250°F (120°C).

3. In a Dutch oven over medium-high heat, melt butter. When butter is foaming, add prepared pork with marinade. Cook, stirring constantly, for 5 minutes, until lightly browned; then add tomatoes, salt and water. Cover tightly with aluminum foil or lid and transfer to preheated oven. Cook for 2 to 3 hours, until meat is tender and falling apart. Remove from oven and, using a fork, mash the meat into the sauce until well combined.

Asafetida

Ferula asafoetida (also known as F. scorodosma)

Names in Other Languages

- **Arabic:** tyib, haltheeth, abu kabeer
- **Burmese:** sheingho
- **Chinese (C):** a ngaih
- **Chinese (M):** a wei
- **Danish:** dyvelsdraek
- **French:** ferule asafoetida
- **German:** Stinkendes, Steckenkraut
- **Greek:** aza
- **Indian:** heeng, hing powder, perunkaya
- **Italian:** assafetida
- **Japanese:** agi, asahueteida
- **Russian:** asafetida
- **Spanish:** assa foetida
- **Swedish:** dyvelstrack
- **Turkish:** seytantersi, setan

Family: Apiaceae (formerly Umbelliferae)

Other Names: asafoetida powder, devil's dung, food of the gods, hing, hingra, laser, yellow asafoetida

Flavor Group: Pungent

Parts Used: sap (as a spice)

Background

The name *asafetida* is derived from the Persian *aza*, "mastic" or "resin," and *foetidus*, Latin for "stinking." This plant was greatly appreciated by the early Persians, who called it "food of the gods." Asafetida is known to be descended from the giant perennial fennels that grow wild in Afghanistan, Iran and northern India at altitudes above 3,300 feet (1,000 m). There is some conjecture about its relationship to laser root (*Ferula tingitana*, often also referred to as silphium, laserpitium or laser), which was treasured for its flavor and health-giving properties in ancient Roman times and shared many of the attributes of asafetida. Laser root grew mainly in Cyrene (North Africa) and is believed to have become extinct by the middle of the first century CE as a result of overgrazing by cattle, its use as a vegetable (the strong flavor

Culinary Information

Combines with

- cardamom
- chile
- cinnamon
- coriander seed
- fennel seed
- ginger
- mustard
- pepper
- tamarind
- turmeric

Traditional Uses

- Indian curries, especially seafood and vegetable
- cooked vegetable and bean dishes
- pappadums and naan bread
- pickles and chutneys
- Worcestershire sauce
- as a general substitute for garlic

Spice Blends

- chaat masala
- curry blends

disappears on cooking) and lack of orderly propagation—one can imagine that this was quite possible in the days when many herbs and spices were simply gathered in the wild and not purposefully cultivated. Alexander the Great was said to have carried laser root west in 4 BCE; at that time it was called "stink finger," the name also used in Afghanistan. Finally deprived of their beloved laser root, the Romans imported the resin of Persian asafetida (thought to be similar to the asafetida we know today) from Persia and Armenia; they introduced it to England around 2,000 years ago. Not surprisingly, considering its challenging aroma, there is scant reference to asafetida in the history of cooking in the British Isles.

The Plant

This is one the world's most maligned spices, particularly by Western writers—its odor has been compared to feces and rotting garlic. Asafetida is a resinous (oleoresin) gum extracted from one of a few species of giant fennel, of which there are about 50 varieties (some of them poisonous). The plant from which most commercial asafetida comes grows to about 10 feet (3 m) tall. It has thick stems and a coarse appearance similar to fennel; the bright yellow flowers appear only after about five years of growth.

The spice asafetida is found in four main forms: tears, blocks, pieces and powder. The aroma is fetid to some noses, hence the name. However, when one considers how many ingredients used to flavor food seem to have strong aromas on first acquaintance, asafetida can certainly be regarded in more benign terms. The bouquet is slightly sulfurous and acrid and resembles fermented garlic, yet it has a lingering sweetness reminiscent of pineapple. There are two major varieties: **hing,** a water-soluble type (from *Ferula asafoetida*), and **hingra** (from *F. scorodosma*), which is oil-soluble and considered inferior. Tears, blocks and pieces of asafetida are the strongest in flavor. They are dark red to brown in color and have the characteristic pervasive aroma of good-quality asafetida. Asafetida is often powdered and mixed with edible starch to make it more manageable.

There are two readily available forms of powder: one is "brown" (actually pale tan) and the other is yellow. The latter has a slightly milder flavor and amalgamates into food easily because of the starch and turmeric added to it.

Processing

Asafetida sap is collected from plants that are at least four years old. The process commences with exposing the roots, slashing them and keeping them shaded from the sun for around 4 to 6 weeks while the resin seeps out and hardens. In some parts of India the plant is tapped at the base of the stem in much the same way that a rubber tree is tapped for its latex. The drying resin is scraped off in pale creamy lumps that turn reddish and finally dark reddish brown as they age. The oleoresin gum is then subjected to further processing to make it manageable. Brown asafetida powder is made by simply grinding the hard gum with some form of starch (usually wheat flour and, more recently, rice flour), resulting in a free-flowing coarse powder. Yellow asafetida is made by mixing the powdered gum with wheat flour, starch, gum arabic, turmeric and sometimes additional coloring such as carotene. Yellow asafetida is not as strong in flavor as brown asafetida; however, the texture is finer and the appearance less threatening and more processed.

Spice Notes

Asafetida resin, which is the solidified sap of the plant, was traditionally compounded with wheat flour to make it easier to use. As a result, many gluten-intolerant people could not use it in cooking. Fortunately, a few of us in the spice trade have convinced some "hingwallas" (the name given to asafetida processors) to produce an asafetida powder compounded only with rice flour and gum arabic.

Buying and Storage

Always try to buy asafetida in a well-sealed, airtight container, for two reasons: first, as with other spices, the volatile oil will escape and the flavor will diminish; and second, the strong aroma will pervade your whole house. The dark reddish brown lumps of resin have the strongest flavor, but unless you are familiar with the substance, buying either the brown or yellow powder will be much more convenient.

Store in an airtight container away from extremes of heat, light and humidity. I sometimes place one container inside another to create a double barrier.

Use

Asafetida is reputed to reduce flatulence, and studies have shown that it is a helpful digestive. It is used regularly in Indian diets high in lentils and beans and other vegetable content that is conducive to gas production. Although asafetida does have a strong aroma, much of that is toned down during the cooking process, resulting in a wonderful flavor that complements whatever dishes you choose to use it in. People belonging to the Brahmin and Jain faiths are prohibited from eating garlic because of its reputed aphrodisiac properties, so asafetida is their substitute for garlic.

Asafetida is particularly good in lentil dishes such as sambar, and it enhances fish and vegetable curries to the extent that I would not make those dishes without it. Some Indian cooks stick a small piece of resin under the lid of the cooking pot and allow the flavor to permeate that way. Apicius, the Roman philosopher and gourmet of the early first century CE from whom the epithet *epicure* derives, was known to keep a chunk of the resin in his storage container for pine nuts; the vapor would seep into the pine nuts sufficiently to provide the desired flavor when they were used as an ingredient. Adding the powder during cooking is probably the simplest method of application. Just think of it as another version of garlic—that way it can be enjoyed with pleasure in dishes other than traditional Indian recipes.

WEIGHT PER TEASPOON (5 mL)
- ground: 4.1 g

SUGGESTED QUANTITY PER POUND (500 g)
- red meats: 1 tsp (5 mL)
- white meats: 1 tsp (5 mL)
- vegetables: 1 tsp (5 mL)
- grains and pulses: 1 tsp (5 mL)
- baked goods: ½ tsp (2 mL)

Vegetarian Sambar

This dish is one of our favorite examples of the vegetarian food of southern India, which is full of goodness and flavor. Asafetida is used in many Indian dishes and plays an important part in Sambar Powder, not only adding that appetizing garlic-like flavor but also decreasing the likelihood of embarrassing moments that can be caused by lentil and bean dishes. Serve over basmati rice or Basmati Pilaf (page 164), garnished with fresh coriander leaves (cilantro).

**Makes
4 servings**

Preparation time:
 30 minutes

Cooking time:
 40 minutes

Tips

Any vegetable you like can be used, such as eggplant, potatoes or carrots, but keep in mind the cooking times. For example, potatoes will take longer than peas to cook.

When two or three vegetables are used, you get a subtle blending of flavors. For a more distinct flavor, use just one type of vegetable, such as carrot or cauliflower.

To cook lentils: Using a fine-mesh sieve, rinse 1 cup (250 mL) dried lentils under cold running water. Transfer to a medium saucepan and add 4 cups (1 L) water and 1 tsp (5 mL) salt. Simmer over medium heat for about 20 minutes or until tender.

2 tbsp	oil	30 mL
2 tbsp	sambar powder (page 761)	30 mL
2 cups	roughly chopped (½ inch/1 cm) mixed vegetables (see Tips, left)	500 mL
2 cups	water	500 mL
½ tsp	fine sea salt	2 mL
1 cup	cooked lentils or yellow split peas (see Tips, left)	250 mL
	Sea salt and freshly ground black pepper	
	Fresh coriander leaves (cilantro)	

1. In a large saucepan over medium heat, heat oil. Add sambar powder and cook, stirring constantly, for 1 minute, until fragrant. Add vegetables and stir-fry for 2 minutes, until just starting to brown. Add water and salt, cover and simmer until vegetables are cooked through (cooking time will vary depending on the vegetables used). Add lentils and simmer for 5 minutes, until heated through. Season with salt and pepper to taste. Serve immediately, garnished with coriander leaves.

Balm

Melissa officinalis

Names in Other Languages

- **Arabic:** turijan, hashisha al-namal
- **Bulgarian:** matochina
- **Chinese (C):** heung fung chou
- **Chinese (M):** xiang feng cao
- **Czech:** medunka
- **Danish:** citronmelisse
- **Dutch:** citroenmelisse
- **French:** baume, melisse
- **German:** Zitronmelisse
- **Greek:** melissa
- **Italian:** melissa, erba limona
- **Japanese:** seiyo-yama-hakka
- **Korean:** remon bam
- **Portuguese:** erva cidreira
- **Russian:** melissa limonnaya
- **Spanish:** balsamita maior
- **Turkish:** ogul out, melisa otu

Family: Lamiaceae (formerly Labiatae)

Other Names: bee balm, common balm, lemon balm, melissa, sweet balm

Flavor Group: Medium

Parts Used: leaves (as a herb)

Background

Balm is native to southern Europe and was introduced to England, probably around 70 CE, by the Romans. It was subsequently cultivated in North America and Asia. The plant's Latin botanical name, *Melissa*, derives from the Greek word for honey. The association with bees goes back more than 2,000 years, when balm was rubbed onto beehives to prevent the bees from swarming and to encourage them to return home. Although it is often referred to as "bee balm," true bee balm is bergamot (page 119), a plant from a different genus.

Culinary Information

Combines with

- allspice
- bay leaf
- coriander seed
- mint
- nutmeg
- pepper
- rosemary
- sage
- thyme

Traditional Uses

- pickled herring and eel
- liqueurs such as Benedictine and Chartreuse
- fruit salads
- green salads
- sauces for lamb and pork
- poultry and fish

Spice Blends

- not commonly used in spice blends

The name *balm* is an abbreviation of *balsam*, a term used to describe a variety of pleasantly scented products derived from plants; it was attributed to this plant because of its sweet aroma. The 16th-century Spanish emperor Charles V was fond of taking a daily tonic called "Carmelite water," an ancient recipe made with balm, lemon peel, nutmeg and angelica root steeped in wine. These days balm is underutilized as a culinary herb; it is grown mainly for decorative purposes and for its fragrance, as an addition to the sweet-smelling collections of dried flowers, exotic oils and spices known as potpourri.

The Plant

Balm is related to mint. In appearance it resembles common garden mint, with rough oval dark green leaves that are serrated around the edges. The plant is compact and leafy, growing to around 32 inches (80 cm) tall, and prefers a sunny garden with moist, rich soil. Balm's thick, matted, shallow roots are less rampant than those of mint, so it is easier to control in the garden. Although a perennial, balm should be cut back in autumn; its root system then remains dormant until spring, when propagation is best carried out by root division. Clusters of small white flowers that attract bees are borne on tall stalks in spring. The leaves of balm have a distinctive penetrating and lingering lemon scent that is tantalizingly refreshing and aromatic, which is why it is often referred to as "lemon balm."

Processing

Balm is best used fresh, as the volatile lemony top notes are easily lost on drying. Should you wish to dry your own for use in pickles or tisanes, be particularly careful to ensure minimal exposure to light or extreme heat and humidity during drying. The best methods for removing moisture and retaining flavor are to spread out the leaves (never overlapping) on paper or hang them upside down in loose bunches in a dark, well-aired place. For best results, dry herbs when the relative humidity is below 50%. When the leaves feel quite crisp and crumbly, the moisture content will be down to about 12%, the ideal level for extended storage.

Buying and Storage

Freshly picked sprigs of balm leaves may be placed in a glass of water (as if in a vase), covered with a plastic bag tent and stored in the refrigerator, where they will last for a few days. Store dried balm in airtight containers in a cool, dark place.

Use

Because balm has a lemony mint flavor, its range of culinary applications is almost endless. Balm has been used traditionally for pickled herring and eel in Belgium and Holland. It forms the basis of the cordial *eau-de-melisse des carnes*, a 17th-century elixir made with herbs and wine also known as "Melissa water." Balm has also been used as an ingredient in several well-known liqueurs, such as Benedictine and Chartreuse. For the home cook, the palate-pleasing lemon flavor is a refreshing addition to fruit salads and adds tang to green salads when only a small amount of vinegar is used in the dressing. Balm is excellent in stuffing for poultry and it complements fish, especially when it is cooked with a little butter and wrapped in foil. You can make an unusual mint and balm sauce to accompany lamb and pork by combining 1 tbsp (15 mL) each chopped fresh balm and mint leaves, 1 tsp (5 mL) sugar, a pinch of fine sea salt, 1 tbsp (15 mL) white wine vinegar and $1/2$ cup (125 mL) hot water.

WEIGHT PER TEASPOON (5 mL)
- rubbed dried leaves: 1 g

SUGGESTED QUANTITY PER POUND (500 g)
- red meats: 4 tsp (20 mL)
- white meats: 4 tsp (20 mL)
- vegetables: 4 tsp (20 mL)
- grains and pulses: 4 tsp (20 mL)

Balm Lemonade

It's lovely to serve homemade lemonade at summer barbecues and picnics. Balm is a wonderful addition, and the syrup in the recipe can also be used for making cocktails (see Tips, below).

½ cup	granulated sugar	125 mL
6 cups	water, divided	1.5 L
	Peel of 3 large lemons, cut into thick slices	
	Freshly squeezed juice of 3 large lemons	
½ cup	lightly packed balm leaves, torn	125 mL

Makes 6 cups (1.5 L)

Preparation time:
5 minutes

Cooking time:
10 minutes, plus 1 hour for infusing

- - - - - - - - - - - - - - - - -

Tips

To make a syrup to use in cocktails, after allowing it to steep for an hour, simply strain the infusion through a fine-mesh sieve into a bottle or jar. The syrup will keep in an airtight container in the refrigerator for up to 2 weeks. To make a gin cocktail, pour 3 tbsp (45 mL) gin into a highball glass, add 3 balm ice cubes (see next Tip) and 2 tbsp (30 mL) balm syrup and top with ⅓ cup (75 mL) soda or tonic water.

To make balm ice cubes, pick 12 small, intact balm leaves and place one in each compartment of an ice-cube tray. Top with water and freeze.

1. In a small saucepan over low heat, combine sugar and 1 cup (250 mL) water and cook, stirring frequently, until sugar is dissolved, about 5 minutes. When sugar has completely dissolved, simmer for 2 more minutes, until syrupy. Remove from heat.

2. Transfer syrup to a heatproof bowl or pitcher. Add lemon peel and juice and balm, then set aside for at least 1 hour to allow flavors to infuse.

3. Add remaining 5 cups (1.25 L) water and stir. Serve with balm ice cubes (see Tips, left).

Balm and Mascarpone Sorbet

This simple recipe is light and refreshing. It can be made to serve as a dessert or as a palate cleanser during a dinner party.

B

Makes 6 to 8 servings

Preparation time:
5 minutes

Cooking time:
10 minutes, plus 3 to 4 hours for freezing

- - - - - - - - - - - - - - -

Tips

Superfine (caster) sugar is a very fine granulated sugar typically used in recipes that require a faster-dissolving granule. If you can't find it in stores, you can make your own by using a food processor fitted with the metal blade to process granulated sugar into a very fine, sand-like consistency.

If balm is not available, you can substitute an equal quantity of fresh mint or applemint.

• **Food processor**

¾ cup	superfine (caster) sugar (see Tips, left)	175 mL
1⅓ cups	water	325 mL
8 oz	mascarpone cheese, at room temperature	250 g
1 cup	lightly packed finely chopped fresh balm leaves (see Tips, left)	250 mL
1½ tsp	freshly squeezed lemon juice	7 mL

1. In a small saucepan over low heat, combine sugar and water. Stir gently until sugar is completely dissolved, about 5 minutes. Remove from heat and set aside to cool completely.

2. In a medium bowl, combine mascarpone, balm and lemon juice and stir until well combined. Add cooled sugar syrup and mix until smooth. Pour into a rectangular or square airtight container (capacity 4 cups/1 L) and freeze for 3 to 4 hours. Using food processor fitted with the metal blade, process just until mixture is broken up, then return to container and freeze for 1 hour before serving.

Barberry

Berberis vulgaris

Names in Other Languages

- **Arabic:** berberis
- **French:** épine vinette
- **Persian:** zareshk
- **Spanish:** agracejo

Family: Berberidaceae

Other Names: berberry, European barberry, holy thorn, jaundice berry, pipperidge bush, sowberry, zareshk

Flavor Group: Tangy

Parts Used: berries (as a spice)

Background

The barberry is believed to have originated in Europe, North Africa and temperate Asia. Decorative members of the *Berberis* family are now grown extensively throughout North America and Australia. The bark and roots have been used medicinally and the close-grained wood is made into toothpicks. A yellow dye made from the bark was used as a coloring for wool, linen, silk and leather before the introduction of chemical dyes in the mid 20th century; in Germany some artisan dyers still use the bark. The name "holy thorn" derives from the Italian belief that it was used in the crown of thorns placed on Christ's head prior to his crucifixion.

Culinary Information

Combines with
- allspice
- cardamom
- chile
- coriander seed
- ginger
- pepper
- saffron
- turmeric

Traditional Uses
- rice pilafs
- stewed fruits, especially apples
- jellies to accompany red meats

Spice Blends
- not commonly used in spice blends

Unfortunately for the barberry shrub, it is host to a strain of rust that affects wheat. When its popularity as a spice led to wider cultivation, its subsequent association with the spread of rust disease in wheat made it extremely unpopular with farmers. Famines in the early 10th century in Spain were largely a result of the damage done to wheat crops by fungal rust. This may go some way to explaining why barberry is so rarely heard of these days, and why some countries still prohibit its importation. It is most commonly used as an ingredient in Afghan and Iranian cooking, where it is used to flavor rice dishes.

The Plant

The ripe berries of barberry (*Berberis vulgaris*) are used in cooking for their pleasantly acidic taste and fruity aroma, which is not unlike tamarind. The barberry bush is deciduous and grows to about 8 feet (2.5 m) tall; it bears clusters of small, bright yellow flowers that are followed by the purple-scarlet fruit, which becomes red upon ripening. Dried ripe barberries are about $1/2$ inch (1 cm) long, oblong in shape and moist to the touch; they look a bit like miniature currants. The red color darkens with age as they oxidize.

Other Varieties
The fruits of **Japanese barberry** (*Berberis thunbergii*), **mountain grape** (*B. aquifolium*) and the berberis common in gardens as a decorative shrub (*B. thunbergii atropurpurea*) should not be eaten, as they are mildly poisonous.

Buying and Storage

You should buy dried barberry only from a reputable merchant. Because of the toxicity of some species, it is not recommended that you purchase fresh barberries, which may come from an uncertain source. Dried barberries are quite moist to the touch (typical of dried fruits) and should be red to dark red in color. After purchasing, store in an airtight container in the freezer to retain maximum color and flavor. Kept this way, your barberries should last for up to 12 months.

Use

Traditionally, barberry was used for its high citric acid content. It was considered a good accompaniment to mutton when made into a jelly (similar to the red currant jelly that so often accompanies game). It has been pickled for serving with curries, and Afghanis and Iranians add barberry to their rice dishes. Barberries are great with dishes flavored with ras el hanout spice blend, and they add an attractive tangy note to couscous and rice. We like to use barberries with fruit, especially apples. They make a particularly pleasing addition to an apple pie, with the extra benefit of delivering occasional fruity bursts of tangy flavor that can also be enjoyed in almost any type of fruit muffin.

WEIGHT PER TEASPOON (5 mL)
- whole: 1.8 g

SUGGESTED QUANTITY PER POUND (500 g)
- red meats: 2 tsp (10 mL)
- white meats: 1½ tsp (7 mL)
- vegetables: 1 tsp (5 mL)
- grains and pulses: 1 tsp (5 mL)
- baked goods: 1 tsp (5 mL)

Zereshk Polo

This classic Persian dish showcases the delicious tang of the barberries.

**Makes
6 servings**

Preparation time:
 2 hours

**Cooking time: 1 hour,
 30 minutes**

Tips

To prepare basmati rice:
In a bowl, cover rice in
cold water and add 1 tbsp
(15 mL) fine sea salt. Mix
well and set aside for
2 hours. This will increase
the tenderness of the rice
and its ability to absorb
the flavors of the dish.
Using a fine-mesh sieve,
drain rice and rinse under
cold running water.

To prepare saffron: In
a small bowl, cover
threads with 2 tbsp
(30 mL) milk and set
aside for 15 minutes to
soak. Remove from milk
before using.

If you can't find slivered
almonds you can use
flaked almonds.

To prepare cooking pot,
coat a large saucepan with
2 tbsp (30 mL) oil.

Discard remaining
marinade after adding
chicken to the dish
(Step 5).

3 cups	basmati rice, soaked (see Tips, left)	750 mL
6 tbsp	olive oil, divided	90 mL
1	medium onion, halved and thinly sliced	1
5	bone-in skinless chicken thighs, trimmed of fat	5
½ tsp	ground turmeric	2 mL
2 tsp	fine sea salt, divided	10 mL
1 tsp	freshly ground black pepper	5 mL
9 cups	water, divided	2.25 L
¾ cup	plain yogurt	175 mL
½ tsp	saffron threads soaked in milk	2 mL
1	egg	1
¼ cup	barberries	60 mL
2 tbsp	slivered almonds (see Tips, left)	30 mL
1 tbsp	granulated sugar	15 mL

1. In a skillet over medium heat, heat 2 tbsp (30 mL)
oil. Add onion and cook, stirring, until golden, about
3 minutes. Add chicken, turmeric, 1 tsp (5 mL) salt and
pepper and cook, stirring, until chicken is browned
on both sides. Add 1 cup (250 mL) water and simmer,
uncovered, for 10 to 15 minutes, until chicken is cooked
through. Remove from heat and transfer chicken to a plate
to cool. Reserve onion and stock.

2. In a bowl, combine yogurt, soaked saffron, and egg. Mix
well. Add chicken, cover, and refrigerate for 1 hour.

3. In a saucepan over medium heat, combine barberries with
2 tbsp (30 mL) oil, almonds and sugar. Cook, stirring,
until golden. Remove from heat and set aside.

4. In a separate saucepan over high heat, bring to a boil
8 cups (2 L) water with 1 tsp (5 mL) salt. Add soaked rice
and cook for 5 minutes, until slightly softened around
edges of grains. Drain and rinse under cold running water.

5. Spread half the cooked rice over bottom of prepared
pot (see Tips, left). Remove chicken from marinade and
lay overtop. Combine barberry mixture with remaining
rice, then spread over chicken. Using a slotted spoon,
distribute reserved onion evenly over rice. Gently pour
reserved stock overtop. Cover with a tight-fitting lid and
cook over low heat for 30 minutes, until rice is tender
and stock is absorbed. Transfer to a serving platter.

Basil

Ocimum basilicum

Names in Other Languages

- **Arabic:** raihan
- **Chinese (C):** lohlahk, fan jyun, gau chahng taap
- **Chinese (M):** jiu ceng ta, lou le, xun sun
- **Czech:** bazalka
- **Dutch:** basilicum
- **Filipino:** belanoi, sulasi
- **French:** basilic
- **German:** Basilienkraut
- **Greek:** vasilikos
- **Indian:** barbar, sabzah, tulsi, gulal tulsi
- **Indonesian:** selasih, kemangi
- **Italian:** basilico
- **Japanese:** bajiru, meboki
- **Malay:** daun selaseh, kemangi
- **Portuguese:** manjericão
- **Russian:** bazilik
- **Spanish:** albahaca
- **Sri Lankan:** suwenda-tala, maduru-tala
- **Swedish:** basilkort
- **Thai:** horapa, manglak, krapow, bai horapa
- **Turkish:** feslegen, reyhan, peslen
- **Vietnamese:** rau que, cay hung que

Family: Lumiaceae (formerly Labiatae)

Varieties: sweet basil (*O. basilicum*), bush basil (*O. basilicum minimum*), Thai basil (*O. cannum* Sims.; also known as *O. thyrsiflora*), holy basil (*O. sanctum;* also known as *O. tenuiflorum*), camphor basil (*O. kilimandscharicum*), lemon basil (*O. citriodorum;* also known as *O. americanum*), perennial basil (*O. kilimandscharicum;* also known as *O. cannum*)

Other Names: bush basil, camphor basil, holy basil, lemon basil, perennial basil, purple basil, sweet basil, Thai basil, hairy basil

Flavor Group: Strong

Parts Used: seeds (as a spice), leaves (as a herb)

Background

The origin of basil goes back 3,000 years to India, where it was and still is considered a sacred herb. It is also native to Iran and Africa and was known in ancient Egypt, Greece and Rome. Basil is certainly a herb that doesn't inspire indifference. Pliny, the celebrated first-century CE Roman scholar, considered it an aphrodisiac, and it was given to horses during the mating season. In Italy basil symbolized love: when a lady left a pot of basil in her window, it signaled that her lover was welcome. In Romania a young man was considered to be engaged if he accepted a sprig of basil from a young lady. However, those less enamored with basil, such as the ancient Greeks, considered it to be a symbol of hatred. Hilarius (yes, that was his name), an early French physician, claimed that merely smelling basil could cause a scorpion to be born in one's brain.

Fortunately, basil's positive elements prevailed; it was introduced to Europe in the 16th century. Basil features most often in Italian and Mediterranean cooking, possibly because the warmer climate there makes it readily available. In the cooler parts of Europe, where it doesn't thrive, it is not nearly as popular as it is in the Mediterranean, North America, Asia and Australia.

The Plant

There are many different types of basil, but succulent, large-leaved sweet basil is by far the most popular variety for culinary use, although deliciously anise-like Thai basil is hard on its heels. Basil's refreshing clove- and anise-like aroma conjures up memories of summer—hardly surprising when one considers that this warmth-loving annual thrives

sweet basil

A Powerful Herb

One theory is that basil's name is derived from *basilikon phyton*, which is Greek for "kingly herb." The belief was that basil's fragrance was so pleasing it was fit for a king's house. Another belief is that it was named after the basilisk, a mythical serpent that could kill with one look.

Culinary Information

Combines with
- garlic
- juniper
- marjoram
- mustard
- oregano
- paprika
- parsley
- pepper
- rosemary
- sage

Traditional Uses
- tomatoes (fresh or cooked)
- pasta sauces
- cooked eggplant
- squash and zucchini
- salads
- herb sandwiches
- poultry stuffing
- sauces and gravies
- herb vinegars

Spice Blends
- Italian herb blends
- Cajun and Creole spices
- meat seasonings
- seasoned stuffing mixes
- spice rubs

Travels in the Spice Trade

Holy basil always reminds me of the time Liz and I visited a 300-year-old spice farm in Mangalore, on the west coast of India, south of Goa. After the obligatory tour that took in pepper vines, vanilla orchids, ginger, turmeric and long pepper, we sat on the cool verandah and drank black tea laced with ginger and cardamom. We were smoothly transported back in time by the sight of a woman crushing fresh spices on a large grinding stone, and the workers making their way to harvest the crops. As we sat conversing about spices, I was acutely aware of a square pot of holy basil, carefully positioned on the eastern side of the house near a doorway, as is the custom. The Indians believe *tulsi* to be sacred and that its prescence will protect the household. On that peaceful morning, with bees buzzing around the *tulsi*'s clusters of flowers, it was easy to imagine that the household was indeed blessed.

in hot conditions and expires with the first chills of winter. Sweet basil plants grow to around 20 inches (50 cm) tall, and even taller in ideal conditions. The stems are tough, grooved and square, with dark green oval, crinkly leaves 1 to 4 inches (2.5 to 10 cm) long. The tiny white long-stamened flowers should be nipped off to prevent the plant from going to seed. As with all annuals, once the plant reaches this stage, its life cycle is virtually finished. Regularly plucking flower heads will also encourage thicker foliage.

The taste of sweet basil is far less pungent than the permeating, heady aroma of the freshly picked leaves would suggest. This means that large quantities can be used without spoiling a recipe. Dried sweet basil leaves are quite different from fresh. The fragrant, fresh-smelling top notes disappear upon drying, although concentration of volatile oils in the cells of the dehydrated leaves gives a pungent clove and allspice bouquet. This is matched by a faint minty, peppery flavor that is ideal for long, slow cooking.

Other Varieties

Bush basil (*Ocimum basilicum mimimum*) has small leaves $1/3$ to $1/2$ inch (8 to 10 mm) long. It grows to about 6 inches (15 cm) tall, and the foliage has a less pungent aroma and less flavor strength than sweet basil. I find bush basil ideal for garnishing dishes, as the small leaves look far more attractive than shredded sweet basil leaves.

The two types of **purple basil** (cultivars of *O. basilicum*)—serrated-leaved 'Purple Ruffle' basil and the smoother 'Dark Opal' basil—are grown mainly for decorative purposes. They have a mild, pleasing flavor and look attractive in salads and as a garnish.

Hairy basil or **Thai basil** (*O. cannum* Sims.) has slender oval leaves with deep serrations on the edges and a more camphorous aroma than sweet basil, with distinct licorice and anise notes. The seeds of this variety (referred to as *subja* in India) have no distinctive flavor, but they swell and become gelatinous in water. They are used to thicken Indian and Asian sweets and drinks and have become increasingly popular as an appetite suppressant.

Holy basil (*O. sanctum*), or *tulsi*, as it is called in India, is a perennial with mauve-pink flowers; it is lightly lemon-scented. **Cinnamon basil** (*O. basilicum* 'Cinnamon') has a distinct cinnamon aroma and long, erect flower heads. An attractive plant, its leaves complement Asian dishes.

The tender perennial **camphor basil** (*O. kilimandscharicum*) is not recommended for use in cooking, but its distinctive camphorous aroma makes it a pleasant decorative herb to have in the garden.

Processing

Basil is possibly one of the most difficult herbs to process. Its moist, crinkly dark green leaves tend to turn black when attempts are made to refrigerate, freeze or dehydrate them. (Such efforts are more likely to work well if you use freshly picked leaves.) To dry basil, harvest the long, leafy stems just before the flower buds start to appear. Spread these out to dry on either paper or wire mesh in a dark, warm, well-aired place. Do not hang them in bunches, as

holy basil

touching leaves will tend to turn black at the edges. When the leaves have shriveled to about one-fifth of their size and are quite crisp to touch, rub them off the stems and store in an airtight container.

Buying and Storage

Avoid buying fresh basil that is wilted or has black marks on the leaves. Freshly picked basil may be frozen and stored reasonably successfully for a few weeks. The best method is to place a small bunch in a clean resealable bag, blow in some air to inflate it, and place in the freezer where it will not get squashed. You will find it quite convenient to nip off a few of these frozen leaves as needed. Another effective way to preserve basil is to pick the larger leaves, wash and dry them and then stack them in a sterilized shallow, wide-mouthed jar (see Tips, page 169), sprinkling a little salt on each leaf as you pile them up. Fill the jar with olive oil so that all the leaves are submerged, screw the lid on firmly and refrigerate. Depending on the quality of the fresh leaves, basil stored this way should last up to 3 months before any blackening occurs.

Store-bought jars of "fresh" basil are generally made from a combination of fresh and dried material. While they are a good substitute for fresh, it should be noted that the amount of food acid used to achieve preservation will impart a more tangy taste. When using these jars of herbs, always reduce the amount of lemon juice or vinegar in the recipe to compensate for the higher acid levels.

It is interesting to note how flavors across the herb and spice spectrum can have similar attributes; it is often these degrees of commonality that indicate the breadth of uses they can encompass. Like basil, cloves and allspice also happen to go well with tomatoes, and many commercially made tomato sauces and canned foods, such as Scandinavian herrings with tomato, contain either cloves or the very clove-tasting allspice.

Dried basil is dark green in color. It is readily available from food stores; however, as for other dried herbs, buy dried basil in good-quality packaging and store away from extremes of heat, light and humidity.

Use

Basil's pervasive clove-like aroma, which comes from the oil eugenol (also found in cloves and allspice), makes it such an ideal complement to tomatoes that it is often referred to as the "tomato herb."

Basil also complements vegetables such as eggplant, zucchini, squash and spinach. When fresh basil is added within the last half-hour of cooking, it enhances the flavor of vegetable and legume soups. My mother often made herb sandwiches with cream cheese and shredded basil leaves—they have a clean, refreshing taste. Most salads, especially those containing tomato, benefit greatly from the addition of fresh basil. The simplicity of basil is best appreciated when it is not cooked at all, such as in salads and pesto-style sauces.

Dried basil goes well with poultry when used in stuffing, included in soups and stews at the commencement of cooking, and added to sauces and gravies. When using dried basil instead of fresh leaves in a recipe, use only one-third of the amount. For example, if 1 tablespoon (15 mL) firmly packed torn fresh leaves is called for in a pasta sauce, only use 1 teaspoon (5 mL) dried basil as a substitute.

Fish brushed with olive oil, dusted with freshly ground black pepper, wrapped in foil with a few basil leaves and barbecued is a simple and effective way to enjoy this versatile herb. Basil is also used in pâtés and terrines, where its volatile notes help counteract the richness of liver and game. You can prepare a tasty vinegar to have on hand for making salad dressings by placing a dozen or more washed and dried (to remove excess water) fresh basil leaves in a bottle of white wine vinegar and setting it aside in a cool place for a few weeks.

Basil leaves are best used whole or torn; most cooks advise against cutting the leaves with a knife, as this tends to dissipate the aroma. To make dried basil taste a little more like fresh when topping tomatoes, zucchini or eggplant for grilling, mix 1 tsp (5 mL) basil with $1/2$ tsp (2 mL) each lemon juice, water and oil and $1/8$ tsp (0.5 mL) ground allspice. Set aside for a few minutes, then spread onto halved tomatoes or slices of eggplant before grilling.

WEIGHT PER TEASPOON (5 mL)
- **whole dry leaves:** 0.8 g

SUGGESTED QUANTITY PER POUND (500 g)
- **red meats:** 2 tsp (10 mL) dried leaves, 8 tsp (40 mL) torn fresh leaves
- **white meats:** 2 tsp (10 mL) dried leaves, 8 tsp (40 mL) torn fresh leaves
- **vegetables:** $1\frac{1}{2}$ tsp (7 mL) dried leaves, 2 tbsp (30 mL) torn fresh leaves
- **grains and pulses:** $1\frac{1}{2}$ tsp (7 mL) dried leaves, 2 tbsp (30 mL) torn fresh leaves
- **baked goods:** $1\frac{1}{2}$ tsp (7 mL) dried leaves, 2 tbsp (30 mL) torn fresh leaves

Figs with Basil Oil

These sweet and savory figs can be served with mascarpone as a dessert, with a little arugula as a starter, or on small squares of toasted focaccia as a canapé. The pairing works wonderfully and is best during the short window in the summer when both fresh figs and basil are in season. The basil oil can also be used as a dressing for salads or pasta.

**Makes
4 servings**

Preparation time:
 24 hours

Cooking time:
 10 minutes

- - - - - - - - - - - - - - - - - -

Tip

Leftover basil oil will keep in an airtight container in the cupboard or refrigerator for up to 2 weeks (it will solidify when cold).

• **Food processor**

BASIL OIL

½ cup	firmly packed fresh basil leaves	125 mL
½ cup	olive oil	125 mL
¼ tsp	freshly squeezed lemon juice	1 mL
Pinch	fine sea salt	Pinch

FIGS

12	ripe fresh figs	12
	Balsamic vinegar (aged, if possible)	
12	very small fresh basil leaves, optional	12

1. *Basil Oil:* In food processor fitted with the metal blade, process basil, oil, lemon juice and salt until smooth (you can also use a mortar and pestle). Transfer basil oil to a small saucepan over low heat and heat gently for 5 minutes. Set aside, covered, overnight; then strain through a fine-mesh sieve, discarding solids.

2. *Figs:* Place oven rack in highest position. Preheat broiler.

3. Using a sharp knife, make crosswise cuts in tops of figs (being careful not to cut all the way through) and pull down the resulting "petals" to make a star shape. Arrange figs, cut side up, on a baking sheet and broil for 2 to 4 minutes or until just beginning to brown. To serve, drizzle figs with basil oil and a few drops of balsamic vinegar. Top each with a basil leaf (if using).

Pasta with Pesto and Clams

On a scorching August day in Puglia, we hired a car to drive us down to the very end of the heel of Italy's boot, the "Italian Maldives." After a refreshing swim in the azure water, we were surprisingly hungry, despite the heat. This local specialty made my day. Beware of store-bought pestos that are full of preservatives and cheaper ingredients, such as peanuts and parsley instead of pine nuts and basil.

Makes 4 servings

Preparation time:
  10 minutes

Cooking time:
  30 minutes

Tips

Trofie is a short, twisted pasta. If not available, use penne or spirals.

To toast pine nuts: Cook in a dry skillet over medium heat, shaking pan gently, for about 3 minutes, until lightly golden. Remove from heat as soon as they start to color.

Pesto is one of the most effective ways to store and use basil. It can be the basis of a quick meal when tossed through freshly cooked pasta or an excellent spread on fresh bread, topped with slices of fresh tomato.

Pesto will keep in an airtight container in the refrigerator for up to 2 weeks, as long as the top is covered with $\frac{1}{16}$ inch (2 mm) olive oil to prevent oxidization.

• **Food processor**

PESTO

2 cups	lightly packed fresh basil leaves	500 mL
$\frac{1}{2}$ cup	pine nuts, lightly toasted (see Tips, left)	125 mL
$\frac{1}{2}$ cup	coarsely chopped Parmesan cheese	125 mL
2	cloves garlic, crushed	2
$\frac{1}{4}$ tsp	finely grated lemon zest	1 mL
$\frac{1}{4}$ tsp	fine sea salt	1 mL
$\frac{1}{4}$ tsp	freshly ground black pepper	1 mL
$\frac{1}{3}$ cup	extra virgin olive oil	75 mL

PASTA

10 oz	trofie pasta (see Tips, left)	300 g
$1\frac{1}{2}$ lbs	small clams (*vongole*), rinsed and drained	750 g
$\frac{1}{4}$ cup	white wine	60 mL
	Sea salt and freshly ground black pepper	

1. *Pesto:* In food processor fitted with the metal blade, roughly chop basil, pine nuts, Parmesan, garlic, lemon zest, salt and pepper. With the motor running, add oil through feed tube and process until pesto mixture is puréed but retains some texture. Set aside.

2. *Pasta:* In a large pot of boiling salted water, cook pasta for 8 to 10 minutes, until al dente. Drain and transfer to a bowl. Stir in pesto until well combined. Set aside.

3. In the same pot over high heat, combine clams and wine. Cover pot and cook for 6 to 8 minutes, shaking pan occasionally, until clams have all opened (discard any that remain closed). Add prepared pesto pasta and cook for 2 minutes, until heated through. Serve immediately.

Variation

For a vegetarian version, substitute 8 oz (250 g) steamed broccoli for the clams.

Thai Basil Chicken

A firm favorite on every Thai menu, Thai basil chicken (*gai pad krapow*) has so few ingredients that you can whip it up at home anytime you like. It is quite popular to serve this dish over steamed rice with a runny fried egg on top, as the Indonesians do with nasi goreng—it makes a delicious breakfast!

**Makes
6 servings**

Preparation time:
  10 minutes
Cooking time:
  10 minutes

- - - - - - - - - - - - - - -

Tips

This dish is often made using ground chicken instead of pieces. You can purchase pre-ground chicken or simply process chicken breasts to the desired consistency by using a food processor fitted with the metal blade.

If you can't find any holy basil, you can substitute Thai basil (avoid Mediterranean basil, as the flavor is completely different). Although best used fresh, holy basil leaves can be frozen and used within 3 months (see page 108).

• **Wok**

2 tbsp	neutral-flavored oil such as vegetable or peanut oil	30 mL
5	shallots, halved and thinly sliced	5
6	cloves garlic, minced	6
2	small red chiles, finely sliced	2
1½ lbs	boneless skinless chicken breast, cut into 1½-inch (4 cm) pieces (see Tips, left)	750 g
5 tsp	fish sauce (nam pla)	25 mL
4 tsp	soy sauce	20 mL
1½ cups	lightly packed holy basil leaves (see Tips, left)	375 mL

1. In wok over high heat, heat oil. Add shallots, garlic, and chiles and stir-fry for 2 minutes, until soft. Add chicken and cook, stirring constantly, for about 5 minutes or until meat starts to brown. Add fish sauce and soy sauce and continue to stir-fry until chicken is cooked through, 4 to 6 minutes. Stir in basil leaves and remove from heat. Serve immediately.

Bay Leaf

Laurus nobilis

Names in Other Languages

- **Arabic:** ghar, waraq ghaar, rand
- **Chinese (C):** yuht gwai
- **Chinese (M):** yue gui, yue gui ye
- **Czech:** vavrin uslechtily
- **Danish:** laurbaer
- **Dutch:** laurier
- **French:** laurier
- **German:** Lorbeer
- **Greek:** dafni
- **Italian:** alloro, lauro
- **Japanese:** gekkeiju, roreru
- **Portuguese:** loureiro
- **Russian:** lavr
- **Spanish:** laurel
- **Swedish:** lager
- **Turkish:** defne agaci
- **Vietnamese:** la nguyet que

Family: Lauraceae

Varieties: "Bay leaf" is used liberally to describe a number of leaves that belong to different families and that are added to recipes much like the European bay leaf. These include Indian bay leaves (*Cinnamomum tamala*); Indonesian bay leaves, or daun salam (*Eugenia polyantha*); Californian bay leaves (*Umbellularia californica*); Mexican bay leaves (*Litsea glaucescens*); West Indian bay leaves (*Pimenta acris*); and boldo (*Peumus boldus*).

Other Names: bay laurel, European bay leaf, noble laurel, poet's laurel, Roman laurel, sweet bay, true laurel, wreath laurel

Flavor Group: Pungent

Parts Used: leaves (as a herb)

Background

The bay tree is native to Asia Minor. Bay trees were cultivated widely in the Mediterranean and had reached Britain by medieval times, probably through Roman influence. The Romans treasured and revered bay leaves. The herbalist John Parkinson wrote in 1629 that Augustus Caesar wore a garland of bryony and bays to protect himself from lightning. In Greek mythology the gods played a mischievous game with Apollo: he was destined to pursue Daphne, who was destined to reject his love. The story ends with the gods turning Daphne into a bay tree to give her respite from Apollo's persistence, and he, devastated, declaring he will wear her leaves forever as a crown.

The Latin name for the bay tree comes from *laurus*, meaning "laurel," and *nobilis*, meaning "famous." Thus we find in Greek and Roman times that the winners of death-defying sports such as chariot races were crowned with a wreath of bay leaves, in the same way as victorious soldiers. The terms "poet laureate" and "baccalaureate" come from the tradition of giving distinguished scholars and physicians laurel berries (*bacca lauri*) in recognition of their achievements.

Culinary Information

Combines with
- basil
- chile
- garlic
- marjoram
- oregano
- paprika
- pepper
- rosemary
- sage
- thyme

Traditional Uses
- slow-cooked dishes
- soups, casseroles and roasts
- terrines
- steamed fish
- vegetable dishes
- tomato-based pasta sauces

Spice Blends
- bouquet garni
- ras el hanout
- steak and white meat seasoning blends
- herbes de Provence
- pickling spices
- spice rubs for red meat

The Plant

The bay tree is a densely foliaged medium-height evergreen that can grow to more than 33 feet (10 m) tall in favorable climates. The leaves are dark green and shiny on top and slightly paler, with more of a matte finish, underneath; they are oblong and tapered, 2 to 4 inches (5 to 10 cm) long and $3/4$ to $1^1/2$ inches (2 to 4 cm) wide. Young leaves are a lighter shade of green; they are soft and have less aroma and flavor than the mature, somewhat leathery, darker green leaves.

Fresh bay leaves, when broken to release their volatile oils, have a pungent, warm aroma with fresh camphor notes and a sharp, lingering astringency. The flavor is pungent, sharp, bitter and persistent. When dried, bay leaves become a lighter green and develop a matte appearance. When crumbled, they release an even more distinctive aroma, with mineral oil–type notes and less bitterness than fresh bay leaves.

Bay trees bear small, waxy cream-colored flowers with distinctive yellow stamens, followed by purple berries that dry to become black and hard. These berries should never be used in cooking, because they are poisonous (they contain laurostearine and lauric acid).

Some gardeners grow bay trees as specimens, with one or two placed strategically in tubs or in the garden. In Australia my parents had a row of about a dozen trees that over 20 years developed into a majestic hedge. Bay trees can be trimmed into a neat ball shape atop a single erect trunk, but if left to grow naturally, many shoots will come up around

the main stem, making for dense, low growth that is more effective as a hedge.

Other Varieties

In some cultures the term "bay leaf" is used liberally to describe a number of different leaves, probably because bay leaves are so popular in the West. None of the following are true bay leaves.

Indian bay leaves (*Cinnamomum tamala*) are quite different than the bay laurel; they come from a variety of cinnamon tree. **Indonesian bay leaves** (*Eugenia polyantha*), also known as daun salam, are another so-called bay leaf that has a slightly clove-like flavor and is used in many Indonesian recipes. **Californian bay leaves** (*Umbellularia californica*) look very similar to *Laurus nobilis* but have a much stronger, eucalyptus-like flavor; they should be used sparingly—say, half the quantity you would use of European bay leaves. **Mexican bay leaves** (*Litsea glaucescens*) and even **West Indian bay leaves**—the leaves of the bay rum berry tree (*Pimenta acris*)—are also added to cooking for their clove-like flavor.

Boldo (*Peumus boldus*) is another strongly flavored camphoraceous leaf, from the Monimiaceae family. It is used in South American cuisine. Indigenous to central Chile, boldo trees have spread to Europe but to my knowledge are not used there for culinary purposes. The leaves are most often blended with herbal teas and used medicinally. Boldo leaves contain the alkaloid boldine, which some sources promote as an antioxidant. However, toxicity concerns have been raised, possibly as a warning against overuse.

Do Not Eat Some Varieties

The bay tree of culinary use should not be confused with the bay rum berry tree or other varieties of laurel tree, many of which are poisonous.

Processing

Bay leaves are best used in their dried form in slow-cooked dishes, because drying dissipates the bitter notes in the fresh leaf and allows the flavor-giving volatile oils to infuse more effectively into the dish. To harvest bay leaves, trim the branches in keeping with how you want the tree to look. Avoid doing this when the tree is in flower—the flowers attract an abundance of bees. Within a few hours of pruning, cut each leaf off the branch with pruning shears. Keep only clean, mature leaves that are free from signs of white wax scale, a pest that deposits a sooty black substance on the leaves.

Like other herbs, bay leaves are best dried in a dark, well-aired place. Allow the water content to evaporate by leaving them to crisp and dry for about 5 days. At that point they will have a moisture content of less than 12%. To avoid curling and to achieve attractive flat leaves, arrange one layer on mesh (insect screening), making sure it is well ventilated, and place another piece of mesh on top, weighted down with some small pieces of wood. When the leaves are crisp and dry, store in an airtight container in a cool, dark place.

Buying and Storage

The majority of dried bay leaves available in stores around the world are produced in Turkey. They come in two main grades: The lowest grade is exported in 110-pound (50 kg)

Spice Notes

One of my most amusing memories about bay leaves comes from when I was a teenager. I had prepared my handsome gray horse Hector for a show. He was spotless, his hooves were painted and he was ready to be transported to the event the next morning. So he wouldn't get dirty, I shut him in a yard where my dad had planted a grove of bay trees. The next morning we were shocked to see that Hector had pruned most of the trees. Those of you who know horses will be familiar with their fresh, hay-scented breath. Imagine the consternation of the ringmasters and judges when this large gray horse breathed bay-leaf breath on them! Every time I cut branches of bay to dry, I still think of Hector.

WEIGHT PER TEASPOON (5 mL)

- **whole average dry leaf:** 0.3 g
- **ground:** 2.5 g

SUGGESTED QUANTITY PER POUND (500 g)

- **red meats:** 2 dry leaves, 3 fresh leaves
- **white meats:** 1 dry leaf, 2 fresh leaves
- **vegetables:** 1 dry leaf, 2 fresh leaves
- **grains and pulses:** 1 dry leaf, 2 fresh leaves
- **baked goods:** 1 dry leaf, 2 fresh leaves

bales and usually contains a considerable amount of extraneous matter, from branches to wire and pieces of rock (presumably to make up the weight). The best grade from Turkey is referred to as "hand-selected." These leaves have a better flavor and are considerably cleaner and more uniform in size and color than the ones in the bales.

When buying dried bay leaves, look for clean green ones— the darker the green, the better the leaf. Yellow leaves are indicative of poor quality at harvest or have been exposed to light for too long. When stored correctly, away from extremes of heat, light and humidity, whole bay leaves will keep their quality for up to 3 years. Powdered bay leaves are convenient to use but should be purchased only in small quantities, or grind them yourself. Once ground, the flavor is lost within 12 months, even when stored in ideal conditions.

Use

Bay leaves are associated mostly with slow-cooked recipes. They are considered to be indispensable in many different soups, stews, casseroles, terrines, pâtés and roast fowl dishes. They are mandatory in a bouquet garni, a traditional French-inspired bunch of herbs also comprising thyme, marjoram and parsley that is placed with the other ingredients in a pot during cooking and removed when ready to serve. Bay leaves are often added to stock while it is cooking.

Always use bay leaves sparingly, as the flavor is strong and amalgamates readily during cooking. For an average-size dish to serve 4 people, use 2 to 3 dried bay leaves, either whole for later removal or crumbled into the dish to soften during cooking. I like to barbecue fish wrapped in foil with a few green dill tips, a bay leaf and a dusting of amchur (green mango) powder.

Bay Rice Pudding

Cooked rice desserts are found all over the world in numerous variations. This is a classic European-style pudding, prepared on the stovetop with the addition of fresh bay leaves, which give the soft, creamy rice a subtle but distinct flavor. It may seem time-consuming, but I just have it on the go while cooking other dishes. And it is so comforting and satisfying that it is worth the time.

**Makes
6 servings**

Preparation time:
5 minutes

**Cooking time: 1 hour,
15 minutes**

Tip

Use "pudding rice" if available, or another short-grain rice such as Arborio or Carnaroli risotto rice.

1 cup	short-grain rice (see Tip, left)	250 mL
2	small fresh bay leaves	2
1	thick slice lemon peel	1
3 cups	water	750 mL
4 cups	whole milk	1 L
½ cup	granulated sugar	125 mL
½ tsp	pure vanilla extract	2 mL
	Freshly grated nutmeg, optional	

1. In a medium saucepan over medium heat, combine rice, bay leaves, lemon peel and water and bring to a boil, stirring occasionally. Once boiling, cover with a tight-fitting lid, reduce heat to low and simmer for about 15 minutes, until most of the water is absorbed. Stir in milk, sugar and vanilla. Simmer, covered, stirring occasionally, for 40 to 50 minutes, until rice is soft and creamy (it should have a slightly soupy consistency). Turn off the heat, remove and discard the bay leaf and lemon peel, and set aside for 10 to 15 minutes to cool slightly. Serve warm, at room temperature or chilled, sprinkled with a little nutmeg (if using).

Bergamot

Monarda didyma

Names in Other Languages

- **Arabic:** munardah
- **French:** bergamote, thé d'Oswego
- **German:** Monarde, Goldmelisse
- **Italian:** bergamotto
- **Japanese:** taimatubana
- **Korean:** perugamotu
- **Spanish:** bergamota

Family: Lamiaceae (formerly Labiatae)

Varieties: lemon bergamot (*M. citriodora*), wild bergamot (*M. fistulosa*), mint-leaved bergamot (*M. menthifolia*)

Other Names: bee balm, fragrant balm, Indian's plume, Oswego tea, red balm

Flavor Group: Medium

Parts Used: leaves and flowers (as a herb)

Background

Bergamot, which is native to North America, was identified in the 16th century by the Spanish medical botanist Nicolas de Monardes. Consequently his name is used to identify this genus of plants. The Oswego people of what is now New York State used to make an infusion of it—hence the name "Oswego tea." It was embraced as a beverage by the American settlers who, after the Boston Tea Party in 1773, boycotted tea from India that was imported by the English.

The Plant

Bergamot, a member of the same family as mint, is the show-off of the herb garden. It defies the aura of humility generally associated with herbs, which are more often than not appreciated for their flavor and medicinal efficacy rather than their looks. Bergamot bears a dozen or more tubular orange-scented flowers clustered in pompom-shaped whorls; they grow atop strong square stems with pairs of hairy oval leaves $3\frac{1}{4}$ inches (8 cm) long and $\frac{3}{4}$ inch (2 cm) wide. The resplendent flowers range from pink and mauve to a rich, vibrant red (the most popular 'Cambridge Scarlet' variety). The flowers are loaded with nectar and attract bees—hence the common name "bee balm" (not to be confused with the culinary herb balm, which also attracts bees).

Other Varieties

Lemon bergamot (*Monarda citriodora*), is used in salads; its flavor is more lemon-like than orange. **Wild** or **purple**

Culinary Information

Combines with
- basil
- mint
- rosemary
- sage
- thyme

Traditional Uses
- salads
- sauces for pork and duck

Spice Blends
- not commonly used in spice blends

Not Earl Grey

Bergamot gets its name from its aroma, which is similar to that of the bergamot orange (*Citrus bergamia*). Oil of bergamot comes from bergamot oranges, and it is that oil, not the bergamot herb, that is used to flavor Earl Grey tea.

SUGGESTED QUANTITY PER POUND (500 g)

- **white meats:** 2 tbsp (30 mL) fresh leaves
- **vegetables:** 2 tbsp (30 mL) fresh leaves
- **grains and pulses:** 4 tsp (20 mL) fresh leaves
- **baked goods:** 4 tsp (20 mL) fresh leaves

bergamot (*M. fistulosa*) also has a slightly lemony aroma but has less culinary use. **Mint-leaved bergamot** (*M. menthifolia*) has crinkly mint-like leaves and is sometimes confused with eau-de-cologne mint (*Mentha* x *piperita citrata*).

Processing

To dry the leaves of bergamot for making tea, hang bunches upside down in a dark, dry, well-aired place until the leaves have become quite crisp and dry. Gently crumble the dry leaves off the stems and store in an airtight container, away from extremes of heat, light and humidity.

Buying and Storage

If you want fresh bergamot you will probably have to grow your own. Harvest the fresh leaves and chop finely, then pack in ice-cube trays topped up with water and freeze. Fresh flowers can also be frozen in the same manner.

Dried bergamot, sold under the name "Oswego tea," may contain some dried flowers as well as leaves. When stored correctly, the flavor will last for 12 to 18 months.

Use

The fresh leaves and flowers are most commonly used in culinary applications, making a fragrant change from mint or basil. The brightly colored soft, honeyed flowers impart a delicate yet pungent taste and are an attractive addition to salads. The leaves contain the volatile oil thymol; as well as orangey notes, they deliver a flavor reminiscent of thyme, sage and rosemary, making bergamot leaves an ideal complementary herb to use with pork and duck, both of which benefit from a hint of orange.

Tomato and Bergamot Loaf

This recipe first appeared in my grandparents' book *Hemphill's Herbs: Their Cultivation and Usage*, which was published in 1983. My mother developed it when she first became interested in vegetarianism. It's a delicious and nutritious alternative to meat loaf, and a family favorite.

**Makes
2 servings**

Preparation time:
5 minutes

Cooking time:
20 minutes

Tip

To make fresh bread crumbs: In a food processor fitted with the metal blade, blitz 5 to 6 slices of day-old bread (if it's too fresh it won't turn into crumbs). Spread crumbs evenly on baking sheets and set aside to dry until crisp, about 20 minutes. Store in a resealable bag in the freezer for up to 6 months.

- **8- by 4-inch (20 by 10 cm) loaf pan, greased**
- **Preheat oven to 350°F (180°C)**

2	eggs, beaten	2
1	can (14 oz/398 mL) diced tomatoes, with juice	1
1½ cups	fresh white bread crumbs (see Tip, left)	375 mL
1¼ cups	shredded Cheddar cheese, divided	300 mL
1 cup	finely chopped celery	250 mL
2 tbsp	chopped fresh bergamot leaves	30 mL
2 tbsp	minced onion	30 mL
2 tbsp	olive oil	30 mL
½ tsp	fine sea salt	2 mL

1. In a large mixing bowl, combine eggs, tomatoes, bread crumbs, 1 cup (250 mL) cheese, celery, bergamot, onion, oil and salt. Spoon into prepared loaf pan, top with remaining cheese and bake in preheated oven for 20 minutes, until golden and cooked through. Serve warm with a green salad.

Black Lime

Citrus aurantifolia

Names in Other Languages

- **Danish:** sort lime
- **Dutch:** zwarte limoen
- **French:** limon noir
- **German:** schwarzer Limette
- **Hungarian:** fekete lime
- **Italian:** limetta nero
- **Spanish:** lima nero

Family: Rutaceae

Other Names: amani, black lemon, dried lemons, dried limes, loomi, noomi Basra, Oman lemons; when fresh, Tahitian lime or Persian lime

Flavor Group: Tangy

Parts Used: fruits (as a spice)

Background

Limes are indigenous to Southeast Asia. Likely, Moorish and Turkish traders introduced them to the Middle East. Citron, the citrus fruit that was familiar before oranges, was known to the Chinese in the fourth millennium BCE and mentioned by the ancient Egyptians. It was cultivated in southern Italy, Sicily and Corsica in the fourth century BCE; most of the citron for candied peel and perfumes still comes from Corsica.

Culinary Information

Combines with

- allspice
- cardamom
- cinnamon
- cloves
- coriander seed
- cumin
- paprika
- pepper
- turmeric

Traditional Uses

- fish stews
- osso bucco
- grilled meats
- roast fowl (placed whole in cavity during cooking)

Spice Blends

- Persian spice mixes
- lemon-and-pepper variants
- seafood seasonings
- spice rubs for poultry

An unexpected use for black limes evolved when a wine educator asked us to find a spice flavor to complement a botrytis (sometimes called "noble rot") dessert wine. Liz made a sugary sorbet flavored with infused black limes. Although its gray color was not appealing, everyone felt the flavor was a marriage made in heaven!

Limes, which fare better in hot climates than lemons, were often confused with lemons, and the history of lime trees is somewhat obscure. There are several types of lime, all of which are borne by trees that are somewhat smaller and bushier than lemon trees and have a varying profusion of prickly spikes. The common lime of India and Asia is thin-skinned, sour and juicy. The limes grown in Europe and America have a different flavor—they are not as sour and are believed to be a hybrid of Mexican lime and citron. Persian limes also have a distinctive taste. This is the variety that was originally dried while still on the tree, possibly an accidental discovery made when a neglected crop that had dried in the parching summer sun was found to have a beautiful taste.

The Plant

The lime trees that bear fruits most commonly harvested for drying are small, uneven-looking evergreen trees that grow up to 16 feet (5 m) tall. The branches have a profusion of small, sharp (and painful if you are pricked) spines. Lime fruits, which develop from small white flowers that are very attractive to bees, are borne for most of the year. The fresh fruits are greenish to yellow, usually have thin skins and are extremely juicy and fragrant. Because limes hybridize easily with other citrus trees, one cannot always be sure which hybrid trees black limes have come from.

Black limes are generally whole sun-dried Tahitian limes that are 1 to $1^1/_2$ inches (2.5 to 4 cm) in diameter. They vary in color from pale tan to very dark brown—almost

Spice Notes

My first encounter with black limes transported me back to my early childhood, when my parents owned a citrus orchard. The grading shed, where the fruits were sorted and crated, always had some stray oranges or lemons that had rolled onto the floor under a bench or grading chute. These dried out—no doubt going moldy and fermenting in the process—and they gave the shed a sweet, pungent aroma that the smell of black limes hauntingly evokes.

black—with up to 10 darker tan longitudinal stripes running from pole to pole. When they are broken open, sticky black remnants of pith are revealed on the inside and a pungent fermented citrus aroma is released. The fragrance of black limes always makes me think of delicious rich homemade marmalades.

Processing

Although limes were originally dried while still on the tree, the more common practice is to harvest the fruit when ripe and boil it in saltwater before drying it in the sun. Humidity conditions must be at a very low level; otherwise, the fruits will dry too slowly, turn quite black and often develop signs of mold. I have been told that a traditional practice was to bury freshly picked limes in the hot desert sands until they had been leached of nearly all moisture.

Buying and Storage

Black limes can be bought from Middle Eastern food stores and specialty spice retailers. *Black* refers to the dried inner membrane; the dried limes do not necessarily have black skin. Dark tan to light brown ones are generally best, but some very dark limes have a greater pungency and depth of flavor—something that is desirable as long as they do not show signs of mold. Always store in an airtight container and avoid extremes of heat, light and humidity.

Use

The highly aromatic, somewhat fermented flavor notes in black limes complement chicken and fish particularly well, similar to the use of preserved lemons in Moroccan and Middle Eastern food. Surprisingly, the addition of one or two pierced black limes to an oxtail stew gives it a welcome degree of piquancy. When adding whole black limes to a dish or putting one in the cavity of poultry before cooking, make a few holes in each lime with a skewer or the tines of a fork, to allow the cooking juices to infuse the tasty treat inside. Before discarding the limes, squeeze out the resulting rich liquid for a particularly satisfying taste sensation.

Black limes may also be pulverized and mixed with pepper to sprinkle on chicken and fish before broiling, as a substitute for lemon-and-pepper spice blends.

Kuwaiti Fish Stew with Black Lime

On one of my parents' many trips to India, they met a couple from Kuwait who were visiting India to photograph and learn more about spices. Bader and Sue were the first people to tell them about black limes, and they kindly shared their family recipe. Serve this fragrant stew with rice garnished with fried onions.

B

Makes 4 servings

Preparation time:
10 minutes

Cooking time:
40 minutes

Tip

For a deeper flavor, add 1 tsp (5 mL) Persian spice blend (page 750) in Step 2.

2 tsp	ground cumin	10 mL
2 tsp	freshly ground black pepper	10 mL
2 tsp	ground cardamom	10 mL
2 tsp	ground turmeric	10 mL
2 tsp	fine sea salt	10 mL
3 tbsp	oil, divided	45 mL
2	onions, quartered	2
3	tomatoes, quartered	3
2	whole black limes, each pierced with a skewer 4 to 5 times	2
1	large green finger chile, finely chopped	1
2 tbsp	tomato paste	30 mL
1 tbsp	minced garlic, divided	15 mL
2 cups	water	500 mL
2 tbsp	all-purpose flour	30 mL
4	skinless fish fillets, such as cod or perch (about 6 oz/170 g each)	4
1 cup	chopped fresh dill fronds	250 mL
1 cup	chopped fresh coriander leaves	250 mL

1. In a small bowl, combine cumin, pepper, cardamom, turmeric and salt.

2. In a large pot over medium heat, heat 2 tbsp (30 mL) oil. Add onions and sauté for 2 minutes, until softened. Stir in tomatoes, black limes, chile, tomato paste, 2 tsp (10 mL) garlic and 2 tsp (10 mL) of the ground spice mixture. Add water and stir. Reduce heat to low and cover to keep warm.

3. In a shallow bowl or plate, combine remaining ground spice mixture with flour. Dredge fish in mixture to coat evenly.

4. In a skillet over high heat, heat remaining 1 tbsp (15 mL) oil. Add fish and cook for 1 minute on each side, until lightly browned. Transfer fish to pot with tomato mixture (the fish should be completely covered; if needed, add more water). Add dill, coriander and remaining garlic. Simmer gently over low heat for 15 to 20 minutes, or until fish flakes easily when tested with a fork.

Borage

Borago officinalis

Names in Other Languages

- **Arabic:** lisaan athaur, hamham
- **Bulgarian:** porech
- **Chinese (C):** lauh leih geuih
- **Chinese (M):** liu li ju, bo li ju
- **Czech:** brotnak
- **Danish:** hjulkrone
- **Dutch:** bernagie
- **French:** bourrache officinale
- **German:** Borretsch, Gurkenkraut
- **Greek:** borantsa, vorago
- **Italian:** borragine
- **Japanese:** borji, ruridisa
- **Korean:** poriji
- **Portuguese:** borragem
- **Russian:** ogurechnaya trava
- **Spanish:** borraja, rabo de alacran
- **Turkish:** hodan, ispit, sigirdili

Family: Boraginaceae
Other Names: bee bread, star flower
Flavor Group: Mild
Parts Used: leaves and flowers (as a herb)

Background

Borage is believed to have originated in Aleppo in the Middle East (the southeastern part of what is now Syria) and was taken to England by the Romans. Large expanses of borage grow on the chalk downs of southern England, and the herb is now widely cultivated in the Mediterranean, North America and many other temperate areas. Borage has traditionally been associated with good spirits and well-being. Pliny is quoted as saying "A borage brew will eliminate a person's sadness and make the person glad to be alive." So strong was belief in the spirit-rousing powers of borage that it was given to Crusaders before they departed on their long journeys and to gladiators prior to blood-curdling skirmishes. In Wales borage is known as *llanwenlys*, which means "herb of gladness."

The Plant

Borage is one of the most photographed herbs and the culinary herb most often represented in tapestries, needlepoint and painted ceramics. These countless renditions

Culinary Information

Combines with
- basil
- chives
- cress
- lovage
- parsley
- salad burnet

Traditional Uses
- cocktails
- fruit punches
- green salads
- herb sandwiches
- soup

Spice Blends
- not commonly used in spice blends

are inspired by the plant's quintessentially "herby" look. Thick, soft, hollow and succulent stems up to 3 feet (1 m) tall are covered with wrinkled deep green leaves up to 6 inches (15 cm) long and topped with an abundance of star-shaped Wedgwood blue flowers with distinguishing black anthers in their centers. The whole plant is covered with fine, bristly hairs, conjuring up a thistle-like "don't touch me" demeanor. Quite often some soft pink flowers appear among the traditional blue borage blossoms, which are full of nectar and attract bees—hence the colloquial name "bee bread." There is also a rare white-flowered variety.

Borage self-sows so easily that, although an annual, it will continue to germinate from its own seeds, except in the harshest of winters. Few garden-scapes are more pleasing to the eye than drifts of self-sown borage: a show of massed azure-blue flowers among a sea of hazy green leaves and downy buds.

Processing

Borage leaves are generally used fresh. They wilt soon after picking, so they can be quite tricky to dry effectively. The best method is to harvest the leaves in the early morning and place them in a single layer on paper or on a frame covered with mesh such as insect screening. Set aside in a dark,

Spice Notes

In the 1950s my mother accidently discovered a quirky phenomenon. She added borage to sandwiches flavored with those typically Australian yeast spreads Vegemite and Promite (the English version is Marmite). The result was a taste sensation that closely resembled freshly shucked oysters!

dry place where the air can circulate freely and allow the moisture content to evaporate. When quite crisp, crumble and store in an airtight container away from extremes of heat, light and humidity. Borage flowers may also be dried using the same method.

An essential oil that is reputed to have anti-inflammatory properties is extracted from the seeds by steam distillation.

Buying and Storage

If you want to enjoy this popular self-sowing culinary herb year-round, your best option is to grow your own. Because borage wilts so soon after picking, it will always be difficult to buy good-quality fresh leaves. Borage flowers are more robust after harvesting and for this reason will often be found in prepared salads along with other exotic leaves and flowers. The flowers freeze well if picked when fully opened and placed carefully, one per compartment, in an ice-cube tray; gently cover with water and freeze. When you want to impress your guests with your panache and originality, drop one of these flowery ice-cubes into a glass of fruit juice, gin and tonic, or any other beverage.

Use

The cucumber flavor of borage makes it a logical addition to any green salad, but be sure to cut up the leaves small enough to negate the whisker-like hairiness. Add the cut-up leaves to cream cheese or cottage cheese and use the borage-flavored cheese, with a little salt and pepper, to make herb sandwiches. Whole tender leaves dipped in batter and fried make a different vegetable to serve as an appetizer or side dish. Borage flowers look attractive floating on refreshing drinks such as fruit punch or Pimm's, and their flavor complements the drinks. A popular dessert and cake decoration is made by dipping borage flowers in beaten egg whites, dusting them with sugar and allowing them to dry.

SUGGESTED QUANTITY PER POUND (500 g)

- **white meats:** 1/2 cup (125 mL) chopped fresh leaves
- **vegetables:** 1/2 cup (125 mL) chopped fresh leaves
- **grains and pulses:** 1/2 cup (125 mL) chopped fresh leaves
- **baked goods:** 1/2 cup (125 mL) chopped fresh leaves
- **flowers added primarily to decorate**

Borage Soup

Excellent served warm or cold, this brilliant green soup is finished off perfectly by bright blue borage flowers.

**Makes
2 servings**

Preparation time:
10 minutes

Cooking time:
20 minutes

- - - - - - - - - - - - - - -

• **Blender**

1	large potato, peeled and quartered	1
2 cups	vegetable broth	500 mL
4 cups	lightly packed fresh borage leaves, roughly chopped	1 L
1/2 cup	table (18%) cream	125 mL
1/2 tsp	freshly grated or ground nutmeg	2 mL
	Fine sea salt and freshly ground black pepper	
6	fresh borage flowers, optional	6

1. In a medium saucepan over medium heat, combine potato and broth and simmer until potato is tender when pierced with a fork, about 15 minutes. Stir in borage leaves and cook for 2 minutes, until wilted and well combined. Remove from heat and set aside to cool slightly. Transfer mixture to blender and purée until smooth. Return mixture to pan over medium heat. Stir in cream and nutmeg, season with salt and pepper to taste, and cook until heated through. Divide into serving bowls and top with borage flowers (if using).

Calamus

Acorus calamus americanus

Family: Araceae

Other Names: flag root, muskrat root, myrtle grass, rat root, sweet calomel, sweet cane, sweet flag, sweet grass, sweet rush, sweet sedge, wild iris

Flavor Group: Pungent

Parts Used: roots (as a spice), leaves (as a herb)

Background

There seems to be little argument that calamus, or sweet flag, as it is often called, is indigenous to the mountain marshes of India. Use of the rhizomes there stretches back to antiquity. Obviously it traveled early: there is evidence of the plant in Tutankhamun's tomb in Egypt. Even after its introduction to Europe and widespread distribution by the Viennese botanist Clausius in the 16th century, the Indian rhizome was reputed to have the strongest and most pleasant flavor. Its first recorded cultivation was in Poland, where it is said to have been introduced by the Tatars.

The name *calamus* is derived from the Greek *calamos*, meaning "reed." In England it was used as a strewing reed for religious festivals in churches and in some homes. It was particularly popular in Norfolk, where much of it was grown. Calamus now grows extensively in the marshes of England and it is not uncommon in Scotland. Although not found in Spain, it grows abundantly throughout the

Culinary Information

Combines with
- allspice
- cardamom
- cinnamon
- cloves
- ginger
- nutmeg
- vanilla

Traditional Uses
- custards and rice puddings
- salads
- Arab and Indian sweet dishes

Spice Blends
- not commonly used in spice blends

rest of Europe and eastward to southern Russia, China and Japan. In the northern United States it is so prolific it is considered indigenous.

Calamus roots were candied in the same way as angelica (see page 76) and used as a sweet addition to cakes and desserts in both England and North America. Its old name, *galingale,* was used to describe both calamus roots and the Asian spice galangal. In parts of Europe the young, tender flowers would sometimes be eaten for their sweetness, and children in Holland would chew the root. The oil extracted from calamus was used in the production of gin and for brewing some beers.

These days, candied calamus is used by the Turks to ward off disease, but it is rarely used in cooking. In recent years it became clear that *Acorus calamus* contains beta-asarone, a carcinogen. As a result, it has been designated "not recommended for culinary use." The American variety, *Acorus calamus americanus*, is said to lack beta-asarone. However, some countries have placed calamus oil from all sources on their prohibited plant and fungus lists. The oil may be banned because any undesirable elements in a plant (as well as potentially beneficial ones) are concentrated when its oil is extracted by steam distillation. Calamus root is still used as an ingredient in the medicinal, cosmetic and perfume industries.

The Plant

The sight of this hardy perennial growing in the shallow, still recesses of streams and watery ditches in the northern hemisphere evokes images of marsh plants, reeds and bulrushes. The long, sword-shaped, slightly crinkled, sweet-scented leaves grow to around 4 feet (1.2 m) tall, and tiny yellow flowers are borne on a solid cylindrical spike resembling a bulrush. Although the plant sometimes produces fruit, propagation is achieved mainly by vigorous growth of the rhizome.

While all parts of the plant are sweet and aromatic—the inner section of the stalk has an orange-like taste—most culinary and medicinal use is made of the root system, or rhizome. The rhizome is about $3/4$ inch (2 cm) in diameter and, when dry, is a pale gray-brown color and scarred from the removal of scores of wormlike rootlets at harvesting. In cross-section the rhizome is pale, almost white, porous

C

and woody. Calamus root has a pungent aroma; the flavor is initially sweet, similar to a mixture of cinnamon, nutmeg and ginger, with a bitter aftertaste.

Processing

Harvesting calamus is a pretty messy business. The matted roots, which are partially buried in the mud about 12 inches (30 cm) below the surface of the water, are cut and raked out of the mire. The leaves are stripped off and separated from the rhizomes, which must be thoroughly cleaned and stripped of the less aromatic rootlets before slicing and drying. Calamus root should not be peeled, because the cells containing the aromatic volatile oil are located in the outer section, near the surface. Appearance has often been considered important. As a result, white peeled German calamus was popular; however, it was not thought to be as good as the unpeeled version, especially for medicinal applications.

Buying and Storage

These days the majority of commercial calamus production seems to be in India and North America. Even when buying for culinary purposes, you will be more likely to find it with the medicinal or ayurvedic spices. Calamus loses its volatile oil easily and is therefore best if not stored for too long. Keep it in the whole sliced form, in an airtight container away from extremes of heat, light and humidity. Stored in this manner, calamus can be kept for up to 3 years.

Use

Caution is recommended when using calamus in cooking because of the possible presence of beta-asarone (see page 133). Also, because of its emmenagogic properties (it promotes menstruation), calamus should not be consumed during pregnancy. The leaves can be harvested and used fresh in an infusion of milk for custards, rice puddings and other desserts, in much the same way a vanilla bean or cinnamon stick is used to impart flavor. Young leaf buds can be added to salads. The powdered root is sometimes used in Indian and Arab sweet dishes for its delicate cinnamon, nutmeg and ginger notes.

WEIGHT PER TEASPOON (5 mL)

- Powdered root: 2 g

SUGGESTED QUANTITY PER POUND (500 g)

See cautionary notes under "Use."

- **red meats:** 1/2 tsp (2 mL)
- **white meats:** 1/2 tsp (2 mL)
- **vegetables:** 1/2 tsp (2 mL)
- **grains and pulses:** 1/2 tsp (2 mL)
- **baked goods:** 1/2 tsp (2 mL)

Candlenut

Aleurites moluccana

Names in Other Languages

- **Burmese:** kyainthee
- **Danish:** candlenut
- **Dutch:** bankoelnoot
- **Filipino:** lumbang bato
- **French:** noix de bancoul
- **German:** Candlenuss
- **Indonesian:** kemiri
- **Malay:** buah keras, kemiri
- **Sri Lankan:** kekuna

Family: Euphorbiaceae

Other Names: buah keras, candleberry, Indian walnut, kemiri kernels, kukui nut tree, varnish tree

Flavor Group: Amalgamating

Parts Used: nuts (as a spice)

Background

Candlenut trees are native to the tropical northern rainforests of Australia, the Molucca (Maluku) Islands and Malaysia and are found on many islands in the South Pacific. The botanical name *Aleurites* is derived from the Greek word for "floury," in reference to the silvery powdered appearance of its young leaves. The common name is derived from the tradition of making a crude lamp by threading the midrib of a palm leaf through the raw nut (like a wick) and lighting it. Because of the high oil content of the nut, this device will burn like a candle. Candlenuts have been used in the

Culinary Information

Combines with

- cardamom
- chile
- cinnamon
- cloves
- coriander seed
- fennel seed
- galangal
- ginger
- mustard
- pepper
- turmeric

Traditional Uses

- Asian dishes (as a thickening agent)
- rice dishes (cut into slivers and roasted)

Spice Blends

- satay sauces
- Malay curries

C

manufacture of paints, varnish and soap and the oil extracted for lamp oil. Roasted candlenuts have also been a source of food for Australian Aborigines and other Pacific peoples.

The Plant

Candlenuts are soft, oily, cream-colored seeds contained within a hard-shelled nut that grows on a magnificent tree. Candlenut trees can be 80 feet (24 m) tall, with large, hand-sized leaves that provide excellent shade. This tropical tree is related to the castor-oil plant. As for many other members of the euphorbia family, the fresh nut is toxic, but it loses its toxicity on roasting or cooking. Uncooked candlenuts have little discernible fragrance and a bland, soapy flavor. Roasted slivers or shavings of candlenut have a pleasing nutty, almond-like flavor without the background bitterness characteristic of almonds. The surrounding flesh of the fruit is not eaten by humans, but it is said to be an important food of the cassowary, a large flightless bird native to Queensland, Australia.

Processing

After harvesting, the nuts are generally roasted. The hard outer shell is removed prior to being sold in the markets of Malaysia and Indonesia.

WEIGHT PER TEASPOON (5 mL)

- whole average nut: 3.2 g

SUGGESTED QUANTITY PER POUND (500 g)

- red meats: 4 nuts
- white meats: 3 nuts
- vegetables: 3 nuts
- grains and pulses: 3 nuts
- baked goods: 3 nuts

Buying and Storage

Because of their high oil content, candlenuts are prone to rancidity, so it is best to buy small quantities and store them in a cool, dry place. You can't be certain that they were roasted prior to being shelled, so before eating be sure to cook them in a preheated 170°F (80°C) oven for 3 minutes to remove any toxicity.

Use

Candlenuts are used as a thickening agent in many Asian dishes. They are most commonly found in Malaysian recipes, especially for satay. When using candlenuts, for best results grind them finely, using a kitchen rasp or nutmeg grater, before adding to other ingredients. An interesting way to use them is to shave off slivers and dry-roast them in a pan for 5 minutes or until golden brown. Add these tasty roasted pieces to curries and satay sauces, or sprinkle them over rice dishes before serving.

Malay Curry

When my sisters and I were preteens, our parents took us on a family holiday to Penang, Malaysia, and although I was a little cautious about heavily spiced food, I remember the amazing Nyonya (Malay) dishes. Candlenut is often considered the secret ingredient in Nyonya cooking, and this unique curry (note the lack of chiles) is a perfect example the whole family will enjoy. Serve with steamed rice garnished with roasted slivered candlenuts.

Makes 6 servings

Preparation time:
15 minutes

Cooking time: 2 hours, 20 minutes

- - - - - - - - - - - - - - - - -

Tip

Makrut lime leaves are sometimes called "kaffir" lime leaves and are available at Asian grocers, fresh, frozen or dried.

• **Preheat oven to 400°F (200°C)**

1 tbsp	ground coriander	15 mL
2 tsp	ground cumin	10 mL
1/2 tsp	ground fennel seeds	2 mL
1/2 tsp	ground turmeric	2 mL
1/2 tsp	ground ginger	2 mL
1/4 tsp	ground cinnamon	1 mL
1/4 tsp	ground cloves	1 mL
1/4 tsp	freshly ground black pepper	1 mL
1/4 tsp	ground green cardamom seeds	1 mL
3 tbsp	oil	45 mL
1	large onion, minced	1
2	cloves garlic, minced	2
2 lbs	stewing beef, cut into 2-inch (5 cm) cubes	1 kg
4	candlenuts, slivered and toasted, divided	4
2	dried makrut lime leaves, torn (see Tip, left)	2
1	can (14 oz/398 mL) whole peeled tomatoes, with juice	1
1 2/3 cups	water	400 mL
2 tsp	palm sugar or lightly packed light brown sugar	10 mL
1/2 tsp	fine sea salt	2 mL
1/4 tsp	kenchur powder	1 mL
	Freshly squeezed juice of 1 lime	
1 cup	coconut milk (see Tip, page 141)	250 mL

Tip

Coconut milk is the liquid extracted from coconut meat and then watered down. The "cream" will sit at the top of the can, so it's best to shake before using to get the right milky consistency.

1. In a dry heavy-bottomed ovenproof pot over low heat, toast coriander, cumin, fennel seeds, turmeric, ginger, cinnamon, cloves, pepper and cardamom for 1 to 2 minutes, until fragrant and colors begin to deepen. Add oil and stir into a paste. Add onion and cook until transparent, about 3 minutes. Add garlic and stir to combine. Working in batches so as not to crowd the pan, add beef, stirring to cover evenly in spices, and cook until lightly browned on all sides, 7 to 8 minutes; transfer cooked meat to a plate as completed.

2. Once all the beef is browned, return to pan and add three-quarters of the candlenuts, lime leaves, tomatoes, water, sugar, salt, kenchur powder and lime juice. Reduce heat and simmer gently, stirring, for about 3 minutes. Cover and transfer pot to preheated oven. Bake for 2 hours, until meat is tender.

3. Stir in coconut milk until well combined. Garnish with reserved candlenut slivers and serve immediately.

Capers

Capparis spinosa (also known as *C. inermis*)

Family: Capparidaceae

Other Names: caper berry, caper bud, caper bush

Flavor Group: Tangy

Parts Used: buds and berries (as a spice)

Background

Capers have been eaten for thousands of years. This hardy perennial grows wild throughout the Mediterranean Basin, in North Africa, Spain, Italy and Algeria. It is often seen in rocky soil, rambling through the cracks of old stone walls and the ruins of buildings. As it grows so readily in these situations, it is difficult to pinpoint exactly where the plant originated. The name *caper* is derived from the Greek word for "he-goat." This suggests that those of us in the spice trade who use the word *goaty* to describe its unique flavor are not being merely fanciful.

The Plant

It is a small—5 feet (1.5 m) tall at best—creeping, bramble-like bush with tough oval leaves and attractive four-petaled white or pink flowers that sport an exuberant spray of long purple stamens. The short-lived flowers—those that bloom

Culinary Information

Combines with

- anise seed
- basil
- bay leaf
- chervil
- dill
- fennel
- garlic
- parsley
- tarragon

Traditional Uses

- puttanesca sauce
- strongly flavored and oily fish
- tartar sauce
- Liptauer cheese
- tomatoes (fresh and cooked)

Spice Blends

- not commonly used in spice blends

in the morning are finished by the afternoon—are about the size of a dandelion. The wild variety (*Capparis spinosa*) bears uncomfortable-looking spines; however, the type grown commercially in France (*C. inermis*) has no spines.

Capers as we know them, either salted or preserved in brine, are the small unopened flower buds. If the flowers are left to mature, they form oval fruits like rose hips that are referred to as caper berries. The taste of fresh caper buds is very bitter and not at all pleasing. However, when pickled, they develop a distinctive acidic, salty, sweaty, lingering metallic flavor and a "goatlike" urea aroma that is surprisingly appealing and refreshing.

Processing

It is critical that caper buds be harvested at the optimum time. Buds that are just the right size (large, overly mature ones will result in a sour, astringent flavor) are gathered in the early morning, before they can open with the rising sun, then put aside in the shade to wilt for a day. The wilted buds, generally with about $1/8$ inch (3 mm) of stem retained, are placed in barrels of heavily salted wine vinegar and left to pickle. During this process, capric acid develops; it is the subtle hint of capric acid that gives pickled capers their characteristic flavor. An alternative process is dry salting, in which the buds are not immersed in vinegar. Dry salting gives a less sharp and somewhat sweeter taste than the pickling method. Caper berries (and sometimes even the leaves and spikes) are also pickled, especially in Cyprus, where capers grow in alarming abundance.

Travels in the Spice Trade

After visiting a large processing facility for bay leaves and dried herbs outside Izmir, Turkey, we left the beaten track. Bumping along a dusty road, we spied caper bushes (*Capparis spinosa*) growing like weeds along the roadside. It's amazing that anyone ever thought of pickling the unpleasant-tasting buds from this spiky, bramble-like bush, producing a condiment that is a natural partner for smoked salmon, among other delights.

A Substitute

The green seeds and buds of nasturtium (*Tropaeolum majus*) have been pickled for use as a substitute for capers; however, these have a sharper, more mustard-like taste. Nasturtium flowers are also used fresh, for decoration in salads.

WEIGHT PER TEASPOON (5 mL)

- whole drained weight: 5.3 g

SUGGESTED QUANTITY PER POUND (500 g)

- red meats: 2 tsp (10 mL)
- white meats: 2 tsp (10 mL)
- vegetables: 1 tsp (5 mL)
- grains and pulses: 1 tsp (5 mL)
- baked goods: 1 tsp (5 mL)

Buying and Storage

The best pickled capers are reputed to be those produced in France. The smallest—around $1/8$ inch (3 mm) in diameter—and most delicate are called *nonpareils*. These are followed in size by four grades: *surfine*, *fine*, *mi-fine* and *capucines*, which may be as large as $1/2$ inch (1 cm). The lowest grade can be up to five times larger than those classified as nonpareils. Dry-salted capers are usually sold as nonpareils and are up to $1/4$ inch (5 mm) in diameter. Capers preserved in salted wine vinegar should always be stored in the refrigerator after opening, covered with their pickling liquid. Never allow them to dry out—just remove what you need from the jar and keep the remainder immersed. Once capers are exposed to air, the flavor rapidly deteriorates. One benefit of dry-salted capers is that they do not need to be refrigerated after opening.

Use

While capers in vinegar are often removed from their liquid and not rinsed prior to application, I prefer to give them a quick wash to dilute both the salty brined taste and the acidity. Salted capers should be rinsed thoroughly and lightly dried on a paper towel before using. The brackish, tangy flavor of capers enhances the appetite and serves as an excellent foil for strong-flavored or oily fish. Capers are an essential ingredient in tartar sauce. They also complement tomatoes (as most things tangy do—see sumac, page 612), enhance salads (particularly along with black olives), and go well with poultry. In Spain, caper berries appear on most tapas menus. Montpellier butter and Hungarian Liptauer cheese use capers as a key ingredient. Another tasty way to prepare capers is to rinse them, dry thoroughly on a paper towel and then deep-fry them. The crunchy, tasty morsels are delicious with cheese and crackers.

Puttanesca Pasta

Puttanata is Italian for "worthless," derived from the word *puttana* ("prostitute"). But this sauce couldn't be further removed from its namesake origins. This humble, salty combination of anchovies, olives and capers mixed with tomatoes, garlic and herbs makes a delicious and satisfying pasta sauce.

C

Makes
4 servings

Preparation time:
  15 minutes
Cooking time:
  30 minutes

- - - - - - - - - - - - - - - -

Tip

Either brined or salted capers may be used. Just be sure to rinse them of excess salt before adding to the sauce.

• **Mortar and pestle**

SAUCE

6	anchovy fillets	6
4	cloves garlic	4
½ tsp	packed light brown sugar	2 mL
18	black olives, pitted and chopped	18
2 tsp	dried hot pepper flakes	10 mL
1	can (14 oz/398 mL) diced tomatoes, with juice	1
⅓ cup	medium- to full-bodied red wine	75 mL
¼ cup	olive oil	60 mL
1 tbsp	capers, rinsed (see Tip, left)	15 mL
1 tbsp	dried Italian herbs (see page 740)	15 mL

PASTA

1 lb	spaghetti or penne	500 g
	Freshly grated Parmesan cheese	

1. *Sauce:* Using mortar and pestle, crush the anchovies, garlic and brown sugar to make a rough paste. Transfer to a saucepan over medium heat. Add olives, hot pepper flakes, tomatoes, wine, oil, capers and Italian herbs. Simmer gently, uncovered, for 30 minutes, stirring occasionally, until liquid has reduced and thickened.

2. *Pasta:* Meanwhile, in a pot of boiling salted water, cook pasta according to package instructions, until al dente. Strain and return pasta to pot. Add prepared sauce and stir through. Top with Parmesan and serve immediately.

Caraway

Carum carvi (also known as *Bunium carvi, Carum aromaticum, C. decussatum, Foeniculum carvi*)

Names in Other Languages

- **Arabic:** karawiya
- **Chinese (C):** yuan-sui, goht leuih ji
- **Chinese (M):** ge lü zi
- **Czech:** kmin, kmin lucni
- **Danish:** kommen
- **Dutch:** karwij, kummel
- **French:** carvi, cumin des près
- **German:** Kummel
- **Greek:** karo, karvi
- **Indian:** shia jeera, gunyan, vilayati jeera
- **Italian:** comino, cumino tedesco
- **Japanese:** karuwai
- **Malay:** jemuju
- **Portuguese:** alcaravia
- **Russian:** tmin
- **Spanish:** alcaravea
- **Swedish:** kummin
- **Thai:** hom pom, tian takap
- **Turkish:** frenk kimyonu

Family: Apiaceae (formerly Umbelliferae)

Varieties: black caraway (*Bunium persicum*, also known as *Carum bulbocastanum*)

Other Names: caraway fruit, Persian caraway, Persian cumin, Roman cumin, wild cumin

Flavor Group: Pungent

Parts Used: seeds (as a spice)

Background

Caraway is acknowledged to be one of the world's oldest comestibles. Seeds have been found in the remains of foods dating back to 3000 BCE. The ancient Egyptians buried their dead with caraway, and it was valued by the early Greeks and Romans for both medicinal and culinary purposes. The Arabs, to whom it has been known since the 12th century, called it *karawiya*, from which the common name is reputedly derived. However, Pliny, the celebrated first-century CE Roman scholar, wrote that its name comes from a former province in Asia Minor called Caria.

Caraway was widely known in the Middle Ages. It was used for centuries as an aid to digestion and was often added to breads, cakes and baked fruit. When used by home cooks, caraway was thought to prevent lovers from straying; as evidence of its "staying" power, caraway in baked dough

Culinary Information

Combines with

- allspice
- cardamom
- cinnamon
- coriander seed
- cumin
- fennel seed
- ginger
- paprika
- pepper
- turmeric

Traditional Uses

- European cheeses
- pork dishes
- breads
- vegetables, especially cabbage and potato

Spice Blends

- garam masala
- sausage seasonings
- harissa paste
- satay spices
- tabil
- tandoori spice blends
- ras el hanout

C

A Confusing Name

The Swedish name for caraway is *kummin*, which causes considerable confusion with the ubiquitous spice cumin, which has a very different, "curry-like" flavor.

is fed to homing pigeons, encouraging them to return to their cotes. In England, after a serious lapse in popularity throughout the 20th century, caraway seems to be enjoying a bit of a resurgence due to the increasing popularity of exotic cuisines, where caraway is regarded as an essential spice—for instance in Indian garam masala (see page 735) and Tunisian harissa (see page 737).

Caraway is indigenous to all of Europe and is claimed to be native to parts of Asia, India and North Africa. Caraway grows so readily in temperate climates that it is now cultivated in many countries.

The Plant

The caraway plant is a delicate biennial that grows to 24 inches (60 cm) tall and has pale green, finely defined leaves on slight, hollow stems that bear white umbrella-shaped flowers. The fruits (as they are most correctly called) split into two crescent-shaped dark brown "seeds" that are $1/4$ inch (5 mm) long, with five strongly defined pale ribs running from end to end. (For the sake of convenience, we'll call them seeds.) The root is long, thick and tapered, like a small carrot; it is pale in color and has a flavor similar to the seeds. The feathery leaf fronds have a mild flavor like dill tips. Caraway seeds have a warm, earthy, robust aroma with hints of fennel and anise and a faint orange-peel quality. The taste is similar, with an initial fresh mintiness combined with anise and eucalyptus flavors, followed by a lingering nuttiness.

Other Varieties

There is another variety of caraway, a perennial that is generally referred to as **black cumin** or **jeera kala** (see page 235), with the botanical names *Carum bulbocastanum* and *Bunium persicum.* The flavor of this seed is more like cumin than caraway. It is generally used in rich North Indian dishes containing cream, yogurt, white poppy seeds and crushed nuts.

Processing

Caraway needs to be harvested in the very early morning, while the dew is still on the fragile umbels; if the sun is shining on them when gathered, the dry heads will shatter, scattering the seeds. After harvesting, complete seed stalks are stored for about 10 days to dry out and finish ripening. Then they are threshed to remove the seeds (the remaining straw is used as cattle feed).

An essential oil, high in the active constituent carvone, is extracted from caraway seeds by steam distillation. This oil is an ingredient in liqueurs such as aquavit, kümmel, gin and schnapps. In addition, it flavors mouthwashes, toothpaste and chewing gums.

Buying and Storage

Dutch caraway is generally considered to be the best, but high grades from Bhutan, Canada, India and Syria are also very good. Whole seeds will last up to 3 years under normal storage conditions. Purchase ground caraway only if you expect to use it fairly quickly, as the volatile top notes dissipate quite rapidly. Store in an airtight container and away from extremes of heat, light and humidity.

Use

Caraway is used in many European cheeses because its fresh anise and fennel notes help to balance fatty richness and robust flavors. It has a special affinity to fruits with cores, such as apples, pears and quinces. Caraway seed is used in pork sausages and complements cabbage surprisingly well. The most famous use for caraway seed is in rye bread. Another carbohydrate that benefits from the addition of caraway is potato; it is especially good as a seasoning for potato soup.

WEIGHT PER TEASPOON (5 mL)
- **whole:** 3.4 g
- **ground:** 2.4 g

SUGGESTED QUANTITY PER POUND (500 g)
- **red meats:** 1½ tsp (7 mL) ground seeds
- **white meats:** 1½ tsp (7 mL) ground seeds
- **vegetables:** ¾ tsp (3 mL) whole seeds
- **grains and pulses:** ¾ tsp (3 mL) whole seeds
- **baked goods:** ¾ tsp (3 mL) whole seeds

Three-Cabbage Coleslaw

The perfect salad for a barbecue, this coleslaw can also be made with a mixture of vegetables (or fruits) such as fennel, carrot or apple. Serve with Pork Belly with Pomegranate Molasses (page 525).

C

**Makes
6 servings**

Preparation time:
10 minutes

Cooking time: **none**

Tip

Use a sharp knife, not a food processor, to slice the cabbage. If the pieces are too thin, the coleslaw may become watery.

1 cup	white cabbage, sliced ¼ inch thick	250 mL
1 cup	red cabbage, sliced ¼ inch thick	250 mL
1 cup	green cabbage, sliced ¼ inch thick	250 mL
⅓ cup	mayonnaise	75 mL
2 tbsp	sour cream	30 mL
1½ tsp	caraway seeds	7 mL
2 tbsp	freshly squeezed lemon juice	30 mL
	Sea salt and freshly ground black pepper	

1. In a large bowl, combine white, red and green cabbage, mayonnaise, sour cream, caraway seeds and lemon juice. Mix well and season with salt and pepper to taste. For the best flavor, cover and refrigerate coleslaw for at least 1 hour before eating. It will keep in the refrigerator for up to 2 days.

Variations

Substitute 1 cup (250 mL) thinly sliced fennel, carrot or apple for one of the types of cabbage.

Travels in the Spice Trade

Caraway plants always remind Liz and me of the time we visited Ura, a small rural town in the Bumthang district of northeastern Bhutan. We were there to research commercial opportunities for low-volume, high-value crops such as brown cardamom, Sichuan pepper and caraway seeds. Crops such as these can provide much-needed revenue to small countries such as Bhutan. Our objective was to help them understand the quality specifications that importing countries require, thereby giving Bhutan opportunities to increase its spice exports. Minjur, the farmer we visited, had a small plot of caraway that looked very healthy. We were interested to learn that caraway plants at that altitude—10,170 feet (3,100 m)—and in that climate grow as perennials for up to five years. I was amused by Minjur's reply when I asked him the price of his caraway seeds. After his long, animated diatribe to our interpreter, I imagined an equally long and involved reply would ensue. However, the answer was a straightforward "500 ngultrum," which is about US$8 per kilogram.

Caraway Seed Cake

Hugely popular in Britain during the Victorian era, recipes for this cake date as far back as the 16th century. This light loaf resembles a simple pound cake enhanced by anise-like caraway and zesty lemon.

Makes 1 loaf cake

Preparation time:
10 minutes

Cooking time:
40 minutes

Tips

If you can't find self-rising flour in stores, you can make your own. To equal 1 cup (250 mL) self-rising flour, combine 1 cup (250 mL) all-purpose flour, 1½ tsp (7 mL) baking powder and ½ tsp (2 mL) salt.

This cake will last up to 3 months in the freezer. To freeze, cool completely, then wrap tightly in plastic wrap. Defrost at room temperature and serve.

- **9- by 5-inch (23 by 12.5 cm) loaf pan, greased and lined with parchment paper**
- **Preheat oven to 350°F (180°C)**

¾ cup	butter, softened	175 mL
¾ cup	granulated sugar	175 mL
3	eggs, lightly beaten	3
2 cups	self-rising flour (see Tips, left)	500 mL
1½ tbsp	caraway seeds	22 mL
1 tsp	freshly grated lemon zest	5 mL
3 tbsp	milk	45 mL
2 tsp	granulated sugar	10 mL

1. In the bowl of an electric mixer at low speed, beat butter and ¾ cup (175 mL) sugar until light and creamy. Add eggs one at a time, beating between each addition. Add flour, caraway seeds, lemon zest and milk and mix until smooth.

2. Pour into prepared loaf pan and sprinkle evenly with 2 tsp (10 mL) sugar. Transfer to preheated oven and bake for 40 minutes or until golden and a tester inserted in the center of the cake comes out clean. Let cool in pan on a wire rack for 10 minutes, then invert cake onto rack to cool completely.

Cardamom – Brown

Cardamomum amomum (also known as *Amomum subulatum*)

Names in Other Languages

- **Arabic:** hal aswad
- **Bhutanese:** elanchi ngab
- **Burmese:** phalazee
- **Chinese (C):** chou gwo, cangus
- **Chinese (M):** cao guo, tsao kuo
- **Danish:** sort kardemomme
- **Dutch:** zwarte kardemom
- **French:** cardamome noir
- **German:** schwarzer Kardamom
- **Indian:** elchi, elaichi, illaichi, badi
- **Indonesian:** kapulaga
- **Italian:** cardamomo nero
- **Japanese:** soka
- **Malay:** buah pelaga
- **Spanish:** cardamomo negro
- **Thai:** luk kravan

Family: Zingiberaceae

Varieties: Indian cardamom (*Cardamomum amomum*), Chinese cardamom (*Amomum globosum*, also known as *A. tsao-ko*)

Other Names: bastard cardamom, Bengal cardamom, black cardamom, Chinese black cardamom, false cardamom, large cardamom, Nepal cardamom, winged cardamom

Flavor Group: Pungent

Parts Used: pods and seeds (as a spice)

Background

The entry on green cardamom (page 158) provides an account of the general history of the cardamom family. Unlike green cardamom, the brown variety is native to the Himalayan region, usually growing in light forest shade alongside cool streams. Plantations have been developed in these areas from what was originally wild stock. Spice gardens of brown cardamom will last for more than 25 years, and there are accounts of plantations in its native Nepal and Bhutan that are more than 100 years old.

Brown cardamom has always been considered at best a poor substitute for green cardamom and has often been

Know Your Cardamom

If your recipe simply states "cardamom pods" without reference to color, always assume that green cardamom is required. Recipes requiring brown or black cardamom will definitely say so.

Indian brown cardamom

Culinary Information

Combines with

- allspice
- chile
- cinnamon
- coriander seed
- cumin
- ginger
- green cardamom
- mustard
- paprika
- pepper
- star anise
- turmeric

Traditional Uses

- marinades for roast meats
- Indian curries
- Chinese master stocks
- Asian soups

Spice Blends

- tandoori spice blends
- Indian curry mixes

Many of my friends who run Indian restaurants have told me that they always count the number of brown cardamom pods put into a dish during cooking. This is so the same number of pods can be removed before serving, as many have had diners complain about a cockroach in their curry when it was only a winged Indian brown cardamom pod!

unscrupulously traded as a substitute. In Scandinavia in the 1970s, when the price of green cardamom was very high, some traders removed the seeds from brown cardamom pods and sold them as green seeds.

The Plant

Like its green relative, brown cardamom is a perennial that grows from a rhizome. It has long, lance-shaped leaves that grow to 6 feet (2 m) tall, with 25 to 30 plain yellow flowers that emerge in a dense cluster close to the ground. The oval pods that form after flowering are about 1 inch (2.5 cm) long and $1/2$ inch (1 cm) wide and deep red to purple in color when ripe; they contain about 40 round, hard, dark brown seeds encased in a soft, sweet-smelling pulp.

Dried Indian brown cardamom pods are dark brown, rough and ribbed on the surface (the furry ribbing is sometimes referred to as wings). Peeling back the leathery skin reveals a mass of sticky tar-colored seeds that release a woody, smoky, camphorous aroma. When chewed, the seeds have an astringent, antiseptic eucalyptus flavor that is refreshing.

Other Varieties

Chinese brown cardamom (*Amomum globosum*) is a similar plant, but the pods are much larger than in the Indian version, being about $1^1/2$ inches (4 cm) long and

C

Don't be put off by some of the names given to this "ugly duckling" of the spice world. When a spice such as brown cardamom is ridiculed with such names as "false" and "bastard," you cannot help but feel this is an offhand put-down of a spice that is too often compared to its popular cousin green cardamom. When brown cardamom is evaluated for its own qualities, the value it has as a condiment can be fully appreciated.

1 inch (2.5 cm) wide. The outer skin of its pods is similar in appearance, though harder and a little smoother. When cut open, segments resembling the layout inside a walnut reveal up to 20 pyramid-shaped seeds covered by a papery membrane. The aroma is more medicinal and less smoky than the Indian variety. The flavor resembles pine and eucalyptus and is sharply astringent, numbing and peppery. It reminds me that the rare and ancient grains of paradise (see page 313), also called Melegueta pepper, is a close relative.

Processing

Harvesting brown cardamom is a fascinating process to observe for the first time, because the uninitiated can see no signs of pods on the plant. They are at ground level, in the deep crown of the plant. The method used to dry Indian brown cardamom pods is crucial to achieving their unique flavor profile. The freshly harvested deep red capsules are spread out on platforms in the shade for about a week. The drying platforms are positioned over a smoldering fire; hot air from the fire hastens the drying process, turning the pods dark brown and imparting the characteristic smoky note. The lack of smoke aroma in Chinese brown cardamom is mainly due to its alternative sun-drying process. The majority of Chinese brown cardamom is supplied from Thailand and may sometimes come from several Indo-Chinese species of *Amomum*.

Travels in the Spice Trade

Liz and I were blessed with the opportunity to visit Bhutan, a totally landlocked country between Nepal, India and Tibet. As our plane landed we could see the Himalayan snows sparkling on the horizon. Our mission, as guests of the Ministry of Agriculture, was to observe spice production and provide insights into the quality and food safety requirements of spice buyers in Western countries. After many hours driving along precipitous mountain roads, we visited a cardamom farm in the remote village of Damphu. I was soon clambering down a steep slope and disappearing into a jungle of plants with two farm workers who were brandishing long, sharp, narrow steel blades. The workers started prodding and hacking at the base of a plant until they extracted a bizarre-looking hoary clump the size of two fists. When we emerged from the undergrowth with our spoils, Kadola, the Ministry of Agriculture officer accompanying us, broke apart the clump to reveal about 20 rough purple pods. When we broke open and tasted one of the just-harvested pods, we were amazed at the fruity sweetness of the soft, translucent fresh pulp surrounding the seeds.

WEIGHT PER TEASPOON (5 mL)
- whole average pod: 1.5 g
- ground: 3 g

SUGGESTED QUANTITY PER POUND (500 g)
- red meats: 2 pods
- white meats: 1 pod
- vegetables: 1 pod
- grains and pulses: 1 pod
- baked goods: 1 pod

Buying and Storage

Don't be put off by the dirty appearance of Indian brown cardamom pods in a pack, as some of the wings will flake off the capsules, giving them a dusty appearance. What's most important is they should be whole, not broken, and have the classic aroma profile described on page 152. Poor-quality pods may contain bits of earth and should be rejected if they have split open. Brown cardamom seeds removed from the pod are sticky and messy to handle; they tend to dry out and lose their best attributes fairly quickly, so keep the pod whole until ready to use. As with all spices, store the pods in an airtight container away from extremes of heat, light and humidity. Stored this way, they will last for up to 3 years.

Use

Cast out any notion that brown cardamom is an inferior version of green cardamom. Consider its flavor strengths, remember that it is a different spice, and you will discover just how useful it can be. The smoky notes of Indian brown cardamom complement many Indian dishes, which is logical when you realize that most traditional Indian meals are cooked in a tandoor or over an open wood fire. Indian brown cardamom is an invaluable spice in any tandoori-style recipe, as its unique woody, smoky notes help to convey the complex array of sensual flavors so readily associated with the tandoor. Similarly, the camphor-like notes in Chinese brown cardamom balance effectively with the strong spices (such as star anise) that are found in so many Southeast Asian recipes. Chinese brown cardamom pods can be added to clear soups, and the seeds, removed and crushed with star anise, make an exotic addition to roasted pork tenderloin and stir-fry dishes of Asian vegetables with strips of beef.

When blending brown cardamom with other spices, first remove the cardamom seeds from the pods and, using a mortar and pestle, crush them with a drier spice, such as coriander seeds, to absorb the stickiness; then add to the spice mix. In wet marinades (for example, those containing yogurt), thump the cardamom pod with the back of a spoon to split it, then add it whole. The flavor will penetrate the dish and the pod can easily be removed before serving.

Chinese brown cardamom

Indian Butter Chicken

This rich, lavish curry, which originated in Delhi in the 1950s, has become one of Indian cuisine's most popular dishes. The ingredient list is very long but it is not a difficult recipe to make. And you will be well rewarded for your efforts when you taste it.

Makes 6 servings

Preparation time:
20 minutes, plus overnight for marinating

Cooking time:
40 minutes

Tips

Ground Kashmiri chile is medium-hot, flavorsome and versatile. You can find it at most Indian markets at varying levels of heat (depending on the amount of seeds and membrane ground with the chile).

Ghee is a type of clarified butter used in Indian cooking. If you don't have any, you can substitute an equal amount of butter or clarified butter.

• **Mortar and pestle**

BUTTER CHICKEN SPICE BLEND

2	brown cardamom pods	2
2½ tsp	sweet paprika	12 mL
1 tsp	ground cumin	5 mL
1 tsp	ground coriander seeds	5 mL
½ tsp	ground ginger	2 mL
½ tsp	ground cinnamon	2 mL
½ tsp	ground fenugreek seeds	2 mL
½ tsp	freshly ground black pepper	2 mL
¼ tsp	ground medium-hot chile (see Tips, left)	1 mL
¼ tsp	ground green cardamom seeds	1 mL
¼ tsp	ground caraway seeds	1 mL

CURRY

1½ cups	plain yogurt	375 mL
6	skinless boneless chicken breasts (about 2 lbs/1kg)	6
2 tbsp	tomato sauce	30 mL
1 tbsp	palm sugar or packed light brown sugar	15 mL
1 tbsp	medium-heat curry powder, such as Madras (page 716)	15 mL
1 tbsp	ground almonds	15 mL
1 tbsp	tomato paste	15 mL
1 tbsp	tomato or mango chutney or mango pickle	15 mL
2 tsp	garam masala (page 735)	10 mL
1 tbsp	ghee (see Tips, left)	15 mL
1 tbsp	ground cumin seed	15 mL
3	onions, finely grated or puréed	3
1 tbsp	minced garlic	15 mL
1	can (3 oz/90 mL) coconut milk	1
1 cup	table (18%) cream, divided	250 mL
1 tbsp	fresh coriander (cilantro) leaves, plus extra for garnish	15 mL
	Fine sea salt	

Tip

The spice blend can be made up to a week ahead and stored in an airtight container.

1. *Butter Chicken Spice Blend:* Using mortar and pestle, roughly grind brown cardamom pods. Transfer to a small bowl and add paprika, cumin, coriander seed, ginger, cinnamon, fenugreek, pepper, ground chile, green cardamom seeds and caraway. Mix well.

2. *Curry:* In a resealable bag, mix yogurt and half of the prepared spice blend, reserving remaining half. Add chicken, seal, and turn to coat chicken thoroughly. Refrigerate overnight.

3. Place oven rack in highest position. Preheat broiler. Line a baking sheet with aluminum foil.

4. Remove chicken from marinade, keeping as much marinade as possible on the chicken (discard excess marinade). Place chicken on prepared baking sheet and broil for 4 to 5 minutes on each side, until chicken is cooked through and well browned.

5. Meanwhile, in a small bowl, combine reserved spice blend, tomato sauce, sugar, curry powder, ground almonds, tomato paste, chutney and garam masala.

6. In a large saucepan over medium heat, melt ghee. Add cumin and cook, stirring constantly, for about 30 seconds, until fragrant. Add onions and garlic and sauté for 2 to 3 minutes, until onions are softened. Stir in prepared tomato sauce mixture, bring to a simmer and cook for 2 to 3 minutes. Add cooked chicken, along with pan drippings, and stir to coat well. Stir in coconut milk, cream, coriander leaves and salt to taste. Simmer gently, uncovered, until slightly reduced, about 10 minutes. Garnish with additional coriander leaves. Serve with basmati rice.

Variation

For a vegetarian version, substitute the same quantity of pumpkin, squash or any root vegetable for the chicken.

Cardamom – Green

Elettaria cardamomum Maton

- **Arabic:** hal
- **Burmese:** phalazee
- **Chinese (C):** baahk dau kau, siu dau kau (*A. krervanh*)
- **Chinese (M):** bai dou kou, xiao dou kou, dou kou (*A. krervanh*)
- **Czech:** kardamom
- **Danish:** kardemomme
- **Dutch:** kardemom
- **French:** cardamome vert
- **German:** Kardamom
- **Greek:** kakoules
- **Indian:** elaichi, illaichi, elaychi
- **Indonesian:** kapulaga
- **Italian:** cardamomo verde
- **Japanese:** karudamon, shozuku
- **Malay:** buah pelaga, ka tepus (*A. krervanh*)
- **Portuguese:** cardamomo
- **Russian:** kardamon
- **Spanish:** cardamomo
- **Sri Lankan:** enasal
- **Swedish:** kardemumma
- **Thai:** kravan
- **Turkish:** kakule tohomu
- **Vietnamese:** truc sa, sa nhan (*A. krervanh*)

Family: Zingiberaceae

Varieties: small cardamom (*Elettaria cardamomum* Maton), Thai cardamom (*Amomum krervanh*), Sri Lankan wild cardamom (*Elettaria ensal*), brown or black cardamom (see page 151)

Other Names: cardamom, small cardamom, queen of spices

Flavor Group: Pungent

Parts Used: pods and seeds (as a spice)

Background

Green cardamom is native to the mountain ranges of the southwestern Indian state of Kerala. In this tropical paradise, cardamom is referred to as the "queen of spices." It thrives in shady monsoon forests enveloped in soft morning mists at altitudes over 3,300 feet (1,000 m) above sea level. Cardamom is also native to Sri Lanka, and up until the 19th century the small cardamom (*Elettaria cardamomum* Maton) and wild cardamom (*E. ensal*) varieties were harvested in India and Sri Lanka from wild plants in the rainforests. Orderly cultivation didn't really take place until the 20th century.

Culinary Information

Combines with

- allspice
- caraway
- chile
- cinnamon
- coriander seed
- cumin
- fennel seed
- ginger
- paprika
- pepper
- star anise
- turmeric

Traditional Uses

- pastries, cakes and cookies
- sweets and milk puddings
- stewed fruits
- rice dishes
- curries
- tagines

Spice Blends

- chai
- curry powders
- ras el hanout
- baharat
- garam masala
- Persian spice blends
- satay spice blends
- tagine spice blends

A Catchall

Cardamom may have been a term loosely used to describe a number of spices. For instance, cardamom is often noted as having grown in the hanging gardens of Babylon, where in 720 BCE climatic conditions may not have been ideal for green cardamom to thrive.

There is a degree of confusion about the history of cardamom: some historical records give sketchy and conflicting descriptions of cardamom, compared to the spice we know and love today. There are descriptions from the fourth century CE that describe cardamom as coming from a vine. Probably the confusion came from its botanical similarity to Melegueta pepper, or grains of paradise (see page 313), another member of the Zingiberaceae family with a peppery taste. Nonetheless, if the spice referred to was indeed cardamom, or something similar, it was mentioned in the fourth century BCE as an article of Greek trade. The Greek word *kardamomum* was used to describe the so-called superior grade, and the ancient Semetic word *amomum*, meaning "very spicy," was used to describe the inferior grade. It is interesting to note that the botanical name for brown cardamom is *Cardamomum amomum*. In the first century CE, Rome was importing large amounts of cardamom and it was one of the most popular Asian spices in Roman cuisine. In addition to its use in cooking, cardamom was valued for its ability to clean the teeth and sweeten the breath after meals, especially those heavily laden with garlic.

The Plant

Green cardamoms are tropical shade-loving perennials with long, lance-shaped light green leaves that grow 3 to

6 feet (1 to 2 m) tall. They are similar in appearance to a ginger plant or a lily. The leaves are slightly shiny on top and dull underneath; when bruised or cut, they release a delicate camphorous aroma reminiscent of ginger and lime. An unusual feature of cardamom is that it grows from a rhizome, as do ginger, turmeric, galangal and zedoary.

Cardamom flowers are borne on stems that emerge at the base of the plant and tend to spread out close to the base, almost on the ground. The small—$1/3$ to $1/2$ inch (8 to 10 mm)—delicate white flowers have about 10 fine purple streaks radiating from the center, almost like a miniature orchid. The pods or capsules of green cardamom form after pollination of the flowers.

When dried, green cardamom pods (*E. cardamomum* Maton) are pale green and oval-shaped, with a knobbly texture. They are about $1/2$ to $3/4$ inch (1 to 2 cm) long. When the papery husk is broken open, three seed segments, each containing three to four oily, pungent brown-black seeds, are revealed. The taste of the seeds is warm, camphorous and eucalypt, pleasantly astringent and refreshing on the palate.

Other Varieties

The pods of **Thai cardamom** (*Amomum krervanh*), when dried, have a papery husk similar to the green variety; however, the shape is more spherical and Thai cardamom

Travels in the Spice Trade

During the cardamom harvesting and drying season, auctions are held in numerous villages. Liz and I followed our noses to one in the aromatic village of Vandamettu, situated in the cardamom-growing hills of Kerala, a state in southwest India. The auction room was about the size of a large classroom, with tables and chairs lined up around the perimeter, facing the center. In one morning, 40 or more lots may be put under the hammer, which could amount to two or three tons of cardamom pods. When a lot comes up, each of the buyers is given a sample of pods in a small plastic bag. He opens it, tips the cardamom into a dish and inspects the quality before bidding. The cardamom auctioneer puts on a theatrical display of salesmanship in that inimitable fashion unique to this profession. A cacophony of shouts in Malayalam (the local language) rings out as the bidding becomes more and more excited as the price rises, then a buyer is nailed with a closure. Quick as a wink, the buyer, the price and the lot number are chalked up on a blackboard, bowls of cardamom pods are tossed onto the red-carpeted floor, and a new batch of bags is handed around. By the end of the auction, the discarded samples of lime-green pods are ankle deep on the floor. You can understand our swooning—the astringent aroma both tantalized our nostrils and cleared our sinuses.

Are you confused
when you see a pack
of dark brown seeds
labeled "green
cardamom seeds"?
You are not alone.
They are called
green cardamom
seeds because they
come from the green
cardamom pod. Old
pods, if not stored
away from light,
will fade to a dull
yellowish tan. Some
people who have
seen only this quality
mistakenly believe
them to be brown
or Thai cardamom,
not green.

pods are usually pale cream in color. Thai cardamom has
a more delicate flavor and aroma than green and is less
camphorous. **Sri Lankan wild cardamom** (*Elettaria ensal*)
is a larger, sturdier plant than Indian green cardamom and is
indigenous to Sri Lanka. It is not as popular commercially
because of its milder flavor.

Processing

In the spice trade, cardamom pods while still on the plant
are called "capsules." These capsules must be harvested just
before maturity; otherwise, the pods will split on drying and
not retain their desirable green color as effectively. Because
the pods don't all develop at the same time, harvesting
occurs over a period of a few months; the pickers are careful
to gather only those that are ready for drying. A basketful
of freshly picked plump, smooth, pea-green cardamom pods
is a wonderful sight to behold. The fresh green pods do not
have a strong aroma. If opened, you would see a very pale,
slightly fleshy interior surrounding several pale seeds. The
full flavor strength develops dramatically upon drying.

The traditional drying process used to take place in a large
shed that had wooden slat flooring with wire mesh stretched
over it to allow the air to circulate freely. There was a wood-
fired furnace at one end and ducting to take the smoke
away, so as not to contaminate the cardamom. Large 12-inch
(30 cm) ducts below the floor provided warm, dry air that
brought the cardamom pods' moisture content down to
below 12%. But progress has caught up with the cardamom
industry. The quaint old aromatic wooden drying sheds sit
sadly abandoned, replaced by efficient computer-controlled
electric or gas-fired drying machines.

Once dried, regardless of the method, the bright green,
highly aromatic cardamom pods are rubbed over a screen to
remove any remaining stalks. Final winnowing and grading
by size is performed before shipment.

Pale cream-colored cardamom pods have been either
picked too late or dried in the sun. White cardamom, which
achieved fashionable status in Victorian times, was created
by bleaching the pods with hydrogen peroxide or exposing
them to the fumes of burning sulfur. Bleached, or white,
cardamom is still found occasionally, as it is desirable to
have white or pale things for some Indian ceremonies.

Buying and Storage

Cardamom pods, and for that matter many whole spices, are added to recipes so the flavor can infuse during cooking and the whole spice can be removed before serving. Unlike me, some diners don't appreciate biting on a whole cardamom pod while eating their meal.

The best-quality green cardamom pods are an even lime-green color and should not look pale or bleached. Avoid pods that are splitting open at the end; this is an indication that they were harvested too late, which results in a lower volatile oil content after drying. Green cardamom seeds are dark brown in color—they are called "green" after the green pod they come from. Look for a distinct, almost eucalyptus aroma and slight oiliness to the touch. The seeds do lose their flavor more rapidly after being removed from the pods, so unless you are a heavy user, buy whole pods.

Powdered cardamom seed should be avoided unless you know it has recently been ground and is packed in a barrier material that keeps the flavor in. Once pulverized, the volatile flavor notes in cardamom will dissipate rapidly, so it is doubly important that the basic rules of spice storage are observed. The color should be dark gray; if too light in color and slightly fibrous in appearance, it is an indication that whole pods, not just the seeds alone, were ground. As the outer husk of the pod has little flavor, this is not desirable. Always keep cardamom in airtight containers and avoid extremes of heat, light and humidity. Stored under these conditions, cardamom should keep for up to 1 year.

Use

Green cardamom is a versatile and useful spice. It is equally complementary to sweet and savory foods. It is a pungent spice and should be added to dishes sparingly, but its fresh top flavor notes make a zesty addition to a wide range of meals. Traditionally cardamom has been used to flavor pastries, cakes, cookies and fruit dishes. Indians include it in many curries, and it adds a brilliant note to Moroccan tagines.

Cardamom pods are usually included in biryani; a wonderful flavor dimension can be added to boiled rice by putting 1 or 2 bruised cardamom pods in the water during cooking. Cardamom complements milk puddings and custards and marries well with citrus fruits and mangoes. Halved grapefruits sprinkled with a little sugar and ground cardamom seeds make a tasty breakfast. We love to add ground cardamom to chocolate recipes such as brownies and cookies.

Many recipes require a bruised cardamom pod. A gentle thump with a rolling pin or pressing down firmly on the pod with the flat of a knife will burst some of the volatile oil–containing cells and allow the flavor to amalgamate more readily with the other ingredients. Even when using seeds removed from the pod, slight bruising is recommended. If you want to grind cardamom seeds (removed from the pod) at home, use a mortar and pestle, pepper mill or clean coffee grinder. If using a coffee grinder, when finished, simply grind about 1 tbsp (15 mL) uncooked rice to clean the contact surfaces. The powdered rice will also carry away any residual flavor.

In the Middle East, cardamom is an enhancement for coffee. There a split cardamom pod is pushed into the narrow spout of the coffee pot. On pouring, the coffee filters past the bruised cardamom, creating a refreshing taste. The next time you make plunger coffee, try putting a few bruised cardamom pods in the pot along with the grounds for a delicious taste.

WEIGHT PER TEASPOON (5 mL)

- **whole seeds:** 4.4 g
- **ground seeds:** 3.5 g

SUGGESTED QUANTITY PER POUND (500 g)

- **red meats:** 2 tsp (10 mL) seeds
- **white meats:** 2 tsp (10 mL) seeds
- **vegetables:** $1\frac{1}{2}$ tsp (7 mL) seeds
- **grains and pulses:** $1\frac{1}{2}$ tsp (7 mL) seeds
- **baked goods:** $1\frac{1}{2}$ tsp (7 mL) seeds

Basmati Pilaf

No Indian meal is complete without rice, and I love a fragrant basmati pilaf with just about everything. There are endless variations on pilaf; this one is simple and delicious, with the key ingredient being green cardamom pods. Remove before serving if you wish, but I quite like unexpectedly biting into the pods and tasting a hit of the pungent seeds.

Makes 6 side servings

Preparation time:
30 minutes, plus
2 hours for soaking

Cooking time:
25 minutes

Tips

To bruise the cardamom pods, give them a gentle tap with a pestle or rolling pin, so the skin splits open just a little.

Soaking the rice before cooking reduces the starchiness of the grain and prevents stickiness. Alternatively, rinse rice well in 2 or 3 changes of water.

1½ cups	basmati rice	375 mL
1 tbsp + ¼ tsp	fine sea salt	15 mL + 1 mL
1 tbsp	butter	15 mL
½	onion, halved and sliced	½
1	3-inch (7.5 cm) cinnamon stick	1
1 tsp	cardamom pods, bruised (see Tips, left)	5 mL
Pinch	saffron threads, soaked in 2 tbsp (30 mL) warm water	Pinch
1	bay leaf	1
2 cups	chicken or vegetable broth	500 mL

1. In a bowl, cover rice in cold water and add 1 tbsp (15 mL) salt. Mix well and set aside for 2 hours. Using a fine-mesh sieve, drain rice and rinse under cold running water (see Tips, left).

2. In a heavy-bottomed saucepan with a tight-fitting lid, melt butter over medium heat. Add onion and sauté for 3 to 4 minutes, just until golden. Add prepared rice and stir to coat well; cook until translucent, about 2 minutes. Add cinnamon, cardamom, saffron with soaking liquid, and bay leaf; stir for 1 minute. Stir in broth and ¼ tsp (1 mL) salt. Bring to a boil, then cover and reduce heat to lowest setting (if using an electric stove, turn off heat). Cook, without removing cover or stirring, for 10 minutes, until al dente (the rice should have just a little bite left). Remove from heat and set aside, covered, until ready to serve (this will ensure a dry, fluffy result).

Cardamom Mangoes

Mangoes make me think of Christmas in Australia, when we would buy trays of the fresh fruit to eat at breakfast, but of course they are wonderful any time of year. This dessert is quick to prepare but tastes exceptionally indulgent, with sweet, cardamom-infused butter adding fantastic flavor to the fruit. Serve with cream, ice cream or plain yogurt.

**Makes
4 servings**

Preparation time:
10 minutes

Cooking time:
10 minutes

4	ripe mangoes, peeled, cored and cut into ½-inch (1 cm) slices	4
¼ cup	butter	60 mL
¼ cup	packed light brown sugar	60 mL
1 tbsp	ground green cardamom seeds	15 mL

1. In a skillet over medium heat, melt butter. Add sugar and stir constantly until completely dissolved. Stir in cardamom seeds. Arrange mangoes in a single layer on bottom of skillet (in batches if necessary) and cook, spooning spiced butter mixture over fruit until just warmed through, about 2 minutes. Transfer mangoes to serving dishes and repeat with remaining fruit, if needed. Drizzle with remaining spiced butter and serve.

Variation

Substitute an equal quantity of apples, bananas, pears or seasonal fruit for the mangoes.

Celery Seed

Apium graveolens

Names in Other Languages

- **Arabic:** karafs, karfas
- **Chinese (C):** kahn choi tsai
- **Chinese (M):** qin cai zi
- **Czech:** celer, mirik celer
- **Danish:** selleri, bladselleri
- **Dutch:** selderij, bladselderij
- **Filipino:** kintsay
- **French:** celeri
- **German:** Sellerie, Eppich
- **Indian:** ajmoda, bariajmud
- **Indonesian:** selderi
- **Italian:** apio, sedano
- **Japanese:** serori
- **Malay:** daun seladri (leaf), daun sop (seed)
- **Portuguese:** aipo
- **Russian:** syel'derey
- **Spanish:** apio
- **Sri Lankan:** salderi
- **Swedish:** selleri
- **Thai:** kin chai, ceun chai farang
- **Turkish:** kereviz, yabani kerevizi
- **Vietnamese:** can tay

Family: Apiaceae (formerly Umbelliferae)

Varieties: celery vegetable (*A. graveolens dulce*), celeriac (*A. graveolens rapaceum*)

Other Names: garden celery, smallage, wild celery

Flavor Group: Pungent

Parts Used: seeds (as a spice)

Background

Native to southern Europe, the Middle East and the United States, smallage—the wild celery from which celery developed and from which the seeds are harvested—was known to the ancients. Around 2200 BCE the Egyptians used it primarily for its medicinal value and for making into garlands. Smallage (wild celery) was often associated with death by the Greeks and Romans, possibly because of its rank odor.

The earliest recorded application of celery as a condiment was in 1623 in France, where the plant was referred to as *ache*. Many varieties of celery are now grown, all without the bitterness of the old original smallage; some are even naturally white and are called "self-blanching." Celery can also be grown as an annual, in which case earth is mounded

Culinary Information

Combines with
- allspice
- bay leaf
- caraway
- chervil
- chile
- cinnamon
- coriander seed
- fennel seed
- ginger
- paprika
- pepper

Traditional Uses
- vegetable juices
- seafood and egg dishes
- cheeses
- salad dressings and mayonnaise
- roast chicken
- breads and biscuits
- crab boil

Spice Blends
- bay seasoning
- celery salt
- meat rubs
- pork spices
- commercial blends for roasting and microwaving meats

C

up around the base to create a blanched bulb that may be used as a vegetable, in the same way as the bulb of fennel.

The Plant

Celery seeds are gathered from an ancient hardy biennial marsh plant known as smallage (wild celery) that bears little similarity to the edible vegetable celery stalks we know so well. The smallage plant tends to be poisonous when raw, and the stalks and jagged leaves have an unpleasant smell. Umbrella-shaped white flowers develop pairs of minute—$\frac{1}{16}$ inch (1 mm) long—seeds that split when harvested. The seeds are so small that there are more than a million of them in 2 pounds (1 kg)!

Dried celery seeds are light brown to khaki in color and have a penetrating hay-like aroma reminiscent of celery stalks. The flavor is strong, bitter, warm, astringent, exceedingly "green" and lingering on the palate. Like caraway, celery seed appears to be a "love it or hate it" spice: very few people feel indifferent to it.

Other Varieties

In the early 18th century the Italians, determined to breed out the extreme bitterness of smallage, developed milder strains for culinary use as a vegetable. This led to the cultivated variety that we know today as **vegetable celery** (*Apium graveolens dulce*), with its thicker juicy, stringless stalks. Another variety, the increasingly popular vegetable known as **celeriac** (*A. graveolens rapaceum*), grows with an edible pale, bulb-shaped root.

Processing

Being a biennial, celery seeds are harvested in the second year after planting, by cutting the seed-bearing stems, allowing them to dry and then threshing to remove the tiny seeds from the husks.

On steam distillation the seeds yield about 2% volatile oil. Celery seed oil is used in manufacturing processed meats, nonalcoholic drinks, confectionery, ice creams and baked products.

Buying and Storage

Celery seeds are generally best purchased in their whole form, which when stored correctly will last for up to 3 years. Being so small, they are most often used in cooking without grinding. Ground celery seed should be used quickly, as the fresh volatile notes will evaporate readily, leaving a less balanced, increasingly bitter flavor after about 1 year. Celery salt is often easier to buy than celery seeds, possibly to make it more appealing to a wider number of people. Celery salt is usually made by mixing 60% salt, 30% ground celery seeds and 10% equal parts of mixed dried herbs such as parsley and dill. Celery seeds and celery salt should be stored like other spices, in an airtight container away from extremes of heat, light and humidity.

Use

The strong flavor of celery seed makes a perfect marriage with tomatoes, hence its use in tomato and vegetable juices and the Bloody Mary cocktail, which inspired the chutney recipe that follows (page 169). Celery seeds are found in recipes for soups, stews, pickles and chutneys. They are excellent with fish and eggs, are sometimes found in cheeses, and go well with salad dressings and mayonnaise for coleslaw. In savory pastries, celery seeds add much the same refreshing, carbohydrate-complementing astringency as do ajowan seeds. Many popular commercial spice blends made for chicken, seafood and red meat contain celery seed along with spices such as paprika, cinnamon, ginger, pepper and salt.

WEIGHT PER TEASPOON (5 mL)
- whole: 2.9 g
- ground: 3 g

SUGGESTED QUANTITY PER POUND (500 g)
- **red meats:** 2 tsp (10 mL)
- **white meats:** 1½ tsp (7 mL)
- **vegetables:** 1 tsp (5 mL)
- **grains and pulses:** 1 tsp (5 mL)
- **baked goods:** 1 tsp (5 mL)

Bloody Mary Chutney

A take on the classic cocktail, this chutney makes the perfect hangover cure when served with fried eggs.

**Makes about
2 cups (500 mL)**

Preparation time:
20 minutes

Cooking time:
50 minutes

- - - - - - - - - - - - - - - - - -

Tips

To roast peppers: Preheat oven to 400°F (200°C). Place peppers on a baking sheet and roast until blackened, about 30 minutes, turning halfway. Alternatively, use tongs to hold the pepper over an open gas flame, turning slowly while it blackens. Transfer roasted peppers to a resealable bag to cool. Remove from bag, peel (the skin should just slip off) and discard seeds. If desired, you can also use store-bought roasted red peppers in this recipe.

To sterilize jars, clean thoroughly in hot soapy water, then drip-dry. Place jars, open end up, on a baking sheet and heat in a preheated 400°F (200°C) oven for 10 minutes. To sterilize lids, place in a saucepan, cover with water and boil for 5 minutes. Be sure to handle lids and jars with clean hands.

2 tsp	oil	10 mL
1	small red onion, finely chopped	1
1	clove garlic, minced	1
3	ripe red tomatoes, diced	3
2	roasted red bell peppers, peeled and seeded (see Tips, left)	2
½	long red finger chile, finely chopped	½
½ cup	cider vinegar	125 mL
3 tbsp	packed light brown sugar	45 mL
1 tbsp	tomato paste	15 mL
1 tsp	celery seeds	5 mL
1 tsp	fine sea salt	5 mL
1 tsp	Worcestershire sauce	5 mL
½ tsp	ground allspice	2 mL
½ tsp	freshly ground black pepper	2 mL
½ tsp	Horseradish Sauce (page 323) or freshly minced horseradish	2 mL

1. In a medium saucepan over low heat, heat oil. Add onion and sauté for 5 minutes, until soft. Add garlic and sauté, stirring constantly, for 2 minutes, until soft. Add tomatoes, roasted peppers, chile, vinegar, sugar, tomato paste, celery seeds, salt, Worcestershire, allspice, pepper and Horseradish Sauce; stir well to combine. Cook, stirring often, for 30 to 40 minutes, until mixture thickens and takes on a jammy consistency. Taste and adjust seasonings, if desired. Remove from heat and set aside to cool.

2. Spoon chutney into sterilized jars (see Tips, left). Once completely cooled, seal and refrigerate for up to 3 months.

Chervil

Anthriscus cerefolium

Names in Other Languages

- **Arabic:** maqdunis afranji
- **Chinese (C):** saan loh baahk
- **Chinese (M):** shan luo bo, hui qin
- **Czech:** kerblik trebule
- **Danish:** korvel
- **Dutch:** kervel
- **French:** cerfeuil
- **German:** Kerbel, Gartenkerbel
- **Greek:** anthriskos, skantziki
- **Italian:** cerfoglio
- **Japanese:** chabiru, shiyaku
- **Portuguese:** cerefolho
- **Russian:** kervel
- **Spanish:** cerafolio
- **Swedish:** korvel
- **Turkish:** frenk maydanoz

Family: Apiaceae (formerly Umbelliferae)

Other Names: French parsley, garden chervil, gourmet's parsley

Flavor Group: Mild

Parts Used: leaves and stems (as a herb)

Background

Chervil is native to eastern Europe; the colonizing Romans spread it further afield. It was once called *myrrhis* because the volatile oil extracted from chervil leaves has an aroma similar to the resinous substance myrrh. Folklore has it that chervil makes one merry, sharpens the wit, bestows youth upon the aged and symbolizes sincerity.

Chervil has tended to be most popular in French cuisine. It is sometimes seen in recipes from other parts of Europe and only occasionally in North American dishes. It was introduced to Brazil by the Portuguese in 1647 and is now grown commercially in California, where it is dehydrated like parsley to be used in packaged soups and fines herbes blends, which are delicate mixes of mild-tasting herbs popular in French cuisine.

The Plant

Pretty, lacy, delicate and decorative, chervil is a shade-loving biennial that cannot tolerate hot, dry conditions. The small plant grows to around 12 inches (30 cm) tall and has bright green frond-like leaves resembling miniature parsley. The flowers are minute and white, producing long, thin seeds that are not used in cooking. The aroma of freshly bruised chervil leaves is grassy and delicately anise-scented; the flavor is similar to French tarragon.

Dried chervil leaves have the hay-like aroma and flavor of parsley, having lost most of their lighter anise notes during dehydration.

Culinary Information

Combines with
- basil
- celery seed
- coriander leaf
- dill fronds
- lovage
- onion and garlic
- parsley
- salad burnet

Traditional Uses
- scrambled eggs and omelets
- cream cheese and herb sandwiches
- green salads
- mashed potatoes

Spice Blends
- fines herbes
- vegetable salts

Other Varieties

Although not a true chervil, there is a plant known as **turnip-rooted chervil**, **bulbous chervil** or **parsnip chervil** (*Chaerophyllum bulbosum*). In the 19th century its edible root was popular as a vegetable, but it is not often seen these days.

WEIGHT PER TEASPOON (5 mL)

- whole dry leaves: 0.8 g

SUGGESTED QUANTITY PER POUND (500 g)

- **red meats:** ½ cup (125 mL) fresh, 4 tsp (20 mL) dried leaves
- **white meats:** ½ cup (125 mL) fresh, 4 tsp (20 mL) dried leaves
- **vegetables:** ¼ cup (60 mL) fresh, 2 tsp (10 mL) dried leaves
- **grains and pulses:** ¼ cup (60 mL) fresh, 2 tsp (10 mL) dried leaves
- **baked goods:** ¼ cup (60 mL) fresh, 2 tsp (10 mL) dried leaves

Processing

When harvesting chervil, the outer, more robust growth should be picked first, allowing the more delicate inner fronds to develop. Frequent gathering encourages abundant new growth and helps prevent seeding and dying off. Drying chervil effectively is quite a challenge because of the fragile makeup of its leaves. They shrivel to almost nothing during dehydration, and in the process they lose the volatile top notes. The best way to dry chervil leaves is to spread them out on a wire rack in a dark place where warm air can circulate freely. After a few days the leaves will be quite crisp and ready to store in an airtight container. Alternatively, fresh chervil leaves may be chopped finely, put into ice-cube trays, covered with a little water and frozen for later use.

Buying and Storage

Fresh chervil is sometimes available from grocery stores. Dried chervil should be dark green and show no signs of the yellowing that results from exposure to light. Store in an airtight container and keep in a cool, dark place, where it should last for up to 1 year.

Use

Subtlety is the keyword when using chervil in cooking. Although chervil will never dominate a dish, many cooks use it to enhance the flavors of the other herbs that accompany it. It is an important inclusion in the traditional French fines herbes blend of tarragon, parsley, chives and chervil. Chervil complements scrambled eggs and omelets, cream cheese and herb sandwiches, salads and even mashed potatoes. Because of its extremely delicate nature, this herb should never be cooked for extended periods or at excessively high temperatures. Add chervil only in the final 10 to 15 minutes of cooking, or use the fresh leaves as a garnish.

Chervil Soup

My grandmother has always been able to create dishes that are simple yet subtly flavored with fresh herbs gathered from her stone-walled herb garden. Dad remembers this soup from balmy summer lunches, often attended by some of Australia's pioneering food, wine, theatrical and literary characters. Cress sandwiches make an excellent accompaniment to this soup.

Makes 4 servings

Preparation time:
10 minutes

Cooking time: 1 hour, 15 minutes

• Blender

1 lb	potatoes, peeled and cut into 1-inch (2.5 cm) dice	500 g
1	onion, chopped	1
4 cups	chicken broth	1 L
	Fine sea salt and freshly ground black pepper	
⅓ cup	lightly packed chopped fresh chervil	75 mL
⅓ cup	reduced-fat sour cream or plain yogurt	75 mL
	Additional fresh chervil leaves	

1. In a saucepan over medium-low heat, combine potatoes, onion and chicken broth. Cover and simmer for 1 hour, stirring occasionally, until potatoes are tender. Transfer to blender and purée until smooth, then return to saucepan. Add salt and pepper to taste and chervil; reduce heat to low and simmer for 10 minutes. Ladle into 4 serving bowls, swirl in sour cream, and top with additional chervil.

Tuna Niçoise with Chervil Vinaigrette

Niçoise salad hails from the French Riviera and comprises tuna, potatoes, green beans, olives and eggs. I love the addition of delicate chervil.

Makes 4 small servings

Preparation time:
40 minutes

Cooking time: 5 to
10 minutes

Tips

To hard-boil eggs: In a large saucepan, arrange eggs in a single layer and cover with 1 inch (2.5 cm) cold water. Bring to a boil over medium heat, then immediately reduce heat and simmer for 6 minutes. Drain eggs in plenty of cold water to stop further cooking, then peel.

To toast sesame seeds: Place in a dry skillet over medium heat and cook, shaking pan constantly, until lightly browned, 2 to 3 minutes. Immediately transfer to a dish to prevent further browning.

If you prefer, use a griddle to sear the tuna.

VINAIGRETTE

1 tbsp	chopped fresh chervil leaves	15 mL
1 tbsp	cider vinegar	15 mL
1 tbsp	freshly squeezed lemon juice	15 mL
1½ tsp	Dijon mustard	7 mL
½ tsp	crushed garlic	2 mL
2 tbsp	extra virgin olive oil	30 mL

TUNA

1	large skinless tuna steak (about 12 oz/375 g)	1
1 tbsp	olive oil	15 mL
	Fine sea salt and freshly ground black pepper	
2	heads baby Gem or Bibb lettuce, leaves separated	2
2	hard-boiled eggs, quartered (see Tips, left)	2
12 oz	new potatoes, cooked, drained and halved	375 g
3½ oz	green beans, cooked and drained	100 g
⅓ cup	niçoise or black olives	75 mL
¼ cup	fresh chervil leaves	60 mL
3 tbsp	sesame seeds, lightly toasted (see Tips, left)	45 mL

1. *Vinaigrette:* In a small bowl, combine chervil, vinegar, lemon juice, mustard and garlic. Whisk in olive oil.

2. *Tuna:* Heat a skillet over high heat. Coat tuna in olive oil and season with salt and pepper to taste. Sear for 3 minutes each side (it will be rare inside; if you prefer, cook for up to 2 minutes longer per side).

3. On 4 serving plates (or use 1 large platter), evenly divide lettuce, eggs, potatoes, beans and olives. Divide cooked tuna into 4 equal portions and flake over the salads. Drizzle each with prepared vinaigrette. Top with chervil and sesame seeds and serve immediately.

Variation

If chervil isn't available, substitute torn fresh basil leaves.

Chile

Capsicum

C

Names in Other Languages

- **Arabic:** filfil ahmar, shatta
- **Burmese:** nga yut thee
- **Chinese (C):** laaht jiu
- **Chinese (M):** la jiao
- **Czech:** pepr cayensky
- **Dutch:** spaanse peper
- **Filipino:** sili, siling haba (long)
- **French:** poivre de cayenne, piment enragé
- **German:** roter Pfeffer
- **Greek:** piperi kagien, tsili
- **Hungarian:** csilipaprika, igen eros apro
- **Indian:** hari mirich (green), lal mirich (red)
- **Indonesian:** cabe, cabai, cabai hijau (green), cabai merah (red), cabai rawit (bird's-eye), lombok
- **Italian:** peperoncino, pepe rosso picante
- **Japanese:** togarashi
- **Korean:** gochu
- **Laotian:** mak phet kunsi
- **Malay:** cili, lombok, cili padi
- **Portuguese:** pimento
- **Russian:** struchkovy pyeret
- **Spanish:** aji, pimenton, pimienta picante, chile, guindilla
- **Sri Lankan:** rathu miris
- **Thai:** prik chee faa, prik haeng pallek
- **Turkish:** aci kirmizi biber, toz biber
- **Vietnamese:** ot

Family: Solanaceae

Other Names: aji, cayenne pepper, chili, chilli, chilly, ginnie pepper, piri piri, red pepper

Flavor Group: Hot

Parts Used: pods and seeds (as a spice), leaves (as a herb)

Background

When Columbus came to the New World in 1492, he was looking for, among other things, new sources of black pepper. This helps to explain why, when he was introduced to the capsicum family—his first experience of another spice that was hot like pepper—he referred to chiles as pepper. To this day, both true pepper from the *Piper nigrum* vine and chiles are referred to as peppers in North America and many parts of Europe. This often leads to confusion.

Unknown to the Old World at the time, there is evidence that *aji* or *axi*, as chiles were called, were eaten by the native Mexican peoples as early as 7000 BCE and possibly cultivated sometime between 5200 and 3400 BCE, making them among the oldest plants cultivated in the Americas.

Culinary Information

Combines with
- allspice
- amchur
- bay leaf
- cardamom
- cloves
- coriander (leaf and seed)
- cumin
- fenugreek (leaf and seed)
- ginger
- lemon myrtle
- makrut lime leaf
- mustard
- paprika
- pepper
- star anise
- turmeric
- Vietnamese mint

Traditional Uses
- Mexican sauces
- Asian stir-fries
- curries of all cultures
- practically every cuisine in the world

Spice Blends
- barbecue rubs
- curry spices
- taco seasonings
- berbere
- pickling spices
- harissa paste
- tagine blends
- chaat masala
- many general-purpose seasoning blends

Upon its discovery, the rest of the world warmly embraced the chile as "poor man's pepper." Even the poorest of people could now procure a ready supply of this easily propagated appetite-enhancing condiment.

By 1650 capsicums were cultivated throughout Europe, Asia and Africa. In Europe, hybridization, along with the influence of soil and climatic conditions, led to a bias toward the milder varieties of *Capsicum annum*, while in the tropics various hotter types of *C. annum* and *C. frutescens* were popular. One explanation for the desire for hot chiles in the tropics is that they raise body temperature, and the resulting perspiration creates a cooling effect as it evaporates off the skin.

Confusion remains about the identification of many chiles, partly because of their ready cross-pollination and hybridization, compounded by the different regional names given to them in dozens of languages and dialects. The history of the chile has been relatively short in many parts of the world, including India, Africa and China. Given the enormous tonnage of chile peppers consumed in these countries, it almost defies logic to try to imagine how they ever survived without them a mere 500 years ago.

The Plant

Five main varieties of chile have hybridized into hundreds of cultivars grown around the world. Entire books have been written on this vast family of plants, and the majority of authors humbly beg the reader's tolerance for imperfect sources. With that in mind, I have attempted to provide condensed information to help demystify chiles and provide details relevant to their culinary use.

Chile plants vary considerably in size and appearance. The most common (*Capsicum annum*) is described as a herb or a small, erect early-maturing shrub with oval leaves and firm, non-woody stems that grow to around 3 feet (1 m) tall. This variety is generally grown as an annual, as its fruiting capacity diminishes after the first year. Some milder versions of *C. annum*, known as paprika, are dealt with in the section on paprika (see page 455). The next most common species is the short-lived perennial *C. frutescens*, which lasts for only 2 to 3 years. Its distinguishing difference from *C. annum* is that the fruits tend to be smaller and hotter, including varieties such as bird's-eye and tabasco. The varieties *C. baccatum*, *C. chinense* and *C. pubescens* are less common. *C. chinense* gives us the extra-hot varieties such as habanero and Scotch bonnet, while the blisteringly hot bhut jolokia is said to be a hybrid of *C. chinense* and *C. annum*.

The chile pod is a many-seeded berry that, depending upon variety, may be pendulous and hide among soft foliage resembling potato or tobacco leaves. Or it may grow erect on cheerful display, waiting to be picked by birds, which carry the seeds in their digestive tracts, providing widespread propagation. Chile pods come in an assortment of shapes, colors and heat levels. They have a shiny skin covering varying thicknesses of flesh, and 2 to 4 almost hollow chambers containing numerous disk-shaped pale yellow to white seeds. Shapes range from small, round fruits only $1/2$ inch (1 cm) in diameter to large pods more than 8 inches (20 cm) long. In between there are elongated mini chiles less than $1/2$ inch (1 cm) wide and about $1^1/2$ inches (4 cm) long; round tomato shapes 1 inch (2.5 cm) in diameter; medium sizes about 4 inches (10 cm) in length; and the unusual Scotch bonnet variety (*C. chinense*), which is shaped like a cross between a tam-o'-shanter and a squash.

The Heat Source

Capsaicin is a crystalline substance contained in its highest concentration in the seeds and the fleshy placenta material that is joined to the seeds. Capsaicin causes the brain to release endorphins, which create a sense of well-being and stimulation.

Most fresh chiles are green until they ripen, after which the color may be red, yellow, brown, purple or almost black. The aroma of fresh chiles is distinctive capsicum-like, and their flavor resembles that of a green bell pepper (which is known as a capsicum in Australia). Ripe chiles have a more full-bodied and fruity flavor, in the same way that a red bell pepper tastes different from a green one. Heat levels, ranging from deliciously tingling to threateningly scorching, are determined by the amount of capsaicin present.

The amount of heat in chiles can usually be estimated on the basis of pod size. Generally (but not always) the smaller the chile, the hotter it will be, because the ratio of seeds and capsaicin-bearing placenta to flesh is relatively high. With ground chiles, the hotter varieties are usually more orange in color than red, because of the higher ratio of pale seeds. It is interesting to note that in the hotter varieties, levels of capsaicin can range dramatically from 0.2% to more than 1%. Much attention has been given to finding a way to

Travels in the Spice Trade

When I was managing a spice company in Singapore in the mid 1980s, I wanted to understand the dynamics of traditional methods of processing spices. With this in mind, I visited a small spice-grinding business in the industrial area of Jurong that was owned by an Indian family. They specialized in grinding chiles imported from India, Pakistan and China and exported many tons of ground chile each year. It was a fascinating experience. The atmosphere in the tropical lichen–stained concrete factory was a cross between a Dickensian workhouse and a 17th-century Malaysian warehouse known as a "godown." The Indian workers were stripped to their waists, wearing only a sarong-like *longyi*.

Five ancient-looking plate grinders churned noisily, reducing sacks full of bright red chiles to a red-orange powder. Because this mechanical action generated a lot of heat, the ground chile had to be cooled when it came out of the grinder; otherwise it could scorch and discolor. Watching the great piles of eye-watering ground chile being spread out to cool on the concrete floor, I found it hard to believe we were in the late 20th century. After it was raked by the sweating, barefooted workers, who were standing ankle deep in it, the ground chile was returned to the grinders for a second grinding to make it extra fine. Another stage of raking out and cooling occurred before final bagging.

I also saw why ground chiles vary from bright red to pale orange in color: you can never be sure just how many pale yellow seeds are in a dried chile. Therefore a batch of chiles that has few seeds will yield a very red powder, while another with a higher proportion of seeds will create ground chile that is orange. After about 20 minutes my ears were ringing from the constant clattering of the grinders, but although my nose and eyes were streaming, I was mesmerized by the sweet, fruity aroma and lingering burning sensation of chile in the air.

measure the heat levels of different chiles. After all, there needs to be some way to differentiate between the searing bhut jolokia, habanero and bird's-eye chiles and the milder, almost paprika-tasting members of the capsicum family.

Measuring Heat

In 1912 the Scoville method was developed to provide food technologists with a quantifiable method of determining the heat levels in chiles. Although subjective until the intervention of modern technology, this method of measuring the pungency of chiles and allocating Scoville units of heat remains the most widely used in the food industry. In the past, panels of tasters would sample greatly diluted quantities of chile, noting at what percentage level the presence of heat could be detected on the palate. Capsaicin is so strong that the palate can detect as little as 1 part in 1,000. Numeric values were then assigned in thousands of Scoville units; for example, 1% of capsaicin detected is equivalent to 150,000 Scoville units. The results can range from 0 to 1,000,000 for the very hottest of palate-searing chiles. With modern technology, the more common scientific method of measuring Scoville heat units is to use high-performance liquid chromatography (HPLC) measures, which require sophisticated equipment but are much more reliable. A user-friendly system for the nonprofessional food lover is to simply quote the heat level on a scale of 1 to 10, with 10 being the hottest.

Dried vs. Fresh

The flavor of dried chile is quite different from that of fresh, in the same way that a sun-dried tomato has a different taste from a fresh tomato. During drying (usually in the sun), caramelization of sugars and other chemical changes create more complex flavors that can dramatically enhance any dish. While fresh chiles have a distinct heat, fresh bell pepper top notes, and sweetness, dried chiles deliver an initial full-bodied fruity, raisin-like sweetness with varying degrees of tobacco and smokiness, depending upon the variety or cultivar.

Many Mexican chiles have different names depending on whether they are fresh or dried. For instance, a poblano chile is called ancho when it is dried, and a jalapeño is called a chipotle when dried and smoked. While the following list of dried chiles is by no means exhaustive, some of the more common varieties are briefly described and heat levels on a scale of 1 to 10 are provided.

The Hottest Pepper

Discovery of the 1-million-Scoville-unit bhut jolokia chile—which I actually don't recommend for cooking—raised the bar on heat levels. The heat level for them could be called 10x3.

In spite of an inordinate preoccupation with the heat in chiles, the tremendous flavor contribution made by dried chiles should not be overlooked.

Other Cultivars

Aleppo pepper (*C. annum*): dark red, coarsely ground, medium-heat chile flakes from Turkey; rich, roasted tobacco–like notes and lingering mild bitterness. A reasonable substitute is made by blending 3 parts medium-heat ground chile with 1 part ground chipotle chile. Chile flakes, dry-roasted in a pan and then ground with a pinch of salt, will also give a similar flavor. **Heat level: 6**

Anaheim (*C. annum*): large, very mild fresh chile popular in both unripe green and ripe red forms. Traditionally eaten stuffed (chiles rellenos); adds a fresh green taste to sauces and salads served with Mexican food. When ripe and red, often referred to as "chile Colorado." **Heat level: 4**

Ancho (*C. annum*): large dried poblano chile about $3\frac{1}{4}$ inches (8 cm) long and $1\frac{1}{2}$ inches (4 cm) wide; deep purple to black in color; mild, fruity flavor with notes of coffee, tobacco, wood and raisins. One of the most frequently used dried chiles in Mexican cooking. **Heat level: 4**

Bhut jolokia (*C. chinense* x *C. annum*): also called "ghost pepper," "ghost chile" or "Naga chile," after the region of Assam, India, where it is mostly grown; reputed to be the hottest in the world, weighing in at over 1 million Scoville heat units. A hybrid developed primarily for commercial purposes, only small amounts of the oleoresin (see page 23) need to be added to processed foods. Used widely in pepper spray, the defensive product also known as Mace (no connection to the spice mace, page 423). **Heat level: 10[3]**

Bird's-eye (*C. frutescens*): small, extremely hot fresh chile; highly pungent. Often called "piri piri" in Africa and used to add "pure" heat to a meal without very much chile flavor coming through. **Heat level: 9**

Cascabel (*C. annum*): round, plum-colored dried chile with light fruity and smoky notes. Used in Mexican recipes. The seeds rattle in the dried fruit, hence the name *cascabel*, which is Spanish for "rattle." **Heat level: 4**

Cayenne pepper (*C. annum*): generally a blend of ground chiles combined to achieve a uniform orange to red color and consistent heat. Some say it gets its name from Cayenne, the capital of French Guiana, but there appears to be no evidence to support this. **Heat level: 8**

Chile flakes (*C. annum*): usually finely chopped dried teja or sannam-type chiles from India; bright red with lots of seeds. Delicious sprinkled over pasta sauces and pizza. **Heat level: 7**

C

Chipotle (*C. annum*): smoked, dried jalapeño with a deep smoky, well-balanced heat. Used in Mexican dishes and by vegetarians as a substitute for ham bones in stews, soups and casseroles; often best known for its canned form in adobo sauce. **Heat level: 5**

Guajillo (*C. annum*): dried chile very similar in appearance and taste to New Mexico chile; about 6 inches (15 cm) long; earthy, cherry-like flavor and distinct but mild heat. Because of their large amount of flesh relative to seeds, guajillo chiles add a pleasing rich red color to food. **Heat level: 4**

Habanero (*C. chinense*): dried chile with a wonderful fragrant, sweet, warm fruitiness and a piquant flavor. Don't be taken in by the heavenly smell—it's devilishly hot! Delicious in salsas and slow-cooked casseroles. **Heat level: 10 +**

Jalapeño (*C. annum*): medium-sized fresh chile usually harvested when green, prior to ripening; fresh green capsicum/bell pepper flavor and reasonably piquant taste. One of the very few chiles that are dried when still green and unripe. Often available canned in brine. **Heat level: 8**

Kashmiri chile (*C. annum*): Indian dried chile available in both whole and powdered forms. Whole chiles have rough, crinkly deep red skin. When ground, powder is bright red, an attribute appreciated in tandoori-style dishes, as is its pleasing sweet, definite chile bite. I like to use the powder in most Indian recipes that require ground chile. **Heat level: 7**

Long chile (*C. annum*): a term loosely used to describe various cultivars of sannam, teja and Chinese chiles (*tien tsin*); about 2$^1/_2$ inches (6 cm) long and bright to dark red in color. Good in Sichuan dishes where you eat the stir-fried whole chiles. **Heat level: 7**

Mulato (*C. annum*): type of dried poblano chile very similar to ancho; dark brown in color; similar taste to ancho—somewhat tobacco-like and smoky—but not smoked like chipotle. **Heat level: 3**

New Mexico chile (*C. annum*): available fresh as green or red; also referred to when dried as "Colorado" or "California" chile; very large dried chile about 6 inches (15 cm) long; earthy, cherry-like flavor and distinct but mild heat. **Heat level: 4**

Pasilla (*C. annum*): dried chilaca chile sometimes called "chile negro"; flavor similar to ancho and mulato, with fruity, herb-like notes and faint licorice tones. One of the triumvirate of chiles traditionally used in making the famous mole poblano dish. **Heat level: 4**

Mexican Chili Powder

This is not a pure chile powder but a blend. It usually consists of ground chile, paprika and ground cumin, with oregano and salt sometimes included. It is what you would sprinkle on tacos and use as a condiment when looking for that characteristic "Mexican" taste. **Heat level:** varies considerably; between 2 and 8, depending on brand.

Another Part of the Plant

Pepper leaves (*C. frutescens*) should not be confused with the Australian native pepperleaf (*Tasmannia lanceolata*, page 508). The leaves of chile plants, most commonly bird's-eye, are used as a piquant herb in Asian dishes. As these leaves may be poisonous, they should always be cooked to neutralize any toxins.

Pequin (*C. annum*): small, shiny, very hot dried chile with a bead-like appearance. Similar to bird's-eye chile but almost spherical in shape. **Heat level: 9**

Piment d'Espelette: highly desirable variety of paprika (see page 455) also often refered to as a chile. It comes from the Basque region of southern France, and as an AOC (Appellation d'origine contrôlée) item, only product grown in Espelette can be called "piment d'Espelette." Its warm, fruity flavor and mild chile heat make this a versatile addition to most savory dishes. Sprinkle on pizzas and pasta, add to scrambled eggs and omelets and even sprinkle over salads.

Piri piri (or peri peri): a name often used loosely to describe chiles in South Africa and some parts of India. Piri piri sauces are essentially chile sauces with a consistent taste profile. Piri piri powder is generally a blend of chiles with a specific tangy, lemon-like flavor that appeals to the South African consumer, an analogy being Europeans' fondness for cayenne pepper. I have also purchased pickled sannam chiles in India that went by the name "piri piri." **Heat level: 9**

Poblano: green unripe pods that when dried are called ancho chiles (see "Ancho," page 180).

Serrano (*C. annum*): similar in appearance to a bird's-eye chile when dried, but larger—up to 2 inches (5 cm) long; available fresh in green and red; pleasant-tasting and fruity. When the ripe red pods are dried, they are called "serrano seco." A good option when a reasonable amount of heat is required. **Heat level: 8**

Tabasco (*C. frutescens*): small yellow, orange or bright red fresh chiles; thin-fleshed and very hot; rarely seen dried. Used to make the searingly hot pepper sauce that goes by the same name. **Heat level: 9**

Tepin (*C. annum*): wild form of pequin chile; thin-fleshed and spherical in shape, much like pequins. These small, quite hot chiles are often collectively referred to as "chiltepin." **Heat level: 8**

Urfa biber: Turkish dried chile very similar to Aleppo pepper, from the Urfa region, 120 miles (200 km) northeast of Aleppo, Syria. Urfa pepper flakes are dark red to almost black, like ancho chiles, and similarly have an almost sweet dried-fruit taste and mild bite. **Heat level: 4**

White chiles: also referred to as "curd chiles"; marinated in yogurt and salt prior to drying; pale yellow in color. Often served in Indian hotels with pickles, as accompaniments to a buffet of curries. Excellent in seafood dishes. May be fried in a little oil and eaten as an appetizer with drinks. **Heat level: 6**

Processing

The drying and processing of chiles is practiced around the world with varying degrees of sophistication; however, the majority of chiles are handled in a fairly basic way. When the peppers are fresh, their moisture content can range from 65% to 80%, depending on how much they have already dried on the plant prior to harvesting. Proper drying must bring the moisture down to around 10% to inhibit any development of mold.

In many parts of India (now reputed to be the world's largest producer of chiles), the process usually begins when the fresh fruits are purchased by a trader. These are heaped together indoors for 2 to 3 days at 68° to 77°F (20° to 25°C) to allow any partially ripe pods to ripen fully and the whole batch to attain a uniform red color. Direct sunlight should be avoided at this stage, as it may cause development of white or yellow patches. The chiles are then put out in the sun, preferably on a concrete floor, the flat roof of a house or woven mats, to protect them from dirt, insects and rodents. At night the drying fruits are heaped into piles and covered with tarpaulins, and then they are spread out in the sun again the next day. Over about three days, the chiles become dry and the larger ones are flattened by trampling or rolling to make them easier to pack into bags for transport. On average, 220 pounds (100 kg) of fresh chiles will yield 55 to 77 pounds (25 to 35 kg) of dried chiles.

Another popular drying method in countries such as Mexico and Spain is to tie bunches of chiles together into garlands, or *ristras*, and hang them on the walls of houses and even on clotheslines to dry. Artificial drying in sheds and kilns is becoming more widespread to overcome the vagaries of weather and produce a more consistent final product.

When drying chiles at home, remember that the glossy outer skin of the fruit does not yield moisture easily, so if the process takes too long, there is a high risk of mold developing inside the pods. To overcome this, slit the chiles in half to allow the moisture to escape more easily, before laying them out on a ventilated screen in a warm, dark place for a couple of days. Then transfer them into the sun for 6 to 8 hours during the warmest part of the day for another 2 to 3 days, or until they feel quite firm and dry.

Buying and Storage

When buying fresh chiles, look for ones that are firm and not wilted. Fresh chiles, whether red, yellow, brown, purple or almost black, should be quite smooth in appearance. Wrinkling of the skin indicates they have started to dry or may not have been ripened on the bush, which is desirable for optimum flavor. Fresh chiles can be stored in the refrigerator for a week or two; in warm, dry (definitely not humid) weather, they may be kept in a fruit bowl for a few days until needed.

Dried chiles will vary greatly in appearance depending upon the variety. The best advice is to buy only from a reputable source where the stock turns over regularly and advice is given about the type and heat level of the chile you are purchasing. Store dried chiles in an airtight container away from extremes of heat, light and humidity. Under these conditions, your dried chiles will keep their flavor for up to 2 years.

Use

Containing more vitamin C by weight than citrus fruits, chiles have become a "must use" condiment in the daily diets of millions of people around the globe. The flavor and heat of chiles are most often associated with Indian, African, Asian and Mexican cooking. An Indian curry or pickle would be incomplete without chiles, and they are fundamental to certain signature condiments such as Tunisian harissa paste and Asian sambal. Chiles are also used throughout the Mediterranean, usually in their dried form. Dried chiles, with their complex flavor notes, complement the robust flavors of garlic, oregano, tomatoes and olives found in many Greek and Italian recipes.

When you're using chiles in cooking, the intensity of the heat and the timing of when it hits you is often affected by the amount of fat in the dish. Oils and fats tend to coat the heat molecules in chile, either flattening them or delaying them. Therefore a stir-fry with chile and Thai spices will be fairly sharp and hot. Add high-fat coconut milk and not only will the heat be tamed, it will hit your palate a little later. Sweetness will also tone down heat, which means that you are likely to reach for more of a sweet chile sauce than an unsweetened one.

Sherry-Pepper Sauce

A friend of my parents who had lived in India for many years always kept on hand a small decanter of dry sherry with 3 or 4 fresh chiles soaking in it. When added to soups, it gave a surprisingly powerful kick. Apparently this was a common practice in English clubs frequented by former residents of India, who found the soups at home insipid. A well-known prepared version is produced in Bermuda by Outerbridge.

WEIGHT PER TEASPOON (5 mL)

- ground: 2.7 g

SUGGESTED QUANTITY PER POUND (500 g)

Based on ground chiles with a heat level of between 6 and 10.

- **red meats:** 1 tsp (5 mL)
- **white meats:** 1 tsp (5 mL)
- **vegetables:** ½ tsp (2 mL)
- **grains and pulses:** ½ tsp (2 mL) whole
- **baked goods:** ½ tsp (2 mL) whole

If you are unsure of the heat level in a chile, start by using a little less; you can always add more later. If you have used too much chile, try adding a little sugar (remembering to maintain the balance of the dish), cream or coconut cream, if appropriate. Adding some chopped potato and removing it after about 30 minutes of cooking is an old remedy, as is adding chopped bell peppers. Leaving the dish in the fridge overnight sometimes helps, as the flavors mature and round out over time; however, the chile heat does not diminish significantly.

When confronted by a volcanic chile experience, don't drink water to put out the fire in your mouth. Water will actually make it worse! A spoonful of sugar provides the quickest relief. Beer is a good accompaniment to hot food, as is the traditional Indian yogurt drink lassi. Cucumber and yogurt raita is also a good cooling aid to have on hand when indulging in hot curries.

When handling fresh chiles, be careful not to touch any sensitive skin areas or your eyes until you have thoroughly washed your hands. Warm, soapy water is usually effective or, if some heat remains, a gentle wipe with some acetone (nail polish remover) will do the trick. Some very hot chiles can even cause fingers to blister, although this is uncommon. Wearing disposable gloves is a wise precaution for those who are unsure just how hot the chiles are. When cooks want to reduce the heat of fresh chiles, a common practice is to remove the seeds and fleshy capsaicin-bearing placenta from the inside. Fresh julienne strips of chile are often used in stir-fries and salads with an Asian influence and to garnish pâtés and terrines.

Dried chiles may be used whole in curries and almost any other kind of slow-cooked liquid, as the flavor and heat will seep out and blend into the dish. Often sauces will call for a whole chile to be pierced and soaked in hot water for 20 minutes, cut open to remove seeds and stem, and then pounded using a mortar and pestle or processed with other ingredients in a food processor. Ground chiles of varying heats are used in a wide range of curries, sauces, pickles, chutneys and pastes. Almost any meal you can think of will be enhanced by the heat and taste of chile. From exotic crustaceans to humble scrambled eggs, the level of extra taste to be derived from a discreet sprinkling of chile is limited only by one's imagination.

Chile Oil

Every cuisine has some kind of hot condiment. Chile oil is most often used as a condiment with Italian food. A simple infused oil using fiery dried red chiles, this adds flavor and heat when drizzled over hot pizzas and pasta.

Makes 1½ cups (325 mL)

Preparation time: none
Cooking time:
10 minutes

- - - - - - - - - - - - - - - -

Tips

Using a blend of oils tames the olive flavor of the olive oil, allowing the chile flavor to shine through.

Rice bran oil is extracted from the seeds and husks of rice. It has a high smoke point and a mild flavor, making it very versatile.

To sterilize the jar, clean it thoroughly in hot soapy water, then drip-dry. Place jar, right side up, on a baking sheet and heat in a preheated 400°F (200°C) oven for 10 minutes. To sterilize lid, place in a saucepan, cover with water and boil for 5 minutes. Be sure to handle lid and jar with clean hands.

1 cup	olive oil	250 mL
½ cup	neutral-flavored oil such as rice bran or vegetable oil	125 mL
6	whole dried red chiles	6
1 tsp	hot pepper flakes	5 mL

1. In a small saucepan over low heat, combine oils, chiles and hot pepper flakes and cook for about 10 minutes, or until small bubbles rise to the surface and oil is fragrant. Remove from heat and set aside to cool completely.

2. Using a funnel, pour infusion, including spices, into a sterilized jar or bottle (see Tips, left). The oil can be used immediately, but the flavor will continue to deepen for up to 3 months. Store in a cool, dark place for up to 1 year.

Lahmucin

Lahmucin is a fabulous Turkish pizza: spiced ground lamb is spread thinly on a crispy base, then topped with pine nuts, minted yogurt and herbs. As far as I'm concerned, it's the best "fast food" you can make at home, and it wouldn't be the same without the kick from flavorsome Aleppo pepper. Tabouli (page 476) is a great accompaniment to this dish.

**Makes
8 servings**

Preparation time:
  30 minutes, plus 1 hour
  for dough to rise

Cooking time:
  10 minutes

Tip

For a much quicker, easier version of lahmucin, use ready-made flatbread.

• **Food processor**

DOUGH

1½ cups	warm water	325 mL
2 tsp	instant active dry yeast	10 mL
1 tsp	granulated sugar	5 mL
3 tbsp	olive oil	45 mL
5 cups	all-purpose flour	1.25 L
2 tsp	fine sea salt	10 mL

TOPPING

¼ cup	lightly packed fresh mint leaves	60 mL
1 cup	lightly packed fresh parsley leaves	250 mL
1 tsp	ground cumin	5 mL
1 tsp	Aleppo pepper flakes, plus extra for sprinkling	5 mL
½ tsp	ground coriander seed	2 mL
½ tsp	ground paprika	2 mL
1 tsp	fine sea salt	5 mL
⅓ cup	tomato paste	75 mL
1½ lbs	lean ground lamb	750 g
½ cup	pine nuts	125 mL
½ cup	packed fresh parsley leaves	125 mL
	Cacik (page 400)	

1. *Dough:* In a measuring cup, combine water, yeast, sugar and oil. Place flour and salt in a large bowl, make a well in the middle and then pour in the yeast mixture. Using a wooden spoon or your hands, combine well. Turn dough out onto a floured surface and knead for about 5 minutes, until smooth and elastic. Return dough to bowl and cover with lightly oiled plastic wrap. Set aside in a warm place for 1 hour, until slightly risen.

Tip

The lamb topping can be made ahead and kept in an airtight container in the refrigerator for up to 2 days, or frozen for up to 1 month.

2. *Topping:* Meanwhile, in food processor fitted with the metal blade, combine mint, parsley, cumin, Aleppo pepper, coriander, paprika, salt and tomato paste; pulse to combine well. Add lamb and pulse 3 or 4 times to make a thick paste.

3. Preheat oven to 475°F (240°C). Place 2 or 3 baking sheets in oven, depending on how many racks you have. Tear 8 sheets of parchment paper the same size as the baking sheets and set aside (do not line trays).

4. On a lightly floured work surface, turn out dough and knead for 1 minute. Divide dough into 8 equal pieces. Working with one piece at a time, place dough on a sheet of parchment and, using a rolling pin, roll out into a thin disk at least $1/4$ inch (5 mm) thick. Spread prepared topping evenly over dough. Holding parchment paper by the edges, place pizza (with parchment) on preheated baking sheet in oven. Repeat with remaining dough and topping. Bake each pizza for 8 to 10 minutes, until lamb is cooked through and dough is crisp and golden.

5. Serve immediately, hot from the oven, sprinkled with additional Aleppo pepper, pine nuts, parsley and cacik.

Chakchouka

Chakchouka is a wonderful breakfast dish found throughout the Middle East, with many regional variations. This version is more Moroccan—the combination of sweet slow-cooked bell peppers with the bite of dried chile in the harissa paste is a perfect showcase for the capsicum family.

Makes 4 servings

Preparation time:
20 minutes

Cooking time:
30 minutes

- - - - - - - - - - - - - - - -

Tip

To reduce the cooking time, bring your eggs to room temperature before using.

2 tbsp	olive oil	30 mL
2	red bell peppers, seeded and cut into ½-inch (1 cm) slices	2
2	green bell peppers, seeded and cut into ½-inch (1 cm) slices	2
2	cloves garlic, minced	2
1	small red chile, seeded and finely diced	1
1	can (14 oz/398 mL) peeled diced tomatoes, with juice	1
1 tsp	harissa (page 737)	5 mL
1 tsp	ground caraway	5 mL
½ tsp	sweet paprika	2 mL
½ tsp	ground cumin	2 mL
¼ tsp	fine sea salt	1 mL
4	eggs	4

1. In a large, deep skillet over medium heat, heat oil. Add red and green peppers and sauté for 5 minutes, until beginning to soften. Stir in garlic and chile and cook for 1 minute. Add tomatoes, harissa, caraway, paprika, cumin and salt; stir to combine. Reduce heat to low and simmer gently for 10 to 15 minutes, until sauce has thickened. Using the back of a spoon, make 4 indentations in the mixture. Break 1 egg into each indentation. Cover and simmer for 5 minutes, until egg whites are cooked and yolks are still runny (or to your liking). Serve immediately with warm pitas or pide.

Variation

For a meaty version, add 2 sliced chorizo or spicy sausages to the skillet while cooking the peppers.

Chipotle in Adobo

Recipes often call for chipotle in adobo, which is an easy way to add some punch to your cooking (it's very hot!). However, a lot of store-bought varieties are high in salt, preservatives and high-fructose corn syrup. Try making your own at home for the very best chipotles in adobo.

Makes about 1 cup (250 mL)

Preparation time:
45 minutes

Cooking time: 1 hour, 15 minutes

Tips

Freeze adobo in an ice-cube tray, then transfer the cubes to a freezer bag and use as needed. The frozen cubes will last for up to 1 year.

To sterilize jar, clean thoroughly in hot soapy water, then drip-dry. Place jar, right side up, on a baking sheet and heat in a preheated 400°F (200°C) oven for 10 minutes. To sterilize lid, place in a saucepan, cover with water and boil for 5 minutes. Be sure to handle the lid and jar with clean hands.

• **Regular or immersion blender**

8	chipotle chiles, stems removed	8
½	white onion, chopped	½
3	cloves garlic, chopped	3
Pinch	dried oregano	Pinch
Pinch	ground allspice	Pinch
¼ tsp	ground cumin	1 mL
¼ tsp	fine sea salt	1 mL
¼ cup	tomato paste	60 mL
¼ cup	cider vinegar	60 mL
2 tbsp	lightly packed light brown sugar	30 mL
½ cup	water	125 mL

1. In a small bowl, cover chiles with boiling water and set aside for 45 minutes, until soft.

2. Using blender, purée ¼ cup (60 mL) soaking liquid with 2 soaked chiles, onion, garlic, oregano, allspice, cumin and salt. Transfer mixture to a saucepan and cook over medium heat for 3 minutes, until heated through. Add remaining chipotles (discard soaking liquid), tomato paste, vinegar, sugar and water and reduce heat to low. Simmer for 1 hour, stirring occasionally, until sauce has thickened and chiles have disintegrated (add more water if necessary to help break down the chiles). Remove from heat and set aside to cool completely. Chipotles in adobo will keep in a sterilized jar (see Tips, left) in the refrigerator for up to 3 months.

Chicken Mole Poblano

Mole poblano is the best known of all the Mexican mole sauces, and most often served at parties and celebrations. Its large variety of ingredients culminates in a complex, utterly delicious sauce, and it's very easy to make. I find it hard to pick a favorite Mexican dish, but let's say this is comfortably in the top three!

**Makes
4 servings**

Preparation time:
25 minutes

Cooking time:
30 minutes

Tips

If the chicken breasts are very big, halve or slice them after cooking (before adding to sauce), if desired.

You can make the sauce ahead and refrigerate it in an airtight container for up to 3 days, or freeze for up to 1 month.

• **Regular or immersion blender**

4	skinless boneless chicken breasts (about 7 to 8 oz/210 to 250 g)	4
4 cups	water or reduced-sodium chicken broth	1 L
2	pasilla chiles, seeded	2
1	small chipotle chile, seeded	1
1 tsp	oil	5 mL
1	onion, chopped	1
1 tsp	lightly packed light brown sugar	5 mL
2	cloves garlic, chopped	2
1 tsp	ground cinnamon	5 mL
½ tsp	paprika	2 mL
¼ tsp	smoked paprika	1 mL
1 tsp	fine sea salt	5 mL
¼ tsp	freshly ground black pepper	1 mL
¼ tsp	ground anise seed	1 mL
Pinch	ground cloves	Pinch
Pinch	dried Mexican oregano	Pinch
6	vine tomatoes, halved and broiled on High until blackened	6
1	soft white corn tortilla, chopped	1
2 tbsp	raw unsalted almonds	30 mL
2 tbsp	chopped pecans	30 mL
3 tbsp	toasted sesame seeds, divided	45 mL
2 tbsp	Thompson raisins	30 mL
1½ tbsp	cocoa powder	22 mL

1. In a large saucepan over medium heat, cover chicken with water and bring to a boil; turn off heat and set aside.

2. In a heatproof bowl, cover pasilla and chipotle chiles with boiling water and set aside for 10 minutes, until soft. Roughly chop (discard soaking liquid) and set aside.

3. In a saucepan or deep skillet over low heat, heat oil. Stir in onion and sugar, cover, and cook, stirring occasionally, for about 5 minutes, until translucent. Add garlic, reserved chiles, cinnamon, paprika, smoked paprika, salt, pepper, anise seed, cloves, oregano, tomatoes and tortilla. Increase heat to medium and cook, stirring often, for 1 minute, until well combined. Add almonds, pecans, 2 tbsp (30 mL) sesame seeds, raisins and cocoa and cook, stirring, for 1 minute. Add 2 cups (500 mL) chicken cooking liquid, stir to combine, and cook for 2 minutes, until heated through. Turn off heat and, using blender, blend at medium speed until sauce is roughly combined (it should retain some texture).

4. Return sauce to pan (if necessary) and add prepared chicken. Cook over medium heat for 5 minutes, until heated through. Serve sprinkled with remaining sesame seeds, with cooked rice on the side.

Variation

Use turkey breasts instead of chicken.

Kimchi

Kimchi is one of the most popular condiments in the world, and it's really easy to make. Our local Korean restaurant does an amazing kimchi rice that I recreate at home with my own kimchi. Korean red pepper flakes (gochugaru) can be found at good Asian grocers and are essential for making kimchi. The coarsely ground sun-dried red peppers have a hot, sweet and slightly smoky flavor and a texture between flakes and powder.

**Makes
6 to 8 cups
(1.5 to 2 L)**

Preparation time:
**24 hours, plus 5 days
for fermenting**
Cooking time: none

- - - - - - - - - - - - - - - - - -

Tips

Some Koreans keep their kimchi for 2 or 3 years, and it keeps on fermenting. I recommend keeping it refrigerated for up to 2 months, but how long you keep it is up to personal taste (and how quickly you use it).

Use kimchi as an accompaniment to Korean food or in dishes such as kimchi rice, kimchi pancakes and stir-fries.

Kimchi is ready when the cabbage leaves are soft and slightly shriveled and the flavors are fully integrated; it should taste pickled and slightly sour. If the kimchi turns white or tastes too sour, it has gone off and should be discarded.

1 lb	napa cabbage	500 g
½ cup	coarse sea salt	125 mL
½ cup	rice flour	125 mL
1 cup	water	250 mL
1	head garlic, cloves minced	1
1 tbsp	minced gingerroot	15 mL
2 tbsp	minced onion	30 mL
1 cup	Korean red pepper flakes (gochugaru) or paste (gochujang)	250 mL
1	bunch green onions, cut into 1-inch (2.5 cm) pieces	1
1	bunch fresh Chinese chives, cut into 1-inch (2.5 cm) pieces	1

1. Using a sharp knife, cut cabbage in half lengthwise. Remove and discard the base core from both halves by cutting it out in a triangle. Slice cabbage leaves into 1-inch (2.5 cm) strips. Rinse well under cold running water. In a large bowl, stack cabbage leaves, sprinkling with salt between each layer and ending with a layer of salt. Cover with about 1 inch of cold water. Cover bowl with a kitchen towel and weigh down with a heavy lid or plate to ensure that cabbage remains submerged. Set aside for 24 hours, until leaves are soft and pliable. Rinse well under cold running water to remove salt; drain well or dry in a salad spinner. Return cabbage to clean bowl.

2. In a small saucepan over low heat, combine rice flour with water; heat gently for 2 to 3 minutes, until it forms a paste. Add garlic, ginger, onion and gochugaru. Remove from heat and pour onto cabbage, stirring to coat leaves completely with spice mixture. Stir in green onions and chives. Transfer to a sterilized airtight container and set aside at room temperature for 3 days to ferment. Open jar to release any built-up gas, then refrigerate for a further 2 days before using (see Tips, left).

Chives

Onion chives: *Allium schoenoprasum*
Garlic chives: *A. tuberosum*

Names in Other Languages

- **Arabic:** thoum muammar
- **Chinese (C):** gau choi, sai heung chung
- **Chinese (M):** jiu cai, xi xiang cong
- **Czech:** patzika, snytlik
- **Danish:** purlog
- **Dutch:** bieslook
- **Filipino:** kutsay
- **French:** ciboulette, civette
- **German:** Schnittlauch
- **Greek:** praso, schinopraso
- **Indonesian:** kucai
- **Italian:** aglio selvatico, erba cipollina
- **Japanese:** nira, asatuki
- **Malay:** ku cai
- **Portuguese:** cebolinha
- **Russian:** luk rezanets, shnitluk
- **Spanish:** cebolleta
- **Thai:** kui chaai
- **Turkish:** frenk sogani, sirmik
- **Vietnamese:** la he

Family: Alliaceae (formerly Liliaceae)

Varieties: blue chives (*A. nutans*), Chinese chives (*A. ramosum*), giant chives (*A. schoenoprasum sibiricum*)

Other Names: rush leek (onion chives); Chinese chives (garlic chives)

Flavor Group: Medium

Parts Used: leaves (as a herb)

Background

Although the history of chives' cousins, such as onions and garlic, goes back over 5,000 years, cooks didn't show much interest in this delicately flavored culinary herb until the 19th century. Native to the cooler parts of Europe and Asia,

Culinary Information

Combines with
- basil
- chervil
- cress
- dill leaf
- fennel fronds
- lovage
- onion and garlic
- parsley
- salad burnet
- sorrel

Traditional Uses
- scrambled eggs and omelets
- sour cream
- salad dressings and mayonnaise
- white sauces
- mashed potatoes
- vichyssoise
- seafood and chicken dishes (as a garnish)

Spice Blends
- fines herbes
- salad herbs

chives now grow wild in Canada and northern areas of the United States. The name is derived from *cepa*, the Latin word for onion, which evolved into the French *cive*.

The Plant

When not in flower, this humble herb more closely resembles a clump of grass than one of the world's most popular culinary herbs. Chives are the smallest member of the onion family, which also includes garlic, leeks and shallots. There are two main varieties of chives—onion chives and garlic chives—which are named for their characteristic onion and garlic flavors, respectively. Only the leaves of these two varieties are eaten, as the small, elongated bulb is virtually non-existent.

Onion chives grow 6 to 12 inches (15 to 30 cm) tall and have slender, grass-like bright green leaves that taper at the top and become more tubular in cross-section as they develop. Masses of mauve-pink pompom-shaped flowers, constructed of cylindrical petals, adorn the plant in summer, making it a favorite with botanical artists. **Garlic chives** grow a little taller than onion chives, and their light green mature leaves are distinctly flat by comparison. Their flowers are white and form on tough stems that are unsuitable for eating. Both varieties are valuable for their subtle onion and garlic flavors, delivered in a fresh-tasting green medium that lacks the pungency and (for some) the "many happy returns" experienced after eating too much onion or garlic.

Other Varieties

Blue chives, also known as **Siberian garlic chives** (*Allium nutans*), have wide, thick, flat gray leaves; they grow in China, Kazakhstan, Mongolia and Russia. Blue chives have a milder garlic flavor than garlic chives. **Chinese chives** (*A. ramosum*) have a flavor that resembles a blend of garlic chives and onion chives. **Giant chives** (*A. schoenoprasum sibiricum*) are not particularly large, in spite of their name. The flowers and the leaves are used, and the bulbs, although small, may be substituted for green onions.

Processing

In the 20th century the invention of freeze-drying had a more profound effect on the popularity of chives than on any other herb or spice. Freeze-drying is a sophisticated, capital-intensive method of dehydration that removes moisture from plant material without damaging delicate cell structures. It relies on the process of sublimation: the shift from a solid directly into a gas. After harvesting and grading by hand, the chives are frozen. Then a vacuum chamber is used to force the frozen moisture to change phase directly to the gaseous state, skipping the liquid stage. Cell- and flavor-destroying latent heat is not produced during dehydration. The finished product has all the color, shape and flavor of fresh chives, lacking only the moisture. Because the moisture in many foods is sufficient to rehydrate freeze-dried chives, they do not need to be reconstituted before using. They can be added directly to foods such as cream cheese, sauces, dressings, mashed potatoes and scrambled eggs.

Buying and Storage

Fresh chives are usually sold in small bunches 1 inch (2.5 cm) in diameter. Many grocery stores do not label chives correctly, but a quick inspection of the cut ends will reveal whether they are tubular (onion chives) or flat (garlic chives) if a gentle sniff does not reveal the variety. Inordinately light-sensitive, chives are best purchased from retailers who keep their stock "under the counter" to prevent deterioration. Avoid chives that look wilted. Fresh chives will keep for up to 1 week when stored in a resealable bag in the refrigerator (do not wash until you are ready to use them).

While it is not practical to dry your own chives, fresh chives can be chopped and frozen, with a little water to cover, in an ice-cube tray. They can also be blended with butter and refrigerated for up to 1 week. Chive butter makes a lovely base for sandwiches and a delicious finish for cooked vegetables.

Most of the dried chives available are onion chives, possibly because the tiny bright green rings are more attractive and their lesser weight fills a container more effectively. Freeze-dried chives (usually labeled as such) are vastly superior in quality to those that have been air-dried.

Always keep dried chives in an airtight container in a cool, dry place away from any source of light. Under those conditions freeze-dried chives will last up to 1 year.

Use

Chives have such a pleasant taste and add such a pleasing hint of freshness that it is almost impossible to overuse them in a savory dish. They are an essential ingredient in the traditional French blend of chives, chervil, parsley and tarragon known as "fines herbes." They also find their way into many commercially produced packaged soups and sauces. Add chives right away to dishes that are being cooked for a short time, such as omelets, scrambled eggs and white sauces. For other applications, don't add them until the final 5 to 10 minutes of cooking, as being subjected to prolonged heat will destroy much of the flavor. Fresh chives are excellent as a garnish on fish and chicken, and they make an attractive and tasty addition to salad dressings and mayonnaise.

WEIGHT PER TEASPOON (5 mL)

- chopped freeze-dried leaves: 0.3 g

SUGGESTED QUANTITY PER POUND (500 g)

- **white meats:** 4 tsp (20 mL) dry, 8 tsp (40 mL) fresh
- **vegetables:** 1 tbsp (15 mL) dry, 2 tbsp (30 mL) fresh
- **grains and pulses:** 1 tbsp (15 mL) dry, 2 tbsp (30 mL) fresh
- **baked goods:** 1 tbsp (15 mL) dry, 2 tbsp (30 mL) fresh

Fines Herbes Omelet

Fines herbes is a classic French combination of fresh herbs, namely chervil, tarragon, parsley and chives. This blend marries well with many dishes, and those containing eggs in particular.

C

Makes 1 serving

Preparation time:
5 minutes

Cooking time:
5 minutes

- - - - - - - - - - - - - -

Tips

To finely chop chives, hold them in a neat, even bunch and snip with scissors or use a sharp knife to cut crosswise.

Be sure to fold the omelet before the egg is completely set; otherwise it won't stay folded.

- **6-inch (15 cm) skillet**

2	large eggs	2
1 tbsp	table (18%) cream	15 mL
1 tsp	finely chopped fresh chervil leaves	5 mL
1 tsp	finely chopped fresh chives (see Tips, left)	5 mL
1 tsp	finely chopped fresh tarragon leaves	5 mL
1 tsp	finely chopped fresh parsley leaves	5 mL
1 tsp	butter	5 mL
	Sea salt and freshly ground black pepper	

1. In a small bowl, lightly whisk together eggs and cream. Add chervil, chives, tarragon and parsley and whisk to combine.

2. In skillet over medium-high heat, melt butter until foaming. Pour in prepared egg mixture. Cook until edges begin to set, about 1 minute. Using a spatula, pull the edges inward to allow the remaining liquid to flow to the outer edges. Repeat once more. When the eggs are almost entirely set but still have a slight wobble, about 2 minutes, fold the omelet in half and turn out onto a plate (see Tips, left). Serve immediately.

Variation

For even more flavor and substance, add 1 to 2 tbsp (15 to 30 mL) soft goat cheese and/or 1 tomato, peeled, seeded and finely diced, in Step 1.

Carrot Soup with Chive Muffins

Fresh chives are indispensable as a garnish for this soup and complement the light, cheesy muffins wonderfully. Together these recipes make a perfect lunch, with plenty of leftover muffins that can be eaten later or frozen.

Makes 4 servings

Preparation time:
20 minutes

Cooking time:
45 minutes

- - - - - - - - - - - - - - - -

Tips

If you can't find self-rising flour in stores, you can make your own. To equal 1 cup (250 mL) self-rising flour, combine 1 cup (250 mL) all-purpose flour, 1½ tsp (7 mL) baking powder and ½ tsp (2 mL) salt.

Once cool, the muffins can be stored in an airtight container for 3 days or frozen for up to 2 months.

- **Regular or immersion blender**
- **12-cup muffin pan, brushed with melted butter and dusted with fine cornmeal**
- **Preheat oven to 350°F (180°C)**

SOUP

2 tbsp	butter	30 mL
1	small onion, chopped	1
4 cups	chicken or vegetable broth	1 L
1 lb	young carrots (unpeeled), sliced into ½-inch (1 cm) rounds	500 g
1 tsp	smoked paprika	5 mL
½ tsp	freshly ground black pepper	2 mL
1 cup	table (18%) cream	250 mL
2 tbsp	fresh chives, chopped into ½-inch (1 cm) lengths	30 mL

MUFFINS

2 cups	self-rising flour (see Tips, left)	500 mL
2 tsp	fine sea salt	10 mL
1 tsp	baking powder	5 mL
1 tsp	sweet paprika	5 mL
2	eggs, lightly whisked	2
1 cup	buttermilk	250 mL
¾ cup	milk	175 mL
½ cup	shredded Cheddar cheese	125 mL
½ cup	freshly grated Parmesan cheese	125 mL
½ cup	oil	125 mL
1	bunch chives, chopped into ½-inch (1 cm) pieces (about ¼ cup/60 mL)	1

Tip

If buttermilk is not available, use plain milk or make your own buttermilk by adding 1 tbsp (15 mL) freshly squeezed lemon juice to 1 cup (250 mL) milk. Set it aside for 20 minutes to curdle.

1. *Soup:* In a saucepan over medium heat, melt butter. Add onion and cook until soft, about 5 minutes. Add broth, carrots, paprika and pepper and bring to a boil. Reduce heat to a simmer and cook for 15 minutes or until carrots are tender. Using blender, purée until smooth. Return to pan (if necessary) and stir in cream. Taste and adjust seasoning, if desired.

2. *Muffins:* In a large bowl, combine flour, salt, baking powder and paprika.

3. In a separate bowl, combine eggs, buttermilk, milk, Cheddar, Parmesan and oil. Slowly add wet ingredients to dry ingredients, stirring until smooth and well-combined. Stir in chives. Pour batter into prepared muffin pan and bake for 15 to 20 minutes, until risen and golden. Remove from oven and set aside to cool in pan for 5 minutes, then turn out onto a wire rack to cool completely.

4. Ladle warm soup into serving bowls and garnish with chives. Serve with muffins alongside.

Cinnamon and Cassia

Cinnamon: *Cinnamomum zeylanicum*; Cassia: *C. cassia*
(also known as *C. burmannii, C. loureirii, C. tamala*)

Names in Other Languages

Cinnamon

- **Arabic:** qurfa
- **Burmese:** thit-ja-boh-gauk
- **Chinese (C):** yuhk gwai, sek laahn yuhk gwai
- **Chinese (M):** jou kuei, rou gui, xi lan rou gui
- **Czech:** skorice, skorice cejlonska
- **Danish:** kanel
- **Dutch:** kaneel
- **French:** canelle, cannelle type Ceylan
- **German:** Zimt, echter Zimt
- **Greek:** kanela
- **Hungarian:** fahej
- **Indian:** darchini, dalchini
- **Indonesian:** kayu manis
- **Italian:** cannella
- **Japanese:** seiron-nikkei
- **Malay:** kayu manis
- **Portuguese:** canela
- **Russian:** koritsa
- **Spanish:** canela
- **Sri Lankan:** kurundu
- **Swedish:** kanel
- **Thai:** ob chuey
- **Turkish:** Seylan tarcini, darcin
- **Vietnamese:** cay que, nhuc que

Family: Lauraceae

Varieties: cinnamon (*C. zeylanicum*), Chinese cassia (*C. cassia*), Batavia cassia (*C. burmannii*), Saigon cassia (*C. loureirii*), Indian cassia (*C. tamala*)

Other Names: cinnamon bark, cinnamon quills, Sri Lankan cinnamon (cinnamon); baker's cinnamon, bastard cinnamon, false cinnamon, Dutch cinnamon, Indonesian cinnamon, Saigon cinnamon (cassia); Indian cassia leaves, Indian bay leaves, tejpat (Indian cassia)

Flavor Group: Sweet

Parts Used: bark and agissa/inner bark (as a spice), leaves (as a herb)

Background

Cinnamon and cassia have had confusing naming conventions since antiquity, because the generic name *cinnamon* has been widely used to describe both cinnamon and cassia. As a result, when researching the history of cinnamon, there is no reliable way to know which variety is being described. For instance, the cinnamon referred to in the Bible may have been any combination of members of the *Cinnamomum* genus, which includes both cinnamon and cassia.

Even the experts differ on the magnitude of this family, naming anywhere from 50 to 250 different types of cinnamon and cassia. What is known for sure is that both cinnamon and cassia were widely traded because neither grew in the Holy Land.

Cinnamon and cassia are said to be among the oldest of spices. References date back 2,500 years to the land of the pharaohs, where what was referred to as cinnamon (and may actually have been cassia) was used in the embalming process. In 1500 BCE the Egyptians voyaged to the "land of Punt" (present-day Somalia) to find precious metals, ivory,

Names in Other Languages

Cassia

- **Arabic:** darasini, kerfee
- **Chinese (C):** gun gwai, gwai sam, mauh gwai
- **Chinese (M):** guan gui, gui xin, keui tsin
- **Czech:** skorice cinska
- **Danish:** kinesisk kanel
- **Dutch:** kassia, bastaardkaneel
- **French:** canelle de Cochinchine, casse
- **German:** chinesischer Zimt, Kassie
- **Greek:** kasia
- **Hungarian:** kasszia, fahejkasszia
- **Indian:** tej pattar (leaf), kulmie dalchini (bark)
- **Italian:** cassia
- **Japanese:** kashia, keihi, shinamonkassia
- **Polish:** kasja, cynamon chinski
- **Portuguese:** canela da China
- **Russian:** korichnoje derevo
- **Spanish:** casia, canela de la China
- **Swedish:** kassia
- **Thai:** bai kravan (leaf), ob choey (bark)
- **Turkish:** cin tarcini
- **Vietnamese:** que don, que quang, que thanh

cinnamon quills

exotic animals and spices, including cinnamon (and/or cassia), which no doubt had reached there via Arab traders, because neither spice grew in Africa at the time. Any search for the true origins of the cinnamon and cassia traded in those times is further shrouded in mystery by the improbable stories promulgated by the traders, who were highly motivated to keep their sources of supply a secret.

For instance, one fable claimed that cinnamon sticks were used by giant birds in the "land of Dionysus" (Greece, India or lands to the east of Europe) to build their nests atop precipitous mountains. To collect this valuable spice, the courageous traders would leave cut-up carcasses of oxen and donkeys near the nests and hide at a safe distance; the birds would swoop down, pick up the heavy joints and take them up to their aeries. Because the nests weren't strong enough to accommodate such weight, they would break and fall to the ground, allowing the spice hunters to collect the valuable cinnamon sticks and trade them to the West. In my opinion, this fable supports the notion that the sticks were actually Sri Lankan *C. zeylanicum*. Delicate hand-rolled cinnamon quills would be far more likely to break under a heavy weight than the strong, somewhat hard sticks of cassia bark.

Culinary Information

Combines with

- allspice
- caraway
- cardamom
- chile
- cloves
- coriander seed
- cumin
- ginger
- licorice
- nutmeg
- star anise
- tamarind
- turmeric

Traditional Uses

- cakes
- sweet pastries and cookies
- stewed fruits
- curries
- beverages such as chai tea
- Moroccan tagines
- preserved lemons

Spice Blends

- curry powders
- pumpkin pie spice
- sweet mixed spice
- ras el hanout
- tagine spice blends
- garam masala
- quatre épices
- barbecue spice blends
- Asian master stocks
- pickling spices
- Cajun spice blends

Both cinnamon and cassia were probably available to the ancient Greeks and Romans. In 66 CE, the Roman statesman Pliny the Elder, already concerned about a balance-of-payments problem in Rome, was horrified when Emperor Nero burned a whole year's supply of cinnamon at his wife's funeral. By the 13th century, travelers were writing about the cinnamon from Ceylon (Sri Lanka); it was around this time that the Chalais—the caste that engaged exclusively in harvesting and peeling cinnamon—emigrated to Sri Lanka from India. Today the majority of cinnamon peelers in Sri Lanka are descendants of those Chalais immigrants.

Records of cassia in China stretch back to 4000 BCE. Because it has never been known to grow wild there, it must have entered China from Assam, the region in northeastern India that borders on China. Batavia, or Java, cassia, grew wild on the Indonesian islands of Sumatra, Java and Borneo. In the first millennium CE, the Indonesians colonized Madagascar, bringing their native cassia with them. There is little doubt that they traded cassia and other spices such as cloves with the Arabs.

One can imagine the network of cinnamon and cassia routes spreading across the known world: from Indonesia to Madagascar, then by Arab, Phoenician and Roman traders to the Mediterranean and overland to Egypt and Africa. At the same time, these spices traveled from Sri Lanka to Rome and Greece and from Assam into China via the famous Silk Road.

cassia quills

Cinnamon was one of the spices most sought after by 15th- and 16th-century explorers. Originally the Portuguese had a virtual monopoly on its supply after they arrived in Ceylon in 1505. They were usurped by the Dutch, who controlled Ceylon from 1636 until they lost it to the British in 1796. Today what is considered to be the world's best cinnamon still comes from Sri Lanka, while various grades of cassia come predominantly from China, Indonesia and Vietnam.

The Plants

Cinnamon and cassia both come from tropical evergreen trees related to the bay laurel, avocado and sassafras. The sections of bark that are stripped from cinnamon and cassia are often confused, even though they are distinctly different in both appearance and flavor profile.

Cinnamon trees, when allowed to grow in their wild state, can reach 26 to 56 feet (8 to 17 m) and develop a girth of 12 to 24 inches (30 to 60 cm). The young leaves of cinnamon trees are an intense red, turning pale green and maturing to a glossy dark green on top. The flowers are pale yellow, small—around $1/8$ inch (3 mm) in diameter—and have a somewhat fetid smell.

Cassia trees are larger than cinnamon trees, reaching 59 feet (18 m) and producing stout trunks up to 5 feet (1.5 m) in diameter. In Vietnam these trees are grown in cassia plantations, and each tree is usually harvested when it is less than 10 years old. This means that to maintain production, a well-stocked nursery of seedlings is essential

Travels in the Spice Trade

On our first visit to a Sri Lankan cinnamon farm, Liz and I were astounded by the skill of the traditional cinnamon peelers. To watch a cinnamon peeler at work is like witnessing a magic show where the hand appears to be quicker than the eye. With extraordinary dexterity the peeler takes a cut stem and, using a crude metal instrument, scrapes off and discards the outer layer of corky-looking bark. Next he rubs the stem with a brass rod, bruising and loosening the remaining paper-thin layer of cinnamon, called *agissa* (inner bark), and preparing it for peeling. Sitting on the ground with one end of the cinnamon stem gripped between big toe and second toe, using a dangerous-looking sharp, pointed knife, he makes two cuts around the stem about 12 inches (30 cm) apart. A longitudinal slit is made along the entire length before he deftly removes the half-cylinders of fine underneath bark. These are put out in the sun for a short time (less than an hour) to firm up, curl and partially dry.

The peeler charged with making the long cinnamon quills telescopes one paper-thin 12-inch (30 cm) length of *agissa* into another until a 3-foot (1 m) quill is formed. Smaller pieces of bark that break or split or come from uneven knots on the harvested branch are placed inside the scroll until it is full of slivers of cinnamon. The still somewhat moist, fragrant and surprisingly lemon-scented quill is rolled until tight and then put aside to dry completely. Drying has to take place in the shade, as sunshine will warp and crack the quills, making them less desirable. We were entranced to see inside the farmer's house, where racks had been created by running strings at ceiling height from wall to wall: the drying cinnamon quills were suspended like a fragrant false ceiling until they were dry and ready to take to the trader. With the sweet aroma of cinnamon permeating the atmosphere, that house certainly didn't require any air fresheners!

for replanting. Cassia trees are grown from seeds gathered beneath the trees; the best seeds for germination are said to be those that have passed through the intestines of birds that have eaten the small green fruits.

Other Varieties

In India the variety *Cinnamomum tamala* (see page 115) is used to produce a low-grade cinnamon bark. The leaves are added to recipes as an ingredient commonly called *tejpat*, or Indian bay leaves; they have a slightly clove-like flavor. In Indonesia the leaves of *C. burmannii* are used in cooking and are often referred to by Westerners as "Indonesian bay leaves." However, strictly speaking, the Indonesian bay leaf, or *daun salam*, is the leaf of *Syzygium polyanthum*, which has a mild clove and cinnamon-like flavor. I would not recommend using European bay leaves (*Laurus nobilis*) as a substitute for either; a better alternative would be to add either a whole clove or a small pinch of ground cloves or allspice to the recipe.

C

Processing

Today the processing of cinnamon in Sri Lanka is possibly one of the most dexterous skills still demonstrated by traditional workers in the spice trade. It is fascinating to watch (see "Travels in the Spice Trade," page 206). Cinnamon peelers work in groups comprising two or three families who supply their labor to farmers under contract.

Two to three years after being planted, cinnamon trees are cut down to approximately 6 inches (15 cm) above the ground and soil is mounded around the stumps to encourage the formation of shoots. Four to six shoots are allowed to develop for up to 2 years before being harvested, when they are about 5 feet (1.5 m) long and $1/2$ to 1 inch (1 to 2.5 cm) in diameter. After cutting, unwanted shoots are pruned, the earth is piled up again and more canes in the stand of cinnamon grow for the next harvest. Harvesting takes place after the first flush of red leaves starts to turn pale green and the sap is flowing freely. The cutter will test these stems to determine when the bark is most easily peeled, and after cutting will transport them to the farmer's house or to sheds where the peeling takes place.

Cinnamon from Sri Lanka is traded in four forms, the highest quality being whole quills roped together in burlap-covered cylindrical bales just over 3 feet (1 m) long and weighing 100 pounds (45 kg). The most perfectly made, tightly rolled and evenly joined quills are considered to be the best and are generally referred to as "C5." In the course of transporting and handling, some quills are damaged; when they are put into bales, these broken pieces are called "quillings." Another grade is referred to as "featherings"; these consist of the inner bark of twigs and small shoots that were not sufficiently large to make into full-sized quills. They are still real cinnamon but they lack the visual appeal of good-quality quills. Most ground cinnamon is made from cinnamon featherings. Cinnamon chips are the lowest grade of true cinnamon. These are made from shavings and trimmings, including pieces of outer bark and the occasional twig or stone. A poor-quality coarse, dark brown cinnamon powder is made from either cinnamon chips or outer and inner bark cut from mature semi-wild trees in the Seychelles or Madagascar, which account for much of the world's supply of "unscraped" cinnamon bark.

Cassia is harvested using a different method from cinnamon. First the lower trunk of the tree is scraped with a small knife to remove moss and the outer cork. The bark is then cut off in sections, the tree felled, and the remaining bark removed in the same way. In southern China the bitter outer material is scraped off after the bark is removed from the tree. Then it is dried in the sun, which causes it to curl into thick scrolled quills that are often confused with cinnamon. In some parts of Vietnam a complicated process of curing, washing, drying and fermenting slabs of cassia produces a more valuable grade of the spice.

Cassia buds, which are sometimes used in sweet pickles, are the dried immature fruits, usually from Chinese cassia. They have a cinnamon-like fragrance and a warm, pungent aroma. As the demand for cassia buds has never been very high, generally only a few trees in a plantation are left undisturbed to produce them.

Buying and Storage

While there are different grades of both cinnamon and cassia, the difference between cinnamon and cassia is easily recognizable whether you are looking at the whole or the ground form. The quality may vary within the types of powdered spice.

Sri Lankan cinnamon is generally available in three main grades. Cinnamon bark is the lowest grade; it is a coarse, slightly bitter dark brown powder and most often the cheapest. Ground cinnamon quills are the best grade of true cinnamon, even though they are made from quillings or featherings. Quillings are broken quills and featherings are the shards of inner bark that were not large enough to incorporate into a quill. Their flavor is just as good as that from a whole quill.

In the past, in some countries such as Australia and England, it was illegal to sell cassia labeled as cinnamon (even though many merchants did). In France, however, one word, *canelle*, refers to both cinnamon and cassia. In the United States there are no restrictions on the naming of cinnamon and cassia; *cinnamon* is the word used most often to describe both. However, some US spice brands now distinguish between them by calling cassia simply "cinnamon" and calling cinnamon "Sri Lankan cinnamon."

Hand-rolled cinnamon quills up to 3 feet (1 m) in length are sometimes seen in the wholesale markets in Sri Lanka. However, consumers most often see quills that are $3^1/_4$ inches (8 cm) long, with many concentric layers

cinnamon quills

of paper-thin bark rolled into cylinders about $1/2$ inch (1 cm) in diameter. The color of cinnamon quills is a uniform light brown to pale tan. When ground, they produce an aromatic powder that is similar in color to the quills and has a very fine, dusty texture. The fragrance is sweet, perfumed, warm and pleasantly woody, with no trace of bitterness or dominating pungency, which helps explain why cinnamon has been regarded for centuries as having aphrodisiac properties.

Cassia bark, by contrast, is generally found in two whole forms. One is flat pieces of dark brown slivers 4 to 8 inches (10 to 20 cm) long and 1 inch (2.5 cm) wide, smooth on one surface and rough and corky on the other. The other form is quills or scrolls. These are smooth and similar in appearance to cinnamon quills, except for the thickness of the curl of bark—about $1/8$ inch (3 mm) as opposed to paper-thin—and the reddish brown color. The aroma of ground cassia (grinding releases the volatile oils and makes the smell more obvious) is highly perfumed, penetrating, sweet and lingering. The flavor has an agreeable bitterness and many people feel it is superior to cinnamon. Cassia powder will usually appear darker and redder than cinnamon, and because the texture is so fine, its flow characteristics are similar to the finest of talcum powders. Ground cassia, often euphemistically called "baker's cinnamon" or "Dutch cinnamon" in Australia, is usually lower-priced than ground cinnamon quills but more expensive than ground cinnamon bark. Many pastry cooks prefer it to cinnamon.

Cinnamon and cassia are not easy to grind yourself, so if a recipe calls for ground cinnamon or cassia, buying a good-quality powder is recommended. The most pleasing and fragrant volatile top notes will evaporate easily, so it is very important to store both ground cinnamon and ground cassia in airtight container protected from extremes of heat and humidity. Under these conditions, they will last for a little over 1 year. Whole cinnamon quills and cassia bark are relatively stable and will keep for 2 to 3 years, as long as they are not exposed to extreme heat.

Use

A whole cinnamon quill, $3^1/_4$ inches (8 cm) long—often referred to in recipes as a "cinnamon stick"—and pieces of cassia bark are used in dishes when the flavor is intended to infuse into a liquid medium. Therefore, when stewing a fruit compote, preparing a curry or a spiced rice dish such as biryani, or even making mulled wine, use the cinnamon or cassia whole. Mexicans are fond of cinnamon tea—*té de canela*—made with broken cinnamon quills, which, like Indian or herbal tea, is left for a few minutes to infuse; the tea is then strained into a cup or glass and drunk hot, with sugar to taste.

The powdered form of cinnamon is most popular in Western countries when mixed with other ingredients to add flavor to cakes, pastries, fruit pies, milk puddings, curry powders, garam masala, mixed spice, pumpkin pie spice and other spice blends. The greater pungency of cassia has become popular in commercial baked goods such as cinnamon doughnuts, apple strudel, fruit muffins and sweet spice cookies. A large proportion of bakeries in North America use cassia instead of cinnamon, possibly because the customer-enticing aroma of baked cassia wafts into the surrounding atmosphere more effectively than that of cinnamon.

Which one you use should simply be a matter of personal preference. Just keep in mind that cassia is more strongly perfumed and pungent than cinnamon, so it is best used with other distinctively flavored ingredients such as dried fruits. Cinnamon, on the other hand, complements fresh ingredients such as apples, pears and bananas. I often mix cinnamon and cassia half and half to get the benefits of both.

The leaves of cinnamon and cassia have a distinctly clove-like aroma and taste and may be used, either fresh or dried, in Indian and Asian cooking. When we were visiting the cassia forests in Khe Dhu in North Vietnam, our hosts picked up some large dry cassia leaves and slipped them into their shoes, as an aromatic odor-fighting insole.

WEIGHT PER TEASPOON (5 mL)

- whole average quill ($3^1/_4$ inches/8 cm): 4 g
- ground: 2.7 g

SUGGESTED QUANTITY PER POUND (500 g)

- **red meats:** 1 quill
- **white meats:** $^1/_2$ quill
- **vegetables:** $^1/_2$ quill
- **grains and pulses:** 1 tbsp (15 mL) ground cinnamon, 2 tsp (10 mL) ground cassia
- **baked goods:** 1 tbsp (15 mL) ground cinnamon, 2 tsp (10 mL) ground cassia

Apple and Cinnamon Teacake

There is nothing I loved more as a child than my granny's hot cinnamon doughnuts. The combination of crunchy sugar with fragrant cinnamon over the warm cakey dough was heavenly. Granny also made a delicious cinnamon teacake, which was in her children's cookbook *Cooking Is Fun*. My young daughter, Maisie, likes to make this cake in a heart-shaped mold, and she loves the cinnamon-sugar topping as much as I do.

Makes one 9-inch (23 cm) cake

Preparation time:
10 minutes

Cooking time:
20 minutes

Tips

Superfine (caster) sugar is a very fine granulated sugar typically used in recipes that require a faster-dissolving granule. If you can't find it in stores, you can make your own by using a food processor fitted with the metal blade to process granulated sugar into a very fine, sand-like consistency.

While any apple will work in this recipe, cooking apples, which are often not as sweet and generally hold their shape better, are best. Look for Braeburn, Honeycrisp or Jonagold apples.

Dropping consistency for cake mix is when a spoonful of batter falls easily back into the bowl within seconds.

- **9-inch (23 cm) cake pan, greased**
- **Electric stand mixer or portable mixer**
- **Preheat oven to 350°F (180°C)**

CAKE

½ cup	superfine (caster) sugar (see Tips, left)	125 mL
¼ cup	butter	60 mL
1	egg	1
1¼ cups	all-purpose flour	300 mL
½ tsp	ground cinnamon	2 mL
1 tsp	baking powder	5 mL
6 tbsp	milk	90 mL
1	large cooking apple, peeled, cored and cut into ½-inch (1 cm) dice	1

TOPPING

1 tbsp	superfine (caster) sugar	15 mL
1 tsp	ground cinnamon	5 mL
1 tbsp	butter, melted	15 mL

1. *Cake:* In a mixing bowl, beat sugar and butter at high speed until light and fluffy. Add egg and mix to combine. Add flour, cinnamon and baking powder and mix to combine. Mix in milk 1 or 2 tbsp (15 or 30 mL) at a time, until batter reaches dropping consistency (see Tips, left). Pour into prepared cake pan and top evenly with apple, pressing fruit gently into batter. Bake in preheated oven for 20 to 25 minutes, until browned on top and a skewer inserted in the center comes out clean. Remove from oven and set aside to cool in pan for about 5 minutes, then turn out onto a wire rack to cool for an additional 5 minutes.

2. *Topping:* In a small bowl, combine sugar and cinnamon. Brush top of cake with melted butter, then sprinkle evenly with cinnamon-sugar mixture. Serve warm or cool. Cake will keep in an airtight container for up to 3 days.

Koshari

Many years ago I went on a backpacker's tour of Egypt. The experience was unforgettable in many ways (mostly good). One highlight was when the tour bus pulled over to the side of the road so we could all enjoy a plastic cup of koshari. In this traditional lentil and rice dish, a spicy tomato and caramelized onion topping is underpinned by sweet, comforting cinnamon and nutmeg in the lentils and rice—it's absolute heaven!

Makes 4 servings

Preparation time:
10 minutes
Cooking time:
45 minutes

Tips

Puy lentils are small green lentils from France. They have a great texture and flavor and do not require such extensive soaking and preparation as other pulses. If you can't find them, you can use regular green lentils.

To cook Puy lentils: Rinse ½ cup (125 mL) lentils under cold running water and drain. In a saucepan over medium heat, combine lentils with 3 cups (750 mL) water and simmer until tender, 20 to 25 minutes. Drain and add to saucepan in Step 2.

ONION TOPPING

2	onions, halved and sliced	2
2 tbsp	oil	30 mL

LENTILS AND RICE

1 tbsp	butter	15 mL
1 tbsp	oil	15 mL
1 cup	cooked Puy lentils (see Tips, left)	250 mL
1 cup	broken rice vermicelli	250 mL
1 cup	basmati rice, rinsed and drained	250 mL
1 tsp	ground cinnamon	5 mL
½ tsp	ground nutmeg	2 mL
½ tsp	fine sea salt	2 mL
3 cups	water	750 mL

TOMATO SAUCE

1	can (14 oz/398 mL) crushed tomatoes, with juice	1
1	clove garlic, minced	1
½ tsp	fine sea salt	2 mL
1 tbsp	white vinegar	15 mL
½ tsp	ground cumin	2 mL
½ tsp	hot pepper flakes	2 mL

1. *Onion Topping:* In a skillet over low heat, heat oil. Add onions, cover with a tight-fitting lid and cook, stirring occasionally, until soft and translucent, about 20 minutes. Increase heat and cook for 5 to 10 minutes, stirring constantly, until dark and crisp. Transfer to a plate lined with paper towels and set aside.

Tip

For a heartier meal, top each serving with a handful of cooked chickpeas.

2. *Lentils and Rice:* In a large saucepan, heat butter and oil. Add lentils, rice vermicelli and rice and stir to coat well. Add cinnamon and nutmeg and cook, stirring constantly, for 2 minutes, until fragrant. Add salt and water and bring to a boil, stirring constantly. Reduce heat to low, cover and simmer for about 15 minutes or until all the liquid is absorbed and rice is tender.

3. *Tomato Sauce:* Meanwhile, in a small saucepan over medium-low heat, combine tomatoes, garlic, salt, vinegar, cumin and hot pepper flakes. Simmer, stirring occasionally, until thickened, about 10 minutes.

4. To serve, divide rice and lentils into 4 serving bowls and top each with a spoonful of tomato sauce and sprinkle with fried onions.

Vietnamese Beef Stew

In Vietnam this fragrant beef dish, known as *bo kho*, is served for breakfast with a toasted baguette. The sweet spices are beautifully balanced and I find this stew very comforting, even if I do eat it mainly for dinner. When it's slow-cooking in the oven, the house smells amazing. I highly recommend serving it as an alternative to traditional beef stew on chilly evenings in front of the fire. Serve it with French baguette or over plain rice or rice noodles.

Makes
6 servings

Preparation time:
20 minutes, plus
2 hours for marinating
Cooking time: 4 to
5 hours

Tip

To make annatto oil: In a small saucepan over medium heat, combine ¼ cup (60 mL) oil and 2 tbsp (30 mL) annatto seeds. Cook, stirring constantly, for about 5 minutes (the color of the seeds will bleed into the oil). Strain infused oil through a fine-mesh sieve and discard seeds.

MARINADE

2	shallots, halved	2
1 tsp	Chinese five-spice powder (page 707)	5 mL
3	whole star anise	3
1	1-inch (2.5 cm) piece gingerroot, peeled and sliced	1
2	cassia quills (about 3 to 4 inches/ 7.5 to 10 cm long)	2
1	stalk lemongrass, halved lengthwise	1
2	cloves garlic, bruised	2
1¾ lbs	beef brisket, cut roughly into 2-inch (5 cm) pieces	800 g

STEW

3 tbsp	annatto oil, divided (see Tip, left)	45 mL
1 tsp	Chinese five-spice powder	5 mL
1	stalk lemongrass, halved lengthwise	1
2 tbsp	tomato paste	30 mL
2	bay leaves	2
3½ cups	beef broth	875 mL
2	carrots, cut diagonally into 2-inch (5 cm) pieces	2
1 cup	lightly packed Thai basil leaves, optional	250 mL

1. *Marinade:* In a resealable bag, combine shallots, five-spice powder, star anise, ginger, cassia, lemongrass and garlic. Add beef, seal and mix well. Refrigerate for 2 hours or overnight, turning bag once or twice to distribute marinade.

2. *Stew:* Preheat oven to 250°F (120°C).

3. Remove beef from bag and pour marinade into a large Dutch oven. Pat beef dry with paper towels.

4. In a skillet over medium heat, heat 1 tbsp (15 mL) annatto oil. Add one-third of the beef and cook for 5 to 7 minutes, until well-browned on all sides. Transfer cooked beef to Dutch oven. Repeat with remaining oil and beef.

5. To Dutch oven, add 1 tsp (5 mL) five-spice powder, lemongrass, tomato paste, bay leaves and beef broth. Stir to combine and bring to a simmer over medium heat. Cover and transfer to preheated oven. Cook for 3 to 4 hours, until meat is tender but not falling apart. Add carrots and cook for 45 minutes more, until carrots are cooked through and meat is very soft. Sprinkle with basil (if using) and serve.

Cloves

Eugenia caryophyllata (also known as *Syzygium aromaticum*)

Names in Other Languages

- **Arabic:** kabsh qaranful
- **Burmese:** ley-nyin-bwint
- **Chinese (C):** ding heung
- **Chinese (M):** ding xiang
- **Czech:** hrebicek
- **Danish:** kryddernellike
- **Dutch:** kruidnagel
- **French:** clou de girofle
- **German:** Gewurznelke
- **Greek:** garifalo, karyofylla
- **Hungarian:** szegfuszeg
- **Indian:** laung, lavang
- **Indonesian:** cingkeh
- **Italian:** garofano
- **Japanese:** choji
- **Malay:** bunga cengkeh
- **Portuguese:** cravo, cravinho
- **Russian:** gvozdika
- **Spanish:** clavo
- **Sri Lankan:** karabu nati
- **Swedish:** kryddnejlika
- **Thai:** kaan ploo
- **Turkish:** karanfil
- **Vietnamese:** dinh huong

Family: Myrtaceae

Other Names: nail spice, nelken, ting hiang

Flavor Group: Pungent

Parts Used: buds and stems (as a spice), leaves (as a herb)

Background

Cloves are native to the eastern Indonesian islands referred to as the Moluccas (which include Ternate, Tidore, Motir, Makian and Batjan). In an extraordinary archaeological discovery in Syria (ancient Mesopotamia), the remains of cloves were found at a domestic kitchen site dating back to around 1700 BCE. One can scarcely imagine the journey those cloves made from the Moluccas, by sea and by land, and the number of hands they passed through on their way to their final destination.

Cloves are believed to have been introduced to China during the Han Dynasty (206 BCE to 220 CE). They were probably the first form of breath freshener: it was recorded that courtiers in that era held cloves in their mouths to sweeten their breath when addressing the emperor.

The Arabs traded cloves from centers in India and Ceylon, keeping the origins of their precious cargo a closely guarded secret. Cloves were a caravan import known to the Romans, and they were also brought into Alexandria, Egypt, in the second century CE. By the fourth century this spice was well

Culinary Information

Combines with

- allspice
- amchur
- cardamom
- chile
- coriander seed
- cumin
- ginger
- kokam
- licorice
- nutmeg
- star anise
- tamarind
- turmeric

Traditional Uses

- cakes
- hams
- sweet pastries and cookies
- stewed fruits
- curries
- mulled beverages such as glüwein
- Moroccan tagines
- preserved lemons
- preserved meats
- pickles

Spice Blends

- curry powders
- pumpkin pie spice
- sweet mixed spice
- ras el hanout
- tagine spice blends
- baharat
- berbere
- garam masala
- Chinese five-spice powder
- mulling spices
- pickling spices
- quatre épices (sweet and savory)

known around the Mediterranean. By the 8th century its reputation and use had spread throughout Europe.

In Europe following the Crusades, disease and plagues were commonplace; there was a constant search for spices that could sweeten the air, which was often ripe with the stench of rotting waste and death. Cloves were found to have a natural antiseptic and anesthetic effect. The pungent clove oil extracted by steam distillation gave quick relief from toothache. By the 13th century people were making pomanders (apples or oranges studded with cloves) to carry with them, in the belief that they would ward off the plague.

On his reputed return from the Orient in 1297, Marco Polo recalled having seen plantations of cloves on East Indian islands in the China Sea. Columbus sailed west in search of these spice islands, but instead he discovered the West Indies. Five years later, Vasco da Gama sailed around the Cape of Good Hope to India on the same search; he obtained cloves in Calicut (Calcutta), a trading center whose supply of the spice probably came from the East Indies.

As of 1514 the Portuguese controlled the clove trade. In those days the search for spices was serious business. In 1522, the only surviving ship of Magellan's circumnavigation fleet returned to Spain with 29 tons (26,000 kg) of cloves, more than enough to pay for the entire cost of the expedition. The captain, Sebastián Elcano, was rewarded with a pension and a coat of arms comprising three nutmegs, two sticks of cinnamon and twelve cloves. The Portuguese monopoly in the Moluccas was broken by the Dutch in 1605. They expelled the Portuguese and ruthlessly maintained control for another 200 years, using cruel and gruesome measures. Part of the Dutch strategy to maintain high prices for cloves was to legally restrict the cultivation of cloves to the island of Gebe, off the coast of Halmahera. As part of this strategy, they uprooted and burned trees growing on other islands. The death penalty was imposed on anyone cultivating or selling the spice in any location other than the Spice Islands. Nonetheless, numerous attempts were made from 1750 to the early 1800s to break this stranglehold on the clove trade. The most successful was executed by an intrepid Frenchman named Pierre Poivre (the original Peter Piper of the nursery rhyme), who was superintendent of Île-de-France (now known as Mauritius). After several attempts he managed to smuggle some clove seedlings out of Gebe and successfully cultivated a small number of trees. Subsequently, with varying degrees of success, clove plantations were established on Réunion, Martinique and Haiti and in the Seychelles.

Meanwhile, the abolition of slavery was gaining momentum in the West, and one result was that Zanzibar had a surplus of slaves. Recognizing that Pierre Poivre's success in breaking the Dutch monopoly on the clove trade represented an opportunity, an Arab named Saleh bin

Travels in the Spice Trade

Zanzibar is one of those place names that conjure up exotic images, rhyming as it does with *bazaar*. I will always remember a little red postage stamp from Zanzibar in my first stamp collection, which I started when I was about 10. It had an illustration of a fisherman casting his net with a dhow in the background, and I found it very exotic. That image was instrumental in drawing me to Zanzibar to see clove trees in bud for the first time. After much searching and following up leads from my spice-trading contacts, I finally found a trader, who explained that Zanzibar was no longer the center of the global clove trade. When Zanzibar achieved independence from Britain in 1968, the Marxist government seized all privately owned clove plantations and gave them to the people. At that point the clove industry went into decline, because the unskilled owners no longer maintained the trees properly. In a relatively short time Zanzibar lost its dominant position in the world market. I subsequently visited the historic clove island of Ternate, in the Indonesian Spice Islands, and saw thousands of healthy clove trees and roads and footpaths strewn with recently harvested clove buds drying in the sun. It was heavenly to inhale the heady aroma of cloves in the steamy tropical air.

Haramil al Abray established clove plantations on the island, where he put those slaves to work. Unfortunately he also attracted the attention of Sultan Said of Oman, who ruled his kingdom (which included Zanzibar) from Muscat. In 1827 the sultan sailed to Zanzibar and made a commercial treaty with the United States, mostly involving trade in ivory. However, he soon realized that to increase Zanzibar's wealth he would have to expand its trade with America and Europe. He identified the clove trade as a means to achieve his objectives. Seeing Saleh bin Haramil al Abray as a political threat, the sultan confiscated all his plantations. Sultan Said then decreed that three clove trees would be planted for every coconut palm on Zanzibar and Pemba. By the time the sultan died in 1856, Zanzibar was one of the world's largest producers of cloves. Despite a major setback from "sudden-death disease," which attacked mature trees in the 1960s, Zanzibar remained, along with Madagascar, one of the world's major clove producers. By the end of the 20th century, though, poor agricultural management in Zanzibar and Pemba had led to the resurgence of Indonesia as the world's largest producer of cloves.

Interestingly, the name *clove* derives from the Latin *clavus*, meaning "nail."

The Plant

Whole cloves as we know them are the dried unopened flower buds of an attractive tropical evergreen that reaches about 33 feet (10 m) in height and has dense, dark green foliage. The trunk of a clove tree is about 12 inches (30 cm) in diameter; it usually forks near the base into two or three main branches of very hard wood with rough gray bark. The lower branches often die back, and when they are closely planted, these conical trees form a magical aromatic canopy. New leaves are bright pink, maturing to a glossy dark green upper surface, the underneath being paler green and dull.

Clove buds are borne in clusters of 10 to 15 and are picked when they have reached full size but are still green, just starting to turn pink—reminiscent of the unopened eyes of baby marsupials. If the buds are not gathered they will flower and turn into drooping oblong fruits known as "mother of cloves," which have no use in the spice trade. When dried, cloves are reddish brown to dark brown in color, approximately $1/3$ to $1/2$ inch (8 to 10 mm) long, nail-shaped and tapered at one end. The bud end has a friable paler ball that appears to sit atop four prongs like a diamond in an engagement ring.

The aroma of cloves is pungent, warm, aromatic, camphor-like and faintly peppery. The flavor is intensely pungent—words such as *medicinal*, *warming*, *sweet*, *lingering* and *numbing* come to mind. When used in moderation, cloves bring a pleasing palate-cleansing freshness and a sweet, spicy flavor to food.

Processing

The first harvesting of cloves takes place when the trees are six to eight years old and continues for up to 50 years, with some trees reportedly living for up to 150 years. The trees are surprisingly sensitive and will usually deliver only one bumper crop in four years; the success of subsequent crops depends largely on the degree of care employed in the previous harvest. Rough handling and breaking branches will generate debilitating shock in clove trees, diminishing succeeding yields.

In Sir James Frazer's famous work *The Golden Bough*, he describes the attitude of the native people to these crops: "When the clove trees are in blossom, they are treated like pregnant women. No noise may be made near them; no light or fire may be carried past them at night; no one may approach them with his hat on, all must uncover in their presence. These precautions are observed lest the tree should be alarmed and bear no fruit, or should drop its fruit too soon like the untimely delivery of a woman who has been frightened in her pregnancy." Although modern attitudes have changed, the planting and harvesting of cloves still has a religious significance in some villages.

Clove clusters are picked by hand when the buds are at full size but before any petals have fallen to expose the stamens. Because they do not all reach the harvesting stage at the same time, a picker must be skilled enough to know the best clusters to pick. The filled baskets are returned to a central area, where the flower buds are removed from their stems by twisting the cluster against the palm of the hand. The snapped-off buds are spread out to dry on woven mats, where the tropical sun dries them to their characteristic reddish brown in a few days. During drying, enzymes are activated that create the volatile oil eugenol, which is also present in lesser concentrations in the dried clove stems. A traditional way to gauge the dryness of cloves is to hold

them tightly in one's hand; if they hurt, the spiky sections are hard, an indication that they have been properly dried. Having lost about two-thirds of their weight on drying, 2 pounds (1 kg) of cloves may consist of up to 15,000 buds.

Clove leaves are also harvested, to produce clove-leaf oil, which is extracted by steam distillation. This volatile oil is used in perfumery and food and beverage manufacturing. Because the harvesting of leafy branches for this oil seriously diminishes yields of cloves and makes the trees susceptible to fungal infection, it is not a common practice among the major producing countries.

Buying and Storage

When buying whole cloves, look for clean, well-presented buds, as this is one of the best indications of how much care has been taken in the harvesting process. Most of the buds should be intact, with the majority still having the small, soft, friable ball on top. If the little ball has broken off, don't worry: the clove itself will retain most of its flavor. However, look out for short clove-sized sticks with no spiky tips; these are in fact clove stems. Clove stems contain only about 30% of the volatile oil found in a clove and are one of the most popular ways for unscrupulous spice traders to adulterate their goods. Another trick of the trade has been to boil cloves in water to extract some of the oil, after which the depleted cloves are dried and sold.

Buy ground cloves only from a reputable establishment that can assure you they have been milled recently, as ground cloves lose their volatile oil fairly quickly (see below). Ground cloves should be dark brown; a light brown powder that is somewhat fibrous and gritty is probably heavily cut with ground clove stems.

Store whole and ground cloves in an airtight container and keep away from extremes of heat, light and humidity. Whole cloves, when stored correctly, will last for more than 3 years. Ground cloves have a storage life of around 18 months.

Use

In Indonesia, ground clove stems are mixed with tobacco to make *kretek* cigarettes, which crackle as they burn and give off a distinctive aroma. Encountering the smell of a *kretek* cigarette anywhere in the world immediately transports me back to the time I sailed around the Indonesian Spice Islands on a chartered ketch.

Cloves are an essential component of a clove orange, or pomander (see page 448), and the fact that the orange does not rot is a dramatic example of the antibacterial qualities of cloves.

Because of their pungency, cloves must always be used sparingly in cooking, or they can easily overpower a dish. Even so, it is hard to imagine many traditional foods, including apple pie, ham, stewed fruit and pickles, without the addition of cloves. In Denmark they are an ingredient in "pepper cake," and they are frequently added to exotic Arabian dishes. A popular mulled wine of the Middle Ages called hippocras was made with cardamom, ginger, cloves, spikenard and other spices; even now the warming spiced wines of Europe and Scandinavia are flavored in the same way. Cloves are also used in Indian and Asian curries. They are a truly international spice that can be found in the kitchens of every continent of the world.

WEIGHT PER TEASPOON (5 mL)
- whole: 2.1 g
- ground: 3.1 g

SUGGESTED QUANTITY PER POUND (500 g)
- red meats: 5 cloves
- white meats: 3 cloves
- vegetables: 3 cloves
- grains and pulses: 2 cloves or ¼ tsp (1 mL) powder
- baked goods: ¼ tsp (1 mL) powder

Herbie's Christmas Ham

For as long as I can remember, this ham has been the Christmas centerpiece at our family dinner. It's prepared a few days before, and excitement builds as the ham cooks, emitting the most heavenly smell. Christmas morning always starts with ham and eggs, and then the ham is eaten at lunch and for days afterward in sandwiches, soups and pies. Dad has finally parted with his secret recipe so it can be shared and loved by other families as much as it is by ours.

C

Makes one 4-pound (2 kg) ham

Preparation time:
20 minutes

Cooking time: 1 hour, 30 minutes

- **Preheat oven to 325°F (160°C)**

3 to 4 lbs	ham leg on the bone	1.5 to 2 kg
20 to 30	whole cloves	20 to 30
1½ cups	kumquat or orange marmalade	375 mL
1½ cups	whole-grain mustard	375 mL
1 tsp	ground star anise	5 mL
2 cups	pineapple juice	500 mL
2 cups	stout beer	500 mL

1. Carefully remove skin from ham, in one piece if possible, and discard skin. Using a sharp knife, score exposed ham fat in a diamond pattern on all sides, drawing the lines about 1 inch (2.5 cm) apart. Using your fingers, press a clove into the center of each diamond. Transfer ham to a deep roasting pan.

2. In a bowl, combine marmalade, mustard and star anise. Spoon liberally over ham to form a thick coating. Pour pineapple juice and stout into bottom of pan. Bake ham in preheated oven for 12 minutes per pound weight (25 minutes per kilogram), basting occasionally with the juices (if ham darkens too quickly, cover it with foil). When ham is golden brown and cooked to an internal temperature of 150°F (70°C), remove from oven, cover with foil and set aside for about 15 minutes before slicing. Keep leftover ham in an airtight container in the refrigerator for up to 1 week, or slice and freeze in portions for up to 3 months.

Mulled Plums

If you are a fan of a festive glass of mulled wine, then you will love these plums. They are simply divine served warm with ice cream or alongside a Christmas pudding, or added to an apple crumble or pie.

**Makes
4 servings**

Preparation time:
5 minutes

Cooking time:
15 minutes

- - - - - - - - - - - - - - - -

Tips

When cooking with wine, remember to use a wine that you also like to drink. Even though the alcohol content will disappear, the flavors in the wine remain. Chose a medium-bodied wine such as Pinot Noir, Shiraz, Merlot or Chianti for this dish.

For a thicker syrup, remove the plums once they are cooked and boil the liquid until it reaches the desired consistency.

1 cup	medium-bodied red wine (see Tips, left)	250 mL
½ cup	granulated sugar	125 mL
8 oz	ripe plums, halved, stones removed (about 10)	250 g
½ tsp	whole cloves	2 mL
1	2-inch (5 cm) cinnamon stick	1
	Peel from ½ orange, thickly sliced	
2	¼-inch (0.5 cm) pieces gingerroot	2

1. In a saucepan over medium heat, combine wine and sugar. Cook, stirring constantly, until sugar is dissolved, about 5 minutes. Add plums, cloves, cinnamon, orange peel and ginger and bring to a soft boil. Reduce heat and simmer for about 10 minutes (time will vary depending on ripeness of plums), until plums are tender but not falling apart (a knife should insert easily but not break the flesh apart). Remove from heat and set pan aside to allow plums to cool in syrup. Serve immediately or refrigerate for up to 1 week.

Variation

To make mulled wine, simply omit the plums.

Coriander

Coriandrum sativum (also known as *C. sativum vulgare*)

Names in Other Languages

- **Arabic:** kuzhbare
- **Burmese:** nannambin (leaf), nannamazee (seed)
- **Chinese (C):** wuh seui (leaf), heung seui (seed)
- **Chinese (M):** yuen sui (leaf), hu sui (seed)
- **Czech:** koriandr
- **Dutch:** koriander
- **Filipino:** ketumbar (leaf)
- **French:** coriandre
- **German:** Koriander (seed), chinesische Petersilie (leaf)
- **Greek:** koliandro, koriandro
- **Indian:** dhania pattar, hara dhania (leaf); dhania kothimbir (seed)
- **Indonesian:** daun ketumbar (leaf), ketumbar (seed)
- **Italian:** coriandolo
- **Japanese:** koendoro
- **Malay:** daun ketumbar (leaf), ketumbar (seed)
- **Portuguese:** coentro
- **Russian:** koriandr
- **Spanish:** cilantro (leaf), coriandro (seed)
- **Sri Lankan:** kothamalli kolle (leaf), kothamalli (seed)
- **Swedish:** koriander
- **Thai:** pak chee (leaf), luk pak chee (seed)
- **Turkish:** kisnis
- **Vietnamese:** ngo (leaf), ngo tay (seed)

Family: Apiaceae (formerly Umbelliferae)

Varieties: coriander seed (*C. sativum vulgare*), Indian coriander seed (*C. sativum microcarpum*), culantro or perennial coriander (*Eryngium foetidum*)

Other Names: cilantro, coriander leaves, Chinese parsley, Japanese parsley, fragrant green

Flavor Group: Amalgamating

Parts Used: seeds (as a spice), leaves, stems and roots (as a herb)

Background

Coriander is native to southern Europe and the Middle East and has been used since ancient times. Evidence of coriander seeds has been found in an archaeological dig in southern Greece, where the stratum reputedly dates back to 7000 BCE. The Ebers Papyrus, from 1550 BCE, mentions coriander, as does the Bible. Coriander seeds have been found in the tombs of the pharaohs, and it was known to be a favorite herb among the Greeks, Hebrews and Romans of antiquity—the Roman physician Hippocrates mentioned it in 400 BCE. Coriander grew in the hanging gardens of Babylon, and in 812 CE Charlemagne, King of the Franks, ordered it to be grown on the imperial farms in central Europe. Love potions were made from coriander in the Middle Ages, and it is mentioned in *One Thousand and One Arabian Nights* as an aphrodisiac.

Culinary Information

Combines with

Leaf (cilantro)
- basil
- curry leaf
- dill leaf
- fenugreek leaf
- garlic
- lemongrass
- lemon myrtle
- pandan leaf
- parsley
- Vietnamese mint

Seed
All culinary spices, but has a special affinity with
- akudjura
- allspice
- caraway
- cardamom
- chile
- cinnamon
- cloves
- cumin
- fennel seed
- ginger
- pepper
- turmeric
- wattleseed

Traditional Uses

Leaf
- Asian and Middle Eastern salads
- Latin American ceviche, salsas, salads and cooked sauces
- stir-fries and curries
- Indian rice dishes (as a garnish)

Seed
- curries
- sweet cakes
- cookies and biscuits
- fruit pies
- chicken and seafood casseroles

Spice Blends

Leaf
- Asian spice blends
- Thai green curries
- seafood seasonings

Seed
- curry powders
- pumpkin pie spice
- sweet mixed spice
- ras el hanout
- baharat
- berbere
- tagine spice blends
- dukkah
- harissa paste blends

Coriander was introduced to Britain by the Roman legions, who carried the seeds with them to flavor their bread. Although popular until Elizabethan times, it seemed to have fallen out of fashion in English cooking by the time of the Industrial Revolution. The plant was taken to the Americas by the early colonists. Both the seeds and leaves have been used for thousands of years in Indian and Chinese cuisine. Today the seeds are used in most cuisines, and coriander is particularly popular in Latin America, where it is used fresh in raw salsas as well as to flavor cooked sauces. The fresh leaves are also used widely in Asian and Middle Eastern cooking.

The Plant

Coriander is an annual plant that flourishes in the temperate zones of the world where other seed crops such as wheat, barley, oats, cumin, caraway, fenugreek and mustard also thrive. It is a vigorous plant that grows to about 32 inches (80 cm) tall. It has fan-shaped dark green leaves that resemble those of Italian parsley. The stems of the coriander plant are slender and branched. The lower leaves are quite round but become more divided and serrated further up the stem. As the plant matures, thick, densely foliaged stems push upward to bear a profusion of small umbrella-shaped pale pink-mauve to whitish flowers. These flowers are the source of the seeds.

Coriander leaves (cilantro) have a fresh, grassy, insect-like aroma and a clean, lemony, appetizing taste. From my experience, about 10% of Westerners do not like the flavor of coriander leaves. Some writers have described its aroma as fetid.

Coriander seeds are small—$1/4$ inch (5 mm) in diameter—and almost spherical. They are ribbed with more than a dozen longitudinal lines, like a tiny Chinese lantern. After drying they attain a completely different character from the leaves, stems and roots. Their delicious taste is reminiscent of orange and lemon peel and sage. Coriander seeds have a papery husk and, even when ground finely, retain a coarse, sand-like texture that should not be gritty. The fiber from the husk absorbs moisture and helps to thicken dishes such as curries and spicy sauces.

Essential oil of coriander is extracted from the seeds by steam distillation. It is used in perfumes; to flavor sweets, chocolate, meat and seafood products, and liquors such as gin; and to mask offensive odors in medicines.

What's in a Name?

The name *coriandrum* was used by Pliny and is derived from the Greek word *koros*, which means "bug" or "insect." One theory suggests that the name was inspired by the insect-like aroma of the fresh leaves, while another is that the smooth, light brown seeds look like small beetles.

Travels in the Spice Trade

One of the advantages of being in the spice business is that Liz and I get to visit unusual places. For instance, once we were invited to an Indian Spices Board research station near Ahmedabad, in the state of Gujarat. This station specialized in the agronomics (all aspects of crop improvement) of seed spices; the researchers used traditional plant-breeding methods to develop cultivars to achieve maximum yield and even natural methods of pest control to reduce dependence on chemicals. It was interesting to see the coriander plants they were developing for optimum seed productivity: they looked quite straggly and very different from the lush parsley-like fronds of homegrown coriander. Still, as we walked between the rows of plantings, the crushed vegetation released that distinctive insect-like aroma that, over our years of working with spices, we have come to love.

Scent Alert

Coriander plants contain organic compounds that include aliphatic aldehydes, which are also found in insects. This may help to explain the sometimes vehement response some people have to the aroma and taste of this herb.

Other Varieties

Two types of seed are generally available. The light tan to pale brown ones (*Coriandrum sativum* var. *vulgare*) are most common and are widely used in cuisines all over the world. They are mild and most typical of coriander seed, and are the variety used in the majority of curries, Moroccan tagines and Southeast Asian dishes. The other is a so-called Indian, or green, variety (*C. sativum* var. *microcarpum*), which is slightly smaller in size, more egg-shaped and pale yellow with a greenish tinge. It tastes a little like the fresh leaf, with lemony overtones. This variety is excellent for making a paste for stir-fries with lots of fresh ingredients. I even like to put some in a pepper mill and grind them freshly over fish and chicken, just the way you'd use fresh-ground pepper on food after cooking.

Perennial "saw-tooth," "saw-leaf" or "long" coriander (*Eryngium foetidum*) is a lesser-known plant whose leaves are used as a herb. Although it tastes like coriander (cilantro), it is actually a different species—it certainly has a different botanical name. This variety has gained some popularity precisely because it is a perennial. Gardeners become impatient with annual coriander (*C. sativum*) because as soon as it starts growing well, it flowers, goes to seed and dies. Perennial coriander is believed to be native to the Caribbean islands and is now widely cultivated in Southeast Asia. We first saw this variety in Vietnam and have since seen it growing at a Spices Board research station in Kerala, in the south of India. "Long coriander" has serrated leaves $2^1/_2$ inches (7 cm) long, which makes them particularly useful in Vietnamese cooking because of its propensity for wrapped food. The aroma, when they are crushed, is similar to conventional coriander leaves, the only drawback being a slightly grassy aftertaste and a sharp, spiky mouthfeel. However, like *C. sativum*, it balances beautifully with dill. I sometimes use it but tend to put the whole leaves in soups and then remove them before serving. Unlike many leaves that become harder as they mature, the largest leaves of perennial coriander are noticeably softer than the young ones.

Processing

Leaves

Coriander leaves (cilantro) are dried the same way as green herbs such as parsley. While a reasonable product can be achieved with sophisticated dehydrators that remove the moisture without damaging the color and losing too much flavor, coriander leaves are difficult to dry at home. The process usually results in a loss of volatile top notes. You can prolong your enjoyment of a bunch of fresh coriander in two ways:

1. Put the bunch, preferably with roots intact, in a glass of water and place a plastic bag over it like a tent. Store in the refrigerator, where it will last for a few days. If you can't use it within that time frame, you can freeze it.
2. To freeze the leaves, wrap freshly washed sprigs in foil, folding in the edges securely. Store the foil packets in the freezer for up to a month. To freeze stems and roots, use the ice-cube tray method (it does not work so well for leaves): Chop the stem, including some root, very finely (or, if you prefer, grate the root). Fill each compartment of the ice-cube tray three-quarters full with coriander, then top with water and freeze. Once frozen, turn out your cilantro ice cubes and store in a resealable bag in the freezer.

With these methods, no part of the coriander plant need ever be wasted—something that happens all too often when a bunch is bought just for its leaves. When cooking a soup with a complementary flavor profile (Asian, Latin American and Middle Eastern are the most likely candidates), simply add a frozen cube of coriander about 10 minutes before the end of cooking. If you want to use frozen roots when making a curry paste, thaw and drain them before using.

Storing Fresh Coriander

Fresh coriander leaves (cilantro) may be stored for a few days in the refrigerator. Homegrown will always last longer than store-bought leaves, which may have been kept in cold storage or harvested many days before you bought them. (See page 230 for more storage details).

When making spice blends, coriander seed is a peacemaker you can use to bring conflicting flavors under control. It is almost impossible to use too much coriander seed. In fact, some North African dishes, such as berbere chicken and goat curry, use it by the cupful rather than the spoonful. If you have made a spice blend and realize you have been too heavy-handed with a pungent spice such as cloves or cardamom, an easy way to fix the mistake is to add twice the amount of ground coriander seed (compared to the quantity of the dominant spice). For example, if you used 1 tsp (5 mL) ground cloves, add 2 tsp (10 mL) ground coriander seed. In most cases the blend will be brought back into balance. Some recipes call for lightly dry-roasting or toasting the whole seeds prior to grinding and adding to a dish. Roasting modifies the flavor, creating a more complex taste profile.

Seeds

Coriander seeds are harvested in the early morning or very late afternoon, when the presence of dew prevents shattering of the fruit. At this stage the seeds are bright green and still taste like the leaves. Upon drying they turn pale brown and develop a pleasing citrus-like flavor. In many countries such as India, the plants are cut, hung to dry and then threshed to remove the seeds. In many developed countries harvesting is carried out using wheat headers, which yields a consistent high-quality material while reducing labor costs considerably.

Buying and Storage

Fresh coriander (cilantro) is best bought in bunches that retain the root system, as they will stay fresher longer (see page 229). Moreover, the roots are particularly useful, especially in Asian cooking. Good-quality dried coriander leaves are underrated because they have almost no aroma. However, when the dried leaves are added at the end of cooking or sprinkled over hot food such as steamed rice, the moisture in the steam is enough to release a surprising amount of flavor, making them a passable substitute for fresh if none is available. To determine the flavor quality of dry coriander leaves, place a couple on your tongue and wait for about a minute. If you don't experience the characteristic taste, they have passed their peak and you shouldn't use them.

Coriander seeds should appear clean; although some may have retained their little tail, which is about $1/16$ inch (2 mm) long, they should be free of sticks and longer stalks. Ground coriander seed is best purchased in small quantities, as the fragrant volatile flavor notes evaporate easily after grinding if not stored properly. Whole seeds, when stored in an airtight container away from extremes of heat, light and humidity, will last for around 2 years. After grinding, the seeds will keep for up to 1 year.

Use

Coriander leaves (cilantro) are used mostly in Asian, Indian, Middle Eastern and Latin American recipes. Because the delicate flavor is driven off by prolonged cooking, for the best flavor, add in the last 5 minutes of cooking.

Coriander seed is one of the most useful spices in any kitchen, because it is an amalgamating spice (see page 682). It mixes well with almost any combination of spices, whether sweet or savory. It is interesting to note that an extract of coriander seed is used to make medicines more palatable, which is not surprising—I have always noticed the way ground coriander seed effectively balances the sweet and pungent spices in blends as diverse as sweet mixed spice, pumpkin pie spice or a fiery Tunisian harissa paste.

Whole coriander seeds are delicious in chicken casseroles, as the flavor infuses while simmering and the cooking time softens the seeds. A few green Indian coriander seeds placed in a pepper mill and ground over grilled fish are delicious. For recipes that call for ground coriander seed, grind the seeds using a mortar and pestle or a more effective method is to use a coffee or pepper grinder. When not finely ground, the husks may seem a little gritty if they are not cooked for long enough to soften, which takes 30 to 40 minutes.

Dry-Roasting

You can dry-roast coriander seeds to create a robust flavor and a darker curry gravy. This works well for dishes such as beef and other red-meat curries and for strong-tasting seafood such as salmon and tuna. Heat a skillet over medium heat, add the seeds and toast, shaking the pan, for up to 3 minutes, until fragrant. Once a spice has been dry-roasted, the oils will oxidize more rapidly and the flavor will deteriorate, so try to use a roasted spice within a few days. It is best not to roast coriander seeds for sweet applications such as cakes, pies and other fruit dishes.

WEIGHT PER TEASPOON (5 mL)
- whole seeds: 1.6 g
- ground seeds: 2 g

SUGGESTED QUANTITY PER POUND (500 g)
- red meats: 5 tsp (25 mL) ground seeds, ½ cup (125 mL) fresh leaves
- white meats: 4 tsp (20 mL) ground seeds, ½ cup (125 mL) fresh leaves
- vegetables: 4 tsp (20 mL) ground seeds, ½ cup (125 mL) fresh leaves
- grains and pulses: 4 tsp (20 mL) ground seeds, ½ cup (125 mL) fresh leaves
- baked goods: 4 tsp (20 mL) ground seeds, garnish with fresh leaves

Ceviche

In Mexico we asked a taxi driver to drop us off where he would eat. It paid off—we ended up in a tiny café by a busy main road feasting on a huge plate of ceviche that cost next to nothing. The simplicity of freshly caught fish, lime juice and coriander needs little else, but regional variations can be found throughout Latin America that include onion, chile, tomato and avocado, so add what you like. Although you do not cook the dish, the acid in the lime juice denatures the proteins in the raw fish in much the same way cooking does.

Makes 2 small servings

Preparation time:
15 minutes
"Cooking" time: 10 to
20 minutes

10 oz	skinless boneless firm-fleshed white fish, such as snapper, cod or halibut, cut into ½-inch (1 cm) pieces	300 g
1	long red finger chile, seeded and finely diced	1
2 tbsp	finely chopped fresh coriander (cilantro) leaves	30 mL
1 tbsp	finely chopped red onion	15 mL
1 tsp	extra virgin olive oil	5 mL
½ tsp	fine sea salt	2 mL
	Juice from 3 freshly squeezed limes	
	Corn chips, for serving	

1. In a non-reactive bowl, combine fish, chile, coriander leaves, onion, oil, salt and lime juice. Mix well and set aside for 10 to 20 minutes. When "cooked" by the lime juice, the flesh of the fish will turn opaque. Serve with corn chips.

Pork Tenderloin in Orange Sauce

Being an amalgamating spice, coriander seed is rarely the main ingredient. In this dish it works perfectly with the orange, soy sauce and sweet onions.

Makes 6 servings

Preparation time:
1 hour, 10 minutes
Cooking time:
40 minutes

- - - - - - - - - - - - - - - - -

Tip

Superfine (caster) sugar is a very fine granulated sugar typically used in recipes that require a faster-dissolving granule. If you can't find it in stores, you can make your own by using a food processor fitted with the metal blade to process granulated sugar to a very fine, sand-like consistency.

3	pork tenderloin fillets (about 8 oz/250 g)	3
MARINADE		
2 tbsp	olive oil	30 mL
	Zest and juice of 2 oranges	
2 tbsp	soy sauce	30 mL
2 tbsp	white wine vinegar	30 mL
1 tsp	fine sea salt	5 mL
2 tbsp	ground coriander seed	30 mL
CARAMELIZED ONIONS		
1/4 cup	olive oil	60 mL
4	onions, finely sliced	4
1/4 cup	superfine (caster) sugar (see Tip, left)	60 mL
1/4 cup	olive oil	60 mL
3/4 cup	dry sherry	175 mL
	Sea salt and freshly ground black pepper	

1. *Marinade:* In a shallow bowl, combine oil, orange zest and juice, soy sauce, vinegar, salt and coriander seed. Add pork and turn to coat well. Cover and set aside in the refrigerator for at least 1 hour.

2. *Caramelized Onions:* In a skillet over low heat, heat oil. Add onions and sugar, stir well, and cover with a tight-fitting lid. Cook, stirring occasionally, for 15 minutes, until soft. Uncover and cook, stirring often, for 2 to 3 minutes, until golden. Set aside.

3. Remove pork from marinade and let excess drain off into bowl, reserving marinade. In a skillet over medium heat, heat oil. Add marinated pork and and cook until an instant-read thermometer inserted in the thickest part of the meat registers 160°F (71°C), 8 to 12 minutes. Transfer to a plate and cover with foil to keep warm.

4. In the same skillet over medium heat, bring reserved marinade to a boil. Cook for 10 minutes, until reduced to a thick syrup. Add sherry and return to a boil. Season with salt and pepper to taste and stir well.

5. Slice pork on the diagonal, 1 inch (2.5 cm) thick, and divide equally among 6 serving plates. Top with caramelized onions and pour sauce overtop.

Apple and Rhubarb Coriander Crumble

Dad recalls Granny writing her books on herbs in the 1950s and '60s. One of his favorites was this crumble, which Mum perfected for us. My sisters and I used to feel as if we'd won the jackpot if we found one of the four cloves in our bowl. Using freshly ground coriander seeds in this crumble showcases the versatility of this wonderful spice. Serve with whipped cream, ice cream or custard.

Makes 6 servings

Preparation time:
20 minutes

Cooking time:
40 minutes

Tip

The crumble can be prepared and frozen before cooking. It will keep in a resealable bag in the freezer for up to 1 month. Bake from frozen for about 35 minutes, until apples are tender and topping is golden brown.

- **9-inch (23 cm) square glass baking dish, greased with butter**
- **Preheat oven to 350°F (180°C)**

6	Granny Smith apples, peeled, cored and sliced	6
1	bunch rhubarb (about 10 oz/300 g), cut into 2-inch (5 cm) pieces	1
4	whole cloves	4
2 tsp	ground cinnamon	10 mL
1 cup	old-fashioned rolled oats	250 mL
1 cup	all-purpose flour	250 mL
½ cup	lightly packed brown sugar	125 mL
2 tsp	ground coriander seed	10 mL
½ cup	butter	125 mL

1. In prepared baking dish, layer apples and rhubarb. Sprinkle with cloves and cinnamon. Set aside.

2. In a bowl, combine oats, flour, sugar and coriander seed. Using your fingertips, rub in the butter until the mixture is crumbly. Spread the crumble mixture evenly and lightly (do not press down) over apples and rhubarb. Bake for about 30 minutes, until apples are tender and topping is golden brown.

Variation

Try substituting an equal quantity of chopped peeled pears for the rhubarb.

Cumin

Cumin: *Cuminum cyminum*; Black cumin: *Bunium persicum*

Names in Other Languages

- **Arabic:** kammun
- **Chinese (C):** siu wuih heung
- **Chinese (M):** kuming, xiao hui xiang
- **Czech:** rimsky kmin
- **Danish:** spidskommen
- **Dutch:** komijn
- **French:** cumin, cumin de Maroc
- **German:** Kreuzkummel
- **Greek:** kimino
- **Indian:** jeera, zeera, safed zeera (cumin seed); jeera kala, shah jeera (black cumin)
- **Indonesian:** jinten-putih
- **Italian:** comino, cumino bianco
- **Japanese:** kumin, umazeri
- **Malay:** jintan puteh
- **Portuguese:** cominho
- **Russian:** kmin
- **Spanish:** comino
- **Sri Lankan:** sududuru
- **Swedish:** spiskummin
- **Thai:** yeeraa
- **Turkish:** kimyon

Family: Apiaceae (formerly Umbelliferae)

Other Names: black cumin, green cumin, jeera, white cumin

Flavor Group: Pungent

Parts Used: seeds (as a spice)

Background

Cumin is believed to be indigenous to the Middle East and was well known to the ancients as far back as 5000 BCE. Cumin seeds have been found in the pyramids of the pharaohs, and it is known that the Egyptians used it in the mummifying process before they started using cinnamon and cloves (cumin is mentioned in an Egyptian medical text, the Ebers Papyrus, from 1550 BCE). In the first century CE, the Roman scholar Pliny referred to cumin as the "best appetizer of all condiments." Both the Old and New Testaments of the Bible reference cumin. In Roman times cumin was a symbol of avarice and greed; a common put-down of misers was to say they had eaten it. Thus the nickname for the avaricious second-century CE Roman emperor Marcus Aurelius was "Cuminus."

Cumin has been used in England since the 13th century and was mentioned in 16th- and 17th-century herbals. It was a popular flavoring in the Middle Ages, although its use had superstitious overtones (it was believed to prevent lovers

Culinary Information

Combines with

- allspice
- cardamom
- chile
- cinnamon
- cloves
- coriander seed
- fennel seed
- fenugreek seed
- ginger
- mustard
- nigella
- paprika
- tamarind
- turmeric

Traditional Uses

- Indian curries and practically all Asian red curries
- chicken and seafood dishes
- rice and vegetable dishes
- breads
- Mexican sauces
- liqueurs such as kümmel

Spice Blends

- baharat
- barbecue spice blends
- curry powders
- berbere
- Chinese master stocks
- chermoula
- dukkah
- harissa paste blends
- Mexican chile powder
- ras el hanout
- panch phoron

Black Cumin Seeds

Black cumin (*Bunium persicum*) seeds are similar in shape to the cumin most people are familiar with (*Cuminum cyminum*), but their color is darker brown, almost black, and when crushed they are highly aromatic—almost piney—and less earthy. The flavor is similarly pine-like, astringent, and bitter. Black cumin should not be confused with nigella (kolonji).

from becoming fickle). At German wedding ceremonies during the medieval period, the bride and groom carried cumin, dill and salt in their pockets to ensure faithfulness to each other. Cumin spread to the Americas when Spanish explorers introduced it along the Rio Grande. It is amusing to read descriptions of cumin in early-20th-century English food texts. It is described as having a "very disagreeable" flavor, "caraway being much preferred"—clearly a testament to the blandness of English food at the time.

Cumin is now grown predominantly in Iran, which has a reputation for producing the best-quality "green" cumin seed. Other major producing countries of cumin seeds are India, Morocco and Turkey.

The Plant

Cumin is a small (about 24 inches/60 cm tall), delicate-looking annual with slender branched stems. Because of their weakness, the stems are weighed down heavily by the fruits that follow its tiny white or pink flowers. These fruits are what are commonly referred to as cumin seeds. The deep, almost blue-green leaves are frond-like and are divided into long, narrow segments similar to those of fennel. Although cumin is a hot-climate plant, it will not do well under extreme heat conditions.

C

Cumin Confusion

There is a perennial variety of caraway (*Carum bulbocastanum*, or *Bunium persicum*) that is generally referred to as "black cumin," or *jeera kala* (see page 236). The flavor of this seed is more like cumin than caraway, and it is generally used in rich North Indian dishes containing cream, yogurt, white poppy seeds and crushed nuts. Don't be fooled: it's not a substitute for true cumin in any recipes. If used elsewhere in the same proportions, it will create a slightly sharp and bitter taste rather than the warm, earthy flavor of cumin seeds.

Cumin seeds average $1/4$ inch (5 mm) in length. Tapered at both ends, they are only slightly curved and measure about $1/8$ inch (3 mm) thick. The seeds range in color from pale brown to khaki and have a fine downy surface that makes them appear dull. Each seed has nine very fine ridges, or oil canals, running along its length and a hairlike tail $1/8$ inch (3 mm) long at one end. Ground cumin seed is a coarse-textured, oily-feeling deep khaki powder.

The aroma of cumin is pungent, warm, earthy, lingering and sweet, and it yields a hint of dry peppermint. The flavor is similarly pungent, earthy, slightly bitter and warming, reminiscent of curry.

Cumin and caraway seeds are somewhat similar in appearance, but they are often confused for two other reasons: the German word for caraway is *Kummel* (which sounds like *cumin* in English), and the Indian word for both caraway and cumin is often *jeera* or *zira*. Since caraway is not used nearly as much as cumin in India (except in good-quality garam masala), this doesn't create problems there, but it can lead to confusion elsewhere.

Processing

Cumin is harvested when the plant has finished flowering and before the ripe fruits begin to fall from its heavily laden umbels. Scythed seed-bearing stems are tied in sheaves and hung in the shade to dry, or simply cut and left to dry in the sun, before threshing to remove the seeds. After threshing, the seeds are rubbed to remove about 90% of the hairlike tails. I was fascinated to see this task still being undertaken manually in the state of Gujarat in northwestern India, where

Spice Notes

From time to time I am asked to assist food companies in developing spice combinations. I once made a mixture to go with fish: it contained turmeric, fresh dill, pepper, coriander seed and lime leaves, but somehow the flavor remained too harsh. With the addition of a small amount of cumin—too little for most people to notice—the mix became full-bodied and balanced. Another company asked me to develop a stuffing mix for poultry. My first attempt contained onion, garlic, thyme, sage, marjoram, bay leaves, mint and paprika. The result was pleasant but not outstanding. Again the judicious addition of a little ground cumin rounded out and balanced the flavor. So keep in mind that cumin is not simply a curry spice; it is a spice with rounded, comforting flavor notes that add balance to a broad combination of spices and food flavors.

A Sweet Surprise

What may come as a surprise to some is that cumin also complements sweet shortbread cookies, a delicacy Liz and I experienced while having afternoon tea on the Nile. Since then I have found that dukkah, an Egyptian blend of nuts, spices and cumin, is delicious when sprinkled on a slice of bread spread with honey. Those of you who like peanut butter and honey sandwiches will appreciate the honey and dukkah combination.

the women were simply rubbing cumin seeds on the palms of their hands and letting them fall past a large industrial-sized fan, which blew away the fine tails while the cumin seeds fell to the ground.

Buying and Storage

Although a pungent spice, cumin will start to lose its most desirable flavor notes after grinding, so if you are buying a powdered version, look for good-quality oily-textured greenish brown, almost khaki-colored, powder in airtight packaging. Because cumin seeds can be quite oily when ground, it is not uncommon for unscrupulous traders to mix in some cheaper ground coriander seed to reduce the cost. If kept in airtight containers away from extremes of heat, light and humidity, whole cumin seeds will keep for up to 3 years and ground cumin for 1 year.

Use

While many cooks may find cumin overtly pungent and tiresomely reminiscent of curries, do keep in mind that its flavor need not dominate. With subtle, judicious application, cumin can be surprisingly effective in balancing and rounding out the bouquet of other spices. Cumin is, of course, used extensively in Indian curries; it is also used with rice and vegetables, in breads and when making pickles and chutneys. The famous Indian seed blend panch phoron contains whole cumin seeds. Middle Eastern dishes often feature cumin because it complements lamb particularly well, and it is an important ingredient in Moroccan spice combinations such as chermoula and harissa. Mexican chile powder, the blend we have all become familiar with in tacos and chili con carne, is usually a simple mixture of chile, paprika, cumin and salt. Cumin also complements orange vegetables (carrots and squash) well, as the seeds may be added to the water when boiling or steaming. Ground cumin is a delicious addition to squash soup and vegetable casseroles.

Recipes often call for dry-roasting cumin seeds or powder, as this brings out a pleasant nutty flavor and reduces some of the bitterness. To roast cumin, heat a dry skillet over medium heat, add the seeds or powder, and stir or shake the pan to keep the cumin moving around so it does not stick or burn. When the cumin begins to give off a toasted aroma and the color begins to darken, remove the pan from the heat and immediately tip out the contents to prevent further cooking from residual heat.

Roasting is appropriate for many Indian and Malay recipes; however, it also changes the flavor, driving off some of the most delicate notes, and this effect may be undesirable in a mild chicken or seafood dish or a chili con carne. For more cumin uses, see "The Art of Combining Spices" (pages 679 to 781), in particular the curry blends.

An essential oil extracted from cumin seeds by steam distillation is an ingredient in perfumes and liqueurs such as the German drink kümmel.

WEIGHT PER TEASPOON (5 mL)
- whole: 2.4 g
- ground: 2.6 g

SUGGESTED QUANTITY PER POUND (500 g)
- red meats: 2 tsp (10 mL) seeds or powder
- white meats: 2 tsp (10 mL) seeds or powder
- vegetables: 1½ tsp (7 mL) seeds or powder
- grains and pulses: 1½ tsp (7 mL) seeds or powder
- baked goods: 1½ tsp (7 mL) seeds or powder

Stir-Fried Beef with Cumin, Onions and Chile

Years ago I assisted Thai expert David Thompson with a cooking demonstration. All of the food was amazing, but it was this beef dish that made the most impact. Usually so much cumin is associated with curry, but it's lovely in this stir-fry.

Makes 4 servings

Preparation time:
20 minutes

Cooking time:
20 minutes

- - - - - - - - - - - - - - - -

Tips

To toast ground cumin: Place it in a dry skillet over medium heat and cook gently, shaking the pan often, for 1 to 2 minutes, until slightly browned and aromatic. Remove from pan immediately.

Many types of chile are dried for use. Basic dried red chiles are generally a bit hotter than their fresh counterparts and have a slightly sweet caramel flavor not found in fresh varieties. Asian grocers carry a variety of dried chiles.

- **Mortar and pestle**
- **Wok**

CHILE PASTE

½ cup	dried long red chiles (see Tips, left)	125 mL
1 tsp	fine sea salt	5 mL
5	shallots, roughly chopped	5
5	cloves garlic, chopped	5
1 tbsp	ground cumin, lightly toasted (see Tips, left)	15 mL

BEEF

1 cup	oil	250 mL
5	dried small red chiles	5
5	shallots, finely sliced	5
1	10 oz (300 g) beef rump, sliced across the grain into 1-inch (2.5 cm) pieces	1
1 tsp	ground cumin	5 mL
Pinch	ground medium-hot chile (see Tip, page 241)	Pinch
Pinch	fine sea salt	Pinch
Pinch	granulated sugar	Pinch
2 tsp	tamarind water	10 mL
2 tsp	fish sauce (nam pla)	10 mL
½	white onion, halved and finely sliced	½
½ cup	lightly packed fresh cilantro, stems and leaves	125 mL

1. *Chile Paste:* In a small bowl, cover dried long chiles with warm water and set aside for 10 minutes to soften; drain well (discard soaking liquid). Using a sharp knife, chop chiles. Using mortar and pestle, combine chopped chiles with salt and pound into a paste. Add shallots, garlic and cumin and pound until well combined. Set aside.

C

Tip

Ground Kashmiri chile is flavorsome and versatile. You can find it at most Indian markets at varying levels of heat, depending on the amount of seeds and membrane ground with the chile.

2. *Beef:* In wok over high heat, heat oil until bubbles appear at the bottom. Add dried small chiles and cook, stirring occasionally, for 2 to 3 minutes, until dark red. Using a slotted spoon, transfer chiles to a plate lined with paper towels. Add shallots and cook for about 3 minutes, until just beginning to brown. Using slotted spoon, transfer shallots to a separate plate lined with paper towels. Discard all but 2 tbsp (30 mL) frying oil from wok and set aside.

3. In a large bowl, combine beef, cumin, ground chile, salt, sugar and fried chiles.

4. In wok, heat reserved oil over high heat. Add beef, with spices, and cook, stirring constantly, for about 2 minutes, until just starting to brown. Add prepared chile paste, breaking it up with the back of a wooden spoon. Add tamarind water and fish sauce. When beef is just cooked through, add sliced onion, cilantro and reserved fried shallots. Cook, stirring, for 1 minute, until heated through. Serve immediately.

Chili con Carne

There may be no dish more disputed than chili; for starters, there are many arguments over the inclusion of beans and even tomatoes. Cumin, however, is an undeniable ingredient, forming an earthy base for rich, smoky dried Mexican chiles. A good chili con carne shouldn't be rushed, since slow cooking brings out its best. Serve simply, over rice sprinkled with fresh cilantro and a spoonful of sour cream, or in tacos or tortillas. This is a perfect make-ahead-and-freeze dish and a genuine crowd-pleaser.

Makes 6 to 8 servings

Preparation time:
45 minutes

Cooking time: 1 hour, 40 minutes

Tip

For extra heat, add 1 tbsp (15 mL) chopped chipotle pepper in adobo sauce with the meat and tomatoes in Step 4.

1	ancho chile pepper	1
2	dried chipotle peppers	2
2 tsp	whole cumin seeds	10 mL
1 tsp	whole coriander seeds	5 mL
2 lbs	lean ground beef	1 kg
2 tbsp	oil	30 mL
1	onion, chopped	1
4	cloves garlic, minced	4
1	long green finger chile, seeded and finely chopped	1
1 tbsp	dried oregano	15 mL
1/4 tsp	ground cinnamon	1 mL
1	can (14 oz/398 mL) crushed tomatoes	1
1 tbsp	tomato paste	15 mL
1 cup	beef stock	250 mL
1 tsp	fine sea salt	5 mL
1	can (14 oz/398 mL) kidney beans (see Tips, page 243)	1
1/4 oz	dark chocolate (70% to 90% cocoa solids)	7 g
	Sea salt and freshly ground black pepper	

1. In a heatproof bowl, cover ancho and chipotle chiles with boiling water and set aside for 30 minutes. Drain, discarding soaking liquid and stems. Chop finely and set aside.

2. In a dry skillet over medium heat, toast cumin and coriander seeds, stirring frequently, until fragrant, about 3 minutes. Transfer to a clean spice grinder or use a mortar and pestle to grind until fine. Set aside.

Tips

If you prefer to make the chili ahead, cool, transfer to an airtight container and refrigerate for up to 3 days, or freeze for up to 3 months.

The canned kidney beans can be replaced with 2 cups of cooked beans.

3. In a large, heavy saucepan or Dutch oven over medium-high heat, brown beef in 2 or 3 batches, being careful not to crowd the pan and using a spoon to break up any large pieces (for best results, the beef should resemble small grains), about 10 to 12 minutes. Using a slotted spoon, transfer cooked beef to a bowl, discarding excess fat in pan. Set aside.

4. In the same saucepan over low heat, heat oil. Add onion, garlic and green chile and cook, stirring occasionally, until onion is softened, about 3 minutes. Stir in ground toasted cumin and coriander, oregano, cinnamon and reserved soaked chiles; cook for another 3 minutes, until well combined. Add reserved meat, tomatoes, tomato paste, stock and salt. Cook, stirring occasionally, for 5 minutes, then cover and simmer for 1 hour, stirring occasionally. Add kidney beans and chocolate and simmer, uncovered, stirring occasionally, for 20 to 30 minutes, until sauce is reduced but not dry. Season with additional salt if necessary and pepper to taste. Serve immediately.

Variation

For a chunkier chili, substitute an equal amount of cubed beef shin or flank steak for the ground beef.

Curry Leaf

Murraya koenigii

Names in Other Languages

- **Arabic:** waraq al-kari
- **Burmese:** pyi-naw-thein
- **Chinese (C):** ga lei yihp
- **Chinese (M):** diao liao, jiu li xiang
- **Danish:** karry blad
- **Dutch:** kerriebladeren
- **French:** feuille de cari
- **German:** Curryblatter
- **Indian:** meetha neem, karipattar, karuvepillay
- **Indonesian:** daun kari
- **Italian:** foglia di curry
- **Japanese:** kare-rihu
- **Malay:** daun kari, karupillay
- **Portuguese:** folhas de caril
- **Russian:** listya karri
- **Spanish:** hoja de cari
- **Sri Lankan:** karapincha
- **Thai:** bai karee
- **Vietnamese:** la ca ri

Family: Rutaceae

Other Names: meetha neem, karipattar, karuvepillay

Flavor Group: Strong

Parts Used: leaves (as a herb)

Background

Curry trees are native to Sri Lanka and India. They are commonly found in forests at low altitudes in the foothills of the Himalayas, from the Ravi to Sikkim and Assam. They are also grown in many domestic gardens, particularly in Kerala, in the south of India, where to my mind they have become a distinctive feature of South Indian cuisine. Curry trees are cultivated on farms in Andhra Pradesh, Tamil Nadu, Karnataka and Orissa. They are also grown on the Andaman and Nicobar Islands, in Sri Lanka, Malaysia and Myanmar, and on many Pacific Ocean islands. The curry tree is a member of the citrus family, so its rootstock has been used in the past for grafting varieties of citrus. It is also related to the well-known decorative mock orange tree (*Murraya paniculata*). Curry trees will grow in most parts of Australia and the southern United States that are free from extreme frosts, as long as they are sheltered from wind.

Culinary Information

Combines with

- allspice
- cardamom
- chile
- cinnamon
- cloves
- coriander (leaf and seed)
- fennel seed
- fenugreek seed
- ginger
- makrut lime leaf
- mustard
- paprika
- tamarind
- turmeric
- Vietnamese mint

Traditional Uses

- garnish for Indian dishes
- Indian and Asian curries
- shrimp moilee
- stir-fries
- seafood marinades

Spice Blends

- curry powders
- sambar powder
- vadouvan curry powder

The Wrong Tree

The curry tree should not be confused with the decorative silvery gray curry plant of European origin (*Helichrysum italicum*), which I believe has no culinary value, although some people claim it has a curry-like flavor.

The Plant

Curry leaves come from the leaflets of a delightfully fragrant small tropical evergreen tree that under favorable conditions grows to about 13 feet (4 m) in height. The trunk is slender and flexible and supports a series of stems with drooping leaves, giving the tree an overall frond-like appearance. Each "frond" carries about 20 leaves growing off the central stem. The leaves vary considerably in size, from 1 to 3 inches (2.5 to 7.5 cm) long and $1/2$ to $3/4$ inch (1 to 2 cm) wide. In summer the leaves are shiny and bright green on top and the underside is dull and pale green. Although the tree is not strictly speaking deciduous, at the beginning of winter in some cooler climates the leaves turn yellow and many of them may drop, but with the first warmth of spring, bright new shoots and leaves appear. In the tropics, leaves are usually available for picking all year round.

Curry leaves do not taste like curry. They get their name from being used in curries, especially in southern India. The curry tree belongs to the same family as oranges and lemons; even inadvertently brushing past one fills the air with heavenly slightly spicy, citrus-like aroma. The flavor is similarly lemony but lacks the fruitiness of lemons and limes.

Travels in the Spice Trade

When Liz and I were living in Singapore, one day we were driving along the East Coast Parkway when we both commented that we could smell curry leaves. We came up behind a truck that we thought must be loaded with them. It turned out, however, that we were simply smelling burning motor oil! As well as having distinct citrus characteristics, curry leaves release a strangely mouthwatering acrid scent that smells bizzarely like burning motor oil.

Other Varieties

There are two types of curry tree. *Murraya koenigii senkambu* has a green midrib and small, narrow leaves, on average 1 inch (2.5 cm) long and $1/2$ inch (1 cm) wide. *M. koenigii suwasini* has a pink midrib and larger leaves; it is much preferred for cooking, as it has a stronger flavor.

Processing

Curry leaves may be successfully dried, provided that care is taken to ensure they retain their color and flavor. Strip the best-looking fresh green leaves from the stem and arrange in a single layer on paper or wire mesh. Place in a dark, well-aired place, avoiding humidity. In a few days the leaves should be dark green, with no blackening or brown patches, and feel quite crisp and dry, which means they are ready to use.

Buying and Storage

When buying fresh curry leaves, ensure that the leaflets are attached to the stems and not at all wilted. Fresh leaves on the stems will keep in a resealable bag in the refrigerator for more than 1 week and in the freezer for up to 2 months.

Good-quality dried curry leaves are difficult to find. Most are quite black in color and lack the characteristic volatile aroma. Look for dry curry leaves that have retained their deep green color. Dried leaves should be stored in an airtight container away from extremes of heat, light and humidity. They will last for up to 1 year.

Use

Curry leaves are used to flavor Indian curries, especially the southern and Madras styles. For best results, fry the fresh or dried leaves in oil before adding other ingredients.

WEIGHT PER TEASPOON (5 mL)
- whole average dried leaf: 0.1 g

SUGGESTED QUANTITY PER POUND (500 g)
- **red meats:** 10 leaves, fresh or dried
- **white meats:** 6 to 8 leaves, fresh or dried
- **vegetables:** 6 leaves, fresh or dried
- **grains and pulses:** 6 leaves, fresh or dried
- **baked goods:** 6 leaves, fresh or dried

Shrimp Moilee

My first trip to India was with Mum and Dad when they were leading one of their Spice Discovery tours. I was enthralled by the amount of fresh seafood available in Cochin, in the southwestern state of Kerala. This recipe from that region is easy to make and tastes amazing. The flavors are fresh, simple and highly characteristic of South Indian cuisine.

Makes
4 servings

Preparation time:
20 minutes
Cooking time:
15 minutes

- - - - - - - - - - - - - - - -

Tips

You can also make this dish using frozen cooked shrimp. Simply thaw and add as directed in Step 3. Reduce the cooking time to 1 minute, just to heat through (be careful not to overcook them or the shrimp will become tough).

Coconut cream tastes the same as coconut milk but is thicker, with less water content.

2 cups	basmati rice	500 mL
16	medium shrimp, peeled and deveined, tails intact (see Tips, left)	16
1 tsp	fine sea salt	5 mL
1½ tsp	ground turmeric, divided	7 mL
2 tbsp	coconut oil	30 mL
20 to 30	fresh curry leaves	20 to 30
1	small onion, sliced	1
3	small green chiles, seeded and diced	3
1	piece (1 inch/2.5 cm) gingerroot, peeled and finely sliced	1
2	cloves garlic, finely sliced	2
2	tomatoes, peeled, cored and diced	2
1 cup	coconut cream (see Tips, left)	250 mL

1. In a saucepan with a lid, cover rice with 2 cups (500 mL) cold water and set aside for about 10 minutes. Bring to a boil over high heat, then reduce heat to low and cook, covered, until water is completely absorbed and rice is tender, about 15 minutes. Remove from heat, cover and set aside.

2. Meanwhile, in a large bowl, sprinkle shrimp with salt and 1 tsp (5 mL) turmeric and toss to coat. Set aside.

3. In a large skillet or wok over medium heat, melt coconut oil and add half the curry leaves; cook until leaves are crisp. Using a slotted spoon, transfer curry leaves to a plate lined with paper towels and set aside. In the pan, combine onion, chiles, ginger and garlic; cook until onion is transparent, about 5 minutes. Stir in tomatoes and remaining curry leaves and simmer for 2 minutes. Stir in remaining ½ tsp (2 mL) turmeric and cook for 1 minute. Stir in coconut cream. Add shrimp and simmer for 2 to 3 minutes, until pink and cooked through.

4. To serve, fluff cooked rice with a fork. Divide among 4 serving plates and top with moilee. Garnish with reserved fried curry leaves.

Dill

Anethum graveolens

Names in Other Languages

- **Arabic:** shibith
- **Chinese (C):** sih loh
- **Chinese (M):** shi luo, tu hui xiang
- **Danish:** dild
- **Dutch:** dille
- **French:** aneth odorant
- **German:** Dill, Gurkenkraut
- **Greek:** anitho
- **Indian:** sowa, anithi
- **Indonesian:** adas manis, adas sowa
- **Italian:** aneto
- **Japanese:** deiru, inondo
- **Laotian:** phak si
- **Malay:** adas china
- **Portuguese:** endro
- **Russian:** ukrop
- **Spanish:** eneldo
- **Sri Lankan:** enduru
- **Swedish:** dill
- **Thai:** phak chee lao
- **Turkish:** dereotu
- **Vietnamese:** tie hoi huong

Family: Apiaceae (formerly Umbelliferae)

Varieties: European dill (*Anethum graveolens*), Indian or Japanese dill (*A. sowa*)

Other Names: dill seed, dillweed, garden dill, green dill

Flavor Group: Pungent (seeds), Strong (tips/fronds)

Parts Used: seeds (as a spice), fronds and tips (as a herb)

Background

Dill is native to Mediterranean regions and southern Russia. It is known to have been cultivated as far back as 3000 BCE by the ancient Babylonians and Assyrians. Dill was known to the Romans, who regarded it as a symbol of vitality: they sprinked it over food given to the gladiators. The first-century CE Roman scholar Pliny wrote of dill. Medieval writers believed it had magical properties that could ward off evil and enhance love potions and aphrodisiacs. It is known to have been cultivated in England since 1570 and was more popular there in the 17th century than it is now. In America, dill seeds were referred to as "meeting-house seeds": members of church congregations often brought along a supply to nibble on during long Sunday sermons.

Culinary Information

Combines with

Tips (Leaf)
- basil
- bay leaf
- coriander leaf
- cress
- fennel fronds
- garlic
- lovage
- parsley

Seed
- allspice
- bay leaf
- celery seed
- chile
- cinnamon
- cloves
- coriander seed
- fennel seed
- ginger
- mustard seed
- pepper

Traditional Uses

Leaf
- cottage and cream cheese flavoring
- white sauces for chicken and seafood
- scrambled eggs and omelets
- fish dishes
- salad dressings and herb vinegars

Seed
- pickles, particularly cucumbers
- rye bread
- carrots
- squash and cabbage (added during cooking)

Spice Blends

Leaf
- salad herbs
- seafood seasonings
- vegetable salts

Seed
- fish and poultry seasonings
- pickling spices
- ras el hanout

The Plant

Tips

The herb dill is a surprisingly hardy delicate-looking, frond-like annual. Dill plants grow to about 3 feet (1 m) tall, with wispy, hairlike leaves at the top of upright smooth, shiny hollow stems. Dill, with its small pale yellow flowers, is a member of the same family as parsley, caraway, anise, coriander and cumin, and it bears similarly umbrella-shaped flower heads followed by seed clusters. Fresh dill tips have a distinct parsley-like aroma and a subtle hint of anise.

Dried green dill tips are dark green and fine, with each piece only $^1/_8$ to $^1/_6$ inch (3 to 4 mm) long. The aroma is grassy but more aromatic than many dried herbs. When placed in the mouth, it softens quickly to release a parsley and anise flavor reasonably close to that of fresh dill.

Seeds

Dill seeds, which are actually the minute fruit divided in two, are pale brown with three fine lighter-colored lines, or oil channels, running the length of the seed. Each seed is about $^1/_6$ inch (4 mm) long and oval. As most split in two after harvesting, the majority of dill seeds look flat on one side and convex on the other, and a few seeds retain their fine $^1/_{16}$-inch (1 mm) stalk. Dill seeds have a more robust aroma and flavor than green dill tips. Upon drying, a distinct anise character and a suggestion of caraway develop, while the parsley overtones found in fresh dill leaves disappear.

Other Varieties

A variant called **Indian dill**, or *sowa* (*Anethum graveolens* var. *sowa*), is grown in India and Japan. *Sowa* is a smaller plant than European dill and has a less agreeable flavor. However, it does provide an oil extracted by steam distillation, which is widely used as a flavoring in the manufacture of pickles and processed foods.

Processing

Tips

When adequate care is taken, the fresh green tips of dill can be readily dried to ensure a supply of this delectable herb all year round. Dill tips, whether gathered for use fresh or for drying, are best harvested when the plant is not yet fully mature and the flower buds are just starting to form. Cut the

Travels in the Spice Trade

During our last trip to the cassia forests in North Vietnam, our entourage sought out a little restaurant in the town that served *com pho*, which we deduced meant Chinese-style rice noodles. The meal was soup-based and accompanied by fresh greens, noodles or rice. We were interested to find a surprising quantity of fresh dill tips among the greenery in the soup. In Australia and many Western countries, we don't usually think of fresh dill (*Anethum graveolens*) as an Asian ingredient; however, when you consider how well it goes with coriander leaf, pepper, cardamom, cumin and turmeric in a Kuwaiti fish stew (see page 127), it's not surprising that it tastes so delicious in Asian dishes. The next time you are making an Asian stir-fry or soup, try adding equal quantities of coriander leaf and dill tips—the dill gives a delightful anise- and parsley-flavored freshness.

stems and snip off the feathery ends with a pair of scissors. Spread out the cut tips in a thin layer on clean absorbent paper (paper towels are suitable) and place in a warm, well-aired dark place for a few days.

Dill can also be dried in a microwave oven (see page 30). Spread 1 cup (250 mL) lightly packed cut tips on a paper towel in the microwave and cook on High for 2 minutes. Continue to microwave for additional bursts of 30 seconds until the leaves feel quite crisp to the touch.

Seeds

Dill seeds are harvested when the plant is mature, has finished flowering and the fruits (seeds) are fully formed. Gathering usually takes place in the early morning or very late afternoon, when there is some moisture from dew on the fruits. This moisture helps to prevent the seeds from shattering and being lost while cutting the seed-laden stems for later threshing.

Buying and Storage

Tips

Fresh green dill is readily available and is easy to store for a few days. Buy bunches that look bright and fresh, without any sign of wilting. Wrap the bottom 2 inches (5 cm) of the stems in foil and place in a container of water in the refrigerator.

Dried green dill tips should always have a crisp feel and be dark green, with no signs of yellowing. This dried herb is best when stored in an airtight container away from any source of light (exposure will bleach out the color and the flavor will diminish rapidly), heat or humidity. Stored well, your dried dill will keep its flavor and color for at least 12 months.

Seeds

Dill seeds are readily available; in their whole form they have a shelf life of up to 3 years when stored away from extremes of heat, light and humidity. The whole seeds are not as light-sensitive as the green tips, so you will have little problem keeping them in a spice rack if so desired.

Powdered dill seeds lose their flavor fairly quickly, so when recipes call for ground dill seeds, I recommend grinding your own, which can be easily done using a mortar and pestle or spice grinder (if you don't have one, a pepper mill works well). In many applications dill seeds will soften during cooking and the flavor will be released, so grinding is not really necessary.

Use

Today dill seed as well as the fresh herb is found in the cuisines of many countries; it seems to be most popular in Scandinavia, Germany and Russia.

Tips

Fresh green dill has a refreshing, refined taste that when used in modest amounts contributes an appetizing flavor to a wide range of foods. Finely chopped dill fronds (as the leaves and stems are called) are particularly good with cottage or cream cheese and in white sauces, seafood and chicken dishes, omelets and scrambled eggs, salads, soups and vegetable dishes, as well as in infused vinegars. Dill fronds and capers have become "must-have" accompaniments to shaved smoked salmon. A few leaves in unflavored yogurt used as a dressing for fresh cucumber makes a perfect side dish for spicy dishes or strong-flavored seafoods.

Seeds

Dill seeds are used for pickles, hence the name "dill pickles" given to American pickled cucumbers. The seeds are found in breads, particularly rye, and go well with other carbohydrates such as potatoes. Dill seeds complement vegetables such as carrots, squash and cabbage. They are an ingredient in the exotic Moroccan spice blend ras el hanout and are often found in commercial spice mixes for seasoning fish and poultry.

WEIGHT PER TEASPOON (5 mL)
- whole dried dill tips: 1 g
- whole seeds: 3 g

SUGGESTED QUANTITY PER POUND (500 g)
- **red meats:** 2 tsp (10 mL) seeds, 1 tsp (5 mL) leaves
- **white meats:** 1½ tsp (7 mL) seeds, 1 tsp (5 mL) leaves
- **vegetables:** 1 tsp (5 mL) seeds, ½ tsp (2 mL) leaves
- **grains and pulses:** 1 tsp (5 mL) seeds, ½ tsp (2 mL) leaves
- **baked goods:** 1 tsp (5 mL) seeds, ½ tsp (2 mL) leaves

Vietnamese Dill and Turmeric Fish

One of my favorite Vietnamese dishes is traditional Hanoi *cha ca*, a fish dish with the intriguing combination of dill and turmeric, heavy with fish sauce and served from a hot skillet at the table. Don't be put off by the amount of shrimp paste—it is very strong but completes the dish. My friend Michael, a fellow foodie whose parents are Vietnamese, has been kind enough to share his family recipe with me, which I now love to cook for my family and friends.

Makes 4 servings

Preparation time:
1 hour, 30 minutes

Cooking time:
15 minutes

1½ lbs	catfish, gray mullet, basa, tilapia or cod, cut into 2-inch (5 cm) pieces	750 g
MARINADE		
¼ cup	oil	60 mL
1 tbsp	granulated sugar	15 mL
2 tsp	shrimp paste	10 mL
2 tbsp	ground turmeric	30 mL
1 tbsp	garlic powder	15 mL
1 tsp	ground ginger	5 mL
SAUCE		
2 tbsp	granulated sugar	30 mL
2 tbsp	warm water	30 mL
2 tsp	shrimp paste	10 mL
	Juice from 2 freshly squeezed limes	
1	clove garlic, minced	1
½	long red finger chile, finely sliced	½
6 oz	rice vermicelli	175 g
3 tsp	oil, divided	15 mL
½	red onion, halved and sliced	½
6	green onions, finely sliced on the diagonal	6
1	bunch fresh dill, chopped	1
½ cup	crushed toasted peanuts, optional	125 mL

1. *Marinade:* In a large bowl, combine oil, sugar, shrimp paste, turmeric, garlic powder and ginger. Add fish pieces and toss to coat thoroughly. Cover and refrigerate for at least 1 hour.

2. *Sauce:* In a small bowl, combine sugar, water, shrimp paste, lime juice, garlic and chile; stir until sugar dissolves. Set aside.

3. In a large pot of boiling water, cook rice vermicelli until soft, about 5 minutes. Using a colander, drain and rinse under cold running water for 2 minutes, until cooled completely. Drain well. Transfer to a serving bowl, cover and set aside.

4. In a large skillet over medium heat, heat 1 tsp (5 mL) oil. Add red and green onions and cook for about 3 minutes, until starting to soften. Using a slotted spoon, transfer onions to a plate and set aside.

5. Add remaining 2 tsp (10 mL) oil to skillet. Add fish and cook for 2 to 3 minutes per side, until it is opaque and flakes easily when tested with a fork. Carefully fold in cooked onions and dill.

6. To serve, divide vermicelli among serving bowls, then top with fish mixture. Garnish with sauce to taste and peanuts (if using). Enjoy immediately.

Yogurt and Dill Cucumbers

My granny wrote this recipe for her book *Herbs for All Seasons*. It reminds me of hot summer days when often the best relief from the midday heat is to have a light lunch in the shade, including this refreshing cucumber dish.

| | Makes 4 small servings | |

Preparation time:
5 minutes

Cooking time:
5 minutes

Tip

For nice thin slices of cucumber, use a Y-shaped vegetable peeler or a mandoline.

2	large cucumbers, peeled and sliced thinly lengthwise (see Tip, left)	2
1 cup	plain yogurt	250 mL
1 tbsp	chopped fresh dill fronds	15 mL
	Sea salt and freshly ground black pepper	
	Additional chopped fresh dill fronds	

1. In a saucepan of boiling salted water, cook sliced cucumbers for 1 minute. Immediately transfer to a colander and rinse under cold running water. Drain well.

2. In a shallow serving dish, combine cooked cucumbers, yogurt and dill. Season with salt and pepper to taste. Chill until ready to serve, garnished with extra dill (best eaten on the day of making).

Elder

Sambucus nigra

Names in Other Languages

- **Dutch:** vlierbes, vlierboom
- **French:** baie de sureau
- **German:** Holunderbeere
- **Italian:** bacca di sambuco
- **Portuguese:** sabugo
- **Spanish:** baya de sauco
- **Swedish:** fladerbar

Litmus Test

A blue coloring substance from elderberries has been utilized as a kind of litmus paper, as it turns green with alkalis and red when detecting acid.

Family: Sambucaceae (formerly Caprifoliaceae)

Varieties: European elder (*S. nigra*); American elder (*S. nigra canadensis*, also known as *S. mexicana*)

Other Names: black elder, bore tree, common elder, elderberry, pipe tree

Flavor Group: Mild

Parts Used: berries (as a spice), flowers (as a herb)

Background

The elder tree is native to Europe, North Africa and western Asia and has been known since Egyptian times. There is hardly any other member of the plant kingdom that can rival the elder tree for superstition and diversity of uses for all its parts. The young shoots have a soft pith that is easily pushed out to form a hollow tube, hence the name "pipe tree" or "bore tree." The 17th-century English herbalist Culpepper referred to their appeal to small boys, who would make them into popguns. The close-grained white wood of old trees was polished and made into butchers' skewers, shoemakers' pegs, needles for weaving nets, combs, mathematical instruments and even musical instruments (probably woodwinds).

Culinary Information

Combines with

Flowers
- angelica
- bergamot
- lemongrass
- lemon myrtle
- lemon verbena
- mint

Berries
- allspice
- cinnamon
- licorice
- star anise

Traditional Uses

Flowers
- cordials for refreshing cool drinks
- vegetable dishes

Berries
- wines
- jellies
- conserves and jams

Spice Blends
- not commonly used in spice blends

Don't Confuse Trees

Elder trees are not to be confused with the dwarf elder (*Sambucus ebulus*), which has fruit that is poisonous and violently purgative.

It was widely believed that the Cross of Calvary was made of elder wood, which perhaps explains why the elder tree became a symbol of death and misfortune. Elder shoots were buried with the dead to protect them from witches and were used to make the whips for hearse drivers. In medieval times, hedgecutters would avoid attacking elder's rampant growth, gypsies would not burn it in campfires, and in many parts of Europe it was associated with magic, especially black magic! It is somewhat puzzling that a tree with such a dark reputation should also have been used so much for practical, medicinal and culinary purposes.

The Plant

There are more than 30 varieties of elder, with varying levels of toxicity, making *S. nigra* the preferred and only variety recommended for eating. The elder tree of culinary use is an attractive, vigorous-growing deciduous tree that reaches 33 feet (10 m) under favorable conditions. Because many cane-like shoots spread out around the base, its appearance is often more like a hedge than a tree. Elder trees have dark green spearmint-shaped leaves $1^{1}/_{2}$ to $3^{1}/_{4}$ inches (4 to 8 cm) long, with finely jagged edges. When bruised, the leaves have a nondescript, faintly grassy aroma.

Elder flowers form in large, flat-topped creamy white clusters more than 3 inches (7.5 cm) in diameter. They look as though they have been painstakingly crafted in lace and designed to support the hordes of bees working busily over them. The fresh flowers have a somewhat bitter taste; however, after they are processed with sweeteners into products such as elderflower cordial, the more pleasant attributes of the flowers become apparent. After flowering, very dark purple, almost black berries develop; when fully ripe, they are $1/3$ inch (8 mm) in diameter.

Fresh elderberries should not be eaten raw: they contain alkaloids and are somewhat bitter. Upon drying or cooking, however, the flavor becomes more agreeable and the toxicity is dissipated. The leaves should not be eaten at all, as they may contain traces of cyanide.

Processing

Flowers

Although the flowering season is a relatively few short weeks in their native Europe, elder trees growing in the warmer parts of the United States and Australia may flower for a couple of months. In Europe, elder flowers are picked in full bloom and thrown into heaps, where they are left to warm for a few hours. This loosens the petals, which are then separated from the stalks and stems by sifting.

To dry your own elder flowers, pick them early in the morning, before the heat of the day has diminished their potency. Place the flower heads on clean paper in a warm, dark, dry place for a few days.

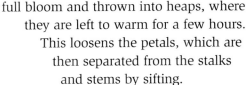

Berries

The berries are harvested when fully ripe and are used fresh only in cooking and processing applications that destroy the alkaloids. Elderberries are sometimes dried for later culinary use in much the same way that currants are. You can dry ripe elderberries, removed from the stems, by spreading them evenly in a single layer on paper or on a frame covered with mesh such as insect screening. Set aside in a dark, dry place where the air can circulate freely and allow the moisture content to evaporate. When dry, they will look like raisins.

Buying and Storage

Elderflower herbal teas are sometimes available from health-food stores, but it is very rare to see elderberries on sale, so you really need to grow the tree if you desire them. Elder is quite attractive in the garden—preferably in a large pot or container, which will prevent it from running amok.

Dried elder flowers should be stored in the same way as dried herbs. They will last for up to 1 year.

Fresh elderberries may be placed in freezer bags and frozen. Use within 6 months. Dried elderberries should be stored in an airtight container, avoiding extremes of heat, light and humidity. They should keep for 3 years.

Use

Both elder flowers and elderberries are used for making wines, although it is more common to use elderberries to color conventional wines, especially port produced in Portugal, than to produce elderberry wine.

The minute petals of elder flowers are used for making infusions such as elderflower cordial and herbal teas. The flowers make a refreshing drink when soaked in lemon juice overnight, and the flower heads, dipped in a light batter and fried, make an unusual side dish. My mother found that the blossoms give a Muscat grape flavor to gooseberry, apple or quince jelly, when tied in a muslin bag and boiled in the fruit syrup for 3 to 4 minutes at the end of the cooking time.

Elderberries, which taste a little like black currants, make lovely conserves and jams and go especially well with apples. Dried berries can be added to pies as you would currants.

SUGGESTED QUANTITY PER POUND (500 g)

NOTE: Double the quantity if using fresh rather than dried berries.

- **vegetables:** 1 cup (250 mL) flowers
- **red meats:** 1 tsp (5 mL) dried berries
- **white meats:** 1 tsp (5 mL) dried berries
- **vegetables:** ½ tsp (2 mL) dried berries
- **grains and pulses:** ½ tsp (2 mL) dried berries
- **baked goods:** 1 tsp (5 mL) dried berries

Elderflower Cordial

My friend Rosie makes batches of this cordial every year with the elder flowers from her country garden, and I am always a willing recipient. Needless to say, it makes a lovely gift as well as a refreshing summer drink when mixed with mineral water or added to punch or cocktails.

Makes about 2½ cups (625 mL)

Preparation time:
25 minutes

Steeping time: 24 hours

Tips

Citric acid is a natural preservative and flavoring. You can find it in well-stocked grocery stores and health-food stores.

To sterilize the bottle, clean thoroughly in hot soapy water, then allow to dry. Place bottle on a baking sheet in a preheated 400°F (200°C) oven for 10 minutes. Place lid in a pan of boiling water on the stove for 5 minutes. Handle carefully, with clean hands.

• **Sterilized resealable glass bottle**

12 to 14	heads fresh elder flowers	12 to 14
	Zest and sliced fruit of 2 large, unwaxed lemons	
1 lb	granulated sugar	500 g
1½ cups	water	375 mL
2½ tbsp	citric acid (see Tips, left)	37 mL

1. In a large bowl, combine elder flowers, lemon zest and lemon slices. Set aside.

2. In a saucepan over low heat, combine sugar and water and cook for 5 to 7 minutes, stirring constantly, until sugar is completely dissolved. Increase heat to high and bring to a boil. Pour the hot sugar syrup over the elder flowers and stir well. Add citric acid, cover bowl with a kitchen towel and set aside at room temperature for 24 hours.

3. Using a fine-mesh sieve lined with cheesecloth, strain infused liquid into bottle (discard solids) and seal tightly. The cordial will keep for up to 3 months in an airtight container at room temperature.

Elderflower Fool

A fool is an English dessert that was around long before ice cream appeared on the scene. It is delicious and easy to make in the summer, when elderberries and elder flowers abound. Serve with crisp biscotti.

Makes 6 servings

Preparation time:
10 minutes

Cooking time:
5 minutes

Tip

When picking elder flowers, ensure that the tiny flowers are fully open and gently shake, upside down, to remove any insects that may be residing. Gently pull the pretty flowers from the stem just before serving.

2 cups	heavy or whipping (35%) cream	500 mL
1 cup	crème fraîche	250 mL
6 tbsp	elderflower cordial (page 261)	90 mL
1/3 cup	confectioner's (icing) sugar	75 mL
1/4 tsp	pure vanilla extract	1 mL
1 1/2 lbs	fresh raspberries, divided	750 g
5	heads fresh elder flowers, flowers gently removed (see Tip, left)	5

1. In a large bowl, lightly whisk together heavy cream, crème fraîche, cordial, confectioner's sugar and vanilla. Stir in three-quarters of the raspberries. Spoon mixture into dessert bowls or martini glasses and top with remaining raspberries and fresh elder flowers.

Epazote

Dysphania ambrosioides (formerly known as *Chenopodium ambrosioides*)

Names in Other Languages

- **Chinese (C):** chau hahng
- **Chinese (M):** chou ching
- **Czech:** merlik, merlik vonny
- **Dutch:** welriekende ganzenvoet
- **Finnish:** sitruunasavikka
- **French:** epazote, thé de Mexique
- **German:** mexicanischer Traubentee
- **Hungarian:** mirhafu
- **Italian:** farinello aromatico
- **Japanese:** Amerika-ritaso
- **Polish:** komosa pixmowa
- **Portuguese:** erva-formigueira, mastruz
- **Russian:** epazot, mar ambrozievidnaya
- **Spanish:** yerba de Santa Maria, epazote
- **Swedish:** citronmalla
- **Turkish:** meksika cayi
- **Vietnamese:** ca dau giun

Family: Chenopodiaceae

Varieties: wormseed (*Dysphania anthelmintica*)

Other Names: American wormseed, goosefoot, Jerusalem parsley, Jesuit's tea, Mexican tea, paico, pigweed, skunkweed

Flavor Group: Strong

Parts Used: leaves (as a herb)

Background

Indigenous to Mexico, epazote has become naturalized as far north as New York City, where it may even grow wild in parks and backyards. It was introduced to Europe in 1732, probably because of its medicinal attributes, as it was at one time recorded in the United States Pharmacopoeia. However, nowadays it is usually only mentioned in American folk medicine.

The increased popularity of Latin American cuisine has seen a resurgence of interest in many traditional South American flavors, with epazote and huacatay leading the charge. The name *epazote* derives from words in the Nahuatl language of southern Mexico and Central America that mean "something dirty and smelling like an animal"—highly descriptive but not all that complimentary!

The Plant

There are many varieties of epazote, but the one featured most in Mexican cooking is a profusely branching annual that resembles overgrown spearmint and grows to 4 feet (1.2 m) tall, with either green or deep red and green leaves. The serrated leaves are 1 to 3 inches (2.5 to 7.5 cm) long and have a less than agreeable aroma and an unusual taste; most people become accustomed to it in much the same way as they acquire a taste for coriander leaf or asafetida. Although considered a weed by many gardeners, epazote is now nurtured in many kitchen gardens.

Culinary Information

Combines with

- chile
- cumin
- oregano
- paprika
- pepper

Traditional Uses

- Mexican casseroles and bean dishes
- tortillas

Spice Blends

- not commonly used in spice blends

Other Varieties

Wormseed (*Dysphania anthelmintica*) is so named because it was grown for its effectiveness against intestinal worms. Wormseed, however, is not used in cooking.

Processing

Epazote is generally used fresh; however, it can be dried in the same way as other green herbs. To dry the leaves for later use, spread them out on either paper or wire mesh and set aside in a dark, warm, well-aired place. When the leaves are crisp and friable, they are ready for use.

Buying and Storage

Epazote grows easily from seed and is widely available from retailers who specialize in Mexican produce. Fresh bunches of epazote can be kept, preferably with the roots intact, in a glass of water covered with a plastic bag like a tent. Store in the refrigerator, where it will last for a few days. You can also freeze it by wrapping freshly washed sprigs in foil, folding in the edges securely. Store the foil packets in the freezer for up to 1 month.

Dried epazote is also available from some spice merchants, and although it is not a perfect substitute for fresh, it can be used in the same way that you would use dried cilantro (coriander) as a substitute for the fresh leaves. Dried epazote will last for up to 1 year when stored in an airtight container away from extremes of heat, light and humidity.

Use

Epazote is favored in the cooking of the Yucatán Peninsula and features in a dish called *mole de epazote*, a soupy red

SUGGESTED QUANTITY PER POUND (500 g)

- **red meats:** 1 tbsp (15 mL) dried leaves
- **white meats:** 2 tsp (10 mL) dried leaves
- **vegetables:** 2 tsp (10 mL) dried leaves
- **grains and pulses:** 2 tsp (10 mL) dried leaves
- **baked goods:** 2 tsp (10 mL) dried leaves

casserole made from goat meat. It is reputed to control flatulence in diets that are high in beans (another similarity to asafetida) and is used in soups, many bean dishes and tacos. Some caution should be exercised with the amount consumed: too much can spoil the flavor of a meal.

Epazote does have some medicinal benefits, and a herbal tea made from epazote is available. However, extremely large doses should be avoided. When excessive amounts are eaten (based on the misconception that consuming more is better), it has been known to cause unpleasant side effects, including nausea.

Mole Verde Sauce

As the name suggests, this Mexican sauce is similar to a classic mole (page 192) but with the addition of more "greenery." It benefits from being eaten immediately after cooking; unlike a regular mole sauce, it doesn't improve over time. Serve with poached fish or chicken and rice.

**Makes
6 servings**

Preparation time:
15 minutes

Cooking time:
45 minutes

Tips

To toast pumpkin seeds, cook them in a dry skillet over medium heat, shaking pan often to prevent burning, for 2 to 3 minutes, until they begin to pop.

Look for Mexican pepper leaves in Latin American markets.

- **Food processor**
- **Blender**

2 cups	unhulled, unsalted raw pumpkin seeds, toasted (see Tip, left)	500 mL
2 cups	chicken broth, divided	500 mL
6 oz	green tomatoes or tomatillos, roughly chopped (about 4 or 5)	175 g
6	large fresh sorrel leaves	6
4	fresh Mexican pepper leaves (hoja santa, see Tips, left)	4
8	large sprigs fresh epazote	8
4	jalapeño chiles, coarsely chopped	4
1/4 cup	oil	60 mL
	Sea salt and freshly ground black pepper	

1. In food processor fitted with the metal blade, chop pumpkin seeds until fine. Transfer to a small bowl and combine with 1/2 cup (125 mL) broth. Set aside.

2. In blender, combine remaining 1 1/2 cups (375 mL) broth, tomatoes, sorrel, pepper leaves, epazote and chiles. Blend at medium speed until smooth.

3. In a heavy-bottomed saucepan over medium heat, cook tomato mixture for 5 minutes, stirring constantly to prevent sticking, until thickened and fragrant. Reduce heat to low and simmer, stirring occasionally, for 20 minutes, until thickened. Add pumpkin seed mixture and cook, stirring often, for 10 minutes, until well combined and heated through. Season with salt and pepper to taste and serve immediately.

Tortilla Soup

When visiting Mexico for the first time, we arrived tired and hungry. It was a revelation to be served this spicy tomato soup topped with crispy strips of tortilla, cubes of avocado and crumbled cheese.

Makes 6 starter servings

Preparation time:
10 minutes

Cooking time:
25 minutes

Tips

To soak the ancho chile: Remove the stem and shake out the seeds. Place chile in a small heatproof bowl and just cover with boiling water. Set aside for 5 minutes, until soft and pliable. Reserve the soaking liquid and add to the soup with the broth.

The dried epazote gives an earthy base note along with the smoky chiles, but if not available, dried oregano can be used.

Queso quesadilla is a creamy Mexican melting cheese created specifically for quesadillas, but it is used in many Mexican dishes that require cheese. If you can't find it, use an equal quantity of shredded Cheddar.

• **Regular or immersion blender**

1 tbsp	oil	15 mL
½	red onion, chopped	½
1	clove garlic, chopped	1
1	ancho chile, soaked and roughly chopped (see Tips, left)	1
1 tsp	dried epazote (see Tips, left)	5 mL
1	can (14 oz/398 mL) tomatoes, with juice	1
4 cups	chicken broth	1 L
	Oil for frying	
3	large corn tortillas, cut into 3- by ½-inch strips (7.5 cm by 1 cm)	3
1 cup	shredded queso quesadilla	250 mL
2	avocados, diced	2
1	lime	1
1 cup	lightly packed fresh coriander (cilantro) leaves, roughly chopped	250 mL
	Sea salt and freshly ground black pepper	

1. In a large saucepan over medium heat, heat oil. Add onion, garlic and chile and cook, stirring, for about 5 minutes, until golden. Add epazote, tomatoes and chicken broth and bring to a boil. Reduce heat and simmer for 15 minutes.

2. Meanwhile, in a skillet, heat 1 inch (2.5 cm) of oil. In batches, fry tortilla strips for about 2 minutes or until golden. Using a slotted spoon, transfer to a plate lined with paper towels.

3. Using blender, blitz soup until smooth. Season with salt and pepper to taste.

4. To serve, ladle soup into serving bowls and top with tortilla strips, shredded cheese, diced avocado, a squeeze of lime and coriander leaves.

Variation

For a heartier soup, add cooked chicken before serving.

Fennel

Foeniculum vulgare

Names in Other Languages

- **Arabic:** shamar
- **Burmese:** samouk-saba
- **Chinese (C):** wuih heung
- **Chinese (M):** hui xiang
- **Czech:** fenykl obecny
- **Danish:** fennilel
- **Dutch:** venkel
- **Finnish:** fenkoli
- **French:** fenouil
- **German:** Fenchel
- **Greek:** finokio, maratho
- **Indian:** saunf, sonf, moti sonf
- **Indonesian:** jinten manis, adas
- **Italian:** finocchio
- **Japanese:** uikyo
- **Malay:** jintan manis, adas pedas
- **Portuguese:** funcho
- **Russian:** fyenkhel
- **Spanish:** hinojo
- **Sri Lankan:** maduru
- **Swedish:** fankal
- **Thai:** yira, pak chi duanha
- **Turkish:** rezene, irziyan, mayana
- **Vietnamese:** cay thi la, hoi huong

Family: Apiaceae (formerly Umbelliferae)

Varieties: common (wild) fennel (*F. vulgare*), Florence fennel (*F. vulgare* var. *azoricum*), Indian fennel (*F. vulgare* var. *panmorium*), sweet fennel (*F. vulgare* var. *dulce*)

Other Names: aniseed, finnichio, Florence fennel, Indian (Lucknow) fennel

Flavor Group: Amalgamating (seeds), Strong (pollen, fronds), Mild (bulb, as vegetable)

Parts Used: seeds and pollen (as a spice), leaves (as a herb)

Background

Much of the history relating to fennel probably refers primarily to the wild perennial, which grows prolifically in Tuscany. Until the 20th century, when Italians migrated to Australia and the United States, the domesticated annual plant had largely been confined to its native Italy.

Fennel is indigenous to southern Europe and the Mediterranean region. Since antiquity the seeds have been used as a condiment by the Chinese, Indians and Egyptians. The Romans used it as a spice and also as a vegetable, which no doubt played a role in its introduction to northern Europe, where it has been known for 900 years. Fennel is mentioned in a record of Spanish agriculture from 961 CE. Charlemagne,

Culinary Information

Combines with

Seed and Pollen
- allspice
- cardamom
- chile
- cinnamon
- cloves
- coriander seed
- cumin
- fenugreek seed
- galangal
- ginger
- mustard
- nigella
- paprika
- tamarind
- turmeric

Fronds
- bay leaf
- chervil
- chives
- coriander leaf
- cress
- dill leaf
- garlic
- parsley

Traditional Uses

Seed
- breads and biscuits
- Italian sausages
- Malay curries
- pasta and tomato dishes
- satay sauces

Pollen
- fish pie
- carbonara pasta
- chocolate desserts

Fronds
- salads
- soups
- terrines (as a garnish)
- white sauces

Spice Blends

Seeds
- curry powders
- garam masala
- Chinese five-spice powder
- pickling spices
- Cajun spice blends
- ras el hanout
- panch phoron

Pollen and Fronds
- not commonly used in spice blends

King of the Franks and Emperor of the West in the eighth century, was an important figure in facilitating orderly plantings of herbs on the imperial farms in Germany. Fennel was one of the plants he cultivated, which helped lead to its diffusion throughout Europe.

The Plant

Foeniculum vulgare var. *dulce*, or sweet fennel, is the variety grown mostly for seed production. On this plant masses of bright yellow umbrella-shaped blossoms appear in summer and are followed by the pale green fruits (seeds) in autumn. Fennel leaves (fronds) have a slight anise aroma.

Fennel Bulbs

Fennel bulbs have been specially grown to be larger than their natural size. When the bulb is about the size of a golf ball, soil is heaped up around the base, and to keep the base covered, soil is continually added as the plant grows. Flower heads are removed as they appear, to stop the plant from going to seed. Fennel bulbs are harvested when they are bigger than a tennis ball; the roots are cut away and the bulb is washed and used within 10 days of cutting.

The dried seeds of sweet fennel are yellow with a green tinge, some more so than others—the greener the seed, the better the quality. On average the seeds are $1/4$ inch (5 mm) long and many will be split in two, making them flat on one side and convex on the other. Pale hair-width ribs run along the length, and occasionally you will notice a seed with its small stalk intact. The aroma is initially wheat-like, with a faint anise freshness. Upon tasting, fennel seeds release a strong anise flavor that is warm, spicy (but in no way hot), menthol-like and breath-freshening. The character of fennel seeds changes upon roasting, which is a common practice in Indian and Malay cooking. Roasting gives them a distinctive sweet flavor, almost as if brown sugar had been added.

Pollen from sweet fennel has traditionally been collected and used in Italy, and it has now begun to travel around the world as a somewhat exotic and expensive ingredient. Proponents claim its flavor is like fennel seed intensified a hundred times. Its rarity and the level of hyperbole surrounding the flavor have elevated it to saffron-like status. Strictly speaking, it is not just pollen; it includes a fair proportion of plant material from the flowers as well. Although fennel pollen is delightfully fragrant and sweet, it is not unlike the small, sweet Lucknow fennel seeds that may be used as an acceptable substitute. In my opinion, its intensity has been a trifle overstated.

Other Varieties

Wild fennel (*F. vulgare*) is a large plant with a less agreeable flavor than **Florence fennel** (*F. vulgare* var. *azoricum*); it grows up to 6 feet (2 m) or more and is often seen in ditches by roadsides and in low-lying moist areas. Florence fennel is an annual plant that is most popular for culinary purposes, producing the distinctive bulb that is eaten as a vegetable. It is a small—35 inches (90 cm)—attractive herb with soft, celery-like stems covered in numerous bright green frond-like leaves, which give the plant a ferny appearance. The bulb, when encouraged by cultivation, is white and firm. Some people erroneously think it is the anise plant, possibly because of its anise-like taste.

Travels in the Spice Trade

One of our more memorable seed-spice experiences was when Dr. Mehta, from Junagadh Agricultural University, in the northwestern Indian state of Gujarat, accompanied us to a spice research station. Liz lost sight of me when in my excitement I disappeared into a stand of fennel (*F. vulgare*). The plant's exotic high-yielding flowers were covered with cloth to prevent cross-pollination with other varieties that were being trialed for high yields. In the warming sun, the sounds of bees and the aroma of crushed foliage as I pushed through row upon row of seed spices reminded me of my childhood spent among herbs and their fragrances. No wonder I always feel so comfortable in these environments.

F

What's in a Name?

The name *fennel* derives from the Roman word for "fragrant hay," *foeniculum*. In 16th-century Italy fennel was a symbol of flattery, leading to the colloquial expression *dare finocchio*, which means "to give fennel." Fennel was a symbol of success in ancient Greece and was referred to as *marathon*, after the battleground on which the Greeks achieved a spectacular victory over the Persians in 490 BCE. Fennel is now cultivated or grows wild in practically every temperate climate in the world.

Indian fennel seed (*F. vulgare* var. *panmorium*) is sourced only from India and is generally referred to as Lucknow fennel seed. These seeds are about half the size of standard fennel seeds and are bright green, similar in color to a good-quality cardamom pod. Lucknow fennel has an intensely anise aroma with mild licorice overtones. The taste is sweet and licorice-like, making it an ideal palate cleanser and breath freshener after meals. This is the type you see sugar-coated in bright colors, usually beside the cash register, in Indian restaurants.

Processing

The bulb and leaves of fennel are rarely processed because their best attributes are appreciated when fresh. The seeds, however, are produced commercially in many countries when the plant has finished flowering and the fruits are fully formed. Like most seed crops, fennel is harvested in the early morning or very late afternoon, when the presence of moisture (dew) helps prevent the seeds from shattering. Prior to threshing, the stalks are cut and dried to remove the seeds. Fennel seeds are best dried in the shade, as this will help them retain higher levels of green color and sweet anise flavor. An essential oil of fennel is made by steam distillation of the seeds; it is used in nonalcoholic drinks, ice creams and liqueurs such as anisette.

Buying and Storage

Fennel bulbs, complete with their frond-like green foliage, can usually be purchased from fruit and vegetable retailers, especially those owned by Italian purveyors, who invariably call this vegetable *finocchio* or (incorrectly) anise. When

WEIGHT PER TEASPOON (5 mL)

- **whole seeds:** 2.1 g
- **ground seeds:** 2.7 g
- **pollen:** 1.7 g
- **fronds and bulb** not available in dried form

SUGGESTED QUANTITY PER POUND (500 g)

- **red meats:** 1 tbsp (15 mL) seeds or fronds, 2 tsp (10 mL) powder
- **white meats:** 1 tbsp (15 mL) seeds or fronds, 2 tsp (10 mL) powder
- **vegetables:** 2 tsp (10 mL) seeds or fronds, 2 tsp (10 mL) powder
- **grains and pulses:** 2 tsp (10 mL) seeds or fronds, 2 tsp (10 mL) powder
- **baked goods:** 2 tsp (10 mL) seeds or powder

storing bulb fennel, for optimum crispness, cover the bulb in water in a bowl in the refrigerator. Then it can be sliced into thin rings and separated like an onion to add to salads. Use within a few days.

Fennel seeds are readily available but the flavor quality and cleanliness vary considerably. Look for seeds that have at least some greenish tinge, and watch out for contamination from small pieces of dirt and, believe it or not, rodent droppings. The shape of fennel seeds makes it difficult to sieve out such foreign matter, so the line of least resistance for some traders is to give them only a cursory cleaning. Whole fennel seeds will keep their flavor for up to 3 years when stored in an airtight container in a cool, dark place.

Ground fennel seeds should be a pale fawn color with a hint of green, coarse-textured and highly aromatic. They will retain their flavor for at least 1 year, provided they are kept in an airtight container and stored away from extremes of heat, light and humidity.

Use

The fresh leaves (fronds) of fennel may be used in very much the same way as fresh green tips of dill weed: in salads and white sauces, with seafood, and to garnish terrines, soups and aspic. Steaming a whole fish on a bed of fresh fennel foliage is a traditional way to impart its aromatic flavor during cooking.

Fennel may be cut in half and cooked as a vegetable, sprinkled with Parmesan cheese or served with a white or cheese sauce. We like to finely shred fresh fennel bulb and fold it through cooked pasta with a little olive oil, torn fresh basil leaves and a dusting of freshly grated Parmesan cheese.

Fennel seeds are added to soups, breads, sausages, pasta and tomato dishes, as well as pickles, sauerkraut and salads. In Indian and Asian cooking, fennel seeds are nearly always roasted, which gives them quite a different sweet, spicy flavor. Although purists may disagree, I am quite comfortable with roasting ground fennel seeds, which is easily done by heating a small pan on the stovetop over medium heat. Add about 2 tbsp (30 mL) powder to the hot pan and shake it slightly to prevent the fennel from burning. When the powder begins to change color and a heavenly aroma wafts into the air, tip the contents into a dish. Roasted fennel seeds will last for around 3 weeks when stored in an airtight container and kept away from extremes of heat, light and humidity.

Rolled Goat Cheese

As it's so delicate, fennel pollen is best cooked very briefly or not at all. The gentle anise flavor of the fennel marries perfectly with goat cheese, making for a very nice appetizer accompanied by pickled beets and a few nasturtium leaves, if handy.

**Makes
2 servings**

Preparation time:
5 minutes
Cooking time: **none**

½ tsp	fennel pollen	2 mL
¼ tsp	freshly ground black pepper	1 mL
5 oz	log soft goat cheese	150 g

1. On a small plate, combine fennel pollen and pepper and spread out in an even layer. Using your fingers, roll goat cheese in seasonings to coat completely. To serve, transfer to a serving plate and cut cheese into ½-inch (1 cm) slices. This can be made ahead and wrapped in plastic wrap or stored in an airtight container for up to 3 days.

Braised Fennel

Braised fennel is a great accompaniment to roasted or grilled meat or fish, and it is a lovely vegetarian dish on its own, with some crusty bread to soak up the juices.

**Makes 4 side
servings**

Preparation time:
5 minutes
Cooking time: **1 hour,
15 minutes**

- **8-inch (20 cm) square glass baking dish**
- **Preheat oven to 350°F (180°C)**

2	bulbs fennel, fronds removed, quartered	2
	Freshly squeezed juice of 1 lemon	
	Sea salt and freshly ground black pepper	
1 tbsp	olive oil	15 mL
1	leek, sliced (about ½ cup/125 mL)	1
1 tsp	freshly grated gingerroot	5 mL
¼ tsp	ground cumin	1 mL
¾ cup	white wine	175 mL

1. In baking dish, arrange fennel bulbs so they fit snugly side by side. Drizzle with lemon juice and season with salt and pepper to taste.
2. In a skillet over medium high heat, heat oil. Add leek, ginger and cumin and sauté for 3 minutes, until golden. Add wine and bring just to a boil. Pour sauce over fennel.
3. Cover baking dish with a lid or foil and bake in preheated oven for 45 minutes, until tender. Uncover and bake for 20 minutes more, until lightly browned. Serve warm or at room temperature.

Grilled Chicken Satay

Chicken satay must be one of my fondest memories of living in Singapore as a child. It was our first port of call at the hawker stalls, and we devoured those tender sticks of chicken dipped in sweet peanut sauce as often as we could. Satay is a great introduction to spiced food for children, and this version lacks the sharp acidity detectable in many prepared satay sauces (it's required for preservation). This satay sauce also makes a good dip for crudités.

Makes 6 servings

Preparation time:
15 minutes

Cooking time:
20 minutes

Tips

If using wooden skewers, soak them in water for at least 30 minutes prior to using, to prevent them from burning while cooking.

You can make the sauce up to 4 days ahead and refrigerate it in an airtight container. If the sauce becomes too thick and dry, simply add more water. If you add too much water, stir over low heat until it thickens.

- **Metal or wooden skewers (see Tips, left)**

SATAY SAUCE

1 tbsp	ground fennel seeds	15 mL
2 tbsp	Malay curry powder (page 718)	30 mL
1½ tsp	palm sugar or packed light brown sugar	7 mL
1 tsp	oil	5 mL
1 cup	crunchy peanut butter	250 mL
1 tsp	soy sauce	5 mL
	Water	

CHICKEN

4	boneless skinless chicken breasts (about 2 lbs/1 kg total) cut into 1½-inch (4 cm) cubes	4
1 tsp	oil	5 mL
	Sea salt and freshly ground black pepper	
1	cucumber, peeled, seeded and cut into 4-inch (10 cm) matchsticks	1
6	green onions, white and green parts, julienned (see Tips, page 275)	6

1. *Satay Sauce:* In a dry saucepan over medium heat, cook ground fennel, stirring constantly, for 30 seconds. Stir in curry powder and cook for 30 seconds. Stir in sugar and oil. Cook, stirring, for 1 to 2 minutes, until a rich, dark paste forms. Add peanut butter and soy sauce and mix well. Add water to reach desired consistency. Remove from heat and set aside.

Tips

Julienne is a term for cutting into matchsticks roughly ⅛ inch (3 mm) thick and 3 inches (7.5 cm) long.

Chicken thighs can also be used. They may require an extra 2 minutes cooking time on each side.

2. *Chicken:* In a large bowl, toss chicken with oil and season with salt and pepper to taste. Thread equal portions onto 6 skewers. Cover and set aside in refrigerator until ready to cook.

3. Heat a barbecue or grill pan to High. Cook skewers until chicken is cooked through and slightly charred (this adds great flavor), 4 to 5 minutes per side. Serve hot, garnished with cucumber and green onion. Serve satay sauce overtop or on the side for dipping.

F

Fenugreek

Trigonella foenum-graecum

Names in Other Languages

- **Arabic:** hulba, hilbeh
- **Chinese (C):** wuh louh ba
- **Chinese (M):** hu lu ba
- **Czech:** piskavice recke seno, senenka
- **Dutch:** fenegriek
- **Finnish:** sarviapila
- **Indian:** methi ka beej, methi ventayam or venthiyam (seed); methi bhaji, methi ka saag (leaf)
- **Indonesian:** kelabet
- **Italian:** fieno greco
- **Japanese:** koroha
- **Malay:** halba
- **Portuguese:** alforva, feno-grego
- **Russian:** pazhitnik grecheski
- **Spanish:** alholva
- **Sri Lankan:** uluhaal
- **Swedish:** bockhornsklover
- **Thai:** luk sat
- **Turkish:** cemen, hulbe
- **Vietnamese:** co cari, ho lo ba

Family: Fabaceae (formerly Leguminosae)

Varieties: blue fenugreek (*T. melilotus-caerulea*)

Other Names: bird's foot, cow's horn, foenugreek, goat's horn, Greek hayseed, methi

Flavor Group: Pungent (seeds), Strong (leaves)

Parts Used: seeds (as a spice), leaves (as a herb)

Background

In fenugreek's Latin botanical name, *Trigonella* is a reference to the triangular shape of the flowers and *foenum-graecum* means "Greek hay," the name given to it by the Romans when they brought it from Greece. The foliage was used there to sweeten the scent of mildewed or sour hay, making it more appealing to cattle, and even today it is used to supplement fodder for cattle and horses—many believe it improves the appetite and adds gloss to their coats. Fenugreek is native to western Asia and southern Europe, where it has grown wild for centuries, courtesy of its hardy nature. It is now cultivated in many parts of the Mediterranean, South America, India and the Middle East. This herb is known to be one of the oldest cultivated plants; there is evidence in medical writings dating from 1000 BCE of its use by the Egyptians in the embalming process. The emperor Charlemagne assisted the popularity of fenugreek by encouraging its cultivation in central Europe in 812 CE.

Culinary Information

Combines with

Leaf and Seed

- allspice
- cardamom
- chile
- cinnamon
- cloves
- coriander seed
- cumin
- fennel seed
- galangal
- ginger
- mustard
- nigella
- paprika
- pepper
- star anise
- tamarind
- turmeric

Traditional Uses

Leaf

- vegetable and fish curries
- spinach and potato dishes

Seed

- Indian curries
- mayonnaise (for a sharp, mustard-like bite)
- extract used in making imitation maple syrup

Spice Blends

Leaf

- not commonly used in spice blends

Seed

- berbere
- curry powders
- hilbeh
- panch phoron
- sambar powder
- zhug

F

The Plant

The flavor of fenugreek reminds me of eating uncooked peas as a child while my grandmother was shelling them.

Fenugreek is a small, slender, erect annual herb that is a member of the pea family and has a similar appearance to alfalfa (lucerne). Its leaves are light green, with three small oblong leaflets. Fenugreek flowers are yellowish white, and the 4- to 6-inch (10 to 15 cm) fruits that form are of a typical legume nature, resembling miniature fava beans and containing 10 to 20 seeds. The common names "goat's horn" and "cow's horn" refer to the hornlike shape of the seedpod.

Fenugreek seeds are like hard golden brown pieces of gravel $1/8$ to $1/4$ inch (3 to 5 mm) long. A pronounced furrow on one side looks as though it's been made by pressure from a thumbnail. The aroma of these seeds is slightly spicy and sharp and the flavor is bitter and leguminous. Fenugreek seeds are often roasted, which highlights the bitterness and releases a somewhat nutty burnt sugar and maple syrup characteristic. Be careful not to over-roast the seeds, as that will make them extremely bitter.

Dried fenugreek leaves are a tangled pale green mass of fine tendril-like stems and triple leaflets. The aroma is grassy and warm, with a hint of coconut, and the leaves taste similar to the seeds but lack their underlying bitterness.

Other Varieties

A lesser-known and milder, less bitter variety of fenugreek, native to the Caucasus and the mountains of southeastern Europe, is **blue fenugreek** (*Trigonella melilotus-caerulea*), so named because of its blue flowers. Culinary use appears to be limited to its place of origin, where it is mostly used to flavor cheese and breads.

Processing

Fenugreek is grown from seed and matures in three to five months. The most common method of harvesting is to uproot the whole plants and dry them in the sun so the seeds can be easily removed by threshing. Then the seeds are dried again, to about 10% moisture content for optimum storage.

Buying and Storage

Fenugreek leaves, or *methi ka saag*, as the Indians call them, are usually available in their dried form from specialty spice shops. The best are pea green in color, with no sign of yellowing, and have a sunny, hay-like aroma and a distinctly beany smell. It is important to store them in an airtight container away from light, which will bleach the color and diminish flavor.

Fenugreek seeds vary little in quality. However, because of their stone-like appearance it is common to find seeds that have not been properly cleaned and are contaminated with actual stones. Check your fenugreek seeds carefully before putting them in a spice or pepper grinder.

Buy ground fenugreek seeds in small quantities: once ground, the flavor tends to dissipate. Store in airtight

Practical Processing

I remember seeing a particularly practical method of threshing fenugreek in the Indian state of Gujarat. A bullock cart was driven round and round in circles over a pile of cut fenugreek to break up the pods and release the seeds. The crushed hay was loaded into a gigantic sieve about 6 feet (2 m) in diameter, which was then shaken by a few young men to separate the seeds from the pods and stems. Soon the shakers were standing ankle deep in golden yellow fenugreek seeds.

Spice Notes

Try this out on your friends sometime: When I am conducting spice appreciation classes, one of my favorite guessing games is to pass around a dish of whole fenugreek seeds and ask people to smell them. Then I ask them to think of an artificial version of a sweet syrup you can buy in supermarkets, because an extract of fenugreek seeds is used with other ingredients to flavor this product. Sometimes I get one or two people out of 20 who guess correctly: the answer is imitation maple syrup! Once you know, it seems incredibly obvious.

WEIGHT PER TEASPOON (5 mL)

Leaf
- whole: 0.4 g

Seed
- whole: 4.5 g
- ground: 3.5 g

SUGGESTED QUANTITY PER POUND (500 g)

Leaf
- **red meats:** 2 tsp (10 mL) dried
- **white meats:** 2 tsp (10 mL) dried
- **vegetables:** 1½ tsp (7 mL) dried
- **grains and pulses:** 1 tsp (5 mL) dried
- **baked goods:** 1 tsp (5 mL) dried

Seed
- **red meats:** 1 tsp (5 mL) whole, 1½ tsp (7 mL) ground
- **white meats:** ½ tsp (2 mL) whole, ¾ tsp (3 mL) ground
- **vegetables:** ½ tsp (2 mL) whole, ¾ tsp (3 mL) ground
- **grains and pulses:** ½ tsp (2 mL) whole, ¾ tsp (3 mL) ground
- **baked goods:** ¼ tsp (1 mL) whole, ½ tsp (2 mL) ground

containers away from extremes of heat, light and humidity. Whole seeds will last for 3 or more years; once ground, the powder will last for up to 1 year.

Use

Fenugreek seeds are often included in sprouting mixes with alfalfa and mung (moong) beans (*Vigna radiata*) or are sprouted on their own for inclusion in salads. The leaves have a unique flavor that complements vegetable and fish curries and goes well in spinach, pea and potato dishes.

Fenugreek seeds are important to the food manufacturing industry, as they provide an extract for making artificial maple syrup and for use in pickles and baked goods. They are often included in curry spices, where they contribute a distinctive sharpness and slightly bitter taste, as found in fiery vindaloo curries. Exercise caution when adding fenugreek seeds to a dish—the bitterness can become overpowering, as is often noted in cheap curries that overuse this relatively inexpensive spice, to the detriment of the blend. Fenugreek seeds are an important ingredient in panch phoron (page 748), a versatile blend of seed spices that is usually fried in oil at the beginning of making a curry or added to spicy pastries and potato dishes.

Ground fenugreek seeds may be added to mayonnaise in the same way that mustard powder is often called for, as it provides a similar taste to mustard but with less heat.

Hilbeh

Hilbeh is a delicious Yemeni fenugreek, cilantro and chile relish. Fenugreek seeds are rarely the hero, and when you eat this, you'll wonder why. After soaking overnight the seeds become gelatinous, which makes for a great texture. Hilbeh can be used similarly to harissa (page 737) and can be added to soups or stews, served alongside falafel or meat kebabs, or simply used as a dip.

Makes 1 cup (250 mL)

Preparation time:
24 hours

Cooking time: none

- **Blender**

2 tbsp	fenugreek seeds	30 mL
3 cups	water, divided	750 mL
2 cups	lightly packed coriander (cilantro) leaves	500 mL
1	green finger chile, seeded and chopped	1
4	cloves garlic, minced	4
2 tbsp	freshly squeezed lemon juice	30 mL
1 tsp	fine sea salt	5 mL
1 tbsp	oil	15 mL
2 to 6 tbsp water		30 to 90 mL

1. In a small bowl, cover fenugreek seeds with 1 cup (250 mL) water and set aside for 24 hours, draining and changing the water twice (when it becomes cloudy). When ready, the seeds will be soft and jelly-like. Drain using a fine-mesh sieve.

2. In blender, combine prepared fenugreek, coriander leaves, chile and garlic. Pulse until puréed. Add lemon juice, salt and oil; pulse to combine. Add 2 tbsp (30 mL) water and pulse to form a paste (add more water if needed to reach desired consistency). The relish will keep in an airtight container in the refrigerator for up to 3 weeks.

Variation

Add 2 peeled, seeded tomatoes in Step 2 with the lemon juice, salt and oil.

Cashew Curry

This dish is a perfect example of how well spices complement the richness of cashew nuts and coconut milk. I developed this recipe after tasting it at Laxmi Vilas Palace, an old shooting lodge surrounded by mustard fields between Agra and Jaipur, India, on my mum and dad's Spice Discovery tour. It makes a wonderful vegetarian meal to share with friends. Serve as part of a banquet or alone with rice, garnished with fresh coriander (cilantro) leaves.

Makes 6 servings

Preparation time: 15 minutes

Cooking time: 1 hour

Tips

You can make the sauce a day ahead, stopping after the addition of the coconut milk in Step 2, and refrigerate in an airtight container until needed. Then simply proceed with the recipe by adding the paneer and fenugreek and warming through.

If you can't find paneer, you can substitute an equal amount of firm tofu.

- **Blender or food processor**

2 tsp	yellow curry powder	10 mL
1 tbsp	oil	15 mL
1	onion, chopped	1
2	cloves garlic, crushed	2
1 tsp	chaat masala (page 704)	5 mL
1 tsp	fine sea salt	5 mL
2½ cups	raw unsalted cashews	625 mL
1 cup	water	250 mL
1	can coconut milk (14 oz/400 mL)	1
2 lbs	paneer cheese, cut into 1-inch (2.5 cm) cubes (see Tips, left)	1 kg
½ cup	lightly packed fresh fenugreek leaves	125 mL
¼ cup	fresh coriander (cilantro) leaves	60 mL

1. In a large, dry skillet over medium heat, cook curry powder for 1 minute, until golden and aromatic. Add oil and onion and sauté until onion is soft, about 2 minutes. Add garlic and sauté for 2 minutes, until softened. Stir in chaat masala and salt. Add cashews and water, reduce heat to low and simmer until nuts are soft, about 45 minutes.

2. Transfer curry mixture to blender or food processor fitted with the metal blade; blend at high speed until smooth. Return sauce to pan over medium heat. Add coconut milk and mix well. Add paneer and fenugreek and heat until warmed through. Garnish with coriander leaves and serve.

Filé Powder

Sassafras officinalis (also known as *S. albidum, S. sassafras, Laurus albida*)

Family: Lauraceae

Other Names: ague tree, gumbo filé, red sassafras, sassafras leaf, silky sassafras, white sassafras

Flavor Group: Mild

Parts Used: leaves (as a herb)

Background

Native to the Gulf of Mexico, the sassafras tree is believed to be the first American medicinal plant to arrive in Europe. It was identified in 1564 by the Spanish medical botanist Nicolas de Monardes, whose name is used to identify a genus of plants. An essential oil extracted by steam distillation from the roots and bark has been used medicinally, as a source for yellow dye, to scent perfumes and soaps, and to flavor soft drinks. In Virginia a root beer was made from young shoots coming off the roots. Sassafras essential oil is now prohibited in food products by the US Food and Drug Administration and in many other countries because of the presence of safrole, which is believed to cause liver cancer. Sassafras powder made from the root is also banned in a number of countries and should never be taken internally.

The culinary interest in filé powder, which is safe to consume, was inspired by the Choctaw people of the southeastern United States. They dried and ground young sassafras leaves and sold them in New Orleans markets to use as a flavoring and thickening agent for soups and stews.

The Plant

Not to be confused with black sassafras (*Antherosperma moschatum*), a tree indigenous to Australia and reportedly toxic, filé powder is made from the young leaves of the American sassafras tree, a 100-foot (30 m) deciduous tree with slender branches, smooth orange-brown bark and broad oval leaves. Small greenish

Culinary Information

Combines with
- basil
- chile
- cinnamon
- coriander seed
- fennel seed
- garlic
- onion
- paprika
- parsley
- pepper
- thyme

Traditional Uses
- gumbo (as a thickening agent)

Spice Blends
- not commonly used in spice blends

yellow flowers form in 2-inch (5 cm) long clusters and develop into dark blue fruits with red stalks. The leaves may be up to 5 inches (12.5 cm) long but the smaller 2- to 3-inch (5 to 7.5 cm) leaves are used for making filé powder. Filé powder is dark green and fine-textured. The aroma is a little like dried savory and the flavor calls to mind a very mild herb mix in which thyme and marjoram notes dominate.

Buying and Storage

Filé powder is not to be confused with sassafras powder or oil, mentioned above (which is usually made from the bark or roots and has a strong, cinnamon-like medicinal taste). Although the sassafras tree contains safrole, a substance toxic to the liver, culinary use of the leaves is not deemed to be a problem. However, culinary or medicinal use of the bark or root is not recommended.

The powder made from the leaves is a dark moss green and very dry and fine. Store in airtight containers away from light, and be particularly careful to avoid humidity, as the powder absorbs moisture readily, hastening its deterioration. When stored under ideal conditions, filé powder will last for more than 1 year.

Use

The most popular use for filé powder is as a thickening agent when making gumbo.

WEIGHT PER TEASPOON (5 mL)
- **ground:** 2.6 g

SUGGESTED QUANTITY PER POUND (500 g)
- **white meats:** 2 tbsp (30 mL)
- **vegetables:** 2 tbsp (30 mL)

Gumbo

Gumbo is a famous Southern American soup/stew that combines the cuisines of regional Native, French, Spanish and African cultures. It was traditionally thickened with okra, but the Choctaw introduced filé powder in the mid 1800s. When my husband and friends went to the New Orleans Jazz Festival, they sustained themselves through the grueling festivities by eating gumbo every single day. He still reminisces about how great it tasted, and while the music at home might not be as lively, he gives this version the thumbs-up.

Makes
4 servings

Preparation time:
15 minutes

Cooking time:
45 minutes

- - - - - - - - - - - - - - - -

Tip

To make fish stock: In a stock pot over medium heat, combine 1 lb (500 g) fish bones, 1 chopped carrot, 1 chopped celery stalk, 1 chopped onion and 3 stalks fresh parsley. Add 8 cups (2 L) water and simmer for 45 minutes, removing any froth floating on top. Strain through a fine-mesh sieve, discarding solids.

2 tbsp	oil	30 mL
1 tbsp	all-purpose flour	15 mL
1	small onion, diced	1
½	green bell pepper, seeded and cut into ½-inch (1 cm) dice	½
2	cloves garlic, minced	2
2	ripe tomatoes, seeded and cut into ½-inch (1 cm) dice	2
¼ cup	tomato paste	60 mL
1 tbsp	Cajun spice mix (page 703)	15 mL
½ tsp	dried thyme	2 mL
1	bay leaf	1
½ tsp	fine sea salt	2 mL
½ tsp	freshly ground black pepper	2 mL
10	okra, sliced into small pieces	10
4 cups	fish stock (see Tip, left)	1 L
4 oz	scallops	125 g
6 oz	medium raw shrimp, peeled and deveined	175 g
6 oz	mixed seafood, such as crab, mussels, oysters or clams	175 g
1½ tsp	filé powder	7 mL
3 cups	cooked long-grain rice	750 mL

Tips

If you are using oysters or crab, add them to the pot just a few minutes before serving so they don't overcook (oysters and crab are done when they are firm and opaque).

Filé will become stringy when reheated, so add it only if you're planning to consume all the gumbo at once.

If preparing gumbo in advance, add the filé just prior to serving. The recommended quantity is 1 to 2 tsp (5 to 10 mL) per 4 cups (1 L) liquid.

1. In a large stainless-steel pot over medium heat, heat oil. Add flour and cook, stirring constantly, until a golden brown paste has formed. Stir in onion, green pepper and garlic and cook until onion is translucent. Add tomatoes and tomato paste and cook over medium heat for 5 minutes, stirring frequently, until well combined and thickened. Add Cajun spice mix, thyme, bay leaf, salt and pepper and stir well. Stir in okra and cook for 5 minutes, until tender. Pour in stock, stir well, and bring to a boil. Reduce heat and simmer for 30 minutes. Add scallops, shrimp and mixed seafood, adjusting heat so soup continues to simmer. Simmer for 5 minutes, until seafood is cooked through.

2. In a small bowl, whisk together 1 cup (250 mL) stock from prepared soup and filé powder (it will become very thick and gluey—this is normal). Add to soup and cook for 2 to 3 minutes, until thickened (see Tips, left).

3. To serve, divide cooked rice evenly among 4 deep serving bowls and ladle gumbo overtop. Serve immediately.

Variation

For a slightly milder but saltier spice mix, subsititute an equal quantity of Creole seasoning (page 709) for the Cajun spice mix.

Galangal

Alpinia galanga

Names in Other Languages

- **Arabic:** khalanjan
- **Burmese:** pa-de-gaw-gyi
- **Chinese (C):** gou leuhng geung, huhng dau kau, saan geung
- **Chinese (M):** hong dou kou, shan jiang
- **Czech:** galgan obecny, kalkan
- **Danish:** galanga
- **Dutch:** grote galanga
- **French:** grand galanga, souchet long
- **German:** Galanga, Galgant
- **Greek:** galanki
- **Indian:** kulanjan, kosht-kulinjan
- **Indonesian:** laos
- **Italian:** galanga
- **Japanese:** garanga, nankyo
- **Malay:** lengkuas
- **Portuguese:** gengibre de Laos
- **Russian:** galgant
- **Spanish:** galanga
- **Thai:** khaa, dok kha
- **Turkish:** galanga
- **Vietnamese:** rieng nep, son nai, cao luong khuong

Family: Zingiberaceae

Varieties: greater galangal (*A. galanga*), lesser galangal (*A. officinarum*), kenchur (*Kaempferia galanga*)

Other Names: galanga, Java root, Laos powder, lengkuas, Siamese ginger (greater galangal); China root, Chinese ginger, colic root, East Indian catarrh root (lesser galangal); kentjur, kencur (kenchur)

Flavor Group: Pungent

Parts Used: rhizomes (as a spice)

Background

Greater galangal (*Alpinia galanga*), the variety most used for culinary purposes, is native to Java. Lesser galangal (*A. officinarum*), which is usually used for medicinal purposes, is native to southern China. Both varieties were recorded as being in Europe in 869 CE, when galangal was listed as an article of trade from the Far East. Galangal was known to the ancient peoples of India, the Arabs gave it to their horses to energize them, and in Asia the powder was taken as snuff (the nasal-cleansing properties of galangal powder can be appreciated if an overenthusiastic sniff is taken). The old term *galingale* was used to describe both galangal and the roots of sweet flag, known as calamus (see page 132).

Culinary Information

Combines with
- allspice
- cardamom
- chile
- cinnamon and cassia
- cloves
- coriander seed
- cumin
- fenugreek seed
- ginger
- mustard
- nigella
- paprika
- tamarind
- turmeric
- zedoary

Traditional Uses
- Thai soups
- Asian curries and stir-fries
- seafood dishes
- sambal pastes

Spice Blends
- Thai red and green curry blends
- rendang curry powder
- laksa spice mixes
- ras el hanout

The Plants

The different varieties of galangal are all members of the ginger family (Zingiberaceae), which is evident from the appearance of these tropical plants, with their long, bladelike green leaves and ginger-like rhizomes.

Greater galangal, the variety used most in cooking, grows to around 6 feet (2 m) tall and has greenish white orchid-shaped flowers with dark red veined tips. The red berries contain seeds that are sometimes substituted for cardamom. The knobbly underground root-bearing stems (rhizomes) have a thin orange-brown skin with lighter and darker "tiger stripe" rings; the creamy pale yellow flesh is on the inside of the rhizome.

The aroma of greater galangal is reminiscent of ginger, with a sharp, sinus-penetrating perfume and similarly biting hot, clean taste. The powder is creamy beige; its texture is coarse, fluffy and sometimes fibrous.

Lesser galangal grows to around 3 feet (1 m) tall, the rhizomes are orange-red to rusty brown with similar stripes, and the flesh is pale brown. This variety has medicinal applications and, aside from limited use in Malaysian and Indonesian recipes, is seldom used in cooking.

A Nice Alternative

Kenchur powder is an interesting alternative to galangal when a milder yet still aromatic taste is desired.

Other Varieties

Kenchur (*Kaempferia galanga*) looks like lesser galangal with its reddish brown skin. However, the inside flesh is not as fibrous. When ground it becomes a creamy white powder with a sweet perfumed aroma reminiscent of orris root powder. Kenchur has a milder taste than greater galangal and very little heat.

Processing

To produce galangal and kenchur powders, the small rootlets are removed from the rhizomes. Some of the outer

skin is scraped off to hasten drying (usually in the sun), which takes a few days. Prior to grinding, the rhizomes are polished. This involves tumbling them in a mesh drum to remove most of the remaining rootlets and skin.

Buying and Storage

Fresh rhizomes of greater galangal are readily available from most Asian markets and other specialty produce merchants. They look like ginger but are encircled by stripes, which are larger and not as orange as the stripes encircling fresh turmeric.

Fresh rhizomes should be plump, firm and clean. Store in an open container in the cupboard the way you keep fresh ginger, onions and garlic; it will keep for up to 1 week. Galangal rhizomes may also be frozen whole; they should be used within 3 months.

Dried galangal slices can usually be purchased from Asian and specialty spice shops. They will keep their flavor for between 2 and 3 years when stored in an airtight container in a cool, dry place.

Purchase ground galangal and kenchur in small quantities. The powder will lose its flavor within about 12 months of grinding. Store in the same way as other ground spices.

Use

Galangal is an important ingredient in many Southeast Asian dishes and is particularly associated with Thai food. Freshly grated or sliced, galangal is found, along with lemongrass and makrut lime leaves, in the popular hot-and-sour soups of Thailand, such as *tom yum kung*.

To prepare fresh galangal for cooking, use a knife to scrape or cut off the skin. Then, depending on the recipe instructions, slice thinly or use a kitchen rasp (such as a Microplane) to finely grate the rhizome.

The powder is included in Thai green and red curries and also features in the cooking of China, Malaysia, Singapore and Indonesia. In a similar way to ginger, the tangy, aromatic flavor of galangal helps to neutralize overly fishy flavors, so it is often used in seafood recipes. Galangal powder also features in sambal, a fiery Asian paste made with chiles, dried shrimp and tamarind water, and is an ingredient in the exotic Moroccan spice blend ras el hanout.

WEIGHT PER TEASPOON (5 mL)
- whole average dried slice: 2.5 g
- ground: 2.3 g

SUGGESTED QUANTITY PER POUND (500 g)
- red meats: 1½ tsp (7 mL) ground
- white meats: 1 tsp (5 mL) ground
- vegetables: 1 tsp (5 mL) ground
- grains and pulses: 1 tsp (5 mL) ground
- baked goods: ½ tsp (2 mL) ground

Shiitake and Galangal Soup

This Thai soup is incredibly tasty and satisfying, and easy to make. The galangal helps bind together the sweet, sour, salty and bitter flavors of the soup.

Makes 4 small servings

Preparation time:
10 minutes

Cooking time:
50 minutes

Tips

Makrut lime leaves are sometimes called "kaffir" lime leaves and can be found fresh, frozen or dried at Asian grocery stores.

If fresh galangal is not available, add 10 dried slices to the broth in Step 2 and cook for an additional 30 minutes.

Coriander roots hold an incredible amount of flavor. Unfortunately they are often cut off before the bunches are sold, in which case double the amount of stems can be used. The roots should be scraped of dirt and washed before chopping.

If fresh shiitake mushrooms are not available, you can substitute an equal amount of dried. You can also use fresh oyster mushrooms instead.

- **Mortar and pestle**

2½ cups	chicken broth	625 mL
1	can (14 oz/400 mL) coconut milk	1
1	6-inch (15 cm) piece fresh galangal, sliced into 10 equal pieces	1
3	fresh coriander roots (see Tips, left)	3
2	shallots, quartered	2
2	makrut lime leaves, halved (see Tips, left)	2
1	stalk lemongrass, coarsely chopped	1
1	clove garlic, halved	1
1	red finger chile, chopped	1
1 tbsp	palm sugar or packed light brown sugar	15 mL
1 cup	fresh shiitake mushrooms (see Tips, left)	250 mL
2 tbsp	fish sauce (nam pla)	30 mL
1 tbsp	freshly squeezed lime juice (approx.)	15 mL

1. In a large saucepan over medium heat, combine broth and coconut milk and bring to a simmer.

2. Meanwhile, using mortar and pestle, vigorously pound galangal, coriander roots, shallots, lime leaves, lemongrass, garlic, chile and sugar into a rough paste. Add spice paste to broth mixture. Bring soup to a boil, then reduce heat and simmer gently for 30 minutes.

3. Using a fine-mesh sieve, strain soup into a bowl (discard solids). Return broth to the pan and add mushrooms, fish sauce and lime juice to taste (you may not need all of it). Serve immediately.

Nasi Goreng

This Indonesian fried rice dish is a national treasure. Recipes vary a lot, as it's traditionally made from leftover rice, meat and vegetables. It's a fantastic standby dish and makes an excellent Sunday night supper in front of the television.

Makes 6 to 8 servings

Preparation time:
15 minutes

Cooking time:
10 minutes

Tips

If not using a wok, cook this dish in a very large skillet, or divide the ingredients in half and cook them in two batches.

To make nasi goreng spice blend: In a bowl, combine 1 tbsp (15 mL) ground red Kashmiri chile, 2 tsp (10 mL) garlic powder, 2 tsp (10 mL) medium-hot chile flakes, 1 tsp (5 mL) granulated sugar, 1 tsp (5 mL) fine sea salt, ½ tsp (2 mL) amchur powder, ½ tsp (2 mL) ground galangal and ¼ tsp (1 mL) ground ginger. Stir well. This recipe makes 10 tsp (50 mL). Store the leftover portion in an airtight container and use to make another nasi goreng.

- **Wok (see Tips, left)**

1 tbsp	oil, divided	15 mL
3	eggs, beaten	3
4 cups	cold cooked long-grain rice	1 L
1½ tbsp	nasi goreng spice blend (see Tips, left)	22 mL
1 cup	green peas, fresh or frozen	250 mL
1	cooked chicken breast (5 to 7 oz/150 to 210 g), shredded, or 1 cup (250 mL) shredded leftover roast chicken	1
8	green onions, white and green parts, finely sliced	8
6 oz	cooked small shrimp, peeled and deveined	175 g
2 tbsp	soy sauce	30 mL
2 tbsp	tomato sauce	30 mL
1 tbsp	fish sauce (nam pla)	15 mL
	Sea salt and freshly ground black pepper	
1 cup	coriander (cilantro) leaves	250 mL
2	limes, quartered	2

1. In wok over medium-high heat, heat 1 tsp (5 ml) oil. Pour in eggs and cook, lifting and swirling wok to get as thin a covering of egg as possible, until completely set, 2 to 3 minutes. Slide egg onto a chopping board and chop roughly; set aside.

2. In same wok over high heat, heat remaining oil. Add rice and nasi goreng spice and stir-fry for 2 minutes, until grains are broken up and coated. Add peas, chicken, green onions, shrimp, soy sauce, tomato sauce and fish sauce and cook, stirring constantly, until well combined and heated through. Stir in reserved egg pieces. Season with salt and pepper to taste. Serve garnished with coriander leaves and lime wedges.

Variations

The eggs are often fried and placed on top when serving. You can also stir them through the rice at the end of Step 2 for a lovely sticky dish.

Garlic

Allium sativum (also known as *A. controversum, A. longicuspis, A. ophioscorodon, A. porrum*)

Names in Other Languages

- **Arabic:** tsoum
- **Burmese:** chyet-thon-phew
- **Chinese (C):** suen tau
- **Chinese (M):** da suan
- **Czech:** cesnek
- **Danish:** hvidlog
- **Dutch:** knoflook
- **French:** ail
- **German:** Knoblauch
- **Greek:** skordo
- **Indian:** lasan, lashuna
- **Indonesian:** bawang putih
- **Italian:** aglio
- **Japanese:** ninniku
- **Korean:** ma neul
- **Malay:** bawang puteh
- **Norwegian:** hvitlok
- **Philippino:** bawang
- **Portuguese:** alho
- **Russian:** chesnok
- **Spanish:** ajo
- **Sri Lankan:** sudu lunu
- **Swedish:** vitlok
- **Thai:** kratiem
- **Turkish:** sarmisak
- **Vietnamese:** toi

Family: Alliaceae

Varieties: elephant garlic (*A. ampeloprasum*), serpent garlic (*A. sativum ophioscorodon*), society garlic (*Tulbaghia violacea*, also known as *T. alliacea*), wild garlic (*A. ursinum*)

Other Names: clown's treacle, poor man's treacle, stinking rose

Flavor Group: Pungent

Parts Used: bulbs and scapes (as a herb)

Background

Garlic has been around for so long the precise details of its origins are obscure. It is thought to have originated in southeastern Siberia and spread to the Mediterranean region, where it became naturalized. There is a firm belief that it was grown in India, China and Egypt before recorded history. Garlic is among the oldest of known cultivated plants—several bulbs were found in the tomb of the Egyptian pharoah Tutankhamun, dating from 1358 BCE. The builders of the pyramids ate it regularly, and the Roman physician Hippocrates noted its medicinal value in 400 BCE. Reference is made to garlic in the Old Testament, in Islamic, Roman and Greek literature and in the Talmud. Although it was

Culinary Information

Combines with

Most culinary herbs and spices, but has a special affinity with

- ajowan
- bay leaf
- caraway
- chives
- coriander (leaf and seed)
- curry leaf
- fennel (fronds and seed)
- makrut lime leaf
- kokam
- mustard
- oregano
- parsley
- pepper
- rosemary
- sage
- tarragon
- thyme
- Vietnamese mint

Traditional Uses

- aïoli
- practically every savory dish imaginable

Spice Blends

- barbecue spices
- Cajun spices
- chermoula
- curry powders
- harissa paste mixes
- Italian herb blends
- laksa spice blends
- seasoning mixes for red and white meats

a common food of the Roman laborer, garlic was largely scorned by the upper classes of the day, who considered its consumption a sign of vulgarity. Nonetheless, it was given to Roman soldiers before going into battle to give them courage—no doubt a touch of "garlic breath" helped them vanquish their barbarian enemies.

Introduced to England by the Romans, garlic began to appear in old English records of plants from the 10th century on. Garlic is mentioned—not always with favorable connotations because of its distinctive aroma—in the writings of Chaucer and Shakespeare. Its many health-giving properties have been well documented: Louis Pasteur reported on its antibacterial activity in 1858, and raw garlic juice was used as a field dressing in the trenches during the First World War. The common names "clown's treacle" and "poor man's treacle" are references to garlic's status as a home cure, a "treacle" being an antidote to poison, stings and bites. Even in the 21st century, garlic is used for its microbiological stability as a preservation aid in food manufacturing, and it is prescribed for a wide range of ailments by reputable health practitioners.

The Plant

Garlic belongs to the same family as onions, chives, leeks and shallots (Alliaceae). It is a hardy perennial with long, flat, solid spear-shaped gray-green leaves 12 inches (30 cm) long and 1 inch (2.5 cm) wide. The name *garlic* derives from the Anglo-Saxon word *garleac*: *gar* meaning "spear" and *leac*, "plant." The most attention-getting part of a garlic plant is its dramatic top-heavy flower, comprising a compact collection of mauve-tinted white petals that rise above the leaves on a tall, rodlike stalk.

The most useful part of garlic is the bulb, which lies beneath the ground. Garlic bulbs may be white- or pink-skinned and vary enormously in size, from the small Asian ones to giant strains grown in California. The garlic bulb is a round, lumpy collection of bulblets encased in a flaky parchment-like outer skin; it looks like tightly clenched knuckles wrapped in tissue paper. The bulblets—commonly called cloves, from the word *cleave*, meaning to split along the grain or separate by dividing—are compacted within the bulb (often called a head) and separated by scaly membranes. Although the garlic clove in its protective husk emits no smell, when it is crushed or peeled, the enzymes within are rapidly activated, producing allicin, which breaks down to become allyl disulfide; the resulting aroma is strong, sulfurous and lingering.

Raw garlic has a sharp, acrid taste and gives a sensation of heat to the palate. Cooked garlic has a sweeter flavor and is not as overpowering as some would have you believe.

Dried garlic is pale yellow and sold either in slices $1/3$ to $1/2$ inch (8 to 10 mm) long, in granules $1/16$ inch (2 mm) in diameter, or as a fine powder.

Garlic scapes are 18-inch (45 cm) flower stalks that are usually gathered from hard-neck garlic (*A. ophioscorodon*). In the past, many gardeners removed them, because a plant with a profusion of curling snakelike scapes will produce smaller garlic bulbs. In recent years, however, they have become a popular culinary delicacy. They have a distinctive garlicky taste that's slightly milder than the bulbs.

Black Garlic

Black garlic is produced by aging raw garlic bulbs in a fermenting oven for about a month at constant levels of heat and humidity. During this time, sugars and amino acids are activated to produce melanoidin, which makes the cloves inside the bulb turn black. The result is a dark, soft, balsamic and tamarind-like paste that can be squeezed from each clove. My favorite way to eat black garlic is with cheese; it also complements pasta, risotto and mushrooms in much the same way as truffles do.

Garlic Breath, Anyone?

They say that one reeks less of garlic when it is consumed with red wine (an excellent idea, in my opinion) and that eating parsley after garlic reduces its lingering effect on the breath. I have also found that chewing a few fennel seeds works particularly well (although the red wine treatment is the most appealing). As an increasing percentage of the population is eating moderate amounts of garlic regularly, sensitivity to garlic breath is less pronounced these days.

Other Varieties

Elephant garlic (*Allium ampeloprasum*) is more closely related to the leek than to standard garlic. Although it has very large bulbs, the flavor is somewhat underwhelming, so it is not really a substitute for true garlic. **Serpent garlic** (*A. sativum ophioscorodon*) is the variety most often propagated to produce garlic scapes, elongated flower stalks that do not actually produce flowers. **Society garlic** (*Tulbaghia violacea*) is a plant with small, star-shaped six-petaled mauve flowers, called society garlic because it was reputed not to produce garlic breath and thus was tolerable in polite society. *Tulbaghia* is not a true garlic, and these days health professionals recommend against eating it. **Wild garlic** (*A. ursinum*) is possibly the most unusual of the 20 or so varieties of plants called garlic even if they are not alliums. Also called "bear's garlic," it is found in much of Europe and western Asia. It has broad leaves that can be eaten, but the bulb is small and considered to be fiddly to harvest, making it less popular with herb and vegetable gardeners.

Processing

The global popularity of garlic has created demand for it in all kinds of processed forms, from fresh refrigerated to preserved garlic in jars and various forms of dehydrated garlic flakes, granules and powders. Dried garlic is the most common because it is easily transported and stored and bears a pleasantly close resemblance to fresh garlic when used in cooking. To produce garlic flakes and granules, the cloves are peeled and either sliced or diced before being passed through a dehydrator, which is warm enough to bring down the moisture content to around 6.75% but not so hot as to drive off the flavor.

Garlic powder is made in one of two ways. One is to grind dried sliced garlic, which typically attracts moisture (technically this is referred to as being hygroscopic), so starch is usually added to prevent it from becoming sticky. The other method involves making a paste from freshly processed garlic that is then spray-dried in the same way instant coffee is made. The result is a powder that dissolves readily on cooking, and for those on gluten-free diets it has the benefit of being free of added wheat starch.

Garlic pastes in jars are made from crushed garlic mixed with either oil or a food acid such as lemon juice or vinegar to achieve preservation. Sometimes these pastes contain a percentage of reconstituted dehydrated garlic, which gives them a deeper yellow color.

Buying and Storage

When buying fresh garlic, look for heads that hold together firmly. The cloves should be hard and showing no signs of shrinking away from the papery sheath. Upon peeling, any spots of discoloration are best cut out, as they will have a rank flavor. Garlic stores best when the heads are kept intact, as separated cloves lose their flavor more rapidly. Keep complete heads in an open container in a cool, dark place away from humidity. Fresh garlic should not be stored in the refrigerator, as it has a tendency to sprout.

Garlic scapes are available from produce markets for a short time in late spring. They should be fresh and tender. Garlic scapes that have grown too large and firm will be somewhat hotter and more fibrous than young ones.

Garlic pastes will usually bear the instruction "refrigerate after opening," which is essential, because even though the food acids and garlic's natural antibacterial qualities aid preservation, prolonged exposure to normal temperatures after removing the lid will cause mold to grow.

All forms of dried garlic are readily available and are best purchased in some sort of high-barrier packaging such as laminated plastic, foil or glass. Never buy garlic powder that looks lumpy; this indicates it has absorbed extra moisture and the flavor will have deteriorated. Always store dried garlic in an airtight container in a cool, dark place. Be particularly careful to avoid extreme humidity; never shake the contents out of the package while holding it over a steaming pot. With this level of care, your dried garlic will last for at least 1 year and maybe 2.

Use

Garlic scapes will vary in flavor strength depending on size. Tender young shoots may be chopped into salads, used as a garnish in the same manner as chives, and sautéed for adding to pasta, omelets and scrambled eggs.

When it comes to using garlic in any form, it is tempting to be glib and ask, "Is there a savory dish that garlic is *not* used in?" But that would be doing this wonderful herb a terrible disservice. There *is* hardly any dish that is not improved by the flavor of garlic, and although its pungency tends to be frowned upon by nonusers, when everyone else is indulging in garlic, its telltale lingering on the breath is barely noticeable among fellow garlicophiles.

When cooked, garlic develops a more moderate and slightly sweeter taste than when it is raw, a transition most noticeable when a whole head is placed on the barbecue to cook slowly for about 30 minutes. The creamy beige flesh inside has none of the hot pungency of raw garlic. It is delicious scooped out of the crisp burnt casing and spread on the accompanying barbecued meats and vegetables (I recommend slices of eggplant).

Garlic need not dominate a dish. It is often surprising the extent to which a small amount can heighten the taste of many foods, including delicate vegetables, and how it can balance with other flavors, be they sweet, pungent or hot. Garlic is found in most cuisines, especially Mediterranean, Indian, Asian and Mexican, and is regularly applied to the manufacture of commercial pâtés, terrines and sausages. Garlic features in many prepared herb and spice blends, such as Italian herbs, pizza seasoning, garlic salt and practically every spice mix designed to sprinkle over white or red meats. It is an ingredient in fiery Tunisian harissa paste and adds depth of character to Moroccan chermoula and Yemeni zhug.

To impart a mild garlic flavor to a salad, rub the inside of the bowl with a cut clove of garlic. This method can also be used on the inside of a pot before making a soup or stew, and lamb or beef roasts and poultry may be similarly rubbed with a cut garlic clove before cooking.

Garlic butter, flavored with freshly crushed garlic, goes well with seafood, as does garlic oil, made by steeping slices of fresh garlic in olive oil. Aïoli, the very rich and thick garlic mayonnaise from the south of France, is a versatile sauce that complements globe artichokes, avocados, asparagus, fish, chicken and snails. A boned leg of lamb stuffed with garlic, rosemary, peppers, apricots and crushed pistachio nuts prior to roasting is one of my favorites.

Some cooks will slice a peeled garlic clove in half and remove the thin, pale green beginnings of the shoot in the center. Depending on how developed the shoot is, it can (when quite green) make the garlic somewhat bitter.

WEIGHT PER TEASPOON (5 mL)

- Whole average fresh clove: 5 g
- Ground dehydrated powder: 4.6 g

SUGGESTED QUANTITY PER POUND (500 g)

- **red meats:** 3 to 4 fresh cloves, 2 tsp (10 mL) powder
- **white meats:** 3 to 4 fresh cloves, 2 tsp (10 mL) powder
- **vegetables:** 2 to 3 fresh cloves, 1½ tsp (7 mL) powder
- **grains and pulses:** 2 to 3 fresh cloves, 1½ tsp (7 mL) powder
- **baked goods:** 2 to 3 fresh cloves, 1½ tsp (7 mL) powder

Garlic Butter

Garlic butter is a versatile butter—perfect for garlic bread and adding to seafood, meat or vegetables before or after grilling—and easy to make. The amount of garlic can be adjusted to one's personal taste, and choosing fresh garlic from a farmer's market will improve the result dramatically.

Makes ½ cup (125 mL)

Preparation time:
10 minutes
Cooking time: none

½ cup	good-quality butter, at room temperature	125 mL
1 to 2	cloves garlic, finely minced	1 to 2
Pinch	fine sea salt	Pinch

1. Using a spoon or the paddle of a stand mixer, beat butter in a mixing bowl until soft. Add garlic and salt and mix well. Spread a large square of plastic wrap on a clean work surface and mound butter in the middle. Tightly wrap butter into a cylinder and refrigerate. The garlic butter will keep in the refrigerator for up to 3 days or in the freezer for up to 3 months. To use, simply slice off the required amount.

Variation

Add 1 tsp (5 mL) Italian herbs (page 740) along with the garlic and salt.

Superfood Salad

Scapes are often the overlooked part of a garlic plant. They are very versatile, lending their garlic flavor to just about any dish. Whenever I'm feeling in need of something virtuous yet tasty, this is my first stop.

Makes 6 servings

Preparation time:
 40 minutes, plus
 soaking overnight
Cooking time:
 5 minutes

Tips

To cook quinoa: Add quinoa to a large saucepan of cold salted water. Bring to a boil, reduce heat and simmer for 10 minutes or until germ separates from seeds (it will look like they have split open, revealing a small white particle, which is the germ). Using a fine-mesh sieve, drain and rinse quinoa under cold running water. Drain well.

To cook mung beans: Drain and rinse soaked beans, then add to a large saucepan of cold salted water. Bring to a boil, reduce heat and simmer for 10 minutes, until tender.

4 oz	mung beans, soaked overnight, cooked and drained (see Tips, left)	125 g
4 oz	quinoa, cooked and drained (see Tips, left)	125 g
4 oz	baby button mushrooms, finely sliced	125 g
4 oz	snow peas, sliced diagonally	125 g
1	large avocado, diced	1
5	garlic scapes, finely sliced	5
¾ cup	freshly squeezed lemon juice	175 mL
⅔ cup	extra virgin olive oil	150 mL
2 tbsp	soy sauce	30 mL
Pinch	fine sea salt and freshly ground black pepper	Pinch
2 tbsp	toasted sesame seeds	30 mL
1 tbsp	pickled red ginger, drained	15 mL

1. In a large bowl, combine mung beans, quinoa, mushrooms, snow peas, avocado and scapes.
2. In a small bowl, whisk together lemon juice, oil and soy sauce. Add to salad and toss to combine. Season with salt and pepper to taste. Serve topped with sesame seeds and pickled ginger.

Variation

For a more substantial salad, add 1 cup (250 mL) flaked cooked trout or salmon.

G

Chicken with 40 Cloves of Garlic

It is worth making this dish purely for the aroma it creates in the house. The quality of both your garlic and your chicken is really important, so find the very best to make this dish the ultimate roast chicken. There is so much pleasure in squeezing out the soft, sweet roasted whole garlic cloves alongside the chicken. Serve with Butternut Squash and Chickpea Salad (page 597), Fattoush (page 618) or Mixed Vegetable Bake (page 673).

Makes 6 servings

Preparation time:
5 minutes

Cooking time: 1 hour, 50 minutes

Tip

Don't discard the wonderful garlic-infused pan juices. Strain into a jar and store in the refrigerator for use in other dishes and dressings.

• **Preheat oven to 350°F (180°C)**

1	large chicken	1
	Fine sea salt	
½ cup	oil, divided	125 mL
40	cloves garlic, unpeeled, divided	40
1	bunch fresh thyme, divided	1
4	fresh bay leaves, divided	4
1	lemon, sliced, divided	1
1	onion, sliced, divided	1

1. Rub chicken with about 1 tbsp (15 mL) of the oil and season with salt, to taste.

2. In a large cast-iron casserole dish or Dutch oven (big enough to fit the chicken whole), combine remaining oil, 30 cloves of garlic, and half each of the thyme, bay leaves, lemon and onion.

3. Stuff chicken with remaining garlic, thyme, bay leaves, lemon and onion. Arrange breast side down in casserole dish on top of garlic cloves. Roast, uncovered, in preheated oven for 45 minutes. Remove from oven and carefully turn chicken over (breast side up). Baste generously with pan juices and return to oven for a further 45 minutes.

4. Remove chicken from oven and increase heat to 400°F (200°C). When oven reaches that temperature, baste chicken and roast for another 15 to 20 minutes or until skin is browned and juices run clear when a skewer is inserted near leg. Transfer to a large platter and serve with garlic cloves alongside.

Wild Garlic and Ricotta Gnocchi

The first time I encountered wild garlic was when my husband and I were walking through the wooded South Downs in England. An unmistakable garlic aroma surrounded me and I suddenly realized the entire undergrowth was wild garlic! I gathered some up and carried home as much as I could to use for cooking. It has since become much more popular and can now be found at many farmers' markets in the spring.

**Makes
4 servings**

Preparation time:
15 minutes

Cooking time:
25 minutes

Tips

If you have bought a whole bunch of wild garlic, add the extra leaves to the pan in Step 4.

If you can't find wild garlic, you can substitute an equal amount of wild arugula.

Type 00 pasta flour is a finely milled white flour. All-purpose flour can be substituted in this recipe, but ensure that it is well sifted beforehand.

2 cups	lightly packed wild garlic leaves, finely chopped	500 mL
2 cups	ricotta cheese	500 mL
¼ cup	grated Parmesan cheese	60 mL
1	egg	1
1 cup	type 00 pasta flour, plus extra for rolling (see Tips, left)	250 mL
	Sea salt and freshly ground black pepper	
1 tbsp	olive oil	15 mL
12 oz	cherry or pomodorino tomatoes	375 g
	Wild garlic flowers, optional	

1. In a bowl, combine garlic leaves, ricotta, Parmesan and egg. Stir in flour, a little at a time, until dough reaches a consistency similar to mashed potatoes. Season with salt and pepper to taste.

2. Place one-quarter of the dough on a clean, well-floured work surface. With floured hands, using your palms, gently roll dough into a long, thin log about 1 inch (2.5 cm) in diameter. Using a floured knife, cut dough into 1-inch (2.5 cm) pieces. Repeat with remaining mixture.

3. In a large pot of boiling salted water, working in batches, cook gnocchi for 3 to 5 minutes (gnocchi are cooked when they float to the surface). Using a slotted spoon, transfer cooked gnocchi to a tray or plate lined with plastic wrap. (Gnocchi can be made ahead up to this point and covered and refrigerated for up to 1 day.)

4. In a large skillet over medium heat, heat oil. Add tomatoes and prepared gnocchi and cook, stirring often, for about 5 minutes, until tomatoes burst open a little and gnocchi are browned. Serve garnished with wild garlic flowers (if using).

G

Ginger

Zingiber officinale

Names in Other Languages

- **Arabic:** zanjabil
- **Burmese:** gin
- **Chinese (C):** saang geung (fresh), geung (dry)
- **Chinese (M):** sheng jiang (fresh), jiang (dry)
- **Czech:** zazvor
- **Danish:** ingefaer
- **Dutch:** gember
- **Finnish:** inkivaari
- **French:** gingembre
- **German:** Ingwer
- **Greek:** piperoriza
- **Indian:** adrak (fresh), sonth (dry)
- **Indonesian:** aliah
- **Italian:** zenzero
- **Japanese:** shoga
- **Malay:** halia
- **Portuguese:** gengibre
- **Russian:** imbir
- **Spanish:** jengibre
- **Sri Lankan:** inguru
- **Swedish:** ingefara
- **Thai:** khing
- **Turkish:** zencefil
- **Vietnamese:** gung

Family: Zingiberaceae

Varieties: torch ginger (*Etlingera elatoir,* also known as *Nicolaia alatior* and *N. speciosa*)

Other Names: gingerroot, ginger stems

Flavor Group: Pungent

Parts Used: rhizomes (as a spice), flowers (as a herb)

Background

The origins of ginger are hazy. Although it is grown in many tropical climates where the inhabitants claim it as their own, it is not known to occur in a genuinely wild state anywhere in the world. Nonetheless, references to its cultivation in both China and India date back to antiquity, suggesting that it may have originated somewhere between northern India and eastern Asia.

Ginger is one of the oldest Asian spices to have reached southeastern Europe. One tale recounts how around 2400 BCE a baker on the island of Rhodes, near Greece, made the first gingerbread. In the fifth century BCE, Persian

Culinary Information

Combines with

- allspice
- cardamom
- chile
- cinnamon and cassia
- cloves
- coriander (leaf and seed)
- cumin
- curry leaf
- fennel seed
- galangal
- lemongrass
- lemon myrtle
- makrut lime leaf
- paprika
- star anise
- turmeric

Traditional Uses

- cakes
- pastries and cookies
- pumpkin scones
- baked squash (sprinkle on before cooking)
- all curries
- Asian stir-fries
- red meats (has a tenderizing effect)
- seafood (counters fishy flavors)

Spice Blends

- barbecue seasoning mixes
- berbere
- Chinese master stocks
- Jamaican jerk spices
- red and green curry spice blends
- curry powders
- mixed spice/pumpkin pie spice/apple pie spice
- tandoori seasonings
- ras el hanout
- quatre épices

Not the Real Thing

There are a number of plants of the Zingiberaceae family that look similar to ginger and may a have a faint ginger aroma. These usually go by the name "wild ginger," but that is somewhat of a misnomer, as they are not wild versions of culinary ginger.

trade missions sent to India by King Darius brought back ginger. The beneficial properties of ginger were mentioned by Confucius (551 to 479 BCE), and in the first century CE the Greek physician Dioscorides similarly extolled its virtues in his *Materia Medica*. Arab traders carried ginger to Greece and Rome, keeping secret their sources of supply.

In the second century CE, ginger was included in the list of imports to Alexandria that were subject to Roman customs taxes. Ginger is mentioned in the Koran, indicating that those virtuous enough to reach Paradise will not be denied the pleasure of ginger-flavored water. Ginger was known in Germany and France in the ninth century, and in England in the 11th century. By the 14th century, ginger was noted as the most common spice in Britain after pepper. Henry VIII noted its medicinal powers and recommended it. Later, gingerbread became a favorite confection of Queen Elizabeth I.

Because ginger could be readily transported growing in pots aboard vessels, the living rhizomes were traded extensively during the Middle Ages. As a result, ginger was transplanted to many areas. Just as the Arabs had taken ginger from India to East Africa in the 13th century, the

Spanish established plantations in Jamaica to grow ginger in the 16th century. By 1547 more than 1,000 tons of ginger were said to have been exported from Jamaica to Spain. Around the same time the Portuguese also established ginger in West Africa. In the Swiss city of Basel, the street where the spice traders conducted their business was called Imbergasse, which means "ginger alley."

The Plant

Ginger is a lush-looking tropical perennial with erect leafy shoots about $1/4$ inch (5 mm) in diameter that grow up to 4 feet (1.2 m) in height. Lance-shaped leafy shoots, which die down annually, sprout laterally from the reedlike stem. The separate flower stem rises directly from the rootstock,

Travels in the Spice Trade

In January 1997 Liz and I spent a month in the South Indian state of Kerala, visiting a number of spice farms and processing facilities. One of our most memorable experiences was a journey to the Kothamangalam area, 28 miles (45 km) north of the city of Cochin, where we visited a ginger-drying facility. After an uncomfortable ride we arrived at a timeless scene spread out over about 12 acres (5 ha) of rocky hillside. Hundreds of farmers, each of whom had leased a small section of the smooth rock-face, were spreading out their harvest of ginger to dry under the burning sun. Small groups were gathered in twos and threes under makeshift shelters of cloth draped over sticks. Their job was to roughly scrape the skin off both sides of the rhizomes to speed up drying. They used a steel sickle held between their feet, so both hands could be used to scrape the ginger against the blade.

Wandering among these people, who were preparing ginger as has been done for centuries, we really did feel as though we had travelled back in time. There was not a mechanical device in sight. The fundamental simplicity was really brought home when we saw a couple of young men cleaning the dried rhizomes. They were standing facing each other, holding both ends of a burlap sack that contained about 6 pounds (3 kg) of dried ginger, vigorously flapping it up and down with alternating arm movements like someone flipping sand from a beach towel. After a few minutes of furious agitation, during which the abrasion against the other rhizomes partially cleaned them, the man holding the open end of the sack let it go. The contents fell onto the ground, revealing a pile of relatively clean ginger surrounded by flaky, easily winnowed-away waste.

We also saw a ginger- and turmeric-cleaning method that was even more charming. Like beached sailors, two men were seated opposite each other in a "boat" about the size of a small dinghy. They had burlap sacking wrapped around their feet, and in between them was a pile of ginger. They were pushing their feet wildly back and forth against each other, the way young children do when facing each other in the bathtub. The result: ginger again cleaned by abrasion.

ending in an oblong spike from which white or yellow blossoms with a purple-speckled lip grow.

Gingerroot, as we commonly call it (the correct term is *rhizome*), is the knobbly section of the root system that grows and spreads underground with tuberous joints. These are referred to in the trade as "races" or—more often and appropriately—"hands," because of their knuckled shape, which resembles an arthritic human hand. The smaller branches of the rhizome are, logically enough, called "fingers." Ginger rhizomes are encircled by scales that form a rough-looking beige skin covering the pale flesh.

The aroma and flavor of ginger may vary depending on the type of cultivar it comes from, the stage at which it is harvested, and the region in which it was grown. Ginger rhizomes can generally be described as having a sweet, pungent aroma and a lemony freshness. The flavor is similarly tangy, sweet, spicy and warm to hot, depending on when it was harvested. To a large degree, early-harvested ginger rhizomes are sweet and tender while later-harvested rhizomes are more fibrous and pungent.

Other Varieties

The ginger flower of Asian culinary use comes from a plant, also from the Zingiberaceae family, known as **torch ginger** (*Etlingera elatior*). While the flower is highly decorative, it is the flower buds that are used in recipes: chopped and served raw as a vegetable or as an ingredient in Nonya cuisine dishes such as laksa. Torch ginger is added to Indonesian, Malay and Thai dishes for its sourness. The flavor is similar to a combination of Vietnamese mint (page 664) and ginger.

Processing

Ginger is processed in two main ways: preserving (in brine or syrup or crystallized to produce stem ginger, for example) and drying (to produce dried sliced ginger or ginger powder).

Preserved Ginger

Preserved or crystallized ginger made from young rhizomes is often called "stem ginger." These forms are particularly sweet because of the sugar used in processing. Like fresh ginger, they may also be mild or hot.

To make preserved ginger, the immature rhizomes (sweeter and less fibrous than mature ones) are harvested and washed and the roots are trimmed. The clean ginger is peeled, cut to

Although consumers won't be aware which grade their ground ginger was produced from, the grading system gives you a very good idea as to why the quality of a spice such as ginger powder can vary so greatly.

the desired shape and sorted into the following three grades for uniformity:

- *First grade*: "young stem" and "choice selected stem" ginger from the ends or fingers of the rhizomes, cut into oval pieces about 1$\frac{1}{2}$ inches (4 cm) long.
- *Second grade*: fingers, which are smaller, oblong pieces.
- *Third grade*: "cargo ginger," which is made from the main stem of the rhizome and sub-graded into three levels determined by size.

The graded pieces are then placed in barrels, salted and covered for 24 hours, after which the liquid that has formed is drained off. A fresh lot of salt is then added, this time with vinegar, and the ginger is left to pickle for seven days. At this stage in the process it is referred to as "ginger preserved in brine" or "salted ginger." Most of it will be further preserved with sugar to make "ginger in syrup" or "dry" and "crystallized" ginger.

To make ginger in syrup, salted ginger is removed from the brine, washed, and soaked in cold water, which is changed several times over two days. Then the washed ginger is boiled in water for 10 minutes. Following that it is boiled in sugar syrup twice, until well impregnated with sugar. Dry or crystallized ginger is made by subjecting the ginger in syrup to a third boil, to evaporate more water. The pieces are then drained, dried and dusted with sugar to make absolutely delicious morsels.

Dried Ginger

Ginger powder (ground ginger) lacks the fresh, volatile aroma of the living rhizomes but retains a spicy, rich fragrance and the characteristic ginger taste.

In the spice trade, dried ginger is sold in seven grades that indicate how it has been prepared prior to grinding.

- "Peeled," "scraped" or "uncoated" ginger refers to whole rhizomes from which the outer skin has been cleanly removed without damaging the underlying tissue. As a result, this grade has the best flavor.
- "Rough scraped" ginger, the second-best grade, has had the skin partially removed—only from the flat sides—to accelerate drying.
- "Unpeeled" or "coated" ginger rhizomes have been dried intact, with the skin still on.

Taste First

Because the pungency of ginger powder can vary quite considerably, before adding it to a dish I recommend smelling it or placing a small taste on the tip of your tongue to test for signs of harshness. If it's noticeably pungent, sharp or hot, reduce the amount called for in the recipe by about a third to a half.

- "Black" ginger is a name that is a little misleading, as it describes whole live hands of ginger that have been scalded for 10 to 15 minutes in boiling water before being scraped and dried. This kills the rhizome, which prevents sprouting, makes scraping easier and tends to darken its color.
- "Bleached" or "limed" ginger describes clean-peeled whole rhizomes that have been treated with sulfur or lime to make them lighter in color.
- "Splits" and "slices" are unpeeled rhizomes that have been split longitudinally or sliced laterally to speed up drying.
- "Ratoons" are the second crop of rhizomes from plants that have been left in the ground for more than a year. They are smaller, darker in color, more fibrous and generally hotter.

Buying and Storage

There are seven main styles of ginger sold for consumer use:

- fresh ginger rhizomes (stems): cleaned but not processed
- minced ginger: preserved in jars
- pickled ginger: most often sliced and colored pink and sold as sushi ginger
- ginger stems in sugar syrup: made from young pickled ginger pieces
- "naked" ginger from Australia: ginger stems in syrup with the syrup drained off
- candied ginger: ginger stems in syrup with the syrup drained off and the pieces dusted with sugar
- ginger powder (ground ginger): ground sliced and dried ginger

Fresh hands of ginger are available from most grocery stores and should be plump, firm and clean. Store fresh ginger in an open container in a cupboard, the same way you would fresh onions and garlic. Stored this way, it will keep for up to 1 week.

Minced or grated ginger can be bought preserved in vinegar or another acid and packed in glass jars; these must be refrigerated after opening. The use-by date on packages varies depending on the manufacturer's preservation methods.

Ginger preserved in syrup and crystallized ginger need to be stored in a cool, dry environment and will keep for

more than 1 year. While most ginger preserved by pickling and steeping in syrup (naked and candied ginger) came from China in the past, from the 1970s onward Australian preserved ginger has been preferred for confectionery and baking because of its sweet, lemony flavor and pleasant, fiber-free texture.

Dried ginger slices and ginger powder may originate from various countries, and the place of origin will influence flavor. Jamaican ginger has a delicate aroma and taste. It is considered one of the better kinds for culinary purposes and is in demand for flavoring soft drinks. A great deal of Jamaican ginger finds its way into European and American supermarkets. Nigerian ginger has a pungent, camphorous note, as does ginger from Sierra Leone. These gingers are sought by the food-processing industry for their volatile oil and oleoresin (see page 23). Indian dried ginger, from Cochin and Calicut, on the Malabar Coast, are widely exported; Cochin is generally considered the better of the two because it has a lemon-like aroma and pleasing pungency and is not bleached (the Calicut grade often is). Although produced in small amounts by world standards, Australian ground ginger has the least amount of fiber and, for my money, gives the best results in cooking. Poor-quality ground ginger has a sharp taste and a hot, biting aroma and often contains a lot of fiber (which may be sifted out with an ordinary flour sifter). Store sliced and ground dry ginger as you would other whole and ground spices: in an airtight container away from extremes of heat, light and humidity. Stored this way it will last for up to 1 year.

Use

Ginger may be classed as one of the more versatile of spices. Its tangy freshness, slight spiciness, warmth and sweetness complement a whole range of dishes from sweet to savory. Fresh, preserved or powdered ginger is often added to cakes, pastries and cookies. Liz makes the most delicious pumpkin scones flavored with a combination of finely chopped pieces of preserved ginger and ginger powder. Ginger goes well with orange vegetables (as does ground nutmeg). Sprinkle ground ginger over squash before baking or toss it in with a little butter after steaming.

Ginger is used fresh in many Asian dishes, where it forms a perfect marriage with the flavors of garlic, lemongrass, chile and makrut lime and coriander leaf. Japanese cooking often features pickled (and colored) pink or red ginger. In a similar manner to galangal, ginger helps to neutralize overly fishy notes; I find it almost mandatory when cooking strongly flavored seafood. Ginger powder is found in most Indian and Asian curries, and when rubbed onto red meats before grilling, it adds a delicious taste and has a slight tenderizing effect.

WEIGHT PER TEASPOON (5 mL)

- **whole average dried slice:** 1.5 g
- **ground:** 2.8 g

SUGGESTED QUANTITY PER POUND (500 g)

- **red meats:** 2 tsp (10 mL) ground, 1 tbsp (15 mL) grated fresh gingerroot
- **white meats:** 2 tsp (10 mL) ground, 1 tbsp (15 mL) grated fresh gingerroot
- **vegetables:** 1½ tsp (7 mL) ground, 2 tsp (10 mL) grated fresh gingerroot
- **grains and pulses:** 1½ tsp (7 mL) ground, 2 tsp (10 mL) grated fresh gingerroot
- **baked goods:** 1½ tsp (7 mL) ground, 2 tsp (10 mL) grated fresh gingerroot

Steamed Salmon with Soy and Ginger

I find the soft steamed juliennes of ginger in this simple dish so delightful. It's perfect on a "diet day" with bok choy or broccoli or served with Coconut Rice with Pandan Leaf (page 454). I like to cook salmon rare, so increase the cooking time to suit your tastes, if necessary.

**Makes
4 servings**

Preparation time:
 10 minutes
Cooking time:
 15 minutes

Tips

The salmon can also be cooked in a steamer lined with parchment, covered with a lid, for 10 to 15 minutes.

To julienne is to cut a vegetable into matchsticks roughly ⅛ inch (3 mm) thick and 3 inches (7.5 cm) long.

- **11- by 7-inch (28 by 18 cm) glass baking dish**
- **Four 12-inch (30 cm) square pieces of aluminum foil**
- **Preheat oven to 350°F (180°C)**

4	8 oz (250 g) boneless salmon fillets	4
4	3-inch (7.5 cm) pieces gingerroot, peeled and finely julienned (see Tips, left)	4
4	green onions, white part only, finely julienned	4
2 tbsp	soy sauce	30 mL
1 tsp	sesame oil	5 mL
	Freshly ground black pepper	

1. Place each fish fillet in center of an aluminum foil square. Divide ginger and green onions into 4 equal portions and scatter over fillets. Sprinkle with soy sauce and sesame oil and season with pepper to taste. Loosely pull up sides of foil around fish (leave it plenty of room) and fold edges closed to seal.

2. Transfer parcels, seam side up, to baking dish and bake in preheated oven for 15 to 20 minutes, until salmon starts to flake (increase cooking time as desired). Serve fish parcels on individual plates or remove from parcels and serve with cooking juices.

Variations

Halibut is also great prepared this way, as are scallops.

If some chile heat is desired, try serving with ½ tsp (2 mL) shichimi-togarashi (page 764) sprinkled over each fillet.

Stem Ginger Pudding

The sweet, warm flavor of stem ginger is delightful in this traditional steamed pudding.

Makes 6 servings

Preparation time:
 15 minutes

Cooking time: **2 hours**

Tips

Plastic pudding molds with lids are available in many cookware stores, as an alternative to covering the mold with foil. If a pudding mold is unavailable, a deep, heatproof bowl that holds roughly the same volume will also work.

You can substitute an equal amount of liquid honey for the golden syrup.

If you can't find self-rising flour in stores, you can make your own. To equal 1 cup (250 mL) self-rising flour, combine 1 cup (250 mL) all-purpose flour, 1½ tsp (7 mL) baking powder and ½ tsp (2 mL) salt.

After cooking for 2 hours, the heat can be turned off and the pudding can be set aside for up to 2 hours before serving, if needed.

- **5-cup (1.25 L) pudding mold, greased, bottom lined with parchment paper**
- **Food processor**

4	1-inch (2.5 cm) pieces stem ginger, finely chopped (see page 305)	4
2 tbsp	syrup from stem ginger	30 mL
4 tbsp	golden syrup (see Tips, left)	60 mL
1 cup	butter, softened	250 mL
1 cup	self-rising flour (see Tips, left)	250 mL
1 cup	superfine (caster) sugar	250 mL
1 tsp	ground ginger	5 mL
3	eggs, lightly beaten	3
2 to 4 tbsp	milk	30 to 60 mL
	Boiling water	

1. In prepared pudding mold, evenly sprinkle ginger over bottom. Drizzle with stem ginger syrup and golden syrup. Set aside.

2. In food processor fitted with the metal blade, combine butter, flour, sugar, ground ginger and eggs. Through the feed tube with the motor running, add milk just until a thick batter is formed (it should drop slowly off a spoon).

3. Scrape batter into pudding mold (over ginger and syrup) and spread evenly. Tear off a piece of aluminum foil large enough to cover the mold and grease one side. Allowing a little bit of give, place foil, greased side down, on top of mold and press around edges to seal. Secure the foil with string (trim off any loose ends).

4. Set a large pot on the stove and place a side plate on the bottom. Place pudding mold on top of plate. Pour boiling water into pot until it reaches halfway up mold and turn heat on low. Cover pot with a tight-fitting lid and steam for 2 hours, ensuring that water does not boil dry by topping up with more boiling water as necessary (see Tips, left).

5. To serve, carefully remove pudding from pot and remove foil. Place a serving plate over the top, then quickly invert mold so pudding turns out onto plate, covered with ginger and syrup.

Sticky Gingerbread

Gingerbread falls into two main categories: the people-shaped crisp cookies that kids adore and a more grown-up cake, rich with molasses and syrup and often more heavily spiced with ginger. This cake improves with age: it is best around the second or third day after baking.

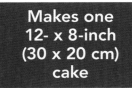

Makes one 12- x 8-inch (30 x 20 cm) cake

Preparation time:
5 minutes

Cooking time:
45 minutes

- - - - - - - - - - - -

Tips

You can substitute an equal amount of liquid honey for the golden syrup.

For an even deeper ginger flavor, add ½ cup (125 mL) chopped crystallized ginger to the batter before baking.

- **12- by 8-inch (30 by 20 cm) cake pan, greased and lined with parchment**
- **Preheat oven to 300°F (150°C)**

1 cup	butter	250 mL
⅓ cup	golden syrup (see Tips, left)	75 mL
½ cup	packed light brown sugar	125 mL
¾ cup	molasses or treacle	175 mL
1¼ cups	milk	300 mL
1½ cups	all-purpose flour	375 mL
1 tbsp	ground ginger	15 mL
1 tsp	ground cinnamon	5 mL
1½ tsp	baking soda	7 mL
2	eggs, lightly beaten	2

1. In a saucepan over low heat, melt butter, syrup, sugar and molasses and stir to combine. Remove from heat and stir in milk. Set aside to cool.

2. In a large bowl, combine flour, ginger, cinnamon and baking soda. Make a well in the center and pour in butter mixture. Add eggs and stir gently, until well combined. Pour into prepared pan.

3. Bake in preheated oven for 40 to 50 minutes or until a skewer inserted in center comes out clean and cake feels quite soft and spongy to the touch. Remove from oven and cool completely in pan before cutting into squares. Cake will keep in an airtight container at room temperature for up to 1 week.

Grains of Paradise

Amomum melegueta (also known as *Aframomum amomum, Aframomum* species, *Amomum* species, *A. grana paradisi*)

Names in Other Languages

- **Arabic:** gawz as Sudan
- **Czech:** aframom rajske zrno
- **Dutch:** paradijskorrels
- **French:** poivre de Guinée, malaguette
- **German:** Malagettapfeffer, Guineapfeffer
- **Greek:** piperi melenketa
- **Italian:** grani de paradiso
- **Japanese:** manigetto
- **Russian:** rajskie zyorna
- **Spanish:** malagueta
- **Turkish:** idrifil

Family: Zingiberaceae

Varieties: alligator pepper or "mbongo spice" (*A. citratum, A. danielli, A. exscapum*)

Other Names: ginny grains, Guinea grains, Melegueta pepper

Flavor Group: Hot

Parts Used: seeds (as a spice)

G

Background

Grains of paradise, a spice often referred to as Melegueta pepper in Europe, is indigenous to the west coast of Africa from Sierra Leone to Angola. The common name Melegueta derives from Melle, an old empire inhabited by the Mandingo people in the Upper Niger region between Mauritania and Sudan. The Portuguese called it Terra de Malaguet, and the coast to its west, often referred to as the Gold Coast, was also called the Grain Coast and the Pepper Coast, after this spice.

The earliest records of grains of paradise date from 1214. In the 13th century the court physician of Emperor John III at Nicea, an ancient city in Asia Minor, prescribed it, likely for its antimicrobial and stimulant properties, and "*grana*

Culinary Information

Combines with

- allspice
- bay leaf
- cardamom
- chile
- cinnamon and cassia
- cloves
- coriander seed
- cumin
- garlic
- ginger
- kokam
- rosemary
- star anise
- tamarind
- thyme
- turmeric

Traditional Uses

- many African dishes (in the same way as pepper)
- Tunisian stews
- game
- slow-cooked casseroles

Spice Blends

This spice is so rare it is not generally added to spice blends; however, it has been included in

- ras el hanout
- tagine spice blends
- mélanges of pepper

paradisi" was listed among spices sold at market at Lyons in 1245. The name was coined by Italian traders who shipped it from the Mediterranean port of Monti di Borea; they had no idea of its origin, since it was transported overland through the desert to Tripoli—hence the assumption that it came from "paradise"! By the mid 14th century, the direct sea routes to West Africa were being plied by ships loaded with ivory and *malaguette*. Although unrelated to pepper, it was seen as an acceptable alternative, and because of its relative accessibility at the time (the sea route to India that provided access to real pepper was not discovered until 1486), it enjoyed popularity in Europe.

In the 16th century the English were actively trading ivory, pepper and grains of paradise from the Gold Coast. An English herbalist of the time, John Gerard, mentions its medicinal virtues—both the seeds and rhizomes were used medicinally in West Africa. The seeds were an ingredient in the spiced wine known as hippocras, and their pungency was exploited to give an artificial strength of flavor to wines, beer, spirits and vinegar. Elizabeth I was reported to have a personal fondness for grains of paradise. By the 19th century the spice had fallen out of favor in Western cuisine, and throughout the 20th century it was generally referred to only as a curiosity. However, in the 21st century, grains of paradise experienced a flurry of popularity in culinary circles because of consumer interest in Moroccan cuisine and its inclusion in the exotic spice blend ras el hanout (page 757).

Grains of paradise has remained difficult to find in Western countries, largely because it has always been wild-harvested. Having no formal farming and harvesting structure seriously limits the supply, and if you're lucky enough to find a source, the import regulations of many countries make them a nightmare to import.

The Plant

Grains of paradise are seeds from a plant that belongs to the ginger and cardamom family. This herbaceous cardamom-like leafy-stemmed shrub grows from a stout rhizome and may vary considerably, depending on where it grows in West Africa. Similar to cardamom, the flowers are borne on 2-inch (5 cm) stems that emerge at the base just above ground level, followed by pear-shaped 4-inch (10 cm) red to orange fruits that contain many small dark brown seeds. The hard, roundish, aromatic and pungent seeds are $1/8$ inch (3 mm) in diameter. Their taste is initially piney, then peppery, hot, biting and numbing, similar to native Australian mountain pepperberry (*Tasmannia lanceolata*); also similarly, a lingering camphor flavor with notes of turpentine is detectable.

Other Varieties

Alligator pepper, or "mbongo spice" (*Amomum citratum, A. danielli, A. exscapum*), is related to grains of paradise. It looks similar to a brown (black) Indian cardamom pod, with a bumpy, reptilian appearance. Alligator pepper has a similar flavor to grains of paradise and is rare even in its native North Africa. Besides ceremonial uses, it finds its way into Tunisian-style beef stews. Alligator pepper is dried and sold in its whole form.

Processing

Unlike its cousins green and brown cardamom and alligator pepper, grains of paradise seeds are removed by hand from their pod and the surrounding sticky pulp to facilitate drying in the sun for up to a week.

Buying and Storage

Grains of paradise is difficult to find in Western countries, as the supply is hampered by three limiting factors: (1) to drug enforcement agencies the name conjures up notions of mind-altering substances; (2) its importation and use as an adulterant for pepper has caused it to be banned in some countries; and (3) the crop has never undergone organized cultivation. Thus, with the exception of small quantities secured from West Africa by spiceophiles, it is likely to remain available only in highly specialized spice shops.

For those lucky enough to obtain these exotic grains, buy the seeds whole and store in an airtight container away from extremes of heat and humidity. Under these conditions, the flavor will last for up to 5 years.

A reasonable substitute for ground grains of paradise can be made by pounding together 6 seeds from a brown cardamom pod, 4 black peppercorns and 1 Tasmanian mountain pepperberry or juniper berry, using a mortar and pestle. Store ground grains of paradise in the same manner as other ground spices: in an airtight container away from extremes of heat, light and humidity. Under these conditions, the ground spice will last for up to 1 year.

Use

Grains of paradise is used in much the same way as pepper. In West Africa it is considered an acceptable alternative to black pepper, and for some local dishes, it is the preferred spice. Exotic Moroccan spice blends such as ras el hanout may contain the crushed seeds, and their peppery notes will be found in Tunisian stews spiced with cinnamon, nutmeg and cloves. It is best to grind grains of paradise before adding it to a dish, as the seeds do not soften readily in cooking, and grinding releases their flavor.

WEIGHT PER TEASPOON (5 mL)
- whole: 3 g
- ground: 2.8 g

SUGGESTED QUANTITY PER POUND (500 g)
- red meats: 1 tsp (5 mL)
- white meats: ¾ tsp (3 mL)
- vegetables: ½ tsp (2 mL)
- grains and pulses: ½ tsp (2 mL)
- baked goods: ½ tsp (2 mL)

Tunisian Beef Stew

Being native to West Africa, grains of paradise features in most African dishes. This beef stew with peanut sauce, called *maafe*, showcases the spice in its everyday use. Serve over mashed potatoes or rice.

Makes 6 servings

Preparation time: 15 minutes

Cooking time: 1 hour

Tip

You can use a mortar and pestle to crush the grains of paradise and the peanuts. Alternatively, use a bowl and the back of a wooden spoon.

2 tbsp	oil	30 mL
1	onion, chopped	1
1½ lbs	stewing beef, cut into 2-inch (5 cm) pieces	750 g
1	red finger chile, chopped	1
1	can (14 oz/398 mL) diced tomatoes, with juice	1
2 tsp	grains of paradise, roughly crushed (see Tip, left)	10 mL
2 tsp	sweet paprika	10 mL
1 tsp	butter	5 mL
½ cup	unsalted roasted peanuts, roughly crushed (see Tip, left)	125 mL
	Sea salt and freshly ground black pepper	

1. In a large, heavy-bottomed saucepan over medium-low heat, heat oil. Add onion and sauté for about 4 minutes, until transparent. Increase heat to medium-high and, in batches so as not to crowd the pan, cook beef until well-browned on all sides, about 8 minutes. Stir in chile, tomatoes, grains of paradise and paprika and bring to a boil. Reduce heat to low, cover, and simmer, stirring occasionally, for about 1 hour, until meat is tender.

2. Meanwhile, in a small skillet over medium heat, melt butter. Add peanuts and, using the back of a wooden spoon, mash into butter to make a rough paste. Add peanut paste to stew. Season with salt and pepper to taste and cook for 5 minutes, until flavors meld. Serve hot.

Variation

To make a vegetarian stew, substitute an equal quantity of cooked chickpeas for the beef and reduce the cooking time to 15 minutes.

Horseradish

Armoracia rusticana (also known as *Cochlearia armoracia, A. armoracia, A. rustica, Cardamine armoracia, Rorippa armoracia*)

Names in Other Languages

Horseradish

- **Arabic:** fujl har
- **Chinese (C):** laaht gan
- **Chinese (M):** la gen
- **Czech:** kren, kren selsky
- **Danish:** peberrod
- **Dutch:** mierikwortel
- **Finnish:** piparjuuri
- **French:** raifort, cranson de Bretagne
- **German:** Meerrettich, Kren
- **Greek:** armorakia
- **Hungarian:** torma
- **Italian:** rafano, barbaforte
- **Japanese:** seyowasabi, hosuradisshu
- **Norwegian:** pepperrot
- **Portuguese:** rabanao bastardo
- **Russian:** khren
- **Spanish:** rabano picante, taramago
- **Swedish:** pepparrot
- **Thai:** hosraedich
- **Turkish:** yaban turbu

Family: Brassicaceae (formerly Cruciferae)

Varieties: wasabi (*Wasabia japonica*, also known as *Eutrema wasabi*)

Other Names: great raifort, Japanese horseradish (wasabi); mountain radish, red cole

Flavor Group: Hot

Parts Used: roots (as a spice), leaves (as a vegetable)

Background

The origins of horseradish are obscure. Some historians claim that the early Greeks knew of it in 1000 BCE and that it was used in Britain before the Romans invaded, but it is curious that Apicius, the Roman epicure of the first century CE, does not mention it. Horseradish is acknowledged to be native to eastern Europe, near the Caspian Sea, and to have grown wild in Russia, Poland and Finland. Because it thrived in temperate zones, it spread easily beyond its native habitat. By the 13th century horseradish was naturalized in Europe, and in the 16th century it was reported as growing wild in Britain, where it was referred to as "red cole." John Gerard refers to it in his 1597 *Herball* as a condiment consumed with meat and fish by the Germans.

Names in Other Languages

Wasabi

- **Chinese (C):** saan kwai
- **Chinese (M):** shan kui
- **Czech:** japonsky zeleny kren
- **Danish:** japansk peberrod
- **Dutch:** bergstokroosi, Japanse mierikswortel
- **Finnish:** japaninpiparjuuri
- **French:** raifort de Japon
- **German:** Bergstockrose, japanischer Kren
- **Japanese:** wasabi, namida
- **Russian:** vasabi
- **Swedish:** japansk pepparrot
- **Thai:** wasabi

Horseradish is one of the bitter herbs eaten during the Jewish Passover seder as a reminder of the bitterness of their enslavement by the Egyptians. Horseradish was highly valued for its medicinal properties and is still popular with natural therapists to help relieve respiratory congestion. The early colonial settlers took horseradish to America, where it is now frequently found growing wild in moist, semi-shade conditions and is considered by many horticulturists to be a vigorous, difficult-to-eradicate weed.

Wasabi, according to Japanese legend, was discovered centuries ago in a remote mountain village. As with most plants whose origins go far back into the mists of time, little is known of its origins; however, it appears that cultivation of wasabi was known around the 10th century in Japan. Wasabi is now cultivated in many countries with the right soil conditions and cold climate, including the United States, Canada, China, New Zealand and Taiwan.

The Plant

Horseradish is a vigorous perennial plant with large, soft, fleshy dark green leaves that resemble those of spinach. The leaves grow to about 24 inches (60 cm) long. Numerous small white aromatic flowers form on upright stems, followed by oblong wrinkled pods that contain mostly unviable seeds—hence, propagation is from the root stock.

Culinary Information

Combines with
- basil
- bay leaf
- dill (fronds and seed)
- fennel (fronds and seed)
- fenugreek seed
- garlic
- lovage
- mustard
- parsley
- rosemary
- sesame seed
- thyme

Traditional Uses
- cold meats (as a sauce)
- seafood sauces containing tomato
- Japanese cuisine in general
- sushi and sashimi
- wasabi peas

Spice Blends
- not commonly used in spice blends

In the 16th century, one of the few condiments that provided a hit of spicy heat was pepper, which was an expensive commodity in those times. Even after the discovery of chiles in the New World, they took a few centuries to be embraced in Europe, so it is not surprising that the locals were thrilled to get a fiery kick from horseradish, a plant that grew in the wild. It has remained a mainstay of English cuisine ever since.

The young leaves can be cooked like spinach, but this is not common, as horseradish is mostly cultivated for the flavor in its root. The root system consists of a main taproot 12 inches (30 cm) long with smaller roots branching out at various angles; it looks similar to a fat carrot but is hairier and more wrinkled, with a yellowish brown skin. The inside flesh is white and fibrous and releases an intense, highly pungent, tear-inducing aroma that goes right up the back of one's nose. These characteristic head-clearing fumes and the strong, biting heat of horseradish are created only when the root is cut or scraped, a process that breaks separate cells and brings together two components—sinigrin, a glucoside, and myrosin, an enzyme—to form a fierce volatile oil identical in chemical terms to that of black mustard seeds. The full intensity is short-lived; even after 15 minutes it will start to diminish unless a souring agent (lemon juice or vinegar) is added. The acidity halts the enzyme reaction, thus stopping the developed heat in its tracks.

Other Varieties

Wasabi, or **Japanese horseradish** (*Wasabia japonica*), is pale green and comes from the tuber of a perennial herb that has a similar aroma and taste to horseradish but is often considered to be more complex and pungent. Over the past 20 years there has been much debate and lobbying by wasabi producers to outlaw misrepresentation of wasabi. A common practice has been for manufacturers to make a fake wasabi by blending horseradish, mustard and green coloring. The European Union has implemented new labeling requirements that permit use of the terms *wasabi* and *wasabi japonica* only on true *W. japonica*, which can now be independently tested for authenticity. As a result of this ruling, a number of fake wasabi products have been removed from supermarket shelves in Switzerland and Germany, with many other countries likely to follow suit.

There is also a tree called the **horseradish tree** (*Moringa oleifera*), which is indigenous to the forests of the western Himalayas. It is cultivated to make ben oil, which is extracted from the seeds for use in cosmetics and as a lubricant for precision instruments. The seed-bearing pods have a meaty taste and are sometimes used to flavor curries. The horseradish tree got its name because the root is pungent like horseradish and has occasionally been used in a similar way to flavor food, although it is not considered to be a good substitute for horseradish.

Processing

Horseradish is best harvested, or "lifted," in late autumn, because the flavor improves with the onset of colder weather. The leafy tops are cut about a week before the roots are dug up (large areas are plowed, smaller holdings are forked). The roots are washed and trimmed, the small lateral ones are cut for processing, and the main taproot is kept for replanting. Prior to chopping or grating for making products such as horseradish sauce, the harvested roots are packed away from light, as exposure will turn them green and make them less desirable in the market. Horseradish has an inner core like that found in carrots. When grating fresh horseradish, use only the outer section of the root, as the inner core has less flavor and, being a bit rubbery, is difficult to grate.

Buying and Storage

Fresh horseradish should be thoroughly washed to clean off any remaining dirt. It may be stored in a resealable bag in the refrigerator for up to 2 weeks or, once grated, in a resealable bag in the freezer for a couple of months. Jars of horseradish relish and paste are available in supermarkets. In the United States these are often colored red with beet juice, primarily for visual appeal, not flavor enhancement. You can usually buy dehydrated horseradish granules, flakes or powder, which are a reasonable substitute for making sauce or to add to dressings. All dehydrated horseradish will taste different from fresh, and the flakes and granules require a long soaking time because of their firm, fibrous texture.

Horseradish and wasabi powders are easier to use, as the heat is activated within minutes of adding cold water. Some wasabi pastes are made using horseradish that has

H

been colored green, a practice that should ultimately cease unless manufacturers of these pastes label their products as imitation wasabi. New Zealand now produces a very high-quality wasabi powder that, believe it or not, is exported in large quantities to Japan. Wasabi powder, like mustard powder, develops its full heat and pungency within seconds of coming into contact with cold water; it is the next best option to fresh wasabi. Store horseradish powder, granules and flakes and wasabi powder in airtight packs, protected from heat, light and humidity.

Use

Horseradish is usually served cold or added to warm foods at the end of cooking, because much of its piquancy is diminished by heat. When using horseradish or wasabi powders, follow these few simple rules to achieve the best results:

- Never add directly to a hot dish; the heat will inhibit the enzyme reaction.
- The powder should be mixed only with cold water to make a thick paste. This activates the enzymes that produce the characteristic heat.
- After making the paste from powder, cover it with plastic wrap and refrigerate for 5 to 10 minutes to allow the heat to reach its full potency.
- Use immediately (even after only 1 hour the strength will have diminished).

The most familiar application of horseradish is to use it as you would mustard with cold meats such as ham, tongue, corned (salt-cured) beef and especially roast beef. Make a simple horseradish sauce or relish by mixing freshly grated or finely sliced root with sugar and vinegar. To complement pork, blend this mix with grated apples, mint and sour cream. Horseradish also goes well with fish and seafood, and many popular red seafood sauces are made by adding grated horseradish to a rich tomato base. In eastern Europe and the Scandinavian countries, horseradish is added to soups and sauces or mixed with cream cheese, and it is regarded as forming a zesty marriage with beets. In Japanese cuisine, wasabi is an ingredient in fillings for sushi, an accompaniment to sashimi (raw fish), and often mixed with Japanese soy sauce for dipping.

WEIGHT PER TEASPOON (5 mL)
- dried chopped pieces: 3 g
- powder: 5 g

SUGGESTED QUANTITY PER POUND (500 g)
- red meats: 1 tbsp (15 mL) freshly grated
- white meats: 2 tsp (10 mL) freshly grated
- vegetables: 1 tsp (5 mL) freshly grated
- grains and pulses: 1 tsp (5 mL) freshly grated
- baked goods: 1 tsp (5 mL) freshly grated

Horseradish Sauce

Freshly made horseradish sauce tastes so much better than jarred varieties, so if you have access to fresh horseradish, give this easy recipe a go. This sauce goes equally well with rare roast beef or smoked cured fish.

**Makes about
1 cup (250 mL)**

Preparation time:
 5 minutes

Cooking time: none

- - - - - - - - - - - - - -

Tip

To finely grate horseradish, use a kitchen rasp such as the type made by Microplane.

3 tbsp	peeled, finely grated fresh horseradish (see Tip, left)	45 mL
1 cup	sour cream	250 mL
1 tsp	Dijon mustard	5 mL
	Sea salt and freshly ground black pepper	

1. In a small bowl, combine horseradish, sour cream and mustard. Season with salt and pepper to taste. The sauce will keep in an airtight container in the refrigerator for up to 1 week.

H

Soba Noodles with Wasabi Dressing

Soba noodles are made from buckwheat and have an earthy, satisfying taste. In Japan, noodles are served all day, every day—at busy train stations and in high-end restaurants, in soups, stir-fries or salads. Wasabi is an indispensable condiment throughout the country and accompanies every type of dish. This chilled noodle salad, livened up with wasabi, is a great alternative to sandwiches in lunchboxes or at picnics.

Makes 4 small servings

Preparation time:
5 minutes

Cooking time:
10 minutes

Tips

In order to activate the enzyme that creates the heat, wasabi powder needs to be mixed with cold water.

To toast sesame seeds: Place in a dry skillet over medium heat and cook, shaking pan constantly, until lightly browned, 2 to 3 minutes. Immediately transfer to a dish to prevent further browning.

10 oz	soba noodles	300 g
2 tsp	sesame oil	10 mL
2 tsp	wasabi powder	10 mL
2 tsp	cold water	10 mL
2 tbsp	rice wine vinegar	30 mL
2 tbsp	oil	30 mL
1 tbsp	soy sauce	15 mL
1 tbsp	freshly squeezed lemon juice	15 mL
1½ cups	snow peas, cut diagonally into 1-inch (2.5 cm) pieces	375 mL
1 tbsp	toasted sesame seeds (see Tips, left)	15 mL
	Pickled red ginger, optional	

1. In a pot of boiling salted water, cook soba noodles until tender, about 5 minutes. Drain and rinse under cold running water. Transfer to a serving bowl and toss with sesame oil (to prevent sticking).
2. In a small bowl, whisk together wasabi powder and water (see Tips, left). Whisk in vinegar, oil, soy sauce and lemon juice. Add dressing to noodles along with snow peas and sesame seeds and toss to mix well. Top with pickled ginger (if using).

Variation

For a hot dish, drain but do not rinse the noodles. In pot over low heat, combine hot noodles with dressing, snow peas and sesame seeds and heat for 2 minutes.

Huacatay

Tagetes minuta (also known as *T. graveolens, T. glandulifera, T. glandulosa*)

Family: Asteraceae or Compositae

Varieties: huacatay (*T. minuta*), papaloquelite (*Porophyllum ruderale*)

Other Names: anisillo, black mint, chijchipa, chinchilla, mastranzo, stinking Roger, southern cone marigold, suico, wacataya, zuico

Flavor Group: Pungent

Parts Used: leaves (as a herb)

Background

Native to the Americas, and so unknown elsewhere in pre-Columbian times, huacatay was used by indigenous people to make a medicinal tea, to flavor food and possibly to control pests in traditional agriculture. The name *Tagetes* refers to the Etruscan prophet Tages. Legend has it that Tages sprang from the earth and revealed to ancient farmers the art of dowsing (also referred to as water divining)—a quite apt description when you consider that an erect huacatay plant looks as though it has literally sprung from the earth. After Spanish colonization it appeared around the world, from Europe to Asia, Africa and Australia, where it is derided as the weed "stinking Roger."

Besides emerging as a culinary herb, huacatay can be used to make a natural dye and an essential oil called tagetes oil, which is extracted by steam distillation. Tagetes oil produced in Brazil is used in perfumes, alcoholic and nonalcoholic beverages, processed foods and baked goods.

The Plant

Huacatay is an annual plant indigenous to the temperate grasslands of southern South America. The plant stands defiantly upright despite often being referred to as a noxious weed. Growing up to 4 feet (1.2 m) tall, with serrated leaves and small creamy yellow flowers at the ends of sticky branches, this plant has some surprises in store for

Repels Insects

In recent times, members of the marigold family have been appreciated for their insect-repelling properties, and none more so than huacatay, which has become popular as a companion plant. Secretions from the roots have an insecticide effect on nematodes such as eel worms, and when used as a strewing herb, it repels cabbage moths and other insects.

Culinary Information

Combines with
- basil
- curry leaf
- dill leaf
- fenugreek leaf
- garlic
- lemongrass
- lemon myrtle
- pandan leaf
- parsley
- Vietnamese mint

Traditional Uses
- ocopa and huacatay sauce
- black mint paste
- marinades for meats
- as a substitute for cilantro

Spice Blends
- not commonly used in spice blends

enthusiastic cooks. The first is a strong, anise-like medicinal aroma that to some is unpleasant, in the same way that cilantro and epazote may be perceived. The second, after closer examination and time to appreciate its aroma, is a scent profile reminiscent of apple, pineapple and anise. Unlike cilantro (coriander), I have found that the leaves have a more agreeable flavor when dried.

Other Varieties

There are many varieties of marigold, some used as a leafy green and others grown primarily for decorative or medicinal purposes. **Papaloquelite** (*Porophyllum ruderale*), also called papalo, is another member of the marigold family with a distinctive flavor that has been likened to cilantro (coriander leaf). The leaves are oval and soft and the flowers, when they go to seed, are like dandelions. It is believed that papaloquelite, along with epazote, was used in Mexican cuisine long before cilantro, as it is one of that region's genuine wild herbs, or *quelites*, as they call them. The flavor is more complex than cilantro and it is used in very much the same way, in salads and as a flavorsome garnish.

Processing

As huacatay is easily plucked from the semi-moist soil it prefers to grow in, I like to pull the whole plant from the ground, wash the roots and then hang it upside down to dry in a dark, well-aired place until the leaves shrivel and feel crisp. Strip the dried leaves off the stems.

Spice Notes

When Liz was a child in rural northern Australia, she never knew that the lanky, scrawny "stinking Roger" weeds growing so abundantly could be eaten. Pulled easily from the ground, the single stem made a handy hobbyhorse, the base end gripped in grubby fists and the feathery top leaves dragging in the red volcanic dust. Liz and her friends galloped barefoot and carefree on their steeds of weeds. Now, six decades later, we pull our car onto the roadside verge to collect stinking Roger leaves, which we now recognize as huacatay, and take them home to our kitchen.

Buying and Storage

The fresh leaves can be purchased in Hispanic markets, where they are generally sold in bundles about 1 foot (30 cm) long and 3 inches (7.5 cm) in diameter. The tightly made bundle comprises cut stalks and leaves that have been folded up and tied with twine.

Fresh leaf-bearing stalks of huacatay are best kept in the crisper drawer of the refrigerator after sprinkling lightly with fresh water. Stored in this manner, they will last for 2 to 3 days, but note that the leaves do wilt rapidly. To freeze, remove the leaves from the stalks and pack them, uncut, into ice-cube trays, barely cover with water, and place them in the freezer. Turn out the ice cubes and store in a resealable bag in the freezer, where they will last for up to 3 months.

As the popularity of this herb increases, both the dried leaves and powder are becoming more available in markets that sell Latin American produce. You can also find "black mint paste" (huacatay made into a paste), which is a useful substitute for fresh huacatay.

Store dried huacatay in the same way as other dried herbs: in an airtight container away from extremes of heat, light and humidity. Under these conditions, the dried leaves will keep their flavor for up to 1 year.

Use

Think of huacatay in the same way that you would cilantro, epazote and asafetida. They all have strong, seemingly odd aromas and flavors on first encounter but are highly appreciated when balanced with other foods. Huacatay complements pork, lamb and goat in Andean, Peruvian and Bolivian marinades and was an important ingredient in *ocopa*, a bagful of peanuts, chiles and herbs that Incan messengers would carry with them to eat when they rested. These days *ocopa* has evolved into a sauce not unlike a mole that contains onion, garlic, huacatay, chile, roasted peanuts, bread and cheese. These are cooked and blended, then enjoyed with hard-boiled eggs and potato. Try using huacatay as a substitute for cilantro (coriander leaf)—you may be surprised.

Use approximately one-third of the amount of dried huacatay as you would fresh.

SUGGESTED QUANTITY PER POUND (500 g)

- **red meats:** $1/2$ cup (125 mL) fresh leaves, 2 tbsp (30 mL) dried
- **white meats:** $1/2$ cup (125 mL) fresh leaves, 2 tbsp (30 mL) dried
- **vegetables:** $1/4$ cup (60 mL) fresh leaves, 1 tbsp (15 mL) dried
- **grains and pulses:** $1/4$ cup (60 mL) fresh leaves, 1 tbsp (15 mL) dried
- **baked goods:** garnish with fresh leaves

Ocopa

When we realized that the wild Australian plant "stinking Roger" was in fact the same as the South American herb huacatay, I had to try making ocopa, a classic Peruvian sauce usually served with hard-boiled eggs and sliced boiled potatoes. I find that it makes a great salad dressing on greens too.

Makes about 3 cups (750 mL)

Preparation time:
10 minutes
Cooking time:
10 minutes

Tip

Aji amarillo is a South American hot yellow chile pepper. It can be found fresh, canned, dried or in paste form, all of which will work in this recipe (1 dried chile is equivalent to 1 fresh or canned or 1 tsp/5 mL paste). Look for it in specialty spice shops or South American grocery stores.

• **Blender**

1 tbsp	oil	15 mL
1	onion, roughly chopped	1
1	large clove garlic, chopped	1
1	dried aji amarillo chile, seeded and chopped (see Tip, left)	1
¼ cup	dried huacatay	60 mL
⅓ cup	raw unsalted peanuts, lightly toasted	75 mL
1 oz	plain crackers (about 4)	30 g
1 cup	ricotta cheese	250 mL
1 cup	evaporated milk	250 mL
¼ tsp	fine sea salt	1 mL

1. In a skillet over medium heat, heat oil. Add onion and sauté until translucent, about 5 minutes. Add garlic, chile and huacatay and cook for 2 minutes, until soft. Transfer to blender and add peanuts, crackers, ricotta, evaporated milk and salt; purée until smooth. Sauce will keep in an airtight container in the refrigerator for up to 3 days.

H

Juniper

Juniperus communis (also known as *J. albanica, J. argaea, J. compressa, J. kanitzii*)

Names in Other Languages

- **Arabic:** hab-ul-aaraar
- **Chinese (M):** du song
- **Czech:** jalovec, jalovcinky
- **Danish:** enebaer
- **Dutch:** jenever, jeneverbes
- **Finnish:** kataja
- **French:** genièvre
- **German:** Wacholder
- **Greek:** arkevthos
- **Hungarian:** borokabogyo
- **Indian:** araar, dhup, shur
- **Italian:** ginepro
- **Japanese:** seiyo-suzu
- **Norwegian:** einer
- **Polish:** scejzjobz, jagody jalowca
- **Portuguese:** junipero
- **Russian:** mozhzhevelnik
- **Spanish:** nebrina, enebro, junipero
- **Swedish:** enbar
- **Turkish:** ardic yemisi, ephel
- **Vietnamese:** cay bach xu

Family: Cupressaceae

Varieties: Syrian juniper (*Arceuthos drupacea*), Californian juniper (*J. californica*), alligator juniper (*J. deppeana*)

Other Names: juniper berries, juniper cones, juniper fruits

Flavor Group: Pungent

Parts Used: berries (as a spice)

Background

Juniper trees are native to the Mediterranean, arctic Norway, Russia, the northwestern Himalayas and North America. Juniper has been regarded as a valuable spice for medicinal purposes for thousands of years, and throughout the ages it has been treated as a magical plant. It is mentioned in the Bible, and the Greek physicians Galen and Dioscorides wrote of juniper's virtues around 100 CE. Because of its air-cleansing piney fragrance, the foliage was used as a strewing herb to freshen stale air. The Swiss burned its berries with heating fuel in winter to sanitize stale classrooms. During the plague, Londoners would burn juniper wood in an unsuccessful attempt to ward off infection (they weren't aware that the disease was transmitted by fleas hitching a ride on rats). Juniper berries were sometimes used as

Culinary Information

Combines with
- allspice
- bay leaf
- marjoram
- onions and garlic
- oregano
- paprika
- rosemary
- sage
- tarragon
- thyme

Traditional Uses
- game and rich, fatty foods
- alcoholic drinks (especially gin)
- soups and casseroles
- roast poultry
- stuffings with bread and herbs

Spice Blends
- game spice blends

a substitute for pepper, and they have also been roasted and used as a coffee substitute. Gin, the spirit that derives its unique flavor from juniper berries, is named from an adaptation of the Dutch word for juniper, *jenever*.

The Plant

There are many different species of juniper, ranging from small shrubs 5 to 6 feet (1.5 to 2 m) tall that provide us with the juniper berry of culinary use to 40-foot (12 m) trees. Juniper bushes are compact, with sharp, ridged needlelike gray-green leaves that protrude at right angles, making the berries painful to harvest unless one is wearing heavy gloves (or using chopsticks!). The greenish yellow flowers are either male or female; however, only one sex is found on any one plant, and pollination is by wind from surrounding plants of the opposite sex. The indistinct flowers are followed by the small—$^1/_4$ to $^1/_3$ inch (5 to 8 mm) in diameter—female seed cones that we refer to as berries. These take two to three years to mature. The male cones, which are small, yellowish and occur at the ends of the foliage, are not used in cooking.

Initially hard and pale green, juniper berries ripen to blue-black, become fleshy and contain three sticky hard brown seeds. When dried the berries remain soft, but if broken open, one will find that the pith surrounding the seeds is quite friable. The aroma of juniper is immediately reminiscent of English dry gin, with a woody, piney, resinous smell that is somewhat flowery and contains notes of turpentine. The flavor is equally pine-like, spicy, refreshing

and savory, making it an excellent foil for rich, gamey or fatty foods. Although juniper is considered harmless for most people, pregnant women and people with kidney disease are advised to avoid consuming it in large quantities.

Other Varieties

There are around 30 varieties of juniper, but the berries from many of them are too bitter to use in cooking. A few notable exceptions are **Syrian juniper** (*Arceuthos drupacea*), found in Turkey, southern Europe and North Africa; **Californian**

Spice Notes

Years ago we had a small juniper tree growing at home. Picking juniper berries, which are nestled within treacherous needled foliage, was so painful that we resorted to removing them with chopsticks and dropping them onto a tray on the ground below. This was an inordinately slow task! At least it had the benefit of greatly improving our chopstick-handling skills.

juniper (*Juniperus californica*), which grows in southwestern North America; and **alligator juniper** (*J. deppeana*), which grows in Arizona, Texas and Mexico. The growing habits, method of pollination and fruiting of these varieties are similar to those of *J. communis*, and the berries are also used in cooking.

Processing

Because juniper berries take two to three years to mature, a tree will bear both immature fruits and ready-to-harvest berries at the same time. The best-quality berries are picked by hand when ripe (usually in autumn), because any form of mechanical harvesting will crush the small, pulpy spheres, allowing them to dry out and lose flavor.

Only ripe fresh or dried berries are suitable for distillation of the oil that is used for making gin (fresh ripe berries are preferred).

Buying and Storage

Juniper berries are at their best when they are still moist and soft to the touch and squash relatively easily between the fingers without crumbling. It is not unusual for some berries to have a cloudy bloom on their blue-black skins. Although this is a harmless mold, berries that have not been properly dried may be excessively moldy and should be avoided. Always wait to crush or grind juniper berries until just before you use them, as the volatile component evaporates rapidly once exposed to the air. Juniper berries have a shelf life of 2 to 3 years when stored in an airtight container away from extremes of heat, light and humidity.

Use

Juniper berries perform a unique role by contributing as much to the character of food through their "freshening" ability as they do by way of their specific taste profile. In addition to seasoning a dish, juniper cuts the strong flavor of game, reduces the fatty effect of duck and pork, and removes the perception of stodginess from bread stuffing. Juniper berries are included in recipes for all sorts of game. They are added to fish and lamb and blend well with other herbs and spices, especially thyme, sage, oregano, marjoram, bay leaf, allspice and onions and garlic.

WEIGHT PER TEASPOON (5 mL)
- whole: 2.3 g

SUGGESTED QUANTITY PER POUND (500 g)
- red meats:
  5 berries
- white meats:
  5 berries
- vegetables:
  3 berries
- grains and pulses:
  3 berries
- baked goods:
  3 berries

Venison Pie

I spend a lot of time in Scotland, where my husband is from and where venison is a prized meat. In this classic preparation the pine-like juniper balances the gaminess of the meat in a hearty, comforting pie. Caribou or other red game meat can also be used in this recipe.

**Makes
6 servings**

Preparation time:
 20 minutes

Cooking time: **3 hours**

- - - - - - - - - - - - - - - -

Tip

To crush juniper berries, use a mortar and pestle, a rolling pin or the back of a wooden spoon. They are fairly soft, so will yield easily.

- **10-inch (25 cm) deep-dish pie plate**
- **Preheat oven to 275°F (140°C)**

2 tbsp	oil, divided	30 mL
2	medium carrots, halved lengthwise and sliced	2
2 cups	button mushrooms, quartered	500 mL
5	shallots, halved	5
2	large cloves garlic, sliced	2
4	slices smoked bacon, chopped	4
1 tbsp	all-purpose flour	15 mL
½ tsp	fine sea salt	2 mL
½ tsp	freshly ground black pepper	2 mL
2½ lbs	stewing venison, cut into 1½-inch (4 cm) pieces	1.25 kg
1 cup	medium-bodied red wine	250 mL
2 cups	chicken broth	500 mL
3	bay leaves	3
1 tbsp	dried juniper berries, lightly crushed (see Tip, left)	15 mL
2	sprigs fresh thyme	2
2 tsp	cornstarch	10 mL
1	sheet (10 by 15 inches/25 by 38 cm) puff pastry	1
1	egg, beaten	1

1. In a large Dutch oven over medium heat, heat 1 tbsp (15 mL) oil. Add carrots, mushrooms, shallots, garlic and bacon; cook for about 5 minutes, until browned (be careful not to burn). Using a slotted spoon, transfer mixture to a bowl and set aside. Set aside pot.

2. In a resealable bag, combine flour, salt and pepper. Add venison, seal bag and shake to coat well.

Tip

The filling can be made a day ahead and refrigerated overnight.

3. In same Dutch oven over medium-high heat, heat remaining 1 tbsp (15 mL) oil. In batches, cook venison until browned on all sides, 5 to 7 minutes; transfer to a bowl. Add wine and cook for 1 minute, stirring to scrape up brown bits from bottom of pan. Add browned venison, reserved vegetables, broth, bay leaves, juniper berries and thyme. Cover and bake in preheated oven for about 2 hours, until tender.

4. Using a slotted spoon, transfer meat and vegetables to pie dish, discarding bay leaves. Add cornstarch to remaining cooking liquid and whisk well. Boil over high heat until reduced by half, about 10 minutes. Pour over pie filling and set aside for 10 to 15 minutes to cool slightly.

5. Preheat oven to 400°F (200°C).

6. Cover pie with puff pastry sheet and pinch edges to seal. Using a knife, cut small crosses in pastry to allow steam to vent. Brush top of pastry with egg. Bake in preheated oven for about 20 minutes or until pastry is golden brown.

J

Kokam

Garcinia indica Choisy

Names in Other Languages

- **French:** cocum
- **German:** Kokam
- **Indian:** kokam, kokum, raktapurka
- **Italian:** cocum
- **Spanish:** cocum

Family: Clusiaceae (formerly Guttiferae)

Varieties: asam gelugor (*G. atroviridis*), cambodge (*G. cambogia*), goraka (*G. gummi-gutta*)

Other Names: black kokam, cocum, fish tamarind, kokum, kokum butter tree, mangosteen oil tree

Flavor Group: Tangy

Parts Used: fruits (as a spice)

Background

This solitary tropical forest tree, indigenous to the Indian states of Karnataka, Gujarat and Maharashtra and the Western Ghats of Kerala, West Bengal and Assam, is difficult to propagate. It is not known anywhere else, although the Portuguese were certainly familiar with it in the Maharashtran city of Goa.

Kokam butter, an edible fat extracted from the seeds on a cottage-industry basis, is an item of commerce that sometimes finds its way into butter and ghee as an adulterant. A number of products are produced from ripe kokam fruit; besides the spice for cooking, rind from unripe kokam is dried in the sun and used as a natural source of red pigment.

Culinary Information

Combines with

- allspice
- cardamom
- chile
- cinnamon and cassia
- cloves
- coriander (leaf and seed)
- cumin
- curry leaf
- fennel seed
- galangal
- lemongrass
- lemon myrtle
- paprika
- star anise
- turmeric

Traditional Uses

- Indian curries, especially Goan fish curry
- cordials

Spice Blends

- not commonly used in spice blends
- asam gelugor powder

The Plant

The kokam tree is a slender, graceful tropical evergreen that reaches 50 feet (15 m) in height and has medium-density foliage of oval light green leaves. The fruit looks similar to a small plum, 1 inch (2.5 cm) in diameter and dark purple when ripe. Kokam trees vary greatly in yield, ranging from around 66 to 280 pounds (30 to 130 kg) per season. The very dark purple dried, flattened rind comes in small, leathery pieces about 1 inch (2.5 cm) long that can be unfolded into a fruit-sized skullcap. The aroma is slightly fruity and faintly balsamic, with notes of tannin. The flavor is immediately sharp, acidic, astringent and salty, leaving a pleasing mouth-freshening dried-fruit sweetness. Kokam's acidity comes from its high levels of malic acid, the same acid found in green apples and the spice sumac. Very small amounts of tartaric and citric acid add to the unique complexity of kokam's flavor.

Other Varieties

A closely related spice grown in Asia is **asam gelugor** (*Garcinia atroviridis*). It has acidic properties similar to kokam and goes by the confusing name "tamarind slices"—

Travels in the Spice Trade

Our first encounter with kokam was in South India when we were greeted with warm rural hospitality by the Sediyapu family, who upon our arrival brought out homemade snacks and kokam water. The food was so absolutely wonderful in South India that it was difficult not to become preoccupied with it. We sat on the shady veranda talking to family members while nibbling spicy tidbits and washing them down with the bright pink kokam water. After initial pleasantries we strolled to a building near the house where their little family business makes cordials, their specialty being kokam cordial (they call it *birinda*). The neat two-room building had one section with stainless-steel vats for boiling the syrup and another for filling the bottles and labeling them. This was the same kokam cordial we had tasted earlier, and we took the opportunity to look at a nearby kokam tree. The Sediyapus said they harvest the fruits when they are ripe, and then it is only the rind, comprising about 50% of the whole fruit, that is preserved by drying it in the sun. Sometimes salt is rubbed onto the rind to speed up drying and assist with preserving the leathery morsels. To make their tangy, refreshing deep purple cordial they boil the kokam with sugar syrup. Our hosts assured us that, taken regularly, it would be beneficial for reducing obesity and cholesterol—a bit of an uphill battle when surrounded by so many beautifully spiced Indian meals!

which it is not. These fruits are sold either sliced and dried or as a powder. I have also seen an asam gelugor spice mix in which it is ground with starch to absorb stickiness and extra citric acid. **Cambodge** (*G. cambogia*) is a similar related tree that grows in the Nilgiri Hills in South India. Concentrates made from the dried rind are used in food manufacturing; however, in India it appears to be reserved mostly for medicinal use. **Goraka** (*G. gummi-gutta*) is a variety that grows in Southeast Asia as well as South India and Africa. The fruit is pale yellow and ribbed like a small pumpkin. The rind and the fruit are dried for their acid taste, and goraka is often sold as a substitute for kokam.

Processing

Kokam fruits are harvested when ripe, and only the rind, comprising about half the entire fruit, is preserved, by drying in the sun. Sometimes salt is rubbed onto the rind to speed up drying and help preserve the tangy leathery morsels. Kokam is also boiled with sugar syrup to make a delicious deep purple to red cordial that, as noted, our Indian hosts assured us is beneficial in reducing obesity and cholesterol. Regardless of any therapeutic effects, on a steamy January afternoon on the outskirts of the lovely city of Cochin (one of my favorite places in India), following a day spent tramping around pepper, nutmeg and clove gardens, the kokam drink was memorably refreshing.

Buying and Storage

Kokam is available from spice retailers who either stock or specialize in Indian spices. Buy small quantities at a time, say 12 to 20 pieces, as the soft, pliable rinds dry out and lose some of their flavor if kept for too long. Should you notice evidence of white crystalline powder on the surface, do not be concerned—it is not mold but most often the result of using a little too much salt during drying. To ensure that a dish will not be overly salty, wash the pieces of kokam briefly in cold water before adding to the recipe. Store kokam in the same manner as other spices, in an airtight container away from direct light and protected from extreme heat and humidity. Under these conditions your kokam will last for more than 2 years.

Use

Kokam is used as a souring agent in much the same way as tamarind. Its slightly fruity flavor produces a milder effect than tamarind or amchur (green mango powder). Pieces of kokam are generally added whole to a dish without being chopped; however, check the pieces first to make sure that no small stones remain within the flattened-out skullcaps of rind. Kokam complements all curries and those made with fish in particular, hence the South Indian common name "fish tamarind." When I make curries, I usually put a few pieces in with the tomato paste and let them infuse while the other preparations are being made.

WEIGHT PER TEASPOON (5 mL)

- **whole:** 1.8 g

SUGGESTED QUANTITY PER POUND (500 g)

- **red meats:** 4 pieces
- **white meats:** 4 pieces
- **vegetables:** 2 to 3 pieces
- **grains and pulses:** 2 to 3 pieces
- **baked goods:** 2 to 3 pieces

K

South Indian Sardines

In the seafood-abundant south of India, kokam is known as fish tamarind. Sardines are sustainable and packed with nutrition, and pairing them with the fruity yet souring attributes of kokam is a perfect way to enjoy them.

**Makes
4 servings**

Preparation time:
10 minutes

Cooking time:
20 minutes

- - - - - - - - - - - - - - - -

Tip

Sardines are cooked when the fins release when gently pulled.

• **Wok, optional**

2 tbsp	oil	30 mL
½ cup	unsweetened shredded coconut	125 mL
4	cloves garlic, crushed	4
4	onions, grated	4
2	green finger chiles, chopped	2
2	fresh or dried curry leaves	2
2	pieces kokam	2
1	piece (1 inch/2.5 cm) gingerroot, peeled and grated	1
1 cup	water	250 mL
8 oz	fresh sardines (about 3 large or 6 small)	250 g
	Sea salt and freshly ground black pepper	

1. In wok or large skillet over medium heat, heat oil. Add coconut, garlic, onions, chiles, curry leaves, kokam and ginger and cook, stirring, for 5 minutes, until softened and fragrant. Add water and sardines. Cover, reduce heat and simmer for about 10 minutes, until sardines are just cooked (see Tip, left). Using a slotted spoon, carefully remove fish and transfer to a plate. Flake off flesh (discard skin and bones).

2. Return fish to pan and cook, stirring, for 2 to 3 minutes, until well combined. Season with salt and pepper to taste. Serve immediately.

Lavender

Lavandula angustifolia (English lavender, also known as
L. spica, L. officinalis, L. vera)

Names in Other Languages

- **Arabic:** khzama, lafand
- **Chinese (C):** fan yi chou
- **Chinese (M):** xun yi cao
- **Czech:** levandule
- **Danish:** lavendel
- **Dutch:** lavendel, spijklavendel
- **Finnish:** tupsupaalaventeli
- **French:** lavande
- **German:** Lavendel
- **Greek:** levanta
- **Italian:** lavanda
- **Japanese:** rabenda
- **Norwegian:** lavendel
- **Portuguese:** alfazema
- **Russian:** lavanda
- **Spanish:** lavanda
- **Swedish:** lavendel
- **Thai:** lawendeort
- **Turkish:** lavanta cicegi
- **Vietnamese:** hoa oai huong

Family: Lamiaceae (formerly Labiatae)

Varieties: French lavender (*L. dentata*), Italian lavender (*L. stoechas*), green lavender (*L. viridis*), cotton lavender (*Santolina chamaecyparissus*)

Other Names: broad-leaf lavender, lavender vera, lavender spica, true lavender (English lavender); fringed lavender (French lavender); Spanish lavender (Italian lavender); santolina (cotton lavender)

Flavor Group: Strong

Parts Used: flowers (as a herb)

Background

All varieties of lavender are native to the Mediterranean regions, and some were known to the ancient Greeks and Romans. Lavender was often added to bathwater—there is

Culinary Information

Combines with
- allspice
- bay leaf
- cardamom
- celery seed
- cinnamon and cassia
- ginger
- marjoram
- parsley
- tarragon
- thyme

Traditional Uses
- ice cream
- shortbread
- cakes and icings
- perfumes and soaps

Spice Blends
- herbes de Provence
- ras el hanout

little doubt that the English word *lavender* came from the Latin *lavare*, "to wash." English lavender was not cultivated in England until around 1568, but it has since thrived there. The quality of lavender grown in England and France was acknowledged as the best in the world until the late 20th century. Since then, under ideal climatic and soil conditions, it has been cultivated in the Australian state of Tasmania, where it is grown for the manufacture of essential oil.

The Plant

Lavender is a particularly attractive aromatic plant. It can be found in most herb gardens, although it is grown more for its fragrance and beauty than its culinary attributes. There are many different types of lavender, and while some are hybrids that have no application in cooking, the most fragrant English variety and the lesser-strength French type are used in recipes from Europe to the north of Africa. English lavender, the preferred variety for culinary use, is a small, bushy shrub that grows to around 3 feet (1 m) tall, with silvery gray–green smooth, pointed leaves. Long, slender, wheat stalk–like stems reach upward, and clustered on their bee-attracting waving tops are $2^1/_2$- to 4-inch (6 to 10 cm) highly perfumed flower heads made up of whorls of tiny mauve petals.

French lavender is distinguished from English by its deeply serrated leaves, thicker quadrangular stems, shorter flower stalks and fatter, fluffy-looking flower heads. It is worth noting that while the flowers of French lavender have much

less aroma than the English variety, its fleshy leaves contain more fragrance. This makes it a practical variety to grow for decorative purposes and to pick for bringing a pleasing scent indoors.

English lavender flower heads are dried for culinary purposes, and only the soft mauve flowers removed from the whorl are used. The aroma of English lavender is penetrating, sweet, fragrant, woody, grassy and floral. Its flavor is camphor-like, piney, floral and similar to rosemary, with an edge of lingering bitterness.

Other Varieties

French lavender (*Lavandula dentata*) flowers prolifically. It is an excellent variety to have in the garden because its flowering period lasts much longer than the spring-flowering English variety. When the flower heads die, cut back the plant heavily and you will be rewarded with an abundance of bee-attracting flowers. **Italian lavender** (*L. stoechas*) has dark purple flowers with upright winged petals at the top. Although it is an attractive variety, it is not suitable for cooking because of its bitterness. **Green lavender** (*L. viridis*) has pale green flowers and less fragrance but it does make an appealing addition to your garden. **Cotton lavender** (*Santolina chamaecyparissus*) has yellow flowers and fluffy foliage; it is most popular for its appearance and is a suitable ground cover.

Processing

Lavender flowers are best harvested in the early morning, before the heat of the day has started to draw out the volatile essence. Flower heads that still have a few buds unopened contain the highest oil content. After cutting the flower-laden stems, tie them in bundles of about 20 and hang upside down in a dark, dry, well-aired place for a few days. When dry, strip or gently thresh to remove the flowers from the stems.

Spice Notes

Just to set the record straight, I find it highly amusing that the beautiful broad fields of lavender growing in Provence, France, are actually high-yielding *Lavandula angustifolia*, or English lavender. Given the centuries of rivalry between these two nations, it comes as no surprise that the French still insist on calling it "French lavender"! I suppose this is justified to a small degree because it is grown in France.

Buying and Storage

Lavender flowers can be bought from some spice retailers and florists. Do not buy lavender for cooking purposes from an establishment that does not specialize in culinary herbs and spices or specialty foods: there is a high risk that it may be contaminated with insecticides and may have other oils, perfumes or nonedible ingredients added to enhance its aroma and appearance. Store dried lavender in the same way as other herbs and spices, in an airtight container protected from extremes of heat, light and humidity. Bowls of lavender flowers may be placed in a room to emit their fragrance; to avoid losing all the aroma in a matter of weeks, put a cover on the container at night and remove it only during the day.

Use

Lavender should be used sparingly in cooking, as its pungency can become overpowering and add unwanted bitterness to foods. Although these days many cooks do not consider lavender a culinary herb, it was used in the 17th century, along with other flowers, to make a conserve that was mixed with sugar and used as a fragrant icing for cakes and cookies. In Morocco, lavender is known as *khzama*. Along with rose petals, orris root powder, saffron and numerous other spices and mind-altering substances, it is added to the exotic spice blend ras el hanout, a name that translates literally as "top of the shop"—the very best concoction a spice trader in the souk has to offer. Lavender is also found in the well-known blend of savory herbs called herbes de Provence. I have been told by a French herb exporter that adding lavender to herbes de Provence began as a practice to boost the flavor of this blend when only poor-quality dried herbs were available. Lavender goes well with sweet dishes that contain cream and adds a colorful and complementary flavor to shortbread. The 17th-century use of lavender in icings remains appropriate today.

WEIGHT PER TEASPOON (5 mL)

- whole dry flowers: 0.7 g

SUGGESTED QUANTITY PER POUND (500 g)

- red meats: 1 tsp (5 mL)
- white meats: 1 tsp (5 mL)
- vegetables: 1 tsp (5 mL)
- grains and pulses: 1 tsp (5 mL)
- baked goods: 1 tsp (5 mL)

Provençal Pissaladière

Provence is one my favorite places in the world—the endless rows of lavender in July are a highlight. The food, of course, is also amazing, and this simple pizza-style dish is sold in every *boulangerie*. It is wonderful eaten warm out of the oven or cold on a picnic, preferably with a glass of rosé! Herbes de Provence is a combination of herbs comprising dried thyme, marjoram, parsley, tarragon and lavender. The floral notes of the lavender go splendidly with the pungent dried herbs, which are added to many French casseroles.

Makes 6 servings

Preparation time:
10 minutes
Cooking time: 1 hour,
30 minutes

Tips

To save time, make the onion mixture a day or two in advance and refrigerate in an airtight container until ready to use.

For a touch of color and spice, sprinkle with piment d'Espelette or red pepper flakes.

To serve as canapés, cut each piece into quarters, to make 24 canapés.

• **Baking sheet, lined with parchment paper**

5	large onions, finely sliced	5
2 tbsp	olive oil	30 mL
1 tbsp	butter	15 mL
2	cloves garlic, minced	2
1/4 tsp	fine sea salt	1 mL
1	sheet (10 by 15 inches/25 by 38 cm) puff pastry	1
2 oz	drained anchovies in oil	60 g
15	niçoise olives, pitted	15
1 1/2 tsp	herbes de Provence (page 739)	7 mL
1	egg, beaten	1

1. In a saucepan with a tight-fitting lid over low heat, combine onions, oil, butter, garlic and salt. Cook for about 1 hour, stirring occasionally, until onions are very soft and resemble jam. Remove lid and increase heat to high. Cook, stirring constantly, for 3 to 4 minutes or until onions are browned. Set aside.

2. Preheat oven to 350°F (180°C).

3. Place puff pastry on prepared baking sheet. Using a knife, gently score a 1-inch (2.5 cm) border around edges of pastry (be careful not to cut through). Spread onion mixture evenly within border. Starting in the top left corner and working across to the bottom right, arrange anchovies in a lattice pattern. Place an olive within each lattice opening. Scatter herbes de Provence overtop and brush border of pastry with egg. Bake for 15 to 20 minutes or until edges are golden. Cut into six rectangular portions and serve. If not eating immediately, cool and store in an airtight container for up to 2 days.

Lavender and Lemon Olive Oil Cakes

These fragrant cakes take me back to the lavender fields of Provence, which stretch far and wide across the incredibly picturesque countryside. Locals like to use lavender in as many applications as possible, and these cakes are a fine example. They are quite dense, so cooking them in a muffin pan makes perfect portions.

Makes 12 small cakes

Preparation time:
10 minutes

Cooking time: 15 to
20 minutes

- - - - - - - - - - - - - - - - -

Tips

Cake flour has a high starch content. If you don't have it, substitute 1¼ cups (300 mL) all-purpose flour plus ¼ cup (60 mL) cornstarch.

Either buy dried lavender (meant for culinary use) or grow and dry your own (see page 343).

For a decadent take on cupcakes, top with a light mauve buttercream icing.

- **12-cup muffin pan, greased and dusted with flour**
- **Preheat oven to 350°F (180°C)**

1 cup	milk	250 mL
	Very finely grated zest and juice of 2 lemons	
1 cup	extra virgin olive oil	250 mL
1 cup	granulated sugar	250 mL
3	eggs	3
1½ cups	cake flour (see Tips, left)	375 mL
1 tbsp	dried lavender (see Tips, left)	15 mL
1 tbsp	baking powder	15 mL

1. In a bowl, whisk together milk, lemon zest and juice and oil.

2. Using an electric mixer, mix sugar and eggs until pale and fluffy. Gradually add milk mixture, whisking lightly to incorporate.

3. In a bowl, combine flour, lavender and baking powder. Gently fold dry ingredients into wet ingredients. Spoon batter into prepared pan and bake in preheated oven for 15 to 20 minutes, until golden and a tester inserted in the centers comes out clean. Remove from oven and set aside to cool in pan for 10 minutes, then carefully invert onto a serving plate. Serve warm or at room temperature with a dusting of confectioners' (icing) sugar and a dollop of whipped cream or crème fraîche. Serve the same day or freeze in an airtight container for up to 1 month.

Lemongrass

Cymbopogon citratus

Names in Other Languages

- **Arabic:** hashisha al-limun
- **Burmese:** zabalin
- **Chinese (C):** heung masu tso, chou geung
- **Chinese (M):** chao jiang, feng mao
- **Czech:** citronovatrava
- **Danish:** citrongraes
- **Dutch:** citroengras, sereh
- **Filipino:** tanglad
- **Finnish:** sitruunaruoho
- **French:** citronnelle
- **German:** Zitronengras
- **Greek:** lemonochorto
- **Hungarian:** citromfu
- **Indian:** bhustrina, ghanda, ghandhtrina, sera
- **Indonesian:** sere, sereh
- **Italian:** erba di limone, cimbopogone
- **Japanese:** remon-su
- **Laotian:** bai mak nao
- **Malay:** serai
- **Philippines:** tanglad
- **Portuguese:** capim santo
- **Russian:** limonnoe sorgo
- **Spanish:** limoncillo, zacate de limon
- **Sri Lankan:** sera
- **Swedish:** citrongras
- **Thai:** takrai, cha khrai
- **Turkish:** limon otu
- **Vietnamese:** xa, sa chanh

Family: Poaceae (formerly Gramineae)

Varieties: Malabar or Cochin grass (*C. flexuosus*), rosha grass (*C. martinii*), citronella grass (*C. nardusi*)

Other Names: camel's hay, citronella, serai

Flavor Group: Strong

Parts Used: stems and leaves (as a herb)

Background

Lemongrass grows throughout tropical Asia. It was used by the ancient Romans, Greeks and Egyptians as a medicine and as a cosmetic. Its popularity in Asia could be linked with the fact that lemons do not grow readily in the tropics. As a result, lemongrass became another source of that fragrant lemon taste that is sought after in practically every cuisine. Lemongrass is cultivated in South America, Central Africa and the West Indies. A particular delight when dining on seafood on the Malabar Coast of India is enjoying the flavor of lemongrass along with ginger, kokam and curry leaves. In Florida it is grown for citral, the oil extracted by steam distillation, which is used as a natural substitute for the flavor of lemon peel, as well as in the manufacture of soaps. The oil from another *Cymbopogon*, rosha grass, has a sweet geranium aroma and is employed to water down attar of roses, an essence of roses used in the manufacture of perfumes.

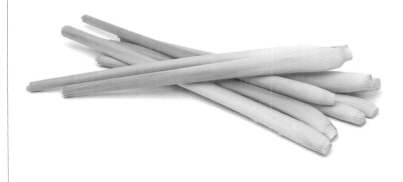

Culinary Information

Combines with

- allspice
- cardamom
- chile
- cinnamon
- cloves
- coriander (leaf and seed)
- cumin
- fennel seed
- fenugreek seed
- galangal
- ginger
- mustard
- nigella
- paprika
- tamarind
- turmeric
- Vietnamese mint

Traditional Uses

- Asian soups
- curries and stir-fries
- steamed seafood
- marinades for fish, pork and chicken

Spice Blends

- Thai and Indonesian seasoning blends
- green curry blends

The Plant

At first glance lemongrass, with its $1\frac{1}{2}$- to 3-foot (0.5 to 1 m) bladelike leaves, does not appear to be overly inviting as a culinary herb. However, once you experience its delicious lemon fragrance, this opinion rapidly changes. Lemongrass grows in tight, dense, tufted clumps that increase in size every year and are rarely seen to flower. The razor-like, slightly sticky blades have a central rib running along them and vary in color from pale green to rust red at the tips during certain stages. While these lance-like leaves have some lemongrass aroma, it is in fact the lower, almost white section of the stem that is most used in cooking. Lemongrass has a tangy flavor similar to the zest of lemon, thanks to the high presence of citral, a substance also found in the outer rind of lemons.

Other Varieties

Malabar or **Cochin grass** (*Cymbopogon flexuosus*) is also known as East Indian lemon grass, as it is indigenous to regions from India to Sri Lanka and Thailand, Burma and

Vietnam. Although used in cooking, it is not considered as suitable as *C. citratus*. Another variety, **Rosha grass** (*C. martinii*), is valued for its oil, which has been used as an insect repellent and antiseptic. **Citronella grass** (*C. nardusi*) has a strong, disagreeable taste and is not used in cooking. It is the most popular variety for extraction of citronella oil, which is an effective insect repellent. Citronella is especially good for keeping mosquitos at bay, although one unexpected feature is that it can entice bees because of its similarity to a bee-attracting pheromone.

Processing

Should you be fortunate enough to have lemongrass growing, remember to divide the clump into two or three smaller ones each year; that way they will thrive and give you better stems. To harvest, cut the stems down low, just above the ground, then remove the sharp, flat leaf section. There are three basic ways of processing lemongrass: the oil is extracted by steam distillation or fresh stems are either dehydrated or preserved in jars. Lemongrass tends to lose

Spice Notes

Many years ago we had a beautiful clump of lemongrass growing at home. With progressive seasons the clump became larger and larger until it was about 3 feet (1 m) in diameter. Then to my horror the lemongrass started to die, which reminded me of what can happen when herbs such as mint, chives and lemongrass get out of control—basically the perimeter growth starves the center of the clump of moisture and nutrients. This leads to dieback in the center, which creates a rot that spreads and kills off the whole mass. That is why you should divide your masses of lemongrass every season or two.

its best volatile character on drying and does not really develop any concentration of flavor or other attributes, as do some herbs such as lemon myrtle. Jars of lemongrass are usually preserved with lemon juice or vinegar. Because their flavors are compatible with lemongrass and appropriate in most recipes using lemongrass, preserved lemongrass makes an acceptable substitute for fresh.

Buying and Storage

Fresh lemongrass is usually sold in bunches of three to four stems about 16 inches (40 cm) long with the tuberous roots removed and the sharp leaves cut off. The stems should be firm and white with a greenish tinge and not look at all dry or wrinkled. The fresh stems can be kept in the refrigerator for a few weeks when wrapped in plastic; they can also be frozen for 6 months. Dried lemongrass is either sliced into small rings $1/4$ to $1/3$ inch (5 to 6 mm) in diameter or finely chopped. Store in the same manner as other dry herbs and spices: in an airtight container away from extremes of heat, light and humidity.

Use

For best results, lemongrass needs to be carefully prepared before adding to most dishes. The only time I don't worry too much is when it is being simmered for later removal. Then I tie the full length in a knot (being careful not to cut my hands on the leaves) and put it in the pot, where the bruised lemongrass releases its flavor during cooking; I remove the spent knotted bunch before serving.

When chopping lemongrass to add to stir-fries and curries, or to crush using a mortar and pestle, strip from the stems any remaining upper section that is at all leaflike and not tightly rolled. Peel off a couple of outer layers, keeping the tender white section, and slice it crosswise into very thin disks. If you don't do this, the remaining longitudinal fibers will produce a hairy appearance and a less than pleasant mouthfeel.

Lemongrass lends its own special character to many Asian dishes. It is well worth considering as an addition to steamed seafood and poultry dishes, marinades for pork, and whole fish barbecued in foil. The citral content in lemongrass is quite robust, so it can withstand long cooking and will not diminish as quickly as, say, lemon myrtle.

WEIGHT PER TEASPOON (5 mL)
- dried and cut: 1.4 g

SUGGESTED QUANTITY PER POUND (500 g)
- **red meats:** $3^{1}/4$ to 4 inches (8 to 10 cm) fresh stem
- **white meats:** $3^{1}/4$ to 4 inches (8 to 10 cm) fresh stem
- **vegetables:** $3^{1}/4$ to 4 inches (8 to 10 cm) fresh stem
- **grains and pulses:** $3^{1}/4$ to 4 inches (8 to 10 cm) fresh stem
- **baked goods:** 2 to $2^{1}/2$ inches (5 to 6 cm) fresh stem

L

Green Chicken Curry

This must be one of the most quintessential Thai dishes—I have yet to eat at a Thai restaurant without someone ordering it. The paste requires some chopping but is really simple, and it can be frozen in portions for future use.

Makes 6 servings

Preparation time:
30 minutes

Cooking time:
25 minutes

Tips

To prepare lemongrass:
Using a sharp knife, cut off the lower bulb end and peel away the outer two or three layers of stem until you reach the soft white interior, which is easier to slice.

Makrut lime leaves are also known as "kaffir" lime leaves and can be found in most Asian markets.

Small red shallots are often used in Asian cooking. If you cannot find them, you can use regular shallots, which have a similar flavor.

- **Blender**
- **Wok**

GREEN CURRY PASTE

5	green finger chiles	5
2 tbsp	finely chopped lemongrass (see Tips, left)	30 mL
1 tsp	finely chopped makrut lime leaves (see Tips, left)	5 mL
5	small red shallots, diced (see Tips, left)	5
1 tbsp	chopped fresh galangal (see Tips, page 353)	15 mL
4	cloves garlic, chopped	4
1 tbsp	chopped fresh coriander (cilantro) root/stem	15 mL
Pinch	freshly grated lime zest	Pinch
½ tsp	shrimp paste	2 mL
½ tsp	ground coriander seed	2 mL
¼ tsp	ground cumin	1 mL
Pinch	freshly ground white pepper	Pinch
Pinch	fine sea salt	Pinch
1 tbsp	water	15 mL

CURRY

2 tsp	oil	10 mL
2 lbs	skinless boneless chicken thighs, trimmed and cut into 1½-inch (4 cm) pieces	1 kg
2 cups	coconut milk (see Tips, page 353)	500 mL
1½ cups	mixed vegetables (button mushrooms, snow peas, green beans)	375 mL
½ cup	packed fresh coriander (cilantro) leaves	125 mL

1. *Green Curry Paste:* In blender, combine chiles, lemongrass, lime leaves, shallots, galangal, garlic, coriander root, lime zest, shrimp paste, coriander seed, cumin, pepper, salt and water. Blend at high speed until a paste forms (add more water if necessary).

Tips

While galangal is slightly sweeter, gingerroot can be substituted if needed.

Coconut milk is a liquid extracted from coconut meat and then watered down. The "cream" will sit at the top of the can, so it's best to shake before using to get the right milky consistency.

2. *Curry:* In wok over medium heat, heat oil. Add chicken and cook, stirring constantly, for 2 to 3 minutes, until lightly browned. Add prepared curry paste and cook, stirring, for about 3 minutes, until chicken is thoroughly coated. Add coconut milk and bring to a boil, then reduce heat and simmer for 10 minutes, until sauce starts to thicken. Add vegetables and cook for 5 to 10 minutes, until vegetables are tender-crisp and chicken is cooked through. Sprinkle with coriander leaves and serve.

Variation

To make a red curry paste, substitute 7 dried red chiles (seeded, soaked in boiling water for 10 minutes, drained and chopped) for the green chiles and add 2 tsp (10 mL) ground paprika in Step 1.

L

Mussels with Lemongrass

Of all of the recipes in this book, this is probably my husband's favorite (and it's something we eat regularly). Fresh mussels are economical and nutritious and they absorb the Vietnamese flavors incredibly well.

Makes 4 starter servings

Preparation time:
15 minutes

Cooking time:
10 minutes

Tips

Rice bran oil is an unhydrogenated oil with little flavor and a high smoke point. If you can't find it, any other neutral oil can be used.

To prepare mussels: Rinse under cold running water. Tap any opened mussels, and if they don't respond by closing, discard. Using the back of a knife, scrape off any barnacles and pull out the tendrils (beards). Store in the refrigerator in a bowl covered with a damp cloth until ready to cook. Mussels are best eaten the day of purchase.

To prepare lemongrass: Using a sharp knife, cut off the tough root end and peel away and discard the outer two or three layers of stem until you reach the soft white interior, which is easier to slice.

1 tbsp	rice bran oil or olive oil (see Tips, left)	15 mL
6	stalks lemongrass, peeled and finely chopped (see Tips, left)	6
2	cloves garlic, thinly sliced	2
3 to 4 lbs	mussels (see Tips, left)	1.5 to 2 kg
2 cups	chicken broth	500 mL
2 tbsp	oyster sauce	30 mL
2 tbsp	fish sauce (nam pla)	30 mL
1	red finger chile, sliced	1
1 cup	lightly packed fresh coriander (cilantro) leaves	250 mL

1. In a large pot over medium heat, heat oil. Add lemongrass and garlic and stir-fry for 1 minute, until fragrant. Add mussels and increase heat to high. Cover tightly with a lid and cook for 5 minutes. Remove lid and stir gently. Add broth, oyster sauce and fish sauce. Cover and cook for 5 minutes, until all the mussels are open (you may need to shake the pot or stir once or twice so the heat is distributed evenly).

2. To serve, ladle mussels into deep serving bowls (discard any that haven't opened) and divide broth evenly among the bowls. Top with chile and coriander leaves and serve immediately.

Lemon Myrtle

Backhousia citriodora

Family: Myrtaceae

Varieties: anise myrtle (*Syzygium anisatum*), cinnamon myrtle (*Backhousia myrtifolia*)

Other Names: lemon ironwood, lemon-scented myrtle, sand verbena myrtle, sweet verbena tree, tree verbena

Flavor Group: Strong

Parts Used: leaves and flowers (as a herb)

Background

Although there are no records that establish the exact antiquity of native Australian herbs and spices, these hardy yet frost-sensitive trees have been growing wild in the coastal

Culinary Information

Combines with

- allspice
- cardamom
- chile
- cinnamon
- cloves
- coriander (leaf and seed)
- cumin
- fennel seed
- fenugreek seed
- galangal
- ginger
- mustard
- nigella
- paprika
- tamarind
- turmeric
- Vietnamese mint

Traditional Uses

- Asian dishes (added in small amounts)
- grilled chicken, pork and fish
- pancakes
- shortbread
- cakes and muffins

Spice Blends

- blends containing native Australian herbs and spices
- barbecue rubs
- stir-fry seasonings
- laksa spice blends
- green curry mixes

areas of northern New South Wales and Queensland for many thousands of years. When these were identified and classified, the botanical name *Backhousia* was given to the genus after a Yorkshire nurseryman, James Backhouse, who visited Australia between 1832 and 1838.

Lemon myrtle trees are now grown in South Africa, the southern United States and southern Europe, and in more recent times, propagation with a view to extracting the essential oil has taken place in China, Indonesia, Thailand and, most actively, in Australia.

Citral

Citral is what gives lemons, lemongrass and lemon verbena their lemony flavor. Lemon myrtle's citral content is much higher than these other sources; it was first identified in the late 19th century. In the early 20th century the essential oil was extracted by steam distillation for use as lemon flavoring. Possibly because lemons were more accessible and had a longer history of being processed for citral, lemon myrtle oil faded into the background until the late 20th century, when scores of enterprising farmers started lemon myrtle plantations.

The Plant

Of all the useful native Australian plants, the magnificent lemon myrtle tree is one of my culinary favorites. These attractive evergreen rainforest trees grow to around 26 feet (8 m) tall and may even reach 60 feet (20 m) in tropical conditions. The growth is bushy, with low branches covered in dark green oval, tapering leaves that resemble bay leaves. In autumn, small white flowers bloom in thick, soft clusters, which makes this an excellent tree to grow for its appearance as well as for its usefulness. Both the flowers and tiny fruits may be eaten, as well as the leaves.

The aroma of lemon myrtle is similar to a blend of lemon verbena, lemongrass and makrut lime leaves, with a haunting eucalyptus background—something that is particularly noticeable after rain. The flavor is lemony and tangy, with distinct lime zest notes and a pleasantly lingering, slightly numbing camphor aftertaste. Lemon myrtle's citral content (the component that gives it the lemon flavor) is around 90%, compared with around 80% for lemongrass and only 6% in lemons. Powdered lemon myrtle leaf is coarse and pale green. When freshly ground it releases all of its appealing aroma and taste attributes.

Other Varieties

Anise myrtle (*Syzygium anisatum*), also known as the ringwood tree, grows in northern New South Wales, Australia. It is a medium to large tree with long, narrow leaves that are originally soft and pink but mature to dark green and glossy. They have a distinct anise and licorice-like flavor that results from their high anethole content. Anise myrtle can be used as a substitute for anise seed and star anise. The oil, extracted

Spice Notes

On the topic of James Backhouse and his connection with Australia (page 356), I was interested to receive an email from Jane Cullen, of York, England, in which she said: "I have been doing some research about *Backhousia citriodora* (lemon myrtle) as I am currently heading a campaign in York to establish a Heritage Centre on the former site of the James Backhouse nurseries; the very same James Backhouse from whom the lemon myrtle derives its name. As well as being a groundbreaking botanist, James Backhouse was a Quaker missionary, and the original 100-acre nursery garden here in York was described as the Kew [Gardens] of the North." One can only hope that Jane's campaign is successful!

by steam distillation, has the ability to mask unpleasant aromas and is used in soaps and cosmetics.

Cinnamon myrtle (*Backhousia myrtifolia*) is so named because it has a distinctly cinnamon and cassia-like flavor. Other common names for this tree are carrol ironwood, neverbreak and grey myrtle. This rainforest tree is widely distributed along the east coast of Australia, from south of Sydney to north of Brisbane. Use the fresh leaves in herbal teas, cookies and even curries, but remember that cinnamon myrtle should be used sparingly, as it has a slightly sharp background note that can be overpowering.

Processing

Lemon myrtle leaves may be picked throughout the year. As with bay leaves, harvest only dark mature leaves that are quite firm, as these will have the best flavor. While lemon myrtle may be used fresh, the flavor intensifies on drying and, unlike many highly fragrant herbs, it seems to lose none of its delicate top-note perfume when carefully dried away from sunlight. The flesh of the fruit is used only when fresh, and it is important to remove the hard core before adding the flesh to a dish.

Like other herbs, lemon myrtle leaves are best dried in a dark, well-aired place. Allow the water content to evaporate and leave them to crisp and dry for about 5 days; at that point they will have a moisture content of less than 12%. To avoid curling and achieve attractive flat leaves, arrange one layer on wire mesh (insect screening), making sure it is well ventilated, and place another piece of mesh on top, weighted down with some small pieces of wood. When the leaves are crisp and dry, they are ready for use.

Buying and Storage

Fresh lemon myrtle leaves can sometimes be bought from specialty suppliers of native Australian foods. Because of its local popularity as a street tree, many Australians now have only to venture out to the "nature strip" beside their sidewalk to pick a few fresh lemon myrtle leaves. However, for those readers not lucky enough to have a supply within easy reach, the more convenient whole or powdered lemon myrtle leaf is readily available from herb and spice shops and many gourmet food retailers. Because of the volatility of the essential oil, it is important to purchase only small quantities—say, less than $1^2/_3$ oz (50 g), for normal household requirements—of freshly ground lemon myrtle powder. Make sure it comes in airtight packaging.

Store dried lemon myrtle leaves in an airtight container in a cool, dark place. Whole leaves will last for up to 2 years, powdered leaves for at least 1 year.

Use

Lemon myrtle has an incredibly varied number of uses, as its aromatic lemony flavor goes with almost any food. There are, however, two basic guidelines worth remembering to achieve the best results: One is to add only a small amount—say, $^1/_4$ to $^1/_2$ tsp (1 to 2 mL), or 1 to 2 leaves—to 1 pound (500 g) of meat or vegetables, then taste before adding more. The other is to put lemon myrtle only in foods that cook for a short time, never subjecting it to extreme temperatures for more than 10 to 15 minutes. When too much lemon myrtle is used, or when it is cooked for too long, the flavor-giving volatile oils become depleted and a sharp, medicinal eucalyptus flavor will dominate.

Lemon myrtle is an excellent substitute for lemongrass. It complements Asian stir-fries, especially those with chicken, seafood and vegetables. Broiled (grilled) chicken, pork and fish are given a lift when a little lemon myrtle is sprinkled on before cooking, as is smoked salmon served cold. Lemon myrtle is a fragrant addition in cakes and muffins, although I generally prefer it in sweet things that are cooked more quickly at a lower heat, such as blini and pancakes. In those quick-cooking applications, infuse lemon myrtle in a little warmed milk or water to bring out the flavor before adding to the rest of the ingredients. Shortbread cookies are particularly delicious when flavored with ground lemon myrtle. However, they are best consumed within a few days of baking (if you can resist them for that long), as the fresh lemon notes deteriorate quite quickly.

WEIGHT PER TEASPOON (5 mL)
- **whole dried leaf:** 0.5 g
- **ground:** 2.2 g

SUGGESTED QUANTITY PER POUND (500 g)
- **red meats:** $^1/_4$ to $^1/_2$ tsp (1 to 2 mL) ground dried leaves
- **white meats:** $^1/_4$ to $^1/_2$ tsp (1 to 2 mL) ground dried leaves
- **vegetables:** $^1/_2$ tsp (2 mL) ground dried leaves
- **grains and pulses:** $^1/_2$ tsp (2 mL) ground dried leaves
- **baked goods:** $^1/_2$ tsp (2 mL) ground dried leaves

Lemon Myrtle Chicken Wrap

As with regular lemon, lemon myrtle works equally well in sweet and savory dishes. It goes particularly well with the mild flavor of chicken, really livening it up. This tasty wrap makes an ideal lunch or light dinner.

**Makes
6 servings**

Preparation time:
 10 minutes

Cooking time:
 10 minutes

4	skinless boneless chicken breasts, cut into 3 strips each	4
2 tsp	ground lemon myrtle	10 mL
2 tsp	olive oil	10 mL
	Sea salt and freshly ground black pepper	
6	soft tortillas	6
12	Slow-Roasted Tomatoes (page 617)	12
2 cups	lightly packed wild arugula leaves	500 mL
½ cup	mayonnaise	125 mL

1. In a bowl, combine chicken with lemon myrtle, oil and salt and pepper to taste. Arrange chicken strips on a baking sheet and broil in the oven for about 4 minutes per side or until cooked through. (Alternatively, you can pan-fry the chicken for about 4 minutes per side or until cooked through.)

2. Spread 2 tbsp (30 mL) mayonnaise along the center of each tortilla. Top with 2 roasted tomatoes, arugula and 2 cooked chicken strips. Roll up and serve immediately (or, if transporting, wrap in foil).

Lemon Myrtle Cheesecake

When I was very young, Mum made cakes to serve at my grandparents' nursery and shop on the weekend. My sisters and I would "waitress." My favorite dessert was a simple unbaked cheesecake. This is a similar cake, with the addition of lemon myrtle in the filling and wattleseed in the base. These Australian native spices work perfectly here, adding a nuttiness to the base and freshness to the filling. Serve with extra lemon zest and fresh raspberries on top, if desired.

Makes 8 servings

Preparation time:
5 minutes

Cooking time:
10 minutes, plus
4 hours for chilling

Tips

The dry ingredients for the base can also be crushed by placing them in a resealable bag (removing all the air) and beating with a rolling pin.

Superfine (caster) sugar is very fine granulated sugar typically used in recipes that require a faster-dissolving granule. If you can't find it in stores, you can make your own by using a food processor fitted with the metal blade to process granulated sugar to a very fine, sand-like consistency.

- **9-inch (23 cm) springform pan, greased and lined with parchment paper**
- **Food processor**
- **Electric mixer**

BASE

7 oz	digestive biscuits or graham crackers (about 15)	210 g
¾ cup	macadamia nuts	175 mL
1 tsp	ground wattleseed	5 mL
½ cup	butter, melted	125 mL

FILLING

1 tbsp	gelatin crystals	15 mL
3 tbsp	water	45 mL
1 lb	full-fat cream cheese, at room temperature	500 g
¾ cup	superfine (caster) sugar (see Tips, left)	175 mL
½ tsp	pure vanilla extract	2 mL
2 tsp	ground lemon myrtle	10 mL
1 tsp	finely grated lemon zest	5 mL
1 cup	table (18%) cream	250 mL

1. *Base:* In food processor fitted with the metal blade, process biscuits, macadamia nuts and wattleseed until fine crumbs form (see Tips, left). Transfer to a bowl, add butter and mix until well combined. Using the back of a spoon, firmly press mixture evenly over base of springform pan. Refrigerate while making filling.

2. *Filling:* In a small saucepan over low heat, combine gelatin and water and mix until dissolved. (To dissolve gelatin in the microwave, combine with water in a heatproof bowl and cook on High for 20 seconds.) Transfer to a mixing bowl and add cream cheese, sugar, vanilla, lemon myrtle and lemon zest. Beat with electric mixer at medium speed until smooth. Add cream and mix until combined. Pour filling over prepared base. Cover and refrigerate for at least 4 hours to set before serving.

Lemon Verbena

Aloysia triphylla (formerly *Lippia citriodora*; also known as *A. citriodora, L. triphylla, Verbena triphylla*)

Names in Other Languages

- **Chinese (C):** nihng mung mah bin chou
- **Chinese (M):** ning meng ma bian cao
- **Czech:** sporys
- **Danish:** jernurt
- **Dutch:** citroenverbena
- **Finnish:** lippia
- **French:** verveine citronelle
- **German:** Zitronenverbene
- **Greek:** louiza, verbena
- **Hungarian:** citrom verbena
- **Japanese:** boshu-boku
- **Polish:** lippia trojlistna
- **Portuguese:** limonete
- **Russian:** verbena limonnaya
- **Spanish:** cedron, hierbaluisa

Family: Verbenaceae

Other Names: lemon beebrush

Flavor Group: Strong

Parts Used: leaves (as a herb)

Background

Lemon verbena is native to South America and was introduced to Europe by the Spanish. For some reason the history of this plant's introduction to Europe is checkered. Some specimens had been secretly imported into Spain by the mid 1700s; then, around 1760, Philibert Commerson, the French royal botanist and naturalist, made its recognition public in Europe. By 1784, following the introduction of lemon verbena to English horticulturalists by a professor

Culinary Information

Combines with
- cardamom
- cinnamon
- ginger
- tamarind
- Vietnamese mint

Traditional Uses
- shortbread
- cakes and muffins
- rice and milk puddings

Spice Blends
- not commonly used in spice blends

of botany at Oxford, it was growing in England, where it quickly became a garden favorite. Because the dried leaves retain their aroma so effectively, lemon verbena was a popular ingredient, along with rose petals, lavender and other dried flowers, in potpourri. Greek folklore has it that tucking some dried lemon verbena in your pillow will ensure sweet dreams. This was the inspiration behind Liz's sleep pillows (see "Spice Notes," page 364), which contained lavender to induce sound sleep, lemon verbena for sweet dreams, and rose petals to help one wake refreshed.

The Plant

Not to be confused with another plant called verbena, or vervain (*Verbena officinalis*), lemon verbena is an attractive deciduous tree that grows to about 15 feet (4.5 m) tall. It has pale green pointed leaves about 4 inches (10 cm) long. If left unpruned, the tree can spread to a width of at least 6 feet (2 m). The highly aromatic leaves feel sticky and almost rough on the underside because of their oil-bearing glands. Delicate pale lavender-colored flowerets form in hazy plumes at the ends of its leaf-covered branches. When the fresh leaves of lemon verbena are crushed, or even when simply brushed against, a heavenly lemon fragrance fills the air. The easiest way to describe the aroma and taste is that they resemble highly perfumed lemons, devoid of acidity and fruitiness.

Processing

Lemon verbena is best harvested a couple of months after the new season's leaves have appeared in spring, as tender young leaves tend to shrivel up and don't retain much aroma. When the tree is about three years old, about 30%

L

Spice Notes

Few plants evoke such powerful recollections of my childhood as lemon verbena. My parents had a grove of trees that we were constantly harvesting in summer. We dried the leaves and put them in ceramic bowls with cork stoppers, along with other ingredients for potpourri, and sold them at Christmastime from our roadside shop. After my wife, Liz, and I built our first home, when our three daughters were little tots, Liz made fragrant pillows using leaves she picked in summer from the same grove and sold them to supplement our income.

of its growth may be cut back the first time you prune it in summer; then do the same degree of pruning in late summer. This encourages abundant new growth and dense foliage; if not harvested or cut back to this extent, the trees can become very leggy and sparse-looking.

It is easiest to strip the leaves off the cut branches before drying, a task done simply by gently pinching the thin end between thumb and forefinger and zipping along to the thick end, by which time you'll have a handful of leaves. Lay the stripped-off leaves on frames of insect screening or sheets of paper in a dark, warm, well-aired place for a few days, until they feel quite crisp and dry.

Buying and Storage

Fresh lemon verbena is rarely available. In dry form it is most often found in fragrant gifts or blended with other herbs for tisanes (teas). Dry lemon verbena leaves should be dark green, crisp and lemon-scented and should not smell at all musty. Store in airtight containers in a cool, dark place until you want to enjoy the fragrance. When the leaves are mixed into a potpourri or some other scented item and left in the open to scent a room, the aroma will evaporate naturally over a year or two.

Use

Fresh lemon verbena leaves will add a tantalizing bouquet to chocolate cake. Place a few leaves in the bottom of the cake tin before spooning in the batter prior to baking. These can be peeled off when the cake has cooled, leaving behind the aromatic oils released during baking. My mother would often put two or three leaves on top of rice puddings and custards before baking. They can also be chopped finely and added to Asian dishes, in much the same way as lemon myrtle.

SUGGESTED QUANTITY PER POUND (500 g)

- **red meats:** 5 fresh leaves
- **white meats:** 4 fresh leaves
- **vegetables:** 4 fresh leaves
- **grains and pulses:** 4 fresh leaves
- **baked goods:** 4 fresh leaves

Lemon Verbena Tea

In the sprawling two-acre (0.8 ha) garden at my grandparents' herb and spice shop and nursery, Somerset Cottage, there was a row of lovely lush, fragrant lemon verbena trees. For pocket money my sisters and I would pick the leaves, which Grandpa would lay on trays to dry, then sell in the shop. The aroma of lemon verbena instantly takes me back to my childhood. This "verveine" tea is refreshing and flavorsome, and it also aids digestion. Serve over ice in the summer.

**Makes
4 servings**

Preparation time:
 5 minutes
Cooking time:
 10 minutes

- - - - - - - - - - - - - - - -

Tip

If using fresh leaves, halve
the quantity.

| 1 cup | dried lemon verbena leaves (see Tip, left, and page 364) | 250 mL |
| 4 cups | boiling water | 1 L |

1. In a large teapot or coffee press, pour boiling water over lemon verbena. Set aside for 10 minutes to steep before pouring.

Variation

Add 1 tbsp (15 mL) dried mint plus 2 strips lemon peel.

Licorice Root

Glycyrrhiza glabra

Names in Other Languages

- **Arabic:** irqu as-sus, sous
- **Chinese (C):** gam chou
- **Chinese (M):** gan cao
- **Czech:** lekorice, sladky drevo
- **Danish:** lakrids
- **Dutch:** zoethout
- **Finnish:** lakritskasvi
- **French:** réglisse
- **German:** Lakritze, Sussholz
- **Greek:** glikoriza
- **Hungarian:** edesfa
- **Indian:** jethi madh, madhuka, mithi lakdi
- **Italian:** liquirizia
- **Japanese:** nankin-kanzo
- **Norwegian:** lakrisrot
- **Portuguese:** alcacuz
- **Russian:** lakrichnik, solodka
- **Spanish:** orozuz, regaliz
- **Swedish:** lakrits
- **Thai:** chaometes
- **Turkish:** meyan koku
- **Vietnamese:** cam thao

Family: Fabaceae (formerly Leguminosae)

Varieties: American licorice (*G. lepidota*), Chinese licorice (*G. uralensis*), Russian licorice (*G. echinata*)

Other Names: black sugar, Spanish juice, sweetroot, sweetwood

Flavor Group: Pungent

Parts Used: roots (as a spice)

Background

Licorice is native to southeastern Europe, the Middle East and Southwest Asia. In those locations, long before its medicinal properties were appreciated, generations enjoyed it as a free source of something sweet to chew on. Licorice root was known to the ancient Greeks, Egyptians and Romans as a remedy for coughs and colds; the botanical name *Glycyrrhiza* is derived from the Greek word for "sweet root." Glycyrrhizin is the sweet-tasting compound that gives licorice its characteristic flavor. The Greek physician Theophrastus wrote in the third century BCE that it quenched one's thirst if held in the mouth. A black juice extracted from the roots, in the same way it is produced today, was taken as a refreshing drink by the Greeks and Romans.

Culinary Information

Combines with

- allspice
- cardamom
- cinnamon and cassia
- cloves
- coriander seed
- fennel seed
- ginger
- mace
- pepper
- star anise
- Sichuan pepper

Traditional Uses

- stewed fruit
- ice cream
- marinades for poultry and pork
- flavoring tobacco

Spice Blends

- Chinese master stocks

Its use as a medicine continued throughout the Middle Ages, although it does not appear to have been cultivated in central or western Europe until the 15th century. The Dominican Black Friars first cultivated licorice in the 16th century at their monastery in Pontefract, Yorkshire, which later became the center of England's licorice confectionery industry. Thus the name "Pontefract cakes" was given to the small black tablets of licorice extract concentrated by evaporation. Licorice root contains about 4% glycyrrhizin, which is reputed to be 50 times sweeter than cane sugar. It is worth noting that the sweetness of licorice root is safe for people with diabetes (not the confectionery, though, which has sugar added). The distinctive flavor of licorice is used to mask the bitter taste of some medicines, and it is an ingredient in alcoholic beverages such as Guinness stout, anesone, raki and sambuca, as well as being used in snuff and to flavor chewing tobacco.

The Plant

The licorice plant is a small herbaceous perennial legume that grows 3 to 5 feet (1 to 1.5 m) tall in a clump of straight, woody stalks. Its frond-shaped leaves are set among the stems, and loose racemes of butterfly-like lilac-blue flowers form in long, spiked clusters, growing where the leaf stalk meets the main stem. Small, bean-like pods, which contain five seeds, develop after flowering; these have no culinary application. The parts used are the large taproot, which can grow as much as 3 feet (1 m) deep, and the numerous horizontal rhizomes that spread out in a meandering tangle underground.

Although there are a few different types of *Glycyrrhiza*, the variety considered best for culinary purposes is *G. glabra*. Its root sections are grayish brown on the outside and have a fibrous yellow middle. The aroma is slightly mild (even when cut or bruised) and sweet, with a dry note resembling new-mown straw. The flavor is initially bitter but develops into very sweet and anise-like in the mouth; the characteristic licorice taste lingers and freshens one's breath. Powdered licorice root is gray-green in color and very fine, like talcum powder; it has an extremely strong flavor.

Other Varieties

American licorice (*G. lepidota*), which is indigenous to North America, has a sweet, lingering licorice flavor and has been used medicinally and to flavor tobacco. However, it is not used as often as *G. glabra*, which has a superior flavor for making confectionary. **Chinese licorice** (*G. uralensis*) is cultivated in China. This flowering plant is quite different from *G. glabra*, with oval rather than frond-shaped leaves. Its use is largely limited to traditional Chinese medicine. **Russian licorice** (*G. echinata*), or wild licorice, is occasionally used as a substitute for *G. glabra* in confectionary, soft drinks, tobacco and snuff.

Processing

Licorice roots are harvested when the plant is in its third or fourth year; the whole root system is taken up in autumn and the crowns and suckers are stored for replanting in spring. After the roots are washed and trimmed, the long, straight pieces are sometimes sold as licorice sticks and the variable-diameter twisted roots are chopped and ground into powder or processed to make extract. Licorice extract is made by crushing the roots to a pulp in a mill, then boiling them in water until a decoction is drawn off and further boiled down to evaporate into a sticky black mass. This may be rolled into sticks and stacked on boards to dry. Some confusion is generated because both the even pieces of rootstock and these lengths of dried concentrate are referred to as "sticks." The waste fiber left over after processing licorice is used for making particleboard.

WEIGHT PER TEASPOON (5 mL)
- **whole chopped pieces:** 2.5 g
- **ground:** 2.8 g

SUGGESTED QUANTITY PER POUND (500 g)
- **red meats:** 1 tsp (5 mL) chopped pieces
- **white meats:** ¾ tsp (3 mL) chopped pieces
- **vegetables:** ½ tsp (2 mL) chopped pieces
- **grains and pulses:** ½ tsp (2 mL) chopped pieces
- **baked goods:** ½ tsp (2 mL) chopped pieces

Buying and Storage

Licorice root is often available from spice specialists in a number of forms, usually in whole pieces, chopped and as powder. It is quite stable and requires no special storage conditions, other than being kept away from extreme heat. The powder, however, is very likely to pick up moisture from the atmosphere, so it must be kept in an airtight container. Humid conditions are best avoided, as they will make the powder sticky and lumpy. Pontefract cakes and licorice sticks made from the concentrate will also get sticky when exposed to humidity, so store them in an airtight container in a cool place.

Use

It is advisable to be conservative when adding licorice to a dish, because its underlying bitterness can be overpowering. When stewing fruits, chopped pieces of licorice may be added along with star anise, cinnamon and vanilla. An Asian "master stock" spice bag may contain pieces of licorice along with brown cardamom, star anise, fennel, mace, Sichuan pepper, cinnamon, ginger and cloves.

Pork Spareribs in Chinese Master Stock

This complex, aromatic master stock (see page 368) has many uses, and arguably one of the best is for making sticky ribs.

Makes 8 spareribs

Preparation time:
3 hours

Cooking time:
1½ hours, plus 1 hour for marinating

Tip

Dried ginger and mandarin peel can be found at Asian grocers. If not available, you can substitute fresh ginger and mandarin peel, although dried will give a more authentic flavor.

- **Cheesecloth or muslin**

MASTER STOCK

3	whole star anise	3
2 tsp	chopped licorice root	10 mL
1	slice dried ginger (see Tip, left)	1
1	piece dried mandarin orange peel	1
½	cassia quill	½
1 tsp	whole Sichuan pepper	5 mL
½ tsp	whole allspice	2 mL
½ tsp	fennel seeds	2 mL
½ tsp	coriander seeds	2 mL
1	dried red finger chile	1
½ cup	granulated sugar	125 mL
2 cups	boiling water	500 mL
⅔ cup	soy sauce	150 mL
8	pork spareribs (about 1 lb/500 g)	8

1. *Master Stock:* In a small bowl, combine star anise, licorice root, ginger, mandarin peel, cassia, Sichuan pepper, allspice, fennel seeds, coriander seeds and chile. Transfer to a 6- to 8-inch (15 to 20 cm) square of cheesecloth and secure top with kitchen string to make a spice bag. In a saucepan over low heat, combine sugar, water and soy sauce. Add spice bag and stir occasionally until sugar is melted. Simmer, uncovered, for 1 hour. Set aside to cool, then remove spice bag.

2. In a resealable plastic bag, combine spareribs and cooled master stock. Refrigerate for at least 1 hour or overnight.

3. Preheat oven to 300°F (150°C).

4. Transfer spareribs and marinade to a baking dish and bake in preheated oven for about 1½ hours, until meat is well cooked and sauce has caramelized.

Lime Leaf (Makrut)

Citrus hystrix (also known as *C. papedia*)

Names in Other Languages

- **Burmese:** shauk-nu, shauk-waing
- **Chinese (C):** fatt fung kam, syun gam
- **Chinese (M):** suan gan
- **Czech:** kaffir citrus
- **Danish:** kaffir lime
- **Dutch:** kaffir limoen
- **Filipino:** swangi
- **French:** limettier hérissé
- **German:** Kaffernlimette, Kaffirzitrone
- **Indonesian:** daun jeruk purut, jeruk sambal
- **Japanese:** kobumikan
- **Malay:** daun limau purut (leaves), limau purut (fruit)
- **Spanish:** hojas de lima cafre
- **Sri Lankan:** kahpiri dehi, odu dehi
- **Swedish:** kafirlime
- **Thai:** makrut, som makrut, bai makrut (leaves), luuk makrut (fruit)
- **Vietnamese:** truc

Family: Rutaceae

Other Names: Indonesian lime leaves, "kaffir" lime leaves, lime leaf, wild lime leaves

Flavor Group: Medium

Parts Used: leaves and fruits (as a herb)

Background

All citrus trees are native to Southeast Asia. They were introduced to Europe in the Middle Ages, probably by Moorish and Turkish invaders. Lemons have been widely used since then; however, limes are often confused with lemons, so the history of lime trees is somewhat obscure. Until recent times there is little evidence of makrut lime trees being known outside Southeast Asia, though with the increasing interest in Asian cooking in general, and Thai and Balinese cuisine in particular, makrut lime leaves are becoming readily available in many Western cities.

L

Culinary Information

Combines with

- basil
- cardamom
- chile
- coriander (leaf and seed)
- cumin
- curry leaf
- galangal
- ginger
- star anise
- tamarind
- turmeric
- Vietnamese mint

Traditional Uses

- salads
- Asian stir-fries
- soups such as laksa
- Asian curries
- refreshing summer drinks

Spice Blends

- red and green curry blends
- Thai spice mixes
- rubs for seafood

What's in a Name?

For many years this tree was called a "kaffir" lime tree because the fruits are rough and seen as inferior. *Kaffir* was a term used to denote inferior persons in South Africa and other nations involved in the slave trade, and in some Asian countries it means "non-believer." This word is now generally considered to be offensive. Consequently I have adopted the name used for these leaves in Thailand—*makrut*—because its cuisine is well known globally and uses these leaves copiously.

The Plant

Makrut lime trees are not to be confused with the common fruit-producing varieties such as Mexican, Tahitian and West Indian limes, nor the lime (linden) trees (*Tilia curopaca*) of Europe and North America.

Makrut lime trees are small, shrubby trees, 10 to 16 feet (3 to 5 m) tall, with numerous needle-sharp spikes and unusual double leaves. Each pair of citrus-looking leaves, joined head to tail, is $3\frac{1}{4}$ to 6 inches (8 to 15 cm) long and 1 to 2 inches (2.5 to 5 cm) wide. Dark green, leathery and glossy on top, they are pale green and matte underneath. When torn or cut, makrut lime leaves emit a heavenly scent that is a cross between lime, orange and lemon, but not like any one of those on its own. The taste of makrut lime leaves is similarly citrus-like, reminiscent of the zest of a mandarin but lacking in the acid tones usually associated with members of that family. The fruit is larger than a Tahitian lime and has a very rough, knobbly surface and thick skin, the outer rind of which is generally the only part used, as these limes yield very little juice.

Processing

Contrary to popular belief, makrut lime leaves dry effectively when sufficient care is taken. The greatest problem when

Spice Notes

Fresh herb leaves vary greatly in moisture content, thickness and size. As a result, it has always been a challenge to find the best method of drying them, especially in the case of thick, leathery leaves such as makrut lime leaves. Before investing in a dehydrator, we used to put all manner of herbs in the well-ventilated, dark ceiling cavity of an iron-roofed shed. When the weather was fine, it provided near-perfect drying conditions.

dehydrating a leathery leaf with a shiny skin is that the surface membranes do not easily yield up their water content. This means deterioration will start before the leaves are dry, and many end up with brown and black patches. However, if too much heat is applied, the leaves will shrivel and turn yellow. To achieve the best result, spread freshly picked leaves on porous paper in a single layer and place in a warm, dark place with low humidity. When the leaves feel quite crisp to the touch and have lost their leathery, pliable feel, they are ready for use.

Buying and Storage

Fresh makrut lime leaves can often be bought from fresh produce retailers. The only time they are not likely to be available is toward the end of winter. Fresh whole leaves may be stored in the freezer, in resealable bags, for about 3 months.

Dried makrut lime leaves should be green, not yellow, and are best kept under the same conditions as other dried herbs. They will keep for up to 12 months in an airtight container, protected from light and extremes of heat and humidity.

Use

Only fresh leaves are suitable for adding to salads. Remove the tough rib that runs down the center of each leaf and chop them very finely to offset their firm, leathery texture. When making a clear soup or stock, either whole fresh or dried leaves may be added, as they will not necessarily be eaten once they have made their contribution to the flavor. Finely chopped fresh or crumbled dried makrut lime leaves are used in dishes such as laksa soup, stir-fried vegetables with chicken or seafood, and curries, especially those containing coconut cream.

WEIGHT PER TEASPOON (5 mL)

- **whole average dried leaf:** 0.5 g
- **granulated dry leaves:** 2.1 g

SUGGESTED QUANTITY PER POUND (500 g)

- **red meats:** 3 to 4 whole fresh or dried leaves
- **white meats:** 3 whole fresh or dried leaves
- **vegetables:** 2 whole fresh or dried leaves
- **grains and pulses:** 2 whole fresh or dried leaves
- **carbohydrates:** 2 whole fresh or dried leaves

L

Thai Fish Cakes

There's a reason why these fish cakes are such a popular street food in Thailand: fragrant makrut lime makes them incredibly addictive. Once the curry paste is made, they are really easy to put together. These juicy morsels make fantastic appetizers or snacks and are best eaten piping hot.

Makes about 20 fish cakes

Preparation time:
40 minutes

Cooking time:
20 minutes

- - - - - - - - - - - - - -

Tip

While galangal is slightly sweeter, gingerroot can be substituted if needed.

- **Blender**
- **Food processor**

RED CURRY PASTE

7	dried red chiles, seeded and soaked in boiling water for 10 minutes	7
2 tsp	ground paprika	10 mL
2 tbsp	finely chopped lemongrass	30 mL
1 tsp	finely chopped fresh makrut lime leaf	5 mL
5	small red shallots, diced	5
1 tbsp	chopped fresh galangal (see Tip, left)	15 mL
4	cloves garlic, chopped	4
1 tbsp	chopped fresh coriander (cilantro) root/stem	15 mL
Pinch	freshly grated lime zest	Pinch
½ tsp	shrimp paste	2 mL
½ tsp	ground coriander seed	2 mL
¼ tsp	ground cumin	1 mL
Pinch	freshly ground white pepper	Pinch
Pinch	fine sea salt	Pinch
1 tbsp	water	15 mL

FISH CAKES

1 lb	firm white fish, such as cod, cut into pieces	500 g
1 tsp	finely chopped fresh makrut lime leaf	5 mL
½ tsp	superfine (caster) sugar (see Tip, page 375)	2 mL
1	egg, lightly beaten	1
20	narrow green beans, trimmed and cut into ¼-inch (5 mm) pieces	20
	Oil	

Tip

Superfine (caster) sugar is very fine granulated sugar typically used in recipes that require a faster-dissolving granule. If you can't find it in stores, you can make your own by using a food processor fitted with the metal blade to process granulated sugar to a very fine, sand-like consistency.

1. *Red Curry Paste:* In blender, combine chiles, paprika, lemongrass, lime leaf, shallots, galangal, garlic, coriander, lime zest, shrimp paste, coriander seed, cumin, pepper, salt and water. Blend at high speed to form a paste.

2. *Fish Cakes:* In food processor fitted with the metal blade, combine fish, lime leaf, sugar, egg and 3 tbsp (45 mL) prepared curry paste. Pulse until combined. Transfer to a serving bowl, add green beans and stir to combine.

3. In a skillet over high heat, heat $1/4$ inch (5 mm) oil until small bubbles begin to appear. Reduce heat to medium. Working in batches and using your hands, shape mixture into round cakes, using about 2 tbsp (30 mL) per cake. Cook for about 3 minutes each side, until golden and cooked through. Transfer to a plate lined with paper towels to drain excess oil and cover to keep warm. Repeat until fish mixture is used up. Serve immediately.

L

Tom Yum Soup

This soup—combining warm galangal, fiery chile, tangy lime and distinctively pungent lime leaves—is utterly good for the soul. It's a fantastic alternative to chicken soup when you are feeling unwell, and the best way to start a Thai meal.

Makes 6 small servings

Preparation time:
10 minutes

Cooking time:
25 minutes

Tips

Makrut leaves are usually called "kaffir" lime leaves (see page 372).

While galangal is slightly sweeter, gingerroot can be substituted if needed.

To prepare the lemongrass: Using a sharp knife, cut off the lower bulb end and peel away the outer two or three layers of stem until you reach the soft white interior, which is easier to slice.

12	large raw shrimp, shelled and deveined, shells reserved	12
1 tsp	oil	5 mL
5 cups	water	1.25 L
5	fresh or dried makrut lime leaves, torn (see Tips, left)	5
1½ tbsp	fresh galangal, peeled and chopped (see Tips, left)	22 mL
1	stalk lemongrass, white part only, chopped (see Tips, left)	1
1	red finger chile, sliced	1
¼ cup	freshly squeezed lime juice	60 mL
1 tbsp	fish sauce (nam pla)	15 mL
1 cup	baby button mushrooms, sliced	250 mL
⅓ cup	fresh coriander (cilantro) leaves, to garnish	75 mL

1. In a large saucepan over medium-high heat, heat oil. Add shrimp and shells and cook, stirring often, for 2 minutes or until shrimp start to brown (they will not yet be cooked through—the browning adds flavor). Add water and bring to a boil. Using a slotted spoon, transfer shrimp and shells to a bowl and set aside. Using a fine-mesh sieve, strain broth into a clean saucepan.

2. To broth in pan, add lime leaves, galangal, lemongrass, chile, lime juice and fish sauce. Simmer for 15 minutes. Add reserved shrimp and mushrooms and simmer for 5 minutes or until shrimp are pink. Taste and adjust seasonings (it may need more lime, fish sauce or chile, depending on your taste). Sprinkle with coriander leaves and serve immediately.

Variation

For a more substantial meal, add 1 cup (250 mL) cooked shredded chicken and 3 oz (90 g) cooked rice noodles before serving.

Lovage

Levisticum officinale (also known as Hipposelinum levisticum, L. levesticum, Ligusticum levisticum, Selinum levisticum)

Names in Other Languages

- **Chinese (C):** yuhn yihp dong gwai
- **Chinese (M):** yuan ye dang gui
- **Czech:** libecek
- **Danish:** lovstikke
- **Dutch:** lavas
- **Finnish:** lipstikka
- **French:** livèche
- **German:** Liebstoeckel, Badekraut
- **Greek:** levistiko
- **Italian:** levistico
- **Japanese:** robejji
- **Norwegian:** lopstikke
- **Polish:** lubczyk ogrodowy
- **Portuguese:** levistico
- **Russian:** goritsvet, gulyavitsa
- **Spanish:** ligustico
- **Swedish:** libsticka
- **Thai:** kot cheyng
- **Turkish:** selam out, deniz maydanozu

Family: Apiaceae (formerly Umbelliferae)

Varieties: mountain lovage (*Ligusticum mutellina*), Scottish lovage (*Ligusticum scoticum*)

Other Names: Cornish lovage, Italian lovage, Old English lovage

Flavor Group: Mild

Parts Used: leaves (as a herb)

Background

Lovage is thought to be native to the Mediterranean, although some experts contend that it may have its origins in China. The Phoenicians first recognized the medicinal attributes of its root, leaves and seeds, and the plant was valued for medicinal, culinary and cosmetic applications by the ancient Greeks and Romans, who were cultivating it at around the beginning of the Common Era (CE). Lovage has been grown commercially in Czechoslovakia, France and Germany since the 12th century and it was used medicinally in England in the 14th century.

Culinary Information

Combines with
- alexanders
- arugula
- chervil
- dill
- garlic
- parsley
- salad burnet
- sorrel

Traditional Uses
- green salads
- scrambled eggs and omelets
- mashed potatoes
- white sauces

Spice Blends
- fines herbes
- salad herbs

Imposters

Two other plants besides true lovage have been referred to as lovage: black lovage, which is actually alexanders (*Smyrnium olusatrum*, see page 57), and ajowan seeds (see page 46), which have been passed off as lovage seeds, possibly because of their similar appearance and spiciness.

The popularity of the peppery foliage of lovage has waned in recent times, possibly because the more subtle flavors of the past have less appeal in the 21st century, when our taste buds are being bombarded by all manner of flavor-enhancing delights, from the natural and spicy to the highly artificial.

The Plant

Lovage is a stout perennial that looks like a sparse version of angelica (page 73). The leaves closely resemble Italian (flat-leaf) parsley. The stems are channeled, similar to those of celery, and grow 3 to 5 feet (1 to 1.5 m) tall. Sulfur-yellow flowers are borne in delicate umbels that are smaller than angelica's great round heads. Lovage has a thick, fleshy gray-brown root shaped like a carrot that is about 4 to 6 inches (10 to 15 cm) long. The root has medicinal properties but no popular culinary use. The flavor of lovage leaves is slightly yeasty and reminiscent of a combination of celery and parsley, with a very mild peppery bite.

Other Varieties

Mountain lovage (*Ligusticum mutellina*) is a variety whose leaves have a less parsley-like appearance. The flowers are purple rather than yellow, but only the leaves are used for their parsley and celery-like taste. **Scottish lovage** (*Ligusticum scoticum*) is sometimes referred to as "sea lovage." It is most similar to true lovage in appearance. The leaves, stems and seeds can be used for their parsley-like flavor.

L

Spice Notes

When my mother, Rosemary Hemphill, was experimenting while developing recipes for her books, I always hoped some tasty morsels would be left over when I came home from school. One of my fondest memories is her delicious herb sandwiches. Mum would blend freshly cut herbs—usually whichever was most abundant at the time—with softened cream cheese and spread it thickly on slices of whole-wheat bread with the crusts removed. Then she would cut each sandwich into triangles. Anyone with access to fresh herbs, especially lovage, can whip these up for a morning or afternoon snack. If wrapped in plastic wrap and refrigerated, the leftovers will keep until the kids come home from school to devour what's left!

Processing

Lovage leaves may be dried in the same way as parsley, in a dark, well-aired place, spread out on paper or wire mesh for a few days so the air can circulate until the leaves are crisp and dry.

To gather seeds, when the plant has finished flowering, carefully cut the stems of delicate seed-laden umbels and hang upside down in a warm, dry place. In a few days the lovage seeds can be threshed and stored for later sowing or culinary use.

Buying and Storage

Because of the lack of demand for lovage as a culinary herb, the fresh or dried leaves are rarely seen for sale. Keen gardeners will find lovage plants available from nurseries that specialize in herbs.

The best way to store freshly picked lovage is to place the leafy stems in a glass of water, cover them like a tent with a clean plastic bag, and keep in the refrigerator. Change the water every few days and use within a week of harvesting. Fresh lovage can be chopped and put in ice-cube trays, covered with a little water, and frozen. Turn out the ice cubes into a freezer bag and store in the bag until required; they will keep for up to 3 months.

Should you be able to buy dried lovage, it must be green like parsley and packed in an airtight container. Store dried lovage in the same way as other dried herbs: in a cool, dark place, where they will keep their flavor for up to 1 year.

Store dried lovage seeds in an airtight container away from extremes of heat, light and humidity.

Use

The subtle flavor of lovage, with its hint of pepper, is a perfect complement to salads when included along with parsley, chervil, dill and finely chopped onions and red peppers. This combination may also be added to omelets, scrambled eggs and mashed potatoes for an attractive appearance and pleasing taste. Potentially bland soups and sauces are given a "safe" lift when lovage is added instead of other, stronger-tasting herbs or spices. My favorite uses for lovage are in herb sandwiches and frittata.

SUGGESTED QUANTITY PER POUND (500 g)

- **red meats:** ½ cup (125 mL) fresh leaves, 1 tsp (5 mL) dried leaves
- **white meats:** ½ cup (125 mL) fresh leaves, 1 tsp (5 mL) dried leaves
- **vegetables:** ½ cup (125 mL) fresh leaves, 1 tsp (5 mL) dried leaves
- **grains and pulses:** ½ cup (125 mL) fresh leaves, 1 tsp (5 mL) dried leaves
- **baked goods:** ½ cup (125 mL) fresh leaves, 1 tsp (5 mL) dried leaves

Lovage Frittata

This frittata can be served warm or cold and makes good picnic fare. The lovage pairs perfectly with eggs and potatoes, but if you don't have fresh lovage on hand, baby spinach can also be used.

Makes 6 to 8 servings

Preparation time:
10 minutes

Cooking time:
35 minutes

- **12-inch (30 cm) deep ovenproof skillet**

¾ cup	olive oil, divided	175 mL
3	onions, halved and sliced	3
14	eggs, lightly beaten	14
2	potatoes, peeled, cut into 1-inch (2.5 cm) cubes and boiled until tender	2
3 cups	lightly packed lovage leaves	750 mL
7 oz	feta cheese, crumbled	210 g
	Sea salt and freshly ground black pepper	

1. In skillet over medium-low heat, heat ¼ cup (60 mL) oil. Add onions and cook for 10 minutes, stirring occasionally, until golden. Place cooked onions in a large bowl, reserving pan.

2. In bowl, combine onions with eggs, potatoes, lovage and feta. Season well with salt and pepper.

3. Preheat broiler.

4. Add remaining ½ cup (125 mL) oil to skillet and heat over medium-low heat. Add egg mixture. After about 30 seconds, stir gently to evenly distribute ingredients. Cook for 2 minutes, reduce heat and cook for a further 5 minutes, until egg begins to set.

5. Transfer skillet to oven and broil under preheated broiler until frittata is just set on top, 3 to 4 minutes. Remove from heat and set aside to cool for 10 minutes, then invert onto a large serving plate.

L

Mahlab

Prunus mahaleb

Names in Other Languages

- **Arabic:** mahlab, mahleb
- **Czech:** visen turecka
- **Dutch:** weichsel
- **Finnish:** veikselinkirsikka
- **French:** mahaleb, cerisier de Sainte-Lucie
- **German:** Steinweichsel, Felsenkirsche
- **Greek:** mahlepi, agriokerasia
- **Italian:** mahaleb, ciliegio di Santa Lucia
- **Japanese:** maharibu
- **Polish:** wisnia wonna
- **Portuguese:** abrunheiro-bravo
- **Russian:** vishnya makhalebka
- **Spanish:** mahaleb, cerezo de Santa Lucia
- **Swedish:** vejksel
- **Turkish:** mahlep, idrisagaci

Family: Rosaceae

Other Names: mach lepi, mahaleb, mahlebi, mahlepi, St. Lucie cherry

Flavor Group: Pungent

Parts Used: kernels (as a spice)

Background

Native to southern Europe, this northern hemisphere tree grows wild in the Mediterranean region across to Turkey. The first written references to mahlab were in the first century CE by the Arabs; subsequent Arab writers mention its cultivation up to the 12th century. Mahlab was first used for perfumes and medicine in the Middle East and Turkey, where it later became a popular culinary spice, especially for flavoring breads. The world's major production of mahlab is now in Iran, followed by Turkey and Syria.

Culinary Information

Combines with
- allspice
- cinnamon and cassia
- cloves
- coriander seed
- ginger
- nutmeg
- poppy seed
- sesame seed

Traditional Uses
- Middle Eastern breads
- cookies and crackers
- cakes and pastries
- Turkish rice dishes
- fruit flans and milk puddings

Spice Blends
- not commonly used in spice blends

A Greek friend of ours gave us a traditional Easter bun called tsoureki, *flavored with mahlab and decorated with brightly colored eggs (the shells were dipped in red food coloring). Not only did this get top marks for presentation, but mahlab's almond- and marzipan-like flavor complemented the bread perfectly.*

The Plant

Mahlab is an unusual fragrant spice made from the husked kernels of a small wild black cherry that comes from a spreading deciduous tree belonging to the same family (Rosaceae) as peaches and plums. The tree grows to about 36 feet (12 m) in height and has $2^1/_2$-inch (6 cm) oval, finely serrated bright green leaves and early-blooming single white flowers. The green fruit is only $^1/_3$ inch (8 mm) in diameter and ripens to become black, at which stage it is harvested. Kernels of mahlab are light tan in color, tear-shaped, $^1/_4$ inch (5 mm) long and creamy white inside. The strange thing about mahlab is that even when you smell it for the first time, it seems incredibly familiar. This familiarity comes from its distinctive aroma, which is cherry-sweet, almond-like and floral, bearing a resemblance to marzipan. The flavor is a combination of fragrant rosewater-like sweetness and a somewhat nutty and surprisingly bitter aftertaste.

Processing

The ripe fruits are harvested and then cut open so the cherry stones can be removed and cracked to reveal the mahlab kernels inside.

Buying and Storage

Although mahlab may sometimes be bought ground, once powdered it goes from creamy white to dirty yellow and loses its flavor and aroma rapidly through oxidization. Therefore I recommend buying the whole kernels only and

M

grinding them just before using, in a mortar and pestle or in a clean coffee grinder.

Store mahlab kernels in an airtight container, partly to lengthen their shelf life but also to prevent the aroma from contaminating other foods in the pantry. Keep away from direct light and extreme heat and humidity. When stored this way, whole mahlab will last for around 1 year. Ground mahlab needs to be used within about a month of grinding.

Use

Mahlab will give an authentic flavor of the Middle East and Turkey to breads, cookies, crackers, cakes and pastries. Mahlab is also an ingredient in Turkish rice, complements fresh fruit flans when added to the pastry, and goes well in milk puddings. Because of its perfumed character and potential for bitterness, only a small amount—$1/2$ to 1 tsp (2 to 5 mL) of the ground spice—is required per 2 cups (500 mL) flour in a recipe.

WEIGHT PER TEASPOON (5 mL)
- whole: 4.7 g
- ground: 2.8 g

SUGGESTED QUANTITY PER POUND (500 g)
- grains and pulses: 2 tsp (10 mL) ground
- baked goods: 2 tsp (10 mL) ground

Arabian Breakfast Breads

These Arabian breakfast breads, *ka'kat*, are delicious with cherry jam and a lovely alternative to croissants. The mahlab in the bread counteracts and complements the sweetness in the cherries.

Makes 16 pieces

Preparation time:
10 minutes, plus
2 hours for rising

Cooking time:
20 minutes

- - - - - - - - - - - - - - - - -

Tips

To toast sesame seeds: Place in a dry skillet over medium heat and cook, shaking pan constantly, until lightly browned, 2 to 3 minutes. Immediately transfer to a dish to prevent further browning.

Stirring in the same direction while combining yeast with flour helps the gluten activate more effectively.

Dough is smooth and elastic when you press a finger into the dough and it quickly springs back into shape.

- **2 baking sheets, lined with parchment paper**

2 tbsp	superfine (caster) sugar (see Tips, page 393)	30 mL
2 tsp	instant active dry yeast	10 mL
2 cups	warm water	500 mL
4 to 5 cups	bread flour	1 to 1.25 L
1/4 cup	unsalted butter, melted	60 mL
1 tsp	fine sea salt	5 mL
1/4 tsp	mahlab seeds, ground to a powder	1 mL
1	egg, beaten	1
3 tbsp	toasted sesame seeds (see Tips, left)	45 mL

1. In a large bowl, dissolve sugar and yeast in warm water. Add flour 1 cup (250 mL) at a time, stirring constantly in the same direction, until a thick dough begins to form (see Tips, left). Once 3 cups (750 mL) have been added, stir for 1 minute, then set aside for 10 minutes to rest.

2. Stir butter, salt and mahlab into dough and resume adding remaining flour, 1 cup (250 mL) at a time, until dough will not take any more without getting too dry. Turn out onto a lightly floured surface and knead for 10 minutes, until smooth and elastic (see Tips, left). Place dough in a clean, lightly oiled bowl, cover with a kitchen towel and set aside in a warm place for 1 1/2 hours, until doubled in size.

3. Turn out onto a lightly floured surface and knead dough until air is pushed out and dough is smooth, about 2 minutes. Divide dough into 16 equal pieces. Using the palms of your hands, roll each piece into a cigar shape, then pinch the ends together to create a circle. Arrange circles at least 2 inches (5 cm) apart on prepared baking sheets. Cover with a kitchen towel and set aside for 30 minutes.

4. Preheat oven to 400°F (200°C).

5. Just before baking, brush cirlces with egg and sprinkle with sesame seeds. Bake for about 20 minutes, until golden. Transfer to a wire rack to cool slightly before serving. Breads will keep in an airtight container for up to 2 days.

M

Mastic

Pistacia lentiscus (also known as *P. lentiscus* var. *chia, Lentiscus massiliensis, Lentiscus vulgaris, Terebinthus lentiscus*)

Names in Other Languages

- **Arabic:** aza
- **French:** mastic
- **German:** Mastix
- **Greek:** mastikha
- **Italian:** lentischio, mastice
- **Spanish:** lentisco, mastique

Family: Anacardiaceae

Other Names: gum mastic, mastiha, mastic tears, masticha, mastika

Flavor Group: Pungent

Parts Used: sap/gum (as a spice)

Background

There are many varieties of mastic trees (*Pistacia lentiscus*) in the Mediterranean and Middle East, but most of the world's production of gum mastic comes from the Protected Designation of Origin trees (*P. lentiscus* var. *chia*) that grow on the Greek island of Chios. On this eastern Greek island, an unsurpassed passion and dedication to the gum mastic tree is evident, so much so that there is even a Gum Mastic

Culinary Information

Combines with
- allspice
- cardamom
- cinnamon and cassia
- cloves
- coriander seed
- cumin
- ginger
- mahlab
- vanilla

Traditional Uses
- Turkish delight
- ice cream
- sweet puddings and cakes
- toothpaste and chewing gum
- slow-cooked lamb
- doner kebabs (shawarma)

Spice Blends
- ras el hanout

Growers Association dedicated to the research, production and promotion of mastic and mastic products.

Mastic has a long history that dates back to classical times. It is mentioned by erudite Greek and Roman authors such as Pliny, Dioscorides, Galen and Theophrastus. Mastic was well known to the pharaohs, and Hippocrates (the Greek doctor known as the "father of medicine") cited it as a cure for all manner of ailments, from baldness to intestinal and bladder problems, as a paste for toothache, and to apply in cases of snakebite. One legend, which I feel is particularly appropriate, has it that when Saint Isidore was tortured to death by the Romans in 250 CE, his body was dragged under a mastic tree. Upon seeing the saint's mutilated form, the tree started to cry real tears.

From the 10th century on, Chios was famous for its *masticha*. The name derives from the Greek word *mastichon*, which means "to chew" and is the root of the English word *masticate*, for mastic was commonly used as a chewing gum and mouth freshener. By the 14th and 15th centuries the production of mastic was highly organized and controlled by the *scribae masticis*, clerks whose job was documenting the production of gum mastic. Such was the importance of mastic that during the Turkish occupation, mastic-producing villages on Chios were given special privileges, such as their own management and permission to ring the church bells. In all there were 21 mastic villages, which paid their tithes with 29 tons (26 tonnes) of mastic and were then free from paying all other taxes. As with most valuable commodities, the penalties for stealing gum mastic were draconian, to say the least, and the severity related directly to the quantity stolen.

M

Receivers of stolen mastic had the same punishments meted out to them. These punitive measures ranged from being branded with red-hot steel on the forehead to losing one's ears, eyes and/or nose. The ultimate penalty was hanging if one was caught with more than 400 pounds (180 kg). Thus the traveller Kyriakus Pitsiccoli of Angona, on one of his many visits to Chios between 1435 and 1440, was heard to say, "If you wish to live in Chios, just keep the gum mastic and never steal it."

Today the Gum Mastic Growers Association lists 64 uses for mastic, extolling among other things its anticancer properties, its use in treatment of duodenal ulcers, its benefits for oral hygiene and, in South Morocco and Mauritania, its use as an aphrodisiac.

The Plant

The gum mastic tree, or *schinos*, as the *chia* variety is called in its native Greek island of Chios, is a slow-growing hardy evergreen tree that averages 6 to 9 feet (2 to 3 m) in height, although some have been known to reach 16 feet (5 m). The mastic tree has shiny dark green leaves resembling those of myrtle. The trunk is rough and gnarled, and when scored it yields a clear resinous substance that coagulates into gum mastic. Full growth of these hardy trees is achieved after 40 to 50 years, and some are reputed to be up to 200 years old. Mastic production commences when the trees are five to six years old, reaching a maximum yield of up to 2 pounds (1 kg) per tree when they are 15 years old. The end of a tree's productive life comes at about 70 years of age. One mastic grower, Stelios, showed us a tree he remembered as mature when he was a boy, more than 65 years before, and it was still in production.

The sappy gum hardens after collection and processing. It is most often seen in large ($1/4$ inch/5 mm) or small ($1/8$ inch/3 mm) pieces referred to as tears. The texture of the tears is brittle and somewhat crystalline. When broken, mastic tears reveal a shiny surface resembling chipped quartz and release a faint pine-like aroma. The flavor is initially bitter and mineral-like, becoming more neutral after a few minutes of chewing, when it takes on the consistency and opaque fawn color of chewing gum. Even after 15 to 20 minutes of chewing, a surprising degree of mouth-freshening flavor remains, unlike today's highly flavored chewing gums that seem to expire in a matter of minutes.

Mastic Tips

Mastic tears are easy to grind to a fine white powder using a mortar and pestle, but grind just before adding to the recipe. Otherwise ground mastic will tend to re-amalgamate into tears or a large clump. Chill the mastic for easier grinding, as that makes it slightly brittle.

If the mortar and pestle you use to grind mastic end up with a sticky, varnish-like coating of mastic (like ours did one very hot day), put them in the freezer for a few hours; you'll be able to chip the mastic residue right off.

Ground mastic infuses best with fats and oil. Adding the powdered tears to warmed olive oil gives any salad dressing the ability to cling to the salad.

In cooking, mastic does contribute to flavor, although its main function is to provide texture and act as a binding agent. Gum mastic oil is also produced, by steam distillation of the leaves and branches of mastic trees; however, few cooks would be familiar with it, as its primary use is in manufacturing sweets, liqueurs and medicines.

Processing

Production of gum mastic is still strictly controlled and occurs between June and September. This begins by first cleaning and leveling the ground around the base of the tree with white kaolin clay, a process called currying. The white clay contains limestone, which promotes drying and contributes to the clarity of the mastic tears that fall onto it. The first cutting, or "hurting"—10 to 20 wounds made on the trunk—is typically done in the morning, which is the best time for maximum flow. The wounds must only score the bark, not cut through to the wood. When the farmer Stelios showed us how he scored the bark, we could see sap droplets form within just a few minutes, looking just like tears forming in the corner of one's eye. The tears ooze and drip, sometimes in stalactite-like strands, before falling to the clay. Up to 100 cuts are made over the season, but too much "hurting" of young trees will inhibit future yields. Over the next 10 to 20 days coagulation takes place as the gum oozes out of the cuts, and soon pearl-like tears, globules and even puddle-shaped pieces of mastic resin adorn the distinctive white carpet of clay beneath each tree.

The tears are then collected, first by using a special tool called a *timitiri* to remove them from the trunk (if they are allowed to remain on the tree, they oxidize and turn yellow, acquiring a bitter taste). Then the mastic on the ground is collected and the tears are put into wooden crates and transferred to the houses, where it is kept cool and sorted, ready for cleaning by the village's womenfolk during winter. After sieving to remove any adhering leaves and soil, the gum is washed in cold soapy water, rinsed thoroughly and spread out on bags inside the houses to dry. After drying, a small knife is used to remove any remaining dirty particles. Much of the winter in the mastic villages is spent carefully cleaning the summer's production by hand, to prepare it for sale.

Clean gum mastic is categorized into three main grades: pitta, large tears and small tears. Pitta is the foam that is created when many drops become one; this grade has the

M

Travels in the Spice Trade

On our first visit to Chios we met with Maria, from the commercial department of the Gum Mastic Growers Association, who gave us an in-depth presentation on the island, its history and the magic of mastic. Visiting an island dotted with the ruins of buildings built between the eighth and fifth centuries BCE is awe-inspiring to say the least. The history of occupation and cruelty meted out to so many populations around the world is always disturbing, and the occupants of Chios have suffered privations under many invaders over the centuries.

Driving around Chios and seeing groves of mastic trees inspired me to write in my notebook: "The mastic tree is a tough-looking, low growing, spreading tree that looks far older than it really is, due to its stressed, gnarled and tortured trunks and limbs. It is reminiscent of old men turned into trees in an enchanted forest. The inhabitants of Chios have endured unspeakable hardships over many centuries, and standing before a mastic tree, shedding its tears of valuable resin, one feels as though one is looking at an anthropomorphization of many hard and tortuous past lives. To gaze on a mastic tree is to look at everything that exemplifies Chios and the perseverance of humans, from being hurt to never giving up, in spite of everything and in finally surviving."

No visit to Chios would be complete without visiting the historic mastic villages. We spent most of our time in the vicinity of Kalamoti and also strolled through the narrow streets of Mesta, Pyrgi, Vessa and Lithi. Visiting a mastic village is akin to stepping back in time, with its quiet, narrow streets (don't try to take car into the village) lined with houses beautifully decorated in black-and-white geometric patterns offset by ristras of bright red tomatoes hanging on the walls to dry.

largest pieces—up to 3 inches (7.5 cm) in diameter—and an oval shape. Large tears measure about $1/3$ to $1/2$ inch (6 to 10 mm) in diameter and small tears average $1/8$ to $1/4$ inch (3 to 5 mm) in diameter. Tiny pieces are classified as powder. Any uncleaned leftovers are usually distilled for use in perfumes and alcoholic drinks such as mastic liqueur, ouzo and raki.

Buying and Storage

Gum mastic can be purchased from Greek and Middle Eastern food stores and specialty food retailers. The most common package size is 1 to 5 grams, because it is relatively expensive and recipes require only a small amount to be used at a time. Tears should be quite transparent, with a slight golden tone resembling Indian moonstone. The best storage is in a cool place; exposure to extreme or prolonged heat will cause the tears to become cloudy and discolor, with a subsequent loss of flavor. Under correct conditions mastic tears will last for more than 3 years.

Use

Mastic has myriad applications, ranging from the medicinal to the functional, including use as a stabilizer in paints and to make varnishes, especially for musical instruments. It has been used in the production of aromatic soaps, toothpaste, insecticides, electrical insulators and tires. Frankincense is produced from gum mastic and rosin, and mastic has been used in the tanning, weaving and beekeeping industries. But it really shines in culinary uses. In addition to being added to chewing gum and confectionery, mastic is an ingredient in liqueurs. When we visited a bar on the waterfront in Chios, we were even treated to a mastic mojito! Mastic is included in the best and most authentic Turkish delight and is found in recipes for breads and pastries, ice creams, sweet puddings and almond cake.

Although purists may disagree, mastic can be an acceptable substitute for the almost impossible to acquire salep (see page 655). Mastic is also used as a binding agent with oil, lemon juice and spices to coat traditional Turkish doner kebab (also known as shawarma), the Middle Eastern equivalent of Greek gyros. A lamb shoulder that has been slow-cooked with ras el hanout and powdered mastic achieves a succulent texture. For many sweet applications in cooking, mastic is pounded with a little sugar and mixed with rose or orange blossom water; the usual ratio is $1/4$ tsp (1 mL) crushed mastic to 4 dessert servings.

WEIGHT PER TEASPOON (5 mL)

- whole tears: 2 g

SUGGESTED QUANTITY PER POUND (500 g)

- **red meats:** $1/2$ tsp (2 mL) ground tears
- **white meats:** $1/2$ tsp (2 mL) ground tears
- **vegetables:** $1/4$ tsp (1 mL) ground tears
- **grains and pulses:** $1/4$ tsp (1 mL) ground tears
- **baked goods:** $1/4$ tsp (1 mL) ground tears

M

Asparagus and Mastic Summer Soup

A lovely appetizer in summer, this asparagus soup is made all the more desirable by the addition of mastic, which makes the texture velvety.

Makes 4 small servings

Preparation time:
5 minutes
Cooking time:
20 minutes

- - - - - - - - - - - - - - - - -

Tip

For an ultra-smooth soup, after blending, strain it through a fine-mesh sieve, then add the cream.

- **Parchment paper**
- **Blender**

1 tbsp	olive oil	15 mL
1	small onion, finely chopped	1
1 tsp	fine sea salt	5 mL
8 oz	fresh asparagus spears (3 to 4 bunches)	250 g
1/4 tsp	ground mastic	1 mL
1 tsp	olive oil	5 mL
1/2 tsp	ground dried jalapeño chile, optional	2 mL
1 cup	chicken broth	250 mL
1/2 cup	table (18%) cream	125 mL
	Sea salt and freshly ground black pepper	

1. In a skillet over low heat, heat 1 tbsp (15 mL) oil. Add chopped onion and cover with a sheet of parchment paper, pressing it down over the pieces (to help the sweating process). Cook for 12 minutes, until onion is very soft (be careful not to brown it).

2. Meanwhile, bring a large saucepan of water to a boil. Add salt and asparagus. Cook for about 2 minutes, just until tender-crisp. Reserve 1/2 cup (125 mL) of the cooking water and drain the asparagus. Cut 8 of the nicest tips off the asparagus spears and set aside to use as garnish.

3. In a small bowl, combine mastic with 1 tsp (5 mL) oil, stirring well.

4. In blender, combine cooked asparagus, mastic oil, cooked onion, reserved cooking water, jalapeño powder (if using) and broth. Purée to a smooth consistency. Return to pan, stir in cream and season with salt and pepper to taste. Warm gently over low heat to serve warm, or chill and serve cold, garnished with reserved asparagus tips.

Orange Blossom Ice Cream

In Egypt, orange blossom ice cream is a delicacy. Its distinctive velvet consistency and wonderfully refreshing flavor are made possible by a combination of mastic and orange blossom water. This mastic recipe is courtesy Tess Mallos, the well-known cookbook author.

Makes
4 servings

Preparation time:
5 minutes

Cooking time: 1 hour,
plus 1 day for freezing

Tips

If you don't have an ice-cream maker, put the mixture in an airtight container and freeze until frozen around the edges. Break up and transfer to a bowl. Using an electric mixer, beat well, return to airtight container and refreeze.

Superfine (caster) sugar is very fine granulated sugar typically used in recipes that require a faster-dissolving granule. If you can't find it in stores, you can make your own by using a food processor fitted with the metal blade to process granulated sugar to a very fine, sand-like consistency.

- **Ice-cream maker (see Tips, left)**

¼ tsp	mastic tears, ground to a powder	1 mL
½ cup	superfine (caster) sugar, divided (see Tips, left)	125 mL
1½ tbsp	cornstarch	22 mL
2 cups	whole milk, divided	500 mL
1¼ cups	heavy or whipping (35%) cream	300 mL
4 to 5 tsp	orange blossom water	20 to 25 mL

1. In a small bowl, combine mastic powder with 1 tbsp (15 mL) sugar and cornstarch. Stir in ½ cup (125 mL) milk. Set aside.

2. In a saucepan over medium heat, combine remaining milk and sugar. Stir in cream and cook until almost boiling, 8 to 12 minutes. Stir prepared cornstarch mixture and add to pan; cook for 30 minutes, stirring constantly, until thick and bubbling.

3. Place pan in a large bowl filled with cold water to cool, stirring often. Once cooled completely, stir in orange blossom water to taste.

4. Pour mixture into ice-cream maker and follow manufacturer's instructions.

5. Transfer ice cream to an airtight container and freeze for 24 hours. Before serving, soften in the refrigerator for 1 hour.

M

Mint

Mentha (also known as *M. crispa, M. viridis*)

Names in Other Languages

Spearmint
- **French:** baume vert, menthe verte
- **German:** grün Minze
- **Indian:** podina, pudeena, pudina
- **Indonesian:** daun kesom
- **Italian:** mentastro verde
- **Japanese:** hakka
- **Laotian:** pak hom ho
- **Malay:** daun kesom, pudina
- **Spanish:** menta verde

Peppermint
- **Arabic:** naana
- **Chinese (M):** yang po ho
- **Dutch:** pepermunt
- **Filipino:** yerba buena
- **French:** menthe anglaise
- **German:** Pfefferminze
- **Italian:** menta pepe
- **Japanese:** seiyo hakka
- **Malay:** pohok
- **Portuguese:** hortela
- **Russian:** myata
- **Spanish:** hierbabuena
- **Sri Lankan:** meenchi
- **Swedish:** pepparmynta
- **Thai:** bai saranae
- **Vietnamese:** rau huong lui

Family: Lamiaceae (formerly Labiatae)

Varieties: spearmint (*M. spicata, M. crispa, M. viridis*), peppermint (*M. piperita officinalis*), Corsican mint (*M. requienii*), applemint (*M. x rotundifolia*), eau-de-cologne mint (*M. x piperita* f. *citrata*), pennyroyal (*M. pulegium*)

Other Names: common mint, green mint, lamb mint, our-lady's-mint, peamint, sage of Bethlehem, spire mint (spearmint); black Mitcham, black peppermint, white peppermint (peppermint)

Flavor Group: Strong

Parts Used: leaves (as a herb)

Background

Peppermint does not seem to have been known in England until the 17th century, when it is thought to have hybridized from watermint and spearmint. Spearmint is native to the temperate regions of the Old World and is mentioned in Roman mythology. Its name is derived from Minthe, a

Culinary Information

Combines with

- chile
- coriander (seed and leaf)
- cumin
- marjoram
- oregano
- parsley
- rosemary
- sage
- savory
- thyme
- turmeric
- vanilla

Traditional Uses

- roast meats such as chicken, pork and veal
- new potatoes and green peas tossed in butter
- tomatoes and eggplant (in small amounts)
- salad dressings
- refreshing sorbets
- yogurt (in raita)
- herbal teas

Spice Blends

- harissa paste mixes
- lamb seasonings
- tandoori spice blends
- special mixed herb blends

charming nymph who inspired a fit of jealousy in Proserpina (the envious wife of Pluto), who transformed Minthe into the lowly, downtrodden mint plant. Hippocrates and Dioscorides mention the medicinal benefits of mint, and in Roman times it was an aromatic and room-freshening strewing herb. The Pharisees in the Bible paid their taxes in mint, anise and cumin. Mint grows so profusely that more than 25 varieties are now found wild in many temperate zones of the world.

Spearmint and peppermint oils are among the most important flavoring ingredients today. It is difficult to recall a day in one's life when the flavor or aroma of mint was not experienced in one form or another. And yet it was not until the 18th century that large quantities of peppermint and spearmint were cultivated in England—in the medicinal herb gardens at Mitcham, in the county of Surrey. By 1796 up to 3,000 pounds (1,350 kg) of oil was being extracted by steam distillation in London from approximately 100 acres (40 ha) of mint grown at Mitcham. The variety of peppermint known as 'Black Mitcham', a hardy variety that produces more high-quality oil than any other variety, remains the backbone of the peppermint oil industry today.

A century later the United States had become a major player in the spearmint and peppermint oil industry through entrepreneurial marketing and large-scale production capabilities. High grades of US-produced mint oil, guaranteed free from contamination by weeds and adulterants, were

M

cleverly marketed while the producers sought to manipulate growers and raw material prices. The mint oil industry experienced incredible highs, prices crashed, and the dynamics that emerge in most developing markets, such as speculation, monopoly and fraudulent advertising, were all apparent. Those early pioneers, many of whom persisted in the face of incredible hardship, would rest more easily if they could see the consumer's love of mint flavorings today.

The Plant

The mint family encompasses a vast array of varieties, a situation brought about by its tendency to hybridize readily within the species. Among all of them, spearmint stands out as the most useful and popular culinary herb. Peppermint is widely favored medicinally and it flavors sweets and is found in many breath-freshening applications, but I don't consider it to be a regular inclusion when cooking.

Spearmint is generally seen in two forms: the mid to light green, narrow-leaved, low-growing classic variety (*Mentha spicata*) and the coarser, crinkly, round-leafed variety we in Australia call common or garden mint (*M. viridis*) and invariably have growing in a shady spot not far from a dripping tap. Spearmint has a distinct mint aroma and a pleasing light flavor that is not pungent, warm or too antiseptic.

Peppermint leaves are more oval than spearmint leaves; they are dark green with an almost peppery heat, an obvious mouth-freshening, germicidal characteristic, and a sweet balsamic taste that instantly evokes peppermint throat lozenges. There are two types of peppermint: "black" peppermint (*M. spicata* x *piperita vulgaris*) has dark, almost purple stems, and "white" peppermint (*M.* x *piperita officinalis*) has green stems.

Other Varieties

Applemint (*Mentha* x *rotundifolia*), also called pineapple mint or woolly mint, has leaves that are crinkly and sometimes variegated and look much like common mint, except for a covering of light down that gives them a soft, fuzzy appearance. Their flavor is similar to spearmint, with a pleasing hint of green apple that complements fruit salads.
Corsican mint (*M. requienii*) has a flavor profile most similar to peppermint; it is used primarily in herbal teas, and an extract produced by steam distillation is used to flavor

liqueurs. **Eau-de-cologne mint** (*M.* x *piperita* f. *citrata*) is taller and more erect than spearmint and peppermint and is grown for decorative purposes and the refreshing eau-de-cologne fragrance it gives off when brushed past in the garden. It is generally not used in recipes, but some cooks enjoy its perfume-like fragrance in Asian dishes. **Ginger mint** (*M.* x *gracilis*) is named for its light ginger fragrance, which goes well with Asian food. **Pennyroyal** (*M. pulegium*) is a low-growing groundcover mint with small, light green leaves; it should not be eaten, but when put under the dog's blanket, it will deter fleas!

You may hear of further varieties. **Corn mint** (*M. arvensis*) has a somewhat bitter taste. **Water mint** (*M. aquatica*) is a variety with a flavor like peppermint. **Japanese peppermint** (*M. arvensis* var. *piperascens*) is another peppermint-tasting variety. **American wild mint** (*M. arvensis* var. *villosa*) grows in North America and has a milder flavor than most so-called wild mints.

Vietnamese mint (*Polygonum odoratum*) is not a true mint; it is covered in more detail in the entry for Vietnamese mint (see page 664). **Horsemint** (*Monarda punctata*) and **coyote mint** (*Monardella villosa*) are related to bergamot (see page 119) and are used more for medicinal than culinary applications.

Processing

Oils of spearmint and peppermint for the food and pharmaceutical industries are extracted by steam distillation. Dried mint is produced in much the same way as other green leaf herbs: by dehydrating in a warm, dark, low-humidity environment until the moisture level is around 10%.

Homegrown mint is easily dried by hanging it upside down in bunches in a dark, well-aired and dry place until the leaves have become quite crisp and dry. Alternatively, you can dry them in a microwave: Place the leaves in a single

M

Travels in the Spice Trade

When Liz and I visited southeastern Turkey to research sumac production near the town of Nizip, we walked across a huge field of spearmint to reach a grove of sumac trees. I could not help thinking how enticing the nymph Minthe must have been. The aroma of fresh mint wafting up through the warm summer air was enough to make one swoon.

layer on a paper towel and microwave on High for 20-second bursts, checking for crispness after each burst. As the leaves become crisp and dry to the touch, remove them and zap the remaining leaves until all are dry. To prevent damage to the magnetron in your microwave, place $^1/_2$ cup (125 mL) water in a microwave-safe cup beside the leaves.

Buying and Storage

Fresh spearmint is readily available from most fresh produce retailers. If you have a choice between the smooth, narrow-leaved or the crinkly, round-leaved varieties, buy the former—it has a better flavor for cooking. Fresh mint stores well if the bunch is stood up in a glass of water in the refrigerator, covered with a plastic bag. Change the water every few days and your fresh mint will last up to 2 weeks.

Dried spearmint is usually sold simply as "mint," and in most cases it will be quite a dark green, almost black in color. Strictly speaking, this is called "rubbed" mint; the

pieces of leaf will be quite small—about $1/8$ inch (3 mm)—because they break up when rubbed off the stem after drying. Good-quality dried mint may be either dark or light green but should not look dusty or be contaminated with pieces of pale yellow stalk. Sometimes you can buy Turkish spearmint, which is light green and has the brightest taste and aroma. Store dried mint in the same way as other dried herbs: in an airtight container away from extremes of heat, light and humidity. Under these conditions, it will last for up to 1 year.

Use

Peppermint is far more limited in the kitchen than spearmint. It will mostly be found in occasional recipes for sweets such as peppermint creams or added as flavoring to baked items such as chocolate cake. Peppermint tea is possibly the most agreeable of all herbal beverages. It is a pleasant-tasting, relaxing tea that aids the digestion and helps clear the head of minor winter sniffles.

Spearmint, on the other hand, has myriad applications, made possible because its light, minty taste brings an element of freshness to the foods it is combined with. Some writers hold the view that mint does not combine well with other herbs; however, when it is added in small amounts, I have seen it complement thyme, sage, marjoram, oregano and parsley very well. When many of us think of mint, the first dish that comes to mind is roast lamb with mint sauce or mint jelly. But mint is also a good accompaniment to chicken, pork and veal and is delicious sprinkled on new potatoes or cooked green peas that have been tossed in a little butter. It goes well with tomatoes and eggplant when used sparingly. Salads and salad dressings benefit from the addition of a little mint, as do cold dishes such as iced cucumber soup and fresh fruit salad. Traditional mint julep, the liqueur crème de menthe and many alcoholic drinks owe their character to the humble mint plant.

Middle Eastern, Moroccan, Indian and Asian cooking all benefit from the inclusion of mint in a variety of recipes that range from stuffed vine leaves, tagines, butter chicken and stir-fried vegetables to chutneys of freshly grated coconut, curry leaves, fried mustard seeds and chile. A favorite of mine is cooling cucumber, yogurt and mint raita, which adds a perfect fillip to spicy Indian meats such as tandoori lamb or chicken and meat koftas.

WEIGHT PER TEASPOON (5 mL)

- rubbed dried leaves: 1 g

SUGGESTED QUANTITY PER POUND (500 g)

- **red meats:** 4 tsp (20 mL) fresh chopped, $1\frac{1}{2}$ tsp (7 mL) rubbed dried leaves

- **white meats:** 2 tsp (10 mL) fresh chopped, $\frac{3}{4}$ tsp (3 mL) rubbed dried leaves

- **vegetables:** 1 tsp (5 mL) fresh chopped, $\frac{1}{4}$ tsp (1 mL) rubbed dried leaves

- **grains and pulses:** 1 tsp (5 mL) fresh chopped, $\frac{1}{4}$ tsp (1 mL) rubbed dried leaves

- **baked goods:** 1 tsp (5 mL) fresh chopped, $\frac{1}{4}$ tsp (1 mL) rubbed dried leaves

M

Mint Sauce

Lamb and mint are a traditional pairing. When I'm not covering my lamb with Moroccan or Indian spices, I do enjoy a good old-fashioned roast leg of lamb with mint sauce and peas.

**Makes about
½ cup (125 mL)**

Preparation time:
10 minutes, plus
30 minutes for soaking

Cooking time: none

1 cup	lightly packed fresh mint leaves, very finely chopped	250 mL
2 tbsp	granulated sugar	30 mL
3 tbsp	boiling water	45 mL
2 to 3 tbsp	white wine vinegar	30 to 45 mL
	Sea salt	

1. In a heatproof bowl, combine mint, sugar and boiling water. Stir until sugar is dissolved. Set aside for 30 minutes to allow mint to infuse liquid. Add vinegar and salt to taste. The sauce will keep in an airtight container in the refrigerator for up to 3 days.

Cacik

Cacik is the Turkish equivalent of Greek tzatziki or Indian raita, a cooling combination of mint, yogurt and cucumber. Cacik can be served as a dip or watered down to make a soup that is refreshing on a hot day. It makes a great accompaniment to Lahmucin (page 188), Eggplant Salad (page 524) and Tabouli (page 476).

**Makes about
1 cup (250 mL)**

Preparation time:
10 minutes

Cooking time: none

Tip

You can substitute 1½ tsp (7 mL) dried mint for the fresh mint.

½	cucumber, approximately 6 inches (15 cm) long	½
1 cup	plain Greek yogurt	250 mL
1	clove garlic, minced	1
½ tsp	fine sea salt	2 mL
1 tbsp	fresh mint leaves, very finely chopped (see Tip, left)	15 mL

1. Using a box grater, grate cucumber. Transfer to a fine-mesh sieve placed over a bowl and set aside for 5 minutes to drain.
2. In a small bowl, combine prepared cucumber, yogurt, garlic, salt and mint. Serve chilled. Best eaten the same day it is made.

Variation

To make a soup: You may wish to grate the cucumber more finely in Step 1. Omit draining the cucumber. Add 1 cup (250 mL) water to the bowl in Step 2 and combine well.

Mint Chocolate Mousse

Chocolate and mint are a wonderful pairing, and I love the simplicity of chocolate mousse for dessert. Don't be fooled—this doesn't seem like a lot of peppermint extract, but the flavor is very concentrated. The mousse is incredibly easy to make and a great dish to prepare ahead when entertaining. I like to serve it in mismatched vintage cocktail glasses or bowls.

Makes 4 small servings

Preparation time:
5 minutes

Cooking time:
10 minutes

Tip

For an attractive presentation, serve with a sprig of mint, a dusting of cocoa or finely grated chocolate or a dollop of whipped cream on top.

3½ oz	70% chocolate, roughly broken	105 g
1 tbsp	butter	15 mL
¼ tsp	pure peppermint extract	1 mL
3	eggs, separated, at room temperature	3

1. Set a heatproof bowl over a saucepan of water over medium heat. Add chocolate, butter and peppermint extract. Bring water to a boil, then turn off the heat (there will be plenty of residual heat to melt the chocolate). Stir chocolate once or twice so it melts evenly. Once it is melted, remove from heat and set aside.

2. In a bowl, using an electric mixer, beat egg whites until stiff peaks form (when beaters are lifted, whites should hold their peaks without drooping).

3. Using a spatula, stir egg yolks into melted chocolate mixture, then fold in egg whites. Work lightly and quickly to incorporate whites into chocolate while retaining as much air and fluffiness as possible.

4. Divide mousse among 4 ramekins or glasses (roughly 4 oz/125 g capacity). Cover and refrigerate for 6 hours or overnight. Mousse will keep in refrigerator for up to 2 days.

M

Mustard

Brassica alba (also known as *Sinipas alba*)

Names in Other Languages

- **Arabic:** khardal abyad (yellow), khardal (black)
- **Chinese (C):** baahk gaai choi (yellow), gai lat, gaai choi (black)
- **Chinese (M):** bai jie cai (yellow), hei jie zi (black)
- **Czech:** horcice bila (yellow), horcice cerna (black), horcice cerna sitinnvita (brown)
- **Dutch:** witte mosterd (yellow), zwarte mosterd (black)
- **Finnish:** keltasinappi (yellow), mustasinappi (black)
- **French:** moutarde blanche (yellow), moutarde noire (black), moutarde de Chine (brown)
- **German:** weisser Senf (yellow), schwarzer Senf (black), indischer Senf (brown)
- **Greek:** moustarda, sinapi agrio (yellow), sinapi mauro (black)
- **Indian:** rai, sarson, lal sarsu, kimcea (black)
- **Indonesian:** biji sawi
- **Italian:** senape bianca (yellow), senape nera (black)
- **Japanese:** shiro-karashi (yellow), kuro-karashi (black)
- **Malay:** biji sawi (black)

Family: Brassicaceae (formerly Cruciferae)

Varieties: yellow (white) mustard (*Brassica alba* or *Sinipas alba*), black mustard (*B. nigra*), brown mustard (*B. juncea*)

Other Names: Chinese mustard, Indian mustard, leaf mustard, mizuna mustard, mustard greens (brown mustard)

Flavor Group: Hot

Parts Used: seeds (as a spice), leaves (as a herb)

Background

Mustard is one of the oldest herbs known to humans: it has been used since the earliest records of history. Much appreciated for its medicinal applications, both internally as a stimulant and diuretic and externally for general muscle relief, it was highly regarded by the ancient Greeks, including Pythagoras, the fifth-century BCE philosopher, and Hippocrates, the famous physician. Mustard is referred to in the Bible as the greatest among herbs. In 334 BCE, King

Culinary Information

Combines with
- allspice
- cardamom
- chile
- cinnamon
- cloves
- coriander seed
- cumin
- fennel seed
- fenugreek seed
- galangal
- ginger
- nigella
- paprika
- pepper
- star anise
- tamarind
- turmeric

Traditional Uses
- pickles
- Indian curries
- salad dressings and mayonnaise
- spiced vinegars
- prepared mustards
- cooking oils

Spice Blends
- curry powders
- panch phoron
- pickling spices
- meat seasonings
- mustard powders
- sambar powder

Names in Other Languages

- **Portuguese:** mostarda branca (yellow), mostarda preta (black)
- **Russian:** gorchitsa belaya (yellow), gorchitsa chyornaya (black)
- **Spanish:** mostaza silvestre (yellow), mostaza negra (black), mostaza de la India (brown)
- **Sri Lankan:** abba
- **Swedish:** vitsenap (yellow), svartsenap (black), brunsenap (brown)
- **Thai:** mastart
- **Turkish:** beyaz hardal tohum (yellow), kara hardal (black)
- **Vietnamese:** bach gioi tu (yellow), hac gioi (black)

Darius III of Persia sent Alexander the Great a bag of sesame seeds, symbolizing the vast numbers of his army. Alexander returned a bag of mustard seeds, to imply not only the number but the power and energy of his men. Mustard was used as a condiment in Roman times, when it was simply sprinkled over food in the same way as pepper; in those days the leaves were commonly eaten as a vegetable. Today mustard greens are most widely used in Asian cuisine and are an important ingredient in American cooking from the Deep South.

In 812 CE, Charlemagne, King of the Franks and Emperor of the West, decreed that mustard was to be grown on the imperial farms in central Europe. Around that time the French were growing mustard on convent lands near Paris as a source of revenue. Human nature being what it is, mustard became the basis for more complex concoctions, once the power of the activated enzyme was appreciated. Thus blends of mustard with honey, vinegar and grape must (the unfermented juice of ripe grapes) became popular. A plausible theory about the derivation of the name *mustard* is that it is from the Latin words for "must" (*mustum*) and "hot" (*ardens*).

M

Mustard was introduced into England by the Romans. In the 13th century Parisian vinegar makers were granted the right to make mustards, and by the 18th century both the English and French were perfecting methods of processing. On the French side it consisted of adding ingredients such as tarragon, mushrooms, truffles, champagne and even vanilla. The English focused on ways of separating the husk from the center, creating superfine mustard powders that often included wheat flour and turmeric. This activity spawned a mustard-manufacturing industry that grew by making accessible to the masses a pleasant-tasting condiment that added zest and interest to what must have sometimes seemed an interminable diet of bland vegetables and salted meats.

Travels in the Spice Trade

Some years ago we were in the Indian state of Gujarat doing research on seed spices when we spied an ox pulling a cart in a circle over what looked like a big pile of straw. When we got closer, we saw that the beast and its driver were threshing brown mustard seeds (*Brassica juncea*). The mustard had been harvested when the seed-bearing pods were fully developed but not yet ripe, to avoid shattering during gathering, which would lose many seeds. After cutting, the mustard "hay" was stacked in sheaves to dry and then threshed by simply laying it on the ground and driving an oxcart over the pile to break the pods and release the dark brown seeds. Off to one side, three young men were holding an enormous sieve about 6½ feet (2 m) in diameter. They were standing in a calf-deep pile of shiny brown mustard seeds as another worker loaded more trampled hay onto the enormous sieve. The young fellows were all smiles, highly amused by our interest in their everyday task.

The Plant

All mustards belong to the former Cruciferae family (now referred to as Brassicaceae), which was so named because the flower petals echo the form of a Greek cross.

White (or yellow) mustard has the smallest growing habit, reaching about 3 feet (1 m) in height, and is distinguished by its hairy appearance. The 1- to 2-inch (2.5 to 5 cm) pods have a pronounced shape like a bird's beak and contain around six seeds, which are yellow. The leaves are pale green, soft and lobed and the bright yellow flowers are relatively large.

Yellow mustard seeds—as I will call them, because they are a creamy yellow color, not white—are close to $^1/_8$ inch (3 mm) in diameter and have the mildest flavor of the mustard triumvirate. The husk of yellow mustard seeds is microscopically pitted; it has such effective moisture-absorbing properties that the seeds were used as an ancient form of the silica gel now widely used to keep chemical preparations and electronics dry.

All mustard seeds have little discernible aroma when whole. In fact, they barely give off fragrance even when ground. Mustard seeds contain an enzyme called myrosinase, and it is this enzyme, which isn't activated until it comes in contact with liquids, that creates mustard's typical hot, pungent taste. The heat of fully developed hot mustard is sharp, irritating and bitingly hot—it rushes up the back of the nose, clears the sinuses and makes the eyes water. Not all prepared mustards are hot, however (see "Processing," below), but mild mustard may still be tangy, savory, smooth and pleasing to the palate.

M

Mustard Oil

Mustard oil, which is often found as an ingredient in Indian recipes, is produced by the cold-pressing method of extraction. Because the oil is cold-pressed, the enzyme is not activated. This means that, traditionally, mustard oil is not hot; it is used simply as a cooking oil in the same ways that other cooking oils are used. However, an enterprising producer in Australia, Yandilla Mustard Seed Oil Enterprises, also makes a hot mustard oil. They presoak their mustard seeds in water just prior to pressing, which creates a lightly spiced mustard oil that is excellent for making curries and Asian stir-fries. In the United States, the FDA specifies that mustard oil should be used only for external purposes because it contains high levels of erucic acid, which laboratory studies indicate may have a negative impact on rats. However, there is no evidence that this substance is harmful to humans.

Other Varieties

A degree of confusion prevails about mustard seeds because three types of mustard are most often used for culinary purposes: white (yellow) mustard, black mustard and brown mustard. In addition there are two other, closely related plants—field mustard (*Brassica rapa*) and rape (*B. napus*)—whose seeds are also pressed to make mustard oil for cooking.

Black mustard (*B. nigra*) is a tall, smooth-looking plant with lance-shaped upper leaves that grows 6 to 9 feet (2 to 3 m) tall. It bears yellow flowers that are similar in appearance to those of yellow mustard, but smaller. The seedpods of black mustard are erect and smooth. They are $3/4$ inch (2 cm) long and hold about 12 dark reddish brown and almost black seeds about $1/2$ inch (1 cm) in diameter. Black mustard seeds are more pungent than the yellow seeds.

Brown mustard (*B. juncea*) is similar to black mustard in size; however, the leaves are large and oval. The flowers are pale yellow and the pods are 1 to 2 inches (2.5 to 5 cm) long. Brown mustard seeds look almost identical to black but have only about 70% of their pungency when the enzyme is activated. **Yellow mustard** (*B. alba*) produces nearly as much heat as black and brown mustard seeds; however, it has less of the deep, nutty pungency that is preferred in Indian cooking. Yellow mustard seeds are traditionally used to make prepared English mustards and mustard pickles.

Field mustard (*B. rapa*) and **rapeseed** (*B. napus*) are often referred to as "canola," a cold-pressed oil used in cooking and processed food manufacturing. The seeds are not generally used as a culinary spice.

Processing

Mustard seeds need to be harvested when the pods are fully developed but not yet ripe, because they burst open easily. Black mustard is particularly difficult to harvest mechanically, so in many countries it has been replaced by the slightly less pungent brown variety, which does not shatter so readily. After cutting, the mustard "hay" is stacked in sheaves to dry, then threshed to remove the seeds. Mustard powders are produced by milling yellow, black and brown seeds to remove the husks (individually or in combinations), then finely sieving them. Occasionally starches and colors are added to achieve the desired flavor and appearance. There is also a de-heated mustard powder that is used in food manufacturing to create a mild mustard

flavor without the burn. This is produced by subjecting the seeds to a humidity and temperature treatment that deactivates the myrosinase enzyme.

Prepared mustards, as the pastes in jars are called, are made by soaking the seeds in cold water to activate the enzyme, then adding an acidic liquid such as vinegar, white wine or verjuice (the juice of unripe fruit, most often grapes). The addition of acid inhibits or stops the enzyme reaction and stabilizes the paste at the desired heat level. Black and brown mustard seeds contain different glucosides than yellow seeds. The reaction of these compounds with the myrosinase makes them more pungent, which is why they are preferred for making hot mustard. However, it is the effects of different liquids on the enzyme that tend to influence the final heat more than the type of mustard seed used. Water produces a sharp, hot taste; vinegar a mild, tangy flavor; wine a pungent, spicy taste; and beer an extremely hot flavor. Even when water has been used to make a hot mustard, vinegar should be added when the mixture has achieved the correct heat level. Its acid will not destroy the volatile oil developed by the enzymes and it will prevent the mustard from deteriorating over time.

Buying and Storage

Yellow mustard seeds are readily available but whole black mustard seeds are comparatively rare, because their wide-scale production has been replaced by that of brown. It is difficult for even an expert to tell the difference between the two. When recipes call for black mustard seeds, brown make an acceptable substitute.

Mustard powder is made by removing the husks from the seeds, grinding the husked seeds and then putting them through a fine sieve. It is most suitable for making hot mustard. Just add a little cold water and let the mixture stand for 15 minutes to develop its heat. Ground yellow mustard seed is simply the whole seed powdered; it contains the husk, which has great moisture-absorbing qualities.

Mustard seeds and powder should be stored in airtight containers protected from extremes of heat, light and humidity. Whole seeds will last for more than 3 years and mustard powder will last for 1 to 2 years.

Myriad varieties of prepared mustard are available, ranging from mass-manufactured to boutique specialty and homemade brands. It is best to avoid jars that show signs of separation. If the vinegar appears on the surface, that is a sign of age; the product could be past its use-by date. Good-quality prepared mustard does not need to be refrigerated after opening, as the natural microbe-inhibiting qualities of mustard will prevent it from going moldy. However, mustard will last longer when kept in the refrigerator. As some mustard manufacturers use different processes, always follow the storage instructions on the label.

Use

Whole mustard seeds are an important ingredient in pickling spice blends and the Indian seed mix panch phoron. They add a nutty taste to steamed vegetables such as their close relative cabbage. When fried in oil at the outset of making a curry, mustard seeds release a deliciously nutty taste and slight piquancy without adding heat (the enzyme has not been activated). It is common in South Indian cooking to fry mustard seeds, curry leaves, cumin seeds and asafetida in oil and then add the tasty concoction to the dish before serving, a process called tempering. (You have to be quick to put the lid on the saucepan to prevent the mustard seeds from popping all over the kitchen.)

Mustard powder should not be added directly to vinegar, as the enzymes will be killed and a bitter flavor will develop; always mix some cold water with the powder first (never hot water, as that also kills the enzyme). To make hot mustard for the table, mix cold water with mustard powder to taste and set aside for 15 minutes to allow the heat to develop. Make only enough for that day, as by the next day the heat will have dissipated. A paste of mustard powder and water is worth adding to oil-and-vinegar salad dressings, as the water-absorbing properties of the retained husk make it act as an emulsifier, preventing the mixture from separating for 10 minutes or more after shaking. An effective coating for roasted red meats can be made by combining 2 tsp (10 mL) brown mustard seed with 1 tbsp (15 mL) each paprika, sumac and oregano, plus salt to taste. As well as making delicious roast meat, a lovely byproduct of this rub is the gravy made from the pan juices, which is rich, dark and full-bodied.

Mild prepared mustard makes an ideal substitute for butter or margarine on sandwiches. It contains almost no fat and has a taste that complements typical sandwich ingredients.

WEIGHT PER TEASPOON (5 mL)
- whole: 4.5 g
- ground: 2.6 g

SUGGESTED QUANTITY PER POUND (500 g)
- red meats: 4 tsp (20 mL) seeds, 1 tbsp (15 mL) powder
- white meats: 4 tsp (20 mL) seeds, 1 tbsp (15 mL) powder
- vegetables: 2 to 3 tsp (10 to 15 mL) seeds, 1½ tsp (7 mL) powder
- grains and pulses: 2 to 3 tsp (10 to 15 mL) seeds, 1½ tsp (7 mL) powder
- baked goods: 2 tsp (10 mL) seeds, 1½ tsp (7 mL) powder

Whole-Grain Mustard

Making your own mustard is relatively easy, and particularly rewarding when you serve it as a condiment or give it as a gift to friends. This recipe is for a full-flavored, coarse-textured mustard. It is ideal for accompanying meats and using as a coating to encrust roast beef or lamb. You can experiment by varying the amounts of spices or adding other ingredients such as chiles and sun-dried tomatoes.

Makes about ½ cup (125 mL)

Preparation time:
10 minutes

Cooking time:
10 minutes, plus 1 to 2 weeks for ripening

Tips

Don't be surprised if this mustard is sharp and bitter after it is first made; a week of storage is required for the flavor to fully develop.

Should the mustard appear too runny after a week or two, regrind the entire mixture to crack more mustard seeds so they will absorb excess moisture, then refrigerate.

• **Mortar and pestle**

1 tbsp	yellow mustard seeds	15 mL
1 tbsp	brown mustard seeds	15 mL
½ tsp	green peppercorns	2 mL
¼ tsp	ajowan seeds	1 mL
¼ tsp	fine sea salt	1 mL
4	allspice berries	4
¼ tsp	packed light brown sugar	1 mL
½ tsp	dried tarragon	2 mL
¼ cup	red wine vinegar	60 mL

1. Using mortar and pestle or a clean spice or coffee grinder, combine yellow and brown mustard seeds, peppercorns, ajowan, salt and allspice. Grind to a coarse consistency (make sure most of the mustard seeds are cracked so they absorb the liquid and create a spoonable mixture). Add brown sugar and tarragon, mixing thoroughly. Add vinegar and stir well for about 3 minutes, until emulsified. Transfer to a sterile airtight container and set aside in a cool, dark place for about 1 week to allow the flavors to develop. The mustard will keep in the refrigerator for up to 1 month.

M

Dosa

When I went on one of my mum and dad's Spice Discovery tours of India, I found myself looking forward to breakfast more than any other meal, thanks to the amazing dosa served at the hotels' breakfast buffets. Crispy aromatic pancakes filled with spiced potato and topped with yogurt make a heavenly combination, and these have become a brunch favorite in our house. Traditionally dosa batter involves grinding and fermenting lentils and rice, but I have developed this quicker and equally tasty version.

**Makes
6 servings**

Preparation time:
 15 minutes

Cooking time: 1 hour,
 20 minutes

- - - - - - - - - - - - - - -

Tips

Ghee is a type of clarified butter used in Indian cooking. If you don't have any, you can substitute an equal amount of butter or clarified butter.

Chickpea flour is also known as gram flour or besan flour. It can be found in Asian and Indian markets and health-food stores.

• **Preheat oven to 350°F (180°C)**

FILLING

2 lbs	white potatoes (about 6 large)	1 kg
1 tbsp	ghee (see Tips, left)	15 mL
½	onion, sliced	½
1 tbsp	freshly grated gingerroot	15 mL
1	green finger chile, sliced	1
1 tsp	brown mustard seeds	5 mL
1 tsp	cumin seeds	5 mL
½ tsp	ground turmeric	2 mL
½ tsp	fenugreek seeds	2 mL
¼ cup	fresh curry leaves	60 mL
	Sea salt and freshly ground black pepper	

BATTER

1½ cups	chickpea flour (see Tips, left)	375 mL
½ cup	white rice flour	125 mL
1½ tsp	brown mustard seeds	7 mL
1 tsp	nigella seeds	5 mL
Pinch	fine sea salt	Pinch
1¾ cups	water	425 mL
2 tbsp	plain yogurt	30 mL
1 to 2 tbsp	oil	15 to 30 mL

GARNISH

1 cup	plain yogurt	250 mL
2 tbsp	finely chopped fresh mint leaves	30 mL
1 cup	lightly packed fresh coriander (cilantro) leaves	250 mL
	Mango chutney	

Tip

The potato and pancake mixtures can be made the day before and refrigerated overnight.

1. *Filling:* Prick potatoes all over with a fork and bake in preheated oven for 1 hour or until very soft. Remove from oven and set aside until cool enough to handle. Peel off skins and crumble potatoes into a bowl (it should resemble a lumpy mash).

2. In a wok or large skillet over medium-high heat, melt ghee. Add onion, ginger, chile, mustard seeds, cumin, turmeric and fenugreek. Cook, stirring constantly, for 5 minutes, until onion is soft and spices are fragrant. Add potato and curry leaves and mix well. Season with salt and pepper to taste. Remove from heat and set aside.

3. *Batter:* In a bowl, combine chickpea flour, rice flour, mustard seeds, nigella and salt. In a measuring cup, whisk together water and yogurt. Make a well in the flour mixture and pour yogurt mixture into center. Stir until a smooth batter forms (it will be very thin).

4. In a large skillet or griddle, heat 1 tbsp (15 mL) oil until shimmery. Using a ladle, pour a spoonful of batter into pan. Immediately tilt and swirl the pan so batter covers as much area as possible as thinly as possible. Cook each side for 2 to 3 minutes, until crisp. Transfer cooked pancakes to a large, heatproof serving plate, cover with foil and place in a warm oven. Repeat with remaining batter, adding more oil to pan as needed.

5. In a small serving bowl, combine yogurt and mint.

6. To serve, reheat potato until piping hot and place on the table with the pancakes, yogurt mixture, coriander leaves and chutney for people to help themselves.

M

Variation

For another vegetarian option, substitute 1 lb (500 g) steamed cauliflower florets, roughly mashed with 1 cup (250 mL) chopped paneer cheese, for the potato.

Myrtle

Myrtus communis

Family: Myrtaceae

Varieties: cape myrtle (*Myrsine africana*, also known as *M. retusa*), bog myrtle (*Myrica gale*, also known as *M. palustris*), box myrtle (*Myrica nagi*, also known as *M. integrifolia*), wax myrtle (*Myrica cerifera*, also known as *M. mexicana*)

Other Names: common myrtle, Corsican pepper, sweet myrtle, sweet gale, true myrtle

Flavor Group: Strong

Parts Used: leaves, branches and flowers (as a spice)

Background

Myrtle is native to southern Europe, North Africa and western Asia and grows widely around the Mediterranean. It is often mentioned in the Bible. In Greek mythology it was considered to be sacred to Aphrodite, which explains why it also has a reputation as an aphrodisiac. Linked with love and feminine allure, myrtle is included in an Israeli bride's wedding bouquet. Myrtle is also connected with fidelity and immortality. In parts of Asia the dried, powdered leaves were made into a dusting powder for babies. The berries were used to flavor wine in the Mediterranean; nowadays they tend to be used in sweet recipes and some liqueurs.

The Plant

On first appearance, evergreen myrtle trees do not conjure up the notion of culinary use. These large shrubs or small trees have tightly clustered shiny, waxy leaves that are 1 to 2 inches (2.5 to 5 cm) in length. Their attractive flowers are white, bursting with an anemone-like abundance of stamens—they look as though their only purpose is to be decorative. The bitterness and astringency of the leaves and the piney juniper and rosemary flavor notes in the berries that form after flowering mean this herb has limited use in flavoring food in the traditional manner. Myrtle should not be confused with crepe myrtle (*Lagerstroemea indica*),

Culinary Information

Combines with

- allspice
- bay leaf
- juniper
- marjoram
- oregano
- pepper
- rosemary
- sage
- savory
- tarragon
- thyme

Traditional Uses

- game
- poultry
- roasted red meats

Spice Blends

- not commonly used in spice blends

a decorative tree, or lemon myrtle (*Backhousia citriodora*), which is described on pages 355 to 357.

Other Varieties

All the varieties of myrtle mentioned here have a similar flavor profile and are used in much the same ways in foods. **Cape myrtle** (*Myrsine africana*) grows in the Himalayas and is found from North Africa to East Asia. The fruits can be eaten fresh or dried, and the seeds, like many small black seeds, have been used to adulterate black pepper. The most common uses for this variety are medicinal.

Bog myrtle (*Myrica gale*) is a deciduous shrub that grows to about 4 feet (1.2 m) tall, with tapering leaves similar to box myrtle. Also referred to as "sweet gale," it should not be consumed by pregnant women, as it has been reported to cause miscarriage. It is found from western Europe to Scandanavia and North America. The leaves and berries can be used to flavor savory foods. The branches were used in beer-making in Yorkshire, England, to produce "gale beer."

Box myrtle (*Myrica nagi*) is a little sweeter and more acidic than the other myrtles, and the fruits tend to be consumed fresh. **Wax myrtle** (*M. cerifera*) is also called "bayberry wild cinnamon." The berries have a waxy coating that is removed by plunging them into boiling water. The wax is then collected to make candles, which when burned release a refreshing pine-like aroma. It should not be confused with barberry (*Berberis vulgaris*, see page 100), a sweet-and-sour tangy fruit used in Persian cuisine.

Processing

Myrtle leaves are not difficult to dry using the same method you would use for bay leaves or makrut lime leaves. Spread freshly picked leaves in a single layer on porous paper and place in a warm, dark place with low humidity. When the leaves feel quite crisp to the touch and have lost their leathery, pliable feeling, they are ready for storage and later use. The ripe berries are best dried in the sun, as the exposure to direct heat helps expel moisture from their leathery skin.

Buying and Storage

The branches, leaves and berries are the parts of the myrtle plant that are most often used. Because they are not readily available from food providers, myrtle is worth growing at home. It needs to be grown in well-drained medium-rich soil in a sunny position. Bunches of fresh myrtle leaves will keep in resealable bags in the freezer for up to 3 months.

Dried myrtle leaves and the deep purple to black berries, in their whole or coarsely crushed form, can be purchased from some specialty spice shops. Store in airtight containers and keep away from extremes of heat, light and humidity.

Use

Because of its bitter taste, myrtle is rarely served with food after it has been cooked. Either meats are wrapped in the leafy branches or the leaves are stuffed into the cavity of poultry before roasting. A few myrtle leaves can be added to casseroles in the same manner as bay leaves, but I recommend removing them before serving.

In the Middle East the fruits, which develop after flowering, are sometimes eaten when ripe, and the dried berries are added to food for their flavor and mild acidity. In Italy the sweet fresh flowers, which taste like orange blossoms, are appreciated in salads. It is as a cooking wood, however, that myrtle appears to be most popular. When used on the fire to grill and roast meats, it imparts a fragrant, smoky note to food that is incredibly appetizing.

An essential oil used in the manufacture of perfumes, soaps and skincare products is made by steam distillation of myrtle's bark, leaves and flowers. A perfumed water known as *eau d'ange* is made from the flowers.

WEIGHT PER TEASPOON (5 mL)

- whole average-size fresh leaf:
  0.5 g

SUGGESTED QUANTITY PER POUND (500 g)

Remove after cooking.

- **red meats:**
  10 leaves
- **white meats:**
  5 leaves
- **vegetables:**
  2 berries
- **grains and pulses:**
  2 berries
- **baked goods :**
  2 berries

M

Veal Osso Bucco with Myrtle

Osso bucco is a sliced veal shank that is delicious slow-cooked. The bone marrow that melts as it is cooking adds a rich decadence to the dish. Here myrtle is used to balance its robustness by imparting a gentle pine-like aroma to the veal. Serve with roasted or mashed potatoes alongside.

Makes
4 servings

Preparation time:
 10 minutes

Cooking time: 1 hour,
 45 minutes

Tip

Veal shank is the lower leg and is generally prepared without the protruding bone, as with lamb shanks. Pieces of veal shank are about 2 inches (5 cm) thick and are best slow-cooked over low heat.

• **Preheat oven to 325°F (160°C)**

1 tbsp	all-purpose flour	15 mL
	Salt and freshly ground black pepper	
4	pieces veal shank with bone, 2 inches (5 cm) thick (see Tip, left)	4
1 tbsp	butter	15 mL
1 tbsp	olive oil	15 mL
1	onion, sliced	1
1 cup	white wine	250 mL
1 cup	beef broth	250 mL
3	sprigs fresh myrtle leaves	3

1. In a resealable bag, combine flour and salt and pepper to taste. Add veal shanks and toss to coat thoroughly.

2. In a large, heavy-bottomed ovenproof saucepan or Dutch oven over medium-high heat, heat butter and oil. Add veal shanks and sauté for 2 to 3 minutes per side, until well browned. Transfer to a plate and set aside.

3. In same pan over medium heat, sauté onion for 5 minutes, until translucent. Add wine and broth and cook for 1 minute, stirring to combine. Turn off heat. Sprinkle myrtle leaves on top of onions, then place prepared veal on top of leaves. Cover with a tight-fitting lid and roast in preheated oven for $1\frac{1}{2}$ hours, until very tender, turning once halfway through cooking time.

4. Discard myrtle leaves before serving. Divide shanks evenly among plates and serve with a spoonful of onion sauce on top.

Nigella

Nigella sativa

Family: Ranunculaceae

Other Names: charnushka, kalonji, devil-in-the-bush, love-in-a-mist (*N. damascena*); black cumin or wild onion seed (incorrectly)

Flavor Group: Pungent

Parts Used: seeds (as a spice)

Background

Nigella is native to western Asia and southern Europe, although it now grows profusely in Egypt, the Middle East and India. There is little recorded history of nigella, but its medicinal properties were known to ancient Asian herbalists. The ancient Romans used it in cooking and the early settlers took it to America, where the seeds were used like pepper, as a seasoning. A great deal of confusion surrounds the naming of nigella, as in India it is occasionally referred to as "black cumin seed." Not only is it a different spice, it has quite a different taste from true black cumin seed (*Bunium persicum*). Nigella is also often called "black onion seed" or "wild onion seed," misnomers made even more confusing by the fact that, although true onion (*Allium cepa*) seeds may physically resemble nigella, they have little flavor and are usually used only for sprouting purposes. On reflection, I believe the majority of recipes that call for onion seeds

Culinary Information

Combines with
- allspice
- cardamom
- chile
- cinnamon
- cloves
- coriander seed
- cumin
- fennel seed
- fenugreek seed
- galangal
- ginger
- mustard
- paprika
- pepper
- star anise
- tamarind
- turmeric

Traditional Uses
- Turkish bread and Indian naan
- savory biscuits
- curries

Spice Blends
- panch phoron
- curry powders

as an ingredient actually intend the cook to use nigella. I have read that in French cookery nigella has been called *quatre épices,* which I find bizarre because quatre épices is a blend of four spices (white pepper, nutmeg, ginger and cloves) traditionally used when making preserved meats such as bacon, ham, sausages, pâtés and terrines in charcuterie (see page 756). Nigella seed oil is used for therapeutic purposes and goes by the unenlightening name "blackseed oil."

The Plant

The nigella of culinary use is an erect annual plant, a member of the buttercup family (Ranunculaceae) and a close relative of the decorative plant known as love-in-a-mist (*Nigella damascena*). Nigella is less attractive. It grows 12 to 24 inches (30 to 60 cm) tall and has wispy, threadlike gray-green leaves and small five-petaled blue or white flowers about 1 inch (2.5 cm) across, which develop spiky-looking capsules that resemble the seed head of a poppy. Each capsule is divided into five seed-bearing compartments crowned by prominent vertical spikes. When ripe they

shatter to disperse the tiny matte jet-black seeds. Each angular, tear-shaped seed is about $\frac{1}{8}$ inch (3 mm) long and has a cream-colored center. The seeds are occasionally confused with and passed off as black sesame (*Sesamum orientale*). Nigella seeds give off little aroma but the flavor is pleasantly sharp and not unlike carrot. It is nutty and has a distinctly metallic, lingering, peppery, throat-drying quality.

Other Varieties

Love-in-a-mist (*Nigella damascena*), also known as "devil-in-a-bush" because of its spiky appearance when in flower, is a decorative annual plant that is also a member of the buttercup family. The flowers are deep to pale blue and are a particularly attractive addition to a herbaceous border, in spite of the fact that the bush looks like it is inhabited by a myriad of cheeky blue devils! Although the seeds of love-in-a-mist have no known toxic effects, they are not generally used in cooking.

Processing

The seed capsules of nigella are harvested as they ripen but before they have had a chance to explode and lose their cargo. After further drying, the pods are threshed to remove the seeds; then they are sieved to clean off any remaining seedpod husks.

Buying and Storage

Nigella seeds are best bought whole. They should be coal black in color. As they are less expensive than black sesame seeds, you are unlikely to be sold black sesame by mistake; more often than not the substitution is the other way around. You can recognize poor-quality uncleaned seeds by the presence of pale, flaky bits of husk from the pods. Nigella seeds are quite stable in their whole form and will keep their flavor for up to 3 years when stored in an airtight container in a cool, dry place.

Use

Because their flavor complements carbohydrates so well, nigella seeds are often seen on Turkish bread and in Indian naan breads. Nigella is an essential ingredient in the five-seed Indian spice blend panch phoron (see page 748), along with cumin, fennel, fenugreek and mustard seeds. Panch phoron also happens to go well with potatoes, another carbohydrate. Lightly roasting or frying the seeds in a little oil before adding to recipes tends to bring out the nutty flavor and reduces some of their metallic sharpness. One of my favorite ways to enjoy nigella seeds is in Spiced Cocktail Biscuits (page 422).

WEIGHT PER TEASPOON (5 mL)
- whole: 3.7 g

SUGGESTED QUANTITY PER POUND (500 g)
- **red meats:** 4 tsp (20 mL) seeds
- **white meats:** 4 tsp (20 mL) seeds
- **vegetables:** 2 to 3 tsp (10 to 15 mL) seeds
- **grains and pulses:** 2 to 3 tsp (10 to 15 mL) seeds
- **baked goods:** 2 tsp (10 mL) seeds

Spicy Fried Cauliflower

This wonderful side dish is coated in panch phoron, an enticing combination of seed spices that complements vegetables particularly well.

**Makes
2 servings**

Preparation time:
 10 minutes
Cooking time:
 15 minutes

Tip

Ghee is a type of clarified butter used in Indian cooking. It has a nutty flavor. If you don't have any, you can substitute an equal amount of melted unsalted butter or oil.

1 tbsp	ghee (see Tip, left)	15 mL
1 tsp	panch phoron (page 748)	5 mL
1	large clove garlic, minced	1
1 tbsp	freshly grated gingerroot	15 mL
$\frac{1}{2}$ tsp	ground turmeric	2 mL
$\frac{1}{2}$ tsp	fine sea salt	2 mL
$\frac{1}{2}$ tsp	garam masala (page 735)	2 mL
1	head cauliflower (about 14 oz/400 g), cut into florets	1
$\frac{1}{4}$ cup	water	60 mL

1. In a wok or large saucepan over low heat, heat ghee. Add panch phoron and cook, stirring occasionally, for 2 minutes, until lightly browned. Add garlic and ginger and cook for 1 minute, until softened. Add turmeric, salt, garam masala and cauliflower and stir to coat well. Add water and cook, stirring constantly, until cauliflower is tender, 5 to 7 minutes.

Spiced Cocktail Biscuits

Mum started making these biscuits not long after Herbie's, my parents' spice business, opened. They have become a family favorite and still feature at many spice-appreciation classes. They make the perfect accompaniment to predinner drinks, and we never seem to have any left over!

Makes about 25 biscuits

Preparation time:
5 minutes

Cooking time:
20 minutes, plus
45 minutes for chilling

- **Rolling pin**
- **2 baking sheets, lined with parchment paper**

1¼ cups	all-purpose flour, plus extra for rolling	300 mL
2 tsp	ras el hanout spice mix (page 757)	10 mL
⅓ cup	butter	75 mL
¾ cup	shredded sharp (old) Cheddar cheese	175 mL
2 tsp	ajowan seeds	10 mL
1 tsp	nigella seeds	5 mL
1	large egg yolk (or 2 small), lightly whisked	1
	Water	

1. In a large bowl, combine flour and ras el hanout. Using your fingers, rub in butter until flour resembles bread crumbs. Add Cheddar, ajowan and nigella; stir to combine. Add egg yolk and stir until a firm dough forms, adding a little water if necessary. Turn out onto a floured work surface and knead lightly until smooth. Wrap dough in plastic wrap and refrigerate for 30 minutes.

2. On a clean floured work surface, roll out dough to ⅛ inch (3 mm) thick. Using a knife, cut dough into 1½-inch (4 cm) strips, then cut diagonally both ways to create diamond shapes (or use a cookie cutter if you prefer). Transfer to prepared baking sheets and refrigerate for 15 minutes.

3. Preheat oven to 375°F (190°C). Bake for 15 to 20 minutes, until bubbling and golden. Cool on baking sheets for 2 to 3 minutes, then transfer to a wire rack to cool completely. Biscuits will keep in an airtight container for up to 1 week.

Nutmeg and Mace

Myristica fragrans Houtt. (also known as *M. officinalis, M. moschata, M. aromatica, M. amboinesis*)

Names in Other Languages

Nutmeg
- **Arabic:** basbasa
- **Burmese:** zalipho thi
- **Chinese (C):** dauh kau syuh
- **Chinese (M):** dou kou shu
- **Czech:** muskatovy orech
- **Danish:** muskatnod
- **Dutch:** notemuskaat
- **Finnish:** muskottipahkin
- **French:** muscade noix
- **German:** Muskatnuss
- **Greek:** moschokarido
- **Hungarian:** szerecsendio
- **Indian:** jaiphal
- **Indonesian:** pala
- **Italian:** noce moscata
- **Japanese:** nikuzuku
- **Malay:** buah pala
- **Norwegian:** muskatnott
- **Portuguese:** noz-moscada
- **Russian:** oryekh-muskatny
- **Sri Lankan:** sadikka
- **Spanish:** nuez moscada
- **Swedish:** muskot
- **Thai:** chan thet
- **Turkish:** hindistancevizi
- **Vietnamese:** dau khau

Family: Myristicaceae

Varieties: Papua nutmeg (*M. argentia*)

Other Names: muskat, muskatnuss (nutmeg); nutmace (mace)

Flavor Group: Sweet (nutmeg), Pungent (mace)

Parts Used: nuts and arils (as a spice), flesh (as a fruit)

Background

Nutmeg is native to the Banda Islands of the Indonesian archipelago, which are also known as the Moluccas or, famously, the Spice Islands. The spice had reached China, Asia and India before the beginning of the Common Era (CE). By 500 CE, nutmeg had arrived in the Mediterranean; during the Crusades it moved north into Europe, so that by the 13th century its use was widely known. During the 16th century the spice trade flourished. The Portuguese, Spanish and Dutch all vied for a piece of the action and took enormous risks to secure their valuable commodities and import them to Europe.

To gaze on a humble nutmeg today it is difficult to imagine how much it influenced the global economy and inspired

Names in Other Languages

Mace

- **Chinese (C):** yuhk dauh kau
- **Chinese (M):** rou dou kou
- **Czech:** muskatovy kvet
- **Danish:** muskatblomme
- **Dutch:** foelie
- **Finnish:** muskottikukka
- **French:** macis
- **German:** Muskatblute, Macis
- **Hungarian:** szerecsendio virag
- **Indian:** jaffatry, javatri, tavitri
- **Indonesian:** sekar pala
- **Italian:** mazza
- **Japanese:** nikuzuku
- **Malay:** kembang pala
- **Portuguese:** macis
- **Russian:** muskatnyi tsvet
- **Spanish:** macis
- **Swedish:** muskotblomma
- **Thai:** dok chand
- **Turkish:** besbase

voyages of discovery from the 15th to 17th centuries. This unique status was the result of geography. Nutmeg trees grew exclusively on Ambon and a few nearby islands in the Banda Sea and were not known anywhere else in the world. In those days, nutmegs, along with cloves (see page 216), were among the most sought-after spices. So strong was the desire to control the market that the Dutch East India Company, or VOC (for Vereenigde Oost-Indische Compagnie), had its own army, which to secure the VOC's pecuniary interests committed unspeakable acts of violence against local populations. By the 17th century the Dutch had lost control of Ambon and consequently access to their lucrative source of nutmegs, a primary revenue source that helped fuel the Golden Age of Holland. The Dutch were determined to get those nutmeg-producing islands back under their control. In what must have been the real estate deal of the millennium, Peter Stuyvesant, governor of New Amsterdam, signed a treaty with the English that swapped the island of Manhattan for a few islands in the Moluccas.

However, the story did not finish there. At the time there was a general view that trees such as nutmeg could not be successfully grown outside their country of origin. The death penalty was imposed on anyone cultivating or selling the spice anywhere except the Spice Islands. Nonetheless, numerous attempts were made from 1750 to the early 1800s to break this stranglehold on the nutmeg and clove trade. The most successful of these entrepreneurs was the superintendent of Île-de-France (Mauritius), an intrepid Frenchman named Pierre Poivre (the original Peter Piper of the nursery rhyme). After several attempts he smuggled some nutmeg and clove seedlings out of the Moluccas and successfully grew a small number of trees on Mauritius. Subsequently, with varying degrees of success, nutmeg and clove plantations were established on the French island

Spice Notes

I was first captivated by the magic of nutmeg when I visited a spice-grower's farm—referred to by the locals as a "spice garden"—in Kerala, southern India, and was lucky enough to find one ripe nutmeg (it was a little early in the season for a full crop). The farmer cut the fruit open, and the flash of shining wet blood-red mace as it opened was breathtaking! Mace is the placenta that conveys nourishment from the fruit to the seed. It clings to the shell of the nutmeg like a hand, its fingers holding so tightly that they leave little indentations to show where they've been on the brittle dark brown shell.

Culinary Information

Combines with

Nutmeg
- allspice
- cardamom
- cassia
- cinnamon
- cloves
- coriander seed
- ginger
- vanilla

Mace
- cloves
- paprika
- pepper

Traditional Uses

Nutmeg
- cooked squash tossed in butter
- squash and potato (before baking)
- pâtés and terrines
- cooked spinach
- cheese sauces
- milk and rice puddings
- sweet, spicy cakes
- cookies

Mace
- seafood (before broiling or pan-frying)
- stock for steaming shellfish
- sauces for veal and in terrines
- fish pies

Spice Blends

Nutmeg
- mixed spice
- pumpkin pie spice
- quatre épices
- some sweet, rich curries

Mace
- pickling spices
- ras el hanout
- spice rubs for seafood

of Réunion, which demonstrated that these trees could be grown in most tropical regions. Nutmegs are now grown in many Southeast Asian countries, India and Sri Lanka, and some of the best-quality nutmegs today are grown on the island of Grenada in the Caribbean.

The Plant

Of all the sweet spices, the strongest-tasting one, nutmeg, shares its parentage with a lesser-known pungent spice, mace. Although there are some similarities in flavor, nutmeg and mace are used in quite different ways and should always be viewed as separate spices.

Nutmeg and mace share the botanical name *Myristica fragrans* Houtt. Both come from a tropical evergreen tree that grows 23 to 33 feet (7 to 10 m) tall. The leaves are shiny and dark on top, with a pale green underside. Nutmeg trees are either male or female. Only one male tree is required to fertilize 10 female trees (which allows them to bear fruit), so culling unwanted male trees is necessary. However, the sex of a tree cannot be determined until it is about five years old. Nutmeg trees become fully mature in 15 years and keep producing fruit for up to 40 years.

Originally a native of the Molucca Islands of Indonesia, nutmeg can now be found growing in most of the tropical spice-growing countries of the world. The nutmeg fruit looks like a firm yellow nectarine and is exactly the same shape. Unfortunately, it's not delicious like a nectarine; it has a sour, rather sharp flavor. The local people use the flesh of the fruit for making pickles, and sometimes it is preserved with salt and sugar and eaten as a tangy confection. Mace is the aril (placenta) of the fruit that surrounds the nutmeg, which is the seed, encased in a hard yet brittle shell.

When a whole nutmeg is cut in half, a symmetrical light and dark brown pattern of oil-containing veins is revealed. The volatile oil in nutmeg and mace contains small amounts of myristicin and elemicin, which are narcotic and poisonous; therefore these spices should never be consumed to excess.

Other Varieties

Papua nutmegs (*Myristica argentia*) come from West Papua. They are more elongated in shape than *M. fragrans* and have less flavor; as a result they are generally considered to be inferior. Papua nutmegs are often sold ground in the hope that consumers will not notice the difference.

Processing

Nutmeg

Nutmeg fruits are picked by using a long bamboo pole that has a spur to dislodge the fruit and a basket-like end that catches the nutmeg when the picker reaches up to pluck a fruit from the tree. When the fruit is cut open, the mace is peeled away from the shell of the nutmeg seed. Sometimes nutmegs are dried in the sun with their shells still on and the mace clinging to them. Once nutmegs are dry, the seed rattles within the smooth outer shell, which bears tracks where the mace used to be wrapped around it. In Indonesia, India and many other nutmeg-producing countries, nutmeg is often sold complete with this brittle outer shell, but in most Western markets you get only the dull brown hard, wrinkled inner nutmeg that has been removed from its tasteless shell. This is the nutmeg spice that we know and love, with its distinctive pungent flavor and aroma.

Nutmeg has also been the subject of adulteration for many centuries, often for practical reasons. Good-quality shelled nutmegs are so high in oil content that they tend to clog a commercial spice grinder, and in extreme cases they come out as slurry rather than a powder. The easiest way for some processors to overcome this excessive oiliness is to add some form of starch to take up the excess oil, which for all intents and purposes becomes indistinguishable from the ground nutmeg itself.

An English spice trader whom I met in India told me they used to leave the bags of whole nutmegs outside overnight. In the morning the nutmegs would be frozen, and in this brittle state they would pass through a grinder without any problems. These days, many spices are ground by either freezing them as they pass through the spice mill (referred to as "cryogenic grinding") or, more economically, by cooling the grinding head of the mill with liquid nitrogen to reduce volatile oil loss from heat generated by friction. Because nutmeg is so high in oil, it retains its flavor well even when ground, so it should be one of those packaged ground spices whose taste is very nearly as good as the freshly ground form.

Mace

After being peeled off the nut, mace is spread out in the sun to dry. During drying it loses the wonderful glistening wet look it has when first peeled off the nut. It shrivels slightly and soon dulls as it oxidizes in the open air. Within a day or two of being placed in the sunshine, it has dried to the dull red-orange of good-quality dried mace. When it is in this whole or roughly broken form, it is referred to in most recipe books as "blade mace." Dried blades of mace need to be handled and packed carefully; otherwise they will break up into small woodchip-sized pieces.

blades of mace

Buying and Storage

Nutmeg

When buying nutmegs, be aware that the quality can vary enormously. When whole nutmegs have been stored for too long—as often happens if farmers think the price is going to rise—they begin to dry out, losing some of the volatile oil; the dry nutmegs then start being attacked by insects that leave behind tiny drill holes. These nutmegs are referred to in the trade as "BWP" (broken, wormy and punky); when ground they yield a dry light brown powder with little flavor.

Travels in the Spice Trade

The Spice Islands played such a significant role in the history of the world, and the spice trade in particular, that it was only a matter of time before Liz and I retraced the steps of the spice merchants who had visited there before us. Even in the 21st century most of these historic islands are difficult to reach. It was fortuitous that we found ourselves on a 12-cabin ketch sailing from Ambon to Banda Neira; we visited the famous volcano of Gunung Api ("fire mountain") and then sailed north across the equator to the clove islands of Tidore and Ternate.

Just before we departed I was telling my 90-year-old mother about the trip. She reminded me that my grandfather, who was a pearling master in Broome, in the northwest of Western Australia, had visited the Banda islands exactly 100 years before. She retrieved a battered old family photo album that included a photo of Gunung Api. Imagine my excitement as we sailed up to this towering volcano 100 years after my grandfather had taken his photo. Its last eruption was in 1988, so when we visited the top of the volcano it was a different shape—one side had been blown away.

A highlight of this trip was exploring the remote spice island of Ai, a quiet and peaceful place with a welcoming population. As we stood among the ruins of Fort Revenge, viewing the remains of dungeons and a rusty cannon that the jungle growth was reclaiming, it was difficult to imagine the conflicts that had occurred there and the economic significance of the island five long centuries before.

Substituting for Mace

If you come upon a recipe that requires mace and you don't have any, a reasonable substitute is about a quarter the amount (or less) of nutmeg, mixed in equal proportions with ground coriander seed.

In whole form, BWPs are useless in a nutmeg grinder, as they will crumble and not yield the even, moist, aromatic shavings we expect.

Whole and ground nutmegs should be stored in airtight containers and kept away from extremes of heat, light and humidity. Whole nutmegs will last for at least 3 years and ground nutmeg will keep its flavor for a little more than 1 year.

Mace

Mace is most readily available in its ground form. Whole mace, referred to as "blades," is not so common. If you've ever seen mace in a delicatessen or supermarket, you might have noticed that it's much costlier than nutmeg. This stands to reason when you think that from one nutmeg fruit you get only a small quantity of mace: about 0.5 gram compared to about 3 grams of nutmeg.

Ground mace, like ground nutmeg, should be stored in an airtight container and kept away from extremes of heat, light and humidity; it will keep like that for up to 1 year. Store whole blades of mace in the same way and they will last for up to 3 years.

Use

Nutmeg

To get the best flavor, many people like to grind or grate their nutmeg fresh (like pepper). A nutmeg mill or grater that will shave fine pieces off the whole nutmeg may be a useful purchase. Otherwise, you can rub it on the finest part of your kitchen grater—being very careful of your fingers!

Nutmeg's warm, aromatic, full-bodied flavor complements a diversity of foods. Although predominantly sweet in character, it should usually be added sparingly. It has long been used in old-fashioned foods such as rice puddings and sprinkled over milkshakes. Once, every milk bar and malt shop had a shaker of nutmeg on the counter—a sprinkle on a shake was as common a practice as today's sprinkle of powdered chocolate or cinnamon over cappuccino. Nutmeg is also included in cookies and cakes. There is a wonderful Dutch recipe for nutmeg cake (see page 431) no doubt inspired by the close association between the Netherlands and Indonesia, the home of nutmeg.

Nutmeg also complements vegetables, especially root vegetables, making microwaved or steamed potatoes, carrots and squash delicious. Just toss them in a little butter and nutmeg after they're cooked. Another popular practice is to season cooked spinach with nutmeg; the robust sweetness seems to neutralize the somewhat metallic taste of spinach.

Mace

Mace has a flavor similar to nutmeg. However, it is more delicate and has somewhat fresher, lighter and less robust notes, making it ideal for use in savory foods such as seafood dishes and with sauces to flavor meats such as chicken or veal. Mace also goes well with carbohydrates such as pasta.

Blades of mace are used whole in cooking to infuse their flavor without leaving particles of ground mace in a dish such as a clear shellfish soup. Although blades of mace are most often removed before serving, they are left in some Indian rice dishes in the same way that pieces of cinnamon, whole cloves and cardamom pods are retained. More frequently, mace is used in a ground form that doesn't need to be cooked for so long, as the ground version releases its flavor more readily.

WEIGHT PER TEASPOON (5 mL)

Nutmeg
- average whole nutmeg: 3.8 g
- ground nutmeg: 3 g

Mace
- average blade: 0.5 g
- ground mace: 2.3 g

SUGGESTED QUANTITY PER POUND (500 g)

Nutmeg
- red meats: 2 tsp (10 mL) ground
- white meats: 1½ tsp (7 mL) ground
- vegetables: 1 tsp (5 mL) ground
- grains and pulses: 1 tsp (5 mL) ground
- baked goods: 1 tsp (5 mL) ground

Mace
- red meats: 1½ tsp (7 mL) ground
- white meats: 1 tsp (5 mL) ground
- vegetables: ¾ tsp (3 mL) ground
- grains and pulses: ¾ tsp (3 mL) ground
- baked goods: ¾ tsp (3 mL) ground

N

Lobster Bisque

This luxurious soup is perfect for a special-occasion dinner. Mace is a traditional element in seafood dishes such as this; its pungency helps balance the richness of the lobster and cream.

Makes 4 small servings

Preparation time:
15 minutes

Cooking time:
45 minutes

• **Regular or immersion blender**

2	lobster tails in shells	2
1 tbsp	butter	15 mL
1 tbsp	oil	15 mL
2	shallots, finely chopped	2
2	tomatoes, chopped	2
	Freshly squeezed juice of 1 lemon	
2	pieces blade mace	2
2 tbsp	cognac	30 mL
3 cups	fish or vegetable broth	750 mL
1	bay leaf	1
1	stalk fresh parsley	1
1 tsp	chopped fresh tarragon leaves	5 mL
3 tbsp	heavy or whipping (35%) cream	45 mL
	Salt and freshly ground pepper	

1. Using a very sharp knife or culinary scissors, split lobster tails in half lengthwise. Remove meat and set aside.

2. In a large, heavy-bottomed saucepan over medium heat, heat butter and oil. Add lobster shells and shallots and sauté for 3 minutes, until shallots are soft and golden brown. Add tomatoes, lemon juice, mace and cognac; cook, stirring often, for 1 to 2 minutes, until alcohol evaporates. Add broth, bay leaf, parsley and tarragon and simmer for 20 minutes. Add reserved lobster meat. Cook, stirring occasionally, for 8 to 12 minutes, until lobster turns white and is cooked through. Transfer cooked lobster to a bowl.

3. Using a fine-mesh sieve, strain soup into blender (discard solids). Add three-quarters of the reserved lobster meat and blend at high speed until smooth (alternatively, use immersion blender in the pan). Return soup to pan, if necessary, and add cream. Heat gently and season with salt and pepper to taste.

4. Using a knife, cut remaining lobster into pieces and divide among serving bowls. Ladle soup overtop and serve.

Nutmeg Cake

This delicious moist, sweet cake is a fine culinary showcase for the unique and wonderful flavor of nutmeg. Nutmeg cake is a traditional European recipe, no doubt inspired by merchandise brought back to Europe by the Dutch East India Company. Serve topped with whipped cream and a little grated nutmeg or dark chocolate.

Makes one 8-inch (20 cm) cake

Preparation time:
5 minutes

Cooking time: **1 hour, 30 minutes**

Tip

If you can't find self-rising flour in stores, you can make your own. To equal 1 cup (250 mL) self-rising flour, combine 1 cup (250 mL) all-purpose flour, 1½ tsp (7 mL) baking powder and ½ tsp (2 mL) salt.

- **8-inch (20 cm) round cake pan, greased and lined with parchment paper**
- **Preheat oven to 350°F (180°C)**

2 cups	self-rising flour (see Tip, left)	500 mL
2 cups	lightly packed brown sugar	500 mL
2 tsp	ground cinnamon or cassia	10 mL
1 tsp	ground allspice	5 mL
1 tsp	ground coriander seed	5 mL
½ cup	butter	125 mL
1	egg	1
2 tsp	ground or freshly grated nutmeg	10 mL
1 cup	milk	250 mL

1. In a large mixing bowl, combine flour, brown sugar, cinnamon, allspice and coriander seed. Using your hands, rub butter into mixture until it resembles coarse bread crumbs. Spoon half of the mixture over bottom of prepared pan.

2. In a small bowl, whisk together egg, nutmeg and milk. Add to remaining flour mixture and stir well (it will make a very runny batter; stir thoroughly to avoid lumps). Pour batter over crumbs in pan. Bake in preheated oven for 1 hour and 20 minutes or until golden brown and springy to the touch in the center. Remove from oven and cool in pan for about 5 minutes, then invert onto a wire rack to cool completely.

N

Olida

Eucalyptus olida

Family: Myrtaceae
Other Names: forest berry herb, strawberry gum
Flavor Group: Medium
Parts Used: leaves (as a herb)

Background

Olida is native to Australia's dry forest and woodland areas on the eastern side of New South Wales's northern tablelands. This region is the traditional home of the Bundjalung people, who have inhabited this area for more than 20,000 years. Olida thrives in shallow, infertile soil and on acid granite.

Olida contains high amounts of methyl cinnamate (cinnamic acid), which has been used for many years in Europe to boost the flavor of fruit jams and conserves. As a natural flavor enhancer, methyl cinnamate allows processors to bulk out manufactured fruit-based products with low-cost, less flavorful ingredients. You could look at it as a sweet-food version of the savory food enhancer MSG (monosodium glutamate, or glutamic acid), which also occurs naturally in food. Excessive use of high concentrations of MSG has

Culinary Information

Combines with
- allspice
- cardamom
- cinnamon
- cloves
- coriander seed
- fennel seed
- ginger
- vanilla

Traditional Uses
- fruit salads
- stone fruits and berries
- whipped cream and ice cream
- cheesecake
- pancakes
- shortbread
- broiled seafood

Spice Blends
- blends containing native Australian herbs and spices
- chicken and seafood seasonings

earned it a dubious reputation. Fortunately, the same cannot be said for using methyl cinnamate in its natural form, as found in olida.

The Plant

Olida has been one of the most confusingly named Australian native herbs since its popularization in the 1990s. Until 2005 its common name was "forest berry herb," so called because of its distinctive berry-like flavor notes. The name was misleading because the part of the tree that is used is actually the leaf; the conical fruits are not eaten, although they may have been used medicinally by the Aboriginal people.

Eucalyptus olida is an attractive 65-foot (20 m) tree with gray-brown bark that sheds in long ribbons to reveal a majestic light gray trunk. The canopy is bushy and covered in dark green tapering oval leaves that resemble bay leaves and other eucalypts. The aroma is distinctly passion fruit–like, with cinnamon and summer berry notes. The flavor is astringent, eucalypt and grassy, while the taste on the palate is numbing and herbaceous.

Processing

Olida leaves were originally wild-harvested. However, because of the risk of endangering the limited population of trees and the increase in its popularity as a condiment, most olida are now plantation grown. The leaves are harvested and dried in the same manner as other herb leaves such as bay leaf, lemon myrtle and anise myrtle, by hanging in a warm, dark place. An essential oil, high in methyl cinnamate, is extracted from the leaves by steam distillation and used in food manufacturing, perfumes and soaps.

Buying and Storage

Fresh olida leaves are rarely available. However, whole dried or powdered leaves, which are more convenient, are becoming more readily available in Australia from herb and spice shops and gourmet food retailers. Most of these purveyors will still refer to olida as "forest berry herb" or "strawberry gum."

Because of the volatility of the essential oil, it is advisable to purchase only small quantities—say, $\frac{1}{3}$ oz (10 g) at a time for normal household requirements—of freshly produced olida powder in airtight packaging. Store as you would other delicate green herbs: in a well-sealed container in a cool, dark place. Olida powder will then last for at least 1 year.

Use

Olida has a wide variety of uses, but it is often best to think of it as a flavor enhancer rather than expecting it to overtly flavor a dish with its own character. There are two basic guidelines worth remembering to achieve the best results with olida:

- Add only a small amount, say $\frac{1}{4}$ to $\frac{1}{2}$ tsp (1 to 2 mL) or 1 to 2 leaves, to 1 lb (500 g) fruit or vegetables, then taste before adding more.
- Add only to recipes that cook for a short time, never subjecting the olida to extreme temperatures for more than 10 to 15 minutes. When too much is used or when it is cooked for too long, the flavor-giving volatile oils will be depleted and a sharp hay-like, less than pleasant eucalyptus flavor may dominate.

Although olida's own flavor will be diminished in a fruit jam, it still enhances the fruit and berry flavors. While olida does go quite well in shortbread, cakes and muffins, I prefer to add it to sweet things that are either not cooked (such as fruit salads) or are cooked faster at a lower heat, such as blini and pancakes. In quick-cooking applications it is most effective to infuse olida in a little warm milk or hot water to bring out the flavor before adding it to the dish.

WEIGHT PER TEASPOON (5 mL)
- **ground:** 2.5 g

SUGGESTED QUANTITY PER POUND (500 g)
- **white meats:** $\frac{1}{2}$ tsp (2 mL)
- **red meats:** 1 tsp (5 mL)
- **fruits and vegetables:** $\frac{1}{2}$ tsp (2 mL)
- **grains and pulses:** $\frac{1}{2}$ tsp (2 mL)
- **baked goods:** $\frac{1}{2}$ to 1 tsp (2 to 5 mL)

Banana Crêpes

As olida benefits from little cooking, this recipe is perfect. Thin, light crêpes filled with lovely sweet olida-scented banana make a pleasant breakfast, brunch or dessert.

Makes 8 crêpes

Preparation time:
1 hour, 15 minutes

Cooking time:
30 minutes

Tips

If you don't have any buttermilk, add 1½ tsp (7 mL) lemon juice to 1¼ cups (300 mL) milk. Let stand for 20 minutes, until it begins to curdle.

If you can't find self-rising flour in stores, you can make your own. To equal 1 cup (250 mL) self-rising flour, combine 1 cup all-purpose flour, 1½ tsp (7 mL) baking powder and ½ tsp (2 mL) salt.

- **Crêpe pan**

CRÊPE BATTER

2	eggs	2
1 cup	buttermilk (see Tips, left)	250 mL
½ tsp	fine sea salt	2 mL
½ tsp	ground olida	2 mL
¾ cup	self-rising flour (see Tips, left)	175 mL

FILLING

2	ripe bananas	2
1 tbsp	heavy or whipping (35%) cream	15 mL
½ tsp	ground olida	2 mL

1. *Crêpe Batter:* In a mixing bowl, beat eggs, buttermilk, salt and olida until well combined. Sift in flour and beat until smooth. For best results, cover and refrigerate for 1 hour before cooking.

2. Preheat oven to 200°F (100°C).

3. *Filling:* In a bowl, using a fork, mash bananas with cream and olida. Set aside.

4. Heat a heavy-bottomed crêpe pan or skillet over medium-high heat. Add a pat of butter and roll around pan until melted and pan is fully greased. Spoon 2 tbsp (30 mL) prepared batter into pan and quickly tilt pan in a circular motion to distribute in a thin layer over the bottom. Cook for about 2 minutes, until top of crêpe is just firm and underside is lightly browned. Turn over and cook other side until lightly browned, about 2 minutes. Turn out onto a plate and transfer to preheated oven to keep warm. Repeat with remaining batter, adding more butter as necessary.

5. When all the crêpes are made, spread filling evenly over each and roll up. Serve warm.

Variations

You can substitute 1 cup (250 mL) mixed summer berries for the bananas.

For extra indulgence, add a spoonful of dulce de leche or caramel sauce to the filling of each crêpe.

O

Oregano and Marjoram

Oregano: *Origanum vulgare*
Marjoram: *O. marjorana* (also known as *Marjorana hortensis*)

Names in Other Languages

Oregano

- **Arabic:** anrar
- **Chinese (C):** ngou lahk gong
- **Chinese (M):** ao le gang
- **Czech:** dobromysl
- **Danish:** oregano
- **Dutch:** wil de marjolein
- **Finnish:** makimeirami
- **French:** origan, marjolaine bâtarde
- **German:** Dosten, Oregano, wilder Majoran
- **Greek:** rigani
- **Italian:** oregano, erba acciuga
- **Japanese:** hana-hakka
- **Portuguese:** ouregão
- **Russian:** dushitsa
- **Spanish:** oregano
- **Swedish:** oregano, vild megram
- **Thai:** origano
- **Turkish:** kekik otu

Family: Lamiaceae (formerly Labiatae)

Varieties: Greek oregano (*O. vulgare hirtum*); Mexican oreganos: *Poliomentha longiflora, Lippia graveolens* (also known as Sonoran oregano); pot marjoram (*O. onites*); winter marjoram (*O. heraclesticum*); Middle Eastern marjoram (*Marjorana syriaca*)

Other Names: wild marjoram, rigani (oregano); sweet marjoram, knotted marjoram, pot marjoram, winter marjoram, rigani (marjoram)

Flavor Group: Pungent

Parts Used: leaves and flowers (as a herb)

Background

The *Origanum* species (*O. vulgare* and *O. marjorana*) are native to the Mediterranean region and for centuries were cultivated as flowering and strewing herbs. They were popular in ancient Greece and Egypt; Apicius, the

oregano

Marjoram

- **Arabic:** marzanjush
- **Chinese (C):** mah yeuk laahn faa
- **Chinese (M):** ma yue lan hua
- **Czech:** majoranka
- **Danish:** merian
- **Dutch:** marjolein
- **Finnish:** meirami
- **French:** marjolaine
- **German:** Majoran
- **Greek:** matzourana
- **Hungarian:** majoranna
- **Indian:** mirzam josh
- **Italian:** maggiorana
- **Japanese:** mayarona
- **Norwegian:** merian
- **Portuguese:** manjerona
- **Russian:** mayoran
- **Spanish:** almaraco
- **Swedish:** mejram
- **Thai:** macheoraen
- **Turkish:** mercankosk

first-century Roman epicure, used these herbs. Both oregano and marjoram became widely distributed in Asia, North Africa and the Middle East, and sweet marjoram was introduced to Europe in the Middle Ages. Marjoram was regarded as a symbol of happiness; to have it growing on a grave signified eternal peace for the departed. The name of the species, *Origanum*, comes from the Greek words *oros* and *ganos* and means "joy of the mountain." This expression derives from the joyous aroma and appearance created by drifts of these herbs growing on the rocky Greek hillsides.

During the Middle Ages, pungent spices such as pepper, grains of paradise, cardamom and cloves were either difficult to procure or too expensive for the average person. For this reason, strong-flavored herbs such as oregano, rosemary and thyme were a popular alternative to the rare and exotic spices indulged in by the privileged and wealthy.

Oregano and marjoram were not well known in Australia and the United States in the early 20th century. That all changed with the influx of post–Second World War immigrants from Italy and Greece, when many parts of the world were introduced to the pleasures of Mediterranean cuisines. It is safe to say that pizzas and pasta sauces flavored with oregano are among the most popular dishes in the West, and I have noticed in recent years that Mediterranean flavors have also spread in popularity among Asian consumers.

Members of the *Origanum* genus are sometimes confused with other plants also referred to as oregano (see below). Oregano is a common ingredient in Mexican cooking, but the oregano grown in South America and exported to many countries is actually Mediterranean *Origanum vulgare*.

Travels in the Spice Trade

During a visit to the Greek island of Chios, we were delighted to see oregano in its native habitat, a tough little plant growing on the rocky hillsides, and to experience how the locals used it. Driving inland, we wondered how such a harsh landscape could produce such a tasty plant. Dried and rubbed Chios oregano seemed to find its way into every meal, especially the Greek salads. I was pleased to see how much the full depth of flavor that develops in a dried herb is appreciated—in stark contrast to many television chefs who extol their own virtue for using only fresh herbs, suggesting that the dried versions are inferior. Although fresh herbs *are* preferred in many dishes, they should never be used at the expense of achieving the most appropriate flavor. When dried oregano is sprinkled over a feta and tomato salad with olives or used to garnish a meal, the effect is not dissimilar to grinding black pepper over your food.

Culinary Information

Combines with

Oregano
- ajowan
- basil
- bay leaf
- chile
- garlic
- marjoram
- paprika
- pepper
- rosemary
- sage
- savory
- thyme

Marjoram
- ajowan
- basil
- bay leaf
- chile
- garlic
- oregano
- paprika
- pepper
- rosemary
- sage
- savory
- thyme

Traditional Uses

Oregano
- pizza
- Italian pasta dishes
- Greek salads
- moussaka
- meat loaf
- roast beef, lamb and pork

Marjoram
- lightly cooked fish and vegetables
- salads
- scrambled eggs
- omelets
- savory soufflés
- stuffings for poultry
- dumplings

Spice Blends

Oregano
- Italian herbs
- mixed herb blends
- seasoning blends for barbecued meats
- stuffing mixes

Marjoram
- bouquet garni
- herbes de Provence
- Italian herbs
- mixed herbs

The Plants

Oregano and marjoram are grouped together here because they are so closely related and similar that it seems unnecessary to classify them separately.

Sweet marjoram, the variety used most often in cooking, is a reasonably dense tender perennial (although in cold climates it will become dormant or die back in winter) that grows 12 to 18 inches (30 to 45 cm) tall. The leaves are deep green, up to 1 inch (2.5 cm) long, lightly ribbed and slightly darker on top and paler on the underside; they are oval to elongated in shape. Both marjoram and

marjoram

oregano have tiny white flowers. Marjoram is characterized by flowers that burst out from tight green knots at the tips of the stems. Its flavor and aroma are mildly savory and grassy, resembling thyme. Dried marjoram leaves are like a mild version of thyme, with an agreeable bitterness and a lingering camphor quality. Strong-flavored **pot marjoram** has an inferior taste to sweet marjoram. It was introduced into England in the 18th century and tends to be grown as a substitute in areas that are too cold for sweet marjoram.

Oregano is more robust and spreading in appearance than sweet marjoram. It thrives as a perennial in most climates. It grows to around 24 inches (60 cm) tall, has much rounder leaves and is covered by a fine down. Oregano has a more piercing scent than marjoram and its flavor is stronger. When dried, oregano has a pleasing depth of taste with a distinctive sharp, peppery element.

Other Varieties

A number of different types of *Origanum* grow wild in Greece, and these wild varieties are variously referred to as *rigani*. The flavors and to a lesser degree the appearance of the different types can vary greatly, depending on climatic and soil conditions. When you return home from Greece, this makes it difficult to find that particular rigani flavor that took your fancy while you were holidaying there.

Pot marjoram (*O. onites*) has a stronger flavor than sweet marjoram and is often used as a substitute for oregano. **Winter marjoram** (*O. heraclesticum*), also called wild marjoram, is a native of Greece; like pot marjoram, it has a strong flavor and is considered a suitable substitute for oregano and rigani. **Middle Eastern marjoram** (*Marjorana syriaca*) is stronger than sweet marjoram but milder than the most pungent oreganos.

Greek oregano, or rigani (*O. vulgare hirtum*), is the variety you will most likely see on sale dried in bunches wrapped in cellophane. It is considered by many to be the only true Greek oregano. **Mexican oregano** (*Poliomentha longiflora*) from Texas is a variety of Mexican oregano. It is a Lamiaceae, from the same family as Mediterranean oregano, and is not to be confused with Sonoran oregano, which is a different plant that is also often referred to as "Mexican oregano."

Sonoran oregano (*Lippia graveolens*) is actually a member of the verbena family (Verbenaceae). It is a small aromatic shrub that goes by the botanical names *Lippia graveolens* and *L. berlandieri*. The leaves have been hand-harvested for

Middle Eastern Marjoram

This variety causes some confusion because it is loosely associated with za'atar. However, *za'atar* is generally used to describe the herb thyme (see page 633) and also a popular mix containing thyme, sesame seeds and sumac.

O

centuries by the Seri people, who live on Mexico's dry north coast. Unlike most herbs, which are dried in the dark, these leaves are dried in the blazing Mexican sunshine and end up with an extremely pungent flavor.

Processing

While fresh marjoram and oregano are excellent additions to salads and mild-flavored foods, they have the best taste and greatest pungency when they are dried. Harvesting should be carried out just before the plants are in full flower, when their vitality is at its greatest and their flavor at its peak. Cut the longest, most densely leaved stems, together with any flower heads that have developed, and hang them upside down in bunches in a dark, well-aired, warm, dry place for a few days. When the leaves are crisp and dry, they may be rubbed off the stalks.

When drying your own oregano and marjoram, always rub the leaves off the stems before storing. Even when the leaves feel crisp and dry, the stalks will still retain some moisture; if you store the stems with the leaves still attached, the retained moisture can migrate back into the leaves. Keep in mind that in the countries where these herbs grow, the humidity is extremely low in summer, and so dehydration is particularly effective (hence the tradition of leaving the dried herbs in bunches for sale).

Buying and Storage

Fresh marjoram and oregano are readily available from fresh produce retailers. When buying in bunches, make sure they

The Dried Herbs

Both oregano and marjoram are more pungent when dried. Both herbs have a more complex flavor profile when dried, which explains why they are used almost exclusively in their dried form in many traditional dishes. Dried oregano has also become popular—along with marjoram, thyme, bay leaf, allspice berries and pepper—for marinating olives.

are not wilted. To keep them fresh, put the stems in a glass of water; they will last comfortably for at least 1 week.

There has been much confusion, especially in the past century, between dried marjoram and oregano. This often had more to do with price and availability than anything else. When oregano is scarce (being by far more popular), traders are tempted to make it go farther by mixing in a percentage of sweet marjoram. To make identification even harder, oregano can vary greatly in appearance and flavor, depending upon its country of origin.

European oregano is generally an intense dark green, almost black, like dried mint, and has a distinctive flavor. Chilean oregano is pale green, very clean, without pieces of stem, and has a strong, savory flavor that is less peppery than the European types. Greek oregano, which may or may not be rigani, is usually sold in dried bunches packed in cellophane bags. This is the most pungent of the oreganos, and the leaves are best rubbed from the stalks as soon as it is purchased, then stored in an airtight container.

Keep your dehydrated marjoram and oregano under the same conditions as other dried herbs, in an airtight container away from extremes of heat, light and humidity. Under these conditions your dried herb will last for more than 1 year.

Use

Oregano is more pungent than marjoram and is a popular ingredient in the regional dishes of many countries. Oregano complements basil—the combination of these two herbs with liberal amounts of tomato has become synonymous in most countries with pizza and Italian pasta. Oregano flavors dishes that contain eggplant, zucchini and bell peppers and is usually found in recipes for moussaka (see page 442) and meat loaf. Roast beef, lamb and pork will develop a full-bodied taste and a mouthwatering crust when rubbed with a mixture of paprika, sumac, oregano and garlic before cooking.

Fresh marjoram adds zest to salads and goes well with delicate-tasting foods such as egg dishes, lightly cooked fish and vegetables. When dried, it has a stronger taste than fresh. It is a traditional ingredient in the classic English blend mixed herbs, along with thyme and sage. Marjoram goes well with pork and veal and complements poultry stuffing, dumplings and herb scones. It is delicious mixed with a little parsley and butter for making herb bread.

WEIGHT PER TEASPOON (5 mL)

- rubbed dried leaves: 0.7 g

SUGGESTED QUANTITY PER POUND (500 g)

- red meats: 2 tsp (10 mL) dried, 5 tsp (25 mL) fresh
- white meats: 1 tsp (5 mL) dried, 1 tbsp (15 mL) fresh
- vegetables: 1 tsp (5 mL) dried, 1 tbsp (15 mL) fresh
- grains and pulses: 1 tsp (5 mL) dried, 1 tbsp (15 mL) fresh
- baked goods: 1 tsp (5 mL) dried, 1 tbsp (15 mL) fresh

Moussaka

As time-consuming as this recipe is, it really is a wonderful, hearty dish and a nice alternative to lasagna. Instead of frying the eggplant, as is sometimes done, I bake it, which has a less oily result. There is probably a no more Greek herb than oregano, and it's used to great effect in this dish.

**Makes
6 servings**

Preparation time: 20 to
 30 minutes
Cooking time: 1½ to
 2 hours

- - - - - - - - - - - - - - - - -

Tips

To save time, prepare eggplant and lamb a day ahead.

For a slightly richer sauce, substitute an equal amount of red wine for the broth.

Kefalytori is a hard, salty sheep's or goat's milk cheese. If not available, substitute an equal quantity of Parmesan or pecorino.

- **2 baking sheets**
- **12- by 8-inch (30 by 20 cm) baking dish**
- **Preheat oven to 350°F (180°C)**

1½ to 2 lbs	eggplant, sliced ½ inch (1 cm) thick (about 3 large)	750 g to 1 kg
2 tsp	fine sea salt	10 mL
¼ cup	olive oil	60 mL
2 lbs	ground lamb	1 kg
1	onion, minced	1
4	cloves garlic, minced	4
1 tbsp	dried oregano	15 mL
1 tsp	ground cinnamon	5 mL
2	bay leaves	2
3 tbsp	tomato paste	45 mL
1	can (14 oz/398 mL) crushed tomatoes	1
¾ cup	chicken or lamb broth (see Tips, left)	175 mL
	Sea salt and freshly ground black pepper	

BÉCHAMEL SAUCE

¼ cup	butter	60 mL
¼ cup	all-purpose flour	60 mL
2 cups	milk	500 mL
¼ tsp	ground nutmeg	1 mL
¼ cup	grated kefalotyri cheese (see Tips, left)	60 mL
	Sea salt and freshly ground white pepper	
2	egg yolks	2

1. On baking sheets, arrange eggplant in a single layer. Sprinkle with salt. Set aside for 15 minutes, then pat dry with paper towels. Brush liberally with oil. Bake in preheated oven for 20 minutes, until soft and golden. Remove from oven and set aside.

2. In a large saucepan over medium heat, cook lamb for 8 to 10 minutes, until brown. Using a slotted spoon, transfer to a plate.

3. In same saucepan over low heat, add onion (there should be plenty of fat from the lamb left in pan) and sauté for 5 minutes. Add garlic, oregano and cinnamon and stir to combine. Add cooked lamb, bay leaves, tomato paste, crushed tomatoes and broth. Simmer, uncovered, stirring occasionally, until liquid has reduced and meat is very tender, about 40 minutes. Remove bay leaves and season with salt and pepper to taste.

4. *Béchamel Sauce:* Meanwhile, in a small saucepan over medium heat, melt butter. Add flour and stir for 1 minute to create a roux. Remove from heat and, very gradually, add milk, stirring continuously until smooth. Return pan to heat and, stirring constantly, bring to a boil. As soon as it boils, turn off the heat (sauce will be thick). Add nutmeg and cheese and season with salt and white pepper to taste. Set aside.

5. *Assembly:* On bottom of baking dish, arrange a single layer of eggplant. Top with half the lamb mixture, followed by another layer of eggplant. Finish with a final layer of lamb.

6. Whisk egg yolks into prepared béchamel sauce and pour evenly over moussaka. Bake in preheated oven for 30 to 40 minutes, until golden brown and cooked through. Remove from oven and set aside for 15 minutes to cool before serving.

Variation

For a vegetarian version, substitute the same amount of cooked red or green lentils for the lamb and use a vegetable broth.

Sautéed Wild Mushrooms with Marjoram and Marsala

When wild mushrooms are in season, this is a divine way to prepare them. My favorites are pretty yellow chanterelles, which pair wonderfully with meaty ceps and sweet marjoram. Serve this dish as an appetizer with toasted sourdough bread, or stir through a cooked plain risotto.

Makes 4 starter servings

Preparation time:
10 minutes

Cooking time:
10 minutes

Tip

Do not wash mushrooms. Instead, dust them carefully with a mushroom brush or pastry brush.

1 tbsp	butter	15 mL
2	shallots, very finely diced	2
1	clove garlic, minced	1
4 cups	wild mushrooms, sliced if large (see Tip, left)	1 L
¼ cup	Marsala wine	60 mL
2 tbsp	fresh marjoram leaves	30 mL
¼ cup	table (18%) cream or crème fraîche	60 mL
	Salt and freshly ground pepper	

1. In a skillet over medium heat, melt butter. Add shallots and garlic and sauté for 3 minutes. Add mushrooms and cook, stirring occasionally, for 4 to 5 minutes, until tender and lightly browned. Pour in Marsala and cook, stirring constantly, for 3 to 4 minutes, until alcohol has evaporated. Stir in marjoram and cream and season with salt and pepper to taste. Serve immediately.

Variation

To make a dip, before adding the cream, drain mushrooms of cooking liquid, then use a food processor to blitz them into a paste. Stir in just enough cream to reach desired consistency.

Orris Root

Iris germanica var. *florentina*

Names in Other Languages

- **French:** racine d'iris
- **German:** florentina Schwertlilie
- **Italian:** giaggiolo
- **Spanish:** raiz de iris florentina

Family: Iridaceae
Varieties: Dalmatian iris (*I. pallida*)
Other Names: Florentine iris
Flavor Group: Pungent
Parts Used: roots (as a spice)

Background

The irises from which orris root powder is produced are native to southern Europe. They extended by propagation into northern India and North Africa and were extensively cultivated for their rhizomes in Italy. Its medicinal qualities were appreciated by the first-century scientists Theophrastus, Dioscorides and Pliny. During the Middle Ages, Florentine iris (*I. germanica* var. *florentina*) and Dalmatian iris (*I. pallida*) were cultivated in northern Italy. As a result, the city of Florence was renowned for growing this plant.

The Plant

The orris root powder of culinary use (and the most fragrant variety) comes from the rootstock (rhizome) of Florentine

A Beautiful Flower

Such is the beauty and variety of colors in this family that it's not surprising they were named after the rainbow goddess, Iris. Orris root was used in perfumery in ancient Greece and Rome. During the 16th and 17th centuries, orris root was used in cooking; however, its popularity as a fragrance—it has a strong scent resembling violet—appeared to outweigh its culinary applications.

Culinary Information

Combines with

- allspice
- caraway
- cardamom
- cloves
- coriander seed
- cumin
- dill seed
- ginger
- fennel seed
- paprika
- pepper
- turmeric

Traditional Uses

- Moroccan tagines
- potpourris
- clove oranges (pomanders)

Spice Blends

- ras el hanout

iris. This flower is one of a vast family of plants grown primarily for their magnificent blooms, which are popular for decorating gardens in spring and early summer. Although sometimes called flag irises, they should not be confused with sweet flag (calamus, see page 132), which is also sometimes called wild iris in the United States.

The Florentine iris is an attractive perennial plant with bluish green flat, narrow swordlike leaves 1 to $1\frac{1}{2}$ inches (2.5 to 4 cm) wide. The flower stems reach to 3 feet (1 m) or more and bear either violet-tinged white flowers with a yellow beard or pure white flowers with no beard. Orris root powder is pale cream to white in color; it is very fine-textured, like talcum powder, and has an aroma distinctly similar to that of violets. The flavor is also floral and has a characteristic bitter taste.

Other Varieties

Dalmatian iris (*Iris pallida*) is indigenous to the Adriatic coast of Croatia. An essential oil used in perfumery, soaps and face creams is extracted from its root by steam distillation.

Processing

The best variety of iris for making orris root powder is *I. germanica* var. *florentina*. It takes three years for the plants

Spice Notes

I could not write about orris root without mentioning two uses that are deeply etched in my memory. One is of my father making potpourri from rose petals, scented geranium leaves, lavender and calendula flowers, and lemon verbena. Our family picked these fragrant ingredients and Dad dried the harvest to make potpourri. It was an act of alchemy, made possible by adding cinnamon and cloves and using orris root powder as a fixative and carrier for the few added drops of essential oils (see page 22). It saddens me to see how the notion of potpourri has become debased. Now it is just another commercial room freshener, redolent with sickly artificial scents.

The other memorable application for orris root involves rolling a clove-orange pomander in the powder. This final garnishing prior to storing it for up to three months while it "mummifies" is crucial to making a long-lasting clove orange.

to mature, after which the rhizomes are dug up. They are peeled and dried for at least three years to achieve optimum pungency; then they are powdered. The degree of care taken in peeling and preparing the rhizomes has an important bearing on quality. Premium-grade Florentine iris is almost white in color; less carefully peeled orris root may yield a powder that is brownish and contains corky reddish brown particles of skin.

WEIGHT PER TEASPOON (5 mL)
- **ground:** 2.3 g

SUGGESTED QUANTITY PER POUND (500 g)
- **red meats:** ¼ tsp (1 mL) powder
- **white meats:** ⅛ tsp (0.5 mL) powder
- **vegetables:** ⅛ tsp (0.5 mL) powder
- **grains and pulses:** ⅛ tsp (0.5 mL) powder
- **baked goods:** ⅛ tsp (0.5 mL) powder

Buying and Storage

Orris root powder was readily available from pharmacies in North America in the past, but it is now necessary to seek out a specialty retailer for a supply. It should be purchased in powdered form; it would not be worth the effort to grind it yourself. Avoid powder that is an off color or has too many lumps. The powder is a magnet for moisture, so it is essential to store it in an airtight container, well protected from humidity.

Use

Because orris root does not instantly make one think of food, I was surprised to find there is no substitute for its haunting floral note in the Moroccan blend ras el hanout. This mixture has a unique aroma and flavor (even without the illegal substances Spanish fly and hashish) that is created by 20-plus different spices, the *pièce de résistance* being orris root powder.

Pomander (Clove Orange)

Pomanders were made in medieval times to ward off evil, prevent disease and discourage insects. A clove orange hanging in a wardrobe gives off a pleasant fragrance and keeps moths at bay. I have my own memories of making clove oranges with my sisters and the sore thumbs from pushing in the cloves. When we moved from our childhood home, the pomanders were still hanging from faded velvet ribbons in the cupboards. They may still be around today!

Makes
1 pomander

Preparation time:
45 minutes, plus 8 to 12 weeks for drying

Cooking time: none

- **Tissue paper, for wrapping**
- **Ribbon, for tying**

2 tsp	orris root powder	10 mL
2 tsp	ground cinnamon	10 mL
1	very fresh orange, picked directly from the tree if possible	1
1 cup	whole dried cloves	250 mL

1. In a bowl big enough to roll the orange, combine orris root powder and cinnamon and set aside.

2. Stud orange with cloves, leaving spaces about as wide as a clove's head between each (this is important—when the orange shrinks it will split if the cloves are too close together). When orange is completely covered with cloves, roll it in spice mixture. Wrap orange in tissue paper and store in a dry place for 8 to 12 weeks.

3. To hang the preserved clove orange, tie a pretty ribbon from top to bottom and around its middle, leaving a loop at the top about 12 inches (30 cm) long to suspend it by. Your pomander will last for many years (as many as 50), gradually shrinking and becoming rock-hard over time.

A Pomander (Clove Orange or Apple)

When Dad was young, the family would make clove oranges at the height of citrus season; my great-grandmother was particularly dextrous, and faster than everyone else! The family created a poem for making pomanders that was printed on a tea towel sold in the Somerset Cottage shop:

Before this task you begin to tackle
Select a ripe, fresh orange or apple
Sharp cloves all around the fruit you stick.
Then on some paper (not too thick)
Mix orris-root powder and cinnamon-spice
For rolling fruit, to keep it nice.

Fold paper round and put it away
For several weeks, rock-hard to stay.
Our recipe is given in all sincerity
This prickly pomander for posterity.

Potpourri

I have fond memories of being a little girl in my grandparents' home, smelling jars of fragrant potpourri. When I grew up, I could never understand why people used artificial room fresheners. This is the recipe for potpourri that Grandpa used to make and was featured in the book *Hemphill's Herbs: Their Cultivation and Usage*, published in 1983.

Makes 10 cups (2.5 L)

Preparation time:
15 minutes, plus
1 month for infusing
Cooking time: none

- - - - - - - - - - - - - - - -

Tip

"Resting" your potpourri by covering it for a while every day or two seems to regenerate its aroma.

• **10- to 12-cup (2.5 to 3 L) glass jar with lid**

4 cups	dried rose petals	1 L
2 cups	dried scented geranium leaves	500 mL
2 cups	dried lavender flowers and leaves	500 mL
1 cup	dried lemon verbena leaves	250 mL
2 tbsp	orris root powder	30 mL
1 tsp	ground cloves	5 mL
1 tbsp	ground cinnamon	15 mL
1 tsp	lavender oil	5 mL
1 tsp	rose geranium oil	5 mL
5	cinnamon sticks	5
12	whole cloves	12

1. In jar, combine rose petals, geranium leaves, lavender and lemon verbena.
2. In a small bowl, combine orris root powder, cloves and cinnamon. Add lavender and rose geranium oils; stir well to ensure they are well combined. Add oil mixture to dried ingredients and, using your hands, gently and thoroughly combine. Seal and set aside in a cool, dark place for at least 1 month.

O

Pandan Leaf

Pandanus amaryllifolius

Family: Pandanaceae

Varieties: Nicobar breadfruit (*P. odoratissimus*), screwpine (*P. fascicularis*)

Other Names: pandanus leaf, screwpine, rampe

Flavor Group: Medium

Parts Used: leaves (as a herb), fruits (as a fruit)

Background

Pandans are native to Madagascar. They are ancient plants whose natural habitat stretches across the Indian Ocean to Southeast Asia, Australia and the Pacific Islands. In those areas they are often seen clinging to the water's edge with masses of stiff aerial roots, which also protect and bind the banks they are growing on.

Australian Aborigines ate the globular, pineapple-sized fruits of the pandan tree by roasting them, then chewing off the flesh. The heat of roasting destroyed the calcium oxalate in them. In the 19th century the Prussian explorer Friedrich Leichhardt, who arrived in Sydney in 1842, discovered—much to his discomfort after incurring a blistered tongue and violent diarrhea—that the fruits could not be eaten without first being processed to neutralize their noxious properties.

Culinary Information

Combines with
- chile
- coriander (leaf and seed)
- galangal
- garlic
- ginger
- makrut lime leaf
- lemongrass
- lemon myrtle

Traditional Uses
- Asian sponge cake
- steamed rice
- green curries

Spice Blends
- not commonly used in spice blends

A Useful Plant

Tough, fibrous pandan leaves were traditionally used for house thatching and were also woven into sails, clothing, floor mats and baskets. The rustling flesh-revealing, ancient-mariner-arousing grass skirts worn by Pacific Island women were made from split and bleached pandan leaves. In many parts of Asia, attractive woven baskets for sticky rice are made from pandan leaves.

The increased popularity of Asian cuisine has made pandan leaf and fruit familiar ingredients.

The Plant

Pandan leaves for culinary use are gathered from the 26-foot (8 m) screwpine tree, a prehistoric-looking ancient species that is neither a pine tree nor a palm. It is characterized by its stiff branches, supported on stilt-like masses of aerial roots, and sharp-edged leaves arranged spirally (the reason for the name "screwpine"). The leaves bend at 45 degrees about halfway along, giving a drooping, windswept look to the dense upper foliage. Fragrant white flowers are followed by fruit heads 8 inches (20 cm) in diameter that look like green pineapples. There are more than 500 species of *Pandanus*, with almost as many variations in the colors of their foliage.

The bouquet of the culinary pandan leaf is sweet, mild and grassy. It always reminds me of the fragrance of rice in Singapore, which has a similarly grass-like sweet and agreeable flavor. Fresh young pandan leaves have a similar appearance to the blades of palm fronds.

Other Varieties

The variety known as **Nicobar breadfruit** (*Pandanus odoratissimus*) is also referred to as the "walking-stick palm." It is not related to the true breadfruit, although its fruit looks similar. A fragrant essence called *kewra* is made from the flowers of this and another variety, *P. fascicularis*. Kewra is a powerful perfume, redolent of musk and jasmine notes; it is the distinctive scent added to *paan*—shavings of areca nut that are chewed with betel leaf.

P

Processing

Because color is one of the key attributes of pandan leaf, it must be dried carefully in a shady place, without exposure to direct sunlight, to retain its bright green appearance and unique fragrance. The leaves are then chopped into pieces large enough to remove from a dish after cooking, or powdered finely so the texture is no longer reedy. Pandan leaf powder is fine, slightly fibrous, aromatic and bright green. Fresh whole leaves are either crushed or boiled to make an extract that is used to color cakes or confectionery.

Buying and Storage

Fresh pandan leaves are available from Asian grocery stores and some specialty produce retailers. The best way to store them is whole, in a resealable bag in the freezer.

Pandan leaf powder can be bought from spice shops. Make sure it is bright green when purchased and keep it stored away from light so it retains its color.

Pandan extract for coloring cakes and confectionery is available in Southeast Asia; however, it usually has artificial color added, and the flavor only barely resembles that of pandan leaf. Kewra extract may be found in a limited number of specialty Asian food stores.

Use

On first sighting, in Singapore and other Southeast Asian countries, slices of bright green pandan cake, a dense yet surprisingly light type of sponge cake, look incredibly artificial. However, their chartreuse color actually comes from the pandan leaf. In many parts of Asia, strips of pandan leaf are added to rice while it is cooking. Sometimes whole leaves are tied in a couple of knots, as one would do with lemongrass, and immersed in a soup or curry while it is cooking. The bruised knotted leaves give up their flavor and are easily removed at the end of cooking. Kewra, the fragrant essence made from the flowers of *P. fascicularis* or *P. odoratissimus*, is referred to as the "vanilla of the East." It is used in sweet dishes and ice creams, as well as in festive Kashmiri dishes and some curries.

WEIGHT PER TEASPOON (5 mL)
- **ground:** 1.3 g

SUGGESTED QUANTITY PER POUND (500 g)
- **red meats:** ½ tsp (2 mL) powder
- **white meats:** ½ tsp (2 mL) powder
- **vegetables:** ½ tsp (2 mL) powder
- **grains and pulses:** ½ tsp (2 mL) powder
- **baked goods:** ½ tsp (2 mL) powder

P

Coconut Rice with Pandan Leaf

Moving to Singapore as a child in the 1980s was an incredible experience, and it didn't take long to feel at home at the markets and hawker stalls. As our palates adapted, rice was always the first thing we chose. We loved this pandan coconut version.

**Makes
6 servings**

Preparation time:
10 minutes
Cooking time:
40 minutes

- - - - - - - - - - - - - -

Tips

To prepare the rice: Wash in a bowl of cool water, rubbing the grains lightly between the palms of your hands to remove the starch. Change the water and repeat twice, then drain thoroughly.

Coconut milk is the liquid extracted from coconut meat and then watered down. The "cream" will sit at the top of the can, so it's best to shake before using to get the right milky consistency.

2	fresh green pandan leaves	2
3 cups	water	750 mL
2 cups	jasmine rice, rinsed well and drained (see Tips, left)	500 mL
1 cup	coconut milk (see Tips, left)	250 mL
1 tsp	fine sea salt	5 mL

1. Working with one pandan leaf at a time, hold down the top of the leaf with one hand, press a fork firmly against the leaf, and use the fork to shred it lengthwise all the way down. Tie shredded pandan leaves in a knot.

2. In a large saucepan over medium heat, combine water, rice, knotted pandan leaves, coconut milk and salt. Cover and bring to a boil. Turn off heat (do not remove lid) and set aside for 30 minutes to allow rice to steam. Fluff through with a fork and discard pandan leaves before serving.

Paprika

Capsicum annum

Family: Solanaceae

Other Names: hot paprika, Hungarian paprika, mild paprika, ñora paprika, pimento, pod pepper, smoked paprika, Spanish paprika, sweet paprika, sweet pepper

Flavor Group: Amalgamating

Parts Used: pods (as a spice)

Background

The origins of paprika go back 7,000 years, to when indigenous Mexicans consumed various chiles—forerunners of paprika—as a regular part of their diet. The New World history of paprika is comparatively short; it was not until Columbus brought back hot and sweet chiles in 1492 that the circumstances were created for the Spanish and Hungarians to create what we now know as paprika. The Spanish first transformed a variety of chile into a deep red powder called *pimentón* (named after the Spanish word for peppers, *pimienta*), which was rapidly embraced as a culinary ingredient. Apparently paprika was first cultivated in Spain at the Jerónimos monastery in Guadalupe, near La Vera. There is now a characteristic Spanish paprika based

Culinary Information

Combines with

Nearly all culinary herbs and spices, but has a special affinity with

- allspice
- basil
- caraway
- cardamom
- chile
- cinnamon
- cloves
- coriander seed
- cumin
- fennel seed
- garlic
- ginger
- oregano
- parsley
- pepper
- rosemary
- sage
- thyme
- turmeric

Traditional Uses

- Hungarian goulash
- chicken
- veal and pork casseroles
- broiled, barbecued or roasted meats (sprinkled on before cooking)
- egg dishes (as a garnish)
- sauces
- meat loaf

Spice Blends

- tandoori spice blends
- barbecue spice blends
- baharat
- Cajun spices
- chermoula mixes
- curry powders
- harissa paste mixes
- Mexican chili powder
- ras el hanout
- tagine spice blends

on subsequent years of cultivation and hybridization and the concomitant development of various methods of drying, smoking and milling.

In Hungary chile peppers were introduced by Turkish conquerors in the mid 16th century. There, since the 17th century, constant breeding of desirable strains, combined with weather and soil conditions, has created a unique cooler-climate paprika renowned for its own special attributes. Today the town of Kalocsa, south of Budapest, and the city of Szeged, further south, are the main paprika-producing regions in Hungary. Hungary was under Turkish occupation in the 17th century, and although the cultivation of "Turkish pepper," as paprika was then called, was prohibited on pain of death, many who had tasted its warmth and piquancy couldn't resist growing it illegally, which goes to explain why it took so long for it to become a recognized condiment there.

The Plant

Paprika is the name commonly given to a wide range of bright red powders made from various strains of *Capsicum annum*, the same family as chile (see page 175). Paprika plants and their fruits vary considerably in size and appearance. All are described as early-maturing erect shrubs with oval leaves, single white flowers and non-woody stems.

Paprika pods, or fruits, may be long (8 inches/20 cm) and thin like a giant chile or small and round ($1^1/_2$ inches/4 cm in diameter), resembling a miniature bell pepper. The fruits may range in color from bright red to dark red and almost brown; all are harvested when fully ripe. Paprika's vivid color is determined by the amount of capsanthin (the red pigment present) and the lack of capsaicin (the heat element in chiles). The varying degrees of heat and bitterness in paprika are determined by the ratio of capsaicin-bearing placenta and seeds and the methods of curing and drying.

In recent years Israel, China and Zimbabwe have become major producers of paprika, and some of their sweet dark red grades have a depth of character, strength of color and agreeable, non-bitter flavor that make them extremely useful. Paprika powder from these sources sometimes finds its way to the market via Hungary and Spain and is incorrectly passed off as paprika from those countries.

Hungarian Paprika

Hungarian paprika is classified into six main grades, each determined by the quality of fruits used; the ratio of seeds, connecting tissue (placenta) and stem to outside flesh; and the degree of thoroughness employed in the grinding process, all of which contribute to the heat level and flavor.

- **Különleges** ("exquisite delicate") is a very mild grade, considered to be the best quality and richest in color. It is made from the flesh of specially selected fruits that have been finely ground to yield an almost silky powder. The removal of seeds, capsaicin-bearing placenta and stem before grinding makes it tantalizingly sweet, with no trace of bitterness or aftertaste.
- **Delicatessen** ("delicate") is less mild than különleges, with a more pronounced bell pepper flavor and a light red color.
- **Édesnemes** ("noble sweet") is the most widely exported variety, valued for its bright red color and sweetness. The sweet flavor, lack of bitterness and full-bodied aroma are

Travels in the Spice Trade

Our research into Hungarian paprika took us to the town of Kalocsa, just south of Budapest. To our good fortune we happened to be there at the time of the annual Paprika Festival. Kalocsa celebrates its connection with paprika to such a degree that it even has a paprika museum. The ceiling is completely blanketed by ristras of paprika, and displays documenting the history of paprika in the region flank the walls, along with antique articles of farm equipment. The following day we attended the Paprika Festival with our host, a delightful woman named Gyorgyi who also showed us around the farms and the paprika-processing facilities. Around much of the festival's perimeter were market stall–like tents where contestants from all walks of life were setting up for the paprika cooking competition. We were offered (and accepted) tastings of paprika *palinka*, a local form of schnapps that gets quite a kick from its 50% alcohol content—just the thing on a cool, wet day.

achieved by grinding the flesh with seeds that have been washed and macerated in water to remove most of the heat-giving capsaicin.

- **Félédes** ("semisweet") is similar to noble sweet, with slight traces of heat. This variety is made from the outer flesh and some placenta, giving it an almost discernible kick.
- **Rósza** ("rose") is made from the whole fruit except for the stem and the section joining the stem to the fruit. Rósza has a less distinctive red color and a little more heat than the grades listed above.
- **Erös** ("strong" or second quality) is made from complete fruits that are not of high enough quality to make the previously mentioned grades. Generally coarser in texture and darker red than the other paprikas, erös has a distinct background bitterness and lingering heat that I liken to a mild ground chile because it is quite hot.

Spanish Paprika

Spanish paprika is graded similarly to Hungarian, but because of its history, cultivation and processing methods it differs markedly from the Hungarian styles. In general the Spanish paprika fruits tend to be smaller and rounder, are darker in color, and have varying degrees of smoky and "cooked" flavor notes, a coarser texture (but not always) and more robust aromas. There are three main types of Spanish *pimentón* (as they call it) and three grades within each type. The grades are **extra**, which contains no seeds milled with the fruit; **select**, containing 10% seeds; and the **ordinary** grade, which contains around 30% seeds. Naturally the percentage of seeds influences the heat level and degree of bitterness in each.

Smoked paprika is produced by smoking the paprika pods as part of the drying and curing process (see "Processing" below). The three main types of smoked paprika from the La Vera region in Spain, which in 2005 was granted Denominación de Origen status, are described according to their levels of sweetness, bitterness and heat:

- **Dulce** (sweet) has a sweet, smoky aroma and a pleasant metallic taste. It is dark red and fine-textured.
- **Agridulce** (bittersweet or semisweet) has a distinct bitterness and an appetizingly sharp edge to its flavor. The color and aroma are similar to those of dulce.

Various grades of loosely named "mild" Spanish paprikas are also on the market, sometimes passed off as Hungarian paprika. A particular dark red, coarse-textured and faintly burnt-smelling one is often regarded as inferior, but I find it complements Moroccan and Middle Eastern foods better than any other.

Ñora paprika from the Murcia region of Spain is made from a small (1 inch/2.5 cm in diameter), dark burgundy-red pepper with a sweet, warm, appetizing aroma and a mild, fully developed bell pepper flavor. This paprika is the same variety as standard Spanish paprika, but the pods are left on the plant until very dark and ripe. Ñora paprika, which is similar to ground guajillo and New Mexico chiles, is my favorite for making the traditional Spanish Romesco sauce.

Piment d'Espelette is a highly desirable variety of paprika, popular for its warm, fruity flavor and slight chile-like bite. It comes from the Basque region of southern France, and as an AOC (Appellation d'Origine Contrôlée) item, only product grown in Espelette can be named "piment d'Espelette." The warm, fruity flavor and mild heat of piment d'Espelette make this unique spice a versatile addition to most savory dishes. Sprinkle on pizzas and pasta, add to scrambled eggs and omelets, and even sprinkle over salads.

Processing

Methods of processing vary among the key producing nations of the world. Given their long history and family businesses that have been in the trade for many generations, Hungary and Spain tend to maintain more traditional practices that involve curing periods, number of times ground, and fineness of the final powder. Less traditional methods simply dry the pods without extended curing and grind them with only one or two passes through an industrial spice mill. Yields from paprika farms can vary from 900 to 3,500 pounds per acre (1 to 4 tonnes per ha); on average it takes 11 pounds (5 kg) of fresh pods to produce less than 2 pounds (1 kg) of paprika powder.

Hungarian Paprika

In Hungary the thick-fleshed, leathery fruits are allowed to ripen fully and to color to bright red before harvesting. After they have been picked, the ripe fruits are cured for 25 to 39 days, which greatly increases their pigment content— studies have shown that the pigment capsanthin can increase by as much as 120% during the curing process. Besides the color, the ascorbic acid (vitamin C) level increases proportionally with the concentration of capsanthin. An interesting point for nutrient watchers is that research has shown that the vitamin C content is lower when the capsaicin (heat) content is high.

Traditionally, curing was achieved by piling the paprika pods in sheltered positions in the windows of houses or by stringing together large garlands of the fruits and hanging them on fences, in open-sided sheds and even on clotheslines. When the dry pods rattled in the wind, the curing process was complete. A more modern method of storage during curing is to place the ripe pods in large cotton-mesh sacks and stack them in open-sided curing sheds. It's an amazing sight to see semitrailer loads of mesh-bagged bright red paprikas arriving at the processing facilities in Kolocsa. After curing, the pods are nearly dry; they are then laid out in the sun for two to three weeks to finish drying. More often these days, the pods are dried in a 120°F (50°C) continuous kiln.

The next critical phase is milling, which creates the different grades of Hungarian paprika referred to above. These are based on the amount of stem, seeds and placenta removed. Grades are also influenced by the quantity of reduced-pungency washed seeds that are ground and added to the paprika powder while it is being milled. Paprikas tend to be much redder than typical chiles because of their thicker flesh, higher capsanthin content and lower quantity of seeds.

Friction in the grinding process generates heat. Although this is often undesirable when grinding, for instance, highly volatile spices such as cardamom, with paprika this heat creates a degree of caramelization, which enhances the

Is It a Paprika or a Chile?

Just keep in mind that paprika and chile are closer than first cousins. You could even say they are siblings! Imagine a line that at the left end has a sweet paprika and at the far right end has a blisteringly hot bhut jolokia chile. From left to right we have a row of paprikas that get increasingly hotter until they become chiles. So when do paprikas become chiles? My observations have led me to the midpoint of the line, where a hot paprika and a mild chile are right beside each other. To all intents and purposes they are identical in heat level; the only differences would be a result of varietal changes or processing methods.

product and forms a key aspect of the bouquet of a well-processed product. However, it's a delicate balance. Too much heat during milling means the powder will take on a sharp, bitter note that is considered undesirable in the best grades of Hungarian paprika. Some of the best and most silky-smooth paprika powder has been roller-milled up to six times.

Spanish Paprika

Spanish paprikas, especially the delicious, aromatic smoked grades from La Vera, in Extremadura, are processed a little differently. The ripe fruits used to make paprika not intended for smoking are piled up on hillsides for about 24 hours to commence curing. Once the moisture content has reduced by 10 to 15% and the capsanthin content has started to increase, they are dried in the searing-hot summer sun for around four days. The pods are then cut into halves or quarters and exposed for a further eight days, until completely dry. The removal of seeds and stem by milling and sifting is done in such a way as to create different levels of sweetness, similar to the methods employed for Hungarian paprika.

The smoked varieties of Spanish paprika are traditionally made by drying freshly harvested ripe fruits in low-lying adobe smokehouses, which are gently heated by smoking grills fired with slow-burning oak wood. The smoking process has to be monitored closely to ensure the peppers dry properly. Too much heat would make the paprika cook in its own moisture and spoil the flavor. Milling is equally painstaking—the first grinding takes up to eight hours—and the heat generated by friction makes a vital contribution to the final flavor, deep red color and smooth, silky texture.

Buying and Storage

With the exception of a few special varieties of paprika such as ñora, which is available from some specialty stores whole, most dried paprika is sold in powdered form. Pickled paprika and paprika paste can be purchased at European delicatessens, and although these are somewhat acidic because of the vinegar required to achieve preservation, they make useful spreads for savories and are a compatible accompaniment to tomato paste in recipes. Fresh paprika pods can be purchased from specialty produce stores; however, be aware that what is sold as a large paprika pod may actually be a large chile, and hotter than you'd expect.

Paprika powder should be labeled to indicate whether it is Hungarian, Spanish or from another source. If not, it should at least state whether it is sweet, mild or hot. Paprika powders range from bright red and silky smooth to dark red and coarse-textured. Paprika powder that is brown has either been exposed to moisture or has discolored with age and should be avoided.

When buying smoked paprika, make sure it is the genuine article; it is a common practice these days to add smoke flavor and MSG to sweet or mild paprika and pass it off as the real thing. Smoked paprika that is dark in color and has a coarse texture is usually an inferior grade containing ground seeds and stem.

Although historically there have been cases where paprika was adulterated with hideous fillers such as red lead and brick dust, current food laws protect the consumer against such flagrant misrepresentation. Consumers with gluten intolerance are advised to seek confirmation from the supplier that the paprika is gluten-free. Gluten in paprika has been documented as caused by processors cleaning their mills by grinding a quantity of wheat, thus leaving residues that may be harmful to some individuals.

Use

Paprika is used extensively to color and flavor food. It is a popular substitute for the artificial red colors commonly added to sausages and preserved meats. Paprika is one of those essential spices that I classify as amalgamating, because its well-rounded and beautifully balanced flavor profile complements most savory flavors. The majority of commercial seasonings designed to be sprinkled on meats prior to cooking will contain paprika. Fast-food barbecued and charcoal-roasted chicken generally gets its mouth-watering color and flavor from seasonings rubbed onto the surface, among them a reasonable amount of paprika.

For home cooking, sweet paprika is the mandatory ingredient that gives Hungarian goulash its characteristic color and flavor: it combines wonderfully with the beef or veal and cream. Paprika also enhances the flavor of pork and chicken. It is often used, with a result that delights both eyes and taste buds, to garnish lobster, shrimp and crabmeat. Eggs, whether scrambled, poached, fried, hard-boiled or made into an omelet, will benefit greatly from a judicious sprinkling of your favorite paprika. Romesco, the famous Catalonian sauce, gets its brilliant color and depth of flavor from the paprika—often ñora—used to make it.

Paprika is an excellent substitute for chile, as it delivers the same flavor profile without the heat. You can make a mild yet tasty and aromatic curry simply by replacing the ground chile with an equal quantity of paprika. Paprika can also be used to tone down the heat of chile if you've been a bit heavy-handed. Adding paprika to a hot chile dish won't upset the flavor but it will help to bring those fiery notes on the palate under control. Add $\frac{1}{2}$ tsp (2 mL) paprika for each fresh chile used, or twice the amount of ground chile or chile flakes used.

Smoked paprika should always be used more sparingly than non-smoked varieties because the flavor is relatively intense. It is an excellent addition to many vegetarian meals, as it imparts a smoky bacon flavor without the meat. It is great in mayonnaise, especially when it accompanies seafood. Grilled cheese sandwiches almost become a meal when sprinkled with smoked sweet paprika before grilling.

WEIGHT PER TEASPOON (5 mL)
- **whole average dried ñora:** 5.2 g
- **ground:** 3.5 g

SUGGESTED QUANTITY PER POUND (500 g)*
- **red meats:** up to $\frac{1}{2}$ cup (125 mL) sweet paprika
- **white meats:** up to $\frac{1}{2}$ cup (125 mL) sweet paprika
- **vegetables:** 4 tsp (20 mL) sweet paprika
- **grains and pulses:** 2 to 3 tsp (10 to 15 mL) sweet paprika
- **baked goods:** 2 to 3 tsp (10 to 15 mL) sweet paprika

*Note: *For hot paprikas, reduce the suggested quantities by about half.*

P

Romesco Sauce

This traditional Catalan sauce hails from Tarragona, in northern Spain. It is perfect served with roasted monkfish or a barbecued leg of lamb, or simply used as a dip with bread or crudités. The smokiness originally came from using ñora paprikas, but as they are increasingly hard to come by, sweet smoked paprika is a wonderful substitution.

Makes about 1 cup (250 mL)

Preparation time:
15 minutes

Cooking time:
5 minutes

- - - - - - - - - - - - - - -

Tips

You can either roast your own red peppers or use the jarred variety.

To roast peppers: Preheat oven to 400°F (200°C). Place peppers on a baking sheet and roast until skin is blackened, about 15 minutes. Transfer to a bag, seal and set aside until cool. Once cool, the skin will easily peel off. Using a knife, scrape out the seeds and discard.

• **Food processor**

4	slices sourdough bread, roughly chopped	4
14 oz	ripe tomatoes, seeded and chopped (about 6)	400 g
3	roasted red peppers (see Tips, left)	3
1 tbsp	sweet smoked paprika	15 mL
2 tbsp	freshly squeezed lemon juice	30 mL
1 tsp	sherry vinegar	5 mL
¼	medium red onion, chopped	¼
2	cloves garlic, roughly chopped	2
2 tbsp	sliced almonds	30 mL
¼ cup	extra virgin olive oil	60 mL
	Sea salt and freshly ground black pepper	

1. In food processor fitted with the metal blade, combine bread, tomatoes, roasted peppers, paprika, lemon juice, vinegar, onion, garlic, and almonds. Process until mixture resembles a rough paste. With motor running, add oil through the feed tube. Season with salt and pepper to taste. Sauce will keep in an airtight container in the refrigerator for up to 1 week.

P

Hungarian Goulash

When Mum and Dad returned from Hungary laden with bags of freshly ground paprika, the first dish we made was this traditional goulash. It can also be made with beef, but I love the delicacy of veal.

**Makes
6 servings**

Preparation time:
15 minutes

Cooking time: 3 hours

- - - - - - - - - - - - - -

Tip

Passata is a smooth, fresh (uncooked) tomato purée. If you don't have any on hand, substitute an equal amount of puréed canned crushed tomatoes.

• **Preheat oven to 275°F (140°C)**

2½ lbs	veal shoulder, cut into 2-inch (5 cm) pieces	1.25 kg
	Salt and freshly ground pepper	
2 tbsp	oil	30 mL
1 tbsp	butter	15 mL
2	onions, halved and thinly sliced	2
4	cloves garlic, minced	4
1	red bell pepper, seeded and cut into 1-inch (2.5 cm) pieces	1
3	carrots, peeled and cut into 1-inch (2.5 cm) pieces	3
3 tbsp	sweet Hungarian paprika	45 mL
1 tsp	caraway seeds	5 mL
½ cup	white wine	125 mL
2 cups	veal broth	500 mL
2½ cups	tomato passata (see Tip, left)	625 mL
2	bay leaves	2
2	potatoes, peeled and cut into 1-inch (2.5 cm) pieces	2
1 lb	fettucine, cooked and buttered	500 g
½ cup	sour cream	125 mL
½ cup	finely chopped fresh parsley leaves	125 mL

1. Using paper towels, pat veal dry and season with salt and pepper to taste. In a large Dutch oven over medium heat, heat oil. Working in batches, cook veal for 8 to 10 minutes, stirring occasionally, until browned on all sides, adding more oil when necessary. Once browned, transfer veal to a plate and set aside.

Tip

Be sure not to add the potato too early. If overcooked it will break down into the soup.

2. In same pan over low heat, melt butter. Add onions, cover with a tight-fitting lid, and cook for 10 minutes, stirring occasionally, until translucent and soft. Uncover pan, add garlic, and sauté for 2 minutes, until softened. Stir in bell pepper, carrots, paprika and caraway. Return browned veal to pan and stir until coated in spices. Add wine, broth, tomato passata and bay leaves and stir to combine. Increase heat to medium and bring to a boil, then cover tightly with lid and transfer pan to preheated oven. Cook for 90 minutes, removing pan from oven to stir every 30 minutes. When meat just becomes tender, add potatoes and cook for 30 minutes longer, until meat is very tender and potatoes are cooked through (see Tip, left).

3. To serve, divide prepared fettucine among deep serving bowls and ladle equal amounts of goulash overtop. Garnish each serving with a swirl of sour cream and a sprinkling of parsley.

P

Parsley

Petroselinum crispum (also known as *P. petroselinum,*
P. vulgare, Selinum petroselinum)

Names in Other Languages

- **Arabic:** baqdunis
- **Chinese (C):** heong choi
- **Chinese (M):** yang yuan sui
- **Czech:** petrzel
- **Danish:** persille
- **Dutch:** peterselie, krulpeterselie (curled parsley)
- **Finnish:** persilja
- **French:** persil
- **German:** Petersilie
- **Greek:** maintano, persemolo
- **Hungarian:** petrezselyem
- **Indonesian:** seledri, peterseli
- **Italian:** prezzemolo
- **Japanese:** paseri
- **Norwegian:** persille
- **Portuguese:** salsa
- **Russian:** pyetrushka
- **Spanish:** perejil
- **Swedish:** persilja
- **Thai:** partasliyat, phakchi farang
- **Turkish:** maydanoz
- **Vietnamese:** rau mui tay

Family: Apiaceae (formerly Umbelliferae)

Varieties: curly parsley (*P. crispum*), Italian parsley (*P. crispum neapolitanum*), Hamburg parsley (*P. sativum tuberosum*), fool's parsley (*Aethusa cynapium*; poisonous)

Other Names: curled parsley, triple-curled parsley, moss-curled parsley (curly parsley); flat-leaf parsley, large-leaf parsley (Italian parsley)

Flavor Group: Mild

Parts Used: leaves (as a herb)

Background

Parsley has been cultivated and developed for so many centuries that its precise origins are difficult to pinpoint. This problem is compounded by the probability that all the parsleys we know nowadays bear little resemblance to their ancestors. Carl Linnaeus, the 18th-century Swedish botanist, considered parsley to be native to Sardinia; however, others have said its origins lie in the eastern Mediterranean region. The botanical name *Petroselinum* comes from the Greek word for "stone," *petra,* which was given to parsley

curly parsley

Culinary Information

Combines with

- arugula
- basil
- bay leaf
- chervil
- chicory
- chives
- dill
- fennel fronds
- garlic
- lovage
- marjoram
- mint
- oregano
- rosemary
- sage
- thyme

Traditional Uses

- chimichurri
- omelets, scrambled eggs and savory soufflés
- mashed potatoes
- tabouli
- soups
- pasta dishes
- parsley sauces for tripe, fish and poultry

Spice Blends

- bouquet garni
- herbes de Provence
- mixed herbs
- Italian herbs
- fines herbes
- chermoula spice mix

Italian (flat-leaf) parsley

because it was found growing on rocky hillsides in Greece. Although the ancient Greeks did not use parsley in cooking, it was revered as a symbol of death and as a funeral herb. In mythology, parsley was believed to have sprung from the blood of a Greek hero, Archemoros, the forerunner of death. It was made into garlands and given to horses as fodder. By the second century CE, the Romans were appreciating parsley's talents as a breath freshener.

In medieval times parsley was surrounded by much superstition. Parsley seeds require a long germination period; as a result, it was believed they needed enough time to travel to hell and back seven times before sprouting. Superstitious farmers would refuse to transplant parsley, and some were afraid to grow it at all. In the 17th century the early colonists took parsley to America and never looked back—once the usefulness and agreeable flavor of parsley had been embraced in the New World, practicality must have overcome any lingering superstitions.

These days, fresh parsley (both curly and flat-leaf) is widely used in cooking, and dehydrated curly parsley is a very popular culinary herb. It is found in home cooking, restaurant meals, fast foods and numerous processed and dried food products.

The Plant

Parsley is a biennial plant grown from seed. As a member of the carrot family, young parsley plants have a striking resemblance to carrot foliage until they come into full leaf, at which point the variety, whether flat-leaf or curly, can be readily identified.

Be patient when growing curly parsley: the seeds can take up to two weeks to germinate. After sowing (curly parsley in particular), the seeds must be kept moist until they sprout. As parsley is a biennial, it is important to prevent the plants from going to seed in the first year, by cutting off the long flower stalks as soon as they appear. If properly pruned, parsley will provide an abundance of leaf growth in the following year.

Parsley has a particularly distinctive aroma, which is interesting since the herb is usually described as mild and subtle. The taste can be described as fresh and crisp and slightly earthy. It is surprisingly unassertive when combined with other herbs; this makes it a perfect partner in blends such as fines herbes, bouquet garni and mixed herbs. Parsley is "blend-friendly" because it complements most flavors it is combined with—it never seems to dominate yet always makes its presence felt.

"Chinese parsley" is a common name often given to fresh coriander (cilantro) leaves (see page 225), but it is a misnomer: there is no such thing as Chinese parsley in the *Petroselinum* genus.

Varieties

Curly parsley (*Petroselinum crispum*) is the variety traditionally associated with the image of parsley, its almost crepe-like frilly leaves being a ubiquitous garnish and the more photogenic of the two varieties. It grows to around 10 inches (25 cm) tall and is easily recognized by its masses of small, tightly bunched bright green leaves. There are more than 30 variations of curled parsley; some kinds may be more tightly curled and others relatively sparse.

Italian parsley (*P. crispum neapolitanum*), also called flat- or large-leaf parsley, grows to 18 inches (45 cm), is a darker green than curly parsley, looks a bit like the tops of celery and cilantro, and has a slightly stronger flavor than curly parsley. Flat-leaf parsley has become the most used culinary variety in recent times because of the rise in popularity of Italian food and fascination with

Parsley Root

Parsley root is a vegetable, not a herb. Like carrots, it is grown for its root, rather than its leaves. It is often found in farmers' markets and is growing in popularity in North America. It greatly resembles parsnips in appearance, although its slightly bitter taste is closer to celery root. Like its carrot relatives, it makes a wonderful addition to soups and stews.

Mediterranean and Middle Eastern cuisines, both of which use copious amounts of Italian parsley. The benefits of its stronger flavor, greater ease of propagation and vigorous growth habit have made this variety appealing to cooks and gardeners alike.

Hamburg parsley (*P. sativum tuberosum*) is grown mainly for its parsnip-like root, which is cooked and eaten as a vegetable in eastern Europe, in much the same way as fennel bulbs. Parsley root is becoming popular in North America as a pot herb, functioning as a thickener and flavor enhancer for soups.

Fool's parsley (*Aethusa cynapium*) is a poisonous plant that looks remarkably similar to Italian flat-leaf parsley; it is found in English gardens, sometimes growing among real parsley. Fool's parsley has a disagreeable flavor; nonetheless, many people have inadvertently gathered it with parsley, consumed it and subsequently become ill. This may explain why the curled varieties are by far the most popular in England.

Processing

Despite its delicate appearance and reputedly subtle flavor, parsley dehydrates quite well. Effective drying of any herb depends on removing the water content within the cell structure of the leaf without driving off the flavor-giving volatile oils. Leaves that lack leathery, shiny, moisture-trapping surfaces often dry easily, and this is the case with parsley. The commercial method for drying this herb is quite astonishing. Washed leaves removed from the stems are blown by a strong air current into a chamber that is heated by something similar to a jet engine. Upon contact with this superheated air (some hundreds of degrees Celsius), the leaves almost instantly lose all but 10% of their moisture. In this lighter state they are sucked up through the top and out of the chamber. Amazingly, the process is so rapid that the surface of the leaves never gets hot enough to diminish flavor. This produces a product that tastes surprisingly like fresh parsley, especially when it is added to moist foods such as egg dishes and even mashed potatoes.

Homegrown parsley is easily dried in an oven at home. Arrange the leaves in a single layer on a baking sheet, preheat the oven to 250°F (120°C) and then turn off heat.

Immediately place the sheet in the oven and dry the parsley using the residual heat, using tongs to carefully turn it a few times. After 15 to 20 minutes the parsley should be crisp and dry. Remove from oven, cool completely and store it in an airtight container in a dark place.

Buying and Storage

Fresh parsley is the most commonly available of all fresh herbs. Choose bunches that are not wilted and have springy, erect, almost bristly leaves. Rinse thoroughly under cold water to remove any grit trapped in the leaves and squeeze dry. To store, either place the bunch in a glass of water (as in a vase) and tent with a plastic bag, then refrigerate, or wrap the fresh sprays in foil and freeze them.

Dried parsley is best purchased in small amounts that are regularly replenished, as it loses its color and flavor rapidly. Look for deep green flakes that are free from pieces of stalk and yellow leaves. Always store dried parsley away from any source of direct light and keep in an airtight container, away from extreme heat and humidity. Stored under these conditions, it will last for up to 1 year.

Use

Parsley's fresh, balanced flavor and crisp mouthfeel make it an ideal accompaniment to most foods. It can diminish the tendency of some foods to linger on the breath, the most notable of these being garlic. It is traditionally featured in well-known herb blends such as the French combination fines herbes (with chervil, chives and tarragon) as well as in a bouquet garni (with thyme, marjoram and bay leaf). Fresh or dried parsley may be used in omelets, scrambled eggs, mashed potatoes, soups, pasta and vegetable dishes and in sauces to go with fish, poultry, veal or pork.

Fresh parsley withstands long cooking times better than most fresh herbs. It is included with garlic and butter when making garlic bread and makes a simple garnish for a juicy, sizzling barbecued steak. Parsley is a key ingredient, along with mint, in the Middle Eastern salad tabouli (see page 476). Flat-leaf parsley features in many Moroccan dishes, from ras el hanout–spiced tagines with preserved lemons to dishes flavored by a chermoula blend that includes coriander leaf, onions, cumin and cayenne pepper.

WEIGHT PER TEASPOON (5 mL)

- dried chopped leaves: 0.3 g

SUGGESTED QUANTITY PER POUND (500 g)

- **red meats:** 5 tsp (25 mL) fresh, 1 to 2 tsp (5 to 10 mL) dried
- **white meats:** 5 tsp (25 mL) fresh, 1 to 2 tsp (5 to 10 mL) dried
- **vegetables:** 5 tsp (25 mL) fresh, 1 to 2 tsp (5 to 10 mL) dried
- **grains and pulses:** 5 tsp (25 mL) fresh, 1 to 2 tsp (5 to 10 mL) dried
- **baked goods:** 5 tsp (25 mL) fresh, 1 to 2 tsp (5 to 10 mL) dried

P

Parsley Sauce

This simple sauce is a classic accompaniment to fish. I particularly love it with steamed smoked cod and mashed potatoes—the epitome of comfort food.

Makes about 1½ cups (375 mL)

Preparation time:
5 minutes

Cooking time:
15 minutes

1½ cups	milk	375 mL
1	shallot, quartered	1
1	bay leaf	1
3	stems fresh curly parsley	3
1 tbsp	butter	15 mL
1 tbsp	all-purpose flour	15 mL
3 tbsp	very finely chopped parsley leaves	45 mL
1 tbsp	table (18%) cream	15 mL
	Sea salt and freshly ground black pepper	

1. In a small saucepan over medium heat, combine milk, shallot, bay leaf and parsley stems. Bring to a simmer (do not allow milk to boil), remove from heat and strain into a bowl through a fine-mesh sieve (discard solids). Set aside.

2. In same pan (rinsed) over medium heat, melt butter. Add flour and cook for 1 minute, stirring, until mixture turns golden and forms a paste (roux). Remove pan from heat and very gradually add milk, stirring continuously until completely incorporated. Return pan to medium heat and bring to a boil, stirring constantly. As soon as it boils, turn off heat and stir in chopped parsley and cream. Season with salt and pepper to taste.

Chimichurri Sauce

Dining at a *churrascaria* in Brazil was a feast I'll never forget: barbecued meats grilled to perfection accompanied by a simple salad and a bowl of chimichurri sauce. Originally from Argentina, this herby, acidic dressing is a welcome change from buttery or tomato-based sauces on meat. It is best when made at least an hour (or more) before serving to allow time for the flavors to develop. Although it's easy enough to make with a food processor, I think lovingly hand-chopping the ingredients makes this recipe a real winner.

Makes about 1 cup (250 mL)

Preparation time:
10 minutes
Cooking time: none

- - - - - - - - - - - - - -

Tip

To finely chop herbs, gather them on a chopping board and, using a sharp knife, chop as if going from 3 to 6 o'clock, keeping the point of the knife stationary.

1 cup	firmly packed flat-leaf (Italian) parsley leaves, finely chopped	250 mL
2 tbsp	firmly packed coriander (cilantro) leaves, finely chopped	30 mL
2	cloves garlic, minced	2
1/3 cup	extra virgin olive oil	75 mL
3 tbsp	red wine vinegar	45 mL
1 tsp	hot pepper flakes	5 mL
1/4 tsp	fine sea salt	1 mL
1/4 tsp	freshly ground black pepper	1 mL

1. In a bowl, combine all of the ingredients. Taste and adjust seasonings, if desired. Set aside for 1 hour to allow flavors to develop. Serve over barbecued vegetables and meat. Sauce will keep in an airtight container in the refrigerator for up to 1 week.

P

Tabouli

I never tire of the fresh flavors of tabouli. It's the perfect summer barbecue salad and a must when serving mezze. Many versions of tabouli are found throughout the world. Lebanese recipes use a higher proportion of parsley to bulgur, which is my favorite way to make it. Serve with Lahmucin (page 188) and Cacik (page 400).

Makes 6 small servings

Preparation time:
20 minutes

Cooking time: none

Tips

Bulgur can be cooked on the stove like rice, but it isn't required—you can simply soak it instead. Place bulgur in a bowl and cover with 2 inches (5 cm) cold water. Add ½ tsp (2 mL) salt and stir to combine. Set aside for 20 minutes to soak. The bulgur will be "cooked." Transfer to a colander, rinse under cold running water and drain well before adding to salad.

If refrigerating for more than 2 days, omit the cucumber and add it before serving—it won't keep as long as the other ingredients.

½ cup	fine bulgur, soaked and drained (see Tips, left)	125 mL
3	ripe vine tomatoes, seeded and diced	3
1	small cucumber, seeded and diced	1
6	green onions, white and green parts, finely sliced	6
3 cups	finely chopped flat-leaf (Italian) parsley	750 mL
½ cup	finely chopped fresh mint	125 mL
½ tsp	ground allspice	2 mL
	Freshly squeezed juice of 1 lemon	
	Sea salt and freshly ground black pepper	
1 tbsp	ground sumac	15 mL

1. In a serving bowl, combine bulgur, tomatoes, cucumber, green onions, parsley, mint, allspice and lemon juice. Season with salt and pepper to taste. Chill before serving. Serve with sumac sprinkled overtop. Will keep in an airtight container in the refrigerator for up to 3 days (see Tips, left).

Variation

For an even healthier salad, add ½ cup (125 mL) cooked white quinoa or use half quinoa and half bulgur.

Pepper – Pink Schinus

Schinus terebinthifolius

Names in Other Languages

- **Chinese (C):** ba sai wuh jiu muhk
- **Chinese (M):** ba xi hu jiao mu
- **Czech:** ruzovy pepr
- **Danish:** rod peber
- **Dutch:** roze peper
- **Finnish:** rosepippuri
- **French:** poivre rose, baies roses, poivre de Bourbon
- **German:** brasilianischer Pfeffer, rose Pfeffer
- **Greek:** roz piperi
- **Hungarian:** rozsaszin bors
- **Italian:** pepe rosa, schino brasiliano
- **Japanese:** kurisuma-beri, sansho-modoki
- **Polish:** owoce schimusowe
- **Portuguese:** pimenta-rosa
- **Russian:** perets rozovyj
- **Spanish:** arveira, pimienta roja
- **Swedish:** rosepeppar
- **Turkish:** pembebiber, yalanci karabiber

Family: Anacardiaceae

Varieties: pepper tree (*S. areira*, also known as *S. molle*; mildly toxic)

Other Names: peppercorn tree, Christmas berry, Brazilian mastic tree

Flavor Group: Pungent

Parts Used: berries (as a spice)

Background

This variety of peppercorn tree is native to the Andean deserts of Peru. In the past, South American native peoples used the peppercorn tree berries to flavor alcoholic beverages. Sometimes the trees are referred to as Brazilian or American "mastic trees" because the whitish sap of the mildly toxic variety *S. molle* was used in South America as a chewing gum. Indeed, peppercorn trees are members of the same family as the tree that yields the resinous sap mastic (see page 386). The *Schinus* genus of trees grows prolifically in arid, well-drained soils in almost any temperate area of the world.

Schinus terebinthifolius—"pink peppercorn" or "Christmas berry," as it is often called—is now grown commercially on the French Indian Ocean island of Réunion. It is either pickled in brine or dried.

P

Culinary Information

Combines with

- allspice
- bay leaf
- chile
- coriander seed
- fennel (fronds and seed)
- juniper
- myrtle
- paprika
- parsley
- rosemary
- sage
- tarragon
- thyme

Traditional Uses

- fish
- game and rich foods (as juniper is used)
- salad dressings

Spice Blends

- some peppermill blends (not recommended)

What's in a Name?

Being "in the pink" refers to two completely different spices when it comes to pink peppercorns. True pink pepper is the ripe peppercorn of the *Piper nigrum* vine (page 492), native to South India, while the other so-called pink peppercorn is a berry from the *Schinus terebinthifolius* tree. Although they are both called "pink peppercorns," I will refer to the Indian vine pepper as "true pink pepper" and the pink pepper in this listing as "pink *Schinus* pepper."

The Plant

The source of peppercorns is a cause of much confusion in my native Australia. Many of us grow up with a "pepper tree" providing shade in the schoolyard, the garden at home or parklands. It is not uncommon to see pepper trees lining the banks of small creeks and in paddocks with cattle huddled underneath, seeking some respite from the blazing sun in rural and outback areas. So it's easy to understand the common Australian assumption that pepper comes from the pepper tree. True pepper actually comes from the vine *Piper nigrum*, which produces the genuine black, white, green and pink peppercorns of commerce (see sidebar, left).

However, several plants produce what might be described as pseudo-pepper. Two varieties of *Schinus* tree bear small red berries that are often sold as pink peppercorns. The variety most often grown for culinary purposes is *S. terebinthifolius*, a dense, short tree with glossy oval leaves that look like bay leaves. The tiny flowers are white and the fruits are borne in thick, upright bunches of relatively large berries that ripen to deep pink or scarlet. *S. terebinthifolius* berries, when dried, are up to $1/4$ inch (5 mm) in diameter. They have a pale to bright pink friable outer husk that has little aroma or flavor; it contains a small ($1/8$ inch/3 mm in diameter), hard, irregular dark brown seed. The seed,

Tummy Problems?

Pink peppercorns became fashionable (more for their appearance than their flavor) to add to clear glass or plastic peppermills along with black, white and green dried peppercorns. In the 1980s some articles linked overconsumption of this type of pink pepper with gastrointestinal problems. Extensive analysis revealed that pink peppercorns were no more toxic than other types of pepper. Some authorities do, however, advise against using *S. ariera* berries, as their toxicity is believed to be greater than that of *S. terebinthifolius* and may have a negative effect on people with intestinal problems.

when crushed, releases a sweet, volatile pine-like aroma that smells faintly like piperine oil, the key component in true black pepper. The flavor burst is similarly sweet, warm, fresh and camphorous, with a lingering astringency but little heat.

Other Varieties

Pepper trees (*Schinus areira, S. molle*), commonly seen in Australia, grow 23 to 66 feet (7 to 20 m) tall, depending on the water supply. They have drooping, frond-like leaves and small yellowish flowers and bear long catkins of berries. The berries are first green, then turn yellow and ripen in chains of rosy pink peppercorns.

Processing

S. terebinthifolius berries are either preserved in brine or dried by harvesting the catkins of berries, threshing to remove them from the stalks and then drying them in the sun. Berries dried in the shade, however, retain a higher degree of color and are more desirable.

Buying and Storage

When buying pink peppercorns in brine it is difficult to identify which species you are purchasing. True pink pepper from the *Piper nigrum* vine is always preserved in brine to prevent activation of the enzyme that turns pink peppercorns black. Ideally the bottle should be labeled "*S. terebinthifolius*" or "*Piper nigrum*" to indicate which species of pink peppercorn it contains. It's a sad indictment of the spice industry that traders usually opt for providing consumers with less rather than more information, using the excuse that it is not wise to confuse people with too many facts.

I recommend buying *Schinus* pepper only in its dried form; that way you can smell it and know what you are being sold. Store dried pink peppercorns in the usual manner, in an airtight container away from extremes of heat, light and humidity. Under these conditions, pink *Schinus* peppercorns will keep their flavor for up to 3 years. As different processors may use a variety of brining methods, always take note of the storage and use-by directions on the jar label.

Use

Schinus pepper is used in many fish recipes in the Mediterranean region. The refreshing, pine-like flavor also complements game and other rich foods, much as juniper berries do. The gel on top of many pâtés often contains pink *Schinus* peppercorns. They are not there only for visual effect—their pine-like, palate-cleansing flavor is a perfect balance for the richness of pâté. Although they may look pretty in a clear peppermill, the friable outer husks tend to clog the mechanism. If you need to grind *Schinus* peppercorns, it is best done using a mortar and pestle.

Brined pink peppercorns, being softer than dried ones, are handy in salad dressings and applications where they won't be cooked. They should be rinsed to reduce saltiness and strained before use.

WEIGHT PER TEASPOON (5 mL)
- whole dried: 1.8 g
- whole brined: 3.5 g

SUGGESTED QUANTITY PER POUND (500 g)
- red meats: 2 tsp (10 mL) whole
- white meats: 1½ tsp (7 mL) whole
- vegetables: 1 tsp (5 mL) whole
- grains and pulses: 1 tsp (5 mL) whole
- baked goods: ¾ tsp (3 mL) whole

Pink Peppercorn Pork Rillette

This is delicious, and though time-consuming, it's very easy to make. Rillettes are a French staple similar to pâté, served at room temperature with toast or crusty bread. I make this every Christmas to have on hand when friends drop by. As well as looking very pretty, the pink peppercorns cut through the richness of the pork wonderfully.

Makes 1½ to 2 cups (375 to 500 mL)

Preparation time: 8 hours

Cooking time: 5 to 6 hours

Tips

Use a mortar and pestle or the back of a spoon to lightly crush the peppercorns.

Pork belly is very fatty, so you will be discarding a lot of fat after cooking—hence the large quantity of meat called for in this recipe.

The amount of oil required will depend upon the size of your cooking vessel.

• **4 small ramekins**

MARINADE

2	shallots, chopped	2
2	cloves garlic, crushed	2
2	slices lemon	2
2 tbsp	olive oil	30 mL
1 tbsp	fine sea salt	15 mL
2 tsp	pink *Schinus* peppercorns	10 mL
½ tsp	juniper berries	2 mL

PORK

2 lbs	pork belly, cut into 2 or 3 pieces	1 kg
2 to 4 cups	olive oil (see Tips, left)	500 ml to 1 L
1 tbsp	dried pink *Schinus* peppercorns, lightly crushed (see Tips, left)	15 mL

1. In a large resealable plastic bag, combine, shallots, garlic, lemon, oil, salt, whole peppercorns and juniper berries; seal and shake well. Add pork belly, seal and set aside in the refrigerator for at least 1 day (not more than 2 days).

2. Preheat oven to 225°F (110°C).

3. Remove pork from marinade and brush off spices (discard marinade). Transfer meat to a Dutch oven or deep baking dish, fat side up. Pour olive oil over pork until fully immersed. Cover with lid (or foil, if using a baking dish) and roast for 4 to 5 hours, until meat is tender and falling apart. Remove from oven and set aside to cool.

4. When pork is cool enough to handle, remove from oil (reserve oil). Using your hands, remove and discard the fat. Using a sharp knife, roughly chop pork and transfer to a bowl. Add crushed peppercorns and 3 to 4 tbsp (45 to 60 mL) reserved cooking oil. Mash with a fork to bind the meat (add more oil if needed). To serve, push the rillette mixture firmly into ramekins. Garnish with a few lightly crushed pink peppercorns. The rillettes will keep, covered, in the refrigerator for up to 1 week. Bring to room temperature before serving.

Pepper – Selim

Xylopia aethiopica

Names in Other Languages

- **Arabic:** fulful as-Sudan, hab az-Zelim
- **Dutch:** granen van Selim
- **French:** grains de Selim, poivre du Sénégal
- **German:** Selimskorner, Negerpfeffer
- **Greek:** afrikaniko piperi
- **Hungarian:** arabbors
- **Polish:** pieprz murzynski
- **Portuguese:** pimenta-da-áfrica
- **Russian:** kumba perets

Family: Annonaceae

Varieties: burro pepper (*X. aromatica*)

Other Names: African pepper, Ethiopian pepper, grains of Selim, Guinea pepper, kimba pepper, negro pepper, Senegal pepper, West African peppertree

Flavor Group: Hot

Parts Used: seedpod (as a spice)

Background

Because both are native to West Africa, Selim pepper is often confused with grains of paradise. It too has been used as a pepper adulterant, as have cubeb peppers. This practice was common around the 16th century, when cheaper substitutes for black pepper were sought during periods of short supply and/or high prices for *Piper nigrum*. In an odd twist of fate, Selim pepper, once despised as an adulterant, is now highly sought after for its rarity, and when available it is far more expensive than black pepper.

Culinary Information

Combines with
- allspice
- bay leaf
- cardamom
- chile
- cinnamon and cassia
- cloves
- coriander seed
- cumin
- garlic
- ginger
- star anise
- tamarind
- turmeric

Traditional Uses
- African dishes (in the same way as black pepper)
- Nigerian stews
- game
- slow-cooked casseroles

Spice Blends
This spice is so rare it is not generally added to spice blends; however, it has been included in
- ras el hanout
- mélanges of pepper

The Plant

Selim pepper, or "grains of Selim," as it is often called, is composed of small seeds about the size of a peppercorn. They are contained within a horn-shaped pod that ranges from 1 inch (2.5 cm) to 2 inches (5 cm) long, with a knobbly appearance like a small broad-bean pod. The tree that the pods grow on is known as the West African peppertree. It is a straggly tree about 24 inches (60 cm) in diameter and up to 65 feet (20 m) tall, with a straight, narrow trunk. It is indigenous to the humid forest zones of West Africa and has many uses beyond its culinary applications. For instance, the highly aromatic roots of the tree are included in West African tinctures taken to expel worms and other parasites from the intestines.

Other Varieties
Burro pepper (*Xylopia aromatica*) is found in South America and used by the indigenous people of Brazil. It is similar to Selim pepper and is not to be confused with the *Schinus* pepper trees that are also native to Brazil.

Processing

The pods containing the seeds grow in clusters and are harvested and dried, usually in the sun but sometimes over a fire, which lends a smoky flavor to the pods and seeds within.

Buying and Storage

Selim pepper is quite rare, and its procurement is made harder by import restrictions in a number of countries. It is generally sold in the whole pod form. When stored in an airtight container, it will keep its flavor for at least 3 years.

Use

Selim pepper is generally used in the same way as black pepper, Sichuan pepper (see page 486) or grains of paradise (see page 313). Like Sichuan pepper, most of the camphor-like, numbing medicinal flavor is in the pod itself, and the seeds actually have very little flavor by comparison. For this reason the whole or ground pod is most commonly added to cooking to get the most out of its taste. Grinding is best done using a mortar and pestle. Discard the stringy fibers that remain after grinding, and add only the residual fine powder to food. In southern Nigeria the dried seedpods add spice to the local fried meat stew, *obe ata*, and a goat's-head soup called *isi-ewu*. Although Selim pepper tastes like a mentholated skin ointment on its own, when combined with rich, gamey or very fatty ingredients, it has the effect of cutting their cloying flavors.

WEIGHT PER TEASPOON (5 mL)

- whole seeds: 3 g

SUGGESTED QUANTITY PER POUND (500 g)

- **red meats:** 1 tsp (5 mL) ground pods
- **white meats:** ¾ tsp (3 mL) ground pods
- **vegetables:** ½ tsp (2 mL) ground pods
- **grains and pulses:** ½ tsp (2 mL) ground pods
- **baked goods:** ½ tsp (2 mL) ground pods

Buka Stew

This Nigerian stew traditionally contains various types of meat, including offal. It has a strong, peppery flavor and a big hit of chile. This version doesn't contain offal, but it can be included in the total weight of meat, if desired (see Tips, below). The hard-boiled eggs are not often seen in more familiar renditions; however, they make this African meal more sustaining.

Makes
4 servings

Preparation time:
15 minutes

Cooking time: 1 hour

- - - - - - - - - - - - - - - -

Tips

To hard-boil eggs: Place in a saucepan in a single layer and cover by at least ½ inch (1 cm) of water. Bring water to a soft boil over medium heat. Reduce heat and simmer for 6 minutes. Remove from heat and rinse eggs under cold running water to stop cooking. For best results, use eggs that are 1 to 2 weeks old.

Beef offal such as heart, liver, tongue or tripe can be used.

- **Mortar and pestle**
- **Blender**

1 tsp	Selim pepper pods	5 mL
10	medium ripe tomatoes, roughly chopped	10
2	red bell peppers, seeded and chopped	2
1	Scotch bonnet chile, chopped	1
2	medium onions, chopped, divided	2
¼ cup	oil	60 mL
1 lb	stewing beef, cut into 2-inch (5 cm) pieces	500 g
1	large clove garlic, minced	1
1 cup	beef broth	250 mL
4	eggs, hard-boiled and peeled (see Tips, left)	4
	Sea salt	

1. Using mortar and pestle, grind Selim pepper into a coarse powder. Set aside.

2. In blender at medium speed, purée tomatoes, bell peppers, chile and half the onion. Add ground Selim pepper and pulse to incorporate. Set aside.

3. In a heavy-bottomed saucepan or Dutch oven over medium heat, heat oil. Add beef (in batches if necessary) and cook for 8 to 10 minutes, until brown on all sides. Transfer cooked beef to a plate and set aside.

4. In same pan over medium heat, cook garlic and remaining onion for 2 minutes, until browned. Add puréed tomato mixture and cook, stirring constantly, for 2 minutes, until combined and thickening. Add reserved beef and broth and bring to a boil. Reduce heat and simmer until meat is tender, about 45 minutes. Add whole hard-boiled eggs and season with salt to taste.

P

Pepper – Sichuan

Zanthoxylum simulans (also known as *Z. bungeanum*)

Names in Other Languages

- **Bhutan:** thingey
- **Chinese (C):** chi faa jiu
- **Chinese (M):** hua jiao
- **Czech:** pepr secuansky
- **Danish:** Sechuan peber
- **Dutch:** Sechuan peper
- **Finnish:** Setsuanin pippuri
- **French:** poivre anise, poivre de Sichuan
- **German:** Anisepfeffer, Szechuan-pfeffer
- **Hungarian:** anizbors, szecsuani bors
- **Indian:** tirphal
- **Indonesian:** andaliman (ripe), mandalling (unripe)
- **Italian:** pepe d'anice
- **Japanese:** kinome (fresh leaf), sansho (dry powdered leaf)
- **Nepalese:** timbur
- **Russian:** Sychuanskij perets
- **Spanish:** pepe di anis
- **Swedish:** sezchuanpeppar
- **Thai:** ma lar
- **Vietnamese:** dang cay

Family: Rutaceae

Varieties: Japanese pepper tree (*Z. piperitum*), northern prickly ash (*Z. americanum),* winged prickly ash (*Z. alatum*, also known as *Z. planispinum*), fagara (*Z. schinifolium*)

Other Names: anise pepper, Chinese pepper, fagara, Japanese pepper tree, prickly ash, sansho (leaves); Sichwan pepper, Szechwan pepper, tirphal (berries)

Flavor Group: Hot

Parts Used: berries (as a spice), leaves (as a herb)

Background

Native to Sichuan, the southwestern province of China that borders on Tibet, Sichuan pepper is thought to have come into culinary use during the first millennium BCE, as a result of Indian cultural influences. Prickly ash trees of the *Zanthoxylum* species are found in China, Bhutan, Korea and Japan. The Japanese make mortars and pestles from the wood of prickly ash trees, claiming that it imparts a distinctive but mild flavor to the food being pounded. North American native peoples employed the bark of a different variety (*Z. americanum*) as a general stimulant and a panacea for toothache; hence *Z. americanum* is referred to as "toothache tree."

Culinary Information

Combines with

- allspice
- bay leaf
- chile
- coriander seed
- fennel (fronds and seed)
- ginger
- juniper
- paprika
- parsley
- pepper
- rosemary
- sage
- star anise
- tarragon
- thyme

Traditional Uses

- rich and fatty foods such as pork and duck
- Peking duck
- salt-and-pepper squid
- dry-roasted with salt as a condiment

Spice Blends

- Chinese master stocks
- Chinese five-spice powder
- salt-and-pepper squid spice mix
- shichimi-togarashi

The Plant

Not to be confused with vine pepper, Sichuan pepper is the dried berries of a number of *Zanthoxylum* trees, commonly called "prickly ash," that belong to the Rutaceae family. Most varieties are small deciduous trees that grow to an average height of 10 feet (3 m) and have sharp spiny prickles on the stem and branches. The one called Sichuan pepper has 12-inch (30 cm) long leaf clusters divided into 5 to 11 oval leaflets resembling small bay leaves. In late spring, small greenish yellow flowers appear before the leaves. These are followed by spherical red berries up to $1/4$ inch (5 mm) in diameter. When dried, the berries split to reveal a tiny black seed that is particularly gritty when crushed. The split berries look somewhat like one seed section of a star anise. One theory is that this likeness led to the often-used name "anise pepper" for this spice.

The aroma of Sichuan pepper is warm, peppery and fragrant, with citrus notes. When crushed it smells of lavender flowers. Its flavor is similarly pepper-like and tangy and leaves a lingering numbing, fizzy sensation on the tongue. The leaves are powdered and used in Japanese cooking as *sansho*.

P

Travels in the Spice Trade

I have had two interesting experiences with these powerful little pepper-like pods. The first was during a trip to Bhutan, visiting the remote town of Damphu. After observing the harvesting of brown cardamom pods, I spied a Sichuan pepper tree covered in ripe red berries that were ready to be harvested. Wondering what these tasted like fresh, and being foolishly curious, I picked one and chewed on it. It was an alarming experience. After about 30 seconds the heat just kept building up in my mouth. Remembering that sugar is one of the best antidotes to an overdose of chile, Liz handed me a packet of cough drops, which I chewed rapidly. The panacea worked, but be warned: make sure you taste plants carefully the first time!

My second experience was during a cooking demonstration by Indonesian chef William Wongso in Ubud, Bali. Until then I had seen only dried Sichuan pepper used in cooking. However, William added fresh berries, complete with seeds, to his dish, which created even more intense heat on the palate. In North Sumatra they call these fresh berries *mandalling*. The taste is intense and numbing. I recommend removing the seeds from the fresh berries; in my opinion, they lend a grittiness to food that Western palates would not find pleasing.

Other Varieties

The **Japanese pepper tree** (*Zanthoxylum piperitum*, also known as *Fagara piperita*) is a deciduous shrub slightly smaller than the Sichuan pepper tree. Like all of the *Zanthoxylum* plants, the flowers may be either male or female; however, only one sex will be found on an individual tree. The seedpod has the same characteristic flavor and numbing heat as the other varieties.

Northern prickly ash (*Z. americanum*) grows on the east coast of North America from Quebec to Florida. It was used by native peoples for its numbing quality, a bit like cloves with a hot bite, when chewed. **Winged prickly ash** (*Z. alatum*, also known as *Z. planispinum*) is a more densely foliaged shrub found in Japan, China and Korea. It is used in cooking in the same way as the other *Zanthoxylum* plants. **Fagara** (*Z. schinifolium*) is also from Japan, China, Korea and other parts of East Asia and is found as far north as Bhutan. Its appearance is similar to that of other *Zanthoxylum* plants.

Processing

Sichuan pepper berries are harvested by hand when ripe and dried in the sun, where they turn from bright red to reddish brown. During drying they split open to reveal the tiny black seed inside. Cleaning (by sieving and winnowing) removes many of the seeds, sticks and sharp thorns from the seedpod.

Sichuan pepper (with seeds)

The leaves are harvested when firm and are dried away from direct light in a warm, dry environment before being powdered for packaging as sansho. As the demand for sansho is quite low in China and other countries where these trees grow, the leaves are often not harvested.

Buying and Storage

Although ground Sichuan pepper may be purchased from specialty spice retailers, to retain the greatest amount of flavor it is better to buy the whole split berries and crush them yourself just before cooking. Before crushing or grinding, take care to remove the small black inner seeds; they have little flavor and will contribute an unpleasant gritty texture when powdered. Prickly pieces of stem and sharp, rose-like thorns are often found, even among good-quality whole Sichuan pepper, because they are difficult to remove with machinery. Therefore, always pick through them and throw out the nasty bits before adding to a dish.

Sansho (the powdered leaf), most often harvested from *Z. simulans*, is available in stores that specialize in Japanese ingredients. It is usually packed in small airtight foil pouches. Buy only a small quantity at a time, as the color and flavor dissipate shortly after opening. I have found that ground native Australian lemon myrtle leaves (see page 355) are an acceptable alternative for sansho; substitute about half the amount of lemon myrtle powder for the quantity of sansho called for in the recipe.

Store both Sichuan pepper and sansho in airtight containers away from extremes of heat, light and humidity. Under these conditions, whole Sichuan pepper will keep its flavor for up to 3 years, and if ground, about 1 year. Sansho powder will keep for about 1 year.

Use

Sichuan pepper was traditionally found in Chinese five-spice blends, but because of its intensity of heat, relatively high cost and (often) the difficulty of sourcing clean, well-ground, non-gritty powder, true pepper (*Piper nigrum*) is usually used. The tangy, sharp flavor of this spice makes it an ideal accompaniment to rich and fatty foods such as pork and roast duck. Peking duck, served with rich, dark, salty sauces and wrapped in paper-thin pancakes, gets much of its unique flavor from Sichuan pepper.

Dry-roasting the split pods enhances their taste. A friend of ours likes to roast Sichuan pepper when it is ground and mixed with salt. It can then be rubbed onto quail and other game prior to roasting, or placed on the table as a condiment in which to dip crisp chicken wings and other delicacies. Salt-and-pepper squid has become a popular Asian restaurant item in recent years; its distinctive flavor is achieved by blending black pepper, Sichuan pepper, chile and salt in equal proportions.

In Japan, Sichuan pepper is an ingredient in the spice blend shichimi-togarashi, along with salt, black sesame seeds and MSG. Sansho is used to season noodle dishes and spicy soups, while the fresh leaves, known there as *kinome*, flavor vegetables such as bamboo shoots and are a garnish for soups.

Sichuan pepper goes well with star anise and ginger, and a small quantity (say, less than one-quarter by volume) adds extra tang to a blend of black, white and green peppercorns (*P. nigrum*) that can be rubbed on meats before cooking.

WEIGHT PER TEASPOON (5 mL)
- whole: 1.8 g
- ground: 2.5 g

SUGGESTED QUANTITY PER POUND (500 g)
- **red meats:** 2 tsp (10 mL) whole
- **white meats:** 1½ tsp (7 mL) whole
- **vegetables:** 1 tsp (5 mL) whole
- **grains and pulses:** 1 tsp (5 mL) whole
- **baked goods:** ¾ tsp (3 mL) whole

Salt-and-Pepper Squid

There must be thousands of versions of spicy fried squid (calamari) out there. To me, Sichuan pepper is a key ingredient that is often left out. It creates a little "fizz" on the tongue, which complements the bang of the chile and the heat from the other peppers. This dish is a crowd-pleaser, guaranteed to quickly disappear.

Makes 6 side servings

Preparation time:
15 minutes

Cooking time: 5 minutes

- - - - - - - - - - - - - - - -

Tip

To clean squid: Gently pull head and tentacles away from the body. Reach into the body and pull out the clear backbone (quill); discard entrails. Using a sharp knife, cut the tentacles from the head just below the eyes; discard head. Cut off side wings and fine membrane. Thoroughly rinse body, tentacles and wings under cold running water and pat dry. On a clean work surface, lay each squid tube flat and cut horizontally along one side so you can open it up and lay it flat. Scrape out any excess slime, rinse under cold running water and pat dry. Make diagonal cuts ¼ inch (5 mm) apart across the flesh, being careful not to cut through. Repeat in the opposite direction. Slice squid into horizontal strips, then into 4-inch (10 cm) lengths.

• **Mortar and pestle**

1 tsp	Sichuan peppercorns	5 mL
1 tsp	white peppercorns	5 mL
1 tsp	black peppercorns	5 mL
1 tsp	ground medium-hot chile, such as Kashmiri	5 mL
4 tsp	fine sea salt	20 mL
2 tsp	garlic powder	10 mL
½ cup	rice flour or cornstarch	125 mL
6 to 8 cups	oil	1.5 to 2 L
1	bunch green onions, white part only, finely sliced	1
1	long red finger chile, sliced	1
1½ lbs	squid, cleaned and sliced into 4-inch (10 cm) lengths (see Tip, left)	750 g
1	lime, cut into wedges	1
¼ cup	roughly chopped coriander (cilantro) leaves	60 mL

1. Using mortar and pestle, combine Sichuan, white and black peppercorns, ground chile, salt and garlic powder; grind until fine. Transfer mixture to a small bowl. Add rice flour and mix well. Set aside.

2. In a wok or deep skillet over medium heat, heat oil until just rippling. Add green onions and sliced chile and cook for 2 to 3 minutes or until beginning to turn golden. Using a slotted spoon, transfer to a plate lined with paper towels.

3. Working in batches, toss squid in seasoned flour to coat generously, shake off excess and drop into hot oil. Cook for 2 minutes, stirring often, until golden and crisp (the squid pieces will curl up, so keep them moving to ensure they cook through). Using a slotted spoon, transfer cooked squid to a plate lined with paper towels.

4. To serve, arrange squid on a serving plate with lime wedges. Scatter with fried chile and green onions and coriander leaves.

P

Pepper – Vine

Piper nigrum

Names in Other Languages

Vine Pepper

- **Arabic:** fulful, fulful aswad (black), fulful abyad (white), fulful akhdar (green)
- **Burmese:** nga-youk-kaun
- **Chinese (C):** wuh jiu, hak wuh jiu (black), baahk wuh jiu (white)
- **Chinese (M):** hua jiao, hei hua jiao (black), bai hua jiao (white)
- **Czech:** pepr, cerny pepr (black), bily pepr (white), zeleny pepr
- **Danish:** peber, sort peber (black), hvid peber (white)
- **Dutch:** peper, zwarte peper (black), witte peper (white)
- **Filipino:** paminta
- **Finnish:** pippuri, mustapippuri (black), valkopippuri (white), viherpippuri (green)
- **French:** poivre, poivre noir (black), poivre blanc (white), poivre vert (green)
- **German:** Pfeffer, schwarzer Pfeffer (black), weiber Pfeffer (white), grüner Pfeffer (green)
- **Hungarian:** bors, feketebors (black), feherbors (white), zoldbors (green)
- **Indian:** kali mirich, gol mirch, gulki, kali mirch (black)

Family: Piperaceae

Varieties: black, white, green, true pink pepper (*Piper nigrum*); cubeb or "tailed" pepper (*P. cubeba*); Indian long pepper (*P. longum*); Indonesian long pepper (*P. retrofractum*); betel leaf (*P. betle*); Mexican pepperleaf (*P. sanctum*); kava (*P. methysticum*); Australian pepper vine (*P. rothianum*, also known as *P. novae-hollandiae*); sa khan (*P. boehmeriafolium*)

Other Names: black pepper, white pepper, green pepper, pink pepper, mignonette pepper, shot pepper

Flavor Group: Hot

Parts Used: berries (as a spice), leaves (as a herb)

Background

Pepper (*Piper nigrum*) is acknowledged as the "king of spices," and its history is almost the history of the spice trade. Over the centuries, no individual spice has had such far-reaching effects on commerce, voyages of discovery, cultures and cuisines as pepper. Native to the Western Ghats of southern India, pepper is referred to in early Sanskrit writings dating back to 1000 BCE. *Pippali* was the Sanskrit word used to describe long pepper (*P. longum*), and it is the name from which the Greek word *peperi*, the Latin *piper* and English *pepper* are derived.

Culinary Information

Combines with

Nearly all culinary herbs and spices, but has a special affinity with

- allspice
- basil
- caraway
- cardamom
- chile
- cinnamon
- cloves
- coriander seed
- cumin
- curry leaf
- fennel seed
- fenugreek (leaf and seed)
- garlic
- ginger
- oregano
- paprika
- parsley
- rosemary
- sage
- savory
- thyme
- turmeric

Traditional Uses

- all savory foods, whether included in cooking or added at the table

Black
- red meats
- game
- strongly flavored seafood
- egg dishes (used in moderation)

White
- sauces
- charcuterie
- soups and casseroles
- Asian stir-fries and curries

Green
- red meats
- poultry
- game
- pork and duck
- pâtés
- terrines
- white sauces

True Pink
- salad dressings
- seafood and poultry
- terrines
- pâtés
- white sauces

Spice Blends

- peppermill blends
- curry powders
- baharat
- berbere
- stuffing mixes
- barbecue spice blends
- Chinese master stocks
- Jamaican jerk spice
- garam masala
- Chinese five-spice powder
- ras el hanout
- Cajun spices
- pickling spices

In the fourth century BCE, Theophrastus described both long pepper and black pepper. In the first century CE Pliny mentioned long pepper, which was known in ancient Greece and Rome before black pepper and was considered to be superior. Around this time Dioscorides referred to white pepper and the belief that it was produced from a different plant than black pepper. Sometime between 100 BCE and

Names in Other Languages

Vine Pepper (continued)

- **Indonesian:** merica, merica hitam (black), merica putih (white), merica hijau (green)
- **Italian:** pepe, pepe nero (black), pepe bianco (white), pepe verde (green)
- **Japanese:** kosho, peppa, burakku-peppa (black)
- **Laotian:** phik noi
- **Malay:** lada, biji lada, lada hitam (black), lada putih (white), lada hijau (green)
- **Portuguese:** pimenta, pimenta-negra (black), pimenta-branca (white), pimenta-verde (green)
- **Russian:** perets, chyornyj perets (black), belyj perets (white), zelyonyj perets (green)
- **Spanish:** pimienta, pimienta negra (black), pimienta blanca (white)
- **Sri Lankan:** gammiris
- **Swedish:** peppar, svartpeppar (black), vitpeppar (white), gronpeppar (green)
- **Thai:** prik thai
- **Turkish:** biber, kara biber (black), beyaz biber (white), yesil biber (green)
- **Vietnamese:** cay tieu, hat-tieu, tieu den (black), tieu trang (white)

600 CE, Hindu colonists took pepper to the Indonesian archipelago. Long pepper and white pepper attracted a customs duty at the port of Alexandria in 176 CE; however, for what are believed to be political reasons, black pepper—the more popular type used by the common citizen—was spared the tax.

Pepper was one of the earliest articles of commerce between Asia and Europe. In their heyday, the ports of Alexandria, Genoa and Venice owed their prosperity to the trade in spices in general and pepper in particular. The search for pepper and faster and safer ways to bring this "black gold" back to Europe prompted the great voyages of discovery, such as Vasco da Gama's voyage in 1498, when he landed on India's Malabar Coast.

By the Middle Ages, pepper was as valuable a commodity as currency, and many landlords, having perhaps little confidence in the coin of the realm, would demand that their tenants pay their rent in peppercorns. Thus the term

Names in Other Languages

Long Pepper

- **Chinese (C):** bat but, cheung jiu
- **Chinese (M):** bi bo, chang jiao
- **Czech:** pepr dlouhy
- **Dutch:** langwerpige peper
- **French:** poivre long
- **German:** langer Pfeffer
- **Greek:** makropiperi
- **Indian:** krishna, pippal, pipar, pippli
- **Indonesian:** cabe bali
- **Italian:** pepe lungo
- **Japanese:** indonaga-kosho
- **Malay:** bakek
- **Russian:** clinnyj perets
- **Spanish:** pimienta largo
- **Swedish:** langpeppar
- **Thai:** dok dipli
- **Turkish:** uzun biber
- **Vietnamese:** tat bat

"peppercorn rent" was coined (in those days it meant quite the opposite of the modern meaning of a very cheap lease). In England at the end of the 10th century, the statutes of Ethelred required "Easterlings"—Germans from the Baltic and Hanseatic towns who traded spices and other Eastern goods in England—to pay a tribute that included 10 pounds (5 kg) of pepper for the privilege of trading with London merchants. It has been suggested that the word *sterling* is derived from "Easterling." Under the reign of Henry II, in 1180, the Pepperers' Guild was formed in London. This was subsequently incorporated into the Spicers' Guild, which in 1429 became the Grocers' Company.

When Constantinople fell to the Turks in 1453, the need for a sea route to Asia via the west became more urgent when the Muslim rulers imposed high duties on the spice trade. This was a key factor in the decision to fund Columbus's voyage to the Spice Islands. His crew was so preoccupied with pepper that when the allspice berry (page 61) was discovered, it was incorrectly named "Jamaica pepper" or *pimienta*, which is the Spanish word for pepper.

A different variety of vine pepper, *P. cubeba*, was never as valuable, because of its pine-like taste and weaker flavor. The East Indians named this variety *cubeb* or "tailed" pepper because of a small spike attached to it. The Arabs recognized this variety as originating from Java as early as the 10th century. The popularity of cubeb pepper has waxed and waned over the centuries. In the 13th century it was popular in Europe as a condiment and for its medicinal qualities, but by the 17th century cubebs were rarely seen. At times when pepper prices were high in the 20th century, if cubebs were available at a low enough cost they were used to adulterate true pepper. This caused the variety to fall into disrepute; it was even banned by some authorities as an admixture to pepper.

Over the centuries the pepper trade waxed and waned much as the nutmeg and clove trades did. Control of the various sources of supply of pepper shifted between the Portuguese and the Dutch. By the time the English were dominant, the value of pepper was considerably less and the trade was not nearly as profitable as it had been for many centuries. In the 18th century the Dutch East India Company collapsed. Entrepreneurial traders with fast schooners turned the ports of Salem and Boston in the United States into key players in the pepper market, a status that endured well into the 20th century.

Names in Other Languages

Cubeb Pepper

- **Arabic:** kabaaba
- **Chinese (M):** bi ji
- **Czech:** pepr cubeba
- **Dutch:** cubebepeper
- **French:** cubebe, poivre de Java
- **German:** Kubebenpfeffer
- **Greek:** koubeba
- **Hungarian:** javai bors
- **Indian:** kabab-chini
- **Indonesian:** tjabe djawa
- **Italian:** cubebe
- **Japanese:** kubeba
- **Malay:** chabai ekur
- **Portuguese:** cubeba
- **Russian:** dikij perets, kubeba
- **Spanish:** cubebe
- **Thai:** prik hang
- **Turkish:** hint biberi tohomu, kubabe
- **Vietnamese:** tieu that

The Plant

Peppercorns are the fruits of a tropical perennial climbing vine that can reach over 33 feet (10 m) in height. There are more than 1,000 species in the Piperaceae family; however, the most important are those that provide peppercorns, cubeb pepper and long pepper (both Indian and Javanese). Pepper vines are an attractive sight in their native southern India; in the Western Ghats (*ghat* is an Indian word meaning "step") of Kerala they are trellised on palm trees (sometimes eucalyptus) in what the locals charmingly call "spice gardens" rather than plantations. The pepper vine is not a parasite—the living tree simply provides an accessible trellis and its canopy of foliage provides shade for the vine and the pickers during harvesting. In some countries, such as Malaysia and Cambodia, pepper vines are grown on poles or accessible trellises.

A pepper vine has dark green oval leaves that are shiny on top and pale on the underside. The leaf size varies by type but tends to average about 7 inches (18 cm) long and 5 inches (12 cm) wide. The minute flowers are borne on catkins 1 to 6 inches (3 to 15 cm) long that hang among the foliage; these cylindrical flower clusters turn into peppercorns after pollination. Pollination of the hermaphroditic flowers—a genetic characteristic of the most commonly cultivated varieties—is assisted by rain, which increases the efficiency of pollen distribution as water flows down the flower cluster. The fruits (peppercorns) form in densely packed spikes 2 to 6 inches (5 to 15 cm) long and more than $1/2$ inch (1 cm) wide at the thickest part of the spike, near the top, tapering to $1/4$ inch (5 mm) or less at the bottom tip. Each spike may produce 50 or more single-seeded fruits, which when fully formed are deep green. The peppercorns then ripen from their green state to yellow and finally to a bright reddish pink when completely ripe. One can always determine the quality of the monsoon by looking at a spike of peppercorns. If the spike has an abundance of fruits, it was a good monsoon. If the clusters are sparse, as if some are missing, it was a poor monsoon that did not facilitate optimum fertilization of the flowers.

Green unripe peppercorns have a fresh, hot bite to them. Even when correctly dried they will yield a more subtle flavor than black, white or true pink peppercorns. Black peppercorns, with their dark brown to jet-black wrinkled skins, are the dried green fruit of *Piper nigrum*. They are

Travels in the Spice Trade

Every time I visit St. Francis Church in Cochin (now known as Kochi), on India's Malabar Coast, which houses the tomb of Vasco da Gama, I imagine what the city's harbor must have looked and smelled like in those frenetic, dizzying days when the spice trade was at its zenith. One place I love to visit is the International Pepper Exchange in Mattancherry, the district in Cochin that is also home to the historic Jewish synagogue, with its amazing display of hand-painted blue Chinese tiles so atmospherically described by Salman Rushdie in his book *The Moor's Last Sigh*. Entry to the Pepper Exchange, just around the corner from the synagogue, is by invitation only, which can usually be arranged for those of us in the spice trade.

The Cochin Pepper Exchange works just like a stock exchange, with speculators, hedgers, futures and all the bourse jargon. The experience is made truly exciting by the traditional "open outcry" system of trading. In what sounds and looks like chaos, all the buyers and sellers shout their contracts and bids in Malayalam (the local language of Kerala) with the cacophony and fury of warriors in battle. Amid the hubbub, they manage to keep in contact with their clients in New York, Rotterdam, London and Singapore—phone receiver in one hand while gesticulating furiously with the other to punctuate their cries. In 1999, when I last visited, computers had been installed, so I thought the melee of traders would have become a thing of the past. However, I am happy to report that in spite of modern technology, the bombastic pepper traders of Cochin still shatter the peaceful afternoon air with their "open outcry" bids and contracts.

A Popular Blend

"Mignonette pepper" and "shot pepper" are terms used to describe a coarsely ground blend of black and white peppercorns that has become popular in France.

by far the most popular form of pepper. Black peppercorns have a warm, oily, penetrating aroma and full-bodied, pungent flavor and lingering heat. White peppercorns are creamy white in color and absolutely smooth on the surface. These are the "heart" of the fruit from which the oil-bearing outer skin (pericarp) has been removed. This makes them less aromatic but hotter and sharper in taste. True pink peppercorns (which differ from those of the *Schinus* pepper tree, page 477) are the fully ripe fruits of *P. nigrum*. They have an almost sweet, ripe, berry-like fruity flavor and appetizing late pepper heat.

Other Varieties

Cubeb or "tailed" pepper (*Piper cubeba*) comes from a tropical climbing vine native to Indonesia. Cubebs are dried until black and are similar in appearance to black peppercorns, except for the $1/8$- to $1/3$-inch (3 to 8 mm) stalk protruding from one end—it looks like a spherical cartoon bomb with its fuse. Cubeb pepper has a small seed suspended inside but does not contain a white core like *P. nigrum*. The aroma is fresh, peppery, piney and citrus-like, while the flavor is distinctly pine-like, hot and pungent.

Indian long pepper (*P. longum*) and **Indonesian long pepper** (*P. retrofractum*) come from slender climbing vines that have sparser-looking foliage than *P. nigrum*. The most noticeable difference between the two is that the fruits of Indian long pepper are smaller and less pungent than those of Indonesian (Javanese) long pepper. Long pepper is so called because the fruits are long cylindrical spikes $^1/_4$ inch (5 mm) in diameter and 1 to $1^1/_2$ inches (2.5 to 4 cm) in length. Each dark brown to black, rough-surfaced spike resembles a male pine flower catkin; when viewed in cross-section, it reveals a cartwheel of up to eight minute dark red seeds. Long pepper has an extremely sweet, fragrant aroma like a cross between incense and orris root powder. The flavor is bitingly hot, lingering and numbing, belying its innocent smell.

Betel leaves (*P. betle*) belong to the same family as all the other vine peppers (Piperaceae). These leaves are used in India for *paan*, a mouth-reddening, tooth-decaying hypnotic concoction that is chewed together with areca nut (*Areca catechu*), which is sometimes incorrectly called betel nut. Betel leaves are also used as a wrapping leaf in many Southeast Asian dishes, especially Thai and Indonesian.

Mexican pepperleaf (*P. sanctum*) comes from a member of the Piperaceae family that is more a shrub than a climber. The oval leaves are similar to betel leaves and are used fresh in Mexican cooking, generally to wrap baked fish. The fresh leaves also find their way into *mole verde*, which is made of mainly fresh ingredients. Mexican pepperleaf is rarely seen outside its country of origin. However, betel leaves can be used as an alternative to wrap food, and when puréed with tarragon, betel leaves provide a reasonable flavor substitute for Mexican pepperleaf.

Kava (*P. methysticum*) is yet another member of the Piperaceae family; its roots are used to make the popular muddy-looking, reputedly intoxicating Polynesian beverage of the same name. To my knowledge this variety is not used to flavor food.

Australian pepper vine (*P. rothianum*, also known as *P. novae-hollandiae*) is not known commercially. Several native species of *Piper* growing in the tropical rainforests of North Queensland are tall climbers with similar leaf structures to the rest of the Piperaceae family. Young native pepper vines attach to tree trunks, but as they mature they eventually grow free of the original support to resemble a stout rainforest liana. The flavor of the dried fruits is a poor substitute for commercially grown pepper. The only recorded edible variety is *P. rothianum*. As yet it has achieved no economic importance.

Sa khan (*P. boehmeriafolium*) is used in nothern Laos, especially around the previous royal capital of Luang Prabang, in the famous stew called *or lam*. The vine, its leaves and its growing habit are very similar to *P. nigrum*. However, it is the stem of this plant that is used to flavor food rather than the peppercorns.

Processing

The processing of vine pepper, especially *P. nigrum*, is pivotal to creation of the green, black, white and true pink peppercorns of commerce. Peppercorns contain an enzyme in the outer skin (pericarp) that is fundamental to the results of the drying or preserving processes used to make the desired final products.

Black Peppercorns

Black peppercorns are traditionally produced by harvesting, six months after flowering, the full-sized green but not yet ripe fruits (berries) of *P. nigrum*. At that point the berries, which have been picked by hand and still adhere to the spikes that bear them, are threshed to separate berry from stem, ready for drying in the sun. During this drying process the enzyme in the pericarp is activated, oxidizing to turn the peppercorns black. Among other pungent components, a volatile oil containing piperine is created, along with oleoresins, all of which contribute to the total complex, mouth-watering fragrance and robust flavor of black pepper.

When traveling in the south of India between December and March, one sees woven mats by the roadside covered with millions of peppercorns at various stages of drying. Those that have just been picked are bright green berries that resemble a sea of miniature peas; the dark brown and jet-black ones are ready to be bagged. Another, more sophisticated method of processing is to plunge the sorted green berries into boiling water for a short period. This accelerates the enzyme reaction. Rather than taking several days in the sun to turn black, scalded peppercorns blacken in about two to three hours. They may then be sun-dried or dried in a kiln to bring the moisture content down to around 12%. Both processes produce an intensely black, highly

aromatic peppercorn that emits a heavenly aroma when freshly ground over food.

There will always be a percentage of black peppercorns that are empty—that is, they lack the firm white heart inside. In the spice trade these are referred to as "light" berries. A specification for whole black peppercorns will usually stipulate a maximum percentage of light berries. Ground black pepper that is particularly black has had, more often than not, an inordinately high ratio of these low-cost light berries added before grinding. It seems quite counterintuitive that pale gray ground black pepper is generally of a better quality than one that is extremely black. That is because the grayer pepper contains mostly full berries with white hearts, while a very black pepper will have been ground using a higher proportion of empty light berries.

Green Peppercorns

Green peppercorns are picked by hand when they have reached full size but have not yet begun to ripen. To keep them green, the enzyme must be prevented from activating and turning the fruit black. The oldest, most traditional process is to put these green peppercorns, either still intact on the stem in attractive spikes or as single peppercorns, in a saltwater solution. The brine inhibits the enzyme from becoming active and turning the fruits black. This is why green peppercorns have traditionally been available only brined, in cans or jars.

To make dried green peppercorns, the freshly harvested green berries are plunged into boiling water for 15 to 20 minutes. This is sufficient time to kill the enzyme and allow the berries to be dried in the sun or in a kiln; they will remain dark green but shrivel up to the texture of black peppercorns while still keeping their characteristic green peppercorn flavor. The most suitable dried green peppercorns for use in peppermills are late-picked berries; these are firmer and less likely to crumble or clog the mechanism than those harvested early in the season. The best high-technology process for producing green peppercorns is freeze-drying, which retains their full, plump appearance and bright green color. Freeze-dried green peppercorns reconstitute soon after coming into contact with moisture, so they are great for cooking. They are not recommended for use in a peppermill, as they are too soft.

White Peppercorns

White peppercorns are produced by removing the enzyme-containing pericarp from the fruits before they are dried. There are two methods for achieving this result. The outer husk may be rubbed off mechanically, in a process called decortication. Because decorticated white pepper is difficult to produce and does not yield as good a final product, the traditional method of soaking and macerating is preferred. This involves picking fruits that are in the process of ripening, when their color is turning to yellow and pink. The berries are tightly packed into burlap sacks and immersed in water—preferably a clean, flowing stream—for between two and three weeks, depending on the ripeness of the fruit. During this period, aided by bacterial activity, the outer husk softens and loosens from the hard core (a process called retting).

After being removed from the water, the peppercorns are macerated: trampled and washed until no pericarp remains. When dried in the sun or in ovens, these peppercorns remain creamy white because they lack the enzyme that turns them black. Thorough drying is crucial at the final stage. If not properly dry, mold will easily form on the white peppercorns, giving them a musty, old-socks smell. Another method for producing white pepper is to harvest only fully ripe berries. These shed their skins more easily in a shorter time, but the practice of collecting only ripe berries is impractical. Ripe berries are prone to shattering, and birds have a fondness for picking them when ripe, resulting in greater losses.

Ground white pepper may be purchased in jars and packages. However, as white pepper is more costly than black, it has not been uncommon for less honest traders to adulterate it with wheat or rice flour.

True Pink Peppercorns

True pink peppercorns are produced by putting the ripe red fruits of *Piper nigrum* into brine in the same manner as the traditional method for green pepper. Unfortunately the pink peppercorns cannot be boiled and dried or freeze-dried, as their pericarp is so soft and friable at this stage that it will only break up if subjected to any process other than immersion in brine. (Dried pink peppercorns from the *Schinus* species of trees are discussed on page 477.)

Pepper Oleoresin

Pepper oleoresin is manufactured principally for the processed food industry. It has a consistent aroma and flavor, is easily mixed with other ingredients, and has no risk of containing any bacteria, all of which are desirable qualities for use in processed foods. Pepper oleoresin is extracted from black pepper using organic solvents such as ethanol. A more recent method of extraction uses carbon dioxide, a process that leaves no solvent residues and produces a superior end product.

Black Pepper Oil

Black pepper oil, used in perfumery and for flavorings, is produced by steam distillation.

Buying and Storage

When buying pepper, keep in mind that the flavor characteristics of peppercorns are influenced primarily by their source. The varieties cultivated and the effects of climatic and soil conditions in different parts of the world all make a contribution to their ultimate aroma and flavor.

The next most important factor is the degree of care taken when drying, storing and grading pepper. Sometimes pepper is not dried sufficiently. This happens when farmers get greedy; by selling a batch of pepper that has 14% moisture content rather than the required 12%, the farmer (who is paid by weight) ends up with more kilos to sell. The problem is that the moister pepper is susceptible to mold, which should make it unsellable. Unscrupulous traders will try to rectify the appearance of moldy pepper with a practice known as reconditioning. This involves spraying the gray

Spice Notes

In January 2005 the Indian Spices Board in Cochin told me about a new process that has been developed for the production of white pepper, called bacterial fermentative skin removal (BFSR). Bacteria capable of degrading pepper skin (the pericarp) so it can be easily removed had been identified in pepper-retting water. The four most potent strains were named PSFB (pepper skin fermenting bacteria) 1, 2, 3 and 4. When these four isolates were used, the degradation time of pepper skin was substantially shortened. This process works because, during bacterial fermentation with equal parts of PSFB1, PSFB2, PSFB3 and PSFB4, pectin (the intercellular cementing substance under the skin) degrades and breaks away from the core of the peppercorn. When cleaned and dried, these white peppercorns have a good flavor and heat level and lack the musty aroma that often comes with conventionally produced white peppercorns. Time will tell if the production of white pepper using the BFSR method becomes widely commercialized.

moldy peppercorns with oil (in some cases even waste motor oil has been used!) and sieving them until the mold disappears and the peppercorns are black and shiny. While shiny, extremely black peppercorns may seem desirable to buy, the patina of good-quality black peppercorns is always slightly matte, never shiny.

Peppercorns from different countries have specific characteristics that relate to soil and climatic conditions, care given to harvesting and processing, and final grading. The following descriptions, while by no means exhaustive, provide some basic guidelines to be aware of when buying pepper.

Indian pepper originates from the Malabar Coast. The two main types of black pepper are named after the centers from which they are traded. Tellicherry, north of Cochin, gives its name to a grade referred to as Tellicherry Garbled Special Extra Bold (TGSEB). To clarify the grading terminology, "garbled" means cleaned to remove stems, stones and most of the light berries; "special" is an indication that this is the best grade based on flavor profile; and "bold" indicates a large peppercorn, this grade being extra large. The other grade important to the Indian spice trade is known as Malabar Garbled No. 1 (MG1). This is a top-grade cleaned peppercorn that used to be known as Alleppey pepper (Alleppey being a picturesque region latticed with manmade canals to the south of Cochin). It is now most often named after the Malabar Coast from which it comes. Indian pepper is regarded by many as the best pepper in the world, esteemed for its high oleoresin and volatile oil content, which explains why the aroma and pungency are so pleasing.

Indonesian peppercorns tend to be smaller than the Indian ones. In recent times Indonesian black pepper has become quite popular in the rest of Asia, Australia and New Zealand for its distinctive lemon-like flavor and competitive prices. There are two main types of Indonesian pepper: Lampong Black, named after a district of southeastern Sumatra, a key pepper-producing area, and Muntok White, a mild-flavored white pepper produced on the island of Bangka and exported from the port of Muntok.

Malaysian black and white pepper is produced almost exclusively in Sarawak and exported from the port of Kuching; both geographic names lend themselves as descriptors. Sarawak pepper has a milder aroma and less pungent flavor than either Indian or Indonesian peppercorns,

Identifying Quality

From time to time you may see the acronym ASTA used to describe pepper, more often than not from Indonesia and Malaysia. This means that the pepper meets the minimum standards for cleanliness, volatile oil content, moisture level and other technical specifications set down by the American Spice Trade Association. Thus it is an indication of a particular quality standard, which may be of significant importance to an industrial spice buyer procuring many tons of pepper. Lower grades that just pass mimimum standards are referred to as FAQ (Fair Average Quality). This term is applied to many other spices as well—more often than not the ones you see overflowing from sacks in atmospheric spice markets.

P

An Unhappy Marriage

Black pepper is found in many spice blends, but—food technologists, please take note—it does have one strange attribute when mixed with ingredients that are high in certain fats and oils, such as coconut: a reaction occurs that creates a distinctly soapy and unpleasant off-taste. I have never experienced this effect in home cooking, but it has occurred in the manufacture of processed foods that are packaged and stored for some weeks during distribution to supermarkets.

but large amounts of it are ground for sale as the familiar standard black and white peppers seen in supermarkets.

Penja white pepper from Cameroon is another style of white pepper that is processed in the same way as other white peppercorns. It has a unique flavor profile because it is grown in very rich volcanic soil. It does have a respectable heat level and the aroma is less musty than that of many other white peppercorns.

Cambodian pepper is increasing in popularity, although Cambodia is a relatively small producer in global terms. The southern Cambodian province of Kampot produces an interesting take on black pepper: the most unusual grade of Kampot pepper is created by a unique process. The pepper berries are harvested when they are ripe and red. When any fruit ripens, its sugars increase as part of the ripening process, and this added sweetness contributes to the overall flavor profile. The same is true of Kampot pepper. The drying process is unusual too. It begins in the shade, slowing down the enzyme activation rate so the piperine does not develop as quickly and the peppercorns are not as black. The result is a black peppercorn with a reddish hue and a ripe, sweet fragrance that is fully appreciated when Kampot peppercorns are freshly ground over food.

Other countries that produce pepper are Sri Lanka, Brazil and Australia. Australian black peppercorns are fruitier in flavor than those from Sarawak, Malaysia, and have a pipe-tobacco aromatic quality.

In a world where regional producers of spices are operating in a highly competitive environment, there is a trend toward marketing some real or perceived level of product differentiation for the commodity. Geographical factors such as soil and climatic conditions and harvesting and post-harvesting procedures will always make a spice taste different from ones grown in other areas. It is thus not unusual for pepper marketers to make a strong case for the difference of their pepper based on these elements of uniqueness.

Use

Pepper has been the world's most popular and most frequently traded spice for thousands of years. Pepper can be classed as one of the few spices that is not only an embellishment for the cook but also a tool in the hands of the diner. A judicious shake, pinch or grind of black pepper may be all that is needed to perk up a not entirely satisfying meal.

Black pepper has the most distinctive flavor of the peppers. It is usually associated with robust foods such as red meat, strongly flavored fish and seafood, and game. When applied in moderation, it complements delicate foods as well. A small sprinkling of freshly ground black pepper will enhance the taste of fresh strawberries and slices of pear served with a soft cheese.

White pepper was often used by European chefs who didn't like the idea of having black specks in their white sauces. White pepper is worth having on hand for occasions when you want a pepper bite without the dominance of black pepper. This is particularly noticeable in Thai and Japanese food, where the light, fresh flavors of ginger, lemongrass, makrut lime leaf, galangal and coriander could be swamped by the robust oiliness of black pepper. Always use white pepper in moderation, as its heat can override more subtle ingredients (you risk a musty, old-socks flavor permeating your food if you are too heavy-handed with an average grade of white pepper). The European blend known as savory quatre épices (see page 756) is a mixture of white pepper, nutmeg, ginger and cloves. Besides being used in charcuterie, savory quatre épices is wonderful on the table in place of ordinary ground white pepper. (Sweet quatre épices is almost identical, except that the white pepper is replaced with ground allspice.)

Green peppercorns complement both black and white pepper and are often included in a blend for peppermills. The flavor of green peppercorns is particularly pleasant in gravies and white sauces for poultry, red meats and seafood. Pâtés and terrines are enhanced by the addition of green peppercorns, as are the majority of rich foods such as pork, duck and game.

True pink peppercorns should be thoroughly rinsed before adding to a recipe to remove the saltiness of their brine. They are delicious crushed in a mortar with a little olive oil and even less vinegar to make a colorful and tasty salad dressing. Pink peppercorns are also appropriate in the applications for green peppercorns noted above.

WEIGHT PER TEASPOON (5 mL)

- whole black: 3.8 g
- ground black: 3.2 g
- whole white: 4.2 g
- ground white: 2.6 g
- freeze-dried green: 1.5 g
- drained green: 6 g
- true pink, drained: 6 g

SUGGESTED QUANTITY PER POUND (500 g)

- red meats: 2 tsp (10 mL) whole
- white meats: 1½ tsp (7 mL) whole
- vegetables: 1 tsp (5 mL) whole
- grains and pulses: 1 tsp (5 mL) whole
- baked goods: ¾ tsp (3 mL) whole

Green Peppercorn Sauce

This is a classic accompaniment to steak, simple yet decadent. Freeze-dried green peppercorns, which are becoming more widely available, can also be used.

**Makes about
1 cup (250 mL)**

Preparation time:
 5 minutes

Cooking time:
 10 minutes

- - - - - - - - - - - - - - - - -

Tip

While cognac is superior, brandy can also be used.

1 tbsp	oil	15 mL
1	shallot, finely chopped	1
1 tsp	minced garlic	5 mL
2 tbsp	cognac (see Tip, left)	30 mL
2 tbsp	drained green peppercorns in brine	30 mL
1 cup	heavy or whipping (35%) cream	250 mL
	Sea salt and freshly ground black pepper	

1. In a skillet over medium heat, heat oil. Add shallot and garlic and cook, stirring, for 2 minutes, until softened. Stir in cognac. Add peppercorns and cream and bring to a boil, stirring constantly, until thickened. Season with salt and pepper to taste and remove from heat. Serve immediately over a cooked beef steak.

Pepper Water

Pepper water is an almost clear, peppery soup that is often sipped from a glass or mug while dining on a devastatingly hot curry. While it doesn't relieve the heat of the curry, this drink has a cleansing effect and is most popular in the south of India. You can use it to moisten the rice that accompanies a dry curry or simply drink it with the meal, the same way you'd enjoy green tea with a Chinese meal.

Makes about 2 cups (500 mL)

Preparation time:
  10 minutes
Cooking time: 1 hour,
  10 minutes

Tips

If using compressed fresh tamarind rather than concentrate, place the piece in a bowl, cover with boiling water and set aside for 10 minutes to soak. Then strain through a fine-mesh sieve, pushing down on the solids with the back of a spoon. Discard remaining pulp and add liquid to the dish.

To serve the soup as a clear liquid, strain it through a fine-mesh sieve before serving. Float a few whole peppercorns in each bowl.

• **Mortar and pestle**

1 tsp	whole black peppercorns	5 mL
1/2 tsp	ground cumin	2 mL
1/2 tsp	brown mustard seeds	2 mL
1	dried red finger chile	1
1/4 tsp	ground turmeric	1 mL
2 tsp	minced garlic	10 mL
1 tbsp	butter or ghee	15 mL
1	small onion, finely chopped	1
6	fresh or dried curry leaves	6
2 cups	beef, chicken or vegetable broth	500 mL
1/2 tsp	tamarind concentrate or 1 piece of tamarind 1 1/2 inches (4 cm) long (see Tips, left)	2 mL

1. Using mortar and pestle, grind together peppercorns, cumin, mustard seeds, chile and turmeric until coarsely powdered. Add garlic and pound into a paste.

2. In a medium saucepan over medium heat, heat butter. Add onion and curry leaves and cook for about 5 minutes, stirring occasionally, until onion is soft and curry leaves are crisp. Add broth, tamarind and prepared spice paste; stir well. Simmer for 1 hour before serving.

P

Pepperleaf and Pepperberry (Tasmanian)

Tasmannia lanceolata

Names in Other Languages

- **Chinese (M):** shan hu jiao
- **Dutch:** bergpeper
- **French:** poivre indigène
- **German:** tasmanischer Pfeffer, Bergpfeffer, australischer Pfeffer
- **Hungarian:** hegyi bors, tasman bors
- **Italian:** pepe di montagna australiano macinate (mountain pepperleaf), bacche di pepe montagna australiano macinate (mountain pepperberry)
- **Russian:** tasmanijskij perets

Family: Winteraceae

Varieties: Dorrigo pepper (*T. insipida*), Mexican pepperleaf (*Piper sanctum*; unrelated)

Other Names: mountain pepper, mountain pepperberry, mountain pepperleaf, Cornish pepperleaf, native pepper, Tasmanian pepper

Flavor Group: Hot

Parts Used: berries (as a spice), leaves (as a herb)

Background

Native to the eastern seabord of Australia, *Tasmannia lanceolata* is found growing wild in the rainforests and wet mountain gullies of Tasmania and Victoria to altitudes of 3,900 feet (1,200 m). Another variety, Dorrigo pepper (*T. insipida*), grows wild in New South Wales, Queensland and the Northern Territory. Although these plants grow prolifically on the east coast of Australia, there is little evidence of their culinary application by the indigenous people. The leaves and berries are antimicrobial, so it is

Culinary Information

Combines with

Leaf
- akudjura
- basil
- bay leaf
- coriander (leaf and seed)
- ginger
- lemongrass
- lemon myrtle
- mustard seed
- wattleseed

Berry
- black pepper
- cardamom
- coriander seed
- cumin
- fennel seed
- garlic
- juniper berries
- marjoram
- parsley
- rosemary
- thyme

Traditional Uses

Leaf
- most foods (in the same manner as black and white pepper)

Berry
- game and rich foods (used sparingly)
- casseroles
- kangaroo fillets

Spice Blends

Leaf
- native Australian lemon pepper
- barbecue spices

Berry
- barbecue spices
- dukkah (Australian version)
- seafood spice blends

Local Interest

Culinary interest in the flavor components of native Australian plants—often referred to as "bush tucker"—is a 20th-century development that has become fashionable and continues to increase in popularity among cooks in Australia.

reasonable to assume that the Aboriginal people used this plant medicinally at one time. It is thought that some 19th-century Australian colonists made use of the bark of *T. lanceolata,* possibly as an external liniment. During the 19th or 20th century, Tasmanian pepper was propagated in Cornwall, England, and the leaves found their way into Cornish kitchens as a pepper substitute. Although its origins in Cornwall are somewhat obscure, in the U.K. in general and Cornwall in particular, the leaves are still often referred to as "Cornish pepper."

The Plant

Tasmanian pepper shrubs are distinguished by the attractive deep red of their young stems and branches, which color in the same way as new crimson gum tips. In ideal conditions

Don't Confuse the Peppers

The *Tasmannia* genus of peppers, native to Australia and including Tasmanian pepper and Dorrigo pepper, should not be confused with native Australian pepper vine (*Piper rothianum*), which belongs to the Piperaceae family.

Tasmanian pepper will grow from 13 to 16 feet (4 to 5 m) tall, so it's basically a small tree. I tend not to call it a tree because it adds to the confusion among the many different types of pepper, including the variety commonly called pepper tree (*Schinus* species, see page 479). The broad-based, tapering leaves on Tasmanian pepper are longer on plants that grow in lowland areas—up to 5 inches (13 cm)—and much shorter on alpine-dwelling ones, which may have leaves that are only $1/2$ inch (1 cm) in length. Small yellow to cream-colored flowers are followed by shiny, plump deep purple to black fruits about $1/4$ inch (5 mm) in diameter that contain a cluster of tiny black seeds inside. The leaves, fruits and even the fresh flower buds all have a distinctive Tasmanian pepper aroma and taste, albeit at varying intensities.

Pepperleaf, which becomes stronger when dried, has a pleasing woody fragrance with vague pepper and dry, cinnamon-like notes. The flavor is similarly woody and camphor-like until its sharp pepper taste and lingering heat become apparent. Pepperberries have an oily, mineral-like, turpentine aroma, and when even minute grains of the ground fruits are tasted, an initial sweet, fruity flavor is quickly followed by an intense biting, tongue-numbing and eye-watering heat that continues to build and will not subside for some minutes. This ongoing development of heat, which is experienced with both the leaves and the berries, is a result of the enzymes contained in Tasmanian pepper being activated by one's saliva.

Tasmanian and Dorrigo pepper plants are similar except that the Dorrigo variety is from a more northerly habitat, the eastern seaboard of New South Wales, and has a less pungent taste—hence the botanical name *T. insipida*. Australian native pepperleaf is not to be confused with Mexican pepperleaf (*Piper sanctum*), which comes from a member of the Piperaceae family.

Processing

Tasmanian pepper leaves are dried in the same way as bay leaves. For best results, cut the leaves off the branches before drying and spread them out on porous material such as insect screening or wire mesh. Place in a dry, dark, well-aired place and set aside for a few days until each leaf is crisp and dry. After drying, the pepper leaves may be ground using a mortar and pestle.

Ripe pepperberries do not need to be sun-dried in the same manner as conventional pepper (*Piper nigrum*) to achieve their flavor; they may be dehydrated for convenient storage by using the same process as for pepper leaves. Pepperberries can also be preserved in brine, which is effective as long as the salty brine is thoroughly rinsed out before using, just as you would with pickled green or pink peppercorns. By far the best-quality and most pleasant-tasting result is achieved by freeze-drying, a capital-intensive industrial process. Freeze-dried pepperberries are not as hot when consumed as the air-dried ones are. They have a pleasant background fruitiness and an appetizing mineral-like flavor that is delicious with red meats and game.

Buying and Storage

Tasmanian pepperleaf is predominantly sold in its powdered form, which looks somewhat granular and has a khaki color. Buy small quantities, because a tiny amount is sufficient to flavor food and, once ground, flavor loss is rapid even under ideal storage conditions. Pepperberries are occasionally available in their frozen form but it is more common to find them ground to a coarse, oily-looking black powder.

P

Freeze-dried pepperberries are reddish black, crumbly and plump. When ground they yield a deep purple powder, a little like ground sumac.

Store both powdered leaves and berries in airtight containers, well protected from extremes of heat, light and humidity. When stored correctly, whole pepperberries will keep their flavor for at least 3 years. Ground pepperberries and pepperleaf will last up to 1 year.

Use

Dried and powdered Tasmanian pepperleaf may be used in the same way as ground black or white pepper (*Piper nigrum*). Because the flavor is relatively sharp and intense, I recommend adding only about half the amount of pepperleaf compared to the amount for black or white pepper. If desired, you can then increase the quantity to suit your taste. Pepperleaf goes well with other native Australian herbs and spices such as lemon myrtle, wattleseed and akudjura (bush tomato). A lemon pepper mix may be made by blending, in proportions to suit your taste, lemon myrtle leaf powder with ground pepperleaf and salt. You can also blend pepperleaf with ground coriander seed, wattleseed, akudjura and salt to sprinkle on lamb, venison or kangaroo fillets before cooking.

Extreme caution is suggested when using air-dried pepperberries. My rule of thumb is to use only one-fifth the quantity of conventional pepper. The freeze-dried berries are milder and may be used a little more generously. Only the brave, foolish or tastebud-deficient would entertain the idea of putting ground air-dried pepperberries directly on food; they are so hot and numbing that, when not cooked, their flavor attributes cannot be fully appreciated. However, I have tasted a modest sprinkling of freeze-dried pepperberries on crème fraîche and fruit, and it was absolutely delicious! Pepperberries work particularly well when added to slow-cooked dishes such as stews and soups, because the extended cooking time tends to dissipate their pungency and the unusual flavor gets a chance to really complement the food. They are also excellent with game meats and, when used sparingly, in marinades for both white and red meat.

WEIGHT PER TEASPOON (5 mL)

- **ground leaf:** 2.4 g
- **ground berry:** 3 g

SUGGESTED QUANTITY PER POUND (500 g)

- **red meats:** 1 tsp (5 mL) ground leaf, ¼ tsp (1 mL) ground berry
- **white meats:** 1 tsp (5 mL) ground leaf, ¼ tsp (1 mL) ground berry
- **vegetables:** 1 tsp (5 mL) ground leaf, ¼ tsp (1 mL) ground berry
- **grains and pulses:** 1 tsp (5 mL) ground leaf, ¼ tsp (1 mL) ground berry
- **baked goods:** 1 tsp (5 mL) ground leaf, ¼ tsp (1 mL) ground berry

Lamb in Tasmanian Pepper Sauce

Tasmanian pepper sauce is very versatile and is often used to accompany lamb. The creamy sauce is light, with an agreeable peppery note that complements the meat nicely.

**Makes
4 servings**

Preparation time:
5 minutes, plus 1 hour
for marinating

Cooking time:
40 minutes

4	lamb fillets, about 6 oz (175 g) each	4
1/4 cup	dry white wine	60 mL
1 tsp	ground Tasmanian pepperleaf	5 mL
1 tbsp	butter	15 mL
SAUCE		
2/3 cup	dry white wine	150 mL
3 tbsp	brandy	45 mL
1/2 cup	chicken broth	125 mL
1 1/4 cups	table (18%) cream	300 mL
1 tbsp	port wine	15 mL
1 tsp	ground Tasmanian pepperleaf	5 mL
4	whole pepperberries	4
	Sea salt and freshly ground black pepper	

1. In a large resealable bag, combine lamb, wine and pepperleaf. Seal, turn to coat and refrigerate for 1 hour or overnight.

2. *Sauce:* In a small saucepan over high heat, combine wine and brandy. Bring to a boil and cook until reduced by two-thirds, 8 to 10 minutes. Add broth, return to a boil and cook for 5 minutes. Add cream, return to a boil and cook, stirring, for 3 to 5 minutes, until sauce has thickened and reduced by one-third. Stir in port, pepperleaf and pepperberries and season with salt and pepper to taste. Set aside and keep warm.

3. In a skillet over high heat, melt butter. Add lamb and sear for 30 seconds each side. Reduce heat to medium-high and cook for 5 minutes each side (meat should be tender and pink in the middle). Slice and serve with sauce.

Variation

If desired, you can substitute an equal amount of kangaroo fillets for the lamb.

P

Perilla

Perilla frutescens

Names in Other Languages

- **Bulgarian:** perila
- **Chinese (C):** hung sou yihp
- **Chinese (M):** hong su ye
- **Czech:** perila krovita
- **Danish:** kinesisk mynte
- **Dutch:** shiso blad
- **Finnish:** veripeippi
- **French:** sésame sauvage
- **German:** Schwarznessel, chinesische Melisse
- **Hindi:** bhanjira (seed)
- **Hungarian:** kinai bazalikom
- **Indonesian:** daun shiso
- **Japanese:** ao-shiso (green), aka-shiso (red)
- **Korean:** deulggae
- **Polish:** pachnotka zwyczajna
- **Portuguese:** perila
- **Russian:** perilla
- **Swedish:** bladmynta
- **Thai:** nga-mon, chicho
- **Vietnamese:** la tia to, rau tia to

Family: Lamiaceae (formerly Labiatae)

Varieties: shiso (*P. frutescens* var. *crispa*), red shiso (*P. frutescens nankinensis*), egoma (*P. frutescens* var. *frutescens*)

Other Names: beefsteak plant, Chinese basil, perilla mint, purple mint, rattlesnake weed, wild sesame

Flavor Group: Mild

Parts Used: leaves (as a herb)

Background

There appears to be some uncertainty about the specific origins of perilla. It was mentioned in the writings of a Chinese physician around 500 CE, which corresponds to the suggestion that it may be indigenous to the Himalayas. Around the eighth century CE perilla was introduced to Japan, where both the green and red varieties have become popular; there they are most often referred to as *shiso*.

Perilla oil, cold-pressed from the seeds of egoma, was used as a lamp oil in Japan around the 16th century but was eventually replaced by more economical lighting oils. The oil is also used for Shinto ceremonies. There has been some renewed culinary interest in it because it is reputed to contain high levels of polyunsaturates.

Culinary Information

Combines with
- arugula
- basil
- chervil
- chicory
- chives
- dill
- fennel fronds
- garlic
- mint

Traditional Uses
- sashimi
- kimchi
- spring rolls
- salads
- soups
- pasta and rice dishes

Spice Blends
- shichimi-togarashi (seed)

Perilla was first introduced to non-Asian gardens as an ornamental plant. Widespread interest in Japanese and Korean cuisine in Western cultures has seen an increase in the cultivation and use of perilla, particularly in sushi restaurants.

The Plant

Perilla is an annual or, in warmer conditions, a perennial. It is a member of the mint family (Lamiaceae) and has spiny-looking serrated oval leaves that are softer and more user-friendly than they appear to be. The plant grows to 2 feet (60 cm) tall in a clump about 1 foot (30 cm) in diameter. Two types are used as herbs and one is grown for seeds. Of those used as herbs, the perilla with bright green foliage is usually referred to in Japan as shiso and the variety with dark red leaves as red shiso. The leaves of both are very similar in appearance, except for their color. In Korea, where green perilla predominates, the leaves are bright green and somewhat larger than those seen in Japan. All types of perilla are aromatic, with hints of basil, cassia, fennel, cilantro and mint, making them a suitable addition to any dish that would benefit from those flavors.

Other Varieties

Egoma (*Perilla frutescens* var. *frutescens*) is the variety grown primarily for its oily seeds, which are gathered for making perilla oil. Its use as an oilseed is probably what led to its being sometimes referred to as "wild sesame," although it is no relation to the sesame plant.

P

Processing

Perilla leaves do not dry successfully, so they are always sold fresh. Perilla oil is made from the cold-pressed seeds of a specific variety (egoma) that are gathered after flowering.

Buying and Storage

Fresh perilla leaves are becoming more readily available in produce stores, especially those specializing in Japanese and Korean ingredients. The leaves wilt easily, so pick them off the stems and wrap in a moist paper towel, place in a resealable bag and refrigerate as soon as you get them home; they will keep for up to 2 days. The leaves can also be picked off the stems and frozen in resealable bags for about 3 weeks; when thawed, they can be used to color and flavor food. However, because freezing wilts and darkens them, thawed perilla leaves are not suitable for salads or garnishes.

Use

Shiso, as perilla is most commonly called in Japanese cuisine, is a traditional accompaniment to sashimi. The leaves are added to many savory dishes in the same way that basil, parsley or coriander leaf (cilantro) are used. In Vietnam the leaves are included in spring rolls and pho. In Korea the leaves are pickled with chile and canned and often added to the pickled condiment kimchi. The flowers are used to garnish food and the dried seeds are sometimes used as an ingredient in shichimi-togarashi (page 764), a spice blend that contains sesame seeds, poppy seeds, chile and salt, among other spices. In Japan, traditional pickled *ume* plums are often dyed with red perilla leaves.

WEIGHT PER TEASPOON (5 mL)
- fresh chopped leaves: 0.5 g

SUGGESTED QUANTITY PER POUND (500 g)
- red meats: 5 tsp (25 mL)
- white meats: 5 tsp (25 mL)
- vegetables: 5 tsp (25 mL)
- grains and pulses: 5 tsp (25 mL)

Herb Summer Rolls

These light Vietnamese spring rolls are the perfect antidote to a regular fried spring roll. Often called a "summer roll," the rice paper wraps around a combination of soft rice noodles, fresh herbs and tofu, pork, crab or shrimp. The rice paper is great for any type of salad filling, and versions of summer rolls are a very popular healthy lunch. Sweet chile sauce makes an ideal dipping sauce.

Makes 20 rolls

Preparation time:
15 minutes, plus
30 minutes for
assembling
Cooking time: none

- - - - - - - - - - - - - - -

Tips

Rice paper can be found in Asian supermarkets and some well-stocked supermarkets.

If you can't find any perilla, you can substitute ¼ cup (60 mL) fresh Vietnamese mint or Thai basil.

For a fun hands-on meal, all the ingredients can be placed on a table and guests can make their own rolls.

3½ oz	rice vermicelli noodles	100 g
½ cup	firmly packed fresh mint leaves, roughly chopped	125 mL
½ cup	firmly packed fresh coriander (cilantro) leaves, roughly chopped	125 mL
½ cup	firmly packed fresh perilla leaves, roughly chopped (see Tips, left)	125 mL
20	round rice papers, 6 to 7 inches (15 to 18 cm) in diameter (see Tips, left)	20
1	head butter lettuce, leaves and main stem/core removed	1
1	carrot, peeled and cut into thin matchsticks	1
40	cooked shrimp	40

1. In a large saucepan over high heat, bring water to a boil. Cook noodles for 3 minutes, until soft. Using a colander, drain well and set aside.

2. In a bowl, combine mint, coriander and perilla. Set aside.

3. In a large, shallow dish, working with batches of 3, cover rice paper rounds in warm water and set aside for 1 to 2 minutes to completely soften.

4. Lift 1 rice paper out of the water, shake off excess and flatten out on a plate or cutting board. Place 1 lettuce leaf in center and top with noodles, 2 tbsp (30 mL) herbs, a few pieces of carrot and 2 shrimp. Fold up bottom edge of circle, fold in sides, then roll up rice paper tightly. Transfer roll to a plate, seal side down, and repeat with remaining rice papers. Cover with plastic wrap and refrigerate until ready to serve (see Tips, left). Summer rolls will keep for up to 6 hours in the refrigerator.

P

Pomegranate

Punica granatum (also known as *P. florida, P. grandiflora* and *P. spinosa*)

Names in Other Languages

- **Arabic:** rumman
- **Chinese (C):** ngon sehk lau
- **Chinese (M):** an shi liu
- **Czech:** granatovnik
- **Danish:** granataeble
- **Dutch:** granaatappel
- **Finnish:** granaattiomena
- **French:** grenade
- **German:** Granatapfel
- **Greek:** rodia
- **Hungarian:** granatalma
- **Indian:** anar (fresh fruit), anardana (dried seeds)
- **Indonesian:** delima
- **Italian:** melagrana
- **Japanese:** zakuro
- **Malay:** delima
- **Portuguese:** roma
- **Russian:** granat
- **Spanish:** granada
- **Swedish:** granatapple
- **Thai:** tap tim
- **Turkish:** nar, rumman
- **Vietnamese:** luu, cay luu

Family: Punicaceae

Varieties: dwarf pomegranate (*P. granatum* var. *nana*), Russian pomegranate (*P. granatum* var. *azerbaigani*), pomegranate Wonderful (*P. granatum* 'Wonderful')

Other Names: grenadier, pomegranate molasses, anardana, Carthaginian apple

Flavor Group: Tangy

Parts Used: seeds (as a spice)

Background

The pomegranate is native to Persia (now Iran), where it was cultivated at least 4,000 years ago. It was known to the ancient Egyptians and later to the Romans by way of Carthage. Some believe that the pomegranate was the original apple in the Garden of Eden. The botanical name given to its family, the genus *Punica*, is derived from the Latin *malum Punicum*, meaning "apple of Carthage," while *poma granata* means "apples with many seeds." Pomegranate is mentioned in the Song of Solomon in the Bible, Mohammed refers to it in the Koran, and it is still used in some traditional Jewish ceremonies. It is mentioned in the Ebers Papyrus, grew in the hanging gardens of Babylon and formed part of the decoration of the pillars of King Solomon's

Culinary Information

Combines with

Seeds
- ajowan
- allspice
- cardamom
- chile
- cinnamon and cassia
- cloves
- coriander (leaf and seed)
- cumin
- fennel
- fenugreek
- ginger
- mustard
- pepper
- turmeric

Molasses
- allspice
- cardamom
- cinnamon and cassia
- cloves
- ginger
- mustard
- pepper

Traditional Uses

Seeds
- curries (similar to using tamarind)

Molasses
- chicken and pork (brushed on before cooking)
- salad dressings
- summer drinks

Spice Blends

Seeds
- Indian masalas
- chicken and seafood seasonings

A Fortune Teller

When traveling in Turkey, we were told about a custom whereby a newlywed bride drops a pomegranate on the ground. When it splits, the number of seeds that fall out indicate how many children she will have.

temple. The Spanish took pomegranate to South America, and it now features as an important ingredient in Mexican cooking, where it is called *granada*.

The bark and root bark of the pomegranate tree have been used medicinally. At one time the rind of the fruit was peeled and dried, producing small orange-yellow chips called "malicorium," which were used for tanning hides and as a medicine. Hundreds of cultivars of pomegranate trees have been developed for appearance, fruit production and desirable flavor characteristics, ranging from quite sweet ones—suitable for eating fresh and making grenadine—to sourer varieties that are preferred for making pomegranate molasses or drying to become the tangy anardana seeds used in Indian cooking.

P

The Plant

The deciduous pomegranate may be either an attractive densely foliaged shrub growing up to 13 feet (4 m) tall or a sparser but splendid tree that reaches 23 feet (7 m). The luxuriant deep green leaves are about $3^{1}/_{4}$ inches (8 cm) long and look similar to bay leaves borne on spiny-tipped branches. The striking orange-vermilion waxy flowers are followed by yellowish brown-red fruits the size of an apple that contain dozens of seeds held in compartments in an inedible bitter, soft pulp. Fresh pomegranate seeds are angular and up to $^{1}/_{3}$ inch (8 mm) long, including their juicy jelly-like pink casing. These fresh seeds give off little aroma but their flavor is pleasantly astringent and fruity.

Dried pomegranate seeds are used in Indian cooking and referred to there as *anardana.* When dry, anardana are dark

Travels in the Spice Trade

My most vivid memory of pomegranate involves an experience in Mexico. After inspecting vanilla plantations in Papantla, nestled shadily among the foothills of the southeast coast, we returned to the former capital city of Queretero. In a small but charming restaurant we were served a meal of chicken poached in a creamy sauce spiced with chile and fresh pomegranate seeds. My delight at experiencing the subtle fruity tobacco notes of pasilla chile in the sauce was exceeded only by the unexpected bursts of flavor from the popping pomegranate seeds that bombarded my taste buds.

My Favorite Salad Dressing

I make a simple salad dressing with pomegranate molasses by combining 3 tbsp (45 mL) each balsamic vinegar and olive oil, 1 tbsp (15 mL) pomegranate molasses and 1 tbsp (15 mL) water in which ½ tsp (2 mL) ground yellow mustard seed has been dissolved. The ground mustard slurry acts as an emulsifier and stops the liquids from separating for at least 10 minutes after shaking.

red to black and exceedingly sticky. They have a delicious fruity, tangy flavor, which makes them an ideal substitute for tamarind. Pomegranate molasses, used extensively in Middle Eastern cuisine, is a deep red, almost black, thick molasses with a rich, berry-like fruitiness and a citric tang. Less intense and concentrated but equally delicious is the nonalcoholic drink grenadine, made from the juice of sweet pomegranates.

Other Varieties

Dwarf pomegranate (*P. granatum* var. *nana*) is grown for decorative purposes. It has very shiny foliage and prolific orange-red flowers and makes a great hedge when trimmed. To my knowledge it is not grown for the fruit. **Russian pomegranate** (*P. granatum* var. *azerbaigani*) is a variety that bears large fruit and is popular for making deep red pomegranate juice. **Pomegranate Wonderful** (*P. granatum* 'Wonderful') produces double red flowers and a good-quality fruit. Exported from California to many countries, this variety has become the world standard. Highly regarded for its rich red color and tangy flavor, it is excellent eaten as a fresh fruit or for making juice.

Processing

The best-tasting pomegranates come from trees that grow where the summers are hot and dry and the winters are cold; they do not fruit as well in humid tropical climates. When the fresh seeds are required, it is important to remove them carefully from the bitter pith and connecting membrane (see Tips, page 524). A traditional way to eat pomegranate was to pick each seed out of the opened fruit with a pin, thus enjoying every flavor-burst of juicy, jelly-like translucent pulp while avoiding the bitter flesh.

P

To make anardana, the seeds are dried with the pulp left on the outside. It is not feasible to grind anardana in anything but a mortar and pestle—the residual stickiness on the surface of the seeds will clog up a spice, pepper- or coffee mill.

Pomegranate molasses is made by boiling down the seeds until the liquid becomes highly concentrated. At that stage it develops its thick consistency and robust flavor.

Buying and Storage

Fresh pomegranates are sold by many produce retailers and are definitely worth buying, especially if you have a good recipe that uses them. Whole fresh pomegranates should be stored in a cool, dark place, where they will last for up to 1 month. The whole fruit, when placed in a freezer bag and frozen, will last for up to 2 months. Pomegranate seeds can be removed and then frozen in resealable bags; they will keep in the freezer for about 3 months.

Anardana are available from Indian food stores and specialty spice shops (which also sell pomegranate molasses, as do Middle Eastern ingredient suppliers). Anardana are best stored in an airtight container; any humidity tends to make the seeds even stickier.

Pomegranate molasses is easy to keep and does not need to be refrigerated after opening; it will keep for at least 1 year. In winter it may become thick in the bottle, but placing it in hot water for a few minutes should make it less viscous and easier to pour.

Use

Fresh pomegranate seeds are added to sauces; they are especially compatible with chicken and seafood. They may be added to fruit salads and sprinkled on pavlova (a very Australian dessert of meringue, fruit and cream). Anardana can be soaked in water like tamarind and the liquid used as a souring agent, or the seeds can be crushed in a mortar, then sprinkled directly onto food for an acidic lift. Pomegranate molasses adds piquancy to salad dressings, and when it is brushed on like a marinade before cooking, it has a tenderizing effect on chicken and pork. In summer a teaspoonful (5 mL) of pomegranate molasses in the bottom of a glass filled with soda water makes a refreshing, thirst-quenching drink.

WEIGHT PER TEASPOON (5 mL)
- whole dried seeds: 3.5 g

SUGGESTED QUANTITY PER POUND (500 g)
- red meats: 1 tsp (5 mL) seeds, 4 tsp (20 mL) molasses
- white meats: 1 tsp (5 mL) seeds, 1 tbsp (15 mL) molasses
- vegetables: 1 tsp (5 mL) seeds, 1 tbsp (15 mL) molasses
- grains and pulses: 1 tsp (5 mL) seeds, 1 tbsp (15 mL) molasses
- baked goods: 1 tsp (5 mL) seeds

Aloo Anardana

This simple spiced *chaat* (potato) side dish is livened up with dried pomegranate seeds (anardana). Serve alongside Delhi Dal (page 651), Indian Butter Chicken (page 156) or South Indian Sardines (page 340).

Makes 6 side servings

Preparation time:
25 minutes

Cooking time:
10 minutes

- - - - - - - - - - - - - - - - -

Tips

Ghee is a type of clarified butter used in Indian cooking. Butter or clarified butter can also be used.

Chaat masala is a quintessential Indian seasoning used in a variety of dishes. It has a high salt content.

Kashmiri chile is a great versatile ground chile to use in this recipe. You can find it at most Indian markets.

• **Wok**

2 lbs	potatoes	1 kg
⅓ cup	ghee (see Tips, left)	75 mL
1 tsp	chaat masala (page 704)	5 mL
1 tsp	ground cumin	5 mL
½ tsp	ground turmeric	2 mL
¼ tsp	ground hot chile (see Tips, left)	1 mL
½ cup	anardana	125 mL
	Sea salt	

1. In a pot of boiling salted water, cook whole potatoes (skin on) just until tender, about 40 minutes. Set aside until cool enough to handle. When cool, cut into roughly $1\frac{1}{2}$-inch (4 cm) cubes.

2. In wok or a large sauté pan over medium heat, melt ghee. Add potatoes and cook, stirring constantly, for 1 minute, until well coated. Add chaat masala, cumin, turmeric and ground chile. Cook, stirring constantly, until potatoes are well coated in spices and beginning to crisp, about 5 minutes. Stir in anardana and cook for 1 minute, until combined. Season to taste with salt, if desired. Serve immediately.

P

Eggplant Salad

In the Middle East, pomegranate is frequently used to dress hot and cold dishes. It gives a spectacular boost of color and flavor to this eggplant salad.

Makes 6 servings

Preparation time:
20 minutes

Cooking time:
30 minutes

- - - - - - - - - - - - - - - -

Tip

Traditionally, pomegranates are seeded by cutting around the "equator" and twisting in half. They are then stretched a little and beaten on the skin side with a wooden spoon to release the seeds. Here's a less messy option: Using a sharp knife, cut pomegranate in half. Fill a large bowl with cold water. Using your hands, submerge the pomegranate and pull apart the membrane (which will float to the top). Use your fingers to gently loosen the arils (seeds). Scoop out the membrane and drain the seeds.

- **Preheat oven to 400°F (200°C)**
- **2 baking sheets**

2 lbs	eggplant, cut into 1-inch (2.5 cm) cubes (about 3 large)	1 kg
2 tsp	coarse sea salt	10 mL
¼ cup	olive oil	60 mL
1 tbsp	whole coriander seeds, lightly crushed	15 mL
2 tbsp	plain Greek yogurt	30 mL
1	pomegranate, seeded (see Tips, left)	1
½ cup	coarsely chopped parsley leaves	125 mL

1. On baking sheets, arrange eggplant in a single layer. Sprinkle with salt. Set aside for 15 minutes, then pat dry with paper towels.

2. Using your hands, cover eggplant thoroughly with oil and coriander seeds. Bake in preheated oven for 20 minutes, until really brown. Remove from oven and set aside to cool slightly.

3. To serve, arrange cooked eggplant on a serving plate. Top with dollops of yogurt and scatter pomegranate arils (seeds) and parsley overtop. This is best served at room temperature.

Variation

Sprinkle ½ cup (125 mL) crumbled feta cheese overtop when serving.

Pork Belly with Pomegranate Molasses

Pomegranate molasses works as a sweet-and-sour element in this simple, delicious dish. Serve with Three-Cabbage Coleslaw (page 149), Basmati Pilaf (page 164) or Mixed Vegetable Bake (page 673). Leftover pork belly makes a wonderful sandwich filling. It's really important to avoid getting any marinade on the skin of the meat, as this will hinder it from crackling perfectly (it's the best part for many people!).

**Makes
4 servings**

Preparation time:
 10 minutes, plus
 2 hours for marinating

Cooking time:
 4½ hours

- **9-inch (23 cm) square metal baking pan, lined with aluminum foil**

3 lbs	pork belly	1.5 kg
1/3 cup	pomegranate molasses	75 mL
1 cup	boiling water	250 mL
5	cloves garlic, bruised	5
1 tsp	fine sea salt	5 mL

1. Place pork belly, skin side up, in prepared pan. Using a sharp knife, cut shallow lines in the skin about 1/4 inch (5 mm) apart.

2. In a heatproof bowl, combine pomegranate molasses and boiling water. Stir in garlic, then pour around base of pork, being careful to avoid the skin. Rub sea salt into scored skin and refrigerate, uncovered, for at least 2 hours or overnight.

3. Heat oven to 300°F (150°C). Bake pork, uncovered, for 4 hours, occasionally nudging pan to swirl marinade around meat. Remove from oven and increase heat to 425°F (220°C). Take pork belly out of sticky pan, discard foil and reline pan with clean foil. Return pork to pan and bake for 25 to 30 minutes, until skin is browned and crisp (crackling). Remove from oven and set aside for 5 minutes before carving.

P

Poppy Seed

Papaver somniferum

Names in Other Languages

- **Arabic:** khashkhash
- **Chinese (C):** ying suhk hohk
- **Chinese (M):** ying su
- **Czech:** mak
- **Danish:** valmue-fro
- **Dutch:** slaapbol
- **Finnish:** uniko
- **French:** graines de pavot, pavot somnifère
- **German:** Mohn, Schlafmohn, Opiummohn
- **Greek:** paparouna
- **Hungarian:** mak
- **Indian:** khas-khas, kus-kus, cus-cus, postdana
- **Italian:** papavero
- **Japanese:** keshi, papi
- **Malay:** kas kas
- **Portuguese:** dormideira
- **Russian:** mak snotvornyj
- **Spanish:** adormidera
- **Swedish:** vallmo
- **Thai:** ton fin
- **Turkish:** hashas tohumu
- **Vietnamese:** cay thuoc phien, vay anh tuc

Family: Papaveraceae

Varieties: blue poppy seed (*Papaver somniferum*); white poppy seed (*P. somniferum album*); field poppy, Flanders poppy, corn poppy (*P. rhoeas*)

Other Names: black poppy seed, maw seed

Flavor Group: Amalgamating

Parts Used: seeds (as a spice)

Background

The opium poppy, which is native to the Middle East, has been cultivated for culinary and medicinal use for more than 3,000 years. Homer refers to the poppy, and it was known to the early Egyptians, Greeks and Romans. By 800 CE it was cultivated in India and China. In India, poppy seeds were made into a confection by mixing them with sugar cane juice.

The plant's specific name, *somniferum*, means "sleep-inducing." The opium poppy's unique narcotic attributes explain why it has been cultivated so widely. As early as the Middle Ages practioners had access to an anesthetic called the "soporific sponge." An infusion of poppy, mandrake,

Culinary Information

Combines with
- allspice
- cardamom
- cinnamon and cassia
- cloves
- coriander seed
- ginger
- nutmeg
- sesame seed
- sumac

Traditional Uses
- breads
- biscuits, crackers and cookies
- pasta (sprinkled over a cheese topping)
- mashed potatoes
- cream toppings on desserts

Spice Blends
- vindaloo curry powder
- shichimi-togarashi

hemlock and ivy was poured over a sponge and held under the patient's nostrils, inducing unconsciousness. In the 18th century, opium, which contains a number of valuable painkilling alkaloids such as morphine, began to be abused because of its mind-altering attributes.

Sadly, however, this plant, which was so useful to the human race for thousands of years, has become something of a pariah.

The Plant

Poppies are straggly-looking, sometimes hairy-stemmed plants that grow to around 4 feet (1.2 m) tall. They are both

Spice Notes

International travelers be warned: the importation of poppy seeds is banned in Singapore, Saudi Arabia and the United Arab Emirates, as they contain up to 50 parts per million (ppm) narcotic alkaloids. And the penalties are strict—I know of one individual who was charged with drug trafficking, then given a pardon and a warning, for inadvertently bringing poppy seeds into Singapore. Because many countries have banned the cultivation of P. somniferum, poppy seeds are often an illegal import. A common practice is to "denature" poppy seeds, either by heat treatment or fumigation, so they will not germinate. Then they can be freely sold.

Although eating poppy seeds in normal culinary quantities will not make you high, some authorities are probably concerned that the imported seeds may be viable and will be used to grow opium poppies! The alkaloid content in poppy seeds is minute and does not have any pharmaceutical effect. However, to the dismay of some athletes who have been tested for drugs, it can be detected in the urine after heavy consumption.

annuals and perennials. The decorative varieties (*Papaver rhoeas*) have attractive flowers that bloom in myriad colors, ranging from white to lilac and pink with reddish purple markings.

After flowering, a rounded parchment-colored, papery-looking woody capsule with a small multipointed crown on top forms. Inside this brittle ribbed casing are several chambers containing hundreds of tiny kidney-shaped seeds. These are the seeds for culinary use. They are essentially a byproduct of poppies grown for opium production. However, once seeds suitable for culinary use have formed within the capsule, very little narcotic content remains.

Two pounds (1 kg) of poppy seeds contains well over 1.5 million seeds. Both the slate blue and creamy white poppy seeds sold for culinary use have a sweet, unassuming aroma and a mild, slightly nutty taste. Blue poppy seeds are a little larger than the white ones, and they are also a bit oilier, with a marginally stronger flavor. This is especially noticeable after roasting.

Varieties

Blue poppy seed (*Papaver somniferum*) is so called because the seeds are blue. They should not be confused with the blue flowering poppy (*Meconopsis grandis*), which is a decorative plant and does not produce seed for culinary applications. **White poppy seed** (*P. somniferum album*) is the variety that yields white poppy seeds, which are used predominantly in Indian recipes. **Field poppy**, **Flanders poppy** or **corn poppy** (*P. rhoeas*), as it is most commonly known, is the bright red decorative variety. As well as the seeds, the flowers and leaves can be eaten; they are often found in salads containing other flowers such as borage, nasturtiums and violets.

Processing

Because opium derivatives such as morphine are still used in a wide variety of painkillers, in a number of countries opium poppies are grown on large-scale plantations under strict government supervision. The opium is gathered by making cuts in the green capsule with a small, sharp implement before the seeds have formed. The latex that oozes out of the incisions is scraped off and collected for further processing. These plants then go on to form pods that fill up with seeds, which are harvested when the heads are ripe and before they burst open. So although the bulk of

revenue from growing *P. somniferum* is from the production of opium, growers get a welcome additional boost from the sale of culinary blue poppy seeds.

Two products are made from the seed oil. One is a clear cold-pressed oil the French call *olivette*, which can be used as a substitute for olive oil in cooking. The other is a further refined, nonedible version for use in artists' paints.

Buying and Storage

Blue poppy seeds are widely available in supermarkets. White poppy seeds can be bought from specialty spice shops and many Indian, Middle Eastern and Asian food stores. Because they contain a fairly high percentage of oil, they are prone to becoming rancid and need to be stored properly, preferably in the refrigerator, and used within a reasonable time. The seeds are also prone to insect infestation, so if you have them in the pantry, make sure the container is well sealed. Buy small amounts of poppy seeds only from shops with high turnover, so you can expect them to be fresh. When stored properly in an airtight container, they will keep for 12 to 18 months.

Use

Blue poppy seeds are often thought of as "European" poppy seeds because those are the kind we see most often on Western bread rolls, buns and bagels and in confectionery. White poppy seeds are sometimes referred to as "Indian," "Middle Eastern" or "Asian" because they tend to feature in those cuisines.

There is little flavor difference between the two kinds of poppy seeds, which means the variety you choose often comes down to aesthetics. Like many seed spices, poppy seeds complement carbohydrates particularly well. If they are not going to be cooked, it is a good idea to lightly toast poppy seeds first (toss them for a couple of minutes in a hot, dry pan to bring out the nutty flavor). Poppy seeds are also delicious when sprinkled over mashed potatoes or pasta, especially when the latter is served with a cheese sauce or tossed in oil.

Because they are so small, poppy seeds are difficult to grind unless you have a handy little mill made in Czechoslovakia. If you don't have one of these mini spice mills, here's a practical method for reducing the seeds to a powder and then making a thickening paste: Pour boiling water over the poppy seeds and allow them to soak for an hour or two. After the seeds have softened and are slightly swollen, they will grind more easily in a blender or food processor.

Poppy seed is known in India as *khus khus*; it should not be confused with the Middle Eastern grain product called couscous. White poppy seeds thicken and add flavor to Indian curries such as vindaloo and may be used as a substitute for ground almonds in North Indian kormas. In Turkey a paste for filling pastries is made from ground poppy seeds mixed with poppyseed oil.

Lemon and Poppyseed Cake

For a delicious lemon and poppyseed cake, follow the recipe for Caraway Seed Cake (page 150) but substitute 3 tbsp (15 mL) poppy seeds for the caraway seeds. Add an extra 2 tsp (10 mL) freshly grated lemon zest.

WEIGHT PER TEASPOON (5 mL)
- whole: 3.7 g

SUGGESTED QUANTITY PER POUND (500 g)
- red meats: 2 tbsp (30 mL)
- white meats: 2 tbsp (30 mL)
- vegetables: 2 tbsp (30 mL)
- grains and pulses: 2 tbsp (30 mL)
- baked goods: 2 tbsp (30 mL)

Poppyseed and Parmesan Soufflés

When I was growing up, Mum would always stir poppy seeds through our macaroni and cheese. We loved the flecks of blue strewn through the creamy sauce, as well as its nutty bite. As an adult making a cheesy soufflé, it felt natural to me to add poppy seeds, and now it's the only way I make soufflés.

**Makes
6 individual
soufflés**

Preparation time:
 10 minutes

Cooking time:
 30 minutes

Tips

Egg whites are at stiff peaks when they do not flop over when held sideways.

A twice-baked soufflé is a great option for preparing ahead. Let soufflés cool, then turn out onto a baking sheet. Cover with 3 tbsp (45 mL) table (18%) cream, 3 tbsp (45 mL) grated Parmesan and an extra 1 tbsp (15 mL) poppy seeds. Bake in preheated 400°F (200°C) oven for 5 minutes. Serve immediately.

- **Six 6- by 4-inch (15 by 10 cm) ramekins**
- **Electric mixer**
- **Preheat oven to 400°F (200°C)**

3 tbsp	butter	45 mL
1/2 cup	fine dry white bread crumbs	125 mL
1/4 cup	all-purpose flour	60 mL
Pinch	dry mustard	Pinch
Pinch	cayenne pepper	Pinch
1 1/4 cups	milk	300 mL
4	eggs, separated	4
1/2 cup	shredded Cheddar cheese	125 mL
1/2 cup	grated Parmesan cheese	125 mL
2 tsp	blue poppy seeds	10 mL
	Sea salt and freshly ground black pepper	

1. In a saucepan over low heat, melt butter. Remove from heat and lightly brush ramekins with some of the melted butter, then dust insides with bread crumbs, tipping out and discarding excess. Return pan to heat and stir in flour, mustard powder and cayenne. Cook for 2 minutes, stirring constantly, until slightly browned (to create a roux). Remove from heat and gradually whisk in milk until smooth, breaking up any lumps. Return to heat and cook, stirring constantly, until sauce boils and thickens, about 5 minutes. Remove from heat and set aside to cool slightly. Whisk in egg yolks, Cheddar, Parmesan and poppy seeds. Season well with salt and pepper.

2. In a clean, dry mixing bowl, beat egg whites just until stiff peaks form (see Tips, left). Add egg whites to cheese mixture and fold in gently, taking care to preserve as much volume as possible. Fill ramekins to within 1/2 inch (1 cm) of rim, then run your finger around inside of rim to help the soufflés attain a good "hat."

3. Bake soufflés in preheated oven for 8 to 10 minutes, until risen and golden (they should still wobble slightly when shaken). Serve immediately—before they collapse!

P

Rose

Rosa damascena

Family: Rosaceae

Varieties: damask rose (*Rosa damascena*); cabbage rose, hundred-leaved rose (*R. centifolia*); China rose (*R. chinensis*); dog rose (*R. canina*)

Other Names: rosa, rose hips, rose petals, roza

Flavor Group: Sweet

Parts Used: flowers (as a herb)

Background

Believed to be indigenous to northern Persia, roses spread across Mesopotamia to Palestine, Asia Minor and Greece. Roses have been cultivated since ancient times: the Persians exported rosewater to China. The word *rose* derives from the Greek word *rhodon*, which means "red," as the blooms were deep red in color (in many languages, in fact, the word for *rose* derives from the word for *red*). Pliny, the Roman naturalist, provided advice on soil preparation for growing the best roses.

An early method of rose oil production was to soak the petals in oil so that it became infused with the aroma of roses. Extracting the volatile oil, on the other hand, is a more involved process. Otto (attar) of roses is said to have been

Culinary Information

Combines with
- allspice
- cardamom
- cassia and cinnamon
- cloves
- coriander seed
- fennel seed
- ginger
- lavender
- mahlab
- mastic
- nutmeg
- poppy seed
- saffron
- vanilla
- wattleseed

Traditional Uses
- rice and couscous
- ice cream
- shortbread and cakes
- Indian sweets (gulab jamun)
- Iranian and Turkish sweets
- Moroccan tagines

Spice Blends
- ras el hanout
- sweet spice blends

discovered during the reign of the Moghul emperor Akbar in the early 17th century. For the wedding feast of Akbar's son Daniyal, a canal was dug surrounding the palace gardens and filled with rosewater for the bridal couple to row upon. Observers noted oil floating on the water, separated by the heat of the sun, and when skimmed off, it had an amazing perfume. The discovery was effectively commercialized; by 1612 distilleries in the ancient Persian city of Shiraz were producing attar of roses on a large scale. To give an idea of the level of concentration, it takes about 220 pounds (100 kg) of fresh rose flowers to produce $1/3$ ounce (10 g) essential oil.

The Plant

More than 10,000 varieties of rose are cultivated. Any scented variety can be used in food. The most popular for culinary use, either as fresh or dried petals or for the manufacture of rosewater, are the damask rose and the cabbage rose. The aroma is slightly sweet, mildly musk-like, floral, dry and comforting. The flavor is grassy and light, with a lingering and appetizing dryness.

The fragrance of rose water is remarkably similar to fresh rose petals. The flavor is initially astringent and rosemary-like but it leaves a refreshing floral dryness on the palate.

This subtle liquid has a flavoring impact far greater than one would expect. Rose water is used in cosmetics and skin-care products. On one of our Spice Discovery tours to India, an enterprising traveler carried a container of rose water to spray on her skin. Before long she was handing it around to the whole group on hot days!

When the flowers are left on certain varieties of rose bushes (especially dog rose), the bulbous red fruit that forms is referred to as a rose hip. Rose hips have a fruity astringency and are appreciated mostly for their high vitamin C content.

Other Varieties

The **cabbage rose** (*R. centifolia*), also known as "hundred-leaved rose," is a hybrid that was developed in Holland around the 17th century. It is sought after for the many tightly clustered petals in each bloom, making it a practical variety to sprinkle over special Indian dishes such as biryani before serving. The **China rose** (*R. chinensis*) is native to southwest China and is grown primarily as an ornamental plant. The **dog rose** (*R. canina*), a wild climbing variety, is most often used for its fruit (rose hips), which are rich in vitamin C. The flower has sparse petals and is therefore of little culinary use.

Processing

Rose petals contain very small amounts of essential oil (less than 1%). They must be harvested in the early morning, before the heat of the day can drive off some of the precious volatiles. Rose petals are dried in much the same way as herbs. Spread out the petals in a thin layer (less than 1 inch/2.5 cm deep) on clean paper or wire mesh. Keep in a warm, dark, well-ventilated area until dry. Within a week the petals will have shriveled and dried but will retain most of their color and develop an agreeable flavor.

Rose oil is produced by steam distillation of the fresh petals, and rose water is made by steeping fresh petals in water. Because the latter retains some flavor components that are lost in steam distillation, rose water is always recommended for culinary use, while rose oil is used mostly for perfumery.

Rose hips are most often made into jams or jellies. These fruits contain hairy fibers, which means they can be an irritant when eaten. This may explain why the most popular preserve using rose hips is a brightly colored clear jelly with the fiber strained out.

You may also see a bright pink product called rose syrup. This is generally made from sugar, water, coloring, citric acid and rose oil or rose hips.

Buying and Storage

When buying either fresh or dried rose petals to use in cooking, make sure they have been grown and produced for culinary use. Many roses are grown specifically for florists, whose main objective is unblemished flowers. As a result, they may have been subjected to heavy doses of pesticides. Dried rose petals are also sold for their appearance and perfume and to make potpourri. Again, many are sold without food-safety considerations. If you want fresh petals for culinary use, you may need to grow your own.

rose hips

Dried rose petals suitable for adding to food and bottles of rose water for cooking are available from many specialty food retailers and spice shops. All rose waters are not created equal, though, and as they are clear liquids, quality cannot be determined by appearance. I have found that most rose waters produced in Lebanon are good.

Rose hips are most commonly sold crushed or powdered for use as a herbal tea popular for its high vitamin C content. Look in the herbal tea section of most stores for rose hip tea.

Rose syrup is used as a dessert topping and for flavoring drinks, most commonly milkshakes. It is intensely sweet and should not be used as a substitute for rose water.

Store dried rose petals and rose hips away from extremes of heat, light and humidity. Rose petals will keep for up to 1 year and rose hips for up to 3 years. Although humidity will not affect rose water, it will last longer when kept away from light.

Use

To many Westerners, the notion of using flowers such as roses and lavender to flavor food seems unusual. However, these traditional flavor enhancers are finding new devotees as a result of ever-broadening exposure to different cultures and cuisines. Rose petals have been used to flavor wines and liqueurs for centuries. Rose petal jam is made fairly extensively in the Balkans, and I remember my mother making rose hip conserve. Crystallized rose petals are used to decorate cakes along with other edible flowers such as violets.

Rose petals are often used in ras el hanout, the Moroccan spice blend. This deluxe mixed spice complements tagines and couscous. Rose vinegar, which can be used in salad dressings, can be made by steeping fresh or dried rose petals in vinegar for a few weeks. Fresh rose petals can be used to garnish salads. They are also appropriate when served as a garnish with tagines, Persian rice dishes and spiced couscous.

Rose water flavors Turkish delight, mastic chewing gum and the Indian sweet *gulab jamun* (*gulab* means "rose"), a dessert of deep-fried balls of condensed milk and flour served with a sweet syrup. It also complements strawberries when added along with a cinnamon stick to sugar syrup—1 tsp (5 mL) rose water to 1 cup (250 mL) water with $\frac{1}{2}$ cup (125 mL) sugar, simmered until sugar has completely dissolved—and used as a glaze.

WEIGHT PER TEASPOON (5 mL)

- dried petals: 0.3 g

SUGGESTED QUANTITY PER POUND (500 g)

- **white meats:** 6 whole fresh petals, 1 to 2 tsp (5 to 10 mL) dried, 1 tsp (5 mL) rose water
- **red meats:** 10 whole fresh petals, 2 to 3 tsp (10 to 15 mL) dried, 1½ tsp (7 mL) rose water
- **vegetables:** 6 whole fresh petals, 1 to 2 tsp (5 to 10 mL) dried, 1 tsp (5 mL) rose water
- **grains and pulses:** 6 whole fresh petals, 1 to 2 tsp (5 to 10 mL) dried, 1 tsp (5 mL) rose water
- **baked goods:** 6 whole fresh petals, 1 to 2 tsp (5 to 10 mL) dried, 1 to 1½ tsp (5 to 7 mL) rose water

Rose Petal Macarons

Macarons are such a treat. They always remind me of the amazing *pâtisseries* in Paris that display a myriad of these colorful delicacies. Adding rose flavoring and petals makes them so pretty that they are an ideal edible gift.

Makes 20 to 25 macarons

Preparation time:
5 minutes

Cooking time:
20 minutes, plus
45 minutes for resting

Tips

Superfine (caster) sugar is very fine granulated sugar typically used in recipes that require a faster-dissolving granule. If you can't find it in stores, you can make your own by using a food processor fitted with the metal blade to process granulated sugar to a very fine, sand-like consistency.

Rose water is a common Middle Eastern ingredient and can be found in major supermarkets and specialty stores.

- **Piping bag with ½-inch (1 cm) nozzle**
- **2 baking sheets, lined with parchment paper**

3 oz	ground almonds	90 g
6 tbsp	confectioners' (icing) sugar	90 mL
3	egg whites	3
¼ cup	superfine (caster) sugar (see Tips, left)	60 mL
2 tsp	chopped dried rose petals	10 mL
4 to 5	drops rose water (see Tips, left)	4 to 5
3	drops pure vanilla extract	3

1. In a small bowl, combine almonds and confectioners' sugar. Set aside.
2. Using an electric mixer, beat egg whites until stiff. Add superfine sugar, 1 tbsp (15 mL) at a time, and beat until mixture is thick and glossy and stiff peaks form. Gently fold in almond mixture, rose petals, rose water and vanilla until well combined. Spoon mixture into piping bag and pipe small rounds, about 1½ inches (4 cm) in diameter, onto baking sheets.
3. When batter is used up, wet your finger in water and gently smooth down any points that are sticking up (so they don't burn). Set pans aside for 45 minutes so rounds can develop a "skin" on top.
4. Preheat oven to 325°F (160°C). Bake macarons for 10 to 15 minutes, until just changing color and you can peel them easily off the baking sheet (they should still be spongy—do not brown). Remove pan from oven and set aside to cool slightly, then transfer macarons to a wire rack to cool completely.

Variation

Mix ½ cup (125 mL) mascarpone or whipped cream with 3 to 4 drops rose water, then use the cream as a filling between two macarons.

R

Moroccan Chicken Bastilla

When visiting Marrkesh, I found it fascinating how you could almost instantly leave behind the mayhem of the city by entering a calm, serene *riad* (a large traditional Moroccan home with a central courtyard). The beautiful pools and gardens hidden from the outside world make very special places to eat, and many riads in Marrakesh are now restaurants. I enjoyed a traditional pigeon bastilla in such a place. It was a truly magical dish with its crisp pastry and a dusting of sugar and cinnamon topped with pretty dried rose petals. The balance of flavors was incredible, with a delicate sweetness that satisfied any craving for dessert. This is a very special dish, often made for celebrations and weddings.

Makes 4 servings

Preparation time:
15 minutes

Cooking time:
50 minutes

- - - - - - - - - - - - - - - -

Tips

Bastilla is usually made with pigeon, although chicken is sometimes used, as I have done here.

A jointed chicken is simply cut into 6 pieces—2 breasts, 2 legs/thighs and 2 wings. Precut chicken pieces can also be used.

• **Baking sheet, lined with parchment paper**

1 tbsp	butter	15 mL
2	onions, finely diced	2
1 tsp	freshly grated gingerroot	5 mL
1½ tbsp	ras el hanout (page 757)	22 mL
½ cup	fresh coriander (cilantro) leaves, divided	125 mL
½ cup	fresh parsley leaves, divided	125 mL
1	medium-size chicken (about 2½ lbs/1.25 kg), jointed (see Tips, left)	1
4	eggs, lightly beaten	4
1 tbsp	freshly squeezed lemon juice	15 mL
¼ tsp	fine sea salt	1 mL
¼ tsp	freshly ground black pepper	1 mL
8	phyllo pastry sheets, 13 by 8 inches (33 by 20 cm) each	8
¼ cup	melted butter	60 mL
¼ cup	toasted flaked almonds	60 mL
1 tsp	confectioners' (icing) sugar	5 mL
½ tsp	ground cinnamon	2 mL
2 tsp	dried rose petals, crumbled	10 mL

1. In a large, heavy-bottomed saucepan or Dutch oven over medium heat, melt 1 tbsp (15 mL) butter. Add onions and cook, covered, for 5 minutes, until translucent. Add ginger and cook for 1 minute, stirring until well combined. Stir in ras el hanout, ¼ cup (60 mL) coriander leaves and ¼ cup (60 mL) parsley. Add chicken and stir to coat well. Pour in just enough water to cover chicken. Reduce heat to low and cover with lid. Simmer for 25 to 30 minutes, until chicken is cooked through. Transfer cooked chicken to a bowl (reserve sauce in pan) and set aside to cool.

Tip

You can make one large bastilla by using a flan ring, pie dish or paella pan as a mold. Cook for an extra 10 to 15 minutes.

2. Increase heat to high and cook sauce for about 8 to 10 minutes, until thickened (it should coat onions well). Reduce heat to medium and add eggs; stir constantly until cooked through. Turn off heat and set aside.

3. When chicken is cool enough to handle, discard skin and bones and roughly chop. In a bowl, combine chicken, lemon juice, salt and pepper.

4. Preheat oven to 400°F (200°C).

5. On a clean work surface, spread out 1 piece of phyllo and brush with melted butter. Using a sharp knife, cut pastry in half vertically. Arrange pieces across each other at right angles and scoop 2 to 3 tbsp (30 to 45 mL) egg mixture into center. Fold two opposite ends of phyllo overtop. Top with one-quarter of the prepared chicken and sprinkle with coriander leaves, parsley and almonds. Fold over other two ends of phyllo. Take a new sheet of phyllo, brush with melted butter and place parcel in one corner (on buttered side). Roll up parcel diagonally across the phyllo, folding in loose edges as you go; tuck in last corner of pastry like an envelope. Using your hands, pat parcel into a round shape. Transfer to prepared baking sheet, herb side up. Brush with melted butter. Repeat with remaining ingredients to make 3 more bastillas. Bake in preheated oven for about 20 minutes, until golden.

6. In a small bowl, combine confectioner's sugar and cinnamon. Sprinkle over bastillas and serve with rose petals scattered overtop.

R

Rosemary

Rosmarinus officinalis

Names in Other Languages

- **Arabic:** iklil al-jabal
- **Chinese (C):** maih diht heung
- **Chinese (M):** mi die xiang
- **Czech:** rozmaryna
- **Danish:** rosmarin
- **Dutch:** rozemarijn
- **Finnish:** rosmariini
- **French:** romarin
- **German:** Rosmarin
- **Greek:** dentrolivano
- **Hungarian:** rozmaring
- **Italian:** rosamaria
- **Japanese:** mannenro
- **Portuguese:** alecrim
- **Russian:** rozamarin
- **Spanish:** romero
- **Swedish:** rosamarin
- **Thai:** rosmari
- **Turkish:** biberiye, hasalban, kusdili
- **Vietnamese:** la huong thao

Family: Lamiaceae (formerly Labiatae)

Varieties: prostrate rosemary (*R. prostratus*)

Other Names: old man, polar plant, compass weed, compass plant

Flavor Group: Pungent

Parts Used: leaves and flowers (as a herb)

Background

Rosemary is native to the Mediterranean region. It gets its botanical name from *ros* ("dew") and *marinus* ("sea"), in reference to the areas around the Mediterranean Sea where it grows so abundantly. Rosemary thrives in sandy, well-drained soils and in misty air filled with sea spray. Dioscorides, a botanist in ancient Greece, recognized the medicinal qualities of rosemary, as did the Roman Pliny. Many legends surround rosemary. One recounts that the plant had plain white flowers until Mary, fleeing into Egypt with the Christ Child, threw her robe over a rosemary bush while she and Joseph were resting beside it. At that point the flowers turned the blue color of her garment; thus the herb was referred to thereafter as "rose of Mary." Another religious fable is that the rosemary bush will never grow taller than the height of Jesus, that is, 6 feet (2 m).

Culinary Information

Combines with
- ajowan
- basil
- bay leaf
- coriander seed
- garlic
- marjoram
- nutmeg
- oregano
- paprika
- sage
- savory
- tarragon
- thyme

Traditional Uses
- scones
- dumplings and breads
- pork
- lamb and duck
- mashed potatoes
- soybeans
- pâtés and game
- zucchini and eggplant

Spice Blends
- Italian herbs
- seasoned stuffing mixes

Enhance Your Memory

On a day when you are finding deep concentration elusive, crush some fresh rosemary leaves and deeply inhale their stimulating aroma. As the penetrating vapor courses through your olfactory cells, a clarity of mind and purposefulness of thoughts will emerge.

It is believed that rosemary was introduced into Britain by the Romans. It was probably cultivated there prior to the Norman Conquest, as its medicinal qualities are mentioned in an 11th-century Anglo-Saxon herbal. By the Middle Ages rosemary was being used in Europe for culinary applications, specifically with salted meats. It was one of the first essential oils distilled by the Catalonian mystic, philosopher and theologian Raimundus Lullus in 1330.

Rosemary twigs were burnt as incense in 17th-century English courtrooms to protect the court officials from diseases, such as jail fevers carried by the unfortunate prisoners brought before them. French hospitals would similarly burn rosemary and juniper to prevent the spread of infections by sanitizing the air.

Rosemary's stimulating and health-giving properties are well documented. Hair rinses containing rosemary are said to promote vigor and growth. Greek scholars used to wear sprigs of rosemary entwined in their locks to help them commit their studies to memory. The association with memory, lovers' fidelity and remembrance is a long one. Ophelia's famous words to Laertes in Shakespeare's *Hamlet*—"There's rosemary, that's for remembrance; pray love, remember"—immortalized a sentiment that prevails today. In Australia, sprigs of rosemary are worn on ANZAC Day, in remembrance of the soldiers who died at Gallipoli in the First World War.

R

Spice Notes

On a personal note, my mother (who wrote Australia's first book on herbs, in the late 1950s) was christened Rosemary in memory of her elder sister, who died just before 1920 at three months of age, after a difficult birth and feeding problems. It was a tragedy for my courageous English grandmother and my swashbuckling pearling-master grandfather in the then remote town of Broome, in the northwest of Western Australia.

Not Everyone's Cup of Tea

In some countries where rosemary grows profusely, the locals would not dream of eating it. They describe the taste as violent and fit only for peasants. For instance, on a visit to the southeastern town of Gaziantep in Turkey, we were surprised to learn that their beautiful rosemary bushes were never used to season the copious quantities of lamb they consume.

The Plant

Rosemary is a hardy, sun-loving perennial shrub. There are two main varieties: an upright plant that grows to 5 feet (1.5 m) tall, with a stiff, bushy appearance that makes it suitable for hedges, and a low-growing (prostrate) variety that is no taller than 12 inches (30 cm). Although there are some other varieties of rosemary, they are rarely seen or used for culinary purposes.

Both upright and prostrate rosemary have similar woody stems and leathery needlelike leaves. Each leaf is dark green and glossy on top, with a longitudinal crease down the middle; its edges have the appearance of being neatly rolled under. The leaf underside is a dull, pale gray-green and concave, with a central rib; when viewed from this angle, its rolled edges make it look like a minuscule canoe. The leaves (often called needles) of upright rosemary are about 1 inch (2.5 cm) long. Prostrate rosemary leaves are identical but shorter, averaging $^1/_2$ inch (1 cm) long.

Rosemary leaves, when bruised, give off an aroma that is fragrant, pine-like, cooling, minty and, with its hints of eucalyptus, refreshingly head-clearing. Their flavor is astringent, peppery, warming, woody and herby, with a lingering camphor-like aftertaste. Upright rosemary is a little more pungent than the prostrate variety; otherwise, their sensory characteristics are the same. When dried, the rolled edges of rosemary leaves curl tightly into minute scrolls; they lose their flat appearance and begin to resemble hard curved pine needles. These are often cut into $^1/_4$-inch (5 mm) lengths to make them easier to use. When dry, the flavor remains pungent, woody and pine-like, but it does lose some of the volatile green notes.

Prostrate rosemary leaves are almost half the size of upright rosemary's, and its flowers are also smaller and a delicate Wedgwood blue. Prostrate rosemary grows particularly well in rockeries and on top of retaining walls.

Processing

Rosemary must be dried immediately after harvesting to prevent the loss of volatile oils. Hang freshly cut bunches upside down in a dark, well-aired, warm place for a few days. When the leaves are quite dry, they can be easily stripped off the stems and crumbled into small pieces to help them soften and disperse their flavor in cooking.

Rosemary oil, a colorless volatile oil used in the manufacture of confectionery, processed meats, beverages, soaps and perfumes, is produced by steam distillation.

Buying and Storage

Because dried rosemary takes so long to soften (if ever) when cooking, buy fresh rosemary whenever possible.

Sprigs of fresh rosemary will keep for a week or more when the stems are immersed in a little water (as if in a vase) that is renewed every few days. Keep it on the counter, as it will not benefit from being refrigerated. Alternatively, sprays of fresh rosemary may be wrapped in foil, placed in a resealable bag and stored in the freezer for up to 3 months.

When stripping fresh rosemary leaves from the stem, always hold the stem at the bottom end with one hand and, with the thumb and forefinger of the other hand, pluck off each leaf with an upward motion. Pulling leaves off with a downward action will remove a strip of coarse outer stem bark, the texture of which is unpleasant to eat.

Dried rosemary is widely available. The little cut pieces have a surprisingly well-concentrated flavor, but if using a dried version I prefer good-quality powdered rosemary, which is quite strong and convenient to use. Normally I would never recommend buying ground dried herbs, because their already delicate volatile oils are all but dissipated by the grinding process. Rosemary, however, does seem to be an exception. Freeze-dried rosemary looks like the fresh herb and softens readily in cooking; however, it lacks the concentration of volatile oil found in conventionally dried rosemary. When stored in airtight containers and kept away from extremes of heat, light and humidity, dried rosemary leaves will last for at least 3 years and ground rosemary for 18 months.

R

WEIGHT PER TEASPOON (5 mL)

- **whole dried leaves:** 1.8 g
- **ground:** 1.6 g

SUGGESTED QUANTITY PER POUND (500 g)

- **red meats:** 2 tsp (10 mL) fresh, 1 tsp (5 mL) dried
- **white meats:** 1½ tsp (7 mL) fresh, ¾ tsp (3 mL) dried
- **vegetables:** ¾ tsp (3 mL) fresh, ½ tsp (2 mL) dried
- **grains and pulses:** ¾ tsp (3 mL) fresh, ½ tsp (2 mL) dried
- **baked goods:** ¾ tsp (3 mL) fresh, ½ tsp (2 mL) dried

Use

The astringent fresh, savory taste of rosemary complements starchy foods, and it is delicious in dumplings, breads and cookies. It also counters the richness of meats such as pork, lamb and duck. The Italians love rosemary. In Italy, butchers often place a complimentary sprig of fresh rosemary in the package with cuts of lamb. Rosemary's powerful flavor does not overpower a dish when it is matched with other strong ingredients, such as garlic and wine.

I like to add ½ tsp (2 mL) finely chopped fresh rosemary to mashed potatoes or legumes. A sprig of fresh rosemary will enhance most casseroles. One of my favorite basic meals is a leg of lamb with sprigs of rosemary and slivers of garlic stuffed into slits in the meat, liberally dusted with sumac and sweet paprika before roasting. Rosemary is used in liver pâté and goes well with game, including venison, rabbit and (if you live in Australia) kangaroo. Vegetables such as zucchini, eggplant, Brussels sprouts and cabbage are all enlivened by the fresh, resinous taste of rosemary.

Rosemary scones are delicious. Make them by adding 1 tbsp (15 mL) finely chopped fresh rosemary to enough mixture for about a dozen savory scones. Serve hot with butter. Not even the crumbs will be left.

Leg of Lamb Stuffed with Olives, Grapes and Rosemary

I find lamb and rosemary to be one of the most heavenly pairings; it's no wonder that the combination is a traditional Greek favorite. The olives and grapes give a sweet and salty fruitiness to this stuffing, and I like to imagine all these ingredients coming together in nature before they appear on the plate. It makes a satisfying Sunday dinner served with roasted rosemary potatoes.

Makes 4 to 6 servings

Preparation time:
 15 minutes

Cooking time: 2 hours

Tips

Ask your butcher to remove the bone from the lamb. This is often referred to as "butterflying."

If you feel like enjoying lamb but don't want to go to the trouble of making a large roast, try one of my father's favorites: sprinkle powdered rosemary over lamb chops before barbecuing.

- **13- by 9-inch (33 by 23 cm) metal baking pan**
- **Ovenproof string**
- **Meat thermometer, optional**
- **Preheat oven to 425°F (220°C)**

1	egg, beaten	1
1	red onion, chopped	1
1 cup	fresh whole-wheat bread crumbs	250 mL
1 cup	red grapes, quartered	250 mL
½ cup	kalamata olives, pitted	125 mL
½ cup	cooked chickpeas, roughly mashed	125 mL
2 tsp	finely chopped fresh rosemary	10 mL
½ tsp	ground cumin seed	2 mL
	Sea salt and freshly ground black pepper	
1	boneless leg of lamb (4 lbs/2 kg), in one piece	1
	Olive oil	

1. In a bowl, combine egg, onion, bread crumbs, grapes, olives, chickpeas, rosemary and cumin. Mix well and season with salt and pepper to taste.

2. On a clean work surface, lay lamb out flat, cut side up. Spoon stuffing evenly over meat, then carefully roll up from one side to the other. Secure roll with several pieces of ovenproof string tied around the circumference, making sure to encase stuffing well. Rub oil all over lamb, season well with salt and pepper, and transfer to baking pan. Roast in preheated oven for 20 minutes, then reduce heat to 375°F (190°C) and roast for 1 hour and 20 minutes, until a meat thermometer inserted in the thickest part of the meat registers 150°F (65°C) for medium rare (the optimum way to serve roast lamb). Roast longer if desired. Remove from oven and set aside for 10 minutes to rest before carving.

R

Rosemary and Lemon Polenta Shortbread

This is a delightful cookie for any occasion. Rosemary and lemon have a long history in savory dishes, but they work equally well in this buttery shortbread.

Makes about 45 cookies

Preparation time:
35 minutes, including chilling

Cooking time:
10 minutes

Tips

The dough can be rolled into a sausage shape and frozen for up to 3 months. To use, simply cut into $1/8$-inch (3 mm) slices and bake as directed in Step 4, adding an extra 5 minutes to the cooking time.

You can substitute 1 tsp (5 mL) dried ground rosemary or 1 tbsp (15 mL) dried chopped rosemary for the fresh rosemary.

Medium cornmeal (polenta) is a fine grain that gives a little texture and crunch to this cookie.

- **2 baking sheets, lined with parchment paper**
- **Cookie cutters**

7 tbsp	unsalted butter, softened	105 mL
$1/4$ cup	granulated sugar	60 mL
1	large egg, beaten	1
	Finely grated zest of 1 lemon	
1 tbsp	finely chopped fresh rosemary leaves	15 mL
$2^1/_2$ cups	all-purpose flour	625 mL
$1/3$ cup	medium cornmeal (see Tips, left)	75 mL

1. In a large bowl, using an electric mixer at high speed, beat butter and sugar until pale and fluffy. Add egg, lemon zest and rosemary; beat until just combined. Stir in flour and cornmeal until mixture comes together. Turn out onto a lightly floured surface and knead gently until smooth. Using your hands, form into two disks and cover with plastic wrap. Refrigerate for 30 minutes or until firm.

2. Preheat oven to 350°F (180°C).

3. On a lightly floured work surface, roll out dough to $1/8$ inch (3 mm) thick. Cut out shapes using cookie cutters and arrange on prepared sheets.

4. Bake in preheated oven for 10 minutes or until lightly golden. Carefully transfer to a wire rack to cool completely. Store in an airtight container for up to 2 weeks.

Variation

Substitute an equal amount of orange zest for the lemon zest.

Safflower

Carthamus tinctorius (also known as *C. glaber* or *Centaurea carthamus*)

Names in Other Languages

- **Arabic:** asfour
- **Chinese (C):** daaih huhng faa
- **Chinese (M):** da hong hua
- **Czech:** svetlice barvirska
- **Danish:** farvetidsel, safflor
- **Dutch:** saffloer
- **Filipino:** casubha
- **Finnish:** varisaflori, saflori
- **French:** carthame, safran bâtard
- **German:** Farberdistel, Saflor
- **Greek:** knikos
- **Hungarian:** magyar pirosito
- **Indian:** kasubha
- **Italian:** cartamo, falso zafferano
- **Japanese:** benibana
- **Portuguese:** cartamo, açafrão-bastardo
- **Russian:** saflor
- **Spanish:** cartamo
- **Swedish:** safflor
- **Thai:** kham nhong
- **Turkish:** aspur, yalanci safran
- **Vietnamese:** cay rum, hong hoa

Family: Asteraceae (formerly Compositae)

Other Names: American saffron, bastard saffron, dyer's saffron, fake saffron, false saffron, flores carthami, saffron thistle, Mexican saffron

Flavor Group: Mild

Parts Used: flowers (as a spice)

Background

The origins of safflower are not known for certain. Some researchers believe it is native to Egypt and Afghanistan, while others say India. The botanical name derives from *kurthum*, the Arabic word for dye, and *tinctor*, meaning "dyer." In many languages the names for safflower make some reference to color or dyeing. The majority of cultivation has been undertaken for the oilseed; it is grown principally for this purpose in the Middle East, China, India, Australia, South Africa and southern Europe, among other places. The flowers are used extensively as a far less expensive substitute for saffron. Be aware: spice traders in fragrantly atmospheric markets around the world will look you in the eye and declare, "Yes, this is real saffron!" Safflower petals have been used as a dye for silk and cotton, and when it is mixed with French chalk (talcum powder),

Culinary Information

Combines with

- all herbs and spices (as a coloring agent)

Traditional Uses

- soups
- rice dishes
- confectionery
- breads
- herbal teas

Spice Blends

- not commonly used in spice blends

the product is known as rouge. Safflower coloring has become popular in processed foods that wish to claim they are 100% natural.

The Plant

Safflower is infamous for its history of being passed off as saffron. It is a stiff, thistle-like, upright plant with a whitish stem branching out near the top. The serrated leaves are oval, spiny, sharp-pointed and about 5 inches (12 cm) long. The $1/2$-inch (1 cm) tubular flowers may be bright yellow, orange or red, depending on the variety. They are made up of many spiky florets, which are followed by small light gray seeds. These seeds produce golden-colored safflower oil, which has become increasingly popular because of its high ratio of polyunsaturated fats.

Dried safflower petals are $1/4$ to $1/3$ inch (5 to 6 mm) long and generally range from yellowish brown and rust red to bright yellow, flaming orange and brick red. The imaginative might say that they resemble a saffron stigma because of their feathery look. The aroma is sweet and leathery, and they possess a somewhat bitter taste that does not linger.

Processing

Safflower petals contain two coloring agents: carthamin, a red dye extracted by treating the flowers with an alkaline solution, and safflor-yellow, a yellow pigment removed by repeated soaking in water. Flowers are gathered twice a week.

For oilseed collection the plants are cut when the seeds are ripe; then they are threshed and winnowed to remove the seeds. On a visit to southeastern Turkey we saw copious amounts of safflower petals spread out on concrete paving,

Travels in the Spice Trade

I was most amused (and proud) when my wife Liz locked eyes with a trader in the covered spice market in Istanbul who was hawking "real Turkish saffron." It was actually safflower, which Liz knew. "That's not saffron," she said with an icy gaze. He immediately replied, "Of course it's not," and then continued shouting to the unaware tourists around us: "Real saffron! Real Turkish saffron!" That said, Istanbul's spice market is one you must see if you have the chance. It's a fascinating place. Even if you are hoodwinked you won't have spent a fortune, you'll make a trader happy, and you will likely have some fun in the process.

drying in the sun. It was testament to the strength of safflower's color, as most brightly colored flowers will fade when exposed to direct sunlight.

Buying and Storage

Unfortunately, in most countries—Australia, England and the United States included—it is a rare spice trader indeed who will sell safflower petals as safflower. Because of its dicey history of being passed off as saffron, it does have some modest uses. The Indians call it *kasubha* and in the Philippines it is known as *casubha*, names that should appear somewhere on a packet of safflower. Store in the same way as other spices, in an airtight container away from extremes of heat, light and humidity, where it will keep for more than 1 year.

Use

Safflower florets are used to color food in the same way that saffron is. The incentive is that safflower costs about one-hundredth the price of real saffron stigmas. However, it has none of the flavor of saffron, although it does color food effectively. In the Philippines, safflower is the coloring ingredient in the traditional soup *arroz caldo,* a type of congee with rice and chicken. In Spain it is added to soups and rice dishes as a saffron substitute. In Poland, safflower colors confectionery and bread. Safflower is also infused as a tea in Bhutan, where it is valued for its reputed efficacy in reducing cholesterol and the risk of heart disease. Because the florets can range from $1/3$-inch (8 mm) pieces to bits of dust, it is advisable to infuse them in a little warm water for five minutes, then drain off the orange-colored liquid before adding the strained liquid to the dish.

WEIGHT PER TEASPOON (5 mL)

- **whole:** 0.6 g

SUGGESTED QUANTITY PER POUND (500 g)

- **red meats:**
  15 florets
- **white meats:**
  12 florets
- **vegetables:**
  10 florets
- **grains and pulses:**
  12 florets
- **baked goods:**
  10 florets

S

Saffron

Crocus sativus

Names in Other Languages

- **Arabic:** za'faran, zafran
- **Chinese (C):** faan huhng faa
- **Chinese (M):** fan hong hua
- **Czech:** safran
- **Danish:** safran
- **Dutch:** saffraan
- **Finnish:** sahrami
- **French:** safran
- **German:** Safran
- **Greek:** krokos, safrani
- **Indian:** zaffran, zafron, kesar, kesari
- **Indonesian:** kunyit kering
- **Italian:** zafferano
- **Japanese:** safuran
- **Malay:** koma-koma
- **Norwegian:** safran
- **Portuguese:** açafrão
- **Russian:** shafran
- **Spanish:** azafran
- **Swedish:** saffran
- **Thai:** ya faran
- **Turkish:** safran, zagferan
- **Vietnamese:** mau vang nghe

Family: Iridaceae

Other Names: azafran, Asian saffron, Greek saffron, Italian saffron, Persian saffron, true saffron

Flavor Group: Pungent

Parts Used: stigmas (as a spice)

Background

Opinions differ on the precise origins of saffron, a spice whose history stretches back to the dawn of civilization. The first reference to the cultivation of saffron dates back to around 2300 BCE, when frescoes in the Knossos Palace of Minoan Crete depicted saffron being harvested by young girls and monkeys. As the date of these frescoes is uncertain, orderly planting may have occurred even earlier. Its cosmetic applications were described in the Ebers Papyrus (1550 BCE), and Alexander the Great discovered it growing in Kashmir in 326 BCE (although it was not indigenous to the region). In ancient Greece and Rome, saffron was scattered on the floors of theaters and public halls, where its pervading fragrance likely sweetened the air.

Saffron was valued as a spice and a dye and for its medicinal properties by the ancient Greeks, Romans, Persians and Indians. It is referred to in the Song of Solomon in the Old Testament, which was written about 1000 BCE. The Greeks called it *krokos*, from the word meaning "weft"—a thread used in weaving on a loom. The name *saffron*, bequeathed by the Moorish traders who introduced it to

Culinary Information

Combines with
- all herbs and spices (used in moderation)

Traditional Uses
- Indian rice dishes
- Italian risotto and Spanish paella
- seafood and chicken dishes
- breads
- couscous

Spice Blends
- ras el hanout
- paella spice mixes

An Intriguing Fact

Although around 90 varieties of crocuses have been identified, all saffron crocuses (*Crocus sativus*) are identical, no matter where they are cultivated. This suggests that they all came from a common source, probably Greece or Asia Minor, where forms of *C. sativus* (notably *C. cartwrightianus*) grow wild. There is a strong belief that human intervention—selection and breeding of the most desirable plants—is responsible for the saffron we know today.

Spain in 900 CE, derives from the Arabic *sahafarn*, "thread," and *za'faran*, meaning "yellow." In the first century CE, the gourmet Apicius described sauces infused with saffron for fish and fowl, as well as its use to enhance wine-based aperitifs. Pliny warned that saffron was "the most frequently falsified commodity," an interesting statement, because in those days the Romans had slaves to do their grunt work. So even when labor was relatively cheap, the fact that the stigmas of about 200,000 flowers are required to produce 2 pounds (1 kg) of saffron was not lost on anyone. Not surprisingly, saffron's value has often been compared to that of gold. In 220 CE, the extravagant Roman emperor Heliogabalus is said to have bathed in saffron-scented water, and in a less wasteful application, Cleopatra enhanced her beauty and prevented blemishes with a face-wash of saffron.

The Phoenicians were great saffron traders. They supplied the Romans with saffron from Corycus (now Korghoz), in the Turkish region of Cilicia (the Romans considered saffron from Cilicia to be of the best quality). Following the introduction of saffron to Spain by the Moors in the eighth or ninth century, the La Mancha region, in the geographic center of Spain, became one of the world's top producers of high-quality saffron. Its searing summer heat and freezing winter provide ideal growing conditions.

Saffron is believed to have been introduced to Italy, France and Germany during the 13th century by the Crusaders. Having developed a liking for saffron on their travels, they brought corms back with them from Asia Minor. Cultivation of saffron commenced in England in Essex in the 14th century. Such was its success that by the 16th century the town of Chypping Walden had been renamed Saffron Walden, and its coat of arms bore three saffron crocuses.

S

Buyer Beware

I have been astounded by the ingenious methods used to falsify saffron stigmas. Dyed lengths of corn silk and coir are not uncommon, but the most creative counterfeit version I've ever seen was made from dark red gelatin shaved into saffron-sized threads. The giveaway was that the strips dissolved after 10 minutes in hot water. I was recently given a sample of saffron that had almost no aroma but looked quite similar to the real thing. When I infused it in a glass of hot water for 10 minutes and held it up to a fluorescent light, I could see that over 50% of the "saffron" was made up of pale mauve shreds. These were crocus flower petals that had been dyed; when the dye leached out, the original petal color was revealed. Safflower petals, turmeric, dyed coconut fiber, corn silk and extruded strands of a red gelatin-like material may all be passed off as saffron, especially to unsuspecting tourists.

As possibly the only true spice ever exported to the East from England, saffron production in Essex thrived for some 400 years, spurred by a global fascination with this exotic spice and the domestic fabric and dyeing industries that developed in the area. By the 18th century, commercial cultivation of English saffron had all but ceased; according to historians its decline was hastened by greater availability of lower-cost imports and the invention of chemical dyes. Though English saffron loyalists may disagree, from my observations of other culinary herbs and spices, I suspect that saffron grown in the harsher climates of Spain, Italy, Kashmir, Iran and the Greek prefecture of Kozani probably had a greater strength of color and pungency of aroma than saffron from Essex.

Consumer protection laws are nothing new, and it seems that offences relating to the adulteration of saffron have earned perpetrators extremely severe punishments. Because of its high value, saffron is the most adulterated, copied and misrepresented spice known. In Germany in the 15th century, adulteration of saffron was taken so seriously that a committee called the Safranschau was established. This group of inquisitors punished "adulterers" and dispensed justice by burning offenders at the stake or burying them alive, along with their impure spice. Although the adulteration of saffron is not such an art form today as it was in the 15th century, there are still many instances of forgery.

The Plant

The saffron crocus is an autumn-flowering ornamental perennial that belongs to the lily family. It grows to only about 6 inches (15 cm) tall. The true saffron crocus must not be confused with an extremely poisonous plant called autumn crocus or meadow saffron (*Colchicum autumnale*), which grows wild in Britain and is an ornamental garden flower in Australia. The saffron crocus has purple flowers, six stamens and three styles, a distinguishing feature being its leafless solitary flower stalks—it bears no leaves until after blooming in autumn.

A saffron crocus's below-ground corms (bulbs)—which, by the way, are poisonous—resemble an onion in appearance. The corms send up long gray-green chive-like leaves that surround the striking lily-like blue to violet flower. This flower has protruding from its center vividly contrasting bright orange stigmas (the pollen-collecting female organs)

Spice Notes

The power of saffron's bouquet was dramatically demonstrated to me not long after we opened our spice shop. On the day our first shipment of saffron arrived from Kashmir, I spent about 30 minutes carefully packing 1-gram lots of saffron from a beautifully decorated 2-pound (1 kg) bulk tin. As soon as I came into the shop from the packing room, which is in a separate building, Liz asked, "Have you been packing saffron?" The semisweet, woody aroma was so strong that it had permeated my clothes in a very short time.

and fluffy yellow pollen-bearing stamens (the male organs). Each flower has three stigmas that are connected to the base of the bloom by a fine pale yellow thread called the style. Dried saffron stigmas separated from the style—these are the spice—are $1/3$ to $2/3$ inch (6 to 12 mm) long, dark red, and thin and needlelike at one end, broadening slightly until they fan out at the tip like a trumpet.

The bouquet, flavor strength and color of saffron vary depending on origin and quality. However, in general saffron may be described as having a tenacious woody, honey-like, oaked-wine aroma and a lingering bitter, appetite-stimulating taste. Its pungent aroma comes from safranal and its earthy, bittersweet flavor from picrocrocin. The color comes from the carotenoid crocin. Some grades of saffron may contain a percentage of pale yellow styles, which although lacking the coloring strength of the stigmas still manage to impart a classic saffron taste.

Processing

The processing of saffron is a centuries-old tradition that is revered because of saffron's high value and importance to the economy of the regions in which it is grown. Because the saffron crocus is sterile, propagation is achieved by dividing the cormlets that form around the plant's main bulb. In some countries saffron is left in the field for five years or more to keep producing; in others, the previous season's corms will be dug up in spring and replanted at the height of summer.

The saffron harvest takes place over a short period— often less than three weeks—during which time nearly every inhabitant of the adjacent towns, including all the generations, works around the clock to bring in the harvest. Each plant produces up to three flowers, on consecutive mornings. The backbreaking work of gathering these blooms commences at dawn, before the sun becomes too hot.

S

After harvesting, the next stage is removing the precious stigmas. This is generally carried out indoors, where nimble-fingered womenfolk, including grandmothers and great-grandmothers, work deep into the night to keep pace with the baskets full of shell-like blue flowers arriving from the fields. The finger-staining wet red stigmas are dexterously plucked by squeezing the style between thumb and forefinger and gently pulling it out of the base of the flower. The three stigmas, with style still attached, are then dried.

There is no noticeable flavor or aroma when the stigmas are fresh. These attributes don't develop until the spice is cured (dried) to a moisture level of 12%. While methods of drying vary somewhat from region to region, the plucked stigmas and their connecting pale styles are usually dried in a sieve over hot charcoal embers. In the case of Greek saffron from Kozani, the wet stigmas are dried on silk-lined trays at room temperature; this process yields a good-quality, very dark red saffron. Whatever the process, care needs to be taken to ensure that the moisture is removed without any overheating or scorching that would cause a loss of aroma and flavor. Fresh saffron stigmas lose about 80% of their weight in the drying process, which means a region that produces 11 tons of saffron in a year has harvested at least 55 tons of fresh saffron!

Buying and Storage

The basic principle to bear in mind when buying saffron is the same one you would apply to purchasing diamonds, gold or any other precious commodity: only buy from a reputable source. The unscrupulous and (perhaps) the ignorant have sold turmeric as ground Indian saffron and safflower petals as saffron threads. True saffron stigmas may be referred to as filaments, threads, strands, silks, fronds, stems, blades, chives or pistils. Like the purveyors of many other valuable commodities, saffron producers have established recognizable standards to help traders know what they are buying.

The two most common grades are filaments with the pale style attached and pure stigmas separated from the style. Saffron with the style attached (you will notice the wiry, threadlike pale yellow strands) should be about 20% cheaper than pure stigmas. Spanish and Kashmiri saffron with the style attached is referred to as "Mancha grade," and in Iran it is called *poshal*. Pure stigmas cut from the style are called *coupe* for Spanish saffron, *mongra* for Kashmiri, *stigmata* for Greek and *sargoal* in the case of Iranian saffron. Within these main grades there are a number of subgrades, each determined by a detailed analysis to establish key characteristics such as picrocrocin and safranal content, crocin (color) and percentage of floral waste and extraneous matter.

Saffron is also available in powdered form, but unless you are absolutely confident as to its grade and purity, I would recommend grinding your own when a recipe specifically calls for saffron powder. Saffron is easily ground by lightly toasting the stigmas in a hot, dry pan, then crushing them using a mortar and pestle or between two nested spoons.

Every producer of saffron will tell you theirs is the best; however, I prefer to say that saffron from different producers tends to have different attributes relating to aroma, flavor, color and relative cost. From my observations, the following characteristics seem to be prevalent. In the second half of the 20th century the Spanish undoubtedly implemented the most effective marketing of saffron. As a result, many food pundits think it is the best, and some even believe the spice originated in Spain. The best Spanish saffron is very good, but in any industry the variation in quality can be significant. For instance, I have seen saffron on sale in Toledo (obviously aimed at tourists) that had much more than the 20% of style that is acceptable in a pack of Mancha grade.

Kashmiri mongra-grade saffron is similar to the premium-grade Spanish. It has a distinctive, somewhat exotic woody odor that is lingering and dry in the nose after being inhaled. Color infusion into warm water is rapid enough to be convenient (5 to 10 minutes) but not so fast as to raise suspicion that artificial dyes have been added. Greek saffron sold by the Saffron Producers Cooperative of Kozani, which is based in the town of Krokos, is strictly controlled. It claims to have the highest crocin content of any saffron. It is dark red, with an aroma and taste profile like saffron from Spain and Kashmir. Most noticeable is the stigma's tendency to retain its dark red color, even after some hours of infusion.

Iran produces in excess of 90% of the world's annual production of 185 to 220 tons of saffron. Southern Khorasan, where largely traditional farming practices are used, is one of the country's principal areas for saffron production. In central Iran they used to construct pigeon towers that had thousands of holes, arranged in such a way that the bird droppings could easily be collected and used as fertilizer.

Sadly, however, this organic farming method cannot be identified as such, because the process of being certified organic is too bureaucratic and expensive for these traditional subsistence farmers.

Iranian sargoal saffron has a distinctive floral note unlike that of the other varieties, and it goes well in Middle Eastern recipes. Iranian saffron stigmas used to cost one-half to two-thirds as much as other high-grade saffron. However, intervention by the Iranian government to maximize revenue has pushed up the prices, which are now almost comparable with Kashmiri. Iranian saffron threads seem somewhat shorter in length than Kashmiri and more brittle in texture, although their color strength is comparable. The brittleness of Iranian saffron makes it relatively easy to crush to a powder.

Limited supplies of saffron from Tasmania, Australia, are becoming available, unfortunately at a very high price, thanks to the high cost of labor. Tasmanian saffron rates

Travels in the Spice Trade

Although it now produces less than 1% of the world's saffron, Spain has achieved a high degree of awareness for its product. Tradition is so entrenched in the village of Consuegra, not far from Toledo, that an annual saffron festival is held in the last weekend of October. I will never forget standing on the plains of La Mancha in a field of deep purple saffron flowers, looking over this picturesque village nestled in front of a ridge topped by *Don Quixote* windmills.

One of the highlights of the Consuegra saffron festival is the saffron-grading (plucking) competition. About a dozen contestants are seated at a long table on a stage in the village square. The first heats begin with the children and by midafternoon it is the adults' turn. Grandmothers who have been doing it for years are locked in a battle for supremacy, tempered by huge smiles and great hilarity. Each contestant is given 30 blooms and a white plate. Once the start signal goes, a dozen dexterous pairs of hands go to work. The first contestant to complete grading her 30 blooms leaps up, waving her arms in the air like a world championship wrestler. Then the judges scrutinize the results. For each valuable stigma left in a flower, one point is lost, and for each worthless stamen accidentally plucked to join the stigmas on the plate, another point is forfeited. I can highly recommend the festival. It's an enjoyable experience, enhanced by the humor and hospitality of the local people.

highly on color strength. However, the stigmas need to be infused in water for up to 8 hours before use to achieve maximum results.

Because of its high cost and the efficacy of such a small quantity, saffron is usually sold in $\frac{1}{2}$-gram or 1-gram packages. The price fluctuates to some degree as a result of supply, which can be affected by climatic conditions and world demand. At the beginning of the 21st century, 1 gram of pure saffron stigma cost about the same as $\frac{1}{2}$ gram of gold.

Store saffron in the same way as other spices: in an airtight container kept away from extremes of heat, light and humidity. Do not store saffron stigmas in the refrigerator or freezer.

For those who use saffron regularly, a quantity may be left to stand in liquid overnight. The next day, strain the solution and pour the saffron water into an ice-cube tray, then freeze until you need a little instant saffron.

Use

When used as a spice, saffron usually needs to be infused in a liquid; the sunlight-colored tincture is then added to the dish to perform its magic. A pinch of saffron (depending on the cook's interpretation, this could be anything from 10 to 30 stigmas, but I would say 10) will deeply color 2 to 3 tablespoons (30 to 45 mL) of warm water, milk, alcohol (for instance, vodka or gin), orange blossom water or rose water. The color will start to leach out of the saffron strands within seconds of being immersed; over a period that may range from five minutes to several hours, each stigma will swell and become pale as it yields its precious pigment. Because more than two-thirds of saffron's color will infuse in the first 10 minutes, it is not essential to let it stand for many hours.

Once I tried to make saffron oil by infusing saffron strands in warm oil, in the same way you would make rosemary or chile oil. It didn't work: the oil acted as a sealant on the stigmas of saffron, locking in the water-soluble color and their flavor.

Saffron is used traditionally to color Indian rice dishes, Italian risotto and Spanish paella. Its unique flavor and radiant color go well with fish, seafood and chicken. The famous Cornish saffron cake, a spicy yeast cake containing dried fruit, is colored with saffron, as is the French seafood soup bouillabaisse. The exotic Moroccan spice blend ras el hanout contains whole saffron stigmas. In North Africa, saffron imparts its flavor to chicken and lamb tagines and is used to color spiced couscous. Rich, creamy Moghul dishes often contain saffron, as do pilaus and biryani, some sweets and ice creams. In those applications I like to infuse the stigmas in rose water. Be careful not to add too much saffron to a dish, as an excessive amount will create a bitter, medicinal taste.

When cooking rice by the absorption method, an interesting way to use saffron is to add it after the water has begun to be absorbed (after about 10 minutes). Infuse a dozen stigmas in warm water when you put the rice on to cook; then, when the rice has absorbed most of the moisture, drizzle the infusion in a figure eight over its surface. Add the strands of saffron, replace the lid and continue to cook without stirring. The moisture and steam will release the color from the saffron and golden veins will bleed down into the white rice, creating an attractive mottled effect when it is served.

Once you start to use saffron, it's easy to appreciate its subtlety and how little is needed to achieve a rewarding result. Its fun to experiment with different infusions, observing how long it takes for various types of saffron to tint selected medium, and how they in turn affect the aroma and taste.

WEIGHT PER TEASPOON (5 mL)

- whole: 0.7 g
- ground: 1.5 g

SUGGESTED QUANTITY PER POUND (500 g)

- red meats: 12 to 18 stigmas
- white meats: 10 to 12 stigmas
- vegetables: 8 to 12 stigmas
- grains and pulses: 8 to 12 stigmas
- baked goods: 8 to 12 stigmas

Persian Halva

Halva is a sweet dessert found throughout the Middle East, Asia, India and Europe. The Iranian version makes use of their undeniably unique saffron by adding it to the sweet, rose-scented, buttery mixture.

Makes 6 to 8 servings

Preparation time:
10 minutes

Cooking time:
25 minutes

Tips

Superfine (caster) sugar is a very fine granulated sugar typically used in recipes that require a faster-dissolving granule. If you can't find it in stores, you can make your own by using a food processor fitted with the metal blade to process granulated sugar to a very fine, sand-like consistency.

To grind saffron, pound it using a mortar and pestle until it resembles a coarse powder.

2 cups	warm water	500 mL
1 cup	superfine (caster) sugar (see Tips, left)	250 mL
½ tsp	lightly packed saffron threads, ground (see Tips, left)	2 mL
¼ cup	rose water	60 mL
1½ cups	butter	375 mL
2 cups	all-purpose flour	500 mL
1 tbsp	pistachios, lightly crushed or chopped	15 mL
1 tbsp	almonds, lightly crushed or chopped	15 mL

1. In a bowl, combine water and sugar; stir until dissolved. Stir in saffron and rose water and set aside.

2. In a deep skillet over low heat, melt butter. Gradually add flour, stirring constantly, and cook for 8 to 10 minutes, until turning brown. Stir in prepared sugar water and cook, stirring constantly, for 10 minutes, until thickened to a smooth paste.

3. Spread mixture onto a serving plate to form a disk roughly 1 inch (2.5 cm) thick. Using a spoon, make indentations around the edge, 1 inch (2.5 cm) apart, all the way around the top and sides of the disk to create a decorative scalloped edge. Sprinkle with pistachios and almonds and set aside to cool completely before serving.

S

Paella

Paella is often thought of as Spain's national dish. Although it is found all over Spain, it actually originated in the Valencia region. There are many variations, but the unmistakable color and flavor of saffron are universal. When visiting Consuegra with Mum and Dad for the saffron harvest and annual festival, we were thrilled to see the "world's biggest paella" being cooked in a gigantic pan and stirred with half a dozen long shovels. Given the size, it was surprisingly tasty, but that version didn't use saffron.

Makes 6 servings

Preparation time:
10 minutes

Cooking time:
30 minutes

Tip

Paella rice is a medium-grain rice that is firm in the middle and soft on the outside. It is widely available in supermarkets and specialty stores.

• **14- to 18-inch (35 to 38 cm) skillet or paella pan**

4 cups	chicken broth	1 L
1 tsp	lightly packed saffron threads	5 mL
2 tsp	mild Spanish paprika	10 mL
2 tsp	sweet Hungarian paprika	10 mL
1 tsp	sweet smoked paprika	5 mL
1/4 tsp	ground dried rosemary	1 mL
1/3 cup	olive oil	75 mL
3	cloves garlic, minced	3
1 1/2 cups	paella rice (see Tip, left)	375 mL
2	boneless skinless chicken breasts, cut in 2-inch (5 cm) pieces	2
1	red bell pepper, seeded and cut into strips	1
2	tomatoes, seeded and cut into 1/2-inch (1 cm) dice	2
1/2 cup	peas	125 mL
1	calamari tube (3 to 4 oz/90 to 125 g), cleaned and cut into rings (see Tip, page 561)	1
1	halibut steak (6 to 7 oz), cut into 2-inch (5 cm) pieces	1
12	large shrimp, heads and tails intact	12
	Sea salt and freshly ground black pepper	
2 tbsp	chopped fresh parsley leaves	30 mL
2	lemons, quartered	2

1. In a small saucepan over medium heat, warm broth. Remove from heat and whisk in saffron, three paprikas and rosemary. Set aside.

Tip

Ask your fishmonger to clean the calamari for you, or follow this method: Gently pull head and tentacles away from the body. Using your fingers, reach into the body and pull out the clear backbone (quill); discard entrails. Using a sharp knife, cut the tentacles from the head just below the eyes; discard head. Cut off side wings and fine membrane. Thoroughly rinse body, tentacles and wings under cold running water and pat dry with paper towels.

2. In skillet or paella pan over medium heat, heat oil. Add garlic and rice and cook, stirring constantly, for 2 minutes, until rice is well coated. Add prepared broth and cook, stirring, for 2 minutes, until heated through. Reduce heat to low.

3. Place chicken, bell pepper and tomatoes on top of rice and cover loosely with aluminum foil (do not stir). Cook for 15 minutes, until rice is tender.

4. Top with peas, calamari, halibut and shrimp (do not stir) and season with salt and pepper to taste. Cover loosely with foil and cook for 10 minutes, until seafood and rice are cooked through (rice should be cooked al dente and form a crust on bottom of pan). Remove from heat, sprinkle with parsley and serve with lemon wedges, ideally straight from the pan at the table.

S

Sage

Salvia officinalis

Names in Other Languages

- **Arabic:** mariyamiya
- **Chinese (C):** louh meih chou
- **Chinese (M):** shu wei cao
- **Czech:** salvej
- **Danish:** salvie
- **Dutch:** salie, tuinsalie
- **Finnish:** rohtosalvia, salvia
- **French:** sauge
- **German:** Salbei
- **Greek:** alisfakia, faskomilo
- **Hungarian:** zsalya
- **Italian:** salvia
- **Japanese:** sage, sezi
- **Portuguese:** salva
- **Russian:** shalfey
- **Spanish:** salvia
- **Swedish:** salvia
- **Turkish:** adacayi

Family: Lamiaceae (formerly Labiatae)

Varieties: clary sage (*S. sclarea*), Greek sage (*S. fruticosa*), Californian black sage (*S. mellifera*), blackcurrant sage (*S. microphylla*), pineapple sage (*S. rutilans*)

Other Names: garden sage, true sage, salvia

Flavor Group: Pungent

Parts Used: leaves (as a herb)

Background

Sage, which is native to the northern Mediterranean coastal areas of southern Europe, has been cultivated for millennia. Its therapeutic virtues were mentioned by Theophrastus, Pliny and Dioscorides, who called it *elelisphakon*, one of the herb's many ancient names, along with *elifagus*, *lingua humana*, *selba* and *salvia*. The botanical name for its genus, *Salvia*, is derived from the Latin *salvere*, which means "to save" or "to heal." It was given to sage because of its medicinal properties.

Culinary Information

Combines with
- basil
- bay leaf
- chives
- garlic
- marjoram
- mint
- oregano
- paprika
- parsley
- pepper
- rosemary
- savory
- tarragon
- thyme

Traditional Uses
- rich, fatty foods such as pork, goose and duck
- bread stuffings
- dumplings
- savory scones
- soups
- casseroles
- roast meats

Spice Blends
- Italian herbs
- mixed herbs
- stuffing mixes

Wild Sage
Sage still grows wild on hills in Dalmatia, the Croatian region of former Yugoslavia on the Adriatic Sea, which is famed for the quality of its sage.

In the ninth century the emperor Charlemagne had sage grown on the imperial farms in central Europe, and during the Middle Ages it was considered indispensable as a medicine. In 16th-century England, before conventional black tea became commonplace, sage tea was a popular beverage; for those desiring something a little stronger, a brew called sage ale was made. The Chinese were so fond of sage tea in the 17th century that Dutch traders could command payment for sage leaves of three to four times their weight in China tea. By the 19th century the benefits of including sage with rich and fatty foods, such as pork and duck, were appreciated.

The Plant

There are around 750 varieties of *Salvia*, but it is garden sage (*S. officinalis*) that is of primary culinary importance. Sage is a hardy erect perennial that grows to around 35 inches (90 cm) tall, with wiry green- and purple-hued stems and a base that becomes woody over two or three years. Sage leaves are about $3\frac{1}{4}$ inches (8 cm) long and $\frac{1}{2}$ inch (1 cm) wide, gray-green and rough but downy and pebbly on top. The underneath is deeply veined and filigreed like an opaque cicada's wing. As the leaves mature and harden, their greenness turns to a soft silvery gray. Long stems bear the purple-lipped flowers in spring, which are a natural

Travels in the Spice Trade

Since my childhood I'd heard my parents referring to Dalmatian sage. As things turned out, Liz and I bought a Dalmatian puppy after our daughters left home. One day when I was taking the spotted puppy for a walk, an old gentleman stopped me and said, "Your dog is from my country." From that unexpected comment and a discussion about the beauty of the Adriatic coast, Liz and I resolved to visit Dalmatia. We wanted to see the sage growing wild—and to find out if there really were Dalmatian dogs there.

We knew that sage grew wild on the protected island of Kornati, and we were fortunate enough to make contact with the Skracic family, who lived there and had permission to harvest wild sage (this small family business markets sage products under the Kadulja brand). I could write a whole chapter about the wonderful experiences we had in Croatia, starting from Dubrovnik, driving along the magnificent Adriatic coast, and taking in spectacular views from picturesque boat rides that took us to Kornati. We stayed in one of the dozen houses on the island; the accommodations were clean and basic. We have rarely been in a more peaceful and beautiful environment, and the hospitality of our hosts was extraordinary.

The next morning we went sage harvesting with the family, cutting small bunches with battery-operated shears and placing the cut stems in a sack to take back to the house. Sometimes I am concerned about wild harvesting because it often prevents plants from re-establishing themselves by natural means, which leads to their extinction. On Kornati the sage is harvested only after flowering. When the sage is in flower, beekeepers arrive with their hives to gather pollen. The landscape is a mass of purple flowers that are visited by millions of bees. Sage honey made by these bees is another not-to-be missed taste experience.

Sage oil is produced on the island by steam distillation, and as a byproduct of the distillation process they also make sage hydrosol, the water-soluble component. These products are used for medicinal purposes and in aromatherapy.

As a footnote (or perhaps I should say pawnote), we saw plenty of pictures of Dalmatians on postcards and T-shirts, but not a single hound. It seems that most of our dog's relatives are mascots in fire departments around the world, especially in the U.S.A.!

attraction to bees. These produce a much-valued sage honey in Dalmatia, where sage is native.

Sage has a high pungency level, similar to that of rosemary and thyme. Its aroma is fresh, head-clearing and balsamic. The flavor is herbaceous, savory and astringent, with hints of peppermint. Dried sage leaves retain the characteristic aroma and flavor of fresh sage very well. These are most often identified as "rubbed" leaves; they are light gray in color, with a fluffy, springy texture.

Other Varieties

Clary sage (*S. sclarea*) is a sparser variety of *Salvia*. It is not used much in cooking these days. It has somewhat rust-colored foliage with bluish white to white flowers. **Greek**

sage (*S. fruticosa*) has a weaker flavor than garden sage. It is used mostly for making a herbal tea. **Purple leaf sage** (*S. officinalis* var. *purpurascens*) makes an attractive addition to the herb garden. It can be used in cooking in the same way as garden sage. **Californian black sage** (*S. mellifera*) grows in the southwest of North America. The leaves can be used as a substitute for garden sage, although they are less pungent. The seeds are ground and used as a thin porridge or grits.

Blackcurrant sage (*S. microphylla*) is from South America. It is used in some Mexican dishes. It has a flavor like sage with a fruity blackcurrant back note. **Pineapple sage** (*S. rutilans*) is indigenous to Central America. It is another of the red-flowered sages and is aptly named for the pineapple-like flavor of its flowers. Pineapple sage has delicate 1-inch (2.5 cm) long, thin, nectar-filled flowers that can be picked and added to salads—or you can just suck the delicious sweet nectar straight from the flower.

Processing

Because sage plants become extremely woody after a few years, even with regular cutting back, they need to be replanted every three years. Layering (see page 28) is an efficient method of propagating sage.

Sage is gathered after flowering. It is hung upside down to dry in dark, well-aired places. The stems are then rubbed to

remove the leaves. Because of their high oil content and the fluffy structure of the leaf, even when dried properly (to less than 12% moisture), rubbed sage leaves will not feel as crisp as many other dried herbs.

An essential oil is extracted from freshly harvested leaves by steam distillation. This is used in seasonings for pork sausages, processed foods, perfumes, confectionery, mouthwashes and gargles.

Buying and Storage

Bunches of fresh sage are readily available from produce retailers. Sage should not look wilted when bought. A bunch standing in a glass of water (as if in a vase) will last for at least a week at room temperature, provided the water is replaced every second day. Sage leaves can also be chopped and put in an ice-cube tray, barely covered with water, and frozen until required (use within about 3 months).

When buying dried sage for making sage tea, try to purchase Dalmatian sage, as this type is undisputedly the best for medicinal purposes. If rubbed, it should be woolly and gray with a greenish tinge and have the characteristic balsamic aroma and savory taste of fresh sage.

Store dried sage in an airtight container and keep in a cool, dark place. It will keep its flavor for more than 1 year.

Use

While some people may find the pungency of sage overpowering, its astringent grease-cutting attributes make it a perfect accompaniment to fatty foods such as pork, goose and duck. Sage often produces the best results when used in moderation and in dishes that are cooked for a long time, such as osso bucco. Its flavor is rarely diminished by exposure to extended cooking times.

Sage goes well with carbohydrates and it is an important ingredient in bread stuffings, dumplings and savory scones. Pea, bean and vegetable soups benefit from sage, as does a mash of potatoes. Sage and onions is a well-known combination, and moderate amounts of sage are excellent with eggplant and tomatoes. Sage is a traditional element in mixed herbs along with thyme and marjoram. Sage will complement any full-bodied soup, stew, meat loaf or roast meat dish. Deep-fried sage leaves make a fashionable garnish.

WEIGHT PER TEASPOON (5 mL)

- whole dried and rubbed leaves: 1.2 g

SUGGESTED QUANTITY PER POUND (500 g)

- **red meats:** 1 tbsp (15 mL) fresh leaves, 1 tsp (5 mL) dried rubbed leaves
- **white meats:** 2 tsp (10 mL) fresh leaves, ¾ tsp (3 mL) dried rubbed leaves
- **vegetables:** 1½ tsp (7 mL) fresh leaves, ½ tsp (2 mL) dried rubbed leaves
- **grains and pulses:** 1½ tsp (7 mL) fresh leaves, ½ tsp (2 mL) dried rubbed leaves
- **baked goods:** 1½ tsp (7 mL) fresh leaves, ½ tsp (2 mL) dried rubbed leaves

Burnt Sage Butter

This is simply the best accompaniment to pasta. My favorite ways to serve it are with ricotta gnocchi, pumpkin ravioli or fresh homemade fettuccine. The first time you make this butter you will wonder why you haven't tried it before. It's a great dinner-party dish that impresses with minimal effort. The soft, almost furry, fresh sage leaves turn light and crispy and are delicious eaten whole (which cannot be said for fresh leaves).

Makes 1 cup (250 mL)

Preparation time:
5 minutes

Cooking time:
10 minutes

Tip

Sage butter can be stored in the freezer for up to 3 months. To freeze, transfer mixture to an airtight container and refrigerate until completely cool. Once cold, using the paddle attachment of a stand mixer, beat until smooth. Divide into desired portions, wrap in plastic wrap and freeze.

1 cup	good-quality salted butter	250 mL
½ cup	lightly packed fresh sage leaves	125 mL

1. In a small saucepan over medium heat, melt butter until it is beginning to foam. Add sage and cook for about 5 minutes, until butter has turned a caramel color and sage leaves have shrunk and become crispy. Serve immediately.

Variation

For a spicy version, add 1 tsp (5 mL) hot pepper flakes to the pan with the sage.

S

Sage Stuffing

Sage has a natural affinity with baked goods. This tasty stuffing mix can be used for chicken or turkey. At Christmas, when stuffing becomes a dish in itself, you can embellish it with good-quality sausage meat and some puréed chestnuts.

Makes enough to stuff 1 large chicken (double the quantity for turkey)

Preparation time:
10 minutes

Cooking time:
5 minutes

Tip

To make fresh bread crumbs, ideally use a loaf of fresh or day-old white bread. Cut into thick slices, then rub between your palms to make fine crumbs. Alternatively, use a box grater or food processor. Fresh bread crumbs will be much larger than dried.

2 tbsp	butter	30 mL
1/2	onion, finely chopped	1/2
1 tbsp	finely chopped fresh parsley leaves	15 mL
2	fresh sage leaves, finely chopped	2
1 tbsp	sweet paprika	15 mL
1 tsp	ground coriander seed	5 mL
1 tsp	dried sage	5 mL
1/2 tsp	dried thyme	2 mL
1/2 tsp	dried oregano	2 mL
1/4 tsp	fine sea salt	1 mL
1/4 tsp	freshly ground black pepper	1 mL
1 cup	soft fresh bread crumbs (see Tip, left)	250 mL

1. In a skillet over medium heat, melt butter. Add onion and sauté for 3 minutes, until softened. Turn out into a bowl and stir in parsley and fresh sage, until well combined. Add paprika, coriander seed, dried sage, thyme, oregano, salt, pepper and bread crumbs. Mix well. (The stuffing may seem dry but it will absorb juices from the meat when cooking.)

Variation

For a Christmas side dish, combine this stuffing with 1 lb (500 g) sausage meat, 1 cup (250 mL) cooked puréed chestnuts and 1/2 cup (125 mL) dried cranberries in a large skillet. Cook over medium heat until meat is cooked through, about 20 minutes.

Sage Shortbread with Goat Cheese

These tasty shortbreads are one of Dad's favorites. They are an excellent platform for rich cheeses because the astringency of sage balances fatty flavors. I serve these in the festive season, topped with a little cranberry sauce and a piece of pecan.

**Makes about
25 shortbreads**

Preparation time:
 10 minutes

Cooking time:
 25 minutes, plus
 30 minutes for chilling

- - - - - - - - - - - - - - - - -

Tip

The dough can be frozen for up to 3 months; bake from frozen and add an extra 3 to 4 minutes to the baking time.

- **Food processor**
- **2 baking sheets, lined with parchment paper**

3½ oz	blue cheese, such as Roquefort or Stilton	100 g
1½ cups	all-purpose flour, sifted	375 mL
⅔ cup	butter	150 mL
3 tbsp	finely chopped fresh sage	45 mL
½ cup	pecans, shelled and finely chopped	125 mL
3½ oz	soft goat cheese (chèvre)	100 g

1. In food processor fitted with the metal blade, process blue cheese, flour, butter and sage until a sticky dough forms. Turn out onto a clean work surface and, using your hands, work in pecans. Divide dough in half and roll into logs about 2 inches (5 cm) in diameter. Wrap tightly in plastic wrap and refrigerate for about 30 minutes, until very firm.

2. Preheat oven to 350°F (180°C). Remove plastic wrap from dough and, using a sharp knife, cut into ¼-inch (5 mm) slices. Arrange slices on prepared baking sheets 1 inch (2.5 cm) apart. Bake in preheated oven for 10 to 15 minutes, until golden. Carefully transfer shortbreads to a wire rack to cool completely. To serve, top each with a pat of goat cheese. Store cooled shortbread in an airtight container for up to 2 weeks.

S

Salad Burnet

Sanguisorba minor (formerly *Poterium sanguisorba*)

Family: Rosaceae

Varieties: garden burnet (*S. officinalis*)

Other Names: lesser burnet, garden burnet

Flavor Group: Mild

Parts Used: leaves (as a herb)

Background

Although the mountainous areas of Europe and the chalk downs of the southern counties of England have been the native habitat of salad burnet for many centuries, it is thought to have originated in the Mediterranean. Its medicinal properties were appreciated by the Roman naturalist Pliny. The old botanic name *Poterium* was derived from the Greek word *poterion*, which means "drinking cup."

Culinary Information

Combines with
- basil
- chervil
- coriander leaf
- lovage
- oregano
- parsley
- Vietnamese mint

Traditional Uses
- salads
- chilled soups
- herb sandwiches
- scrambled eggs and omelets
- fruit drinks

Spice Blends
- not commonly used in spice blends

(The leaves were added to wine cups and beverages.) The rest of the name, *sanguisorba*, comes from *sanguis* ("blood") and *sorbere*, meaning "to staunch," alluding to its styptic properties: it was used to stop bleeding. The early settlers took salad burnet to America, and it is also a familiar sight in herb gardens in Australia.

The Plant

Salad burnet is a delicate perennial herb that grows to around 12 inches (30 cm) in height. It has small, round, serrated deep green leaves that look as though they have been cut with pinking scissors. These leaves are borne in pairs about 1 inch (2.5 cm) apart, on slender stems that droop evenly when long and heavy, giving a fern-like appearance. In summer, tall stalks rise from the center of the plant and are crowned with reddish pink berry-like flowers with long purple stamens. The aroma and flavor of salad burnet are like that of cucumber: cool, light and refreshing.

Other Varieties
Garden burnet (*Sanguisorba officinalis*) has coarser leaves than salad burnet and is used mostly for medicinal purposes. Toxicity information is sketchy, so caution is advised when consuming this variety.

Processing

Salad burnet is only used fresh, as it does not dehydrate satisfactorily.

S

SUGGESTED
QUANTITY PER
POUND (500 g)

- **red meats:** ¾ cup (175 mL) fresh leaves
- **white meats:** ¾ cup (175 mL) fresh leaves
- **vegetables:** ½ cup (125 mL) fresh leaves
- **grains and pulses:** ½ cup (125 mL) fresh leaves
- **baked goods:** ½ cup (125 mL) fresh leaves

Buying and Storage

Fresh bunches of salad burnet can be purchased occasionally from produce retailers; however, they are prone to wilting so are best bought the day they are to be used. After washing, store in the same manner as lettuce, wrapped in plastic wrap and placed in a crisper at the bottom of the refrigerator, where they will last for 3 to 5 days.

To ensure a ready supply for dropping into beverages, pull the small leaves from the stalks and place them whole in ice-cube trays, top up with water and freeze. Once frozen, turn out into resealable bags; they will keep for up to 2 months in the freezer.

Use

Salad burnet is always best used fresh. As the name suggests, the cucumber-like taste and delicate appearance go well in salads, chilled soups and herb sandwiches with ricotta or cream cheese. Scrambled eggs serve well with a garnish of salad burnet and chervil, and like borage, salad burnet leaves enhance the cooling appearance of summer fruit punches.

Salad with Toasted Seeds and Grains

Its cucumber-like taste and attractive leaves make salad burnet a great choice for summer salads. The crunchy topping on this salad gives substance and texture to the cooling salad burnet and sweet tomatoes.

Makes 4 servings

Preparation time:
5 minutes

Cooking time:
5 minutes

Tips

If salad burnet is not available, any other salad leaf, such as arugula or chicory, will suffice.

Precooked spelt and quinoa are available at some supermarkets and health-food stores. Alternatively, simmer quinoa in a pot of boiling salted water for 10 minutes or until the germ separates from the seed (it will look like they have split open, revealing a small white particle, which is the germ). Spelt needs to be simmered for 25 minutes or until tender. The seed and grain mixture can be kept in an airtight container in the refrigerator for up to 2 weeks and used for snacking, as a topping on dips, or in sandwiches.

2 tsp	extra virgin olive oil, divided	10 mL
1 tbsp	chia seeds	15 mL
1 tbsp	pumpkin seeds	15 mL
1 tbsp	raw unsalted sunflower seeds	15 mL
2 tbsp	cooked spelt (see Tips, left)	30 mL
2 tbsp	cooked quinoa (see Tips, left)	30 mL
Pinch	ground rosemary	Pinch
Pinch	fine sea salt	Pinch
2 cups	lightly packed salad burnet leaves (see Tips, left)	500 mL
2 cups	baby spinach	500 mL
1 cup	yellow cherry tomatoes, halved	250 mL
1 tsp	freshly squeezed lemon juice	5 mL

1. In a skillet over medium heat, heat 1 tsp (5 mL) oil. Add chia, pumpkin and sunflower seeds, spelt, quinoa and rosemary. Cook, stirring constantly, for about 5 minutes, until grains are toasted and lightly browned. Season with salt and set pan aside to cool.

2. In a shallow serving bowl, toss salad burnet, spinach and tomatoes with 1 tsp (5 mL) oil and lemon juice. Top with toasted seeds and grains. Serve immediately.

S

Salt

Sodium chloride (NaCl)

Other Names: common salt, halite

Flavor Group: classed on its own, as Salty

Parts Used: crystals (as a spice)

Background

In a classic "Which came first, the chicken or the egg?" scenario, no one knows for sure exactly where the salt in the sea came from. Was it in rocks that were eroded over millions of years and carried down to the sea, or was it already in the ancient seas that left huge underground deposits—such as the layer of salt 3,300 feet (1,000 m) deep that lies under the mud and sand on the bottom of the Mediterranean?

Highly valued for its taste and preserving capabilities, there is evidence of salt gathering ("winning") that dates back to Neolithic times. Plutarch described salt as "the noblest of foods, the finest condiment of all," and Jesus

Culinary Information

Combines with
- all herbs and spices (when not excessive)

Traditional Uses
- all savory dishes
- some sweet dishes

Spice Blends
The majority of herb and spice blends designed to be sprinkled on meats before cooking and at the table, such as

- barbecue seasonings
- steak, fish and poultry sprinkles
- seasoned salts

Kosher Salt

Kosher salt is simply salt with large absorbent crystals, which was originally used for "koshering" meat (making it kosher by drawing out the blood from its surface). Ideally it should contain no additives, which gives it a fresher, cleaner taste than table salt, which is usually iodized. However, today some brands of kosher salt contain anticaking agents.

referred to his Apostles as "the salt of the earth." One of the first major Roman roads was called Via Salaria (Salt Street). Roman troops abroad received a salt ration as part of their remuneration, which eventually developed into a cash payment and became *salary*. Traders understood the value of salt to communities remote from underground salt deposits or the sea, and rulers quickly appreciated the benefits of taxing the trade in salt. In the first century CE, the Roman naturalist Pliny wrote that the rulers of India and China earned more revenue from their salt taxes than they did from their goldmines.

Salt has been regarded as pivotal to the existence of humanity. It is seen as a commodity that is essentially pure and never deteriorates (damp salt can always be dried out again, with no loss of taste); consequently, numerous superstitions about salt have become entrenched in our psyche. When salt is spilled, it is not unusual to throw a pinch over one's left shoulder to smite the devil in the eye. Lot's wife was turned into a pillar of salt, and in Leonardo da Vinci's painting of the Last Supper, a spilled saltcellar is under Judas's elbow. A classic tale that I like to "take with a pinch of salt" is of the courageous Marquis de Montreval, who died of fright in 1716 after the contents of a saltcellar were accidentally spilled over him. To this day numerous religious rites involve the symbolism of salt. But in all its history, it seems that salt has never suffered as much criticism as has been leveled at it in recent years, perhaps as a consequence of its abuse. Nonetheless, salt remains one of the five fundamental tastes (sweet, sour, salt, bitter and umami), and without it, in balance, our diets would be bland in the extreme.

Why Salt?

Although it is not a spice, salt was undoubtedly the first seasoning; its history dates back to the dawn of humanity. Salt is one of the fundamental tastes, along with sweet, sour, bitter and umami. Salt performs the essential function of maintaining the equilibrium of our body fluids, a balance so critical that one can be at greater risk of dehydration from lack of salt than from a shortage of water. It must be said that healthy adults need only about 6 to 8 grams of salt a day, an amount largely provided by seasoning the food we eat. Excessive use, most of which is provided by processed foods, can lead to health problems.

Salt is a mineral. As a result, it may or may not contain a number of impurities, including minerals, algae and other elements from the environment. These affect color and flavor. The component responsible for the salty taste is sodium chloride (NaCl), while various other minerals, such as salts of iron, soda or magnesium, contribute to the flavor characteristics of salts from different parts of the world.

The main types of salt come from underground deposits or are harvested from the sea. Whether fine or coarse, salt is always crystalline and dissolves readily upon coming into contact with moisture. This makes it easy to add, even to dry foods that are moistened only just before consumption.

Varieties of Salt

There are many different types of special salts. Each is distinguished by its origins and the traditional methods of winning that are used, which generally involve hand-raking.

Indian black salt is a true rock salt that is sold in either large—1$\frac{1}{2}$ to 2 inches (4 to 5 cm)—dark purple to red chunks or ground into a fine pink powder, which is infinitely easier to use. Black salt has a particularly sulfurous aroma, much of which dissipates during cooking, and is in my opinion the best salt for seasoning Indian recipes. Black salt complements seafood and combines well with asafetida, cumin, garam masala and amchur powder in that deliciously spiced salt blend chaat masala (page 704).

Black Mediterranean sea salt is made by blending sea salt with activated volcanic charcoal. It makes an attractive finishing salt that claims health benefits from the presence of beneficial trace minerals, notably magnesium.

Fleur de sel is from the saltpan areas in France, which have been producing salt for more than 1,500 years. It is an expensive, almost sweet, floral-tasting salt harvested from

Seasoned Salts

Seasoned salts (see page 762), such as celery salt, garlic salt and onion salt, are simply blends of herbs and spices that contain a large amount of salt. A trend today is to sell various kinds of flavored salts. In my opinion, most of them are a waste of money—you can make your own in seconds. Why pay an exorbitant price for a chile salt, a lemon myrtle salt or a herb salt when you can add 10% of any of those ingredients to salt you already have? Salt is relatively cheap and it is heavy; it has become the dry-food manufacturer's answer to water, often acting as a bulking agent at the expense of other, more subtle flavors.

S

Black Mediterranean sea salt

Smoked Salts

Smoked salts are produced by smoking salt flakes or crystals over the embers of a fire. With increased consumer interest in flavored salts, some smoked salts are also being made by adding smoke flavoring and MSG to plain salt.

natural saltpans on the islands of Ré and Noirmoutier and in parts of Brittany.

Celtic sea salt (or gray salt, as it is sometimes called) comes from the same vicinity as fleur de sel. It is hand-raked and has a coarse look and moist texture. It is not as convenient to sprinkle over food as fleur de sel, but the flavor hints of the ocean and it goes wonderfully in most cooking applications.

Maldon sea salt is from Maldon in Essex, England. Its characteristic flaky texture is achieved by spreading the concentrated solution (after initial evaporation) over flat surfaces, on which it is finally dried before being scraped up. It has become fashionable to put Maldon sea salt in china crucibles on tables in restaurants, as the texture and slightly sweet taste are best suited to being added at the end of cooking or at the table. **South African caviar salt** is produced in a similar way to Maldon sea salt, except that instead of being flat and flaky, the pieces are tiny caviar-shaped balls.

Australian Murray River salt comes in various forms, including flakes and pink salt. It is produced by extracting salt from groundwater with high salinity and is marketed as a gourmet product. In an area where salinity has become

Travels in the Spice Trade

When Liz and I were in Turkey to research sumac, we walked a few blocks from our hotel in Izmir to an old street that had escaped the disastrous fires that razed many of the city's wooden structures in 1924. Charming balconies and vine-covered trellises flanked each side. At night the cobbled roadway was closed to traffic and filled with tables and chairs from the streetfront restaurants. When we sat down for dinner, our hosts suggested the fish baked in salt, an impressive dish because the salt sets hard like a shell during baking. With much fanfare the waiter brought the encrusted fish to the table and bashed it, breaking away the crust and sending shards of salt and brittle fins flying across the table and onto the cobblestones. Inside was a beautifully cooked delicate fish that flaked easily from the bone, seasoned only with lemon juice and freshly ground black pepper. We washed it down with a light, dry Turkish red wine. Delicious!

Salt Mills

Salt mills look attractive on the table; the twist of the mill and the crystalline rain of crunchy salt add a pleasing dimension to any meal. Take care, though, when selecting a salt grinder. Because salt is highly corrosive, most metals (even stainless steel) have enough impurities in them to oxidize when they come in contact with it. Wood and plastic mechanisms work well, although they wear out quickly. The best types of salt grinders have ceramic parts that will not rust or succumb to salt's abrasive nature.

an environmental issue, with land lost to agricultural production at the rate of one football field per hour, this process has enabled re-vegetation of previously useless land, with positive ecological results. **Hawaiian pink salt** has a sweetness not found in most other salts and is available in a range of textures and shades of pink.

Processing

The process of gathering salt is called "winning," a term also used for mining coal or extraction of ore. Salt is processed by three main methods: agricultural, mining and industrial (methods vary depending on where the salt is produced). **Agricultural** methods involve diversion of seawater into evaporative ponds, salt marshes or saltpans. The process often involves several stages of evaporation. In **mining**, rock salt, which is found in large underground halite deposits formed by the evaporation of ancient seas, is mined from huge galleries like the one in Wieliczka, Poland, which is 1,300 feet (400 m) below the surface; the main gallery is the size of a cathedral. Mining was more common in the past. It has been largely replaced by the **industrial** technique, which involves injecting water into rock salt deposits. This dissolves the salt, which is then filtered and evaporated by boiling.

Refined salt is simply salt that has been dissolved in water to remove impurities that affect the color and flavor. Once these elements are refined out, the salt is redried and made available in varying crystal sizes. In refined salt the minerals have been stripped out, and additives such as iodine and free-flow agents to prevent clumping are included.

Health Note

There is strong medical evidence that most of us are consuming levels of salt in excess of our daily requirements, leading to a number of health issues. The prevalence of salt in processed and fast foods is largely responsible for concerns about the quantity of sodium in contemporary diets. I use salt in cooking, but if you are in the habit of salting food heavily, you can reduce this dependence by substituting herbs and spices that add flavor without adding sodium.

Buying and Storage

The distinguishing features of the many different kinds of salt are taste characteristics that underpin the basic saltiness; the texture, which affects mouthfeel and how it dissolves or reacts in cooking; and the color, which can help to distinguish one kind of salt from another.

There is an expectation of purity when it comes to salt. The most popular forms are pure white; even a microscopic amount of foreign matter or discoloration is not tolerated. Curiously, some fashionable salts, such as Celtic salt and Himalayan pink salt, are perceived as more natural than, say, Maldon salt flakes because they come in varying shades of off-white.

Common salt (cooking salt, kitchen salt, ordinary household salt) is refined salt from mines or the ocean. Because the majority of impurities have been removed, it delivers an uncomplicated standard taste. It may be coarse or fine, and sometimes magnesium carbonate or sodium aluminosilicate is added to make it free-flowing. **Table salt** is a more refined version of common salt. It is finely ground and often has some form of anticaking agent added. Iodized salt was produced to supplement iodine-deficient diets and reduce the incidence of thyroid problems. Iodine naturally occurs in sea salt but diminishes during storage. **Rock salt** is the name given more often than not to coarse sea salt, a reference to its chunky shape. Strictly speaking, rock salt is halite, the salt mined from underground deposits. Non-food-grade rock salt is used to make old-fashioned ice-cream churns cold, and in saltwater swimming pools where electrolysis creates chlorine. It is the salt used for melting ice on winter roads.

Herb and vegetable salts are formulated using plants or extracts of plants, such as seaweed, that have high levels of natural mineral salts. Unfortunately, many consumers think they are buying a product produced solely from vegetable matter. However, the majority of these salts may contain substantial amounts of common salt. In the 1980s, when the salt scare was as its peak, substitutes made from potassium chloride were marketed. These salt imitations were bitter and imparted an unpleasant taste if too much was added. They had the additional complication of causing adverse physiological reactions in some people. Those on a low-salt diet should check with their physician about the appropriateness of any salt substitute they plan to use.

Salt is best stored in airtight containers to protect it from high humidity. It won't deteriorate if it gets damp, but it will go lumpy and be inconvenient to use.

Use

When it comes to adding the right amount of salt to food, everyone's an expert. We have control over salt—we can add it at the table and use just as much as we like. The paradox with salt is that there is no point in being timid with it, but if you've added too much, you can't take it out.

Salt should generally be added toward the end of cooking, because if you taste a dish and think the salt is just right at the beginning, any reduction during cooking will concentrate the salt content in relation to the volume of ingredients in the dish. The only way to reduce saltiness is to dilute the proportion of salt by adding more ingredients. Adding sugar, as some food writers have advised, will not counteract too much salt.

Salt enhances the flavor of vegetables when it's added to cooking water, because it raises the salinity level, which means that less of the vegetables' natural mineral salts will be leached out. Salt sprinkled over slices of zucchini, eggplant and similar vegetables prior to cooking will draw out the bitter juices. Salting vegetables before pickling them leaches out excess moisture and toughens them to create a crisp texture. Salt is an important element in the process of preservation. For instance, by drawing out moisture and inhibiting microbial activity it dries fish effectively, and numerous pickles rely on its antiseptic and enzyme-deactivating attributes.

WEIGHT PER TEASPOON (5 mL)

Salts vary in bulk density depending on the particle size and moisture content, hence these examples:

- **Celtic gray salt:** 6.8 g
- **Maldon flaky salt:** 4.6 g
- **table salt:** 7.2 g

SUGGESTED QUANTITY PER POUND (500 g)

- **red meats:** 1/2 tsp (2 mL)
- **white meats:** 1/2 tsp (2 mL)
- **vegetables:** 1/2 tsp (2 mL)
- **grains and pulses:** 1/2 tsp (2 mL)
- **baked goods:** 1/2 tsp (2 mL)

S

Preserved Lemons

In Morocco, preserved lemons are an indispensable ingredient in tagines and stews. I love how the flavor of a lemon can change so much—and the reversal of roles (the rind is eaten and the flesh is generally discarded). Small lemons picked straight from the tree are ideal, but any will work.

**Makes
8 preserved
lemons**

Preparation time:
10 minutes, plus 3 to
4 weeks for preserving

Cooking time: none

Tip

After scrubbing the lemons, use the heel of your hand to roll them firmly on a clean work surface to release the juices.

• **4- to 6-cup (1 to 1.5 L) sterilized canning jar**

8	unwaxed lemons, scrubbed (see Tip, left)	8
½ cup	coarse sea salt	125 mL
2	2-inch (5 cm) cinnamon sticks	2
2	bay leaves	2
	Freshly squeezed juice of 2 lemons	

1. Cut lemons in half and rub generously with salt. Place 8 lemon halves in jar, pushing down to compact and squeeze out juice. Add cinnamon and bay leaves. Top with remaining 8 lemon halves, followed by any remaining salt and lemon juice (lemons should be completely covered). Seal tightly with lid and set aside in a cool, dark place for 3 to 4 weeks, turning jar upside down every few days. Add more lemon juice if needed to ensure lemons remain covered in liquid. After 3 to 4 weeks lemon rind should be very soft.

2. Refrigerate once jar is opened. Preserved lemons will keep in the refrigerator for up to 6 months. To use, rinse off excess salt under cold running water and add to dish as needed.

Salt-Baked Snapper

My parents first ate this dish in Turkey. The method produces a beautifully cooked delicate fish, seasoned only with lemon juice and pepper, that flakes easily off the bone. We all now find it a great way to serve fish at home—with a bit of theater when cracking the crust.

Makes 2 to 4 servings

Preparation time:
10 minutes

Cooking time:
40 minutes

- **13- by 9-inch (33 by 23 cm) baking dish**
- **Preheat oven to 400°F (200°C)**

2	whole snappers (12 oz/375 g), scaled and gutted	2
1	lemon, sliced	1
	Freshly ground black pepper	
2	egg whites, beaten	2
3 lbs	coarse sea salt	1.5 kg

1. Tuck an equal number of lemon slices into cavity of each fish. Season generously with pepper.

2. In a large bowl, combine egg whites and salt. Spread a $1/2$-inch (1 cm) layer of mixture evenly on bottom of baking dish. Place fish on top. Completely cover fish with remaining mixture. Bake in preheated oven for 40 minutes, until salt forms a hard crust. Serve at the table, cracking crust with the back of a knife. Remove flesh from bones, shaking off excess salt.

S

Saltbush

Atriplex nummularia (also known as *A. johnstonii*)

Names in Other Languages

- **Croatian:** soli bush
- **Czech:** sul bush
- **Dutch:** zout bush
- **French:** sel brousse
- **German:** Salzbusch
- **Hungarian:** so bokor
- **Indonesian:** garam semak
- **Italian:** cespuglio sale
- **Malay:** garam belukar
- **Portuguese:** sal mato
- **Spanish:** orgaza
- **Turkish:** tuz cali
- **Vietnamese:** muoi bui

Family: Chenopodiaceae

Varieties: old man saltbush (*A. nummalaria*), wheelscale saltbush (*A. elegans*), silverscale saltbush (*A. argentea* var. *expansa*), Nuttall's saltbush (*A. nuttalli*), sack saltbush (*A. saccaria*), wedgescale saltbush (*A. truncata*)

Other Names: giant saltbush, bluegreen saltbush

Flavor Group: Medium

Parts Used: leaves (as a herb)

Background

There are more than 250 species in the *Atriplex* genus, often referred to simply as "saltbush." These grow in subtropical and temperate regions of the world. Saltbush is indigenous to Australia, where Aboriginal peoples collected the seeds for making damper, an iconic Australian bread now made with wheat flour. Saltbush has been naturalized in North America and Mexico. Most of these plants are recognized only for their value as fodder for animals. In southern

Culinary Information

Combines with

- ajowan
- akudjura
- basil
- bay leaf
- coriander seed
- garlic
- lemon myrtle
- marjoram
- mint
- nutmeg
- oregano
- paprika
- rosemary
- sage
- thyme
- wattleseed

Traditional Uses

- seafood
- soups
- casseroles
- terrines
- sausages

Spice Blends

- spice rubs for fish
- in spice blends as a salt substitute

Australia, saltbush is one of the most common forage shrubs; it provides a food source for livestock when feed is scarce during times of drought.

Saltbush contains around 20% of the sodium found in common salt. If salt was scarce, it is believed, some people consumed saltbush just for its salty taste. In recent times, following the demonization of salt as an overused food additive, those wishing to reduce salt in their diets have turned to herbs such as saltbush, which have a low naturally occurring sodium content but can provide a salty taste.

The Plant

There are around 60 species of saltbush growing in semiarid areas around Australia. The largest is the one we call "old man saltbush." It is an evergreen shrub that can grow to 10 feet (3 m) tall and may have a diameter almost equal to its height. The leaves are $1/2$ to $1 1/4$ inches (1 to 3 cm) long and have a scaly coating that gives them an attractive gray appearance, a little like sage. The shape of the leaves can range from quite round to elliptical. The plant has very small flowers (the male and female flowers occur on different

S

plants) that are pollinated by wind. Saltbush is tolerant of droughts and will grow in areas of high salinity.

Other Varieties

The numerous other varieties mentioned on page 584 are all very similar to *Atriplex nummularia*. They are used primarily as fodder for livestock. The leaves and stems have the same salty taste.

Processing

Saltbush is harvested and dried in the same way as the majority of culinary herbs, except that it is not as critical that it be protected from sunlight as it is for very green herbs. Once dry, the leaves are usually rubbed to create small—$\frac{1}{16}$ to $\frac{3}{16}$ inch (2 to 4 mm)—flakes that will soften readily when added to food.

Buying and Storage

Spice shops that sell Australian native produce and some specialty food stores will sell dried saltbush. Store in the same way as other herbs and spices, in a dark place protected from extremes of heat and humidity. Dried saltbush will keep its flavor for more than 1 year.

Use

Besides saltbush's use as a salt substitute, in an interesting marketing twist, some lamb producers in Australia are selling "saltbush lamb." The assertion is that lamb fed on saltbush will yield a particularly tasty and succulent meat. Saltbush lamb is indeed delicious; however, at this stage I am unsure how much influence the saltbush has on the flavor. It may be that the excellent result is due to the quality of animal husbandry.

When it comes to cooking with saltbush, in addition to its obvious sodium content, its flavor is a little like thyme and parsley. Saltbush can be added to all savory foods such as soups, casseroles and roasts, with or instead of salt. I like to include it in a spice rub with paprika, pepperberry, wattleseed and lemon myrtle for seasoning seafood.

WEIGHT PER TEASPOON (5 mL)
- rubbed leaves: 1.5 g

SUGGESTED QUANTITY PER POUND (500 g)
- red meats: 1 tsp (5 mL)
- white meats: ¾ tsp (3 mL)
- vegetables: ½ tsp (2 mL)
- grains and pulses: ½ tsp (2 mL)
- baked goods: ½ tsp (2 mL)

Savory

Satureja hortensis

Names in Other Languages

- **Arabic:** nadgh
- **Chinese (C):** fung leuhn choi, heung bohk hoh
- **Chinese (M):** feng lun cai, xiang bao he
- **Czech:** saturejka
- **Danish:** bonneurt
- **Dutch:** bonenkruid, kunne
- **Finnish:** kesakynteli
- **French:** sarriette, poivrette
- **German:** Bohnenkraut, Pfefferkraut, Saturei
- **Greek:** throubi, tragorigani
- **Hungarian:** csombord
- **Indian:** salvia-sefakups
- **Italian:** santoreggia
- **Japanese:** seibari
- **Norwegian:** sar, bonneurt
- **Portuguese:** segurelha
- **Russian:** chabyor
- **Spanish:** sabroso
- **Swedish:** kyndel
- **Turkish:** dag reyhani, zatar

Family: Lamiaceae (formerly Labiatae)

Varieties: summer savory (*S. hortensis*), winter savory (*S. montana*; also known as *S. illyrica*, *S. obovata*), lemon-scented winter savory (*S. montana citriodora*), thyme-leaved savory (*S. thymbra*), creeping savory (*S. spicigera*)

Other Names: garden savory, sweet savory

Flavor Group: Pungent

Parts Used: leaves (as a herb)

Background

Savory is native to the Mediterranean and has been an important culinary herb for thousands of years. The ancient Romans valued it as a potherb and as a seasoning, and at their feasts they served a sauce made of vinegar steeped with savory. Savory's peppery taste was appreciated, as

S

Culinary Information

Combines with

- ajowan
- basil
- bay leaf
- coriander seed
- garlic
- marjoram
- nutmeg
- oregano
- paprika
- rosemary
- sage
- tarragon
- thyme

Traditional Uses

- beans
- peas
- lentils
- egg dishes
- soups and casseroles
- bread stuffings
- pork
- veal
- poultry
- fish

Spice Blends

- bouquet garni
- fines herbes
- za'atar

early records attest, before the Romans imported pepper from India; Virgil noted it as "among the most fragrant of herbs." The botanical name, *Satureja*, is believed to have sprung from the belief that savory was a plant chosen by the satyrs; this explains why it is thought to have aphrodisiac properties. As *Banckes's Herbal* in the 16th century stated, "It is forbidden to use it much in meats since it stirreth him to use lechery."

The Romans introduced savory to England 2,000 years ago, after which it grew abundantly in herb gardens throughout the countryside. Savory was sometimes used as a substitute for black pepper, which explains why in some languages its name suggests it is a kind of pepper. The Germans and Dutch took to savory; they especially enjoyed it in bean dishes, possibly for its reputation for reducing flatulence. Widespread use of savory by the Germans gave rise to the often-used names *Bohnenkraut* and *Bonenkruid*, which literally mean "bean herb." Savory was one of the first herbs taken to the New World by the Pilgrims, and even today savory is a traditional ingredient in the stuffing made for Thanksgiving turkey.

The Plant

The annual herb summer savory is the variety preferred by cooks, while the perennial winter savory is a favorite with gardeners. Summer savory is a small, slender herbaceous plant with hairy branching stems that grow to 18 inches (45 cm) tall. The leaves are $1/4$ to $1/2$ inch (0.5 to 1 cm) long and range from green to bronze-green (they look a little like small, soft, oval tarragon leaves). Summer savory bears small lavender, pink or white flowers in late summer that are often harvested with the leaves. The bouquet is fragrant, piquant and thyme-like, with a hint of marjoram. Savory's peppery taste is reminiscent of ajowan. It's this spiciness within savory that adds an appetizing bite to this relatively pungent herb.

Dried summer savory, which includes the leaves and flowering tops, is gray-green in color and looks quite scruffy. The nonuniform appearance is due to the inclusion of small and large leaves, petals, buds and a relatively high amount of fine leaf particles. The flavor is strong and characteristic of fresh summer savory.

Other Varieties

Winter savory (*Satureja montana*) is a hardy woody perennial with a stiff appearance, like thyme; it is a useful substitute for summer savory when it is out of season. More often than not, dried savory leaves are from winter savory plants, probably because they are perennial and can be harvested for most of the year. **Lemon-scented winter savory** (*S. montana citriodora*) is a subspecies that is popular in Slovenia and tastes like lemon thyme. Its narrow leaves are green and glossy, averaging $1/2$ inch (1 cm) long. Small lipped white flowers bloom in late summer and early autumn. It is smaller than summer savory, growing to around 12 inches (30 cm) tall, and makes an attractive border in gardens.

Thyme-leaved savory (*S. thymbra*) is a wild variety of shrub from Spain. It has a flavor strongly reminiscent of thyme when used in cooking. **Creeping savory** (*S. spicigera* or *S. repandra*) is a perennial small-leaved compact, prostrate type of savory that is grown for decorative purposes. Soft, cushiony mounds of it are an ideal fill-in for rustic stone paving.

Processing

Savory is a herb that retains its distinctive flavor when dried. As is the case with many strong-tasting herbs, the dry form is preferred in numerous cooking applications. The commercial harvesting of summer savory takes place 75 to 120 days after sowing and sometimes before flowering has commenced, as the flavor is reputed to be somewhat stronger at that stage. The cut leafy stalks, and flowering tops, if applicable, are tied into bunches and hung upside down in a dark, well-aired environment to dry. After a few days the leaves become crisp. At that point they are removed from the stems by threshing, followed by winnowing to remove any remaining hard pieces of stalk.

Buying and Storage

Fresh summer savory is seasonally available from specialty produce retailers. It keeps quite well, so bunches of fresh savory should never appear wilted. Savory maintains its freshness if the bunch is stood up in a glass of water in the refrigerator, with a plastic bag forming a tent over it. Change the water every few days and your fresh savory will last for more than 1 week. Alternatively, the sprays can be wrapped in foil and frozen, or the leaves can be picked off, placed in ice-cube trays and barely covered by water before freezing.

Dried savory is generally winter savory. It can be purchased all year round. Good-quality savory kept in a cool, dark place in an airtight container will last for nearly 2 years.

Use

Savory's wonderfully distinctive piquancy brings an agreeable tasty element to relatively mild foods without overpowering them. The classic blends fines herbes and bouquet garni (the traditional bunch of herbs used in casseroles) often contain savory. Savory complements egg dishes, whether chopped finely and added to scrambled eggs and omelets or treated as a garnish along with parsley. Beans, lentils and peas all benefit from the addition of savory in almost any situation. Its robust flavor holds up well in slow-cooked dishes such as soups and stews. Savory combines well with bread crumbs for stuffings and is an ideal seasoning when making coatings for veal and fish. Sprinkle savory on roast poultry and pork before cooking and include it in meat loaf and homemade sausages.

WEIGHT PER TEASPOON (5 mL)

- whole dry rubbed leaves: 1.3 g
- ground: 1.1 g

SUGGESTED QUANTITY PER POUND (500 g)

- red meats: 5 tsp (25 mL) fresh leaves, 2 tsp (10 mL) dry rubbed leaves
- white meats: 4 tsp (20 mL) fresh leaves, 1½ tsp (7 mL) dry rubbed leaves
- vegetables: 2 tsp (10 mL) fresh leaves, ¾ tsp (3 mL) dry rubbed leaves
- grains and pulses: 2 tsp (10 mL) fresh leaves, ¾ tsp (3 mL) dry rubbed leaves
- baked goods: 2 tsp (10 mL) fresh leaves, ¾ tsp (3 mL) dry rubbed leaves

Cannellini Bean and Summer Savory Gratin

This gratin makes an excellent side dish with roast chicken instead of potatoes. Try it with Lemon Myrtle Chicken Wrap (page 360) or Chicken with 40 Cloves of Garlic (page 300). If you are lucky enough to have this hardy herb in your garden, use fresh; otherwise, use dried.

Makes 4 side servings

Preparation time:
10 minutes

Cooking time:
40 minutes

Tip

If you have only full-fat crème fraîche, use ½ cup (125 mL) mixed with ¼ cup (60 mL) water to achieve the right consistency.

- **9-inch (23 cm) round or rectangular baking dish**
- **Preheat oven to 400°F (200°C)**

2½ cups	cooked cannellini beans	625 mL
¾ cup	reduced-fat crème fraîche (see Tip, left)	175 mL
1 tsp	Dijon mustard	5 mL
2 tbsp	fresh or dried summer savory leaves	30 mL
1 tsp	fresh or dried thyme leaves	5 mL
½ tsp	sweet smoked paprika	2 mL
¼ tsp	fine sea salt	1 mL
1 cup	fresh dry bread crumbs	250 mL
2 tbsp	grated Gruyère cheese	30 mL

1. In baking dish, combine beans, crème fraîche, mustard, savory, thyme, paprika and salt. Top with bread crumbs and Gruyère and bake in preheated oven for 40 minutes, until golden brown.

S

Sesame

Sesamum indicum

Names in Other Languages

- **Arabic:** simsim, tahina
- **Burmese:** hnan si
- **Chinese (C):** ji mah (white), hak ji mah (black)
- **Chinese (M):** zhi ma
- **Czech:** sezam
- **Dutch:** sesamzaad
- **Filipino:** linga
- **Finnish:** seesami
- **French:** sésame, teel
- **German:** Sesam, Vanglo
- **Greek:** sousami
- **Hungarian:** szezamfu
- **Indian:** til (seed), gingelly (oil)
- **Indonesian:** wijen
- **Italian:** sesamo
- **Japanese:** muki goma (white), kuro gomah (black)
- **Korean:** keh
- **Malay:** bene, bijan
- **Portuguese:** gergelim
- **Russian:** kunzhut
- **Spanish:** ajonjoli
- **Sri Lankan:** thala
- **Swedish:** sesam
- **Thai:** nga dee la
- **Turkish:** susam
- **Vietnamese:** cay vung, mè

Family: Pedaliaceae

Other Names: black sesame, white sesame, benne, gingelly, semsem, teel, til

Flavor Group: Amalgamating

Parts Used: seeds (as a spice)

Background

Sesame is native to Indonesia and tropical Africa, and some experts contend it is also indigenous to India, where even today it is regarded as an oilseed crop rather than a spice. Sesame is possibly the oldest crop grown for edible oil extraction.

There are many ancient records of its use. A 4,000-year-old drawing on an Egyptian tomb depicts a baker adding sesame seeds to dough. Sesame was valued by the ancient Greeks, Egyptians and Romans, and there are records of its production in the Tigris and Euphrates Valleys that date back to 1600 BCE. It is mentioned in the Ebers Papyrus of around 1550 BCE, and an archaeological dig indicated that sesame was grown in Armenia between 900 and 700 BCE and pressed to extract oil. The remains of sesame seeds were found in excavated ruins of the Old Testament kingdom of Ararat, in the Anatolian region of Turkey. The use of

Culinary Information

Combines with

- allspice
- cardamom
- cinnamon and cassia
- cloves
- coriander seed
- ginger
- nutmeg
- paprika
- sumac
- thyme

Traditional Uses

- breads
- biscuits
- tahini
- hummus
- salads (when lightly toasted)
- halva

Spice Blends

- za'atar
- dukkah
- shichimi-togarashi

Folk Tale Famous

In the tale "Ali Baba and the Forty Thieves," the magic password was "Open sesame"— an easily remembered phrase for those in the know, since a fully ripe sesame pod shatters open dramatically at the slightest touch.

sesame became widespread in Africa, and in the 17th and 18th centuries enslaved Africans took it to America; *benne*, their name for it, still means "sesame" in parts of America's South. Nutritionally beneficial, sesame became an important food in the Middle East, where it remains a primary ingredient in halva and tahini, which is often used to make chickpea hummus.

The Plant

The sesame plant is an erect annual that grows 3 to 6 feet (1 to 2 m) tall. It may have either bushy growth or slender, unbranched stems. Its irregular long, oval leaves are hairy on both sides and exude a surprisingly unpleasant smell. White, lilac or pink flowers are borne along its stems from quite low down and are followed by the fruits, or capsules. Sesame seeds are contained within four-sided oblong capsules that are 1 inch (2.5 cm) long. When fully ripe, they shatter and spread their contents.

Unhulled sesame seeds are mostly black or golden brown (the latter are easily confused with toasted sesame seeds). Sesame seeds are flat, tear-shaped and no more than $1/8$ inch (3 mm) long. White sesame seeds, from which the husks have been removed, are actually off-white in color. They look and feel waxy because of their high oil content and give off a faint nutty aroma. Black and brown unhulled sesame seeds have almost no aroma, but when chewed, their texture is more crunchy than white sesame; their flavor is equally nutty but with an extra hint of sharpness.

S

Travels in the Spice Trade

The wonderful thing about visiting India regularly is the opportunity to see traditional practices as they've been performed for thousands of years. On a drive to Deogarh, a town on the far western side of Uttar Pradesh, we saw sesame oil being extracted in the most ancient of ways. Imagine a huge rock mortar about 4 feet (1.2 m) in diameter. A large wooden pestle was connected, via a series of rods and ropes, to a blindfolded Brahman bullock that was circling the enormous mortar, which was overflowing with recently harvested sesame seeds. The constant crushing and squeezing of the seeds in this giant mortar was producing fresh, rich sesame oil. One of the workers produced a small jug of the oil for us to taste. It was a flavor sensation we'll never forget.

Processing

Sesame seeds must be harvested before the pods are fully ripe; otherwise they will burst open and the contents will be wasted. To aid in the now widespread practice of machine harvesting, hybrids have been developed with pods that do not shatter so easily. Traditional processing methods involve cutting the stems and hanging them upside down over mats to dry and drop their seeds. The seeds are then decorticated (hulled) either mechanically or by using chemicals to dissolve and remove the husks. Because so much sesame seed is consumed in North America, organically grown sesame from Mexico that has been hulled without the use of chemicals is experiencing an increase in demand.

Along with peanuts, sesame is classed as a known allergen that can harm some sensitive individuals. This is why, when buying prepared food products, you may see a statement on the label that reads something like "Manufactured on equipment used to process nuts and sesame seeds."

Buying and Storage

Sesame seeds are best purchased regularly and should not be kept for too long before using, as their high oil content can lead to rancidity. White sesame seeds are readily available in supermarkets, health-food stores and spice shops. Black sesame seeds are rarer and can be found in spice shops and Asian food stores. Because of the similarity in appearance, black sesame seeds are often confused with nigella seeds; however, the flavor is quite different.

Store both white and black sesame in an airtight container away from extremes of heat, light and humidity. When

It's an Oil Seed

I know the oiliness of sesame well. My father first started buying white sesame seeds in burlap bags in the 1960s. After a couple of weeks the wooden floorboards in our storeroom bore huge oil stains from where the bags of sesame seeds had been stacked.

WEIGHT PER TEASPOON (5 mL)

- **whole:** 4 g

SUGGESTED QUANTITY PER POUND (500 g)

- **red meats:** 4 to 6 tsp (20 to 30 mL)
- **white meats:** 4 to 6 tsp (20 to 30 mL)
- **vegetables:** 4 to 6 tsp (20 to 30 mL)
- **baked goods:** 4 to 6 tsp (20 to 30 mL)

stored this way, unhulled sesame seeds will last for up to 18 months and hulled white sesame seeds for up to 1 year.

Sesame oil should be stored in an opaque glass bottle and kept away from extremes of heat and light. Manufacturers will put a best-before date on the label, which is usually less than 2 years.

Use

White sesame seeds are sprinkled on breads and biscuits in much the same way as poppy seeds. Their pleasing nutty taste develops during baking. Sesame seeds are ground and compressed with sweet syrups and honey to make the wonderfully indulgent Middle Eastern confection halva. Toasted sesame seeds are delicious sprinkled over salads and, believe it or not, ice cream. Toasted white sesame seeds crushed with salt make the tasty Japanese vegetable seasoning called *gomasio*.

Most of the world's production of sesame seeds is for the extraction of sesame oil (sometimes referred to as "gingelly oil"). Sesame oil is a cooking oil with a distinctive aroma and flavor. It is relatively stable, even in hot climates. Sesame oil works well in Asian stir-fries. It has quite a strong flavor, so only a little is required. Salad dressings with Asian flavors (lemongrass, lime, chile and ginger) are also enhanced by a little sesame oil.

When ground to a paste, sesame seeds are called *tahini*, which is used extensively in Middle Eastern cooking. Black sesame seeds are popular in Asian cooking. They are used in Chinese desserts such as toffee bananas, and the Japanese mix them with salt and MSG to use as a sprinkle-on condiment. However, black sesame seeds do not take well to toasting; it tends to make them bitter. I have seen black sesame seeds on Turkish bread (some makers interchange them with nigella seeds).

S

Hummus

No meze is complete without hummus. Delicious and nutritious, it's a mealtime staple throughout the Middle East and popular the world over. Tahini, often used on its own as a spread, dressing or dip, adds a rich creaminess to this hummus. We make a batch of it every week (it was the first recipe my kids learned by heart)—it tastes so much better homemade than bought.

Makes about 2 cups (500 mL)

Preparation time:
5 minutes

Cooking time: none

Tips

If desired, you can use two 14-oz (398 mL) cans of chickpeas, drained and rinsed.

Tahini, a paste made from ground sesame seeds, is available in well-stocked supermarkets.

• **Food processor**

3 cups	cooked chickpeas (see Tips, left)	750 mL
2	cloves garlic	2
1 tsp	fine sea salt	5 mL
½ tsp	ground cumin	2 mL
2 tbsp	tahini (see Tips, left)	30 mL
7 tbsp	extra virgin olive oil	105 mL

1. In food processor fitted with the metal blade, combine chickpeas, garlic, salt, cumin, tahini and oil and process for at least 5 minutes, until smooth. Hummus will keep in an airtight container in the refrigerator for up to 1 week.

Variation

For a spicy kick, add 1 tbsp (15 mL) harissa paste (page 737) before processing.

Butternut Squash and Chickpea Salad

This fantastic autumnal salad is delicious warm or cold. I like to use lovely large Spanish chickpeas from a jar or soak and cook my own—the extra effort results in tender pulses perfect for salads. The dukkah, made of nuts, cumin and sesame seeds, imparts a wonderful texture and flavor to the salad.

Makes 6 servings

Preparation time:
10 minutes

Cooking time:
30 minutes

Tip

If desired, sprinkle salad with crumbled feta cheese before serving.

• **Preheat oven to 375°F (190°C)**

2 tbsp	olive oil	30 mL
½ tsp	ground coriander seed	2 mL
½ tsp	fine sea salt	2 mL
1	butternut squash (about 1½ lbs/750 g), peeled, seeded and cut in 1-inch (2.5 cm) cubes	1
2 tbsp	tahini	30 mL
3 tbsp	oil	45 mL
	Freshly squeezed juice of 1 lemon	
½ tsp	fine sea salt	2 mL
2½ cups	cooked chickpeas	625 mL
2 tbsp	dukkah (page 731)	30 mL
2 tbsp	finely chopped fresh flat-leaf (Italian) parsley leaves	30 mL

1. In a bowl, combine 2 tbsp (30 mL) olive oil, ground coriander and salt. Add squash cubes and toss to coat, then arrange evenly on a baking sheet. Bake for 30 minutes, turning once, until golden and tender.

2. In a small bowl, whisk together tahini, 3 tbsp (45 mL) oil, lemon juice and salt. Set aside.

3. In a large bowl or serving dish, gently combine chickpeas, roasted squash and tahini mixture. Sprinkle salad with dukkah and parsley and serve.

Variation

You can substitute an equal quantity of pumpkin or carrots for the squash.

S

Sesame Tuna

I adore Japanese food; many of the dishes are so light and flavorsome and rely on incredibly fresh fish. This recipe, inspired by one of my favorite experiences at our local Japanese restaurant, uses sesame in both seed and oil form. It can be served individually or on a large shared plate.

**Makes
4 servings**

Preparation time:
5 minutes

Cooking time:
10 minutes

Tips

The combination of reduced-sodium soy sauce and regular soy sauce prevents the dressing from being too salty.

If you prefer your fish cooked through, simply dress it 10 minutes before serving. The acidity of the dressing will "cook" the fish, as in ceviche.

2 tbsp	black sesame seeds	30 mL
2 tbsp	white sesame seeds	30 mL
2	sushi-grade skinless tuna fillets (about 1¼ lbs/625 g)	2
12	shiso leaves, optional	12
DRESSING		
6 tbsp	reduced-sodium soy sauce (see Tips, left)	90 mL
2 tbsp	regular soy sauce	30 mL
6 tbsp	freshly squeezed lemon juice	90 mL
¼ cup	freshly squeezed lime juice	60 mL
2 tsp	sesame oil	10 mL

1. In a shallow dish, combine black and white sesame seeds. Using your hands, roll tuna in seeds, pressing gently until completely coated.

2. In a nonstick skillet over high heat, sear tuna for 2 minutes on each side. Remove from heat and slice ⅛ inch (3 mm) thick.

3. In a small bowl, whisk together soy sauces, lemon and lime juices and sesame oil.

4. Arrange shiso leaves (if using) over serving plate and overlap tuna slices on top. Drizzle with dressing and serve immediately.

Variations

Substitute salmon for the tuna.

For a spicy crust, add 1 tbsp (15 mL) shichimi-togarashi (page 764) to the seed coating.

Spikenard

Nardostachys grandiflora (also known as *N. jatamansii*)

Family: Valerianaceae

Other Names: muskroot, nard, nardin

Flavor Group: Pungent

Parts Used: rhizomes (as a spice)

Background

Spikenard was used to flavor food in ancient Rome, so perhaps it is not surprising that it is mentioned in recipes of the renowned gourmet and philosopher Apicius. It was apparently used in Europe in the medieval period and was one of a number of exotic ingredients used in hippocras, a mulled wine also containing cloves, cardamom, ginger and other spices. Spikenard is mentioned in the Bible's Song of Songs along with "saffron, calamus and cinnamon, with every kind of incense tree; myrrh and aloes, with all the best spices." It appears, though, that it was mostly used to prepare a medicinal and devotional oil that was extracted from the roots and young stems of the plant. Although

S

Culinary Information

Combines with
- allspice
- cardamom
- cinnamon
- cloves
- ginger
- grains of paradise
- juniper
- sage
- thyme
- turmeric
- zedoary

Traditional Uses
- casseroles
- mulled wine
- spiced hare
- stuffed dormouse
- sea urchin

Spice Blends
- not used in spice blends

spikenard may turn up in religious rites these days, its use as a condiment is largely unheard of.

The Plant

A member of the same family as the medicinal herb valerian (Valerianaceae), spikenard is indigenous to eastern Asia, from the Himalayas to southwest China. It is a perennial that grows to about 1 foot (30 cm) tall, with bell-shaped pink hermaphroditic flowers that bloom in late summer.

Other Varieties
American spikenard (*Aralia racemosa*), **Californian spikenard** (*A. californica*) and **ploughman's spikenard** (*Inula conyza*) are unrelated plants that to my knowledge have never been used for culinary purposes.

Processing

The rhizomes (subterranean stems) are harvested after the plant has finished flowering. They are used to make a highly aromatic essential oil by steam distillation.

To dry the rhizomes, wash thoroughly after lifting and put out in the sun to dry for several days. When the tangled, hairy-looking rhizomes snap easily and have lost their leathery feel, they are ready for use. The best way to grind spikenard is to chop the rhizomes into a small pea-sized dice and then grind using a mortar and pestle.

Buying and Storage

The closest you will get to spikenard in stores is valerian root, a massive tangle of rhizomes sold by some Middle Eastern grocers and herbalists. Keen gardeners can buy spikenard seeds online. Although germination rates are low, careful attention to the seed merchant's sowing instructions will improve the chances of success.

Store spikenard in airtight containers kept away from extremes of heat, light and humidity. Dried spikenard rhizomes will keep for 3 to 4 years. Ground spikenard will keep for 1 year.

Oil of spikenard is the only product of this plant that can be purchased nowadays. I do not recommend using it in food—it is highly concentrated and reported to be toxic.

Use

Spikenard rhizome is reputed to have a flavor similar to a mixture of cinnamon and star anise, with a deep musky aroma. In small quantities it adds an exotic note to game along with grains of paradise, cubebs, long pepper and ginger. Whole spikenard may be added to a slow-cooked dish and then removed at the end of cooking. Ground spikenard is added in the same way you would add ginger or turmeric powder to a dish.

WEIGHT PER TEASPOON (5 mL)
- ground: 2.5 g

SUGGESTED QUANTITY PER POUND (500 g)
- **red meats:** ¾ tsp (3 mL) ground
- **white meats:** ½ tsp (2 mL) ground
- **vegetables:** ½ tsp (2 mL) ground
- **grains and pulses:** ½ tsp (2 mL) ground
- **baked goods:** ¼ tsp (1 mL) ground

S

Star Anise

Illicium verum (also known as *I. anisatum*)

Family: Illiaceae (formerly Magnoliaceae)

Varieties: Japanese star anise (*I. religiosum*; poisonous), Florida anise (*I. floridanum*; poisonous)

Other Names: anise stars, badian, Chinese anise, Chinese star anise, star aniseed

Flavor Group: Pungent

Parts Used: fruits (as a spice)

Names in Other Languages

- **Arabic:** raziyanjekhatai
- **Chinese (C):** baat gok, pak kok
- **Chinese (M):** ba jiao
- **Czech:** badyan, cinsky anyz
- **Danish:** stjerne anis
- **Dutch:** steranijs
- **French:** anis de Chine, anise étoilé, badiane
- **German:** Sternanis, Badian
- **Greek:** anison asteroeides
- **Indian:** badian, anasphal
- **Indonesian:** bunga lawang, adas cina
- **Italian:** anice stellato
- **Japanese:** daiuikyo, hakkaku
- **Malay:** bunga lawang
- **Norwegian:** stjerneanis
- **Polish:** anyz gwiazdkowaty
- **Portuguese:** anis estrelado
- **Russian:** badyan, zvezdchatatyj anis
- **Spanish:** anis estrellado, badian
- **Swedish:** stjarnanis
- **Thai:** poy kak bua
- **Turkish:** cin anasonu
- **Vietnamese:** bat giac huong, cay hoy, hoi

Background

Star anise is indigenous to southern China and North Vietnam and is grown in India, Japan and the Philippines. The trees do not bear fruit until they are about six years old, after which they can supposedly produce for up to 100 years. Centuries of trade carried star anise to India from the Far East; I have experienced many delectable dishes in Kerala, southern India, that were spiced with star anise. However, it wasn't seen in Europe until the 16th century. It is astounding to think that it took until 1588 for a sample (which came from the Philippines) to reach London. Once discovered in the West, the essential oil of star anise, extracted by steam distillation, found its way into confectionery and liqueurs, most notably anisette.

The Plant

Star anise is the dried star-shaped fruit of a small Asian evergreen tree that grows to about 16 feet (5 m) tall. The star anise tree, a member of the magnolia family, has shiny, aromatic leaves approximately 3 inches (7.5 cm) long. Its unscented flowers are narcissus-like and greenish yellow. After blooming they are followed by rayed fruits composed of eight seed-holding segments (whenever I see a bowl of star anise, it looks to me as if it's full of funnel-web spiders, a nasty Australian species!).

A careful look at the eight rough, dark brown, arched pods of an upside-down star reveals that each section has split (some more than others), creating a canoe shape that contains a light brown tick-shaped, extremely shiny seed

Culinary Information

Combines with

- allspice
- cardamom
- chile
- cinnamon and cassia
- cloves
- coriander seed
- cumin
- fennel seed
- ginger
- mace
- nutmeg
- pepper
- Sichuan pepper

Traditional Uses

Many savory Chinese dishes, including

- Peking duck
- pork ribs and belly
- soups
- stir-fries

Spice Blends

- Chinese five-spice powder
- Chinese master stocks
- curry powders

Don't Confuse Spices

Never refer to star anise as "star anise seed"—it only causes confusion. Anise seed (page 78) is gathered from an annual herb, and the seeds of the anise plant have a very different flavor.

of no particular culinary significance. The aroma of whole star anise is distinctly anise-like. Although it is not related to the herb from which anise seed is collected (see page 78), star anise and anise seed contain essential oils of similar chemical composition. Star anise has a strong, sweet, licorice-like character and deep, warm spice notes that are reminiscent of clove and cassia. The flavor is similarly licorice-like, pungent, lingering and numbing, leaving the palate fresh and stimulated. The seeds, if consumed separately, have a less intense flavor than the woody boat-shaped spokes of the star, but they do convey an interesting nuttiness to food.

Other Varieties

Japanese star anise (*I. religiosum*) is a closely related species with poisonous leaves and fruits (caused by their content of sikimitoxin). It has been used as an adulterant of true star anise in the past and is called "mad herb" in China. It is used in Japanese funeral rites and can be identified by its lack of anise smell and turpentine-like flavor. I have seen stars that fit this description; they are generally smaller than true star anise and may have up to 12 segments. **Florida anise** (*I. floridanum*) is another poisonous plant, also known as "purple anise" or "stink bush." Although a close relative of star anise, it is toxic and should never be eaten.

S

Processing

In a process very similar to those used to harvest cloves, allspice, pepper and even vanilla, star anise fruits are harvested when green (that is, before they have ripened) and are dried in the sun. During drying they turn a deep reddish brown and their characteristic aroma and flavor fully develop as a result of enzyme activation. Ground star anise is made by grinding the complete dried stars, including seeds, to a fine dark, smooth-textured powder.

An essential oil for use in food and drink manufacturing is produced by steam distillation.

Buying and Storage

Whole star anise can be bought from some supermarkets and most specialty food stores. Although the intact eight-segment stars are attractive, the presence of some broken stars is not necessarily a sign of low quality but rather indicates less than fastidious packing, rough handling or both. The freshness of whole star anise can be determined by breaking off a segment, squeezing it between thumb and forefinger until the brittle seed pops, then sniffing for the distinctive anise/licorice aroma. If you don't experience the scent immediately, the spice is probably past its optimum storage life, which is 3 to 5 years if kept in an airtight container away from extremes of heat, light and humidity.

It is best to buy whole star anise for most uses. However, if you require a ground version, purchase it already ground: home grinders are not as effective as industrial grinding machines. Ground star anise should be purchased in small quantities. When stored in an airtight container away from extremes of heat, light and humidity, it will last for a little more than 1 year.

Use

Star anise is, in my opinion, one of the signature flavors of Chinese savory cooking. It combines particularly well with pork and duck and is an important ingredient in a Chinese master stock, a ball of spice-filled muslin that looks like a giant bouquet garni (see page 368). Star anise is the dominant spice in a Chinese five-spice mixture.

Because star anise is pungent, only a very small quantity is required to achieve a pleasing result.

WEIGHT PER TEASPOON (5 mL)

- **average whole star:** 1.7 g
- **ground:** 2.7 g

SUGGESTED QUANTITY PER POUND (500 g)

- **red meats:** 2 whole stars, 1¼ tsp (6 mL) ground
- **white meats:** 2 whole stars, 1¼ tsp (6 mL) ground
- **vegetables:** 1½ whole stars, 1 tsp (5 mL) ground
- **grains and pulses:** 1 whole star, ½ tsp (2 mL) ground
- **baked goods:** ½ tsp (2 mL) ground

Pho

Pho is a much-loved traditional soup that originated in northern Vietnam, where it is freshly prepared in front of you by street vendors. The key ingredient in the aromatic broth is star anise, which blends well with the fresh herbs and other flavors to create a stunning dish.

**Makes
4 servings**

Preparation time:
15 minutes
Cooking time:
15 minutes

Tip

Kecap manis is a thick, soy-based sauce that has been sweetened with palm sugar and has garlic and star anise added. It is commonly used throughout Asia and is available in major supermarkets and Asian grocers.

4 oz	dried flat rice noodles	125 g
5 cups	beef broth	1.25 L
1	¼-inch (5 mm) piece gingerroot, peeled and sliced	1
2	whole star anise	2
1 tbsp	kecap manis (see Tip, left)	15 mL
3 oz	shiitake mushrooms	90 mL
12 oz	rump steak, finely sliced	375 g
1	red finger chile, finely sliced	1
1 cup	bean sprouts	250 mL
4	green onions, white and green parts, finely sliced	4
¼ cup	lightly packed fresh coriander (cilantro) leaves	60 mL
½ cup	lightly packed fresh Thai basil leaves	125 mL
½ cup	lightly packed fresh mint leaves	125 mL
1	lemon, cut into wedges	1

1. In a heatproof bowl, cover noodles with boiling water and set aside to soften for 10 to 15 minutes.

2. In a large saucepan over medium heat, combine broth, ginger, star anise and kecap manis; bring slowly to a simmer. Add mushrooms and steak and simmer until meat is just cooked through, 7 to 10 minutes.

3. Drain noodles and divide equally among 4 bowls. Ladle broth overtop. Garnish with bean sprouts, green onions, coriander leaves, basil, mint and a wedge of lemon, or serve garnishes at the table so people can help themselves.

Spiced Chocolate Brownies

Brownies are one of those universally popular recipes that can be made in no time without any fuss. The warm licorice flavor of star anise complements chocolate fantastically. These brownies make a great grownup treat.

Makes 20 to 25 brownies

Preparation time:
10 minutes
Cooking time:
50 minutes

Tips

Superfine (caster) sugar is a very fine granulated sugar typically used in recipes that require a faster-dissolving granule. If you can't find it in stores, you can make your own by using a food processor fitted with the metal blade to process granulated sugar to a very fine, sand-like consistency.

The fruity notes in ground pasilla or ancho chile would work well with the chocolate flavor, but a regular ground mild red chile such as Kashmiri can also be used.

For easy individual portions, the batter can be poured into paper muffin cups (filled halfway) and cooked for 20 minutes.

- **8-inch (20 cm) square baking pan, greased and lined with parchment paper**
- **Preheat oven to 350°F (180°C)**

²⁄₃ cup	unsalted butter	150 mL
8 oz	dark (70%) chocolate, broken into pieces	250 g
1 cup	superfine (caster) sugar (see Tips, left)	250 mL
3 tbsp	pine nuts	45 mL
1 tsp	pure vanilla extract	5 mL
¹⁄₂ tsp	ground star anise	2 mL
¹⁄₄ tsp	ground mild chile, optional (see Tips, left)	1 mL
2	eggs	2
1	egg yolk	1
²⁄₃ cup	all-purpose flour	150 mL

1. In a heatproof bowl set over a saucepan of water (to create a double boiler), place chocolate and butter. Bring water to a bowl, then turn off the heat (there will be plenty of residual heat to melt the chocolate). Stir chocolate until smooth. Remove bowl from heat and add sugar, pine nuts, vanilla, star anise and ground chile (if using); stir until well combined. Stir in eggs and egg yolk. Sift in flour and stir to form a smooth batter.

2. Pour batter into prepared baking pan and bake in preheated oven for 35 minutes, until a tester inserted in center comes out clean. Transfer pan to a wire rack to cool completely, then turn out and cut into equal squares.

S

Stevia

Stevia rebaudiana-Bertoni

Family: Asteraceae (formerly Compositae)

Other Names: candy leaf, sugar leaf, sweet herb of Paraguay, sweet honey leaf

Flavor Group: Pungent

Parts Used: leaves (as a herb)

Background

Stevia is native to Paraguay, Brazil and Argentina. Stevia leaves appear to have been used medicinally and as a sweet by Indians of the Guaraní tribe long before Europeans came to the Americas. Stevia was first researched by Petrus Jacobus Stevus, a 16th-century Spanish botanist whom the plant is named after. The later so-called discovery of stevia and identification of its use as a sweetener has been attributed to a South American natural scientist, Moises Santiago Bertoni, who identified it in 1887; his name now appears in the botanical name that identifies the variety used in food.

Sweeter Than Sugar

In 1931 two French chemists isolated the constituent they named stevioside and found it to be 300 times sweeter than sugar. In the 1950s Japan banned the use of artificial sweeteners in beverages, pickles, meat and fish products, baked items, soy sauce and low-calorie foods, no doubt as an incentive to develop its stevia-growing industry. Stevioside extracted from stevia leaves is widely used as a sweetener in manufactured products in Japan, Korea, China, Taiwan, Malaysia, Brazil and Paraguay.

Culinary Information

Combines with

- allspice
- caraway
- cardamom
- chile
- cloves
- coriander seed
- ginger
- licorice
- nutmeg
- star anise

Traditional Uses

- beverages
- cream and cream cheese
- desserts
- stewed fruit
- ice cream
- rice pudding

Spice Blends

- only as a sugar substitute

I find it interesting that stevia, which is a natural product, should taste so distinctly of artificial sweetener. Most of its sweetness comes from two compounds: stevioside, which can make up to 10% of the dry leaf weight, and rebaudioside, up to 3%.

The Plant

Stevia is a humble spindly, soft green plant with lightly serrated wide leaves borne in simple pairs off the main stem. It looks like a small weed, growing on average to less than $1^1/_2$ feet (45 cm) in height. Stevia leaf powder is deep green and has a slightly grassy aroma. The taste is intensely sweet and has a background bitterness that can be lingering if too much is eaten.

Processing

Dry stevia leaves on screens in a dark, dry, well-aired place until the leaves are quite crisp to the touch, indicating a moisture level of around 10%.

The compound stevioside is extracted by proprietary processes that yield a white powder product 300 times sweeter than sugar: $^1/_4$ tsp (1 mL) of stevioside extract replaces 1 cup (250 mL) of sugar. A simple, less potent—and therefore easier to use—extract may be made at home by putting $^1/_2$ tsp (2 mL) stevia leaf powder in $^1/_2$ cup (125 mL) warm water. Set aside to steep overnight, then strain through a coffee filter to produce a particle-free liquid. Store the liquid in the refrigerator for up to 1 month.

Buying and Storage

Stevia plants are available from some herb nurseries. They can be grown in semihumid subtropical conditions with

S

temperatures ranging from approximately 70° to 100°F (20° to 40°C).

Dried stevia leaves and stevia leaf powder can be found in health-food stores and some specialty spice shops.

Stevioside extract is usually sold as white stevia powder and may vary considerably, depending on the quality of plants used for extraction. The presence of additives such as maltodextrin to dilute the intensity and make the powder more user-friendly will also affect the flavor strength.

Use

The first and most important thing to remember about stevia is that although its sweetness is heat stable and won't deteriorate during cooking, it does not caramelize like sugar. As a result, it cannot be used to make meringues or other recipes that depend on large quantities of sugar. But using homemade stevia extract to sweeten beverages, sauces, muffins, ice cream, cheesecakes and rice puddings is quite feasible. When using commercial stevioside powders, it is best to be guided by the sugar equivalent given on the package. By experimenting with small quantities of stevia in familiar foods and drinks, you will soon be able to identify the quantity that suits your taste. Stevia does have a slight licorice flavor and, very strangely, tastes similar to aspartame (E951), an artificial sweetener, which does not appeal to everyone.

WEIGHT PER TEASPOON (5 mL)

- **ground leaves:** 2.5 g

SUGGESTED QUANTITY PER POUND (500 g)

- **vegetables:** 1 tsp (5 mL) ground leaves
- **baked goods:** 1 tsp (5 mL) ground leaves

Spelt Stevia Muffins

I love being able to make sugar-free muffins for children, because their diet invariably has more sugar in it than it should. Stevia sweeteners are now widely available and are excellent for baking. And spelt flour is a lot more wholesome and flavorsome than regular flour. It is worth looking for in your supermarket or health-food store.

**Makes
12 muffins**

Preparation time:
10 minutes

Cooking time:
20 minutes

- - - - - - - - - - - - - - - -

Tip

If you can't find self-rising flour in stores, you can make your own. To equal 1 cup (250 mL) self-rising flour, combine 1 cup (250 mL) all-purpose flour, 1½ tsp (7 mL) baking powder and ½ tsp (2 mL) salt.

- **12-cup muffin pan, greased**
- **Preheat oven to 350°F (180°C)**

2 cups	self-rising flour (see Tip, left)	500 mL
1 cup	spelt flour	250 mL
½ tsp	baking soda	2 mL
½ tsp	baking powder	2 mL
¼ cup	stevia powder/sweetener	60 mL
¼ cup	butter, melted	60 mL
2	eggs, beaten	2
1 tsp	pure vanilla extract	5 mL
1 cup	milk	250 mL
½ cup	mashed ripe banana (1 small)	125 mL
1 cup	blueberries (fresh or frozen)	250 mL

1. In a large bowl, combine self-rising flour, spelt flour, baking soda, baking powder and stevia.

2. In a small bowl, combine butter, eggs, vanilla, milk and banana. Stir well.

3. Pour wet mixture into dry mixture, add blueberries and stir until smooth. Divide batter equally among prepared muffin cups (fill to just below top), then bake in preheated oven for 20 minutes, until browned and tops are firm to the touch. Remove from oven and set aside to cool in pan for 5 minutes, then transfer to a wire rack to cool completely. Store in an airtight container for up to 3 days. To freeze, cool completely, then transfer to resealable bags and freeze for up to 3 months.

S

Sumac

Rhus coriaria

Names in Other Languages

- **Arabic:** summak
- **Czech:** sumah, koreni sumac
- **Danish:** sumak
- **Dutch:** sumak
- **French:** sumac
- **German:** Farberbaum, Sumach
- **Greek:** roudi, soumaki
- **Hungarian:** szomorce
- **Indian:** kankrasing
- **Italian:** sommacco
- **Japanese:** sumakku
- **Russian:** sumakh
- **Spanish:** zumaque
- **Turkish:** sumak, somak

Family: Anacardiaceae

Varieties: elm-leaved sumac (*R. coriaria*), lemon sumac (*R. aromatica*), smooth sumac (*R. glabra*), poison sumac (*R. vernix*, also known as *R. venenata, Toxicodendron vernix*)

Other Names: Sicilian sumac, sumach, sumak, tanner's sumac

Flavor Group: Tangy

Parts Used: berries and outer flesh of berries (as a spice)

Background

Sumac trees grow wild in the Mediterranean region and in North America. They are found in southern Italy and much of the Middle East, especially southeastern Turkey and Iran. Sumac berries were used by the Romans, who referred to them as "Syrian sumac." At the time, lemons were unknown in Europe; sumac was a pleasing souring agent, less sharp than vinegar and more agreeable than tamarind. All parts of the tree yield tannins and dyes that have been used for centuries in the leather industry. American native peoples used to make a sour drink from the berries of smooth (scarlet) sumac (*Rhus glabra*). **Poison sumac** (*R. vernix*),

Culinary Information

Combines with
- chile
- garlic
- ginger
- oregano
- paprika
- parsley
- pepper
- rosemary
- sesame seed
- thyme

Traditional Uses
- tomatoes
- avocado sandwiches
- salads (as garnish)
- doner kebabs (shawarma)
- Turkish pide
- broiled and roasted meats (sprinkled on before cooking)
- roasted vegetables
- fish and chicken

Spice Blends
- za'atar
- seasoning rubs for meat

Do Not Consume

Most varieties of sumac have some degree of toxicity. Although they cannot be consumed, they are useful. Poisonous varieties are used to make varnish—it's a principal component of Japanese lacquerware—and for this reason it is sometimes known as the "varnish tree."

from eastern North America, is also known as "poison ivy tree." It has the alternative botanical names *R. venenata* and *Toxicodendron vernix*. It is distinguished by white fruits, and the sap of this tree is used to make ink and varnish. This variety should never be eaten. Western markets have been introduced to sumac by immigrants from the Middle East who have opened doner kebab (shawarma) restaurants, where this tangy powder is sprinkled over freshly sliced onions.

The Plant

There are at least 150 varieties of rhus trees, but only six bear berries suitable for culinary use. Many of the remainder can cause severe skin irritation, and cases of poisoning from eating the berries have also been reported. For this reason I would not recommend trying to identify and use sumac in its natural state without expert guidance. Instead, purchase it from a reputable purveyor.

The edible sumac tree is a member of the same family as the mango. The first time I encountered it was in southeastern Turkey. Growing in what looked like barren, rocky soil, flanked by gnarled olive trees and prolific pistachio and walnut groves, the sumac trees were 6 to 10 feet (2 to 3 m) tall. They had reasonably dense dark green, frond-like foliage that resembled that of the surrounding olive trees. Although sumac trees are deciduous, Ibrihim, the farmer, assured us that the leaves of the edible

Travels in the Spice Trade

When I first heard about sumac being used as a spice, I was uneasy about the relationship between this variety of rhus tree and other varieties that are poisonous. Back in the 1980s, one of our employees came to work with an extreme allergic reaction. She had been cutting back a rhus tree at her home over the weekend, and every inch of visible skin was bright red and horribly inflamed. Naturally we sent her home to recover, which she did in a few days. However, that image of her reaction to the tree remained in my mind, and it motivated Liz and me to visit a sumac farm in Nizip, a small town near the southeastern border of Turkey. We wanted to see sumac production firsthand.

The experience was highly educational. Viewing the entire process from harvest to final product gave me the confidence to write about this spice. After our sumac experience, our spice-trader hosts took us for lunch in a small town nearby called Biraçik, on the banks of the Euphrates. The restaurant was in the open air, with a splendid view across the fast-running river. The specialty was a local fish, quite oily and strong, which benefited greatly from the refreshing tang of sumac.

Although there are many delectable souring spices, such as tamarind and pomegranate, the refreshing fruity sourness of sumac is unique. In recent years it has become increasingly well known in Western cooking.

variety *R. coriaria* never turn bright scarlet like those of many decorative rhus trees. In addition, he said he had never known anyone to suffer an allergic reaction from contact with the leaves or fruits. There were a few male trees among the grove; they do not bear fruit but their leaves are harvested and added to ground sumac spice or mixed with thyme and oregano to make a kind of za'atar (see page 781).

Sumac berries stand out from the foliage like optimistic Christmas decorations. They are tightly bunched in conical clusters $3^{1}/_{4}$ to 4 inches (8 to 10 cm) long and about $^{3}/_{4}$ inch (2 cm) across at the widest point, near the base. Each berry—they develop from a similarly dense bunch of small white flowers—is a little larger than a peppercorn. When fully formed, the berry is green and covered with a hairy down, like kiwifruit. (Most of the nonpoisonous varieties of rhus have hairy berries, while the fruits on some decorative types are smooth.) The berries ripen to a pinkish red and are deep crimson when harvested. Sumac berries have a very thin outer skin; the flesh surrounds an extremely hard tick-shaped seed.

Sumac powder is a deep burgundy color, coarse-textured and moist. The aroma is fruity, like a cross between red grapes and apple, with a lingering freshness. The taste is initially salty (from salt added after processing), tangy (from malic acid in the downy covering of the berries, which is also found in sour apples) and pleasantly fruity, with no sharpness.

Other Varieties

Although there are instances of sumac leaves, bark and roots being eaten, I would suggest caution, as the levels of toxicity are uncertain. For this reason I would use berries only from the three edible varieties mentioned here. I would use leaves only from male trees of *Rhus coriaria*.

Elm-leaved sumac (*R. coriaria*) is the variety most used in recipes. **Lemon sumac** (*R. aromatica*) is indigenous to the eastern half of North America, from Quebec to Florida and over to Texas. This variety has a distinct lemon flavor, and the ripe berries can be soaked in cold water to make a refreshing lemony drink (it is best not to use hot water, as that will release more tannic acid, making the beverage somewhat bitter). **Smooth sumac** (*R. glabra*) is found in North America and, like lemon sumac, it is one of the varieties used by indigenous peoples. It has been used to make a tangy drink in the same way as lemon sumac.

Processing

Clusters of ripe crimson sumac berries are harvested by hand, then placed in the sun to dry and ripen further for two to three days. (Berries from the second harvest of the season are said to have the strongest flavor.) After drying, these bunches of fruits are put through a stone mill that pulverizes the berries. At the same time it separates their acid-containing outer skin and the thin, deep crimson underlayer of flesh from the hard, stony seed, pieces of stem and any remaining flowers. The powder that comes out of the mill is sieved to yield the darkest, most uniform and sweetest-tasting spice. Salt is added as a preservative, and it also enhances sumac's natural flavor. Sometimes cottonseed oil is mixed in to create a darker color and desirable moist texture. Material remaining on the sieve is scraped off and put through the mill again, then sieved for a second time to further extract any useful sumac, which falls through the mesh.

S

The next step separates the hard seeds from stems, leaves and stalks by sieving on a larger screen that lets the seeds through but leaves unwanted material behind. These seeds are ground separately in a conventional grinder to yield a light brown powder. Different grades of sumac are made by blending the first sieving with varying proportions of second and third sievings and powdered seeds. The best quality has the highest ratio of outer flesh to pulverized stem and seed. It can be recognized by its deep color and coarse, uniform texture.

Buying and Storage

As mentioned, sumac should be purchased only in its powdered form from reputable merchants; attempts to identify, grow and pick it yourself are definitely not recommended.

Sumac powder varies in color, texture and moistness. Color and texture are good indications of quality: the darker, more uniform material has less stem and pulverized seed than lighter-colored grades. It is worth noting that some buyers prefer lighter-colored sumac, possibly because it is what they are used to. Moisture sometimes causes lumps to form, but this soft "feel" is due to added cottonseed oil, not water activity, so there should be no risk of mold forming, even in fairly lumpy powder. Sumac is best stored in airtight containers away from extremes of heat, light and humidity. It will last for at least 1 year.

Use

In the Middle East, sumac is used extensively as a souring agent instead of lemon juice or vinegar. It is sprinkled on kebabs before cooking and used to garnish salads, particularly those containing tomatoes, parsley and onions. Sumac is delicious on roast meats (especially lamb) when mixed with paprika, pepper and oregano. Grilled fish and chicken are greatly enhanced by a light dusting of sumac prior to cooking. A half-and-half mixture of sumac and coarsely ground black pepper makes an excellent substitute for lemon pepper at the table. The Middle Eastern blend za'atar is made by combining thyme, toasted sesame seeds, sumac and salt (see page 781). Traditionally za'atar is sprinkled on flatbread that has been brushed with olive oil and then lightly toasted.

WEIGHT PER TEASPOON (5 mL)

- ground: 3.1 g

SUGGESTED QUANTITY PER POUND (500 g)

- **red meats:** up to 2 tbsp (30 mL)
- **white meats:** up to 2 tbsp (30 mL)
- **vegetables:** up to 2 tbsp (30 mL)
- **grains and pulses:** up to 2 tbsp (30 mL)
- **baked goods:** up to 2 tbsp (30 mL)

Slow-Roasted Tomatoes

Fresh tomatoes and sumac are a fantastic combination. When the tomatoes are roasted slowly, their flavor is intensified. This dish has long been a favorite at Herbie's spice-appreciation classes. The tomatoes are wonderful served warm or cold, as finger food or in salads or sandwiches (especially Lemon Myrtle Chicken Wrap, page 360).

Makes 24

Preparation time:
5 minutes

Cooking time: 3 hours

- - - - - - - - - - - - - - - -

Tip

Because of the high water content of tomatoes, it may be necessary to open the oven door to release steam once or twice during cooking.

• **Preheat oven to 210°F (100°C)**

12	ripe plum (Roma) tomatoes, halved lengthwise	12
½ tsp	granulated sugar	2 mL
½ tsp	fine sea salt	2 mL
½ tsp	freshly ground black pepper	2 mL
1 to 2 tbsp	sumac	15 to 30 mL
2 tbsp	olive oil	30 mL

1. On a baking sheet, arrange tomatoes cut side up. Sprinkle evenly with sugar, salt and pepper. Season liberally with sumac and drizzle with oil. Roast in preheated oven for about 3 hours, until tomatoes lose moisture and shrink but are still soft (see Tip, left). Serve warm or cool. Tomatoes will keep in an airtight container in the refrigerator for up to 3 days.

S

Fattoush

This salad is traditionally made with day-old bread in homes around the Levant. Tangy sumac elevates this dish, making it a wonderful accompaniment to roast meats or a tasty meal on its own.

Makes 6 side salads

Preparation time:
10 minutes

Cooking time:
15 minutes

Tips

Use toasted pitas in place of chips with dips such as hummus (page 596) and baba ganoush.

Toasted pitas can be kept for up to 1 week in an airtight container.

• **Preheat oven to 350°F (180°C)**

2	whole-wheat pitas	2
2 tbsp	extra virgin olive oil	30 mL
½ tsp	sumac	2 mL
½ tsp	fine sea salt	2 mL
1	medium cucumber, peeled and diced into ½-inch (1 cm) pieces	1
½	small red onion, finely chopped	½
2	large red tomatoes, diced	2
½ cup	packed fresh flat-leaf (Italian) parsley leaves, roughly chopped	125 mL
10	mint leaves, roughly chopped	10
½	head iceberg lettuce, sliced into ½-inch (1 cm) ribbons	½

DRESSING

5 tsp	freshly squeezed lemon juice	25 mL
5 tsp	oil	25 mL
1	clove garlic, crushed	1
Pinch	fine sea salt	Pinch
1 tbsp	sumac	15 mL

1. Using scissors, cut pitas into 1-inch (2.5 cm) squares and arrange in a single layer on a baking sheet.

2. In a small bowl, combine oil, sumac and salt. Drizzle pita pieces liberally with oil mixture. Bake in preheated oven for 10 minutes or until crisp. Set aside.

3. In a serving bowl, combine cucumber, onion, tomatoes, parsley, mint, lettuce and prepared pitas.

4. In a small bowl, whisk together dressing ingredients and pour over salad. Sprinkle salad with extra sumac and serve immediately.

Variation

If desired, add ½ cup (125 mL) chopped celery or radish to the salad.

Sweet Cicely

Myrrhis odorata

Family: Apiaceae (formerly Umbelliferae)

Other Names: anise chervil, British myrrh, Spanish chervil, fern-leaved chervil, giant sweet chervil

Flavor Group: Mild

Parts Used: leaves and unripe seed heads (as a herb), roots (as a vegetable)

Background

Native to Europe, where it was once cultivated as a pot shrub, sweet cicely was called *seseli* (the way it is pronounced) by the first-century CE Greek physician Dioscorides. The botanical name comes from *myrrhis*, which means "perfume," and *odorata*, "fragrance." Its common name is prefixed by "sweet" because the taste has a distinctive sugary sweetness. Its old-fashioned names, which incorrectly imply it is a type of chervil, were attributed to sweet cicely because of its similar anise-like finish and ferny leaf structure, suggesting a giant version of chervil. The oil-rich ripe seeds were once gathered and crushed to a powder for polishing wooden floors and furniture, which gave them a high gloss and an agreeable scent.

The Plant

Sweet cicely is a relatively tall, particularly attractive perennial herb that grows 2 to 5 feet (0.6 to 1.5 m) in height in cool climates and mountain regions. Thick, hollow branching stems, similar to those of angelica, bear dense foliage of fern-like green leaves that have a soft texture due to their silky down covering. The leaves are about 12 inches (30 cm) long and are paler on the underside. The plant is highly ornamental when in bloom: the $1/2$- to 2-inch (1 to 5 cm) umbels of white flowers make a dramatic display, covering the plant like flecks of ocean foam among the upright green seed heads, which from a distance look like a type of lavender. When mature and ripe, the seeds are ridged, elongated and dark brown, like large grains of wild rice. The leaves and fresh seeds of sweet cicely have an

S

Culinary Information

Combines with
- allspice
- cardamom
- chervil
- cinnamon and cassia
- mint
- nutmeg
- parsley
- vanilla

Traditional Uses
- salads
- tart fruits such as acidic berries

Spice Blends
- not commonly used in spice blends

agreeable warm anise aroma, reminiscent of myrrh, with a pleasing sweet taste. The roots have a similar flavor; they may be shaved into salads like fennel bulb or cooked as a winter soup vegetable.

Processing

Sweet cicely is nearly always used fresh; therefore, it is rarely dehydrated. If you are growing your own, the leaves may be picked in late winter and late summer. The unripe seed heads may be harvested while still green, although they do not freeze well. Ripe seeds—they will have turned brown—can be collected and hung upside down to dry. When the plant has died back in autumn, the roots may be lifted for drying. Drying the roots for later culinary use is best undertaken by first slicing the root into circles about $1/4$ inch (5 mm) thick to facilitate the release of moisture. Place the slices in a dry, warm, dark place for several days, until they are firm and not at all leathery.

Buying and Storage

Although easily grown from seed in cool, moderate climates that are not humid, sweet cicely is not readily available from fresh produce retailers, so it is best to grow your own. After picking the fresh leaves, wash and store them in the same manner as lettuce, preferably wrapped in plastic wrap and placed in a crisper at the bottom of the refrigerator, where they will last for 3 to 5 days. Dried ripe seeds and roots are best stored in airtight containers away from extremes of heat,

SUGGESTED QUANTITY PER POUND (500 g)

- **red meats:** 5 tsp (25 mL) chopped fresh leaves and seed heads
- **white meats:** 5 tsp (25 mL) chopped fresh leaves and seed heads
- **vegetables:** 5 tsp (25 mL) chopped fresh leaves and seed heads
- **grains and pulses:** 5 tsp (25 mL) chopped fresh leaves and seed heads
- **baked goods:** 5 tsp (25 mL) chopped fresh leaves and seed heads

light and humidity. Under those conditions they will last for up to 1 year.

Use

The roots of sweet cicely, when cut up and boiled like carrots or turnips, were a popular vegetable in the past, and the hollow stems have been candied in the same manner as angelica. But the leaves and finely chopped unripe seed heads have the greatest culinary significance, because they are delicious in salads. When a few sweet cicely leaves are added to the cooking water of sharp fruits such as rhubarb or acidic berries, their natural sweetness counters the tartness of the fruit. Sweet cicely is a safe sweetener for diabetics and goes well with cream and yogurt and in cooling summer drinks. The Carthusian monks who created the liqueur Chartreuse (named after the mountains where they dwelled) used sweet cicely to flavor it.

S

Tamarind

Tamarindus indica

Names in Other Languages

- **Arabic:** sbar, tamr al-hindi
- **Burmese:** ma-gyi-thi
- **Chinese (C):** daaih mah lahm, loh fong ji
- **Chinese (M):** da ma lin, luo huang zi
- **Czech:** tamarind
- **Danish:** tamarind
- **Dutch:** tamarinde, indische dadel, assem
- **Filipino:** sampalok
- **Finnish:** tamarindi
- **French:** tamarin
- **German:** Tamarinde, indische Dattel
- **Greek:** tamarin
- **Hungarian:** tamarindusz gyumolcs
- **Indian:** pulee, amyli, chinch, imlee, imli
- **Indonesian:** assam, assam jawa, asam kuning
- **Italian:** tamarindo
- **Japanese:** tamarindo
- **Laotian:** mal kham
- **Malay:** assam, assam djawa
- **Portuguese:** tamarindo
- **Russian:** finik indiskiy
- **Spanish:** tamarindo
- **Sri Lankan:** pulee, siyambala
- **Swedish:** tamarind
- **Thai:** makahm, som ma kham, mak kham peak
- **Vietnamese:** cay me, me chua, trai me

Family: Fabaceae (formerly Leguminosae)

Other Names: assam, Indian date

Flavor Group: Tangy

Parts Used: pods (as a spice)

Background

Tamarind trees are indigenous to tropical East Africa and possibly southern Asia. They grow wild in India, where they flourish as if it is their native habitat. The hardy tamarind tree also grows in many other tropical and subtropical countries, such as Australia and Mexico. Tamarind was used by the Arabs and in Europe in the Middle Ages.

The common name for tamarind in Asia, *assam*, simply means "acid," in recognition of its high tartaric acid content. The cleaning effect of this acid is so pronounced that in India tamarind pods have been used to polish brass and copper. In the past, tamarind leaves have been used to make red and yellow dyes, mostly for fabric.

Tamarind trees were a popular decorative element in colonial gardens, especially on the west coast of India. There a local belief held that evil spirits lived in tamarind pods. Taking advantage of this superstition, British people living in Goa in the 19th century would often wear a tamarind pod behind one ear (like a carpenter's pencil) when going to the marketplace, so they would not be bothered by the locals. As a result the British in Goa were nicknamed *lugimlee*

Culinary Information

Combines with

- ajowan
- allspice
- asafetida
- caraway seed
- cardamom
- chile
- cinnamon and cassia
- cloves
- coriander seed
- fennel seed
- fenugreek seed
- ginger
- mustard
- nigella
- paprika
- turmeric

Traditional Uses

- Asian soups
- curries and any dish requiring an acidic tang
- Indian pickles
- chutneys
- curry pastes

Spice Blends

- assam powder

("tamarind heads") by the locals, and I believe the name has remained a vernacular reference to foreigners in the region to this day.

Tamarind has been appreciated for its medicinal properties in Arabic countries, India and Asia. It is said to cool and cleanse the system and is reputed to be particularly good for one's liver and kidneys.

The Plant

The tamarind tree is huge and spreading. It rises up on a thick trunk covered in gray bark to 60 feet (20 m) high, and its pale green foliage units of 10 to 15 curry-leaf-shaped leaflets provide a wonderful canopy of shade. When in bloom, the foliage is punctuated by small clusters of red-striped yellow flowers. The 4-inch (10 cm) fruits of the tamarind tree are knobbly light brown pods with a brittle shell. When broken away, the shell reveals a sticky pale tan mass with longitudinal strings and fibrous veins—this is the pulp. The pulp surrounds about 10 shiny, smooth dark brown angular seeds, each measuring roughly $1/8$ by $1/3$ inch (3 by 8 mm). Upon coming into contact with the air, the pulp begins to oxidize, turning dark brown, almost black.

Its aroma is vaguely fruity and sharp, while the flavor is intensely acidic, tingling and refreshing, reminiscent of dried stone fruit.

Processing

When one stands beneath these grand spreading, very tall trees, it is difficult to imagine how the pods could possibly be picked. We saw tamarind harvesting in action when we visited the Sediyapu family's organic spice gardens near Mangalore, in the south of India. Our hosts told us to look up, and all of a sudden the upper foliage of a majestic tamarind tree began to quiver furiously. High in the tree, a farmworker was shaking the branches to dislodge the fully developed tamarind pods, which began falling to the ground in a clattering hailstorm. The pods were then gathered up and taken to the house, where we enjoyed a delicious lunch with the family.

Mrs. Sediyapu showed us how they peel off the outer skin of the pod to reveal the soft, sticky light brown tamarind pulp laced with fine string-like strands. She then proceeded

Travels in the Spice Trade

I have a vivid recollection of the majesty of the tamarind tree. Liz and I were leading a spice tour to India in 1991 when, after a hot and dusty drive, we were looking for a place to picnic. Just outside Hyderabad we found an ideal spot, beneath the cooling shade of a tamarind tree. There is a belief that tamarind trees emit harmful acrid vapors. Not only would that make it unsafe to sleep under them, it is believed that plants will not grow there to avoid inhaling the vapors. This may explain why there is usually little vegetation around the base of a tarmarind tree. However, it does create an ideal picnic spot in the middle of a hot day.

Hiding in Plain Sight

The Indians make a refreshing drink from tamarind called *imli panni*, and in the Middle East a version with added sugar is sold in attractive cordial bottles. In parts of Asia a delicious confection is made of sweetened balls of tamarind rolled in sugar and sometimes spiced with chile. Although a surprising number of Westerners are not aware of tamarind, many consume it regularly without realizing—it is one of the key ingredients in Worcestershire sauce.

to remove the seeds in a wonderfully dexterous, almost medieval manner. Using a hard dried-out scoop from the base of a coconut frond as a container, she took the mass of tamarind pulp in one hand and pressed it against a fierce-looking sickle held upturned in her other hand. The shiny black seeds dropped like marbles into the palm-frond dish while a growing ball of seeded tamarind pulp filled her left hand. The bulk of commercially produced tamarind is still hand-peeled; however, it would be rare to find this degree of care being taken to remove the seeds.

Tamarind concentrate is a thick black molasses-type liquid made by boiling down an extract of oxidized tamarind paste that has been strained to remove the seeds and fiber. Tamarind paste is made from the fresh, unoxidized pulp, mixed with salt and some food acid to prevent oxidation.

Buying and Storage

Tamarind can be bought from spice shops and Asian and Indian grocery stores. It is sold in block form: a sticky, plastic-wrapped slab of oxidized pulp and varying proportions of rock-hard seeds. Tamarind block from India has a fairly dry texture interspersed with thumbnail-sized papery flakes of inner pod skin. The type from Asia, most often Thailand, is cleaner looking and very sticky. There is not a huge difference in flavor between the two; while some cooks prefer the aesthetics of Thai tamarind, others find the Indian material easier to handle, as it is less sticky. Because of the amount of acid in tamarind, it is quite stable and requires no special storage conditions; just keep the block in an airtight container to prevent it from drying out.

Tamarind concentrate is convenient to use and can be bought in jars that range from about $3^1/_2$ oz (100 g) to 18 oz (500 g). Tamarind concentrate requires no special storage conditions because of its high acid content. However, always follow the storage instructions on a package, as the manufacturer may have added ingredients that compromise the stability when stored at ambient temperatures.

Tamarind paste is pale brown, has a salty taste and comes in containers similar in size to the concentrate. Store tamarind paste in the same manner as tamarind concentrate (above).

Another, less common form of tamarind is a powder called "cream of tamarind" or "assam powder." This is made by mixing tamarind extract with a carrier such as dextrose to form a free-flowing powder. Assam powder is sold in Indian and Asian markets. It should be stored in airtight containers and kept away from extremes of heat and humidity, as humidity will make the powder quite hard.

A member of the kokam family known as *asam gelugor*, although acidic in taste, is sometimes incorrectly referred to as "tamarind slices." In South India, kokam (page 336) is often referred to as "fish tamarind," which is a bit confusing, as the only similarity kokam has to tamarind is its acidity.

Use

Because of its high tartaric acid content, in the majority of tropical countries tamarind is one of the most popular souring agents for foods. Recipes generally call for a quantity of tamarind water (typically 2 tbsp/30 mL to $^1/_2$ cup/125 mL) to be added during cooking. To make tamarind water from a block, break off a walnut-sized piece ($^3/_4$ inch/2 cm in diameter) and add to $^1/_2$ cup (125 mL) hot water. Stir well, press it a bit with a spoon, and set aside for about 15 minutes. Strain the liquid, squeezing the remaining pulp as dry as possible before discarding it. Tamarind water can also be made from the concentrated liquid by dissolving 2 tsp (10 mL) in $^1/_2$ cup (125 mL) water. If you think of tamarind water as another form of lemon juice and use it in roughly the same proportions, the flavor strength should be just about right in any cooking application.

Tamarind paste is pale brown in color and used in Asian stir-fries; it should be added sparingly because of its high salt content. It is not a substitute for tamarind water—the unoxidized paste has a different, saltier and less acidic flavor.

Tamarind powder is added to dishes while they are cooking for an easy acidic touch, in much the same way as we use amchur powder (page 68).

WEIGHT PER TEASPOON (5 mL)

- walnut-sized piece: 12 g

SUGGESTED QUANTITY PER POUND (500 g)

Made by soaking 1 walnut-sized piece in $^1/_2$ cup (125 mL) hot water:

- **red meats:** $^1/_2$ cup (125 mL) tamarind water
- **white meats:** $^1/_3$ cup (75 mL) tamarind water
- **vegetables:** $^1/_3$ cup (75 mL) tamarind water
- **grains and pulses:** $^1/_2$ cup (125 mL) tamarind water
- **baked goods:** $^1/_2$ cup (125 mL) tamarind water

Sweet Tamarind Shrimp

This lovely shrimp dish is based on the North Indian recipe for prawn *patia*, which has Persian origins.

Makes 6 small servings

Preparation time:
20 minutes

Cooking time:
20 minutes

- - - - - - - - - - - - - - - -

Tips

The tamarind is used where in other recipes you might find lemon or lime juice, balancing the sweet, salty and hot flavors.

Ground Kashmiri chile could be used in this recipe. It is flavorsome and versatile. You can find it at most Indian markets in varying levels of heat (depending on the amount of seeds and membrane ground with the chile).

If you don't have palm sugar, substitute an equal quantity of packed light brown sugar.

• Mortar and pestle

1 cup	tamarind pulp	250 mL
1½ cups	hot water	375 mL
8	green finger chiles, seeded and chopped	8
5	cloves garlic, minced	5
2 tsp	cumin seeds	10 mL
¼ cup	oil	60 mL
3	onions, chopped	3
2 tsp	ground cumin	10 mL
2 tsp	ground coriander seed	10 mL
2 tsp	garam masala (page 735)	10 mL
1½ tsp	ground medium-hot chile (see Tip, left)	7 mL
1 tsp	ground turmeric	5 mL
4	tomatoes, diced	4
4 tsp	palm sugar (see Tips, left)	20 mL
20	fresh or dried curry leaves	20
	Sea salt	
12 oz	raw medium shrimp, peeled and deveined	375 g
½ cup	lightly packed fresh coriander (cilantro) leaves	125 mL

1. In a small bowl, cover tamarind with hot water; set aside for 15 minutes. Strain into a bowl through a fine-mesh sieve, squeezing pulp before discarding.

2. Using mortar and pestle, grind chiles, garlic and cumin seeds. Set aside.

3. In a large skillet, heat oil over medium heat. Add onions and cook for 5 minutes, until softened. Add prepared chile mixture and cook for 2 minutes, until fragrant and well combined. Stir in ground cumin and coriander, garam masala, ground chile and turmeric. Cook, stirring constantly, for 1 minute, until combined. Add tomatoes and cook, stirring often, for 5 minutes or until tomatoes are sauce-like. Stir in tamarind water, sugar and curry leaves; season with salt to taste. Bring to a boil, reduce heat, add shrimp and simmer for 4 to 5 minutes, until shrimp are pink and cooked through. Remove from heat and garnish with coriander leaves. Serve immediately.

Tarragon

Artemisia dracunculus

Family: Asteraceae (formerly Compositeae)

Varieties: French tarragon (*A. dracunculus*), Russian tarragon (*A. dracunculus dracunculoides*)

Other Names: winter tarragon, Mexican tarragon, Spanish tarragon (*Tagetes lucida*)

Flavor Group: Strong

Parts Used: leaves (as a herb)

Background

Few references to tarragon have been found that predate the 13th century, when Ibn Baitar, a respected 13th-century Arabian physician living in Spain, described its virtues and called it *tarkhun* (Arabic for "dragon"). It was not until the 16th century that it became more widely known as a condiment and was cultivated by the French, who named it *estragon*, meaning "little dragon." The dragon reference in its nomenclature is believed to come from either the appearance of its coiled serpent–like root system or the belief that tarragon was an antidote to the venom of serpents.

Tarragon was introduced to England in 1548; Gerard's *Herball* (1597) mentions it. It is most popular as a culinary herb in France, where it is found in many traditional recipes. Tarragon had appeared in the United States by 1806.

Culinary Information

Combines with
- basil
- bay leaf
- chervil
- dill
- garlic
- lovage
- marjoram
- paprika
- parsley
- savory

Traditional Uses
- tartare and béarnaise sauces
- salad dressings and vinegars
- fish and shellfish
- chicken
- turkey
- game
- veal
- egg dishes

Spice Blends
- fines herbes
- salad herbs

The Premium Herb

French tarragon, which is preferable for culinary use, is native to the Mediterranean region, while Russian tarragon, which has an insipid, less agreeable taste, is indigenous to Siberia. French tarragon has long been cultivated commercially in California, which means that when the Western world had its mid-20th-century love affair with French cuisine, good-quality dried French tarragon was readily available.

The Plant

French tarragon is a small herbaceous perennial. It has smooth, glossy, dark green long, narrow leaves shooting from opposite sides of wiry stalks, which form a tangle of stems 35 inches (90 cm) tall. The small yellowish buds rarely develop into flowers, and it is said that even in the unusual circumstance of their setting seed, they are often sterile. For this reason, what is referred to as "true tarragon" can be propagated only by root division or from cuttings (see page 27). It must be grown in well-drained soil, protected from hard frost and positioned where it gets plenty of sunshine, but with a bit of afternoon shade. French tarragon is worshipped by cooks for its characteristic licorice-anise aroma and tart, lingering appetite-appealing flavor.

Other Varieties

Russian tarragon (*A. dracunculus dracunculoides*) has neither the pungency nor the fragrance of French tarragon. It can be recognized easily, as it grows twice as tall and has larger, paler, indented leaves and seed-bearing flowers.

Winter tarragon (*Tagetes lucida*), also referred to as Mexican tarragon or Spanish tarragon, is a member of the marigold family, like huacatay (page 325). It bears bright yellow flowers; is sturdy and neat-looking, with firm dark green leaves; and has a reasonably strong, spicy aroma similar to French tarragon. Winter tarragon grows from seed and is often incorrectly sold as French tarragon.

T

Processing

We visited a herb farm just outside Canterbury, New Zealand, where the field of French tarragon was adjacent to the dehydration facility. This meant that the grower's freshly chopped leaves were in the dryer within half an hour of being harvested, which helped them to retain their characteristic flavor.

When growing French tarragon, it's important to remember that it needs to be replanted at least every third year, preferably from tip cuttings. In the Australian climate in particular, after three years the fragrance and flavor of the foliage on a French tarragon plant deteriorate until it resembles the inferior Russian variety.

French tarragon dries surprisingly well, which is fortunate when you consider how this perennial withers away in winter. As with parsley, it is possible to dry the herb at home, but a carefully dried commercial product is generally superior.

To dry tarragon from your own garden, cut the stems when they are in abundance (preferably before the unlikely appearance of the sterile flower buds) and continue to harvest until the first sign of yellowing in autumn. Hang the cut stems upside down in small separate bunches in a dark, warm, dry, well-aired place, with enough space between to allow the air to circulate freely. Within a few days the leaves should have turned dark green, show no signs of blackening and be quite crisp to the touch. Remove the leaves by running your thumb and forefinger down the stem.

Oil of tarragon, which is extracted by steam distillation, is used in perfumes, beverages, confections, commercially produced mustards and salad dressings.

Buying and Storage

As French tarragon is not always easy to come by, it is wise to be a tad cautious when buying it fresh. When there is no distinctive anise aroma or tangy taste, it is probably Russian tarragon. Masses of delightful yellow blooms are a giveaway that it is another variety, winter tarragon.

Fresh tarragon will last for a few days when the stems are placed in water (as if in a vase) that is changed every day and kept in the refrigerator with a plastic bag tented over the container. Finely chopped leaves can also be put in an ice-cube tray, barely covered with water, and frozen until required (use within about 3 months).

Dried tarragon leaves are readily available and should always be suitably aromatic and tangy in taste. Look for a dark green color, never dark brown or khaki. Store in an airtight container, shielded from light and extremes of heat and humidity. Dried tarragon leaves will keep their flavor for at least 1 year.

Use

French tarragon lends its unique flavor profile to French sauces such as tartare and béarnaise and is an essential component (along with chives, chervil and parsley) in the subtle blend known as fines herbes. Tarragon has a particular ability to flavor vinegar, which is achieved by placing a complete washed stem with leaves in a bottle of good-quality white wine vinegar for a few weeks. Tarragon vinegar is a useful ingredient for salad dressings and homemade mustards. Tarragon complements fish and shellfish. It goes well with chicken, turkey, game and veal and most egg dishes. The chopped leaves (or rehydrated dry ones) are attractive and tasty in mayonnaise, melted butter sauce and French dressing.

WEIGHT PER TEASPOON (5 mL)

- dried whole and cut leaves: 0.8 g

SUGGESTED QUANTITY PER POUND (500 g)

- **red meats:** 1 tsp (5 mL) dried, 4 tsp (20 mL) fresh chopped
- **white meats:** ¾ tsp (3 mL) dried, 1 tbsp (15 mL) fresh chopped
- **vegetables:** ½ tsp (2 mL) dried, 2 tsp (10 mL) fresh chopped
- **grains and pulses:** ½ tsp (2 mL) dried, 2 tsp (10 mL) fresh chopped
- **baked goods:** ½ tsp (2 mL) dried, 2 tsp (10 mL) fresh chopped

French Tarragon Chicken

Tarragon, chicken and cream are a match made in heaven, as shown by this simple, classic dish. The distinctively anise-like tarragon cuts through the richness of the cream, and there is no competition from the chicken for flavor. Ask your butcher to joint your chicken, or buy eight separate chicken pieces. Serve with mashed potatoes or rice.

Makes
4 servings

Preparation time:
10 minutes

Cooking time:
50 minutes

Tip

For a richer, creamier sauce, replace the chicken broth with an equal amount of table (18%) cream and adjust seasoning with salt and pepper to taste.

- **13- by 9-inch (33 by 23 cm) ceramic or glass baking dish**
- **Preheat oven to 350°F (180°C)**

1 tbsp	butter, divided	15 mL
3	shallots, finely chopped	3
1	chicken, jointed into 8 pieces	1
	Sea salt and freshly ground black pepper	
2/3 cup	white wine	150 mL
2/3 cup	chicken broth	150 mL
2/3 cup	table (18%) cream	150 mL
1/2 cup	lightly packed fresh tarragon leaves, divided	125 mL
1 tbsp	freshly squeezed lemon juice	15 mL

1. In a skillet over medium heat, melt $1^1/_2$ tsp (7 mL) butter. Add shallots and sauté until golden, 3 to 4 minutes. Using a slotted spoon, transfer shallots to baking dish. Reduce heat to medium-low and melt remaining butter.

2. Pat chicken dry with paper towels and season with salt and pepper. Place, skin side down, in skillet and cook over medium heat until browned, 5 to 8 minutes. Turn pieces over and cook for 2 minutes, until lightly browned. Transfer chicken, skin side up, to baking dish.

3. Add white wine and broth to skillet, stirring to scrape up brown bits from bottom of pan. Pour into baking dish and add cream, $1/_4$ cup (60 mL) tarragon and lemon juice. Bake in preheated oven for 40 minutes, until juices run clear from leg pieces when pierced with a fork.

4. Remove from oven and top with remaining tarragon. Season with salt and pepper to taste. Serve immediately.

Variation

Leftover chicken can be taken off the bone and mixed with mayonnaise for a delicious sandwich filling, or used in a pot pie.

Thyme

Thymus vulgaris

Names in Other Languages

- **Arabic:** alkil, satar, zatar
- **Chinese (C):** baak leih heung
- **Chinese (M):** bai li xiang
- **Czech:** materidouska, tymian
- **Danish:** timian
- **Dutch:** tijm
- **Finnish:** tarha-ajuruoho
- **French:** thym
- **German:** Thymian
- **Greek:** thimari
- **Hungarian:** timian
- **Indonesian:** timi
- **Italian:** taimu
- **Japanese:** jakoso
- **Norwegian:** timian, hagetimian
- **Portuguese:** tomilho
- **Russian:** timyan
- **Spanish:** tomillo
- **Swedish:** timjan
- **Thai:** taymat
- **Turkish:** zatar, dag kekigi
- **Vietnamese:** hung tay

Family: Lamiaceae (formerly Labiatae)

Varieties: garden thyme (*T. vulgaris*), lemon thyme (*T. citriodorus*), wild thyme (*T. serpyllum*), larger wild thyme (*T. pulegioides*)

Other Names: common thyme

Flavor Group: Pungent

Parts Used: leaves (as a herb)

Background

Thyme is indigenous to the Mediterranean; many species of this plant come from an area that encompasses southern Europe, western Asia and North Africa. The Egyptians (who used thyme in the embalming process) and the ancient Greeks (who employed it as a fumigant) both appreciated its antiseptic properties. Dioscorides, the first-century Greek physician, mentioned its value as an expectorant, and Pliny also recommended it for fumigating. The name *thyme* derives from the Greek *thymon*, meaning "to fumigate," although various interpretations have been made using similar words

25

Culinary Information

Combines with

- ajowan
- basil
- bay leaf
- coriander seed
- garlic
- marjoram
- mint
- nutmeg
- oregano
- paprika
- rosemary
- sage
- savory
- tarragon

Traditional Uses

- soups
- casseroles
- meat loaf
- pâtés
- terrines
- sausages
- potato salad
- stuffing for poultry
- rich sauces and gravies

Spice Blends

- bouquet garni
- Cajun spice mixes
- herbes de Provence
- Italian herbs
- Jamaican jerk seasoning
- mixed herbs

Not for Cooking

Ornamental types of thyme are rarely used in cooking. These include Westmoreland thyme (*T. vulgaris* 'Westmoreland'), golden thyme (*T.* x *citriodorus* 'Aureus'), silver posie thyme (*T. vulgaris* 'Silver Posie'), gray woolly thyme (*T. pseudolanuginosus*), variegated lemon thyme (*T. citriodorus* 'Variegata') and caraway thyme (*T. herba-barona*).

that mean "courage" and "sacrifice"—other attributes that thyme was associated with. Among the Greeks, the phrase "to smell of thyme" was a sincere compliment implying gracefulness. The botanical suffix for wild thyme, *serpyllum*, derives from a Greek word for "to creep," likely in reference to the low-growing entwined, snakelike habit of the groundcover thymes. The ancient Romans found the palate-pleasing taste of thyme a useful complement to fatty cheeses, and they also used it to flavor alcoholic beverages. One legend has it that thyme was included among the hay used to make a bed for the Virgin Mary and the Christ Child.

Thyme was introduced to England by the Romans and was common there in the Middle Ages. By the 16th century thyme had become naturalized in England (Gerard mentions it in his 1597 *Herball*), although the flavor of English thyme never achieved the pungency of thyme grown in hot Mediterranean climates. The famous Hymettus honey of Greece has its characteristic flavor because the bees that produce it gather pollen from the abundance of wild thyme flowering on Mount Hymettus, near Athens.

In 1725 the German apothecary Neumann isolated the essential oil of thyme, thymol. However, it is worth noting that until the early 20th century the majority of the world's thymol was actually extracted from ajowan seeds (see page 46), not the herb thyme.

The Plant

Although there are more than 100 varieties of thyme, including many hybrids, it is really only common garden thyme (*Thymus vulgaris*) and lemon thyme that are of culinary significance.

Garden thyme is a small perennial shrub that may vary widely in appearance, depending on the soil and climatic conditions it grows under. Generally this variety of thyme is stiff and bushy in appearance. It has many thin, erect stalks no taller than 12 inches (30 cm) that are covered by pairs of small, narrow, elliptical gray-green leaves, $1/4$ to $1/3$ inch (5 to 6 mm) long, which are sometimes rust-colored on the underside. The pinkish white-lipped flowers, borne in whorls at the tips of the branches, are particularly attractive to bees.

The aroma of thyme is pungent, warming, spicy and agreeable. Its flavor is similarly pungent and warming with a lingering medicinal, mouth-freshening sharpness that comes from the presence of an important volatile oil, thymol.

Other Varieties

Lemon thyme (*Thymus citriodorus*), a cross between garden thyme and larger wild thyme, is a smaller plant of similar structure that grows to only 6 inches (15 cm) tall. Its leaves are greener than those of garden thyme, and although less pungent in flavor, they have a particularly appealing lemon tang. **Wild thyme** (*T. serpyllum*) is arguably the best known of the low-growing groundcover thymes seen in abundance in rockeries and filling gaps in sandstone flagging. **Larger wild thyme** (*T. pulegioides*) is grown only for decorative purposes. It is not a low groundcover like *T. serpyllum* and is equally at home in garden beds and rockeries.

Processing

When grown under what many believe to be the most suitable conditions, thyme is already close to being dry when it is picked. I remember seeing thyme growing in arid-looking conditions among sumac trees in southeastern Turkey and thinking how small and desiccated the tiny plants seemed. Yet their flavor, concentrated by the lack of moisture and the abundance of sunshine, was incredibly powerful.

Thyme is dried in the same way as other firm-leaved herbs such as sage, oregano and rosemary: in the shade where it is warm and the humidity low. The leaves can easily be

Travels in the Spice Trade

When we visited thyme farms in Provence, we were introduced to a group of farmers who grow thyme, savory and rosemary and are making a concerted effort to propagate the wild thyme of Provence. Driving through some of the wilder parts of Provence in spring, you will see brave little outcrops of pink-flowered wild thyme (*Thymus vulgaris*). The unique characteristic of this wild thyme is that it has a much higher volatile oil content than other strains of *T. vulgaris*. However, since it wasn't cultivated commercially, wild thyme was at risk of dying out. Over the centuries, many plants that have been harvested only from the wild have experienced a similar fate. Gatherers pick the flower heads and seeds as well as the leaves. As a result, the plants are not able to self-sow and continue multiplying. For several years the farmers' cooperative we met with had been collecting the seeds of wild thyme and cultivating it for commercial production. Although cultivating wild species sounds like an oxymoron, organic farmers and heritage seed collectors are doing just that. The taste intensity of this wild thyme is so sought-after that each year's harvest, which exceeds 16 tons, is exported, and every year orders are still left waiting to be fulfilled.

removed from the stems by rubbing them over a large sieve that lets the tiny leaves through while keeping out the pieces of woody stalk. Some years ago I was told of one ingeniously simple method that involved placing dried thyme bushes on a slab of concrete and running a tennis-court roller over them. The bushes sprang up again, making them easy to pick up, and the leaves were swept into a pile for collection.

The best-quality dried thyme leaves are often winnowed to remove the last remaining pieces of stem. Winnowing is an ancient agricultural method for separating unwanted parts of plant material. Tossing it in the air lets the wind separate out the light particles while the desired heavier parts fall directly to the ground. In the case of thyme, the stems fall to the ground in front of the winnower and the leaves collect a little farther away, depending on the intensity of the breeze. These days winnowing is carried out by machines that have a series of screens to separate different sizes and weights of material without waste.

Buying and Storage

Fresh garden thyme and lemon thyme can usually be purchased in bunches from produce retailers. The robustness of this plant makes the prospect of buying wilted thyme almost inconceivable. If thyme is kept too moist, the leaves will start to blacken and lose their flavor. Sprays of thyme will keep for more than a week in a container of water (as if in a vase) in the refrigerator. The leaves can also be stripped off and frozen with a little water in ice-cube trays, where they will keep for up to 3 months. Sprigs wrapped in foil will freeze and keep for up to 3 months.

Dried thyme is readily available in supermarkets and specialty food stores. Good-quality dried garden thyme leaves are gray-green in color. They should not have any pieces of stem among them, as these will not soften in cooking and can be most uncomfortable if consumed.

In the Middle East, their quite green, tantalizingly pungent thyme is referred to as *zatar*, a term that is also used to describe a spice blend. If you are buying thyme from a Middle Eastern store, ask for "zatar herb"; if you want the blend with sumac, request "za'atar mix."

Lemon thyme is rarely seen in its dry form, more because of a lack of demand than its ability to keep its flavor when dried.

Thyme should be stored in the same way as other dried herbs: in an airtight container protected from extremes of heat, light and humidity. Thyme, when stored correctly, will last for longer than most dried herbs—from 18 months to 2 years.

Use

It would be an overstatement to say that it is easier to list the recipes thyme is *not* used in than those where it is. However, in Western and Middle Eastern cuisine, thyme finds its way into many traditional dishes. Its distinctive savory pungency brings an agreeable depth of flavor to soups, stews and casseroles and almost any dish containing meat. Thyme is traditional in bouquet garni along with marjoram, parsley and bay leaf, and in mixed herbs, which most often contain thyme, sage and marjoram. Thyme nicely complements the flavor of chicken; one of our favorite ways to cook chicken is to coat pieces with za'atar mix prior to grilling, pan-frying or baking. Thyme is excellent in pâtés and terrines and adds a delicious savory flavor to meat loaf, ground beef and sausages. It has an affinity for tomatoes and potatoes as well, being especially effective in potato salad, and complements the flavor of corn and green beans. Thyme works well in rich sauces and is an important ingredient in making pickles and for flavoring spiced olives.

WEIGHT PER TEASPOON (5 mL)

- whole dried and rubbed leaves: 1.5 g
- ground: 1.3 g

SUGGESTED QUANTITY PER POUND (500 g)

- **red meats:** 1 tsp (5 mL) dried, 1 tbsp (15 mL) fresh leaves
- **white meats:** ¾ tsp (3 mL) dried, 2 tsp (10 mL) fresh leaves
- **vegetables:** ½ tsp (2 mL) dried, 1½ tsp (7 mL) fresh leaves
- **grains and pulses:** ½ tsp (2 mL) dried, 1½ tsp (7 mL) fresh leaves
- **baked goods:** ½ tsp (2 mL) dried, 1½ tsp (7 mL) fresh leaves

T

Sausage and Thyme Cassoulet

This rustic, hearty French casserole is one of my all-time favorite things to cook for friends, and I will often make an enormous batch for a winter party. Instead of champagne and canapés I serve bowls of cassoulet topped with crunchy herb crumbs. People can eat it with a fork or a spoon while mingling or sitting in front of the fire with a lovely glass of Cabernet or Shiraz. For a heartier meal, serve over mashed potatoes.

**Makes
4 servings**

Preparation time:
20 minutes

Cooking time:
45 minutes

- - - - - - - - - - - - - - -

Tip

Toulouse sausage is best in this dish, but if you can't find it, any full-flavored pork sausage will do. You might also try merguez, chorizo or Cumberland sausages.

• **Preheat oven to 400°F (200°C)**

CRUMB TOPPING

1 cup	fresh sourdough bread crumbs	250 mL
1	clove garlic, very finely chopped	1
½	small red onion, very finely chopped	½
1 tbsp	fresh thyme leaves	15 mL
1 tbsp	finely chopped fresh parsley leaves	15 mL
1 tsp	freshly grated lemon zest	5 mL
2 tbsp	olive oil	30 mL

CASSOULET

2 tsp	olive oil	10 mL
1	red onion, finely chopped	1
2	cloves garlic, minced	2
1	red bell pepper, seeded and chopped	1
4	pork sausages, sliced into ½-inch (1 cm) pieces (see Tip, left)	4
2	anchovy fillets, chopped	2
1	confit duck breast, shredded (see Tip, page 639)	1
1	can (14 oz/398 mL) diced tomatoes, with juice	1
1 cup	lima beans, cooked and drained	250 mL
1 cup	black-eyed peas, cooked and drained	250 mL
1 cup	dry red wine	250 mL
1½ tbsp	dried thyme	22 mL
1 tsp	dried rosemary	5 mL
1 tsp	paprika	5 mL
1 tsp	smoked sweet paprika	5 mL
1 tsp	piment d'Espelette (see page 459)	5 mL
	Sea salt and freshly ground black pepper	

1. *Crumb Topping:* In a bowl, combine bread crumbs, garlic, onion, thyme, parsley, lemon zest and oil, mixing well to ensure that crumbs are well coated in oil. Spread evenly over a baking sheet and bake in preheated oven for 5 minutes, until golden. Remove from oven and set aside.

2. *Cassoulet:* In a large casserole dish or Dutch oven over medium heat, heat oil. Add onion and sauté until translucent, about 5 minutes. Add garlic and red pepper and sauté for 2 minutes, until softened. Add sausages and cook until browned on both sides, about 6 minutes. Add anchovies, duck, tomatoes, lima beans, black-eyed peas, wine, thyme, rosemary, two paprikas, and piment d'Espelette. Stir well, reduce heat to low and simmer for about 30 minutes, until sauce has thickened and sausages are tender. Season with salt and pepper to taste. To serve, ladle into bowls and top with crunchy crumbs.

Tonka Bean

Dipteryx odorata (also known as *Coumarouna odorata*)

Family: Fabaceae (formerly Leguminosae)

Other Names: tonkin bean, tonquin bean

Flavor Group: Pungent

Parts Used: seeds (as a spice)

Background

Tonka beans are indigenous to the northern part of South America. The majority come from Venezuela, although Colombia, Brazil and Nigeria also produce them. The most interesting and controversial aspect of tonka's history has been the focus on its potential toxicity. The beans contain about 3% coumarin, which if consumed in large quantities can cause liver damage. Coumarin also occurs in cassia (*Cinnamomum cassia, C. burmannii* and *C. loureirii*), licorice (*Glycyrrhiza glabra*, also a Fabaceae member) and lavender (*Lavandula angustifolia*). When used in normal culinary quantities, it will have no ill effects on normally healthy people. In Australia and many parts of Europe, tonka has experienced a heightened level of popularity among chefs and food lovers. This newfound celebrity status has

Culinary Information

Combines with
- allspice
- cardamom
- cassia
- cinnamon
- cloves
- coriander seed
- ginger
- vanilla

Traditional Uses
- milk-based desserts
- baked goods
- stewed fruits
- compotes of dried fruits

Spice Blends
- not commonly used in spice blends

The Coumarin Problem

In 1954, relying on early and apparently erroneous data on the effect of coumarin as a blood thinner (which it is not), the U.S. Food and Drug Administration imposed a ban on the importation of tonka beans for flavoring. To my knowledge that restriction is still in place.

been driven largely by media exposure extolling its unique flavor attributes, and likely heightened by the frisson of danger associated with its illegality in the United States. Nonetheless, the general advice from food safety authorities in most countries still remains "Use with caution."

The Plant

Tonka trees grown for fruit production are imposing, generally dense and glossy-foliaged trees that reach more than 65 feet (20 m), with a diameter of up to 3 feet (1 m). The trees grow in moist, well-drained soils that are relatively poor. However, the density of growth and fecundity of flowering and pod production is enhanced by good-quality soils, fertilizer and compost. The wood from the tree is quite hard and is used for flooring. Around three months after flowering, the green, then light brown to yellowish pods form; they look like small ripening mangoes. It is within these pods that the seed, or bean, is found. Tonka beans are extremely pungent; their highly complex aroma is reminiscent of marzipan, bitter almonds, cinnamon and vanilla.

Processing

Fully ripe pods fall from the trees and are picked up from among the leaf matter and taken in wicker baskets to be processed. Each pod is cut or broken open with a hammer to reveal a wrinkled-looking oblong brown seed (the tonka bean) about 1 inch (2.5 cm) long; when cut to reveal its cross-section, the bean reveals a creamy white center. These beans, which are the whole seed, are placed in the sun to dry. The naturally occurring enzymes activated by the process of drying turn the beans black on the outside. The centers turn pale brown and the pungent flavor is created. To my knowledge, the flesh of the pod has no culinary use.

Buying and Storage

Tonka beans are available in some specialty spice shops. They should always be purchased whole and in small quantities, as you require only a little when adding to recipes. Some beans may exhibit a slight bloom on the surface, a little like juniper berries. This is not a problem; it is simply some of the coumarin that has crystallized on the surface. Store in a very well-sealed airtight container, as the aroma is extremely pervasive and will easily cross-contaminate other ingredients close by. Whole tonka beans, kept away from extremes of heat, light and humidity, will last for 3 years or more.

Use

The key word when using tonka is "sparingly"—a little definitely goes a long way. I have found that the best way to add tonka bean to a recipe is to grate it, exactly the same way you would grate nutmeg. The powder, which resembles freshly ground nutmeg, is highly aromatic. These notes complement ice cream, panna cotta, poached pears, crème brûlée, sponge cakes, shortbread cookies, fruit cakes and Christmas puddings. Tonka bean can also be added to game, pâté and foie gras, as the rich taste of tonka balances with rich foods in the same way that star anise works well with duck and pork.

Non-culinary uses for tonka beans include as a flavoring for pipe tobacco and, in extracts made by steam distillation, an ingredient in lotions and perfumes.

WEIGHT PER TEASPOON (5 mL)
- average whole tonka bean: 2 g
- ground: 2.5 g

SUGGESTED QUANTITY PER POUND (500 g)
- red meats: 1/3 tsp (1.5 mL) ground
- white meats: 1/4 tsp (1 mL) ground
- vegetables: 1/4 tsp (1 mL) ground
- grains and pulses: 1/4 tsp (1 mL) ground
- baked goods: 1/4 tsp (1 mL) ground

Crème Brûlée

Crème brûlée is a classic dessert that never seems to date. Traditionally made with vanilla beans, this version uses tonka, which has a similar flavor profile. The trick to this dessert is not to overcook the custard, or you'll end up with scrambled eggs.

**Makes
4 servings**

Preparation time:
5 minutes

Cooking time:
30 minutes

Tips

Superfine (caster) sugar is a very fine granulated sugar typically used in recipes that require a faster-dissolving granule. If you can't find it in stores, you can make your own by using a food processor fitted with the metal blade to process granulated sugar to a very fine, sand-like consistency.

If you do not have a blowtorch, place custards on the very top rack in the oven, as close to the heat as possible, and broil, watching carefully, until sugar melts and turns a deep golden brown, about 3 to 5 minutes.

- **Four 4-inch (10 cm) diameter ramekins**
- **9-inch (23 cm) square glass baking dish**
- **Muslin-lined sieve**
- **Kitchen blowtorch (see Tips, left)**
- **Preheat oven to 340°F (170°C)**

1¼ cups	heavy or whipping (35%) cream	300 mL
2	tonka beans, roughly chopped	2
4	egg yolks	4
1 tbsp	superfine (caster) sugar, plus extra for brûléing (see Tips, left)	15 mL

1. In a saucepan over medium heat, combine cream and tonka beans. Bring just to a simmer (do not boil). Remove from heat, cover and set aside for 10 minutes.

2. Meanwhile, in a mixing bowl, beat egg yolks with sugar until light and fluffy. Stir in infused cream. Set a muslin-lined sieve over a heatproof bowl and strain mixture to remove eggy threads and tonka bean bits.

3. Arrange ramekins in baking dish and pour in custard egg mixture. Slowly pour hot water into baking dish until it reaches halfway up the ramekins. Bake in preheated oven for about 20 minutes, until tops of custards form a light golden skin but still wobble. Carefully remove baking dish from oven and take ramekins out of the water. Set aside for about 30 minutes to cool, then, being careful not to break the skin, cover and refrigerate for at least 3 hours or (ideally) overnight.

4. Before serving, sprinkle each custard with ½ to 1 tsp (2 to 5 mL) sugar, about ¼ inch (5 mm) thick. Using kitchen blowtorch, hold flame 2 to 3 inches (5 to 7.5 cm) from top of custard and heat sugar, using even movements, until sugar melts and turns deep golden brown (do this quickly to avoid "cooking" the custard). Repeat with remaining custards. Set brûlées aside for about 5 minutes to allow sugar to cool and harden before serving.

T

Turmeric

Curcuma longa (also known as *C. domestica*)

Names in Other Languages

- **Arabic:** kurkum, kharkoum
- **Burmese:** sa-nwin
- **Chinese (C):** wohng geung, wat gam
- **Chinese (M):** yu jin, huang jiang
- **Czech:** kurkuma, indicky safran
- **Danish:** gurkemeje
- **Dutch:** geelwortel, kurkuma, tarmeriek
- **Filipino:** dilaw, dilao
- **Finnish:** kurkuma, kurkum
- **French:** curcuma, safran des Indes
- **German:** Curcuma, Kurkuma, indischer Safran, Gelbwurz
- **Greek:** kitrinoriza, kourkoumi
- **Hungarian:** kurkuma
- **Indian:** haldee, halad, haldi, kaha, manjal
- **Indonesian:** kunjit, kunyit; daun kunyit (leaves)
- **Italian:** curcuma
- **Japanese:** ukon, tamerikku
- **Malay:** kunyit, kunyit basah
- **Norwegian:** gurkemeie
- **Portuguese:** açafrão-da-terra
- **Russian:** zholty imbir
- **Spanish:** curcuma
- **Sri Lankan:** munjal, kaha
- **Swedish:** gurkmeja

Family: Zingiberaceae

Other Names: Madras turmeric, Alleppey turmeric, Indian saffron, yellow ginger

Flavor Group: Amalgamating

Parts Used: rhizomes (as a spice)

Background

Turmeric is not known in a truly wild state, but it is believed to have evolved from wild curcuma. Through a process of continuous selection of wild curcuma and cultivation by vegetative propagation of the fingers (similar to the propagation of ginger), turmeric as we know it has evolved. Curcuma is indigenous to southern Asia, where it was domesticated and featured prominently in both medicinal and religious applications. Turmeric was listed in an Assyrian herbal in 600 BCE as a coloring; it had reached China by the seventh century CE. Marco Polo described its use in Koncha, China, in 1280, noting its similarity to saffron. One wonders whether he was also sampling some other interesting substances, for besides color, there is little that saffron and turmeric have in common. Even the bright yellow of turmeric is quite different from the golden orange-yellow of infused saffron.

Culinary Information

Combines with

- allspice
- caraway
- cardamom
- chile
- cinnamon and cassia
- cloves
- coriander (leaf and seed)
- fennel seed
- fenugreek seed
- galangal
- garlic
- ginger
- lemongrass
- lemon myrtle
- makrut lime leaf
- mustard
- nigella
- paprika
- parsley
- tamarind
- Vietnamese mint

Traditional Uses

- Asian and Indian curries
- Moroccan tagines
- stir-fried chicken
- seafood and vegetables
- pickles
- sauces
- rice dishes

Spice Blends

- curry powders
- Indian masalas
- chermoula spice mix
- ras el hanout
- Persian spice mixes
- tandoori spice blends

Names in Other Languages

- **Thai:** khamin
- **Turkish:** sari boya
- **Vietnamese:** nghe

Turmeric was known in the Malagasy Republic (Madagascar) in the eighth century, and by the 13th century it was being used as a dye in West Africa. As a spice, turmeric features in ayurvedic medicine, the traditional "natural" medicine of India. Its healing properties have been well documented in folk medicine and are now being studied by scientists. Ointments containing turmeric are applied as an antiseptic, and in some parts of Asia turmeric water is used as a cosmetic.

Turmeric is used extensively as a coloring in foods (including confectionery and pharmaceuticals) in response to the increasing consumer demand for natural colors. Yellow turmeric paper can be used as a test for alkalinity. The textile industry has used turmeric for many years as a dye, even though by today's standards it is not at all colorfast. It is likely that as the price of turmeric is pushed up by greater culinary use, longer-lasting synthetic dyes will replace it.

T

The Plant

Turmeric is the rhizome (the part of the root system that grows off the primary tuber) of a tropical perennial plant that belongs to the ginger family (Zingiberaceae). For harvesting purposes it is grown as an annual. Turmeric has long, flat bright green leaves that grow up from the base to a height of 3 feet (1 m). With its pale yellow flowers it looks similar to ginger and some lilies. The rhizomes, which are commonly referred to as "fingers," are ginger-like in appearance and 2 to $3^1/_4$ inches (5 to 8 cm) long. They are rounder in cross-section than ginger, measure $^1/_2$ inch (1 cm) thick and are deep orange-yellow in color.

Powdered turmeric is bright yellow and has a distinctive earthy aroma and a surprisingly pleasing sharp, bitter, spicy, lingering depth of flavor.

Processing

After the turmeric rhizomes have been lifted, they are plunged into boiling water for about an hour. This speeds up the drying time and denatures them so they will not sprout. It also aids even distribution of color in the rhizome—when

Travels in the Spice Trade

When writing about turmeric, I can't help recalling one visit to the state of Kerala, in the south of India, where we visited a large turmeric plantation. Until then we had only seen turmeric in smallholding spice gardens, growing among pepper vines and nutmeg and clove trees. One day, after we had looked at ginger-drying on a massive scale, we were informed that there were large turmeric plantations in the same area. We had already traveled for hours over rough roads to find the ginger, but that was only the beginning. After a fairly harrowing drive over roads that were more regularly traversed by bullock cart, we arrived in an open area just as the sun began to set. The driver pointed out a biblical-looking mud-brick shed that housed the harvested turmeric waiting to be cleaned and sent to market. We asked where the turmeric plantation was. He replied that this was the plantation and all the turmeric had just been harvested!

I am sure few people have traveled as far and as long as we did that day to gaze upon a turmeric plantation with no turmeric growing. At least we carry a timeless image in our minds (it was too dark to take photos) of the undulating landscape studded with coconut palms. I loved inhaling the aromas (sharp earthiness and pungency) given off by the stored turmeric. At first I thought it was the smell of turned soil and dirt clinging to the rhizomes; now, whenever I smell good-quality turmeric, it takes me back to the earthy smell of that storage shed in the south of India.

fresh turmeric is cut, you notice that the orange-yellow color is not evenly distributed throughout the cross-section. The fingers are then dried in the sun.

Once dry, the fingers are polished to remove the outer skin, rootlets and any remaining soil particles. The traditional way to polish them was for workers to rub the turmeric vigorously with hands or feet wrapped in several layers of burlap sacking to provide abrasion (and as protection for the worker). Another method was to put the turmeric fingers in a long gunnysack with some stones. Two workers would shake the bag between them (the same way you would flap a beach towel to get the sand out), transforming the dirty brown rhizomes into smooth, dark yellow fingers ready for market. Nowadays polishing is carried out in large wire or perforated metal drums that are rotated on an axle; the rubbish falls out through the holes and the polished fingers are left behind in the drum.

Ground turmeric is made by crushing the slate-hard fingers in a hammermill, then transferring them to a grinder set up to produce the familiar bright yellow powder. (Gelatinization of the starches during boiling makes them rock-hard, which is why they are almost impossible to grind domestically.)

Turmeric oleoresin is extracted for use as a natural color (E100) in the food and pharmaceutical industries, where it is sometimes referred to as "curcuma oleoresin."

Buying and Storage

An increase in the popularity of Asian foods in North America has helped cooks become aware of the virtue of using fresh turmeric rhizome for its color and flavor. Fresh turmeric is often available from specialty produce merchants, particularly those that cater to the Asian market. The rhizomes should be plump, firm and clean. Store fresh turmeric in an open container in the cupboard the same way you keep your fresh onions and garlic, where it will last for up to 2 weeks.

Turmeric leaves (used in Malay and Indonesian cooking) and the tender young shoots for Thai dishes are also available from Asian produce stores. Store these quite firm leaves in the crisper section of your refrigerator, where they will last for a little more than 1 week.

There are two main types of turmeric powder, Madras and Alleppey. It is interesting to note that although many spices have prefixes derived from geographic regions, this does not

necessarily mean that is where they are grown. The name may have been given because a certain grade or type of the spice was always available from traders in that particular area, or perhaps because the district the spice was named after became better known for its production than other areas. For example, Madras turmeric is grown in Tamil Nadu but traded mostly in Madras. Alleppey turmeric is produced in Kerala but takes its name from the beautiful waterway-laced Alleppey district near Cochin, where much of this turmeric is traded.

Madras turmeric is light yellow and is the most commonly available variety for culinary use. The English regarded it as the superior grade, probably because it colors without contributing much flavor. Madras turmeric is used primarily to color curries, mustards and pickles. It has a curcumin content (the coloring agent) of around 3.5%.

Alleppey turmeric is much darker in color. Its curcumin content may be as high as 6.5%, making it a more effective coloring. It also has superior fresh turmeric flavor notes, even when dried. Alleppey turmeric more closely resembles the flavor of fresh turmeric, with a somewhat earthy aroma and surprisingly delicate top notes of lemon and mint, reminiscent of its cousin ginger. The texture is oily because of its higher curcumin content; when you're blending it with other spices, I suggest sieving it through a small strainer to prevent clumping.

Turmeric powder should be stored in the same way as other ground spices: in an airtight container protected from light and extremes of heat and humidity. Under these conditions, both the Alleppey and Madras varieties will keep their color and full flavor for 12 to 15 months.

Use

Once you get over the notion that turmeric is used mainly to color food, it is remarkable how versatile it seems. It is, of course, most often associated with curries, where the right amount, especially of Alleppey turmeric, makes a significant contribution to flavor. A Moroccan chermoula spice blend is dependent upon the warm earthiness of turmeric to amalgamate spices such as cumin, paprika, chile and pepper with onion, garlic, parsley and coriander leaf. Our Kuwaiti Fish Stew with Black Lime (page 127) relies on turmeric to harmonize its cardamom, pepper, cumin and chile notes with cilantro leaves and fresh dill. Turmeric works well in stir-fries with lime leaf, galangal, chile and native Australian lemon myrtle. Kapitan chicken, a delicious dish that European colonials enjoyed in Malaya, has onions, garlic, chile and turmeric as its prime flavor constituents.

Although often called "Indian saffron," turmeric should never be used as a substitute for true saffron in a recipe, because the flavor is quite different. However, you can make an attractive and tasty yellow rice dish with turmeric. When cooking by absorption, for every 1 cup (250 mL) of rice covered with water, add $\frac{1}{2}$ tsp (2 mL) turmeric powder, a $1\frac{1}{2}$-inch (4 cm) piece of cinnamon stick, 3 whole cloves and 4 green cardamom pods.

Always be very careful not to spill turmeric on your clothes, as it will leave stains that are almost impossible to remove.

WEIGHT PER TEASPOON (5 mL)

- **ground:** 3 g

SUGGESTED QUANTITY PER POUND (500 g)

- **red meats:** 1 tbsp (15 mL) ground
- **white meats:** 1 tbsp (15 mL) ground
- **vegetables:** 2 tsp (10 mL) ground
- **grains and pulses:** 1 tsp (5 mL) ground
- **baked goods:** 1 tsp (5 mL) ground

T

Chermoula Paste

Many recipes call for the addition of "Moroccan spice," which could be anything from a tagine spice mix to ras el hanout or berbere. However, chermoula is really the default Moroccan spice. This heavenly blend can be made using either dried spices or fresh, if a light, salsa-style dressing is desired. It is low on chile heat and full of flavor and goes with just about everything, from breads to grilled meats. My favorite way to use chermoula is to mix it with a little plain yogurt and use it to liberally coat swordfish steaks before grilling.

Makes about 1 cup (250 mL)

Preparation time:
10 minutes

Cooking time:
5 minutes

Tip

Fresh turmeric will stain easily, so wear gloves when grating.

• **Food processor**

1	clove garlic, chopped	1
1	shallot, chopped	1
1 tbsp	ground cumin	15 mL
½ tsp	ground coriander seed	2 mL
2 tsp	paprika	10 mL
2 tsp	grated fresh turmeric root (see Tip, left)	10 mL
1 tsp	grated fresh gingerroot	5 mL
Pinch	cayenne	Pinch
1 tbsp	finely chopped fresh coriander (cilantro) leaves	15 mL
2 tbsp	finely chopped fresh parsley leaves	30 mL
¼ tsp	fine sea salt	1 mL
2 tbsp	olive oil	30 mL
1 tbsp	freshly squeezed lemon juice	15 mL

1. In food processor fitted with the metal blade, combine garlic, shallot, cumin, ground coriander, paprika, turmeric, ginger, cayenne, coriander leaves, parsley and salt. Pulse to combine. With the motor running, add oil and lemon juice through the feed tube and process to create a paste, scraping down sides of bowl if necessary. It will keep in an airtight container in the refrigerator for up to 1 week.

Variation

To make a marinade for meat or fish, combine ¼ cup (60 mL) chermoula with 2 tbsp (30 mL) plain Greek yogurt.

Delhi Dal

The use of red kidney beans is commonplace in northern India, and they make this red lentil dish extremely satisfying. This is my mum's favorite dish to eat when she's in Delhi, and she has me hooked on it too—I always try to have a portion or two in the freezer for a rainy day. Serve with steamed basmati rice or pilaf (page 164).

**Makes
6 servings**

Preparation time:
40 minutes
Cooking time:
20 minutes

Tip

Red lentils are ideal for dal, as they soften and go mushy, creating a wonderful soupy consistency. While not essential, soaking them for about an hour reduces cooking time and aids digestion.

• **Food processor**

PASTE

1 cup	lightly packed fresh coriander (cilantro) leaves and stems	250 mL
1	small onion, roughly chopped	1
1 tbsp	peeled and roughly chopped gingerroot	15 mL
1 tbsp	minced garlic	15 mL
1	green finger chile, seeded and chopped	1
2 tbsp	lentil and dal spice mix (page 715)	30 mL
1 tbsp	oil	15 mL

DAL

1 tbsp	oil	15 mL
2 cups	red lentils, soaked in 3 cups (750 mL) water (see Tip, left)	500 mL
1½ cups	cooked red kidney beans (see Tips, page 779)	375 mL
2	cans (14 oz/398 mL) diced tomatoes, with juice	2
Pinch	sugar	Pinch
2 tbsp	fresh curry leaves	30 mL
1 tsp	fine sea salt	5 mL
	Freshly ground black pepper	
	Additional fresh coriander (cilantro) leaves	

1. *Paste:* In food processor fitted with the metal blade, combine coriander leaves, onion, ginger, garlic and chile. Process to a smooth paste. Add lentil and dal spice mix and 1 tbsp (15 mL) oil. Pulse to combine well.

2. *Dal:* In a large saucepan over medium heat, heat 1 tbsp (15 mL) oil. Add paste and cook, stirring constantly, for 3 minutes, until fragrant and beginning to brown. Add lentils and soaking water, kidney beans, tomatoes, sugar, curry leaves and salt. Bring to a boil, then reduce heat and simmer for 15 minutes, stirring occasionally, until lentils and beans are very soft. Season with salt and pepper to taste. Garnish with coriander leaves.

T

Vanilla

Vanilla planifolia

Family: Orchidaceae

Varieties: vanilla (*V. planifolia*, also known as *V. fragrans*), West Indian vanilla (*V. pompona*), Tahitian vanilla (*V. tahitensis*), salep (*Orchis latifolia, O. mascula, O. maculata, O. anatolica*)

Other Names: vanilla bean, vanilla pod, vanilla extract, vanilla essence, vanilla bean paste

Flavor Group: Sweet

Parts Used: pods (as a spice)

Background

Vanilla is indigenous to the southeast of Mexico and parts of Central America, where it grows in well-drained soils that are high in humus from the surrounding tropical vegetation. Although it is not known when the Aztecs started using vanilla, its production had reached a considerable degree of sophistication by the time the Spanish were introduced to the spice in 1520. A drink of chocolate and vanilla sweetened with honey was given to Cortés by the Aztec emperor Montezuma. So impressed were the Spanish by this discovery that they imported vanilla beans and established factories in Spain to manufacture chocolate flavored with vanilla. Quite apart from its flavor, vanilla apparently earned a reputation as a nerve stimulant and an aphrodisiac. It was also used to scent tobacco.

Although plants were taken to England as early as 1733 and were reintroduced at the beginning of the 19th century, all serious attempts to get them to produce pods outside their natural habitat failed. In the middle of the 19th century, botanists discovered that the plants were barren because they lacked natural pollinators. In an amazing twist of fate, a 12-year-old slave by the name of Edmund Albius on the island of Réunion found he could hand-pollinate vanilla flowers. Thereafter a satisfactory method of hand-pollination was devised and spread around the world. By the early 20th century vanilla was being cultivated in Réunion, Tahiti and parts of Africa and Madagascar.

Culinary Information

Combines with

- allspice
- angelica (crystallized)
- cardamom
- cinnamon and cassia
- cloves
- ginger
- lavender
- lemon myrtle
- lemon verbena
- licorice
- mint
- nutmeg
- pandan leaf
- poppy seed
- rose petals
- sesame seed
- wattleseed

Traditional Uses

- ice cream
- dessert creams and sauces
- cakes
- cookies
- sweets
- liqueurs
- vanilla sugar

Spice Blends

- sugar and spice blends

Sadly, the invention of artificial vanilla—made from the waste sulfite liquor of paper mills combined with coal-tar extracts or eugenol, the oil from cloves—nearly ruined the natural vanilla industry. Imitation vanilla was about one-tenth the price of real vanilla, and although inferior in flavor profile, it soon accounted for the lion's share of vanilla flavoring used in the manufacture of ice cream, confectionery and beverages. By the end of the 20th century, however, consumer demand for natural flavors and an appreciation of the superior flavor nuances in real vanilla had created some resurgence in the Mexican industry, as well as opportunities for new producers such as India, Papua New Guinea and Indonesia.

The Plant

Vanilla is a member of the orchid genus, which forms part of the largest family of flowering plants in the world, encompassing some 20,000 species. There are about 100 varieties of vanilla. It is one of the only genera in Orchidaceae that have any culinary significance, the other being the obscure and hard-to-find salep (*Orchis latifolia*, see page 655). The most important variety of vanilla, *V. planifolia*, is a tropical climbing orchid. Its succulent stems, $1/3$ to $3/4$ inch (1 to 2 cm) in diameter, reach upward 33 to 50 feet (10 to 15 m) by clinging to host trees with long aerial roots. The leaves are flat, fleshy and large, $3^1/4$ to 10 inches (8 to 25 cm) long and $3/4$ to $3^1/4$ inches (2 to 8 cm) wide. They are rounded at the base and taper abruptly to a pointed tip like a cowlick. The slightly fragrant pale greenish flower is yellow-lipped and averages $3^1/4$ to 4 inches (8 to 10 cm) in diameter. The almost cylindrical 4- to 10-inch (10 to 25 cm) angled capsules that follow hang in clusters—these are referred to as pods (or beans). When fresh, the pods have no aroma or taste; curing activates the enzymes that naturally occur in a vanilla bean, creating the flavor component vanillin (the active ingredient responsible for vanilla's flavor). There are two other varieties of vanilla but their flavor is generally considered to be inferior to that of *V. planifolia* because of their lower vanillin content.

A cured vanilla bean is dark brown to black in color, averages 7 to 8 inches (18 to 20 cm) in length and has a shriveled appearance, with many longitudinal ridges and indentations. It is as flexible as a strip of well-oiled bridle leather. A dusting of sugary white powder known as *givre* sometimes appears on the surface; this is vanillin that has crystallized. When split lengthwise, a sticky black mass of millions of minute seeds is revealed, each one no larger than a speck of ground black pepper. The aroma of a vanilla bean is fragrant, floral, sweet and highly agreeable. Similarly its taste is rich, smooth and appealing, although the flavor can be fully appreciated only in tandem with its seductive smell.

Travels in the Spice Trade

When Liz and I were in Papantla, Mexico, we were told that the high price of vanilla makes it vulnerable to theft. Bandits would steal vanilla pods that were ready to harvest and cure them in secret before selling them on the black market. To counter this theft, our hosts told us about an ingenious (albeit labor-intensive) process that was helping to make the problem a thing of the past. Many farmers now brand each vanilla pod, using a cork embedded with pins to scratch a pattern that remains even after curing. So if you see a vanilla pod with a little dotted pattern at one end, you are looking at one of the most unusual applications of agricultural branding! Apparently this measure has resulted in a significant drop in the rate of theft and the capture of a number of bandits.

Other Varieties

West Indian vanilla (*Vanilla pompona*) resembles *V. planifolia* but has larger leaves and flowers and shorter, thicker pods. It has less flavor than *V. planifolia* and *V. tahitensis* and is rarely used commercially. **Tahitian vanilla** (*V. tahitensis*) is a hybrid produced by cross-breeding *V. pompona* with *V. planifolia*. It was introduced to Tahiti in 1848 by Admiral Ferdinand-Alphonse Hamelin and is now cultivated in Hawaii and many other tropical countries, including Réunion and Niue. Tahitian vanilla has slender stems, narrow leaves and small pods that taper at either end. Although lower in vanillin content than *V. planifolia*, Tahitian vanilla has a unique aroma and flavor profile that makes it highly sought after these days by many chefs.

Processing

Processing vanilla pods is an extraordinarily labor-intensive process, beginning with fertilizing the flowers, which must be done by hand to ensure pollination and a good crop. The flowers are pollinated in their natural habitat by little bees of the genus *Melipona*, and because there are either not enough of these bees around to pollinate the vanilla flowers or the vines are growing in regions where the bees do not exist, pollination has to be performed by hand. To complicate things further, there is a small membrane in the vanilla flower that prevents the stigma and stamen from touching and pollinating. Consequently, to ensure that all the flowers produce a vanilla bean, the painstaking process of bending the two filaments so they touch (generally done with a small implement like a toothpick) must be carried out on every flower in the plantation.

You may have noticed that most vanilla beans are uniform in length and look quite straight. On a plantation we visited in Papantla, Mexico, the farmer told us he always removes any curved pods, leaving only the good straight ones on the vine to mature. Because the vanilla pods don't mature at the same time, the harvest can take place over a period of about three months. The pods are picked and then taken into town, where they are cured.

When harvested, the beans are green, and at this stage they are odorless and tasteless. They are laid in boxes and placed in a wood-fired kiln to start the drying and curing process. After about 24 hours in the kiln, the beans are spread out in the sun to absorb heat (they become so hot

V

you could burn your fingers picking one up). At the end of the day the pods are gathered up and wrapped in woollen blankets or straw mats. Then, on multitiered racks in a large shed protected from the weather, they are put to bed for the night to sweat.

The vanilla beans go through this process daily for up to 28 days. At that point they are stored for up to six months, until they have turned a very dark brown or black and the head curer is satisfied that the curing process is complete. During this time a vanilla bean may have been handled 100 times or more. What began as 10 pounds (5 kg) of green, uncured beans becomes 2 pounds (1 kg) of properly cured vanilla beans. The beans are then graded according to quality and strung together in tight bundles of 60 to 100 pods, ready for export.

Vanilla beans are not always perfect; some may be very short or twisted. In the village of Papantla, the womenfolk cleverly and painstakingly braid the pliable beans that don't make the cut into charming little figures and flower designs. Another local product is a delicious liqueur made from vanilla beans. It tastes a little like Tia Maria, only instead of the distinctive coffee taste it has a strong, almost smoked, woody, sweet vanilla flavor.

Natural vanilla extract is made when finely chopped cured vanilla beans are soaked in alcohol, water and a little sugar to extract the fragrance and flavor components of the bean. A proportion of the water is then distilled off, leaving an essence of soluble vanilla extractives in a solution that contains up to 35% alcohol. This is called "single-fold" extract. It's a standard based on approximately $3^1/_2$ oz (100 g) of beans extracted in 4 cups (1 L) of alcohol. Two-fold extract is made with twice the quantity of vanilla beans in 4 cups (1 L) of alcohol. Three- and four-fold extracts are also produced; however, these stronger distillations tend to be reserved for commercial use because of their strength and degree of concentration. Some so-called thick vanilla essences contain added sugar, glycerin, propylene glycol and dextrose or corn syrup. It always pays to read the labels!

More recently, vanilla bean pastes have been developed by some producers. These are generally composed of ground spent vanilla beans (waste material from the extraction process), vanilla extract, corn syrup and thickeners. These pastes are popular with restaurants because they give patrons the impression that the dish was prepared using seeds scraped from whole beans. However, most of these pastes tend to be less effective in cooking than pure extract or actual seeds, because you are getting a product that is very different from seeds scraped out of a whole vanilla bean. The best vanilla bean paste I have seen is from the Pacific island of Vanuatu. It is made by grinding vanilla beans and adding organic raw sugar and a very small amount of lemon juice; there is nothing else, not even alcohol, in the paste. The sugar contributes to the paste's consistency and the lemon juice assists in preservation.

Buying and Storage

Vanilla beans are readily available from specialty food retailers. However, when buying whole vanilla beans, regardless of their country of origin, it is important to make sure they have not dried out and lost their flavor and aroma. A good vanilla bean is dark brown or black, moist to the touch and as pliable as a piece of confectionery licorice. It is immediately fragrant. Size is no indication of flavor quality, though traders will always tell you that the longest beans (7 inches/17 cm or more) are the premium grade. When smelling and touching a soft black aromatic vanilla bean, you can almost sense the hundreds of times it was handled to bring it to its perfect state. You can taste the sunshine and the balmy nights of sweating that accelerated the enzyme reactions to create its seductive flavor and true character.

There are five main types of vanilla on the market, and within each type there are grades (as with most spices) that reflect overall quality.

Mexican vanilla, with its deep history and 300-year monopoly of the trade (it lasted until the 19th century), has long been regarded as possessing the finest aroma and flavor. Some cooks who have experienced only artificial vanilla may feel that Mexican vanilla lacks a certain depth of flavor, but they fail to appreciate the delicate top notes that are characteristic of this type.

Bourbon vanilla comes from three main sources: Madagascar, the Comoro Islands and Réunion. Its depth of body is a little more pronounced than Mexican vanilla, which makes Bourbon vanilla a preferred variety for the extraction industry. However, in my opinion it lacks the fine aroma of the best vanilla from Mexico.

Indonesian and Papua New Guinean vanilla carries a deep, full-bodied flavor but has traditionally been of variable quality. This is not so critical when real vanilla is used for

Seed Mass and Quality

We like to do our own little test for one attribute of vanilla quality: the volume of sticky seed mass as a proportion of total bean weight. Full, plump beans are sometimes shy on contents (as we noticed with some very fat beans offered to us in a market in Sri Lanka). When we tested the volume of seed mass for batches of beans from different sources, we found quite dramatic differences in the ratios. When scraped out, the sticky black seed mass could make up as little as 6% and as much as 20% of the total bean weight. From my observations, the beans with the highest percentage of seed mass had the best flavor.

V

Essence or Extract?

I am often asked to explain the difference between an essence and an extract. An extract is made by extracting the desired attributes of a substance. For example, soaking vanilla in alcohol extracts the vanilla flavor. Just to make things confusing, an extract may be called an essence because the qualities that have been extracted capture the essence of the flavor. Still with me? Although it is confusing, an essence is either a distilled or concentrated extract or an artificial facsimile of the product's distinctive characteristics. In the case of vanilla, you might say it is the manufactured essence of its flavor. Note that an artificial essence cannot be called an extract because it has not been extracted from the item, in this case vanilla. This explains why artificial vanilla is generally labeled "imitation vanilla essence."

blending with synthetic vanillin and syrups, which is the most popular application for this type. Recently, greater care in curing and bean selection for the top grades has seen Indonesian vanilla become more readily available, and it has met with some success on the whole-bean market.

West Indian vanilla (*V. pompona*) is of a lower grade than Mexican or Bourbon vanilla. It is produced principally on the formerly French island of Guadeloupe. It has a low vanillin content and is mostly used in making perfumes because the flavor is considered too poor to be suitable for vanilla extract.

Tahitian vanilla (*V. tahitensis*) was propagated in Tahiti and is produced in Hawaii and other tropical countries, including Papua New Guinea and the Pacific island of Niue. It has a lower vanillin content than *V. planifolia*. Some consider its taste to be rank (a stigma possibly promulgated by competitors), and this perception makes it less popular for flavoring purposes than Mexican and Madagascar vanilla. Personally, I find the aroma and flavor of Tahitian vanilla exotic and pleasing. Not surprisingly, proponents of Tahitian vanilla claim that the later harvesting of this hybrid delivers a superior vanilla. As with many flavors, you are the best judge of your own preferences.

Vanilla beans should be stored in an airtight container and protected from extremes of heat, light and humidity. Under these conditions, a vanilla bean will keep for up to 18 months.

When buying vanilla essence or extract, look closely at the label to determine what the product actually contains. As previously mentioned, there are many blended concoctions that may contain other flavors and artificial vanillin. Depending on the packaging laws in the country concerned, true vanilla extract is most likely to be labeled "natural vanilla extract," with some reference to the alcohol content, such as "less than 35% alcohol by volume." Vanilla extract should be stored in a dark place away from extreme heat. Under these conditions it will keep for up to 18 months.

Under rare circumstances a vanilla powder is made by scraping off the sugary crystalline powder that naturally forms on the surface of some vanilla beans after curing. This is a very expensive form of vanilla! More often than not a product sold as vanilla powder will be a mixture of powdered vanilla beans and vanilla extract mixed with a food starch and sugar. Artificial vanillin powder is commonly blended with fine sugar to make the vanilla sugar seen in supermarkets. There is now a trend toward making upmarket

New Ways of Using Vanilla

Vanilla is also delicious in savory cooking because it is not overtly sweet. An innovative Mauritian restaurant in Sydney served a delicious vanilla chicken in a creamy sauce flavored with finely chopped vanilla beans and a hint of black pepper. It was aromatic, delicate and beautifully balanced.

These days, people are experimenting with new techniques such as adding finely chopped vanilla beans to recipes to make them infinitely more interesting. Some cooks like to slit the vanilla bean in half, scrape out the sticky pulp and seeds, and add this concentrate to their recipes. When adopting this approach, I still like to infuse the remnants of the scraped-out bean in the wet ingredients whenever possible. There are important taste attributes in the leathery black skin of a vanilla bean that are worth retaining.

vanilla sugar that contains only ground-up vanilla beans and sugar. This gourmet-style vanilla sugar is riddled with the characteristic black specks of vanilla; it is the best-quality vanilla sugar.

Use

Vanilla essence is used to flavor ice cream, cookies, cakes, sweets and liqueurs. It also adds fragrance to perfumes. True natural vanilla has a pervasive sweet fragrance balanced by a slight caramel taste and a faint smoky back note. By comparison, artificial vanilla tends to have a sharp, bitter flavor with distinctly "chemical" overtones. That's why using too much artificial vanilla will ruin a dish, whereas a slightly heavy hand with the real thing can be forgiven. All vanilla essences and extracts are quite strong, so 1 teaspoon (5 mL) will be sufficient to flavor a typical cake.

Whole vanilla beans can be put in a sugar canister to ensure a supply of delicately flavored vanilla sugar (one bean to 2 cups/500 mL sugar is sufficient). Vanilla beans can flavor custards and fruit compotes; one of our family favorites is Vanilla Poached Pears in sparkling wine (page 663). Simply put a whole bean in the pot during cooking; afterwards, take out the bean and wash and dry it carefully before returning it to the sugar canister for future use. This method may be used a few times before the flavor from a bean is no longer effective. Please keep in mind that if you have infused a vanilla bean in a liquid that contains protein, such as milk, after washing and drying it you should wrap the bean in plastic wrap and store it in the refrigerator. Use the reserved bean within a week; otherwise it will go moldy.

WEIGHT PER TEASPOON (5 mL)

- whole average bean: 3 to 4 g

SUGGESTED QUANTITY PER POUND (500 g)

- white meats: 1 bean
- grains and pulses: 1 bean, ½ to 1 tsp (2 to 5 mL) extract
- carbohydrates: 1 bean, ½ to 1 tsp (2 to 5 mL) extract

Vanilla Salmon Salad

Even though most of the vanilla plantations have vanished from Mauritius, vanilla has left its mark on the cuisine. I was lucky enough to holiday there and enjoyed the fantastic variety of food the island has to offer from its various cultural influences. The seafood is outstandingly fresh, as you'd expect, and I had a version of this salad nearly every day for lunch.

**Makes
2 servings**

Preparation time:
 10 minutes
Cooking time:
 15 minutes

1	vanilla bean	1
¼ cup	freshly squeezed lime juice	60 mL
1½ tbsp	lightly packed light brown sugar	22 mL
1	red finger chile, seeded and very finely chopped	1
½ tsp	freshly grated gingerroot	2 mL
1 tbsp	olive oil	15 mL
7 oz	Belgian endive, cut into roughly 2-inch (5 cm) pieces	210 g
2	ripe tomatoes, seeded and finely chopped	2
2 tbsp	fresh coriander (cilantro) leaves	30 mL
1 tsp	oil	5 mL
12 oz	sushi-grade skinless salmon fillet, cut in 2 pieces	375 g

1. Using a sharp knife, split vanilla bean lengthwise. Scrape seeds into a small saucepan and add vanilla pod, lime juice and sugar. Heat gently over low heat, stirring constantly, until sugar has dissolved, about 3 minutes. Transfer 3 tbsp (45 mL) of the sauce to a small bowl (reserve remaining sauce). Add chile, ginger and olive oil to bowl and combine. Set aside.

2. In a serving bowl, combine endive, tomatoes and coriander leaves. Add prepared vanilla-chile dressing and toss to coat well. Divide salad evenly among serving plates. Set aside.

3. In a skillet over medium-high heat, heat 1 tsp (5 mL) oil. Add salmon and cook for 2 minutes each side or until done to your liking (it should be quite rare for the best flavor). Arrange salmon on top of salad and drizzle with reserved vanilla sauce.

V

Yogurt Vanilla Cream

Just about every dessert benefits from a little cream on the side. When I'm feeling very indulgent, I spoon this vanilla cream over granola with berries, too.

**Makes about
2 cups (500 mL)**

Preparation time:
overnight
Cooking time:
5 minutes

Tips

Superfine (caster) sugar is a very fine granulated sugar typically used in recipes that require a faster-dissolving granule. If you can't find it in stores, you can make your own by using a food processor fitted with the metal blade to process granulated sugar to a very fine, sand-like consistency.

Add yogurt vanilla cream to breakfast granola, stir it into stewed fruits, or serve atop apple pie or pancakes.

• **Cheesecloth**

2 cups	plain yogurt	500 mL
2 tsp	superfine (caster) sugar (see Tips, left)	10 mL
½ cup	heavy or whipping (35%) cream	125 mL
2	vanilla beans	2

1. Line a colander with cheesecloth and set over a bowl. Place yogurt in colander and refrigerate overnight.
2. Transfer drained yogurt to a clean bowl (discard liquid). Add sugar and heavy cream. Using a sharp knife, slit vanilla beans lengthwise and scrape the tiny black seeds into yogurt cream mixture. Stir well to combine, then cover and refrigerate for at least 1 hour before serving (it will keep for up to 1 week in the refrigerator).

Vanilla Poached Pears

After leaving home and learning to fend for myself, this became one of my first dinner-party desserts. It's a classic dish that never fails to impress. I find it especially refreshing after a heavily spiced meal.

**Makes
6 servings**

Preparation time:
5 minutes

**Cooking time: 25 to
35 minutes**

Tips

Choose pears that hold their shape when cooked, such as Bosc or Bartlett.

For a thicker syrup, after removing pears from pan, boil liquid for about 15 minutes, until reduced to desired consistency.

3 cups	off-dry Riesling wine (1 bottle)	750 mL
2 to 3 cups	water	500 to 750 mL
½ cup	granulated sugar	125 mL
6	pears, peeled, stem left intact (see Tips, left)	6
1	2-inch (5 cm) cinnamon stick	1
2	vanilla beans, split lengthwise and opened	2
	Yogurt Vanilla Cream (page 662) or vanilla ice cream, optional	

1. In a saucepan over low heat, combine wine, water and sugar. Cook, stirring occasionally, until sugar completely dissolves, 7 to 10 minutes. Add pears, cinnamon and vanilla beans. Gently simmer for 15 to 20 minutes, until pears feel tender when pierced with a skewer or knife (the time will vary depending on ripeness of the pears).

2. To serve, cut pears in half lengthwise. Arrange 2 pear halves upright in a pool of cooking liquid on each serving plate. Top with a dollop of yogurt vanilla cream or a scoop of ice cream (if using).

V

Vietnamese Mint

Polygonum odoratum (also known as *Persicaria odorata*)

Names in Other Languages

- **Chinese (C):** yuht naahm heung choi
- **Chinese (M):** yue nan xiang cai
- **Czech:** kokorik vonny
- **Danish:** vietnamesisk koriander
- **Hungarian:** vietnami menta
- **Indonesian:** daun kesom, daun laksa
- **Malay:** daun laksa, daun kesom
- **Laotian:** phak pheo
- **Portuguese:** hortela-vietnamita
- **Russian:** kupiena lekarstvennaya
- **Thai:** phak phai, phrik maa, chan chom, hom chan
- **Vietnamese:** rau ram

Solitary Confinement

If you are planning to grow Vietnamese mint in the garden, make sure you plant it in its own garden bed or restrict it to a pot. This plant can be so rampant that it will take over completely, giving it the unflattering epithet of "weed."

Family: Polygonaceae

Varieties: water pepper (*Persicaria hydropiper*; also known as *Polygonum hydropiper*)

Other Names: Asian mint, Cambodian mint, hot mint, knotweed, laksa leaf, smartweed, Vietnamese coriander

Flavor Group: Strong

Parts Used: leaves (as a herb)

Background

Polygonum, the name of the genus to which Vietnamese mint belongs, literally means "many-kneed." It is a direct reference to the jointed and angled appearance of the stems of this herb. There are more than 200 species of *Polygonum*, some of which have been included in medical pharmacopoeias from Switzerland, France and Russia since Renaissance times. Although its early uses are unrecorded, it is interesting to note that its popularity in Asian cuisine is not dissimilar to the way Europeans use sorrel. Fresh Vietnamese mint gives a similar biting, somewhat bitter taste that is appreciated for its appetite-enhancing properties.

Culinary Information

Combines with
- basil
- cardamom
- chile
- coriander (leaf and seed)
- cumin
- curry leaf
- galangal
- ginger
- pepper
- star anise
- tamarind
- turmeric

Traditional Uses
- Asian soups such as laksa
- Asian curries and stir-fries
- fresh green salads
- dipping sauces

Spice Blends
- not commonly used in spice blends

The Plant

This herbaceous perennial is not a member of the mint family at all but belongs to the same family as sorrel (Polygonaceae). Most commonly referred to as "Vietnamese mint" or "laksa leaf," it bears long pink or white flowers at the top of slender stems that are 14 inches (35 cm) tall, with swollen-looking joints $1/3$ to 2 inches (1 to 5 cm) apart. The deep green tapering 2- to $3^1/_4$-inch (5 to 8 cm) leaves shoot out from these joints. The color of the leaves may appear dark thanks to random black smudging in their pigmentation, which seems less pronounced in plants that grow in the shade. The aroma is fragrant, minty and insect-like. It resembles coriander leaf (cilantro) and basil, with an overtone of citrus zest. These attributes are also apparent in the taste and are accompanied by a warming biting, peppery sensation that is surprisingly hot.

Other Varieties
Water pepper (*Persicaria hydropiper*) is also called "smartweed" in Australia. It is considered semiaquatic, growing in marshes and generally moist environments. It is found in Australia and New Zealand, as well as most of Asia and the warmer parts of Europe. Water pepper has a very similar appearance to Vietnamese mint but looks more straggly and unkempt. The leaves have a peppery bite, hence its common name.

V

Processing

Vietnamese mint does not dry satisfactorily. It tends to shrivel down to almost nothing and forfeit its characteristic flavor notes more dramatically than even dried coriander leaf, so it is always used fresh.

Buying and Storage

Vietnamese mint can be grown easily, even in a pot or a window box. In temperate climates growing your own is a way to ensure a steady supply for most of the year; like mint, its namesake, it can be prolific and rampant (see "Solitary Confinement," page 664). Vietnamese mint is readily available from specialty shops and Asian markets, where it is most likely to be called "laksa leaf" or "Cambodian mint." Bunches of Vietnamese mint will keep for a couple of days when stood up in water (as if in a vase) and kept in the refrigerator. Alternatively, I have found that a bunch placed loosely in a large plastic bag and kept in the freezer will last for a few weeks. When required, break off the appropriate amount and use in the same way as fresh.

Use

As well as complementing Asian soups, Vietnamese mint flavors and garnishes fresh salads. It also works well in dipping sauces with coriander leaf (cilantro), lime leaf, ginger and fish sauce. It makes an interesting contribution to Malay curries when half a dozen leaves are added during cooking.

The aroma of Vietnamese mint always causes me to salivate with fond memories of delicious Singapore laksa, a spicy fragrant soup with noodles and chicken or seafood.

SUGGESTED QUANTITY PER POUND (500 g)

- **red meats:** 6 to 8 fresh leaves
- **white meats:** 6 to 8 fresh leaves
- **vegetables:** 6 to 8 fresh leaves
- **grains and pulses:** 6 to 8 fresh leaves
- **baked goods:** 6 to 8 fresh leaves

Shrimp Laksa

This popular Malaysian/Singaporean noodle dish has hundreds of variations and has become a staple takeout dish in Australia. As much as I love the speed of takeout, its depth of flavor and generous quantities of vegetables make this homemade version a lot more satisfying. If you grow your own Vietnamese mint, it will be much appreciated when making this laksa.

**Makes
4 servings**

Preparation time:
 15 minutes
Cooking time:
 20 minutes

Tip

To butterfly shrimp, peel off the head and shell, leaving the tail on. Using a sharp knife, carefully cut lengthwise along the curved back of the shrimp, deeply but without cutting right through. You can then open and flatten the shrimp to create the "butterfly" effect.

1 tbsp	oil	15 mL
1	onion, chopped	1
¼ cup	laksa spice mix (page 741)	60 mL
2½ cups	coconut milk	625 mL
1¼ cups	chicken, vegetable or fish broth	300 mL
2 tsp	fish sauce (nam pla)	10 mL
20	shrimp (tails on), peeled, deveined and butterflied (see Tip, left)	20
10 oz	baby bok choy, halved lengthwise (about 8 small)	300 g
1 cup	enoki or halved button mushrooms	250 mL
10 oz	rice noodles, cooked and drained	300 g
2 cups	lightly packed bean sprouts	500 mL
2 tbsp	fresh Vietnamese mint leaves, torn	30 mL
2 tbsp	fresh coriander (cilantro) leaves	30 mL
1	lime, quartered	1

1. In a large skillet or wok over medium heat, heat oil. Add onion and sauté until transparent, about 3 minutes. Add laksa spices and cook, stirring, for about 2 minutes to make a paste. Add coconut milk, broth and fish sauce and bring to a boil. Reduce heat and simmer, uncovered, for about 10 minutes. Add shrimp, bok choy and mushrooms and simmer for about 5 minutes, until shrimp are pink, firm and opaque and vegetables are just cooked through.

2. Divide noodles among 4 deep serving bowls and ladle laksa overtop. Top with bean sprouts, Vietnamese mint and coriander leaves. Add a lime wedge on top for squeezing. Serve immediately.

Variations

You can replace the shrimp with an equal amount of chicken or firm tofu.

V

Wattleseed

Acacia aneura

- **French:** graines d'acacias
- **German:** Akaziensamen
- **Italian:** semi di acacia australiano macinate

Wattle Trees

Australian acacias were called "wattle trees" because the early colonists used their thin branches and trunks, along with mud and clay, in the construction of houses—in Europe this method is known as "wattle and daub." Wattle is sometimes referred to as mimosa; however, although related, it is not the true mimosa.

Family: Fabaceae (formerly Leguminosae)

Varieties: mulga (*A. aneura*), coastal wattle (*A. sophorae*), gundabluey wattle (*A. victoriae*), golden wattle (*A. pycnantha*)

Other Names: acacia, mimosa

Flavor Group: Pungent

Parts Used: seeds (as a spice)

Background

Australian Aborigines have understood the nutritional benefits of wattleseed for thousands of years. They used the seeds, roots, gum and bark of various types of acacia for medicinal purposes. Acacia gum, which oozes from cracks in the bark, can be sucked like a lollipop or soaked in water to make a kind of jelly. Dark gums are mostly astringent and unpalatable, but the paler golden-hued resins have quite an agreeable taste.

Culinary Information

Combines with
- akudjura
- allspice
- cardamom
- cinnamon and cassia
- coriander seed
- lemon myrtle
- pepper
- pepperleaf
- thyme
- vanilla

Traditional Uses
- ice cream and sorbet
- yogurt
- cheesecake
- whipped cream
- grilled salmon
- chicken
- kangaroo
- game

Spice Blends
- native Australian barbecue spice blends
- seafood seasonings
- roast vegetable seasonings

Wattle bark was recognized as an important source of tannin. By the end of the 19th century, up to 22,000 tons of wattle bark was being exported from Australia for use in the leather-tanning industry. By the late 20th century Australia's burgeoning bush-food industry had created an appreciation for the taste of roasted wattleseed in ice creams, pancakes, chocolates and desserts.

The Plant

Though acacias are indigenous to Australia, Africa, Asia and America, it is Australia's acacias that are of culinary use. Australian acacias are also the most decorative: they burst into fluffy, glowing masses of blossoms in various shapes and colors that range from creamy white to vibrant yellow. The wattleseed of culinary importance comes from a relatively small number of acacia trees that bear edible leguminous seedpods. There are more than 700 species of acacia, and the majority of them have poisonous seeds, so one must be absolutely sure the variety selected for culinary use is not toxic.

One variety considered a "food wattle" is mulga (*Acacia aneura*). Its nutritious seeds contain potassium, calcium, iron and zinc in fairly high concentrations, as well as protein, much of which is contained in the tail-like connecting tissue attached to the seed. Mulga trees grow in outback Australia to heights of 20 feet (6 m). They seem to be thoroughly unlikely members of the pea family (Fabaceae) until you observe their pealike pods, which contain seeds typical of

W

legumes. Many acacias do not have leaves at all, but rather stalks that are flattened into a leaflike shape and act as leaves, a structure that makes them resistant to prolonged drought. A parasitic insect that attacks the mulga causes swollen lumps to appear on its branches. These chunks are sweet and juicy inside and are referred to as "mulga apples."

Although Australian Aborigines ate cooked green wattleseed for sustenance, it is only the roasted and usually ground wattleseeds that are used as a spice to flavor food. The whole roasted spice is spherical, dark brown and about the size of a small coriander seed. Ground wattleseed is easier to add to food; it is a grainy powder that resembles ground coffee in appearance. It has a distinctive light, coffee-like aroma and a pleasing slightly bitter, nutty coffee taste.

Other Varieties

Most of the wattleseeds gathered for culinary purposes come from mulga trees (*Acacia aneura*) or the following three varieties, which are common in Australia. **Coastal wattle** (*A. longifolia* var. *sophorae*) grows $1^1/_2$ to 10 feet (0.5 to 3 m) tall. It is similar to Sydney golden wattle (*A. longifolia*). The seeds have been ground to make flour for damper, a quintessential Australian bread, and are also roasted to use as a spice. **Gundabluey wattle** (*A. victoriae*) is found around most parts of Australia. It flowers in early summer. The seeds of the pods are often collected and used to produce flour for making damper, as well as being roasted to make the spice. **Golden wattle** (*A. pycnantha*) is Australia's national flower. For many years those of us who grew up in Australia would think of September 1 as National Wattle Day. Although it was informally recognized while I was at school, it wasn't until 1992 that the golden wattle was officially recognized as the national flower.

Processing

While wattle trees grow and bear pods prolifically, the task of gathering and preparing the seeds for consumption is painstaking and labor-intensive. The seed-bearing pods are harvested when green and immature. The traditional method of processing, used by the Aborigines, is simply to throw the pods on an open grass-fire, where they are steamed. This produces something akin to an edible but almost tasteless pea. Steaming reduces a certain amount of background

Spice Notes

I was introduced to the wonders of *Acacia aneura* by an unlikely source: a geologist, Frank Baarda, who was working in Central Australia. Frank told me that the root systems of acacia trees can reach down 100 feet (30 m) as insurance against prolonged droughts. The geologist in him could not resist telling me how he knew this, so he launched into a fascinating explanation about gold prospecting and acacia trees.

Gold prospectors now have equipment so sensitive that it can measure what is called "gold value" in minute proportions, as low as several parts per billion. Frank said they had discovered gold values at the surface that indicated there might be deposits below, but at 30 feet (9 m) down they found nothing. When an exploratory borehole was made, gold was discovered at 100 feet (30 m) below the surface and, interestingly, so were the fossilized roots of acacia trees. The puzzle was then solved. The roots of the acacia trees had transported minute amounts of gold to their leaves, which had accumulated over centuries and left a small but discernable gold value on the surface. Who says money doesn't grow on trees?

Another snippet of information I found equally interesting is that arsenic is found in high concentrations in gold deposits and is one of the key indicators of its presence. Why then was there no indication of arsenic along with the surface gold value? Because arsenic is poisonous, and the acacia tree has the ability to resist taking up the arsenic present in the deposits.

Speaking from an Australian perspective, the flavor of wattleseed is far more appealing to me than the popular natural hickory-smoke flavor traditionally associated with barbecue, which always tastes artificial to those of us who grew up in the Australian countryside.

astringency and makes the seeds and attached membrane easier to remove from the pod. The next step is roasting the steamed whole seeds. This involves adding them to a dish filled with glowing hot embers and setting them aside until the coating on all the seeds shows signs of cracking. Next the roasted seeds are removed from the dying embers and left to cool. After cooling they are sieved to separate them from the remaining ash—an extremely dusty, sooty task. Finally the cleaned roasted seeds are milled to make "roasted and ground wattleseed," ready to use in cooking.

Buying and Storage

Roasted and ground wattleseed is available from specialty spice shops, adventurous delicatessens and food outlets that sell native Australian foods. Wattleseed is relatively expensive when compared to the majority of spices (about five times the price of ground nutmeg) because of the many steps involved in processing. In addition, it has mostly been wild-crafted (gathered from its wild state) and not commercially cultivated. In recent years, because of the increase in demand for native Australian ingredients and concerns about endangering populations of native plants

W

WEIGHT PER TEASPOON (5 mL)

- ground: 4.2 g

SUGGESTED QUANTITY PER POUND (500 g)

- **red meats:** ¾ tsp (3 mL) roasted and ground seeds
- **white meats:** ½ tsp (2 mL) roasted and ground seeds
- **vegetables:** ½ tsp (2 mL) roasted and ground seeds
- **grains and pulses:** ½ tsp (2 mL) roasted and ground seeds
- **baked goods:** ½ tsp (2 mL) roasted and ground seeds

by wild harvesting, commercial cultivation has intensified. In the longer term this ordered cultivation will make wattleseeds more readily available at a reduced cost.

Buy small amounts of wattleseed regularly. Even though its flavor profile is quite stable, it is always best if not stored for longer than 2 years. Keep roasted ground wattleseed in an airtight container, just as for other ground spices, and avoid extremes of heat, light and humidity.

Use

Wattleseed flavors sweet dishes such as ice creams, sorbets, mousses, yogurt, cheesecakes and whipped cream. It is delicious in pancakes and goes well with breads. In these applications, roasted ground wattleseed should be infused with the liquid ingredients, preferably at a boil, or at least heated. The resulting infusion may be strained or the softened wattleseed grounds may be included for extra color and texture.

Wattleseed complements chicken, lamb and fish (it is particularly delicious with salmon steaks), especially when a small amount is blended with ground coriander seed, a pinch of lemon myrtle leaf and salt to taste. Sprinkle this mixture over the food and pan-fry, grill or barbecue. The wattleseed adds a subtle barbecued note.

Mixed Vegetable Bake

Root vegetables take on herb flavors fantastically. Sadly, this has been exploited commercially by herbal seasonings that are high in salt and MSG. In this dish, the sumac and wattleseed add depth to the traditional mixed herbs, making a versatile mix that can be sprinkled over any combination of vegetables while roasting. This bake makes an excellent side dish with Leg of Lamb Stuffed with Olives, Grapes and Rosemary (page 545) or Chicken with 40 Cloves of Garlic (page 300).

**Makes
6 servings**

Preparation time:
 15 minutes

Cooking time:
 45 minutes

Tips

To make this dish more similar to a dauphinoise (and a little bit naughty!), replace the broth with table (18%) cream.

For very finely sliced vegetables, use a mandoline.

Store any leftover herb mix in an airtight jar and use it to season other roasted vegetables and even meats.

- **9-inch (23 cm) square glass baking dish, greased with butter**
- **Preheat oven to 350°F (180°C)**

HERB MIX

¼ cup	sumac	60 mL
3 tbsp	fine sea salt	45 mL
1½ tbsp	dried oregano	22 mL
1 tbsp	dried thyme	15 mL
1 tbsp	garlic powder	15 mL
2 tsp	ground wattleseed	10 mL
1 tsp	dried basil	5 mL
1 tsp	dried sage	5 mL
1 tsp	dried parsley	5 mL
½ tsp	dried ground rosemary	2 mL

VEGETABLES

1 lb	potatoes, peeled and finely sliced	500 g
1 lb	pumpkin or butternut squash, peeled and finely sliced	500 g
1 lb	sweet potatoes, peeled and finely sliced	500 g
1 cup	chicken broth	250 mL
1 cup	shredded Gruyère, Comté or Cheddar cheese	250 mL

1. In a small bowl, combine sumac, salt, oregano, thyme, garlic powder, wattleseed, basil, sage, parsley and rosemary.

2. In prepared baking dish, layer potatoes, pumpkin and sweet potatoes, sprinkling each layer with about ½ tsp (2 mL) prepared herb mix and about 1 tbsp (15 mL) cheese. Pour broth into dish. Sprinkle top layer with 1 tsp (5 mL) herb mix and remaining cheese. Cover loosely with aluminum foil or parchment and bake in preheated oven for 40 minutes, until vegetables are fork-tender. Remove foil and bake for about 10 minutes more, until browned on top.

W

Chocolate and Wattleseed Truffles

Truffles aren't as difficult to make as you'd think, although they can get a little messy. They're certainly an impressive way to end a dinner party. The wattleseed adds a richness to the chocolate that marries perfectly with espresso.

Makes about 30 truffles

Preparation time:
5 minutes

Cooking time:
30 minutes, plus 1 hour for chilling

- - - - - - - - - - - - - - - -

Tip

If the truffles begin to melt in your hands when rolling, run your hands under very cold water or place them in an ice bath for 30 seconds, then dry hands and continue rolling.

- **Electric mixer**

8 oz	dark (70%) chocolate, broken into pieces	250 g
6 tbsp + 2 tsp	heavy or whipping (35%) cream	100 mL
1¼ tsp	ground wattleseed, divided	6 mL
2 tbsp	unsalted butter, at room temperature	30 mL
⅓ cup	unsweetened cocoa powder	75 mL

1. Place chocolate in a heatproof bowl set over a saucepan of water (to create a double boiler). Bring water to a boil, then immediately turn off heat (there will be plenty of residual heat to melt chocolate). Stir chocolate until smooth. Remove from heat and set aside.

2. In a small saucepan over low heat, combine heavy cream and 1 tsp (5 mL) wattleseed. Cook for 3 to 5 minutes, stirring often, until steaming and small bubbles form around edge of pan (do not let it boil). Remove from heat and set aside to cool.

3. Using electric mixer at medium speed, beat butter until very soft and creamy, about 3 minutes. Add chocolate and beat until smooth. Using a spatula, stir in cream until combined. Cover and refrigerate for at least 1 hour, until firm.

4. Sift cocoa powder into a shallow baking dish and stir in remaining ¼ tsp (1 mL) wattleseed. Working quickly, scoop up chocolate mixture in rounded teaspoonfuls (5 mL) and roll between the palms of your hands into balls. Gently roll balls in cocoa mixture and transfer to a plate. Truffles will keep in an airtight container in the refrigerator for up to 1 week.

Zedoary

Curcuma zedoaria, C. zerumbet

Names in Other Languages

- **Arabic:** zadwaar
- **Chinese (C):** ngoh seuht, wat gam
- **Chinese (M):** e zhu
- **Czech:** zedoar
- **Dutch:** zedoarwortel
- **French:** zédoaire
- **German:** Zitwer
- **Hungarian:** feher kurkuma, zedoaria-gyoker
- **Indian:** kachur, amb halad, shoti
- **Indonesian:** kencur zadwar, kunir putih
- **Italian:** zedoaria
- **Japanese:** gajutsu
- **Portuguese:** zedoaria
- **Russian:** zedoari
- **Spanish:** cedoaria
- **Swedish:** zittverrot
- **Thai:** khamin khao
- **Turkish:** cedvar
- **Vietnamese:** nga truat

Family: Zingiberaceae
Other Names: shoti, white turmeric, wild turmeric
Flavor Group: Pungent
Parts Used: rhizomes (as a spice)

Background

Zedoary is native to India, the Himalayas and China. It was first taken to Europe in the Middle Ages by Arab traders. It is now grown in Indonesia and thrives in tropical and subtropical regions. Although popular in Europe in the 16th century, the culinary use of zedoary waned over the centuries. One explanation for its declining use is that it takes two years to be harvested after propagation. This makes it less economical than its cousins ginger and galangal. Another plausible reason is that its flavor profile is generally regarded as inferior to ginger and galangal, which are both popular and readily available.

The Plant

Zedoary is a member of the same family as galangal, turmeric and ginger (Zingiberaceae). Its long, light green leaves sprout from a rhizome (root-bearing stem), the interior of which is yellow and resembles lesser galangal. The large leaves reach up about 3 feet (1 m), growing in clumps rather like a lily. The flowers are yellow and burst from the bright red leaf sections.

There are two kinds of zedoary: long and round (*Curcuma zedoria*) and oval (*C. zerumbet*). The only difference between them is the shape of the rhizome, which is reflected in their common descriptions. Zedoary has a distinctive warm, aromatic, ginger-like smell with definite musky camphor overtones and a slightly bitter aftertaste.

Dried zedoary rhizomes look like ginger, but they are a little grayer in color and somewhat larger and rougher in texture.

Z

Culinary Information

Combines with

- allspice
- cardamom
- chile
- cinnamon and cassia
- cloves
- coriander seed
- cumin
- fenugreek seed
- ginger
- mustard
- nigella
- paprika
- tamarind
- turmeric

Traditional Uses

- Southeast Asian curries
- Indonesian seafood dishes
- Indian curries (as a thickener)

Spice Blends

- curry powders
- rendang curry

Processing

In the same manner as ginger and turmeric, zedoary is harvested after flowering. The rhizomes are generally sliced and dried to facilitate storage and shipment. When zedoary is ground, the powder is a yellow-gray color and quite fibrous. The level of fiber is determined by the age of the rhizomes when they were lifted. As with ginger, the older the rhizome, the more fiber it has.

Buying and Storage

Zedoary is usually available only in its sliced and dried form. However, it can sometimes be bought from Chinese herbalists as a powder. The sliced rhizomes will keep for 3 years or more stored under ideal conditions: in an airtight container kept away from extremes of heat, light and humidity. The powder should be stored under the same conditions, where it will last for more than 1 year.

Use

Although the application of zedoary in cooking has been largely replaced by ginger and galangal, it is still used to flavor some Southeast Asian curries. A similar spice, known as kenchur (see page 288) and used in Indonesia, is made from a smaller rhizome and has a more camphorous aroma. Whole dried zedoary slices are added to soups and generally removed before serving. Zedoary powder is added to curries and sauces in the same way that you would add ground ginger or galangal.

Zedoary adds its mild flavor to seafood dishes, and the leaves are sometimes found in Javanese cooking, where they are used as a herb. The root is high in starch. It is called *shoti* in India, where it is sometimes valued as a thickener and used as a substitute for arrowroot.

WEIGHT PER TEASPOON (5 mL)

- ground: 2.7 g

SUGGESTED QUANTITY PER POUND (500 g)

- red meats: 1½ tsp (7 mL) ground
- white meats: 1 tsp (5 mL) ground
- vegetables: 1 tsp (5 mL) ground
- grains and pulses: ½ tsp (2 mL) ground
- baked goods: ½ tsp (2 mL) ground

Zedoary Pickle

This is a popular spicy condiment served with Indian meals. The zedoary and fresh ginger give it a strong ginger aroma and flavor. Serve with Dosa (page 410), Delhi Dal (page 651) or any of the Indian curries in this book.

Makes ¼ cup (60 mL)

Preparation time:
10 minutes, plus 1 hour for chilling

Cooking time: none

Tips

If fresh zedoary is available, use an equal amount, freshly grated.

You can find small ginger graters at kitchen supply stores that can also be used for zedoary, garlic or galangal, or use a kitchen rasp such as one made by Microplane or the finest side of a box grater. Remove skin before grating.

Ground Kashmiri chile is flavorsome and versatile. You can find it at most Indian markets in varying levels of heat (depending on the amount of seeds and membrane ground with the chile).

2 tbsp	freshly squeezed lemon juice	30 mL
4 tsp	ground zedoary (see Tips, left)	20 mL
2 tsp	freshly grated gingerroot (see Tips, left)	10 mL
1 tsp	minced garlic	5 mL
½ tsp	ground medium-hot chile (see Tips, left)	2 mL

1. In a small bowl, combine lemon juice, zedoary, ginger, garlic and ground chile. Cover and refrigerate for at least 1 hour before serving. The pickle will keep in an airtight container in the refrigerator for up to 1 week.

Part Three

The Art of Combining Spices

The Principles of Making Spice Blends

When I make a spice blend, I seek to create a distinctive taste. Sometimes the blend bears little resemblance to any of the individual spices used. In others a few characteristic flavors may dominate, for example, in mixed spice (North American apple pie or pumpkin pie spice), where cinnamon and cloves are often the first detectable aromas.

OFTEN ONE OF THE GREATEST PLEASURES in using spices is combining them with each other to create completely different tastes. Spice blends, also called seasonings, mixes, masalas or rubs, are a convenient and effective way to add flavor when cooking. Anyone can make their own blends with only a basic understanding of how to combine a variety of spices. Like any artist, the spice blender will bring a range of components together to create a homogeneous result that is uniquely personal.

Spice blending is indeed an art as much as a science. Every professional spice blender will have his or her own approach to making a blend. The requirements may vary considerably, depending on the end user. A multinational food company that wants a blend to use in fast-food outlets will require a flavor profile that doesn't offend anyone. It will also be concerned about cost and whether ingredients of consistent quality are readily available. In the mid 20th century the majority of these blends were high in salt, sugar and monosodium glutamate (MSG). By the 1990s they still tended to be high in salt (after all, it is cheap and heavy, the dry food–maker's answer to water); wheat flour, used as filler; and free-flow agents, required to prevent clumping. (*Clumping* is the term used in the spice trade to describe the formation of lumps. It occurs when spice blends contain hygroscopic, or water-attracting, ingredients and are stored for long periods in less than ideal conditions.) In the 2000s the better spice blends reduced their dependence on ingredients such as salt, MSG and wheat and began including a higher proportion of completely natural herbs and spices.

Once you become familiar with the panoply of herbs and spices, it is apparent that most of those we use have distinctive and often strikingly different characteristics. Some are strong and—if sampled in isolation—could even be described as unpleasant. Others (such as two of my favorites, cinnamon and paprika) are a delight to experience even on their own.

Although the following guidelines will help you to understand the basic principles of making spice blends, there are really no hard-and-fast rules. Use your own creativity and instincts to create a range of unique tastes that you will enjoy.

The Art of Blending Spices

The art of making a successful spice blend involves bringing together a range of different tastes and textures to create an ideal balance. It's a bit like balancing sweet, salty, sour and bitter taste elements when preparing a meal. When combining spices, we balance their different attributes. For this purpose I group spices into five basic categories: sweet, pungent, tangy, hot and amalgamating.

Balancing Sweet, Pungent, Tangy and Hot in a Typical Blend

The following guide (page 683) is to help you gain an instinct for the relative strengths of key spices. The suggested quantities of the most commonly used sweet, pungent, tangy and hot spices, combined with an appropriate amalgamating spice, will produce a spice blend that is uniquely yours. The quantities called for (in teaspoons/mL) approximate the proportion of the various types of spices by volume found in a typical blend. Remember, this is an approximate guide only. For instance, within the pungent group, ground star anise is stronger than ground caraway seed, so if you were using it, you would likely want to reduce the quantity.

Sweet Spices

The sweet spices are those with varying degrees of inherent sweetness. They tend to be associated mostly with sweet foods such as puddings, cakes and pastries. It is worth remembering, though, that sweet spices also have a role to play in balancing savory foods.

Pungent Spices

When smelled individually, pungent spices have very strong aromatic top notes that may be somewhat camphor-like and astringent. The pungent spices are valuable because, even in small proportions, they contribute a freshness that may otherwise be lacking in the blend. Use all pungent spices sparingly.

Tangy Spices

Just as sourness is important in balancing dishes (think of the number of times lemon juice is used in recipes), the astringency of the tangy spices makes an important contribution to the balance of a spice blend. Tamarind is not used in spice blends because it is messy to handle and will not blend readily with dry spices. However, sumac makes an excellent tangy addition to a dry spice blend, as does amchur (green mango) powder.

Hot Spices

Spices belonging to this category are added judiciously to blends, in the smallest proportions. However, they can make or break a dish. These spices, which are relatively few in number, are essentially responsible for the overused term "spicy food." Hot spices such as black pepper and chiles stimulate the taste buds and also encourage the body to release endorphins, which give us a sense of well-being. You don't need much spicy heat to make food appetizing; hot spices should be used in only tiny amounts.

Amalgamating Spices

Only a few amalgamating spices are regularly used, but they are found in the majority of (but not all) common spice blends. It is worth keeping in mind that it is almost impossible to use too much coriander seed (page 225). If you have been too heavy-handed with one of the other categories of spice, a little extra coriander seed can save a blend from ruin. Sweet paprika is similar to coriander seed in terms of the amount you can use.

Fooling the Customer

Meat-pie manufacturers in Australia add quite a lot of white pepper to their pies, so even when a pie is cooling off, the pepper's heat fools the diner into thinking the pie is still warm from the oven!

Imperial/Metric Measurement Equivalents

¼ teaspoon	1 mL
½ teaspoon	2 mL
1 teaspoon	5 mL
2 teaspoons	10 mL
1 tablespoon (3 teaspoons)	15 mL
¼ cup	60 mL
⅓ cup	75 mL
½ cup	125 mL
1 cup	250 mL

Proportions of Spice Types

Spice Group: Sweet
Typical quantity: $4^{1}/_{2}$ tsp (22 mL)

- allspice
- anise seed
- cassia
- cinnamon
- nutmeg
- rose
- vanilla

Spice Group: Pungent
Typical quantity: $^{7}/_{8}$ tsp (4 mL)

- akudjura
- ajowan
- asafetida
- calamus
- caraway
- cardamom
- celery seed
- cloves
- cumin
- dill seed
- fenugreek seed
- galangal
- ginger
- juniper
- licorice root
- mace
- nigella
- orris root
- pink *Schinus* pepper
- star anise
- wattleseed
- zedoary

Spice Group: Tangy
Typical quantity: $2^{1}/_{2}$ tsp (12 mL)

- amchur
- barberry
- black lime
- capers
- kokam
- pomegranate
- sumac
- tamarind

Spice Group: Hot
Typical quantity: $^{1}/_{4}$ tsp (1 mL)

- chile
- horseradish
- mustard
- black pepper

Spice Group: Amalgamating
Typical quantity: 12 tsp (60 mL)

- coriander seed
- fennel seed
- paprika
- poppy seed
- sesame seed
- turmeric

Keep an Eye on Texture

If you are blending ingredients that have varying textures—such as ground cumin, chile flakes, cracked pepper and paprika—there is another phenomenon to take into account. In the spice business it is known as "stratering." Over a period of time, the different particle sizes form layers (strata) that look like a cross-section of sedimentary rock. Ultimately they separate to such a degree that one spoonful of the spice blend will have a much different flavor from the next. Should you encounter a blend that has stratered, shake or remix it before using to ensure uniformity of flavor.

Making Your Own Rub for Steak

Use these proportions to make your own rub to sprinkle on steak before grilling:

- 4½ tsp (22 mL) ground cinnamon
- ⅞ tsp (4 mL) ground ginger
- 2½ tsp (12 mL) amchur powder
- ¼ tsp (1 mL) freshly ground black pepper
- ¼ tsp (1 mL) ground chile
- 12 tsp (60 mL) sweet paprika
- salt to taste

Note that although pepper and chile are both hot spices, the relative differences in their flavor and heat strength mean that some variation in quantity is appropriate. Please keep in mind that these proportions can be varied as you experiment and become familiar with the spices. However, treating the suggested quantities as a starting point will help you avoid any major mistakes.

Measuring: Volume versus Weight

When making a spice blend, it is important to be consistent in the method you use for measuring the various spices. Either measure by volume (volumetric) or by weight (mass); do not use both styles for the same mix. And never use a recipe that gives the ingredients in weights and then make it up in the same proportions by volume, say, making every one-third ounce (10 g) equal 2 teaspoons (10 mL). Most spices have a different "bulk index"—the weight-to-volume relationship best illustrated by the old riddle "What weighs the most, a ton of sand or a ton of feathers?" Naturally they both weigh the same, but the same weights of sand and feathers would occupy vastly different volumes.

The same principle applies to using individual spices. A measure of ground coriander seed may weigh ⅓ oz (10 g) while the exact same measure of ground cloves may weigh ⅔ oz (20 g), because its density is greater. That is why, when you buy spices, the package sizes may appear the same but the weights can vary from a few grams to a hundred grams. These variables are compounded by whether the ingredients are whole, chopped, sliced or ground—all factors that affect the weight per teaspoon, that is, the bulk index.

When I make a blend, I start with volume, as we tend to relate more easily to a visible unit of measure than to weight. For commercial purposes, I weigh each quantity of spice as it is added, so when the blend is completed I have a record of the weight of each ingredient used. I then calculate the percentage of each ingredient in the recipe, so that every time it is made up with equivalent-quality herbs and spices, it will be exactly the same. Another benefit to always using volume is that it is easier to extrapolate into larger quantities. All the spice blends in this book are measured in teaspoons (mL) for consistency. Should you want to make a larger quantity, instead of a teaspoon measure you could use a tablespoon, a cup or even a bucket!

Using Herbs in Blends

Herbs are Savory

I have not grouped the herbs into flavor categories, like the spices, because I consider them all to be savory. Instead they have been grouped based on relative pungency.

Dried rubbed (crumbled) herbs can be incorporated into some spice blends. I generally use herbs for color, texture and the savory notes they add to a mix. Some blends are made up of herbs only, such as mixed herbs and bouquet garni. When herbs are included in a spice blend, I tend to use a little less than the amount of a sweet spice, say about 3 tsp (15 mL) instead of the $4^1/_2$ tsp (22 mL) suggested on page 683. For example, to give a herbaceous note to the steak spice mentioned earlier (page 684), add 3 tsp (15 mL) dried rubbed oregano leaves.

Balancing Herbs in a Typical Blend

The following guide shows the appropriate proportions of various dried herbs (and/or spices) for using in herb blends.
Typically, a balanced blend contains

- 2% hot spices
- 4% pungent spices and/or herbs
- 12% tangy spices and/or strong herbs
- 22% sweet spices and/or medium herbs
- 60% amalgamating spices and/or mild herbs

The suggested ratios of herbs and spices are based on using dried herbs and spices. If incorporating fresh herbs, multiply the quantities by a factor of 3.

Storing Herb Blends

If you are making a blend that will be stored for more than a day or two, be sure to use dried herbs. Fresh herbs are unsuitable because they have a comparatively higher water content than dried (up to 80% more than a dried herb). This added moisture would make a blend become lumpy, accelerate deterioration of the volatile oils in the spices, and possibly even make the blend develop mold.

Proportions of Herb Types

Mild Herbs

Typical quantity: 5 tsp (25 mL)
- alexanders
- angelica
- borage
- chervil
- elder flower
- filé powder
- lovage
- parsley
- salad burnet
- sweet cicely

Medium Herbs

Typical quantity: 2 tsp (10 mL)
- balm
- bergamot
- chicory
- chives
- makrut lime leaf
- pandan leaf

Strong Herbs

Typical quantity: 1 tsp (5 mL)
- basil
- coriander leaf (cilantro)
- curry leaf
- dill
- fennel fronds
- fenugreek leaf
- lavender
- lemon myrtle
- lemon verbena
- lemongrass
- marjoram
- mint
- myrtle
- tarragon
- Vietnamese mint

Pungent Herbs

Typical quantity: $\frac{1}{2}$ tsp (2 mL)
- bay leaf
- garlic
- oregano
- rosemary
- sage
- savory
- stevia
- thyme

Keep Fresh Cold

Any blend containing fresh material should be stored in the refrigerator and used within a day or two.

Let It Rest

A phenomenon that often goes unrecognized with spice blends is that they "round out" and become better balanced when cooked or after about 24 hours of storage. In other words, a blend of, say, curry powder may initially have a slightly harsh fragrance. A day later, all its complexities will have amalgamated and you will have a balanced blend, with no remaining sharp notes.

Herb Blend for Ground Beef

A simple blend to enhance meat loaf, hamburger patties or your favorite shepherd's pie could include these herbs:

- ½ tsp (2 mL) dried thyme
- ½ tsp (2 mL) dried sage
- 1 tsp (5 mL) dried marjoram

If you prefer to use fresh herbs, substitute finely chopped leaves in 3 to 4 times the quantities. To make a blend suitable for adding to casseroles such as osso bucco, add to the above

- ½ tsp (2 mL) crushed bay leaves
- 5 tsp (25 mL) finely chopped fresh parsley leaves

Remember, if you're using fresh herbs, the blend should be used within a day or two.

A Typical Balanced Rub for Roast Meat

Here is a blend, based on the typical principles for blending herbs and spices, that is excellent for coating meat before roasting:

- 2% hot spices = 2 tsp (10 mL)
  1 tsp (5 mL) ground chile + 1 tsp (5 mL) black pepper

- 4% pungent spices and herbs = 4 tsp (20 mL)
  2 tsp (10 mL) ground cumin + 1½ tsp (7 mL) ground ginger + ½ tsp (2 mL) dried rosemary

- 12% tangy spices = 12 tsp (60 mL)
  10 tsp (50 mL) sumac + 2 tsp (10 mL) amchur powder)

- 22% sweet spices = 22 tsp (110 mL)
  14 tsp (70 mL) ground cinnamon + 8 tsp (40 mL) ground allspice

- 60% amalgamating spices and mild herbs = 60 tsp (300 mL)
  30 tsp (150 mL) ground coriander seed + 23 tsp (115 mL) sweet paprika + 7 tsp (35 mL) rubbed dried parsley

The Spice and Herb Combination Pyramid

The Spice and Herb Combination Pyramid is a convenient "ready reckoner" for the proportions of spices and/or herbs to use when making blends. The pyramid shows each category of herbs and spices grouped by their approximate relative flavor strengths. At the top of the pyramid are the strongest ingredients; at the base are the mildest. The percentages shown are an indication of the approximate quantity by volume that can be combined to form a balanced blend.

Hot Spices (2%)
chile, horseradish, mustard, pepper

Pungent Spices and Herbs (4%)
ajowan, akudjura, asafetida, bay leaf, calamus, caraway, cardamom, celery seed, cloves, cumin, dill seed, fenugreek seed, galangal, garlic, ginger, juniper, licorice, mace, nigella, oregano, orris root, pink *Schinus* pepper, rosemary, sage, savory, star anise, stevia, thyme, wattleseed, zedoary

Tangy Spices and Strong Herbs (12%)
amchur, barberry, basil, ground black lime, caper, coriander leaf (cilantro), curry leaf, dill, fennel fronds, fenugreek leaf, kokam, lavender flowers, lemon myrtle, lemon verbena, lemongrass, marjoram, mint, myrtle, pomegranate, sumac, tamarind, tarragon, Vietnamese mint

Sweet Spices and Medium Herbs (22%)
allspice, anise seed, balm, bergamot, cassia, cinnamon, chives, makrut lime leaf, nutmeg, rose, pandan leaf, vanilla

Amalgamating Spices and Mild Herbs (60%)
alexanders, angelica, borage, chervil, coriander seed, elder flower, fennel seed, filé powder, lovage, paprika, parsley, poppy seed, salad burnet, sesame seed, sweet cicely, turmeric

The Spice Blends

Using Spice Blends as Rubs

To use a spice blend as a dry rub (marinade), coat the meat, fish or vegetable in an appropriate quantity of the blend (see box, right) before cooking. Some blends do not contain salt, in which case you may also season with salt to taste. Even curry powders can be used as rubs. Try adding salt to a curry powder and using it as a rub—I think you'll be pleasantly surprised.

The following recipes for spice blends use volume measures. Thus 1 tsp (5 mL) oregano may be considered as 1 part oregano. You may use a teaspoon (5 mL), a tablespoon (15 mL), a cup (250 mL) or a quart jug (1 L) of ingredients, but just be sure to use the same vessel for everything—it all depends on how much you want to make at a time. I suggest using a teaspoon (5 mL) as your standard measure. That way you will not make too much at first. You can always make more later on if you are happy with the result. If you make any variations, make a note of them so the result, if pleasing, can be replicated.

Storage

When the mix is complete, store it in an airtight container, away from direct light and extremes of heat and humidity. Spice blends stored in this way will keep their flavor for up to 1 year. Don't store blends in the fridge or freezer. Condensation will form when you take them out of this chilled environment, the added water will cause volatile oils to oxidize and the blends will deteriorate more rapidly.

Using Spice Blends

While the uses for some spice blends, such as curry powders and sambar, are very specific, the majority may be used to flavor a wide range of dishes in a variety of ways. Although the blends vary in strength of flavor, as a basic rule of thumb all can be used either as rubs or as recipe additions, in the following quantities:

SUGGESTED QUANTITY OF SPICE BLEND PER POUND (500 g)
- red meats: 1 tbsp (15 mL)
- white meats: $2\frac{1}{2}$ tsp (12 mL)
- vegetables: $1\frac{1}{2}$ tsp (7 mL)
- grains and pulses: $1\frac{1}{2}$ tsp (7 mL)
- baked goods: 1 tsp (5 mL)

Asian Stir-Fry Seasoning

Stir-frying has become a popular method for quickly preparing a nutritious meal. The addition of this Asian spice blend will make an enormous difference to any stir-fry.

Makes about ¼ cup (65 mL)

Tips

Superfine (caster) sugar is a very fine granulated sugar typically used in recipes that require a faster-dissolving granule. If you can't find it in stores, you can make your own by using a food processor fitted with the metal blade to process granulated sugar to a very fine, sand-like consistency.

Ground long chiles, preferably the type known as tien tsin, suit this spice blend well. If you like things extra-hot, use ground Scotch bonnet or habanero chile.

2 tsp	ground star anise	10 mL
2 tsp	fine sea salt	10 mL
1½ tsp	ground cumin	7 mL
1½ tsp	ground ginger	7 mL
1 tsp	ground cassia	5 mL
1 tsp	superfine (caster) sugar (see Tips, left)	5 mL
1 tsp	ground licorice root	5 mL
¾ tsp	ground allspice	3 mL
¾ tsp	ground red chile (see Tips, left)	3 mL
¾ tsp	ground fennel seed	3 mL
½ tsp	freshly ground black pepper	2 mL
½ tsp	ground coriander seed	2 mL

1. Combine ingredients in a bowl and stir well to ensure even distribution. Transfer to an airtight container and store, away from extremes of heat, light and humidity, for up to 1 year.

How to Use Asian Stir-Fry Seasoning

Use this blend to enhance your wok-cooked meals by sprinkling 2 to 3 tsp (10 to 15 mL) per 1 lb (500 g) meat and vegetables during cooking. This blend is also excellent as a dry rub on fish, chicken and red meats before barbecuing, broiling/grilling or even roasting.

Aussie Bush Pepper Mix

Australian native herbs and spices have unique flavor profiles that evoke the vast outback and the distinctive atmosphere of the Australian bush. These flavors include the nutty, caramel-like taste of akudjura combined with roasted coffee–like notes from wattleseed, all enhanced by the freshness of lemon myrtle.

Makes 10½ tsp (50 mL)

Tips

If you prefer, use more or less salt to taste.

I like the flavor so much that I often sprinkle this blend on tomato sandwiches or eggs instead of using salt and pepper.

4½ tsp	ground coriander seed	22 mL
2 tsp	akudjura	10 mL
2 tsp	fine sea salt (see Tips, left)	10 mL
½ tsp	ground wattleseed	2 mL
½ tsp	ground pepperleaf	2 mL
½ tsp	ground pepperberry	2 mL
½ tsp	ground lemon myrtle leaf	2 mL

1. Combine ingredients in a bowl and stir well to ensure even distribution. Transfer to an airtight container and store, away from extremes of heat, light and humidity, for up to 18 months.

How to Use Aussie Bush Pepper Mix

This bush pepper mix is versatile enough to be used as a dry rub on meat before broiling/grilling, roasting or barbecuing. It can also be used to season potato wedges and vegetables such as eggplant before cooking. It works brilliantly as a change from plain salt and pepper.

Australian Flavors

Migration has had a huge influence on Australia's history. As a result, Australian cuisine uses nearly every culinary spice and herb in some way. The following list of spices and herbs is a selection of the flavors, some indigenous, that suggest a quintessentially Australian food experience. These spices, used individually or in combinations on red meats, white meats, vegetables and grains, evoke the stark, uncontrived openness of the Australian psyche. They are generally listed in order of amount used.

- coriander seed
- ginger
- akudjura (bush tomato)
- lemon myrtle
- olida (forest berry herb)
- wattleseed
- Tasmanian pepperleaf
- anise myrtle
- Tasmanian pepperberry

Baharat

Baharat (also known as *advieh*) is the name given to a classic blend of aromatic spices that is used widely in Arab and Iraqi cooking. Baharat may be best described as an exotic blend that fills your head with diverse aromas. It is not hot, yet it conveys all the romantic fragrances of everything we associate with spices. The result is a beautifully balanced combination: it has a woody bouquet, aromatic bay rum notes, mellifluous cinnamon-cassia sweetness, deep pungency and an apple-like fruitiness. The flavor is round and full-bodied, sweet and astringent, but with a satisfying and appetite-stimulating peppery bite. While each spice makes its own distinctive contribution and may leave a lingering hint of its individuality, no single flavor should dominate in a well-made baharat. The proportions may vary depending upon taste preferences, but a typical baharat may be made by carefully blending the following ground spices.

Makes 10½ tsp (50 mL)

It's Probably Not the Blend

When visiting spice markets in Istanbul, it can be puzzling to see large signs reading "baharat" above the traders' stalls. To the locals, *baharat* means simply "flowers and seeds" or, loosely translated, "herbs and spices." These offerings are not likely to be the baharat blend.

4 tsp	sweet paprika	20 mL
2 tsp	freshly ground black pepper	10 mL
1 tsp	ground cumin	5 mL
1 tsp	ground coriander seed	5 mL
1 tsp	ground cassia	5 mL
½ tsp	ground cloves	2 mL
½ tsp	ground green cardamom seed	2 mL
½ tsp	ground nutmeg	2 mL

1. Combine ingredients in a bowl and stir well to ensure even distribution. Transfer to an airtight container and store, away from extremes of heat, light and humidity, for up to 1 year.

How to Use Baharat

Baharat is added to recipes in much the same way that Indians add garam masala as a universal flavor enhancer. Baharat adds a nuance of the exotic Middle East to winter-warming dishes. It is delectable rubbed onto braised lamb shanks before browning. In fact, it complements lamb so well that virtually any cut, including chops and roasts, is improved greatly when the meat is dusted with baharat and a little salt to taste and allowed to dry-marinate in the fridge for an hour before being cooked. It is also good with robust beef dishes such as oxtail stew. Any beef casserole gains a full-bodied taste and deep, rich color if baharat is added the same way as for lamb. Baharat features in classic Middle Eastern recipes for tomato sauces, soups, fish curries and barbecued fish.

Baharat Beef with Olives

Baharat spice mix makes this stew wonderfully comforting—it's a winter staple in all the Hemphill households. Mum started making this stew with beef cheeks, which can be hard to get but are extremely tender when cooked this way. Serve over creamy mashed potatoes for the ultimate in comfort food.

**Makes
4 servings**

Preparation time:
15 minutes

Cooking time:
3½ hours

Tip

If using beef cheeks, you may need to increase the cooking time to 5 hours. Cheeks contain more connective tissue, which needs longer cooking to break down and soften, but the extra time is worth the meltingly tender result.

• Preheat oven to 200°F (100°C)

1 tbsp	olive oil	15 mL
3	cloves garlic, chopped	3
2 lbs	beef shin or cheek, cut into 2½-inch (6 cm) pieces (see Tip, left)	1 kg
1½ tbsp	baharat spice mix (page 692)	22 mL
1	can (14 oz/398 mL) whole tomatoes, with juice	1
½ cup	dry red wine	125 mL
¼ cup	pitted black olives, such as kalamata	60 mL
½ cup	water	125 mL
	Salt and freshly ground black pepper	

1. In a Dutch oven over low heat, heat oil. Add garlic and sauté for 3 to 4 minutes, until softened but not browned.

2. Meanwhile, coat beef in baharat spice mix.

3. Increase heat to medium-high and add spiced beef to pan. Cook for 8 to 10 minutes, stirring often, until browned on all sides (work in batches if necessary). Add tomatoes, wine, olives and water and bring to a simmer, stirring occasionally. Cover with a tight-fitting lid and bake in preheated oven for 3 hours, until beef is very tender (check it after 2½ hours). Season with salt and pepper to taste before serving.

Barbecue Spices

In the 1980s a barbecue spice blend was most likely a mixture of salt, paprika and other spices intended to enhance the color and flavor of red meats. Since then, barbecuing has mushroomed in popularity, with the result that a vast range of spice blends—featuring spices typically associated with cuisines such as Indian, Thai and Moroccan—are now considered appropriate for barbecuing. Rather than including citric acid, a highly processed ingredient, I have opted to add some acidity by including that versatile Middle Eastern spice sumac. The following recipe is for a classic modern barbecue spice.

Makes 18 tsp (90 mL)

Tips

Superfine (caster) sugar is a very fine granulated sugar typically used in recipes that require a faster-dissolving granule. If you can't find it in stores, you can make your own by using a food processor fitted with the metal blade to process granulated sugar to a very fine, sand-like consistency.

You want the dried herb leaves to be crushed, but not to the point where they are powdered. The best way to achieve this is to rub them through a coarse sieve.

Use more or less black pepper to suit your taste.

Be particularly watchful that your container is airtight, as the salt content will attract moisture. Also, be sure to store barbecue spices away from light so the paprika does not bleach and lose flavor.

7 tsp	sweet paprika	35 mL
3 tsp	coarse sea salt	15 mL
2 tsp	ground sumac	10 mL
1 tsp	garlic powder	5 mL
1 tsp	superfine (caster) sugar (see Tips, left)	5 mL
1 tsp	crushed dried parsley or chervil (see Tips, left)	5 mL
1 tsp	dried rubbed oregano	5 mL
1 tsp	freshly ground black pepper (see Tips, left)	5 mL
½ tsp	ground cinnamon	2 mL
½ tsp	ground ginger	2 mL

1. Combine ingredients in a bowl and stir well to ensure even distribution. Transfer to an airtight container (see Tips, left) and store, away from extremes of heat, light and humidity, for up to 1 year.

How to Use Barbecue Spices

I prefer to use this spice blend (and others) as a dry rub on meats to be barbecued, instead of the ubiquitous wet marinades. Contrary to common belief, soaking a piece of meat in a sea of liquid marinade for hours does not necessarily make it more tender, nor does it absorb a great deal of flavor. In some cases a marinade high in salt will actually leach out some of the meat's natural succulence. A barbecue blend is best sprinkled over the meat about 20 minutes before cooking (the moisture on the meat's surface is sufficient to make it stick). Set the meat aside at room temperature and allow to dry-marinate. If desired, squeeze a little lemon juice over the meat while it is cooking; this helps prevent the spices from burning and enhances the flavor.

Bay Seasoning

This blend is based on a popular American combination known as Old Bay seasoning, which is traditionally used to season a range of seafood dishes. Commercial versions are often high in salt. Cooks who want to reduce their sodium intake can do so by making their own version that uses less salt.

Makes 15 tsp (75 mL)

Tips

You can tweak the heat level of bay seasoning by using more of your favorite ground chile. However, it is best to avoid chiles that have distinctive flavors, such as pasilla, ancho or mulato, as their fruity notes are not as compatible with the other spices as, say, ground Kashmiri chile.

Bay leaf is easily ground by crushing it first with your fingers, then grinding the crushed leaf using a mortar and pestle.

8 tsp	fine sea salt	40 mL
2½ tsp	sweet paprika	12 mL
2 tsp	ground celery seed	10 mL
¼ tsp	ground red chile (see Tips, left)	1 mL
¼ tsp	ground bay leaf (see Tips, left)	1 mL
¼ tsp	ground mace	1 mL
¼ tsp	ground yellow mustard seed	1 mL
⅛ tsp	ground allspice	0.5 mL
⅛ tsp	ground ginger	0.5 mL
⅛ tsp	freshly ground black pepper	0.5 mL
⅛ tsp	ground cardamom seed	0.5 mL
⅛ tsp	ground cinnamon	0.5 mL

1. Combine ingredients in a bowl and stir well to ensure even distribution. Transfer to an airtight container and store, away from extremes of heat, light and humidity, for up to 1 year.

How to Use Bay Seasoning

In addition to its inclusion in classic crab boils (see page 696), bay seasoning is truly a general all-purpose flavor-enhancer. Sprinkle on food prior to cooking, or even use it to season french fries and steamed vegetables after cooking.

Crab Boil

A seafood boil is an American tradition from New England and the South—a group feast, eaten off a table covered with layers of newspaper, that generally comprises shellfish, potatoes, corn and sausage. Bay seasoning gives great flavor to this dish.

**Makes
4 servings**

Preparation time:
 15 minutes

Cooking time:
 25 minutes

Tip

If desired, you can substitute 2 lbs (1 kg) raw jumbo shrimp (in the shell) for the crabs. Cook for 5 to 7 minutes.

- **50-quart (47 L) stock pot or similar**
- **Newspaper for serving**

12	new potatoes, scrubbed and halved	12
¼ cup	bay seasoning	60 mL
2 tbsp	fine sea salt	30 mL
2	lemons, quartered	2
4	ears corn, halved	4
1 lb	smoked sausages, cut in half	500 g
12 cups	water	3 L
8	live crabs (see Tip, left)	8
1 tbsp	bay seasoning, for sprinkling	15 mL
1 cup	melted butter	250 mL

1. Place potatoes in bottom of pot and top with bay seasoning, salt, lemons, corn and sausages. Pour in water, cover and bring to a boil over medium heat. Once it is boiling, carefully drop crabs into pot and immediately cover with lid. Boil for 10 to 12 minutes, until crabs are cooked through (color will change to pink/red and claws should release easily when pulled).

2. Cover serving table with at least 4 layers of newspaper. Using tongs, transfer cooked crabs to paper. Using a colander, drain vegetables and sausages and arrange on newspaper with crabs. Sprinkle 1 tbsp (15 mL) bay seasoning overtop and serve with bowls of melted butter for dipping.

Berbere

This Ethiopian spice blend (pronounced *ber-beray*) has a coarse, earthy texture and pungent yet fragrant spice notes. It can be extremely hot, depending on the amount of chile included. Berbere is also the basis of a paste used similarly to curry paste.

Makes 13¾ tsp (70 mL)

2 tsp	whole cumin seeds	10 mL
2 tsp	whole coriander seeds	10 mL
1 tsp	whole ajowan seeds	5 mL
¾ tsp	whole fenugreek seeds	3 mL
1 tsp	whole black peppercorns	5 mL
½ tsp	whole allspice	2 mL
4 tsp	fine sea salt	20 mL
1 tsp	ground ginger	5 mL
½ to 1 tsp	ground bird's-eye chile (1 tsp/5 mL or more will be very hot)	2 to 5 mL
½ tsp	ground cloves	2 mL
½ tsp	ground nutmeg	2 mL

1. In a dry skillet over medium heat, combine cumin, coriander, ajowan and fenugreek seeds, peppercorns and allspice. Roast lightly, stirring constantly, until fragrant, about 2 to 3 minutes. Transfer to a mortar or a spice grinder and grind coarsely.
2. Transfer mixture to a bowl. Add salt, ginger, chile, cloves and nutmeg. Stir well to ensure even distribution. Transfer to an airtight container and store, away from extremes of heat, light and humidity, for up to 1 year.

Variation

Berbere Paste: In a skillet over medium heat, heat 1 tbsp (15 mL) oil. Add 1 finely chopped onion and cook, stirring constantly, until beginning to brown. Add 1 tbsp (15 mL) sweet paprika and 3 tbsp (45 mL) berbere spice mix. Cook, stirring often, for 5 minutes, until onion softens. Remove from heat and set aside to cool. Transfer to an airtight container and refrigerate for up to 2 weeks.

How to Use Berbere

In Western cooking, the dry mix adds a tantalizing spiciness when rubbed over meats before cooking. Berbere paste adds flavor to stews and casseroles when treated as a delicious curry paste–like base. Use 1 tbsp (15 mL) berbere paste to 1 lb (500 g) meat.

Biryani Spice Mix

Rice is a staple in tropical regions, and dishes based primarily on rice feature in the cuisines of tropical and subtropical countries around the world. When we are in India, we always look forward to having a biryani, preferably home-cooked. Every family has its own take on how this dish should taste. This spice mix makes it possible to have a fragrant biryani meal at home anytime the mood strikes. We tend to make a large batch so we have some to put in the refrigerator to heat up for lunch the next day.

Makes 15 tsp (75 mL)

Tip

As this is an Indian spice blend, I suggest using chile flakes made from long teja or Kashmiri chiles.

3 tsp	ground coriander seed	15 mL
2½ tsp	ground cinnamon	12 mL
2 tsp	ground ginger	10 mL
1½ tsp	freshly ground black pepper	7 mL
1½ tsp	ground fennel seed	7 mL
1 tsp	ground cumin	5 mL
¾ tsp	ground Kashmiri chile	3 mL
¾ tsp	ground cardamom seed	3 mL
¾ tsp	ground nutmeg	3 mL
¾ tsp	whole cumin seed	3 mL
½ tsp	medium-heat chile flakes (see Tip, left)	2 mL
¼ tsp	ground cloves	1 mL

1. Combine ingredients in a bowl and stir well to ensure even distribution. Transfer to an airtight container and store, away from extremes of heat, light and humidity, for up to 1 year.

How to Use Biriyani Spice Mix

Use this blend to make Chicken Biryani (page 699).

Chicken Biryani

Originally a Persian dish, biryani has made its way into India, Sri Lanka, Indonesia and Malaysia. What I find so wonderful about it is that it is a complete dish, containing meat, rice, spices and vegetables, making it utterly satisfying.

Makes
4 servings

Preparation time:
 15 minutes
Cooking time:
 50 minutes

Tip

Ghee is a type of clarified butter used in Indian cooking. If you don't have any on hand, you can substitute an equal amount of butter or clarified butter.

- **11- by 7-inch (28 by 18 cm) casserole or baking dish with lid**
- **Preheat oven to 325°F (160°C)**

1 tbsp	ghee (see Tip, left)	15 mL
1	onion, finely chopped	1
1 tbsp	biryani spice mix (page 698)	15 mL
1 lb	skinless boneless chicken breasts, cut into 1-inch (2.5 cm) pieces	500 g
2	tomatoes, peeled and chopped	2
1/3 cup	plain yogurt	75 mL
1 cup	basmati rice	250 mL
1 cup	chicken broth	250 mL
3	whole cloves	3
3	whole green cardamom pods	3
1	3-inch (8 cm) cinnamon stick	1
1/2 cup	fresh or frozen peas, thawed	125 mL
1 tbsp	butter	15 mL

1. In a skillet over low heat, melt ghee. Add onion and spice mix and cook, stirring often, for 3 minutes, until fragrant. Increase heat to medium and add chicken. Cook, stirring often, until browned on all sides, about 5 minutes. Add tomatoes and yogurt and stir to combine. Reduce heat to low and cook for 5 minutes, until sauce begins to thicken. Remove from heat and set aside.

2. Meanwhile, in a saucepan over medium heat, combine rice, broth, cloves, cardamom and cinnamon. Bring to a boil, reduce heat to low and cover with a tight-fitting lid. Simmer for 7 minutes, until broth has been absorbed by the rice. Remove pan from heat, discard whole spices and fluff rice with a fork. Add peas and stir to combine.

3. Grease casserole or baking dish. Spread half the rice evenly over bottom of dish. Top with chicken mixture, then remaining rice. Dot with butter, cover tightly with aluminum foil and cover with lid (using both foil and lid results in beautifully steamed and tender rice). Bake in preheated oven for 20 minutes, until rice is very soft and fluffy (be careful of steam when removing foil). Serve immediately.

Bouquet Garni

Bouquet garni has a familiar balanced flavor, not unlike mixed herbs but mellower, because of the inclusion of parsley, and less pungent, because it contains no sage. The name essentially means "bunch of herbs"—traditionally it consists of a sprig each of thyme, marjoram and parsley plus a few bay leaves, tied together in a bunch. A dried version is made by encasing the blend in a square of cheesecloth that it is removed and discarded after cooking, or it can simply be added to the dish so that the small dried leaves soften and amalgamate with the rest of the ingredients.

**Makes
1 bouquet**

**Makes 9 tsp
(45 mL)**

Tip

Dried bay leaves are easily crushed by whizzing them for about 30 seconds in a food processor fitted with the metal blade, or until the average crushed leaf size is less than $1/4$ inch (5 mm).

FRESH BOUQUET GARNI

1	sprig fresh thyme	1
1	sprig fresh marjoram	1
1	sprig fresh curly or flat-leaf parsley	1
3	fresh bay leaves (attached to stem)	3

1. Using cooking string, tie together thyme, marjoram, parsley and bay sprigs. Use immediately.

DRIED BOUQUET GARNI

4 tsp	dried thyme	20 mL
$2\frac{1}{2}$ tsp	dried marjoram	12 mL
$1\frac{1}{2}$ tsp	dried parsley flakes	7 mL
1 tsp	crushed bay leaves (see Tip, left)	5 mL

1. Combine ingredients in a bowl and stir well to ensure even distribution. Transfer to an airtight container and store, away from extremes of heat, light and humidity, for up to 1 year.

How to Use Bouquet Garni

Bouquet garni is added to soups, stews or casseroles during cooking to infuse the flavor of the herbs into the dish. If you are using a fresh bouquet garni, most of the leaves will soften and fall off during cooking, leaving the hard stems and large leaves, which can easily be removed and discarded at the end of cooking. A dried bouquet garni is more effective in slow-cooked dishes, though it is not as attractive as a fresh bunch. If tied in a square of cheesecloth, the dried version can be easily discarded once the dish is cooked.

Brazilian Spice Mix

Some years ago I was approached by members of the Australian Mushroom Growers Association, who wanted to position their product as "meat for vegetarians." They had brought a Brazilian chef to Australia to demonstrate how to make mushrooms tasty and accessible, and asked me to develop a Brazilian spice mix that would suit this purpose. This mildly spiced blend uses herbs and spices found in many Brazilian recipes. Note how the sweetness of cinnamon and allspice balances perfectly with the earthiness of cumin and the heat of pepper and chile.

Makes 15 tsp (75 mL)

Tip

Mild ground chiles that would be suitable for this blend include New Mexico, guajillo and pasilla.

3½ tsp	sweet paprika	17 mL
2½ tsp	ground ginger	12 mL
2 tsp	fine sea salt	5 mL
1¾ tsp	garlic powder	8 mL
1½ tsp	onion powder	7 mL
¾ tsp	ground cumin	3 mL
¾ tsp	ground coriander seed	3 mL
½ tsp	dried coriander (cilantro) leaves	2 mL
¼ tsp	ground allspice	1 mL
¼ tsp	ground cinnamon	1 mL
¼ tsp	freshly ground black pepper	1 mL
¼ tsp	freshly ground white pepper	1 mL
¼ tsp	ground red chile (see Tip, left)	1 mL

1. Combine ingredients in a bowl and stir well to ensure even distribution. Transfer to an airtight container and store, away from extremes of heat, light and humidity, for up to 1 year.

How to Use Brazilian Spice Mix

In addition to complementing mushrooms, this lightly spiced blend makes an excellent dry rub for fish and chicken. My favorite use is to sauté mushrooms in a little butter and sprinkle this blend overtop while they are cooking. Use about 2 tsp (10 mL) blend per ½ lb (250 g) mushrooms.

Cajun Spice Mix

Cajun spice mix is an excellent example of combining a herb such as basil, which we traditionally associate with Italian cooking, with spices more often associated with Latin American, Indian and Asian cuisines. Its distinctive flavor comes from the somewhat unexpected combination of paprika, basil, garlic, onion, thyme, salt and cayenne pepper with varying quantities of black and white pepper, depending on your heat preferences.

**Makes about
½ cup (125 mL)**

Tip

If you prefer a hotter Cajun spice mix, increase the quantity of white or cayenne pepper to suit your taste.

4 tsp	sweet paprika	20 mL
4 tsp	dried basil	20 mL
3 tsp	onion flakes	15 mL
3 tsp	garlic powder	15 mL
2 tsp	fine sea salt	10 mL
2 tsp	freshly ground black pepper	10 mL
2 tsp	ground fennel seeds	10 mL
1½ tsp	dried parsley flakes	7 mL
1½ tsp	ground cinnamon	7 mL
1½ tsp	dried thyme	7 mL
½ tsp	freshly ground white pepper (see Tip, left)	2 mL
½ tsp	cayenne pepper	2 mL

1. Combine ingredients in a bowl and stir well to ensure even distribution. Transfer to an airtight container and store, away from extremes of heat, light and humidity, for up to 1 year.

How to Use Cajun Spice Mix

This hot, peppery blend is a traditional New Orleans favorite for making Cajun blackened fish or chicken. Sprinkle the blend onto chicken, fish or beef and set aside to dry-marinate for up to 20 minutes before cooking. Either pan-fry, broil/grill or barbecue. To achieve the traditional blackened appearance, fry the seasoned meat in butter—it is the butter burning during cooking that creates the classic blackening effect. Cajun spice is also often added to gumbo (page 284).

Chaat Masala

Masala simply means "mix." In India, chaat masala is used in everyday cooking to salt food prepared at home or to season snacks and street food.

Makes 18½ tsp (90 mL)

Tips

The most appropriate ground chiles for this blend are the bright red Kashmiri or teja.

Chaat masala is my spice of choice for salting practically every Indian recipe. I call it an Indian "all-purpose sprinkle."

8 tsp	ground cumin	40 mL
3 tsp	fine sea salt	15 mL
3 tsp	powdered black salt	15 mL
3 tsp	ground fennel seeds	15 mL
1½ tsp	garam masala (page 735)	7 mL
Pinch	asafetida	Pinch
Pinch	ground red chile (see Tips, left)	Pinch

1. Combine ingredients in a bowl and stir well to ensure even distribution. Transfer to an airtight container and store, away from extremes of heat, light and humidity, for up to 1 year.

How to Use Chaat Masala

Chaat masala makes a good general seasoning on meat and vegetables, either before or after cooking. Because of its high salt content, it is used to season potatoes (*chaat*) and fried pulses such as chickpeas. Used in curries in place of ordinary cooking salt, it adds a wonderfully authentic fragrance. The classic yogurt drink lassi can be ordered sweet or salty. The sweet version uses mango juice and the salty version adds ¼ tsp (1 mL) chaat masala per cup (250 mL). Supposedly the salt helps maintain your saline balance in hot high-humidity climates.

Chai Tea and Coffee Masala

The recent Western passion for Indian food not only created an interest in specific recipes, it also made people aware of the many tasty delights that are so much a part of Indian life. Travelers to India return home with the desire to recreate some of their experiences, and one of those is drinking chai—sweet, milky spiced tea. The spices that flavor chai are often cinnamon, cloves and cardamom, and as a special treat a few saffron stigmas are occasionally included.

Makes 2 cups (500 mL)

Preparation time:
5 minutes

Cooking time:
5 minutes

1	1-inch (2.5 cm) cinnamon stick	1
2	green cardamom pods	2
3	cloves	3
1 cup	milk	250 mL
1 cup	water	250 mL
1 tbsp	Indian black tea leaves	15 mL
4 tsp	granulated sugar (approx.)	20 mL

1. In a saucepan over medium heat, combine spices, milk, water, tea and sugar (use more sugar if you want your tea to be very sweet). Heat until just beginning to bubble around the edges. Remove from heat and set aside for a few minutes. Strain into individual cups.

Variation

These spices are equally complementary to coffee, which is why I call it a "tea *and* coffee masala." To add a spicy fragrance to after-dinner coffee, use the same quantities of spices per cup (250 mL). Add along with the ground coffee to a plunger-type coffeemaker before pouring in the boiling water.

Chermoula

Chermoula is a classic Moroccan mix that combines many of the spices we find in Indian cuisine with the added fresh notes of parsley and cilantro (coriander leaf). The popularity of Moroccan food has made it a regular feature on urban restaurant menus. Regarded by many as being more user-friendly than some hotter spice blends, chermoula is a clever combination of robust flavors such as cumin, mild Spanish paprika and turmeric balanced by the freshness of onion, parsley and cilantro, with hints of garlic and cayenne pepper. Chermoula is often made with fresh herbs (mostly garlic and onion), like a salsa, then lightly spiced and used as a dressing or to marinate fish and chicken before lightly cooking (see Chermoula Paste, page 650).

Makes 9 tsp (45 mL)

Tip

Alleppey turmeric has a higher curcumin content and deeper flavor than regular turmeric. It balances perfectly with the other spices in this blend.

3 tsp	ground cumin	15 mL
2 tsp	sweet paprika	10 mL
1 tsp	dried coriander leaf	5 mL
1 tsp	Alleppey turmeric (see Tip, left)	5 mL
1 tsp	dried parsley leaf	5 mL
1/2 tsp	garlic powder	2 mL
1/2 tsp	onion powder	2 mL
Pinch	cayenne pepper	Pinch
Pinch	freshly ground black pepper	Pinch
Pinch	fine sea salt	Pinch

1. Combine ingredients in a bowl and stir well to ensure even distribution. Transfer to an airtight container and store, away from extremes of heat, light and humidity, for up to 1 year.

How to Use Chermoula

This blend is versatile enough to be used as a rub (dry marinade) on meat or firm fish such as tuna. I particularly enjoy it on roasts and barbecued chops, including lamb. Sprinkle the blend onto the meat or fish and set aside for up to 20 minutes before cooking, then pan-fry, broil/grill or barbecue.

Chinese Five-Spice Powder

This distinctive blend is redolent with the aroma of star anise (a spice found in many Chinese recipes), combined with the sweetness of cassia and cloves, the bite of pepper and plenty of ground fennel seed to amalgamate the flavors. Few spice blends are as dominated by one spice as Chinese five-spice is by star anise.

Makes 10¾ tsp (55 mL)

6 tsp	ground star anise	30 mL
2½ tsp	ground fennel seeds	12 mL
1½ tsp	ground cassia	7 mL
½ tsp	ground Sichuan or black pepper	2 mL
¼ tsp	ground cloves	1 mL

1. Combine ingredients in a bowl and stir well to ensure even distribution. Transfer to an airtight container and store, away from extremes of heat, light and humidity, for up to 1 year.

How to Use Chinese Five-Spice Powder

Chinese five-spice powder is used in many Asian recipes. Its sweet, tangy profile goes particularly well with greasy meats such as pork and duck. Stir-fried vegetables are greatly enhanced by a sprinkling of Chinese five-spice during cooking. With a little salt, it also makes the ideal rub (dry marinade) for chicken, duck, pork and seafood.

Cinnamon Sugar

This version of the old classic is a bit special because it contains more than just cinnamon and sugar. In my books, that makes it one of the ultimate sweet-spice indulgences!

Makes 15 tsp (75 mL)

Tip

Superfine (caster) sugar is a very fine granulated sugar typically used in recipes that require a faster-dissolving granule. If you can't find it in stores, you can make your own by using a food processor fitted with the metal blade to process granulated sugar to a very fine, sand-like consistency.

¼ cup	superfine (caster) sugar (see Tip, left)	60 mL
1 tsp	ground cinnamon	5 mL
1 tsp	ground cassia	5 mL
¼ tsp	ground cardamom seed	1 mL
¼ tsp	ground cloves	1 mL
¼ tsp	ground ginger	1 mL
¼ tsp	vanilla bean powder	1 mL

1. Combine ingredients in a bowl and stir well to ensure even distribution. Transfer to an airtight container and store, away from extremes of heat, light and humidity, for up to 1 year.

How to Use Cinnamon Sugar

This is a true family favorite for sprinkling over donuts, toast, porridge, desserts and fresh fruit salads. Try it on Apple and Cinnamon Teacake (page 211).

Creole Seasoning

This Creole spice blend is quite similar to Cajun Spice Mix (page 703). However, it is a bit milder.

Makes 14 tsp (70 mL)

Tips

Dried herbs are easily ground using a mortar and pestle, or they may easily be powdered by rubbing through a fine sieve.

Bay leaves are easily ground by crushing them first with your fingers, then grinding the crushed leaves using a mortar and pestle.

3½ tsp	sweet paprika	17 mL
3 tsp	fine sea salt	15 mL
2 tsp	onion powder	10 mL
2 tsp	garlic powder	10 mL
1 tsp	ground dried oregano (see Tips, left)	5 mL
½ tsp	ground dried basil	2 mL
½ tsp	freshly ground black pepper	2 mL
½ tsp	freshly ground white pepper	2 mL
¼ tsp	ground dried thyme	1 mL
¼ tsp	ground bay leaf (see Tips, left)	1 mL
¼ tsp	ground allspice	1 mL

1. Combine ingredients in a bowl and stir well to ensure even distribution. Transfer to an airtight container and store, away from extremes of heat, light and humidity, for up to 1 year.

How to Use Creole Seasoning

In this blend all the ingredients are finely powdered, which makes it an ideal spice rub for meats. This blend may also be used instead of Cajun spice mix in gumbo (page 284).

Curry Powders

The notion of curry powder is believed to have originated in India, where the locals would have referred to it as *masala,* which means "mix." After being posted back home, colonials who wished to replicate the exotic flavors of the subcontinent would have simplified these masalas into what we now call curry powders. They are made into powders for convenience, because many of the spices have a very firm texture and need to be pounded or broken up to yield their flavors and aromas.

Curry powders are blends of sweet, pungent, hot and amalgamating spices. They can be mixed in literally hundreds of different proportions to make blends to suit particular tastes. They may also take into account how well the blend complements individual foods; for instance, beef might require a stronger-flavored blend than fish or lentils.

How to Use Curry Powders

The versatility of curry powders can be surprising. For example, mayonnaise blended with curry powder makes a tasty salad dressing. An almost indiscernible amount of curry powder can successfully lift a bland creamy vegetable soup. We tend to think of "curry" as a stew or chopped-up meat and vegetables in a sauce, but the dry powder can easily be blended with a little salt and rubbed on meat as a dry marinade. The moisture in the meat makes the powder cling, and a squeeze of lemon juice before and during broiling/ grilling or barbecuing gives a bit of added zing and stops the spice from burning if the barbecue is very hot.

The principal components of a basic Madras-style Indian curry powder—the type you use when a recipe just calls for "curry powder"—are the sweet spices similar to those found in a mixed spice: cinnamon, allspice and nutmeg. Pungent spices such as cloves, cardamom and cumin add depth of character, while hot spices such as chile, pepper and bitter fenugreek give it bite. These all come together in harmony with the addition of amalgamating spices: fennel, coriander seed (very important) and turmeric. All homemade curry powders should be blended thoroughly and stored in airtight containers away from extremes of heat, light and humidity. They will keep their flavor for up to 1 year.

Roasting Spices

A popular technique for making curry powder is to roast the spices. Roasting modifies the flavor and adds another dimension to the art of making curry powder. The traditional method is to dry-roast the whole spices and then grind them together. Each spice is roasted for a different length of time, depending on the desired flavor or its individual characteristics. For example, over-roasting fenugreek can create extremely bitter, unpleasant notes.

If you want to add extra depth and richness of flavor to a prepared curry powder, here is an easy method: Heat a dry skillet over medium heat and add the appropriate amount of curry powder (for convenience, use the skillet or pot the curry will cook in). The pan must be dry, with no oil; the natural oils in the spices will prevent them from sticking or burning. Stir constantly so the powder toasts evenly. When it starts to change color (likely in 30 to 60 seconds) and gives off a toasted aroma, remove from the heat. You can roast enough curry powder for an individual curry or, if you prefer, make a larger quantity for later use. If making a batch for storage, allow to cool completely, then transfer to an airtight container. Curry powders made with roasted spices have a shorter storage life than regular versions; they should be used within 1 month of making.

Spice Notes

When I'm eating curry, I am often reminded of the time we were having a meal in Mangalore, in southern India, with the Sediyapu family. They were pleased to see us eating with our fingers in the traditional way because, as they said, "How can you know what you are eating unless you feel the food first?" In the West we think we are civilized because we use knives and forks. However, to the Indian way of thinking, we are foolish to put food into our mouths that we have not felt to see how hot or cold or how hard or soft it is. Some Indian people tell me that their senses are so developed they can feel the heat of the chile in a dish through their fingers. Such a talent would have saved many of us from searing experiences in the past.

Amok Curry Powder

This Cambodian curry powder is used for fish. It is a perfect example of the influence Indian migrants have had on cuisines in Asia to the east of India. It is rich and spicy but, surprisingly, does not overpower the flavor of the seafood it is cooked with.

Makes 18 tsp (90 mL)

Tip

Alleppey turmeric has a higher curcumin content and deeper flavor than regular turmeric. It balances perfectly with the other spices in this blend.

2½ tsp	ground red chile	12 mL
2 tsp	ground Alleppey turmeric (see Tip, left)	10 mL
2 tsp	ground Madras turmeric	10 mL
1½ tsp	garlic powder	7 mL
1½ tsp	ground ginger	7 mL
1½ tsp	sweet paprika	7 mL
1¼ tsp	ground cumin	6 mL
1¼ tsp	ground coriander seed	6 mL
1 tsp	ground galangal	5 mL
1 tsp	ground dried makrut lime leaf	5 mL
1 tsp	ground kenchur	5 mL
¾ tsp	freshly ground black pepper	3 mL
¾ tsp	ground dried lemon myrtle leaf	3 mL

1. Combine ingredients in a bowl and stir well to ensure even distribution. Transfer to an airtight container and store, away from extremes of heat, light and humidity, for up to 1 year.

How to Use Amok Curry Powder

This blend is excellent as a dry rub (marinade) not only on fish but on chicken as well, before barbecuing, broiling/grilling or even roasting. Use this blend to make Cambodian Fish Curry (page 714).

Cambodian Fish Curry

Mum and Dad first tasted *amok* at a hole-in-the-wall Cambodian restaurant in Sydney, where they were impressed by the balance of flavors and how well they suited seafood. Dad immediately worked out an accessible spice combination so anyone could make the dish at home. Serve with steamed jasmine rice topped with sliced chile.

Makes
4 servings

Preparation time:
10 minutes

Cooking time:
15 minutes

- **Mortar and pestle or small blender**
- **Wok**

2	small red shallots, finely chopped	2
½ tsp	fine sea salt	2 mL
1 tbsp	amok curry powder (page 713)	15 mL
½ tsp	fish sauce (nam pla)	2 mL
1 tbsp	palm sugar or packed light brown sugar	15 mL
1	can (14 oz/400 mL) coconut milk	1
1 lb	skinless firm white fish fillets	500 g
12	medium raw shrimp, peeled and deveined	12
½ cup	sliced green beans	125 mL
1	fresh long red chile, finely sliced	1

1. Using mortar and pestle or small blender, grind shallots, salt, curry powder, fish sauce and sugar to make a paste, adding a drop or two of water if necessary.

2. In a wok over medium heat, cook paste, stirring, for 2 to 3 minutes, until fragrant. Stir in coconut milk and bring to a simmer. Add fish, shrimp and beans and simmer for 10 to 12 minutes, until seafood is opaque and cooked through. Sprinkle with fresh chile and serve immediately.

Lentil and Dal Spice Mix

We always say that if you ever wanted to be a vegetarian, India would be the place to become one. Grains and pulses (legumes) are good for us, and with the addition of this spice mix, a simple can of red kidney beans (or any other canned beans) is transformed into a nutritious delight. I love to use this blend to make Delhi Dal (page 651).

Makes 15 tsp (75 mL)

Tips

Alleppey turmeric has a higher curcumin content and deeper flavor than regular turmeric. It balances perfectly with the other spices in this blend.

Chile flakes made from long teja chiles or Kashmiri chiles would be suitable for this Indian dish.

2½ tsp	ground coriander seed	12 mL
2¼ tsp	ground cumin	11 mL
2 tsp	whole brown (black) mustard seeds	10 mL
2 tsp	whole cumin seeds	10 mL
1½ tsp	garam masala (page 735)	7 mL
1½ tsp	ground Alleppey turmeric (see Tips, left)	7 mL
1 tsp	ground ginger	5 mL
1 tsp	asafetida powder	5 mL
1 tsp	medium-hot chile flakes (see Tips, left)	5 mL
¾ tsp	garlic powder	3 mL

1. Combine ingredients in a bowl and stir well to ensure even distribution. Transfer to an airtight container and store, away from extremes of heat, light and humidity, for up to 1 year.

How to Use Lentil and Dal Spice Mix

As well as complementing all legumes, this spice mix is the perfect flavor enhancer for vegetables. It is a wonderful addition to potato and cauliflower soup, baked root vegetables and even sweet corn fritters. Use around 3 tsp (15 mL) per 1 lb (500 g) base ingredient.

Madras Curry Powder

Earthy yet fragrant, this is the default curry powder to use when a recipe simply says to add a quantity of curry powder.

Makes 17 tsp (85 mL)

Tip

Add more or less ground chile to suit your taste. The most appropriate type for this blend would be long teja chiles or Kashmiri chiles. If you prefer it hotter, use ground bird's-eye chile.

7 tsp	ground coriander seed	35 mL
3 tsp	ground cumin	15 mL
3 tsp	ground turmeric	15 mL
1 tsp	ground ginger	5 mL
¾ tsp	freshly ground black pepper	3 mL
½ tsp	ground yellow mustard seed	2 mL
½ tsp	ground fenugreek seed	2 mL
½ tsp	ground cinnamon	2 mL
¼ tsp	ground cloves	1 mL
¼ tsp	ground cardamom seed	1 mL
¼ tsp	ground red chile (see Tip, left)	1 mL

1. Combine ingredients in a bowl and stir well to ensure even distribution. Transfer to an airtight container and store, away from extremes of heat, light and humidity, for up to 1 year.

How to Use Madras Curry Powder

Madras curry powder is one of the most popular and versatile Indian spice mixes. It can be used in a variety of dishes, both meat and vegetarian, whenever "curry powder" is called for.

Herbie's Saturday Curry

After conducting weekly spice-appreciation classes at Herbie's, Dad would often be left with a bowl of curry powder he had made while demonstrating the principles of blending spices, so he started making this dish on Saturdays. Serve with Basmati Pilaf (page 164) or plain steamed rice.

**Makes
4 servings**

Preparation time:
15 minutes

Cooking time:
2½ hours

Tips

Many types of chiles are dried for use. These basic dried long red chiles are generally a bit hotter than their fresh counterparts and have a slightly sweet caramel flavor not found in fresh varieties. Asian grocers carry a variety of dried chiles.

This recipe is relatively simple and a good basis for experimenting with different souring agents—try kokam, amchur or tamarind instead of lemon juice and compare the difference.

• **Preheat oven to 250°F (120°C)**

2 tbsp	Madras curry powder (page 716)	30 mL
2 tbsp	oil	30 mL
1 tbsp	panch phoron (page 748)	15 mL
1	onion, chopped	1
1 lb	lamb leg, cut into 1-inch (2.5 cm) cubes	500 g
2 tsp	freshly squeezed lemon juice	10 mL
1	can (14 oz/398 mL) whole tomatoes, with juice	1
2 tsp	garam masala (page 735)	10 mL
2 tsp	chaat masala (page 704)	10 mL
3	dried long red chiles (see Tips, left)	3
2 tbsp	large dried garlic flakes	30 mL
2 tbsp	tomato paste	30 mL
8	fresh or dried curry leaves	8
1 tsp	methi (dried fenugreek leaf)	5 mL
1 to 2 cups water		250 to 500 mL

1. Heat a large, heavy saucepan or Dutch oven over medium heat. Add curry powder and cook, stirring constantly with a wooden spoon, for about 2 minutes, until fragrant (be careful not to burn). Add oil and stir to make a paste. Add panch phoron and cook, stirring constantly, until seeds start popping. Add onion and cook, stirring constantly, for 2 minutes, until lightly browned. Add lamb and, working in batches of about 6 pieces at a time, cook for 8 to 10 minutes, until browned and coated with spices (transfer pieces to a plate as they cook). Return cooked lamb to pan and add lemon juice and tomatoes, roughly chopping tomatoes with spoon while stirring. Cook for 5 minutes, until tomatoes have softened. Sprinkle garam masala, chaat masala, whole chiles and garlic flakes overtop. Add tomato paste, curry leaves, methi and water. Stir well and turn off heat. Cover with a tight-fitting lid and bake in preheated oven for about 2 hours, until tender. Serve immediately or allow to cool completely and refrigerate overnight to allow flavors to develop.

Malay Curry Powder

Malay curries are similar to the Madras style but contain ground fennel seed. If you see a Nonya, Singapore or Malay curry recipe that simply calls for "curry powder," this would be the one to use.

Makes 18 tsp (90 mL)

Tip

Add more or less ground chile to suit your taste. The most appropriate ground chile for this blend would be Kashmiri. However, any medium-hot ground red chile will also work.

6 tsp	ground coriander seed	30 mL
3 tsp	ground cumin	15 mL
3 tsp	ground fennel seed	15 mL
1½ tsp	ground Alleppey turmeric	7 mL
1 tsp	ground ginger	5 mL
1 tsp	ground cinnamon	5 mL
¾ tsp	freshly ground black pepper	3 mL
½ tsp	ground yellow mustard seed	2 mL
¼ tsp	ground cloves	1 mL
¼ tsp	ground cardamom seed	1 mL
¼ tsp	ground chile (see Tip, left)	1 mL

1. Combine ingredients in a bowl and stir well to ensure even distribution. Transfer to an airtight container and store, away from extremes of heat, light and humidity, for up to 1 year.

How to Use Malay Curry Powder

Malay curry powder may be used in the same universal manner as Madras curry powder. The main difference is that Malay curry powder is less sharp-tasting because of the omission of ground fenugreek. The addition of fennel seed adds a somewhat brighter, sweeter flavor.

Spices in Malaysian and Singaporean Cuisines

Malaysian and Singaporean cuisines represent some of the greatest examples of fusion. Many of their typical characteristics have been influenced by Chinese, Portuguese, Indian and Sri Lankan cooking. The Strait of Malacca's tasty cooking style, known as Nonya, has become increasingly popular with tourists, perhaps because of how it fuses Chinese, Malay, Portuguese, Indian and Burmese traditions. Although there are many variations, the following are some of the key spices used in Malaysia and Singapore.

- coriander (leaf and seed)
- fennel seed
- cinnamon and cassia
- turmeric
- lemongrass
- cumin
- ginger
- Vietnamese mint
- pepper (black and white)
- galangal
- cardamom (green and white)
- tamarind
- chile
- star anise

Massaman Curry Powder

This is a Thai curry powder with a difference: instead of the expected light, sharp flavors we often see in Thai green and red curries, massaman curry powder borrows its heritage from a distinctly Malay influence. This combination of deep-flavored spices combined with galangal and star anise, usually seen in Malay and Indian curries, results in a sumptuous, rich curry.

Makes 15 tsp (75 mL)

Tip

For those who like their curries hot, I'd suggest using ground bird's-eye chile. If you prefer something a little milder, use a readily available ground mild Kashmiri chile or hot paprika. For younger diners the amount of chile can be reduced or even eliminated without loss of flavor, by replacing it with the same amount of sweet paprika.

5 tsp	ground coriander seed	25 mL
4 tsp	ground cumin	20 mL
1½ tsp	ground fennel seed	7 mL
1 tsp	ground Alleppey turmeric	5 mL
¾ tsp	sweet paprika	3 mL
¾ tsp	ground ginger	3 mL
¾ tsp	ground red chile (see Tip, left)	3 mL
½ tsp	ground galangal	2 mL
½ tsp	ground cassia	2 mL
½ tsp	ground star anise	2 mL
¼ tsp	ground cardamom seed	1 mL

1. Combine ingredients in a bowl and stir well to ensure even distribution. Transfer to an airtight container and store, away from extremes of heat, light and humidity, for up to 1 year.

How to Use Massaman Curry Powder

Massaman curries are traditionally made with beef. However, this curry powder can also be used with pork, chicken and even fish.

Spices in Thai Food

Thai food evokes images of dishes that are aromatic and fresh, yet hot and sour. These flavors are beautifully balanced with palm sugar and, in the southern part of Thailand, the taste of coconut. In broad, grossly oversimplified terms, Thai cuisine could be described as either predominantly light, sharp and fresh or full-bodied, rich, spicy and nutty, such as in massaman or jungle curries. Although there are many variations, the following are some of the key spices used in Thai cuisine.

- coriander leaf (cilantro)
- makrut lime leaf
- lemongrass
- chile (green and red)

- turmeric
- garlic
- ginger
- galangal

- cloves
- cardamom (green and Thai white)
- pepper (white)

Massaman Beef Curry

Massaman curries, which tend to be associated with northern Thai cuisine, are generally milder and sweeter than their Indian counterparts. The addition of peanuts helps to make this style of curry a popular meal for all age groups. For younger diners, the chile can be reduced or even eliminated without loss of flavor by replacing it with the same amount of sweet paprika.

Makes 4 servings

Preparation time:
15 minutes
Cooking time: 2 hours

Tips

Coconut cream tastes the same as coconut milk but is thicker, with less water content. Coconut milk is liquid extracted from the coconut meat that has been watered down. The "cream" will sit on the top of the can, so it's best to shake before opening to get the right milky consistency. Both coconut cream and milk are used in this recipe to achieve the best creamy consistency.

If desired, this curry can be cooked for a similar amount of time in a 250°F (120°C) oven.

2 tbsp	oil	30 mL
1½ lbs	chuck or round steak, trimmed and cut into 2-inch (5 cm) pieces	750 g
2 tbsp	massaman curry powder (page 719)	30 mL
2 tbsp	coconut cream (see Tips, left)	30 mL
1	large potato, peeled and cut in 1-inch (2.5 cm) pieces	1
1 cup	coconut milk (see Tips, left)	250 mL
1 cup	chicken broth	250 mL
2 tbsp	palm sugar or packed light brown sugar	30 mL
½ cup	roasted unsalted peanuts	125 mL
1 tsp	fine sea salt	5 mL

1. In a large, heavy saucepan over medium heat, heat oil. Working in batches, add beef and cook, stirring often, for 8 to 10 minutes, until browned on all sides. Transfer beef to a plate when browned.

2. To same pan, add curry powder and coconut cream and cook, stirring constantly, for 1 minute, until a thick paste forms. Return beef, with any juices that have collected, to pan and add potato, coconut milk, broth, sugar and peanuts. Stir to combine, cover with a tight-fitting lid and reduce heat to lowest setting. Simmer, covered, for 1 hour, stirring occasionally, until beef just becomes tender. Uncover and simmer, stirring occasionally, for about 30 minutes more, until sauce has thickened and beef is very tender (see Tips, left). Serve immediately.

Rendang Curry Powder

No one really knows where rendang curry originated. However, the curry made with this blend is a traditional dish that is made in infinite variations by thousands of families. The secret of a good rendang curry is that it is cooked for a long time—up to eight hours—until the coconut milk splits and the oil separates. The result is a relatively dry curry that is quite rich (see page 722 for a delicious recipe).

Makes 10¾ tsp (55 mL)

Tip

The most appropriate ground chiles for this blend include Kashmiri, bird's-eye or any medium-hot ground chile.

4 tsp	ground coriander seed	20 mL
2 tsp	ground cumin	10 mL
1 tsp	ground fennel seed	5 mL
1 tsp	ground ginger	5 mL
¾ tsp	medium-hot ground chile (see Tip, left)	3 mL
½ tsp	ground galangal	2 mL
½ tsp	ground Alleppey turmeric	2 mL
½ tsp	ground cassia	2 mL
¼ tsp	ground cloves	1 mL
¼ tsp	freshly ground black pepper	1 mL
¼ tsp	ground cardamom seed	1 mL

1. Combine ingredients in a bowl and stir well to ensure even distribution. Transfer to an airtight container and store, away from extremes of heat, light and humidity, for up to 1 year.

How to Use Rendang Curry Powder

Use rendang curry powder in any dish that calls for curry powder. This blend works particularly well when you reduce the amount of liquid in your regular curry recipe, resulting in a drier and richer curry.

Spices in Indonesian Cuisine

Indonesian cuisine does not retain a huge legacy from the native spices that could be sourced only from there until the 17th century. Cloves, nutmeg, mace, cubeb and long pepper all feature in varying degrees, but their use was overtaken by the influence of Arab, Indian, Chinese, Portuguese and Dutch traders. Various cooking styles and cultural influences had an impact as well. Although there are many variations, the following are some of the key spices.

- fennel seed
- coriander seed
- cumin seed
- cassia

- turmeric
- ginger
- galangal
- nutmeg

- pepper (black, cubeb and long)
- tamarind
- star anise

Beef Rendang

This delicious beef curry is simple to make, and the addition of ground long pepper gives it an authentic Indonesian flavor.

Makes
4 servings

Preparation time:
10 minutes

Cooking time: 2 to 2½ hours

- - - - - - - - - - - - - -

Tips

For finely ground salt, process in a clean spice or coffee grinder.

To toast coconut: Place in a dry skillet over medium heat and cook, stirring often, for 3 to 4 minutes, until golden.

If using fresh compressed tamarind, place in a small bowl, cover with boiling water and set aside for 10 minutes to soak. Strain into a bowl through a fine-mesh sieve, pushing the solids with the back of a spoon to squeeze out as much liquid as possible. Discard remaining pulp.

• **Preheat oven to 250°F (120°C)**

3 tbsp	rendang curry powder (page 721)	45 mL
1 tbsp	sesame oil	15 mL
1 tbsp	oil	15 mL
1	onion, finely chopped	1
2	cloves garlic, minced	2
1 lb	stewing beef, cut in 3-inch (7.5 cm) cubes	500 g
1 tsp	ground dried long pepper	5 mL
1 tsp	tamarind concentrate or 2-inch (5 cm) piece fresh tamarind	5 mL
2 tsp	salt, finely ground (see Tips, left)	10 mL
½ cup	water	125 mL
¼ cup	unsweetened shredded coconut, toasted (see Tips, left)	60 mL

1. In a dry heavy-bottomed, ovenproof dish or Dutch oven over medium-low heat, toast curry powder for about 2 minutes, shaking pan occasionally, until aromatic. Add both oils, onion and garlic; cook, stirring often, for 1 minute, until combined. Add beef, a few cubes at a time, and cook for about 6 minutes, until browned on all sides. Add long pepper, tamarind and salt and stir to combine. Add water and bring to a simmer. Cover and bake in preheated oven for 2 hours or until very tender. Stir in toasted coconut and set aside for 5 minutes before serving.

Sri Lankan Curry Powder

While there are many similarities between the curry powders of India and its neighbor Sri Lanka, there are definite differences. In a Sri Lankan curry blend there is much more cinnamon—which isn't surprising, since the spice is native to the country—and more chile. However, there is no fenugreek to add a bitter component. One would think a Sri Lankan curry would taste sweeter, but the cinnamon balances so well with the other spices that it produces a richness and depth of flavor that make this style of curry so very appealing.

Makes 11 tsp (55 mL)

Tip

Add more or less ground chile to suit your taste. The most appropriate type for this blend would be bird's-eye chile (Sri Lankans prefer their curries quite hot). However, ground Kashmiri chile or any medium-hot ground red chile will certainly work too.

3 tsp	ground coriander seed	15 mL
2 tsp	ground cumin	10 mL
1½ tsp	ground fennel seed	7 mL
1 tsp	ground red chile (see Tip, left)	5 mL
1 tsp	ground Alleppey turmeric	5 mL
1 tsp	ground cinnamon	5 mL
¾ tsp	ground cloves	3 mL
½ tsp	ground cardamom seed	2 mL
½ tsp	freshly ground black pepper	2 mL

1. Combine ingredients in a bowl and stir well to ensure even distribution. Transfer to an airtight container and store, away from extremes of heat, light and humidity, for up to 1 year.

How to Use Sri Lankan Curry Powder

Use Sri Lankan curry powder in the same way that you would use any curry powder in a curry recipe. This blend works well with beef, chicken and pork.

Sri Lankan Curry

My father first experienced Sri Lankan curry in the early 1980s. At that point he had a delightful employee, Elmo, who was Sri Lankan. Every lunchtime when Elmo opened his tiffin tin, filled with a delicious curry his wife had made the night before, the most heavenly aromas permeated the air. After some cajoling Elmo revealed his wife's secrets, which were the inspiration for my father's blend and this curry. Serve with Basmati Pilaf (page 164) or plain steamed rice.

Makes 4 servings

Preparation time:
15 minutes

Cooking time:
2½ hours

- - - - - - - - - - - - - - - -

Tips

Many types of chile are dried for use. Basic dried red chiles are generally a bit hotter than their fresh counterparts and have a slightly sweet caramel flavor not found in fresh varieties. Asian grocers carry a variety of dried chiles.

You can serve this curry immediately after cooking, but for best results allow to cool completely and refrigerate overnight to allow flavors to fully develop.

● **Preheat oven to 250°F (105°C)**

2 tbsp	Sri Lankan curry powder (page 723)	30 mL
2 tbsp	oil	30 mL
1	onion, chopped	1
1 lb	lamb shoulder, cut in 1-inch (2.5 cm) pieces	500 g
2 tsp	freshly squeezed lemon juice	10 mL
1	can (14 oz/398 mL) whole tomatoes, with juice	1
2 tsp	garam masala (page 735)	10 mL
2 tsp	chaat masala (page 704)	10 mL
3	dried long red chiles (see Tips, left)	3
2 tbsp	large dried garlic flakes	30 mL
2 tbsp	tomato paste	30 mL
8	fresh or dried curry leaves	8
1 tsp	methi (dried fenugreek leaf)	5 mL
1 to 2 cups	water	250 to 500 mL

1. Heat a large, heavy saucepan or Dutch oven over medium heat. Add curry powder and cook, stirring constantly with a wooden spoon, for about 2 minutes, until fragrant (be careful not to burn). Add oil and stir to make a paste. Add onion and cook, stirring constantly, for 2 minutes, until lightly browned. Add lamb, working in batches of about 6 pieces at a time, and cook for 5 to 7 minutes, until browned and coated with spices (transfer cooked pieces to a plate).

2. Return all the cooked lamb to pan and add lemon juice and tomatoes, roughly chopping tomatoes with spoon while stirring. Cook for 5 minutes, until tomatoes have softened. Sprinkle garam masala, chaat masala, whole chiles and garlic flakes overtop. Add tomato paste, curry leaves, methi and water. Stir well and turn off the heat. Cover with a tight-fitting lid and bake in preheated oven for about 2 hours, until lamb is tender.

Vadouvan Curry Powder

The British colonials embraced Indian cuisine by creating the somewhat ubiquitous Madras style of curry powder. The French, however, who colonized Pondicherry (on the eastern Coromandel Coast of India), developed their own take on a curry blend, called *vadouvan*. This is a particularly pleasing curry powder, as its sweetness derives from the inclusion of onion and garlic powders, mild heat from chile, and classic South Indian fragrances from cardamom and curry leaves.

Makes 16 tsp (80 mL)

Tip

The most appropriate ground chile for this blend would be Kashmiri. However, ground teja or any ground medium-hot red chile will certainly work too. This is a very family-friendly curry powder. If you want to make it for younger diners, you may substitute an equal amount of sweet paprika for the ground chile.

4 tsp	onion powder	20 mL
3 tsp	garlic powder	15 mL
3 tsp	ground cumin	15 mL
1½ tsp	ground coriander seed	7 mL
1½ tsp	ground Madras turmeric	7 mL
1 tsp	finely chopped dried curry leaf	5 mL
¾ tsp	freshly ground black pepper	3 mL
½ tsp	ground fenugreek seed	2 mL
½ tsp	ground ginger	2 mL
½ tsp	ground Kashmiri chile (see Tip, left)	2 mL
¼ tsp	ground cardamom seed	1 mL
¼ tsp	ground cloves	1 mL

1. Combine ingredients in a bowl and stir well to ensure even distribution. Transfer to an airtight container and store, away from extremes of heat, light and humidity, for up to 1 year.

How to Use Vadouvan Curry Powder

Vadouvan goes equally well with vegetables as it does with meat, and it is especially good with cauliflower. A spiced butter for dressing cooked beans can be made by mixing 1 tsp (5 mL) vadouvan curry powder and ¼ cup (60 mL) butter.

Chicken Vadouvan Curry

One day a customer came into my father's shop with a little package of curry powder she had purchased in France. She wanted to know what it was and if my dad could make it. Always up for a challenge, he went to work. After much sniffing and a little tasting, he recognized it as a vadouvan curry powder and forthwith decided to replicate it, with some slight improvements of his own. This is such an easygoing curry that it has become a family favorite for adults and children alike. Serve alongside steamed rice.

**Makes
4 servings**

Preparation time:
10 minutes
Cooking time:
30 minutes

- - - - - - - - - - - - - - -

Tip

You can substitute the freshly squeezed juice of 1 lemon for the tamarind paste, if needed.

2 tbsp	oil	30 mL
1	onion, finely chopped	1
2 tbsp	vadouvan curry powder (page 725)	30 mL
1½ lbs	skinless boneless chicken thighs, trimmed and cut into 2-inch (5 cm) pieces	750 g
1 tsp	fine sea salt	5 mL
	Water	
1 tsp	tamarind paste (see Tip, left)	5 mL
1 cup	plain yogurt	250 mL
½ cup	lightly packed fresh coriander (cilantro) leaves, roughly chopped	125 mL

1. In a large saucepan over medium heat, heat oil. Add onion and sauté for 2 minutes, until lightly browned. Add curry powder and cook, stirring constantly, for 1 minute, until well combined. Add chicken and cook for 5 minutes, stirring often, until chicken is browned on all sides and coated in spices. Add salt and just enough water to cover chicken. Stir in tamarind paste until well combined. Bring to a simmer, reduce heat to medium-low and cook for 20 minutes, until chicken is cooked through. Remove from heat, stir in yogurt and serve immediately, garnished with cilantro.

Vegetable Curry Powder

This curry powder is quite different from the others because it is designed to complement and enhance the flavor of vegetables without dominating them. It has no chile or pepper, which makes it mild enough for the most conservative of tastes without compromising on overall flavor.

Makes 15 tsp (75 mL)

4 tsp	ground coriander seed	20 mL
2 tsp	sweet paprika	10 mL
1½ tsp	ground Alleppey turmeric	7 mL
1½ tsp	whole cumin seeds	7 mL
1½ tsp	whole yellow mustard seeds	7 mL
1½ tsp	whole brown (black) mustard seeds	7 mL
1 tsp	ground cumin seed	5 mL
½ tsp	ground fennel seed	2 mL
½ tsp	ground cassia	2 mL
½ tsp	ground ginger	2 mL
¼ tsp	ground cardamom seed	1 mL
¼ tsp	asafetida powder	1 mL

1. Combine ingredients in a bowl and stir well to ensure even distribution. Transfer to an airtight container and store, away from extremes of heat, light and humidity, for up to 1 year.

How to Use Vegetable Curry Powder

Use this blend to enhance your vegetable dishes, especially stir-fries, by sprinkling 2 to 3 tsp (10 to 15 mL) per pound (500 g) of vegetables during cooking. As well as complementing vegetables, this very tasty yet mild curry blend is ideal with seafood. To make a quick fish curry, coat cubes of firm-fleshed fish with vegetable curry powder and stir-fry with a little oil in a wok over medium heat. When the fish is cooked (it will turn opaque and flake easily with a fork), add 2 to 3 tbsp (30 to 45 mL) coconut milk and bring to a boil, stirring to scrape up any brown bits stuck to pan. Serve over rice.

Vindaloo Curry Powder

Goa is an ancient seaport on the west coast of India that was inhabited by the Portuguese in the 16th century. It is famous for its vindaloo curry—a seriously hot experience. The name *vindaloo* is believed to come from the addition of red wine (*vinho*) vinegar, which makes this taste quite different from the many curries that get their acidic tang from tamarind.

Makes 13½ tsp (70 mL)

Tip

Add more or less ground chile to suit your taste. The most appropriate type for this blend is bird's-eye chile. However, if you prefer less heat, ground Kashmiri chile or any ground mild red chile will certainly work too.

3 tsp	ground bird's-eye chile (see Tip, left)	15 mL
2 tsp	white poppy seeds	10 mL
2 tsp	ground cumin seed	10 mL
2 tsp	hot paprika	10 mL
1 tsp	ground cassia	5 mL
1 tsp	ground ginger	5 mL
1 tsp	crushed dried bird's-eye chile	5 mL
½ tsp	amchur powder	2 mL
½ tsp	freshly ground black pepper	2 mL
¼ tsp	ground cloves	1 mL
¼ tsp	ground star anise	1 mL

1. Combine ingredients in a bowl and stir well to ensure even distribution. Transfer to an airtight container and store, away from extremes of heat, light and humidity, for up to 1 year.

Vindaloo Curry

In the early 1990s my father attended a spice conference in Goa, on the west coast of India. He was enchanted by an amazing pork vindaloo curry he ate at a small local restaurant. The heat was almost debilitating, so, believe it or not, my father has reduced the amount of chile in this version of the classic dish.

Makes 4 servings

Preparation time:
15 minutes

Cooking time:
2½ hours

Tips

Vindaloo is most often made with pork, although it is equally tasty with other meats.

Many types of chile are dried for use. Basic dried red chiles are generally a bit hotter than their fresh counterparts and have a slightly sweet caramel flavor not found in fresh varieties. Asian grocers carry a variety of dried chiles.

• **Preheat oven to 250°F (120°C)**

2 tbsp	vindaloo curry powder (page 728)	30 mL
2 tbsp	oil	30 mL
1	onion, chopped	1
1 lb	pork shoulder, cut in 1-inch (2.5 cm) pieces	500 g
2 tsp	freshly squeezed lemon juice	10 mL
1	can (14 oz/398 mL) whole tomatoes, with juice	1
2 tsp	garam masala (page 735)	10 mL
2 tsp	chaat masala (page 704)	10 mL
3	dried long red chiles (see Tips, left)	3
2 tbsp	large dried garlic flakes	30 mL
2 tbsp	tomato paste	30 mL
8	fresh or dried curry leaves	8
1 to 2 cups	water	250 to 500 mL
½ cup	red wine vinegar	125 mL
1 tsp	methi (dried fenugreek leaf)	5 mL

1. Heat a large, heavy saucepan or Dutch oven over medium heat. Add curry powder and cook, stirring constantly with a wooden spoon, for about 2 minutes, until fragrant (be careful not to burn). Add oil and stir to make a paste. Add onion and cook, stirring constantly, for 2 minutes, until lightly browned. Add pork, in batches of about 6 pieces at a time, and cook for 5 to 7 minutes, until browned and coated with spices (transfer cooked pieces to a plate).

2. Return all the cooked pork to pan and add lemon juice and tomatoes, roughly chopping tomatoes with spoon while stirring. Cook for 5 minutes, until tomatoes are softened. Sprinkle garam masala, chaat masala, whole chiles and garlic flakes overtop. Add tomato paste, curry leaves, water, vinegar and methi. Stir well and turn off the heat. Cover with a tight-fitting lid and bake in preheated oven for about 2 hours, until tender. Serve immediately or, for best results, allow to cool completely and refrigerate overnight to allow flavors to fully develop.

Yellow Curry Powder

Yellow curries are dominated by turmeric. However, it is somewhat surprising to find that the earthy taste of turmeric is not generally overpowering in yellow curries. When used with paneer and cashews, for instance, as it is in Cashew Curry (page 281), you will see how well turmeric balances with the other flavors.

Makes 16 tsp (80 mL)

Tips

The most appropriate ground chiles for this blend would be Kashmiri or any dried medium-hot long chile. However, as this is a mild curry powder, sweet paprika will certainly work too.

Before using, set aside the prepared curry powder for a couple of days to allow time for the spice notes to amalgamate. Do not be concerned if the mixture has a harsh aroma when you first make it; it will mellow and become "rounder" after about 24 hours.

4 tsp	ground coriander seed	20 mL
4 tsp	ground Madras turmeric	20 mL
1½ tsp	ground Alleppey turmeric	7 mL
1½ tsp	sweet paprika	7 mL
1½ tsp	ground cumin seed	7 mL
1 tsp	ground fennel seed	5 mL
1 tsp	ground ginger	5 mL
¾ tsp	ground cassia	3 mL
½ tsp	ground chile (see Tips, left)	2 mL
¼ tsp	ground cardamom seed	1 mL

1. Combine ingredients in a bowl and stir well to ensure even distribution. Transfer to an airtight container and store, away from extremes of heat, light and humidity, for up to 1 year.

How to Use Yellow Curry Powder

Use this blend in Thai and other Asian dishes when a mild curry flavor is desired. This blend is particularly good with seafood and helps to neutralize the overly strong flavors of some fish.

Dukkah

Dukkah is an Egyptian specialty that is not, strictly speaking, a spice blend but rather a blend of roasted nuts seasoned with spices. While many different nuts may be included in dukkah, the combination I have found to be most appealing contains hazelnuts and pistachios.

Makes 1½ cups (375 mL)

Tip

The coriander and cumin seeds may be roasted whole and then ground, but I find the flavor to be lighter when plain, unroasted ground coriander seed and cumin are used.

- **Food processor**

¼ cup	hazelnuts	60 mL
¼ cup	pistachio nuts	60 mL
⅔ cup	white sesame seeds	150 mL
⅓ cup	ground coriander seed	75 mL
2½ tbsp	ground cumin	37 mL
1 tsp	fine sea salt (or to taste)	5 mL
½ tsp	freshly ground black pepper	2 mL

1. In a skillet over medium heat, toast hazelnuts and pistachios, stirring constantly, until fragrant, about 3 minutes. Transfer to food processor fitted with the metal blade and pulse until chopped. Transfer to a mixing bowl.

2. In same pan, toast sesame seeds, stirring constantly until golden. Remove from heat and immediately add to bowl, along with coriander seed, cumin, salt and pepper. Mix well and set aside. Once completely cooled, transfer to an airtight container and store, away from extremes of heat, light and humidity, for up to 6 months.

How to Use Dukkah

The most popular way to consume dukkah is to break off a piece of Turkish or crusty bread, dip it in virgin olive oil and then dip the oiled bread in the dukkah. This is a tasty snack that goes well with drinks. Dukkah also makes a good crunchy coating for chicken and fish (coat it before pan-frying) and adds a pleasing crunch when sprinkled over fresh salads, such as Butternut Squash and Chickpea Salad (page 597), preferably along with a little sumac. Tsire powder (page 777) is a similar spice blend from West Africa.

Fried-Chicken Spice

Chicken probably benefits more than any other protein from the addition of spice. Many years ago, my father, a master herb and spice blender, was commissioned to make a spice blend that would mimic a certain retired military gentleman's fried chicken. Dad made a blend, minus the MSG, that has remained a family favorite for more than 50 years. My update is a contemporary incarnation that also works as a rub for roasting poultry.

Makes 15¾ tsp (80 mL)

Tips

Superfine (caster) sugar is a very fine granulated sugar typically used in recipes that require a faster-dissolving granule. If you can't find it in stores, you can make your own by using a food processor fitted with the metal blade to process granulated sugar to a very fine, sand-like consistency.

Leaves of dried parsley can sometimes be quite large. In order to get them to blend well with other ingredients, rub them through a coarse sieve, which should yield something similar to a powder but with more texture.

5 tsp	sweet paprika	25 mL
4 tsp	fine sea salt	20 mL
1 tsp	garlic powder	5 mL
1 tsp	superfine (caster) sugar (see Tips, left)	5 mL
1 tsp	ground dried oregano	5 mL
1 tsp	ground dried parsley flakes (see Tips, left)	5 mL
1 tsp	ground ginger	5 mL
¾ tsp	freshly ground black pepper	3 mL
½ tsp	ground dried rosemary	2 mL
½ tsp	ground cinnamon	2 mL

1. Combine ingredients in a bowl and stir well to ensure even distribution. Transfer to an airtight container and store, away from extremes of heat, light and humidity, for up to 1 year.

How to Use Fried-Chicken Spice

Fried-chicken spice is an all-purpose seasoning. Sprinkle on any meats or roasted vegetables before cooking. It's also delicious sprinkled over french fries as soon as they are drained from the deep-fryer.

Fried Chicken

This is a classic preparation for fried chicken. The buttermilk lends a mild tang to the coating and renders the chicken very tender, with a light crust. Be careful when deep-frying, as the oil is extremely hot. Serve with Three-Cabbage Coleslaw (page 149).

**Makes
4 servings**

Preparation time:
5 minutes, plus
6 hours or overnight
for marinating

Cooking time:
40 minutes

Tip

To test if the oil is hot enough, drop in a piece of crustless bread. It should brown without burning in 60 seconds.

4	bone-in, skin-on chicken drumsticks	4
4	bone-in, skin-on chicken thighs	4
2 cups	buttermilk	500 mL
1 cup	all-purpose flour	250 mL
1 tbsp	fried-chicken spice (page 732)	15 mL
	Oil for deep-frying	

1. In a resealable bag, combine chicken with buttermilk. Seal and turn to coat well, then refrigerate for 6 hours or overnight.

2. At least 1 hour before cooking, remove chicken from refrigerator and bring to room temperature (this will allow chicken to cook more quickly and reduce the chance of burning).

3. In a shallow bowl, combine flour and fried chicken spice. Set aside.

4. Remove chicken from buttermilk, discarding liquid (chicken should be coated with a layer of buttermilk for the seasoning to stick to).

5. In a deep skillet over medium heat, heat $1^1/_2$ inches (4 cm) oil until it reaches about 350°F (180°C) (see Tips, left). Dredge each piece of chicken liberally in flour mixture, coating both sides, then carefully drop into hot oil (depending on size of skillet, you can cook 3 or 4 pieces at a time). Cook for 5 minutes each side, until golden brown and an instant-read thermometer inserted in the thickest part registers 165°F (74°C). Transfer to a wire rack to rest for 2 minutes before serving.

Game Spice

The rich taste of game is well balanced by the pine-like notes of juniper and the pungency of cloves in this blend of spices. When I make this blend, I place all the whole ingredients in a mortar and crush them roughly with the pestle. That way the oils from the juniper berries, which are quite moist, are absorbed by the other spices.

**Makes 5 tsp
(25 mL)**

2	whole cloves	2
1	whole dried bird's-eye chile	1
1	dried bay leaf	1
2 tsp	juniper berries	10 mL
1 tsp	whole allspice	5 mL
1 tsp	whole black peppercorns	5 mL
½ tsp	coriander seeds	2 mL

1. Combine ingredients in a bowl and stir well to ensure even distribution. Transfer to an airtight container and store, away from extremes of heat, light and humidity, for up to 1 year.

How to Use Game Spice

This blend has a pleasant amalgamation of flavors that complements stuffings, casseroles, homemade sausage or even a meat loaf. Rub onto meat as a dry marinade and set aside for about 30 minutes before cooking. Use 1 tsp (5 mL) or more game spice blend per 1 lb (500 g) meat or use it as a substitute for juniper berries (equal to the amount of juniper berries you would have used).

Garam Masala

Garam masala is a traditional Indian blend of spices. Some even regard it as the linchpin of a diverse range of dishes, including curries and butter chicken. *Masala* means "blend" or "mixture" and *garam* means "spices," but a garam masala is a distinctive blend in its own right. Although there are many interpretations, they should all have the same taste characteristics. I find it interesting how often Indian cooks add garam masala rather than the individual ingredients—this is, of course, for simplicity, because it's ready-made.

Makes 10½ tsp (55 mL)

4 tsp	ground fennel seed	20 mL
2½ tsp	ground cinnamon	12 mL
2½ tsp	ground caraway seed	12 mL
½ tsp	freshly ground black pepper	2 mL
½ tsp	ground cloves	2 mL
½ tsp	ground cardamom seed	2 mL

1. Combine ingredients in a bowl and stir well to ensure even distribution. Transfer to an airtight container and store, away from extremes of heat, light and humidity, for up to 1 year.

How to Use Garam Masala

This balanced, almost sweet blend with its touch of black-pepper bite lacks the characteristic curry notes of cumin, coriander and turmeric, which makes it enormously versatile as a spicing agent across a wide cross-section of Indian dishes. Although most often associated with curries, garam masala is delicious when used as a rub for barbecued fish, along with as much ground dried chile as you like and salt to taste. One of my favorite uses for garam masala is in Herbie's Saturday Curry (page 717).

Garlic Steak Rub

Garlic-flavored steak rubs are extremely popular, and this blend is versatile and easy to use.

Makes 15¼ tsp (75 mL)

Tip

Red and green capsicums (bell peppers) are diced and dried to make bell pepper granules. Although these are used mostly in processed foods and packaged dry meals and soups, you can purchase them from some supermarkets and bulk food stores. They provide a nice texture along with a sweet paprika taste. If you can't find them, you can sieve the seeds from red chile flakes (discard the seeds) and then crush the dried chile flesh coarsely using a mortar and pestle.

4 tsp	garlic powder	20 mL
3 tsp	onion powder	15 mL
2½ tsp	fine sea salt	12 mL
1½ tsp	red bell pepper granules (see Tip, left)	7 mL
1½ tsp	sweet paprika	7 mL
1 tsp	ground ginger	5 mL
1 tsp	freshly ground black pepper	5 mL
½ tsp	ground yellow mustard seed	2 mL
¼ tsp	ground cinnamon	1 mL

1. Combine ingredients in a bowl and stir well to ensure even distribution. Transfer to an airtight container and store, away from extremes of heat, light and humidity for up to 1 year.

How to Use Garlic Steak Rub

The flavor of garlic combined with onion, salt and subtle spices complements red meats and adds both color and succulence. I rub this blend onto steaks before barbecuing, broiling/grilling or roasting.

Harissa

Harissa is a traditional Tunisian paste that is often used as a condiment. If you are at a meal where it is being passed around, use with extreme caution—the key ingredient is an abundance of chile. Harissa is made with dried chiles because their flavor is stronger and more complex than that of their fresh counterparts. Another Tunisian blend, tabil, is made in the same way except that it contains no paprika or cumin—which makes it relatively hotter.

Makes about 1 cup (250 mL)

Tips

As this is meant to be a hot paste, my preference is to use dried bird's-eye chile flakes. You can also use flakes made from Kashmiri chiles, piment d'Espelette or rich, full-flavored Aleppo pepper.

To dry-roast cumin seeds: Place in a hot, dry skillet and cook, shaking pan constantly so the seeds will not stick or burn, until darkened and aromatic. Remove from heat and transfer seeds to a dish to cool. Once roasted, cumin seeds will last for about 1 month if stored in an airtight container (cool completely before storing). Keep protected from extremes of heat, light and humidity.

• Mortar and pestle

¼ cup	dried chile flakes (see Tips, left)	60 mL
¼ cup	hot water	60 mL
6	fresh spearmint leaves, finely chopped	6
5 tsp	crushed garlic	25 mL
5 tsp	sweet paprika	25 mL
2 tsp	whole caraway seeds	10 mL
2 tsp	whole coriander seeds	10 mL
1 tsp	whole cumin seeds, dry-roasted, then ground (see Tips, left)	5 mL
1 tsp	fine sea salt	5 mL
1 tbsp	olive oil (approx.)	15 mL

1. In a bowl, combine chile flakes and hot water and set aside for 10 minutes, until quite soft. (Do not drain off the water; it helps form the paste and will be absorbed by the dry spice ingredients.) Add spearmint, garlic, paprika, caraway, coriander and cumin seeds, and salt. Transfer to mortar; crush and mix thoroughly with pestle. Gradually add oil, mixing until a thick paste forms (the amount will depend on desired consistency). Transfer to an airtight container and refrigerate for up to 2 weeks.

How to Use Harissa

Traditionally harissa is used as a condiment with cooked meats such as kebabs. It appears on the table in a small dish and is ubiquitous in the Middle East, just as chile sauce is in Singapore. Harissa makes a nice alternative to sweet Thai chili sauce and sriracha. I love to use it on cold meat sandwiches as a spicy alternative to mustard. Harissa is delicious on crusty bread or pita that has been spread with hummus. It is also wonderful in the Middle Eastern dish chakchouka (page 190).

Herbes de Provence

Herbes de Provence is a traditional blend of dried herbs found in French and European recipes. It has some of the pungency of mixed herbs and bouquet garni, but what might otherwise be overt is fine-tuned by balancing ingredients. The anise freshness of tarragon, the lightness of celery and the floral notes of lavender counter the strength of thyme and marjoram. Make small amounts of herbes de Provence regularly from the best-quality ingredients available (it will taste better and last longer). My favorite combination follows.

Makes 10 tsp (50 mL)

Tip

Crushing bay leaves releases their flavor into cooking, and small crushed pieces will soften in dishes that are cooked for over 1 hour. As a properly dried bay leaf is quite crisp, you can simply crush it between your fingers until you have pieces of less than $1/4$ inch (5 mm). Alternatively, you can chop them using a sharp knife or a spice grinder—just be careful to stop before it becomes a powder!

4 tsp	dried thyme	20 mL
2 tsp	dried marjoram	10 mL
2 tsp	dried parsley flakes	10 mL
1 tsp	dried tarragon	5 mL
$2/3$ tsp	dried lavender flowers	3 mL
$1/2$ tsp	celery seed	2 mL
1	crushed dried bay leaf (see Tip, left)	1

1. Combine ingredients in a bowl and stir well to ensure even distribution. Transfer to an airtight container and store, away from extremes of heat, light and humidity, for up to 1 year.

How to Use Herbes de Provence

Herbes de Provence is used like mixed herbs (see page 745) in casseroles for game and poultry; 2 to 3 tsp (10 to 15 mL) is sufficient in a recipe that serves 3 to 4 people. Think of this as a type of mixed herbs for bread stuffings, and try it in Provençal Pissaladière (page 345).

Italian Herb Blend

In North America a packaged blend known as "dried Italian seasoning" is ubiquitous. In fact it has been suggested that for many people (not, of course, residents of Italy) its flavors define Italian food. Despite its broad-brush generalization, an Italian blend should contain a combination of herbs that effectively complement traditional Italian recipes such as Bolognese sauce, pasta dishes and pizza.

Makes 14 tsp (70 mL)

4 tsp	dried basil	20 mL
3 tsp	dried thyme	15 mL
2 tsp	dried rubbed marjoram	10 mL
2 tsp	dried rubbed oregano	10 mL
1 tsp	dried rubbed sage	5 mL
1 tsp	dried garlic flakes	5 mL
1 tsp	dried rosemary	5 mL

1. Combine ingredients in a bowl and stir well to ensure even distribution. Transfer to an airtight container and store, away from extremes of heat, light and humidity, for up to 1 year.

How to Use Italian Herb Blend

Sprinkle this blend over pizza before cooking and include it as a general seasoning in warming vegetable and meat soups, stews and casseroles. Add 2 to 4 tsp (10 to 20 mL) Italian herb blend per 1 lb (500 g) ground beef when making a Bolognese sauce.

Laksa Spice Mix

Laksa is a classic Asian noodle soup that has become one of Australia's favorite takeout meals. Although this spice blend contains a lot of ingredients, it is well worth the effort. It will add a full, robust flavor to fresh ingredients, far better than most store-bought versions.

Makes 12 tsp (60 mL)

Tips

Superfine (caster) sugar is a very fine granulated sugar typically used in recipes that require a faster-dissolving granule. If you can't find it in stores, you can make your own by using a food processor fitted with the metal blade to process granulated sugar to a very fine, sand-like consistency.

For those who prefer a hotter, spicier laksa, use bird's-eye chile flakes.

3 tsp	ground coriander seed	15 mL
1½ tsp	ground cumin	7 mL
1½ tsp	ground fennel seed	7 mL
1 tsp	fine sea salt	5 mL
¾ tsp	ground turmeric	3 mL
¾ tsp	ground galangal	3 mL
¾ tsp	medium-hot chile flakes (see Tips, left)	3 mL
½ tsp	garlic powder	2 mL
½ tsp	dried and finely crushed makrut lime leaf	2 mL
½ tsp	ground ginger	2 mL
½ tsp	ground cinnamon	2 mL
½ tsp	freshly ground black pepper	2 mL
½ tsp	superfine (caster) sugar (see Tips, left)	2 mL
¼ tsp	ground dried lemon myrtle leaf	1 mL
¼ tsp	ground yellow mustard seed	1 mL
⅛ tsp	ground cloves	0.5 mL
⅛ tsp	ground cardamom seed	0.5 mL

1. Combine ingredients in a bowl and stir well to ensure even distribution. Transfer to an airtight container and store, away from extremes of heat, light and humidity, for up to 1 year.

How to Use Laksa Spice Mix

Use this mix in Shrimp Laksa (page 667) or any Asian seafood and noodle soup.

Mélange of Pepper

Unlike the peppermill blend on page 749, which should be freshly ground over food, this blend is meant for use in cooking and is not suitable to put in a pepper mill. Kate and I were captivated by a mélange of pepper we saw for sale in the markets of Cavaillon, in the south of France. Over many centuries this part of France was influenced by traders from Marseilles, who were in contact with North Africa and had access to many spices from the Near and Far East. I could not resist replicating this highly fragrant blend.

Makes 27½ tsp (140 mL)

9 tsp	whole black peppercorns	45 mL
5 tsp	whole white peppercorns	25 mL
4½ tsp	pink *Schinus* pepper	22 mL
3 tsp	green peppercorns	15 mL
3 tsp	cubeb pepper	15 mL
3 tsp	Sichuan pepper	15 mL

1. Combine ingredients in a bowl and stir well to ensure even distribution. Transfer to an airtight container and store, away from extremes of heat, light and humidity, for up to 3 years.

How to Use Mélange of Pepper

This blend is an excellent addition to most slow-cooked dishes. Add 3 tsp (15 mL) per 1 lb (500 g) meat at the beginning of cooking. Do not grind, as the whole spices add color and texture to the dish and soften during cooking. We love it in a chicken casserole made with red wine and in winter-warming beef dishes. Lamb stews take on a new dimension with this fragrant pepper mix. Whenever we use it, I'm transported back to our Cavaillon market experience.

Mexican Chili Powder

This is a simple blend of chile, cumin and paprika that many people find more agreeable than ground red chile and commercial chili powders, which often contain artificial ingredients. This is because of its mildness and the earthy balance created by the addition of cumin, which is fundamental to its characteristic "Mexican" flavor. The inclusion of sweet paprika, which belongs to the same family as chiles, adds a dimension of sweetness. I find it interesting (but not surprising) that cumin—which we associate with Indian curries and Moroccan and Middle Eastern food—when used with sweet paprika creates a recognizable Mexican flavor. This highlights how subtle variations in the use of spices can create completely different meanings. As in art, music and literature, the outcome depends on what you do with what you have available.

Makes 12 tsp (60 mL)

Tips

A wide range of Mexican chiles can be used in this blend, from blistering habaneros to mild and sweet New Mexico and Colorado to fruity ancho, pasilla and mulato—all will do the trick, depending on your personal taste preferences.

You may prefer to use less or more salt to suit your taste.

5 tsp	mild, medium or hot ground red chile (see Tips, left)	25 mL
3 tsp	ground cumin	15 mL
2 tsp	sweet paprika	10 mL
1 tsp	dried rubbed oregano, optional	5 mL
1 tsp	fine sea salt (see Tips, left)	5 mL

1. Combine ingredients in a bowl and stir well to ensure even distribution. Transfer to an airtight container and store, away from extremes of heat, light and humidity, for up to 1 year.

How to Use Mexican Chili Powder

Mexican chili powder flavors North American chili con carne and provides the keynote for many other Tex-Mex recipes. Taco seasonings are often made with Mexican chili powder that has been padded out with starchy fillers, including some that contain gluten (to reduce the cost), monosodium glutamate (MSG) and extra salt. This blend may be used as an excellent all-natural taco seasoning and added to cheese quesadillas.

Middle Eastern Seafood Spice

This spice blend captures tastes that are unique to the Middle East. Of particular note is the inclusion of acidic sumac, which enhances the color and flavor of any seafood.

Makes 10 tsp (50 mL)

Tips

Alleppey turmeric has a higher curcumin content and deeper flavor than regular turmeric.

For a more authentic flavor, use a Middle Eastern style of ground red chile, such as Aleppo pepper.

Black limes are generally purchased whole, so you will need to grind them yourself. Place 2 or 3 black limes in a bag and, using a rolling pin, pound into ¼ inch (5 mm) pieces. Transfer to a mortar and grind thoroughly with the pestle.

2 tsp	ground cumin	10 mL
2 tsp	ground Alleppey turmeric (see Tips, left)	10 mL
1 tsp	ground red chile (see Tips, left)	5 mL
1 tsp	freshly ground black pepper	5 mL
1 tsp	ground dried black lime (see Tips, left)	5 mL
1 tsp	ground ginger	5 mL
1 tsp	sumac	5 mL
½ tsp	ground cardamom seed	2 mL
½ tsp	sweet paprika	2 mL
	Salt, to taste	

1. Combine ingredients in a bowl and stir well to ensure even distribution. Transfer to an airtight container and store, away from extremes of heat, light and humidity, for up to 1 year.

How to Use Middle Eastern Seafood Spice

Strongly flavored fish and seafood, such as salmon, tuna, shrimp and oily fish such as mullet, benefit greatly from being rubbed with this dry spice mix and set aside for about 30 minutes prior to cooking.

Spices in Middle Eastern Cuisine

"Middle East" is a relatively loose term applied to the vast area that includes Israel, Palestine, Lebanon, Jordan, Syria, the Gulf States and Yemen. These cuisines have been influenced by Arabic, Persian, Indian and European cultures, and all use, in varying degrees, nuts, fruits, yogurt and sesame (both as oil and in the paste tahini) along with spices. The following are some of the key spices of these cuisines.

- paprika
- coriander seed
- sumac
- parsley
- thyme

- cumin
- cassia
- pomegranate (seeds and molasses)
- black pepper

- cloves
- cardamom (green)
- mahlab
- mastic

Mixed Herbs

In Australia this combination of mixed herbs would have to be the quintessential pre-1970s ingredient (it was then the most commonly used herb blend in Australia). When I was young, many of the people who visited my parents' herb shop had cooked only with mixed herbs and pepper. The packaged mixed herbs available in supermarkets at the time were usually a blend of equal proportions of thyme, sage and marjoram, along with a generous helping of twigs, stones and dirt—it was low-grade product. My first encounter with herb and spice blending took place when my parents developed a very high-quality mixed herbs blend. Mother experimented with the blend in meat loaf, changing the proportions of the traditional triumvirate and adding parsley, oregano and mint. I will never forget eating meat loaf every night for two weeks until she got the proportions right! In my opinion, her mixed herbs blend remains the best, and I'd like to share her recipe with you. All these ingredients are herbs that can be gathered from your own herb garden (if you have one) and dried.

Makes 10 tsp (50 mL)

4 tsp	dried thyme	20 mL
2½ tsp	dried rubbed sage	12 mL
1½ tsp	dried rubbed oregano	7 mL
1 tsp	dried spearmint	5 mL
¾ tsp	dried rubbed marjoram	3 mL
½ tsp	dried parsley flakes	2 mL

1. Combine ingredients in a bowl and stir well to ensure even distribution. Transfer to an airtight container and store, away from extremes of heat, light and humidity, for up to 1 year.

How to Use Mixed Herbs

Hamburger patties benefit greatly from the addition of mixed herbs, as do the majority of soups, stews and casseroles. An equivalent quantity of this blend may be used in recipes in place of store-bought mixed herbs. Add approximately 2 to 3 tsp (10 to 15 mL) per 1 lb (500 g) ground meat.

Mixed Spice (Apple Pie Spice/ Pumpkin Pie Spice)

This popular blend of sweet spices is often confused with an individual spice—allspice (page 61). In Australia we call this blend simply "mixed spice." In North America it generally goes by the names "apple pie spice" and "pumpkin pie spice," after its common uses. Mixed spice has its origins in European cooking but has migrated around the world under these different names. It is the most popular way to flavor fruitcakes, shortbread, sweet pies and a wide variety of delectable pastries. The quantity of ground coriander seed may seem surprising, but coriander is an amalgamating spice, bringing together the sweet and pungent spices in a fragrant delicacy that wouldn't be achieved otherwise.

Makes 10 tsp (50 mL)

4 tsp	ground coriander seed	20 mL
2 tsp	ground cinnamon	10 mL
2 tsp	ground cassia	10 mL
½ tsp	ground nutmeg	2 mL
½ tsp	ground allspice	2 mL
½ tsp	ground ginger	2 mL
¼ tsp	ground cloves	1 mL
¼ tsp	ground cardamom seed	1 mL

1. Combine ingredients in a bowl and stir well to ensure even distribution. Transfer to an airtight container and store, away from extremes of heat, light and humidity, for up to year.

How to Use Mixed Spice

To impart a delicious sweet spice flavor to cakes, pies, cookies and pastries, add 2 tsp (10 mL) mixed spice per 1 cup (250 mL) flour when blending the dry ingredients. Fruitcakes, mince pies and rich or sweet foods require more—up to twice the amount if you're looking for a distinct spiciness.

Moroccan Spice

The traditional flavors of Morocco are not unlike those that are typically Indian, such as cumin, turmeric, coriander, chile and cardamom. One difference is in the proportions used. For instance, the spice blends of Morocco tend to be milder in heat and less sharp in taste.

Makes 23¼ tsp (115 mL)

8 tsp	ground cumin	40 mL
6 tsp	sweet paprika	30 mL
3 tsp	dried minced onion flakes	15 mL
2 tsp	ground coriander seed	10 mL
1½ tsp	ground Alleppey turmeric	7 mL
1 tsp	cayenne pepper	5 mL
¾ tsp	garlic powder	3 mL
½ tsp	freshly ground black pepper	2 mL
½ tsp	ground allspice	2 mL

1. Combine ingredients in a bowl and stir well to ensure even distribution. Transfer to an airtight container and store, away from extremes of heat, light and humidity, for up to 1 year.

How to Use Moroccan Spice

Use this Moroccan spice as the default spice whenever you see a recipe that calls for a dry Moroccan spice mix. When a little salt is added, this blend is also excellent as a dry rub on chicken and full-flavored seafood before barbecuing, broiling/grilling or even roasting.

Spices in Moroccan Cuisine

Much of Moroccan cuisine borrows from its long history of trading with its North African neighbors, such as Ethiopia, Egypt and Tunisia. In the West, flavors borrowed from these areas are usually described as "Moroccan." Although there are many variations, the following are some of the key spices used in Moroccan cuisine.

- coriander seed
- turmeric
- paprika
- cumin
- cinnamon and cassia
- ginger
- cloves
- pepper
- chile

Panch Phoron

Panch phoron, said to be of Bengali origin, is a blend of five seed spices that produces a characteristic result. Panch phoron traditionally combines the seeds of brown mustard, nigella, cumin, fenugreek and fennel; it is encountered most often in the north of India, where the majority of seed spices are grown. This clever blend has a unique flavor profile that beautifully illustrates what can be achieved by judiciously blending diverse spice flavors. It should not be confused with Chinese five-spice powder, even though the name comes from the Hindustani word for "five," which is *panch*, and *phoron*, meaning "seeds." In Indian and Western spice shops it is sometimes called *panch puran*, *panch phora* or *panch pora*.

Makes 10 tsp (50 mL)

Tip

If you are adventurous, try experimenting by varying the ratios of the spices to create subtle differences that may better suit your palate. For example, increase the nigella for more tang, the fennel for more sweetness, or the fenugreek to add a touch of bitterness. We know a chef who coarsely grinds panch phoron and uses it as a coating on roast meats, liberally sprinkling it over the meat before cooking. We like to put 3 tsp (15 mL) whole panch phoron seeds in ground beef when making meat loaf. For classic recipes using panch phoron, see Spicy Fried Cauliflower (page 421) and Herbie's Saturday Curry (page 717).

3 tsp	brown mustard seeds	15 mL
2½ tsp	nigella seeds	12 mL
2 tsp	cumin seeds	10 mL
1½ tsp	fenugreek seeds	7 mL
1 tsp	fennel seeds	5 mL

1. Combine whole spices in a bowl and stir well to ensure even distribution. Transfer to an airtight container and store, away from extremes of heat, light and humidity, for up to 3 years.

How to Use Panch Phoron

This classic Bengali spice blend is used in vegetable, dal and fish curries, generally sautéed in oil at the commencement of making the dish. Seed spices complement carbohydrates. With that in mind, we like to use panch phoron with that ubiquitous carbohydrate the humble potato. We "bloom" (sauté) a bit of ground panch phoron in oil, then add partially cooked diced potato and cook, stirring, until browned. It makes a delicious accompaniment to any meat.

Peppermill Blend

This combination of various types of peppercorns and whole allspice is designed to be placed in a pepper mill and freshly ground over food. In making this blend, I have selected the combination of peppercorns for their flavor, not just their appearance. The following whole spices make a fragrant, delicately balanced blend that suits most occasions calling for a twist of freshly ground pepper.

Makes 9 tsp (45 mL)

Tip

When including a spice that comes in variable sizes (such as allspice), it is advisable to remove pieces larger than 1/8 inch (3 mm) in diameter. They will probably not go through the pepper mill.

5 tsp	black peppercorns	25 mL
1 tsp	white peppercorns	5 mL
1 tsp	whole allspice	5 mL
1 tsp	green peppercorns	5 mL
1 tsp	cubeb pepper	5 mL

1. Combine whole spices in a bowl and stir well to ensure even distribution. Transfer to an airtight container and store, away from extremes of heat, light and humidity, for up to 3 years, or until you are ready to top up your peppermill.

Variations

You can tweak this combination to suit your tastes. Increase the proportion of white pepper to make it hotter, or use a combination of Indian, Malaysian and Kampot black peppercorns to lend a slight sweetness and a lemon-like profile.

Adding 4 tsp (20 mL) coriander seeds to the mix creates a blend that is tantalizingly fresh when ground over chicken and fish at the table.

Persian Spice

From time to time you discover a particular spice blend that breaks the rules. Persian spice, a blend I created, is one example. This aromatic combination includes unusually large proportions of pungent and hot spices to capture a taste of Persia, but the flavors marry so well that the blend can be used directly on seafood or meat before cooking.

Makes 8 tsp (40 mL)

2 tsp	freshly ground black pepper	10 mL
2 tsp	ground cumin	10 mL
2 tsp	ground Alleppey turmeric	10 mL
1 tsp	ground cardamom seed	5 mL
1 tsp	amchur powder	5 mL
	Salt, to taste	

1. Combine ingredients in a bowl and stir well to ensure even distribution. Transfer to an airtight container and store, away from extremes of heat, light and humidity, for up to 1 year

How to Use Persian Spice

This blend is excellent as a dry rub on seafood and red meats before barbecuing, broiling/grilling or even roasting. Alternatively, use it to season all-purpose flour to use as a coating for red meats before browning when starting casseroles and stews. We like to coat pieces of swordfish with Persian spice and pan-fry them with a little olive oil.

Pickling Spice

There is nothing quite like making a trip into the country to buy seasonal vegetables and enjoying the satisfaction of pickling them yourself. When pickling fruits and vegetables, it is usually preferable to use whole spices. Unlike ground spices, they won't leave powdery residues that might spoil the appearance of the finished product.

Makes 22 tsp (110 mL)

5 tsp	whole yellow mustard seeds	25 mL
4 tsp	whole black peppercorns	20 mL
3 tsp	dill seeds	15 mL
3 tsp	fennel seeds	15 mL
3 tsp	whole allspice	15 mL
2 tsp	whole cloves	10 mL
1½ tsp	crushed bay leaf	7 mL
1	1½-inch (4 cm) cinnamon stick, broken	1
1 tsp	diced dried bird's-eye chile (or to taste)	5 mL

1. Combine ingredients in a bowl and stir well to ensure even distribution. Transfer to an airtight container and store, away from extremes of heat, light and humidity, for up to 3 years.

How to Use Pickling Spice

Use this blend in any recipe calling for pickling spice. You'll need about 3 tsp (15 mL) pickling spice per 2 lbs (1 kg) vegetables. Some cooks tie the blend in a square of cheesecloth so they can remove the spices when cooking is completed. Others prefer to leave them and bottle with the pickled ingredients. If left in, their flavor continues to infuse the pickles, and the myriad colors and textures add aesthetic appeal.

Pickling spice can also be used to make an infusion to add zest to clear soups. Combine 4 tsp (20 mL) spice blend and 4 cups (1 L) dry sherry in a sterilized decanter or resealable glass jar. Set aside for a week or two, then strain the infusion through a fine-mesh sieve. Before serving soup, stir 1 tsp (5 mL) into each serving. The infusion will keep indefinitely when stored in a cool, dark place.

Pickling spices also impart a particularly complementary flavor when added to the boiling water used to cook crustaceans such as crab.

Peri Peri Spice Mix

This powder is a blend of hot chile with a distinctive tangy, lemon-like flavor that appeals to the South African consumer, and to those who have developed a taste for the Portuguese-style barbecued chicken that has co-opted the name.

Makes 15 tsp (75 mL)

10 tsp	ground bird's-eye chile	50 mL
1½ tsp	sweet paprika	7 mL
1 tsp	ground cumin	5 mL
1 tsp	fine sea salt	5 mL
1 tsp	ground ginger	5 mL
½ tsp	amchur powder	2 mL

Tip

The name *peri peri* is often used loosely to describe chiles in South Africa and some parts of India. Therefore, peri peri (also called piri piri) sauces are essentially chile sauces that have a consistent taste profile.

1. Combine ingredients in a bowl and stir well to ensure even distribution. Transfer to an airtight container and store, away from extremes of heat, light and humidity, for up to 1 year.

How to Use Peri Peri Spice Mix

Use this blend as an alternative to ground chile, or just keep some on hand to sprinkle on foods such as pasta and pizza. Peri peri spice mix is excellent as a dry rub on chicken and pork before barbecuing, broiling/grilling or even roasting. To make a delicious peri peri chicken, rub the mix on chicken and set aside in the refrigerator to dry-marinate for up to 1 hour before cooking. Shelled and deveined shrimp, dusted with peri peri spice mix and sautéed with butter and garlic, make a quick, easy and very tasty dish.

Spices in Southern Africa

African cuisine south of the Sahara Desert is typified by the foods of Nigeria, Ethiopia and the Republic of South Africa. Indian migration to Africa made an impact on the spices used in these areas, as did Malay influence, which is evident in the Cape Malay–style cooking of South Africa. Like the rest of the world, Africans warmly embraced chiles after the early voyages to the Americas. For the first time in their history, people of any socioeconomic group could enjoy their own spicy hit with just a few easily grown, prolific chile plants. The following are some of the key spices used in these regions.

- coriander seed
- chile
- cumin
- allspice
- ginger
- pepper
- grains of paradise
- fenugreek seed

Pork Seasoning

Pork is quite rich and has a very distinctive taste and depth of flavor. That richness is well balanced by the addition of celery seeds to this blend, which is used as a seasoning rub. This combination also goes well with the richness of duck and goose.

Makes 16 tsp (80 mL)

7 tsp	ground celery seeds	35 mL
3 tsp	ground dried oregano	15 mL
3 tsp	sweet paprika	15 mL
2 tsp	freshly ground black pepper	10 mL
1 tsp	fine sea salt	5 mL

1. Combine ingredients in a bowl and stir well to ensure even distribution. Transfer to an airtight container and store, away from extremes of heat, light and humidity, for up to 1 year.

How to Use Pork Seasoning

Use this blend as a dry rub (marinade) to add color and flavor to pork loin chops before pan-frying or broiling/grilling. Rub a generous amount on the scored skin of pork before roasting.

Portuguese Seasoning

Portuguese chicken, a tasty fried or barbecued chicken similar to peri peri chicken (see page 752), has become popular in Australia as both a dine-in and takeout meal. Sadly, too many fast-food outlets rely heavily on excessive amounts of salt, MSG and flavor enhancers such as hydrolyzed vegetable protein (HVP). Here's a healthier, more flavorful alternative.

Makes 10 tsp (50 mL)

6 tsp	sweet paprika	30 mL
1 tsp	ground cumin	5 mL
1 tsp	ground cinnamon	5 mL
1 tsp	ground ginger	5 mL
½ tsp	ground allspice	2 mL
½ tsp	ground bird's-eye chile	2 mL

1. Combine ingredients in a bowl and stir well to ensure even distribution. Transfer to an airtight container and store, away from extremes of heat, light and humidity, for up to 1 year.

How to Use Portuguese Seasoning

Use this seasoning mix as a dry rub on either spatchcocked chicken (see Tips, page 755) or chicken pieces before broiling/grilling or barbecuing to make classic Portuguese chicken. Alternatively, use it to make a delicious wet marinade, as in Portuguese Roast Chicken (page 755).

Portuguese Roast Chicken

This recipe is a wonderful alternative to regular roast chicken. The paprika gives it great color, and the chile and other spices provide a depth of warm spiciness.

Makes
4 servings

Preparation time:
20 minutes, plus
2 hours for marinating

Cooking time:
50 minutes

Tips

The chicken can also be cooked over medium heat on a charcoal or gas barbecue. Turn every 10 minutes, basting once on the skin side, until cooked through.

Portuguese chicken is most often prepared by "spatchcocking" a whole chicken—removing the backbone and flattening the bird, which allows for quicker, more even cooking. The vegetables underneath the chicken soak up all the wonderful flavors and cooking juices.

• **Blender**
• **13- by 9-inch (33 by 23 cm) baking pan**

CHICKEN

1	whole chicken, about 3 lbs (1.5 kg)	1
1	large potato, unpeeled, finely sliced	1
1	large sweet potato, unpeeled, finely sliced	1

MARINADE

2 tbsp	Portuguese seasoning (page 754)	30 mL
½	onion, chopped	½
2	cloves garlic, roughly chopped	2
1 tsp	red wine vinegar	5 mL
2 tbsp	freshly squeezed lemon juice	30 mL
3 tbsp	oil	45 mL

1. *Chicken*: On a cutting board, place chicken breast side down. Using kitchen scissors, remove backbone by cutting along each side of the bone (discard bone). Turn chicken over and flatten with the palm of your hand. Using a knife, make slashes in the skin $1/16$ inch (2 mm) deep and 1 inch (2.5 cm) apart to allow marinade to penetrate. Set aside.

2. *Marinade*: In blender, combine spice blend, onion, garlic, vinegar, lemon juice and oil. Blend at high speed until smooth. Divide marinade in half. Place half in a resealable bag with the chicken; seal and turn to coat. Refrigerate for at least 2 hours or overnight. Refrigerate remaining marinade in an airtight container.

3. Preheat oven to 400°F (200°C). Lightly oil baking pan.

4. Arrange potato and sweet potato slices evenly over bottom of baking pan. Place chicken, skin side down, on top. Bake in preheated oven for 20 minutes (see Tips, left). Remove pan from oven, turn chicken over and baste with reserved marinade. Bake for 20 to 30 minutes, until chicken is cooked through (an instant-read thermometer inserted in the thickest part registers 165°F/74°C) and skin is blackened. Remove from oven and set aside for 5 minutes. Cut chicken into pieces and serve with cooked potatoes.

Quatre Épices

The name *quatre épices* literally means "four spices." Like many simply named spice blends, it is a traditional combination used in French cuisine. The only complication is that there are both savory and sweet versions. Savory quatre épices is most often used in charcuterie; the sweet version is associated with puddings and cakes.

Makes 11 tsp (55 mL)

SAVORY QUATRE ÉPICES

6 tsp	freshly ground white pepper	30 mL
2½ tsp	ground nutmeg	12 mL
2 tsp	ground ginger	10 mL
½ tsp	ground cloves	2 mL

SWEET QUATRE ÉPICES

6 tsp	ground allspice	30 mL
2½ tsp	ground nutmeg	12 mL
2 tsp	ground ginger	10 mL
½ tsp	ground cloves	2 mL

1. Combine ingredients in a bowl and stir well to ensure even distribution. Transfer to an airtight container and store, away from extremes of heat, light and humidity, for up to 1 year.

How to Use Savory Quatre Épices

The classic use of this savory blend is for spicing meats when making charcuterie (cured meats, predominantly pork, and preserved sausages such as salami). I also find savory quatre épices a pleasant alternative to plain ground white pepper in a pepper shaker. The pungency of the other spices masks the musty aroma that white pepper tends to have.

How to Use Sweet Quatre Épices

Sweet quatre épices adds an extra level of richness to fruit cakes and puddings. It is the classic spice combination used in tarte Tatin, that delicious apple tart caramelized with butter and sugar.

Ras el Hanout

This traditional Moroccan mix is the pinnacle of all spice blends. The sometimes more than 20 ingredients merge to form a balanced, full-bodied blend with no sharp edges. It is arguably the finest example of how well a collection of diverse spices can form a blend immeasurably greater than any of its individual parts.

Makes 40 tsp (200 mL)

Tips

Alleppey turmeric has a higher curcumin content and deeper flavor than regular turmeric. It balances perfectly with the other spices in this blend.

Bay leaves are easily ground by crushing them first with your fingers, then grinding the crushed leaves using a mortar and pestle.

15	whole saffron stigmas	15
5 tsp	sweet paprika	25 mL
4 tsp	ground cumin	20 mL
4 tsp	ground ginger	20 mL
2 tsp	ground coriander seed	10 mL
1 tsp	ground cassia	5 mL
1 tsp	ground Alleppey turmeric (see Tips, left)	5 mL
¾ tsp	ground fennel seed	3 mL
¾ tsp	ground allspice	3 mL
¾ tsp	ground green cardamom seed	3 mL
¾ tsp	whole dill seed	3 mL
¾ tsp	ground galangal	3 mL
¾ tsp	ground nutmeg	3 mL
¾ tsp	ground orris root	3 mL
¼ tsp	ground bay leaf (see Tips, left)	1 mL
¼ tsp	ground caraway seed	1 mL
¼ tsp	cayenne pepper	1 mL
¼ tsp	ground cloves	1 mL
¼ tsp	ground mace	1 mL
¼ tsp	ground cubeb pepper	1 mL
¼ tsp	ground brown cardamom pod	1 mL

1. Combine ingredients in a bowl and stir well to ensure even distribution. Transfer to an airtight container and store, away from extremes of heat, light and humidity, for up to 1 year.

How to Use Ras el Hanout

Although this blend is by no means pungent, it has such a pervasive effect on food that you need only half the amount compared to other spice blends. Ras el hanout is extremely versatile. It adds an enticing flavor to chicken and vegetable tagines (casseroles) and to Ras el Hanout Chicken (page 758). Sprinkle over chicken or fish before pan-frying, grilling or baking or add to couscous while cooking (see Tip, page 758).

Ras el Hanout Chicken

This balanced and flavorsome casserole was one of the first dishes my children ate when they switched to solid foods, and it is still one of their favorites (although not puréed anymore!). It is definitely a dish for the whole family. Serve with spiced couscous (see Tip, below).

**Makes
4 servings**

Preparation time:
15 minutes

Cooking time:
45 minutes

Tip

To make spiced couscous, add ½ tsp (2 mL) ras el hanout to 1 cup (250 mL) couscous, while cooking.

6	skin-on, bone-in chicken thighs	6
2 tbsp	ras el hanout (page 757)	30 mL
1 tbsp	olive oil	15 mL
2	small onions, quartered	2
4	cloves garlic, halved	4
1½ cups	chicken broth, divided	375 mL
2	small carrots, peeled and cut in ½-inch (1 cm) pieces	2
1 cup	fresh or frozen peas	250 mL
12	small button mushrooms, halved	12
	Salt	

1. Coat chicken in ras el hanout.

2. In a heavy-bottomed saucepan over medium heat, heat oil. Add prepared chicken and cook for 3 to 5 minutes each side, until browned on both sides. Stir in onions, garlic and ¼ cup (60 mL) broth. Reduce heat to lowest setting, cover pan with a tight-fitting lid and cook for 15 minutes (do not remove lid). Add carrots and remaining 1¼ cups (300 mL) broth; cover and cook for 10 minutes, until carrots are almost tender. Add peas and mushrooms and season with salt to taste; stir to combine. Cook for 5 to 10 minutes, until vegetables are tender. Serve immediately.

Roast Meat Spice Rub

One of the main objectives when serving roast meat (in addition to brilliant flavor) is to carve from a succulent cut that has a colorful and tasty crust. This rub could also be called a crusting mix, because it adds both color and texture as well as flavor.

Makes 16 tsp (80 mL)

Tips

Don't be put off because mustard seeds have been included in this blend. The heat of cooking stops the heat-making enzyme in mustard from developing, which means the component just adds a nutty taste while enhancing the crusting effect.

Superfine (caster) sugar is a very fine granulated sugar typically used in recipes that require a faster-dissolving granule. If you can't find it in stores, you can make your own by using a food processor fitted with the metal blade to process granulated sugar to a very fine, sand-like consistency.

4 tsp	ground coriander seed	20 mL
4 tsp	sweet paprika	20 mL
2 tsp	whole brown mustard seeds (see Tips, left)	10 mL
2 tsp	sumac	10 mL
1½ tsp	fine sea salt	7 mL
¾ tsp	ground ginger	3 mL
½ tsp	superfine (caster) sugar (see Tips, left)	2 mL
½ tsp	rubbed dried oregano	2 mL
½ tsp	freshly ground black pepper	2 mL
¼ tsp	ground allspice	1 mL

1. Combine ingredients in a bowl and stir well to ensure even distribution. Transfer to an airtight container and store, away from extremes of heat, light and humidity, for up to 1 year.

How to Use Roast Meat Spice Rub

In addition to using this blend as a dry rub for roast meat, I always sprinkle some on the vegetables that are being roasted in the pan alongside it (potatoes, squash, carrots and beets are favorites). Be sure to make a simple gravy with the pan juices—you will be surprised by how great it tastes.

Salad Dressing Seasoning

Salad dressings are the best way to liven up many of those healthy leafy greens we turn into salads. Most commercial salad dressings are likely to be very high in salt; they may also include unwanted preservatives and often contain emulsifiers made from alginates. These additives give many dressings a somewhat slimy mouthfeel, which in my opinion counteracts the whole purpose of enjoying a fresh, crisp salad. This seasoning contains mustard powder, which is an emulsifying agent without any unpleasant side effects. When you make the dressing, the vinegar inhibits the enzyme in the mustard, so the result will not be overly hot.

Makes 4 tsp (20 mL)

Tips

You want the dried herb leaves to be crushed, but not to the point where they are powdered. The best way to achieve this result is to rub them through a coarse sieve.

Because the dried herbs used in this seasoning have a very low moisture level, there is no need to refrigerate this blend. It can be stored at room (ambient) temperature for at least 3 months. If you substitute fresh herbs for the dried parsley and dill, you will need to refrigerate the seasoning and use it within 3 weeks.

2 tsp	ground yellow mustard seed	10 mL
1 tsp	crushed dried parsley flakes (see Tips, left)	5 mL
½ tsp	dried green dill leaf tips	2 mL
¼ tsp	coarsely ground black pepper	1 mL
¼ tsp	ground allspice	1 mL

1. Combine ingredients in a bowl and stir well to ensure even distribution. Transfer to an airtight container and store, away from extremes of heat, light and humidity, for up to 1 year.

How to Use Salad Dressing Seasoning

In a cup with a pouring spout, combine 4 tsp (20 mL) salad dressing seasoning, ⅓ cup (75 mL) olive oil and ¼ cup (60 mL) vinegar. Stir well and transfer to a sterilized bottle or jar. Store at room temperature for up to 3 months (see Tips, left).

Sambar Powder

Sambar is a South Indian soup that can be a meal in itself (see Vegetarian Sambar, page 93) or it can be ladled over rice to accompany a curry. The basis for a good sambar is the spice mix, called sambar powder or sambar masala. This version is quite mild, but more chile can be added if desired.

Makes 17 tsp (85 mL)

Tips

If you are using this powder immediately, you can substitute fresh curry leaves. Otherwise, use dried curry leaves, as this will enable storage of the mix for up to 12 months.

Chickpea flour is also known as gram flour or besan flour. It can be found in Asian and Indian markets and health-food stores.

8	dried curry leaves, chopped (see Tips, left)	8
5 tsp	ground coriander seed	25 mL
5 tsp	chickpea flour (see Tips, left)	25 mL
2 tsp	ground cumin	10 mL
1 tsp	coarsely ground black pepper	5 mL
1/2 tsp	fine sea salt	2 mL
1/2 tsp	ground fenugreek seed	2 mL
1/2 tsp	amchur powder	2 mL
1/2 tsp	whole brown mustard seeds	2 mL
1/2 tsp	ground mild chile	2 mL
1/4 tsp	ground cinnamon	1 mL
1/4 tsp	ground Alleppey turmeric	1 mL
1/4 tsp	asafetida powder	1 mL

1. Combine ingredients in a bowl and stir well to ensure even distribution. Transfer to an airtight container and store, away from extremes of heat, light and humidity, for up to 1 year.

How to Use Sambar Powder

Sambar powder makes an excellent coating for chicken and seafood when dusted on before pan-frying. I have found that the chickpea flour in it helps to thicken curry gravies. Simply stir 2 tsp (10 mL) sambar powder per 1 lb (500 g) meat or vegetables into the curry while it is cooking.

Seasoned Salt

Flavored salts were among the world's first mass-marketed spice blends. They combined the most common seasoning (salt) with a variety of agreeable flavors such as onion, garlic and celery to produce a product that could be readily sprinkled into dishes while cooking or over food at the table. Next came seasoned salts. These had more complex flavors and distinctive characteristics that were similar to barbecue spices (see page 694). They included sweet paprika, onion, garlic, parsley and other flavors, as well as MSG, making them quite different from the earlier vegetable salts. In the second half of the 20th century, a trend toward reducing salt intake for health reasons fuelled the popularity of vegetable salts such as Herbamare, which contains sea salt, celery leaf, leek, cress, onion, chive, parsley, lovage, garlic, basil, marjoram, rosemary, thyme and kelp with trace iodine, and salt substitutes such as potassium chloride. Until that time these products had been regularly consumed mostly by health-conscious consumers.

Makes about 1 cup (250 mL)

| 1 cup | fine sea salt | 250 mL |
| 1 tsp | ground dried spice or herb | 5 mL |

1. In a bowl, combine salt and seasoning. Mix thoroughly. Transfer to an airtight container and store away from extremes of humidity for up to 1 year.

Tip

Because homemade seasoned salts don't contain anti-clumping agents, lumps may form, but these can be easily crushed without any loss of flavor in the mix.

Variations

Garlic or Onion Salt: Follow the method for making seasoned salt but use equal portions of salt and garlic or onion powder. More or less of each can be experimented with to suit taste preferences.

What Are Vegetable Salts?

A vegetable salt aims to replace a high concentration of sodium chloride with naturally occurring salts found in certain vegetables, herbs and seaweed. However, many of these products are mislabeled, so people on low-sodium diets should exercise caution when embracing them as a salt substitute—even a glance at the ingredients on the label will often identify salt as the major component. Substituted in equal quantities for table salt, a proper vegetable salt (one that isn't predominantly sodium chloride) will help to lower salt intake. The flavor-enhancing attributes of the herbs, spices and other ingredients should be equally satisfying.

Shichimi-Togarashi

This Japanese blend of whole and ground spices is also known as "seven-flavor seasoning." There are many variations (sometimes various types of seaweed are included), but this is a typical shichimi-togarashi.

Makes 14½ tsp (70 mL)

Tips

Chile flakes made from dried long red chiles work best in this recipe.

Powdered tangerine or orange peel can be made by buying dried tangerine, orange or mandarin peel pieces from an Asian grocery store, then using a mortar and pestle to grind them into a coarse powder.

6 tsp	medium-hot chile flakes (see Tips, left)	30 mL
3 tsp	powdered Sichuan pepper leaf (sansho)	15 mL
2 tsp	powdered tangerine or orange peel (see Tips, left)	10 mL
1 tsp	black sesame seeds	5 mL
1 tsp	white sesame seeds	5 mL
½ tsp	hemp seeds	2 mL
½ tsp	white poppy seeds	2 mL
½ tsp	brown mustard seeds	2 mL

1. Combine ingredients in a bowl and stir well to ensure even distribution. Transfer to an airtight container and store, away from extremes of heat, light and humidity, for up to 1 year.

How to Use Shichimi-Togarashi

Shichimi-togarashi is used as a seasoning in cooking and as a condiment on the table, for soups, noodle dishes, tempura and many other Japanese dishes (see Sesame Tuna, page 598). In Western cooking it is effective for seasoning barbecued, broiled/grilled or pan-fried seafood—just mix with a little salt and rub on before cooking. A cooked cob of corn, buttered while hot and sprinkled with shichimi-togarashi, is far more interesting than one seasoned simply with salt and pepper.

Spices in Japanese Cuisine

Japanese cuisine is known for its simplicity and aesthetic appeal. The flavors are usually dictated by the main ingredients and the way they are cooked. Other than sushi, Japanese food is typified by broiling, simmering, steaming or deep-frying, using predominantly fresh ingredients. Spices and herbs tend to be used subtly while the proteins and vegetables retain their characteristic flavors. The following are some of the key spices in Japanese cuisine.

- sansho (Sichuan pepper leaf)
- black sesame seed
- mustard seed
- Sichuan pepper
- white pepper
- wasabi

Shish Kebab Spice

Shish kebabs—meat and vegetables cooked on skewers—always benefit from a spice rub before cooking. This blend contains classic Middle Eastern spice combinations that add depth of flavor and color. The inclusion of parsley, mint and cardamom provides fresh notes.

Makes 15 tsp (75 mL)

Tip

Black limes are generally purchased whole, so you will need to grind them yourself. The easiest method is to place 2 or 3 black limes in a resealable bag and, using a rolling pin, pound until they are broken into pieces no larger than 1/4 inch (5 mm). Transfer to a mortar and grind thoroughly with the pestle.

You want the dried herb leaves to be crushed, but not to the point where they are powdered. The best way to achieve this is to rub them through a coarse sieve.

3 1/2 tsp	ground cumin	17 mL
3 tsp	ground Alleppey turmeric	15 mL
2 tsp	ground dried black lime (see Tips, left)	10 mL
2 tsp	sweet paprika	10 mL
1 tsp	freshly ground black pepper	5 mL
1 tsp	fine sea salt	5 mL
1 tsp	ground cardamom seed	5 mL
1/2 tsp	onion powder	2 mL
1/2 tsp	crushed dried parsley (see Tips, left)	2 mL
1/2 tsp	dried spearmint	2 mL

1. Combine ingredients in a bowl and stir well to ensure even distribution. Transfer to an airtight container and store, away from extremes of heat, light and humidity, for up to 1 year.

How to Use Shish Kebab Spice

Shish kebab spice is a versatile dry rub for red meats, predominantly lamb, whether broiling/grilling, barbecuing, pan-frying or roasting. To make a tasty dip for corn chips, combine 2 tsp (10 mL) shish kebab spice and 1 cup (250 mL) sour cream, then cover and refrigerate for 30 minutes.

Lamb Kebabs

Lamb kebabs are a summer barbecue staple that benefit from the light charring of a grill or barbecue. They can be served with couscous and salad or wrapped in a soft tortilla with cacik (page 400).

**Makes
2 servings**

Preparation time:
25 minutes

Cooking time:
15 minutes

Tip

If using wooden skewers, soak them in water for at least 30 minutes prior to using, to prevent them from burning when cooking.

• **Metal skewers, oiled, or wooden skewers, soaked (see Tip, left)**

8 oz	lean lamb, cut into 1½-inch (4 cm) pieces	250 g
1 tsp	freshly squeezed lemon juice	5 mL
1 tsp	shish kebab spice (page 765)	5 mL
1	red bell pepper, seeded and cut into 1½-inch (4 cm) pieces	1
1	onion, quartered, layers separated	1

1. In a large bowl, combine lamb, lemon juice and spice mix. Cover and set aside for at least 15 minutes or refrigerate overnight.
2. Preheat barbecue or grill pan to high.
3. Alternating pieces of lamb, red pepper and onion, thread meat and vegetables onto prepared skewers. Cook kebabs on preheated barbecue or grill pan for 10 minutes, turning to cook evenly on all sides (the meat should still be pink inside). Remove from heat and set aside for 5 minutes to rest before serving.

Sichuan Chile Spice

When I was managing a spice company in Singapore in the mid 1980s, the restaurant I visited most often specialized in Sichuan cuisine. My favorite dish was their chile chicken, which was simply stir-fried with a combination of spices that resembled this blend. Toward the end of cooking they threw on a small handful of dried tien tsin chiles—about a tablespoonful (15 mL) per ½ lb (250 g) chicken. This blend is a must for the chile addict!

Makes 16 tsp (80 mL)

Tips

For the best flavor, use tien tsin chile flakes. If you don't have any on hand, flakes of guajillo or Colorado chile will also impart a delicious flavor.

4 tsp	sweet paprika	20 mL
4 tsp	medium-hot chile flakes (see Tips, left)	20 mL
3 tsp	superfine (caster) sugar (see Tips, page 780)	15 mL
2 tsp	fine sea salt	10 mL
1 tsp	ground ginger	5 mL
1 tsp	garlic powder	5 mL
1 tsp	freshly ground white pepper	5 mL

1. Combine ingredients in a bowl and stir well to ensure even distribution. Transfer to an airtight container and store away from extremes of heat, light and humidity, where it will keep its flavor for only 6 months. (The sugar and onion and garlic powders, along with the salt, will attract moisture.)

Spices in Chinese Cuisine

Chinese cuisine does not employ a wide range of spices. Instead, a great deal of the flavor in Chinese food comes from the stocks created during cooking. Of all the cuisines in the world, Chinese is the only one I have experienced that is so dominated by a single spice—star anise. This may be because star anise, along with Sichuan pepper, is one of the few culinary spices native to China. Although there are many variations, the following are some of the key Chinese spices:

- star anise
- fennel seed
- coriander leaf (cilantro)
- dill leaf
- cassia bark
- ginger
- Sichuan pepper
- black pepper
- chile
- cloves
- licorice root

Stuffing Mix

Experimenting with spice combinations never ceases to surprise. Cumin's ability to go well with flavors that are distinctly not curry was borne out quite dramatically when we were developing a blend to season a stuffing mix for a roast-chicken producer. We had the basic elements you would expect to go with the bread crumbs, such as onion, garlic, thyme, sage, marjoram, parsley, oregano, bay leaf and sweet paprika. However, when we cooked it, the result seemed a little sharp and lifeless until we added a pinch of cumin. This addition—so small that very few people could identify it in the final dish—transformed the stuffing, making it beautifully balanced and full-bodied. This stuffing mix is also an excellent example of a situation in which dried herbs produce a more effective result than fresh.

Makes 10 tsp (50 mL)

5 tsp	Hungarian sweet paprika	25 mL
2 tsp	ground coriander seed	10 mL
1 tsp	dried sage	5 mL
1 tsp	dried thyme	5 mL
½ tsp	ground cumin	2 mL
½ tsp	dried oregano	2 mL
¼ tsp	freshly ground black pepper	1 mL
	Salt	

1. Combine ingredients in a bowl and stir well to ensure even distribution. Transfer to an airtight container and store, away from extremes of heat, light and humidity, for up to 1 year.

How to Use Stuffing Mix

In a large bowl, combine 1 recipe (10 tsp/50 mL) stuffing mix, 1 finely chopped onion and 4 tsp (20 mL) finely chopped fresh parsley leaves. Add 4 cups (1 L) fresh 1-inch bread cubes and ½ cup (125 mL) melted butter. Mix well. Stuff into poultry cavity (the stuffing will be moistened by the juices as it cooks). It's delicious in Thanksgiving Day turkey as well as chicken and game birds.

Taco Seasoning

Tacos are the ultimate family favorite. I can barely recall the countless times that Kate and her sisters enjoyed tacos with Liz and me when they were young. Commercial taco seasonings contain who-knows-what, so I made our own, all-natural family blend.

Makes 15½ tsp (80 mL)

Tips

Anchos are the most popular mild chiles in Mexican cooking. While guajillo provides good color and flavor, ground ancho chile, which is readily available, would give this blend a certain authenticity.

Taco seasoning is relatively mild because of the inclusion of paprika and cumin.

4 tsp	sweet paprika	20 mL
3 tsp	ground cumin	15 mL
2 tsp	fine sea salt	10 mL
1½ tsp	smoked sweet paprika	7 mL
1 tsp	ground coriander seed	5 mL
1 tsp	amchur powder	5 mL
½ tsp	ground Mexican chile (see Tips, left)	2 mL
½ tsp	ground cinnamon	2 mL
½ tsp	dried coriander leaf (cilantro)	2 mL
½ tsp	dried rubbed oregano	2 mL

1. Combine ingredients in a bowl and stir well to ensure even distribution. Transfer to an airtight container and store, away from extremes of heat, light and humidity, for up to 1 year.

How to Use Taco Seasoning

Use this to season ground meat (3 tsp/15 mL per 1 lb/500 g) for tacos and Mexican dishes, especially those with beans. Give barbecued meat a lift by using it as a dry rub before cooking.

The Latin American Influence

With the possible exception of spices exported from India, Mexican and Latin American ingredients have had the greatest impact on cuisines around the world. Until the Spanish traveled to the Americas, allspice, vanilla, chiles, chocolate, tomatoes, potatoes and beans were unknown to the rest of the world. Europe, and especially Spain, in turn influenced the cuisines of Argentina, Chile, Nicaragua, the West Indies and Mexico. The following are some of the key spices used in Mexican and Latin American cuisine.

- paprika
- cumin
- coriander leaf (cilantro)
- oregano
- chile (pasilla, ancho, mulato, guajillo, pequin, jalapeño, habanero, New Mexico)
- cinnamon (Sri Lankan)
- epazote
- huacatay
- annatto

Tagine Spice Mix

In the simplest terms, a tagine may be described as a Moroccan casserole. The highly aromatic blend of sweet and hot spices that bears its name has an uncanny similarity to baharat (page 692), minus the black pepper. The flavors in a typical tagine spice mix go particularly well with lamb, especially if it has a strong, almost gamey taste. These spices help to neutralize that punch.

Makes 10 tsp (50 mL)

5 tsp	sweet paprika	25 mL
2½ tsp	ground coriander seed	12 mL
1 tsp	ground cassia	5 mL
1 tsp	ground red chile	5 mL
½ tsp	ground allspice	2 mL
¼ tsp	ground cloves	1 mL
¼ tsp	ground cardamom seed	1 mL

1. Combine ingredients in a bowl and stir well to ensure even distribution. Transfer to an airtight container and store, away from extremes of heat, light and humidity, for up to 1 year.

How to Use Tagine Spice Mix

This blend is ideal to season any stew featuring red meat or game, including beef cheeks and oxtail. Use 4 tsp (20 mL) per 1 lb (500 g) meat. The best way to experience how well this unusual spice blend complements lamb is to try Lamb Shanks Tagine (page 771).

Lamb Shanks Tagine

This rich, hearty tagine is the ultimate in winter-warming comfort food. Serve with couscous.

Makes 4 servings

Preparation time:
15 minutes

Cooking time: 2 hours

• **Preheat oven to 325°F (160°C)**

8	lamb shanks	8
¼ cup	tagine spice mix (page 770)	60 mL
1 tbsp	oil	15 mL
6	prunes, pitted	6
4	carrots, peeled and cut in 1-inch (2.5 cm) pieces	4
2	onions, finely chopped	2
2	parsnips, peeled and cut in 1-inch (2.5 cm) pieces	2
1	can (14 oz/398 mL) whole crushed tomatoes, with juice	1
4 cups	water	1 L
2 cups	orange juice	500 mL
2 tbsp	garlic purée	30 mL
2 tbsp	tomato paste	30 mL
¼ tsp	freshly ground black pepper	1 mL
	Sea salt	

1. Coat lamb shanks with tagine spice mix.
2. In a skillet over medium heat, heat oil. Add lamb and cook for 5 to 7 minutes per side, until browned all over. Transfer to a large ovenproof pot or Dutch oven. Add prunes, carrots, onions, parsnips, tomatoes, water, orange juice, garlic purée, tomato paste and pepper. Cover with a tight-fitting lid and bake in preheated oven for $1\frac{1}{2}$ to 2 hours or until meat is very tender. Season with salt to taste and serve.

Tandoori Spice Mix

Tandoori dishes are cooked in a very hot cylindrical clay or metal oven called a tandoor. A key element of this style of cooking is the mouth-watering smoky flavor imparted by the charcoal-burning oven. Enjoy this blend for its great taste.

Makes 9½ tsp (50 mL)

3 tsp	sweet paprika	15 mL
1½ tsp	ground cumin	7 mL
1 tsp	ground coriander seed	5 mL
1 tsp	ground ginger	5 mL
1 tsp	smoked sweet paprika	5 mL
½ tsp	ground cinnamon	2 mL
½ tsp	ground fenugreek seed	2 mL
½ tsp	ground green cardamom seed	2 mL
½ tsp	ground brown cardamom pod	2 mL

Tip

Avoid ready-made tandoori pastes, as most contain artificial colors to achieve an almost luminous bright red appearance. Freakishly bright color does nothing for the flavor.

1. Combine ingredients in a bowl and stir well to ensure even distribution. Transfer to an airtight container and store, away from extremes of heat, light and humidity, for up to 1 year.

How to Use Tandoori Spice Mix

This blend is excellent, with added salt to taste, as a dry rub on meat before barbecuing, broiling/grilling or even roasting. If you are slightly more ambitious, use it to make a marinating paste for roast meats. In a resealable bag, combine 2 tsp (10 mL) tandoori spice mix and 1 cup (250 mL) plain yogurt. Add meat, seal bag, turn to coat and refrigerate overnight. A leg of lamb is particularly delicious when marinated this way.

Spices in Indian Cuisine

Indian cuisine arguably uses more spices than any other. It tends to be categorized as either North or South, each being influenced by what grows in the region and the cultural impact of immigrants, invaders and colonizers. These are some of its key spices.

- coriander (leaf and seed)
- turmeric
- cinnamon
- cumin
- fenugreek (leaf and seed)
- ginger
- pepper
- chile
- nutmeg
- mace
- cloves
- tamarind
- kokam
- cardamom (green and brown)
- saffron

Tangia Spice Mix

Traditionally a Moroccan bachelor takes his tangia to a butcher who specializes in preparing ingredients for clay-pot cooking. The vessel is filled with appropriate combinations such as veal shanks on the bone cut into 2-inch (5 cm) pieces, oil, spices and preserved lemons. A paper lid is tied over the top. The pot is then carried to the local bathhouse, where the men tending the furnace place the tangia on a bed of hot coals for five or six hours. The bachelor returns in the evening and collects his tangia. The result is an amazing slow-cooked dish—his evening meal to share with family and friends. Today many people engage in tangia-style cooking, using more sophisticated clay pots that can be used in the oven, or even that ubiquitous appliance the slow cooker. Use this spice mix to give veal shanks and other cuts of meat a deep, rich flavor.

Makes 7½ tsp (40 mL)

Tips

A tangia is an amphora-shaped clay cooking pot about 18 inches (45 cm) deep, traditionally used in Morocco. It is deeper than a tagine and can contain more liquid, making it better suited to slow cooking (a tagine is quite shallow and the ingredients would dry out if cooked for as long).

Aleppo pepper is a mild chile pepper that is widely used in Middle Eastern cooking.

3 tsp	sweet paprika	15 mL
2 tsp	ground coriander seed	10 mL
1 tsp	ground cassia	5 mL
½ tsp	ground cloves	2 mL
½ tsp	ground cardamom seed	2 mL
½ tsp	Aleppo pepper, or to taste (see Tip, left)	2 mL

1. Combine ingredients in a bowl and stir well to ensure even distribution. Transfer to an airtight container and store, away from extremes of heat, light and humidity, for up to 1 year.

How to Use Tangia Spice Mix

This spice mix is versatile, complementing the flavor of all red meats when slow-cooked. Use 4 tsp (20 mL) per 1 lb (500 g) meat. To make a dry rub for chicken and veal, combine 1 recipe tangia spice mix with 2 tsp (10 mL) sweet paprika, 1 tsp (5 mL) smoked sweet paprika, 1 tsp (5 mL) ground black lime and salt to taste.

Tangia of Veal

This simple tangia is a perfectly balanced dish of delicate veal, aromatic spices and preserved lemon. Serve with mashed potato or couscous.

**Makes
4 servings**

Preparation time:
15 minutes

Cooking time:
3½ hours

- **Preheat oven to 250°F (120°C)**
- **Tangia cooking pot, flameproof casserole or Dutch oven**

4	veal shanks, about 2 inches (5 cm) thick (3 lbs/1.5 kg)	4
2½ tbsp	tangia spice mix (page 773), divided	37 mL
1 tbsp	olive oil	15 mL
2	onions, finely chopped	2
1	can (14 oz/398 mL) crushed tomatoes, with juice	1
1	preserved lemon (page 582), rind only, finely chopped	1
3 cups	water	750 mL
1 tsp	fine sea salt	5 mL

1. Coat veal with 1½ tbsp (22 mL) spice mix.
2. In a skillet over medium-high heat, heat oil. Add veal and cook for 6 to 8 minutes each side, until lightly browned. Reduce heat to low. Add onions, tomatoes, preserved lemon, remaining spice mix, water and salt; stir to combine. Increase heat to medium and bring to a simmer. Cover and bake in preheated oven for 3 hours, or until very tender. Serve immediately.

Tempero Baiano

Just as mixed herbs are ubiquitous in Western food, garam masala in Indian dishes and herbs de Provence in French cuisine, tempero baiano could be considered the all-purpose seasoning of Brazil. As with all widely used herb-and-spice combinations, the variations are almost as diverse as the people who make it. Tempero baiano originated in the Brazilian state of Bahia. However, its popularity has spread throughout the country, probably because it is so versatile.

Makes 13¾ tsp (70 mL)

Tips

Dried parsley leaves can sometimes be quite large. In order to have them blend well with other ingredients, rub them through a coarse sieve, which should yield something similar to a powder, but with more texture.

Chile flakes made from dried long red chiles work best in this recipe. For those who prefer a milder seasoning, use ground pasilla chiles.

Bay leaves are easily ground by crushing them first with your fingers, then grinding the crushed leaves using a mortar and pestle.

4 tsp	rubbed dried parsley (see Tips, left)	20 mL
3 tsp	rubbed dried oregano	15 mL
2 tsp	rubbed dried basil	10 mL
1 tsp	ground nutmeg	5 mL
1 tsp	ground Madras turmeric	5 mL
¾ tsp	freshly ground black pepper	3 mL
¾ tsp	freshly ground white pepper	3 mL
¾ tsp	medium-hot chile flakes (see Tips, left)	3 mL
½ tsp	ground bay leaf (see Tips, left)	2 mL

1. Combine ingredients in a bowl and stir well to ensure even distribution. Transfer to an airtight container and store, away from extremes of heat, light and humidity, for up to 1 year.

Variation

You can make a fresh version of tempero baiano using 1 packed tbsp (15 mL) each fresh parsley, oregano, basil and chile instead of 1 tsp (5 mL). Leave the remaining spices, including the bay leaf, in their ground dried form. Using a food processor fitted with the metal blade, process the ingredients into a paste, adding just enough oil to achieve a smooth consistency. The amount of oil needed will vary depending on the succulence of the fresh herbs. Store in an airtight container in the refrigerator for up to 2 days.

How to Use Tempero Baiano

This seasoning is excellent as a rub (dry marinade) on fish and chicken before barbecuing, broiling/grilling or even roasting. It is lovely added to a fish soup: use 2 tsp (10 mL) per 1 cup (250 mL) soup. When sprinkled on vegetables before roasting, tempero baiano adds great flavor and depth of color.

Crumbed Lamb Cutlets

The inclusion of the Brazilian spice blend tempero baiano in this dish delivers light herbaceous flavors with a touch of spice that is not overpowering. In addition, the colors and textures make the crust on these lamb chops visually appealing. They need nothing more than a wedge of lemon and a green salad alongside.

**Makes
4 servings**

Preparation time:
10 minutes

Cooking time:
10 minutes

Tips

Lamb chops or cutlets are cut from a rack of lamb. They are a prime lean cut that requires quick cooking.

To make fresh bread crumbs: Cut a loaf of fresh or day-old white bread (sourdough gives an excellent flavor) into thick slices. Rub each slice between your palms to form crumbs. Alternatively, grate using a box grater or, for best results, pulse in a food processor fitted with the metal blade. If bread is very fresh, spread crumbs evenly over a cutting board or tray to dry slightly.

¼ cup	all-purpose flour	60 mL
1	egg, lightly beaten	1
1 cup	fresh bread crumbs (see Tips, left)	250 mL
1 tsp	tempero baiano (page 775)	5 mL
8	trimmed lamb chops or cutlets (about 2 oz/60 g each; see Tips, left)	8
	Oil, for frying	
1	lemon, cut into wedges	1

1. To prepare the breading station, place flour in a shallow bowl. In another bowl, whisk egg. In a bowl large enough to dip the lamb in, combine bread crumbs and tempero baiano.

2. Dip a lamb chop (meat end only) into flour, shaking off excess, then dip into egg, allowing excess to drip off, then coat generously in spiced bread crumbs. Transfer to a wire rack (this prevents one side from getting soggy). Repeat with remaining lamb.

3. In a skillet over medium heat, heat ¼-inch (5 mm) oil until small bubbles appear on bottom of pan. Cook prepared lamb for 3 minutes each side. Transfer to a clean wire rack to rest for 2 minutes. Serve with lemon wedges on the side.

Tsire

Tsire powder is a West African blend of crushed roasted peanuts seasoned with salt and spices, including varying amounts of chile. It is traditionally used as a coating for meat.

Makes 4 ounces (125 g)

Tip

Chile flakes made from bird's-eye chile would be suitable for this recipe.

3½ oz	roasted unsalted peanuts, crushed	100 g
1 tsp	fine sea salt	5 mL
1 tsp	ground cinnamon	5 mL
1 tsp	hot chile flakes (see Tip, left)	5 mL
½ tsp	ground allspice	2 mL
½ tsp	ground ginger	2 mL
½ tsp	ground nutmeg	2 mL
¼ tsp	ground cloves	1 mL

1. Combine ingredients in a bowl and stir well to ensure even distribution. Transfer to an airtight container and store, away from extremes of heat, light and humidity, for up to 2 weeks.

How to Use Tsire

The traditional way to use tsire is to dip meat in oil or beaten egg and then coat it with the nut and spice blend. The result resembles an extremely tasty breading. The most readily available meat in West Africa is chicken, and just as the peanut flavor of satay goes well with chicken and lamb, so does tsire.

Tunisian Spice Mix

One of my favorite North African spice mixes is harissa (page 737). That combination of dried chile with garlic, caraway and mint is an unusual and particularly appetizing addition to many meals. However, I have many friends who don't enjoy heat, so I felt challenged to find a way they could enjoy the benefits of these flavors without the high heat of the chile—that was my inspiration for this blend. It is similar to harissa but less "hot" and without any flavor compromise.

Makes 16 tsp (80 mL)

Tips

Chile flakes made from dried long red chiles work best in this recipe. For those who prefer a milder seasoning, use ground pasilla chiles.

Dried mint leaves can sometimes be quite large. In order to have them blend well with other ingredients, rub them through a coarse sieve, which should yield something similar to a powder, but with more texture.

5½ tsp	sweet paprika	27 mL
5 tsp	garlic powder	25 mL
1½ tsp	ground caraway seed	7 mL
1 tsp	ground coriander seed	5 mL
1 tsp	ground cumin	5 mL
1 tsp	fine sea salt	5 mL
½ tsp	medium-hot chile flakes (see Tips, left)	2 mL
½ tsp	rubbed dried spearmint (see Tips, left)	5 mL

1. Combine ingredients in a bowl and stir well to ensure even distribution. Transfer to an airtight container and store, away from extremes of heat, light and humidity, for up to 1 year.

How to Use Tunisian Spice Mix

Use this blend as a rub (dry marinade) on chicken before broiling/grilling, roasting or barbecuing. You can also use this mix in Tunisian Lentil Hotpot (page 779), a quick and healthy vegetarian meal.

Tunisian Lentil Hotpot

This is a satisfyingly hearty and wholesome dish, whether served alone or with toasted flatbread. If chile heat is desired, swirl 1 tsp (5 mL) harissa through before serving.

**Makes
4 servings**

Preparation time:
  10 minutes
Cooking time:
  25 minutes

- - - - - - - - - - - - - - - - -

Tips

To cook lentils: Using a fine-mesh sieve, rinse 1 cup (250 mL) dried lentils under cold running water. Transfer to a medium saucepan and add 4 cups (1 L) water and 1 tsp (5 mL) salt. Simmer over medium heat for about 20 minutes or until tender.

To cook dried chickpeas and kidney beans: Soak overnight in a large bowl, covered by at least 1 inch (2.5 cm) of water. Drain and rinse well under cold running water, then place in a large saucepan, covered by at least 5 inches (12.5 cm) of salted water. Simmer over medium-low heat for 1½ hours or until tender, then drain. They will keep in the refrigerator for up to 1 week or in the freezer for up to 3 months.

1 tbsp	olive oil	15 mL
1	onion, finely chopped	1
2	stalks celery, cut into small dice	2
1	carrot, cut into small dice	1
3 tbsp	Tunisian spice mix (page 778)	45 mL
1	potato, diced	1
2 cups	water or vegetable broth, divided	500 mL
1 cup	canned whole tomatoes, with juice	250 mL
2 cups	cooked brown lentils (see Tips, left)	500 mL
1 cup	cooked chickpeas (see Tips, left)	250 mL
⅓ cup	cooked red kidney beans	75 mL
3 tbsp	small dried pasta, such as macaroni or small conchiglie	45 mL

1. In a skillet over medium heat, heat oil. Add onion, celery and carrot and sauté for 2 to 3 minutes, until lightly browned. Add spice mix and potato and cook for 2 minutes, until fragrant. Add 1 cup (250 mL) water and tomatoes. Bring to a simmer and cook for 5 minutes. Add lentils, chickpeas, beans and remaining 1 cup (250 mL) water; mix well. Stir in pasta, return to a boil and cook for 10 minutes or until pasta is al dente. If a soupier consistency is desired, add more water to taste. Serve immediately.

Vanilla Bean Sugar

Many prepared vanilla sugars are made with artificial vanillin flavors, so years ago I decided to make my own, using quality vanilla. I prefer to mix ground vanilla beans with superfine (caster) sugar. However, if you are unable to buy good-quality vanilla bean powder, you can use whole vanilla beans and the infusion method below. (Vanilla beans are soft and pliable and are not easy to grind because of their high level of moisture.)

Makes 3⅓ tbsp (50 mL)

3 tbsp	superfine (caster) sugar (see Tips, left)	45 mL
1 tsp	vanilla bean powder	5 mL

1. In a bowl, combine sugar and vanilla bean powder. Stir well to ensure even distribution. Transfer to an airtight container and store, away from extremes of heat, light and humidity, for up to 1 year.

Tips

Superfine (caster) sugar is a very fine granulated sugar typically used in recipes that require a faster-dissolving granule. If you can't find it in stores, you can make your own by using a food processor fitted with the metal blade to process granulated sugar to a very fine, sand-like consistency.

When you have scraped the seeds from a vanilla pod, never discard the skin. Pop it into a jar of sugar—the flavor of vanilla will infuse into the sugar until the skin has completely dried out.

Infusion Method

Place 2 soft vanilla beans in an 8-ounce (250 mL) jar with a tight-fitting lid. Cover with 1 cup (250 mL) superfine (caster) sugar and seal jar tightly. Store in a cool, dark place for 3 weeks to allow the vanilla flavor to infuse into the sugar. Shake before using. You can top up the sugar several times as you use it over the next year.

Za'atar

The term *za'atar* tends to create some confusion in the marketplace. This Arabic word is used in many Middle Eastern countries to describe both the herb thyme and a seasoning blend made of thyme, sesame, sumac and salt. Like many spice blends, za'atar varies considerably from region to region. Different areas prefer different proportions, and in some areas ingredients such as the leaves of sumac may be added.

Makes 7 tsp (35 mL)

Tips

You want the dried herb leaves to be crushed, but not to the point where they are powdered. The best way to achieve this is to rub them through a coarse sieve.

To toast sesame seeds: Place in a dry skillet over medium heat and cook, shaking pan constantly, until lightly browned, 2 to 3 minutes. Immediately transfer to a dish to cool and prevent further browning.

3 tsp	dried thyme leaves, crushed (see Tips, left)	15 mL
2 tsp	dried parsley flakes, crushed	10 mL
1 tsp	sumac	5 mL
1/2 tsp	toasted sesame seeds (see Tips, left)	2 mL
1/4 tsp	dried oregano leaves	1 mL
1/4 tsp	fine sea salt	1 mL

1. Combine ingredients in a bowl and stir well to ensure even distribution. Transfer to an airtight container and store, away from extremes of heat, light and humidity, for up to 1 year.

Variation

A deliciously fresh-tasting version of za'atar can be made by substituting 9 tsp (45 mL) finely chopped fresh thyme or lemon thyme for the dried thyme. When made with fresh thyme, za'atar should not be kept for more than a few days.

How to Use Za'atar

Za'atar complements carbohydrates in general. Za'atar bread can be made in the same way as garlic bread, by mixing 2 to 3 tsp (10 to 15 mL) of the blend with 1/2 cup (125 mL) butter; spread the seasoned butter on slices of French bread, wrap them in foil and heat in a preheated 350°F (180°C) oven for about 15 minutes. The more traditional Middle Eastern method is to brush flatbread (such as Lebanese or pita bread) with olive oil, sprinkle it with za'atar and toast lightly. Za'atar is delicious mixed into mashed potatoes or as a seasoning for baked potato wedges. It is an attractive and tasty coating for roast chicken or pan-fried or broiled/grilled chicken pieces. It also makes a delicious dry rub (marinade) for lamb chops before grilling.

Bibliography

The Australian New Crops Newsletter. Queensland, Australia: University of Queensland, Gatton College. Available online at www.newcrops. uq.edu.au.

Botanical.com. "A Modern Herbal." Available online at http://botanical.com.

Bremness, Lesley. *Herbs.* Dorling Kindersley Handbooks. New York: Dorling Kindersley Publishing, 1994.

Brouk, B. *Plants Consumed by Man.* London, England: Academic Press, 1975.

Burke's Backyard. "Burke's Backyard Fact Sheets." Available online at http://www. burkesbackyard.com.au/index.php.

The Chef's Garden. Available online at www.chefs-garden.com.

Cherikoff, Vic. *The Bushfood Handbook: How to Gather, Grow, Process and Cook Australian Wild Foods.* Balmain, NSW, Australia: Ti Tree Press, 1989.

Corn, Charles. *The Scents of Eden: A History of the Spice Trade.* New York: Kodansha America, 1998.

Cribb, A.B., and J.W. Cribb. *Wild Food in Australia.* Sydney, Australia: William Collins, 1975.

Dave's Garden. "Plant Files." Available online at http://davesgarden.com/guides/pf.

Duke, James A. *Handbook of Edible Weeds.* London, England: CRC Press, 1982.

Encyclopedia of Life. "Plants." Available online at http://eol.org/info/plants.

Farrell, Kenneth T. *Spices, Condiments and Seasonings.* 2nd ed. New York: Van Nostrand Reinhold, 1990.

Feasting at Home. Blog. "Eggplant Moussaka." Available online at http://www.feastingathome. com/2013/03/rustic-eggplant-moussaka.html.

Gernot Katzer Spice Pages. Available online at www-uni-gray.at/ ~ katzer/engl.

The Guardian. "Nigel Slater's Winter Recipes." Available online at http://www.theguardian. com/lifeandstyle/2011/jan/23/nigel-slater-recipes.

Gourmet Traveller. "Meyer Lemon and Olive Oil Cakes." Available online at http://www. gourmettraveller.com.au/recipes/recipe-search/ fare-exchange/2011/9/meyer-lemon-and-olive-oil-cakes.

Greenberg, Sheldon, and Elisabeth Lambert Ortiz. *The Spice of Life.* London, England: Mermaid Books, 1984.

Grieve, M. *A Modern Herbal.* Vol. 1 and 2. New York: Hafner Publishing, 1959.

Heal, Carolyn, and Michael Allsop. *Cooking with Spices.* London, England: David and Charles, 1983.

Hemphill, Ian. *Spice Travels: A Spice Merchant's Voyage of Discovery.* Sydney, Australia: Pan Macmillan, 2002.

Hemphill, Ian, and Elizabeth Hemphill. *Herbaceous: A Cook's Guide to Culinary Herbs.* Melbourne, Australia: Hardie Grant, 2003.

———. *Spicery: A Cook's Guide to Culinary Spices.* Melbourne, Australia: Hardie Grant, 2004.

Hemphill, John, and Rosemary Hemphill. *Hemphill's Herbs: Their Cultivation and Usage.* Sydney, Australia: Lansdowne Press, 1983.

———. *Myths and Legends of the Garden.* Sydney, Australia: Hodder Headline, 1997.

———. *What Herb Is That? How to Grow and Use the Culinary Herbs.* Sydney, Australia: Lansdowne Press, 1995.

Hemphill, Rosemary. *Fragrance and Flavour: The Growing and Use of Herbs.* Sydney, Australia: Angus & Robertson, 1959.

———. *Herbs for All Seasons.* Sydney, Australia: Angus & Robertson, 1972.

———. *Spice and Savour: Cooking with Dried Herbs, Spices and Aromatic Seeds.* Sydney, Australia: Angus & Robertson, 1964.

Herbivoracious. "Make Your Own Kimchi." Available online at http://herbivoracious. com/2013/05/making-your-own-kimchi-recipe. html.

Hot. Sour. Salty. Sweet. And Umami. Blog. "Holy Basil." Available online at http:// holybasil.wordpress.com/2008/01/09/bo-kho-vietnamese-beef-stew.

Humphries, John. *The Essential Saffron Companion.* Berkeley, CA: Ten Speed Press, 1998.

Jaffrey, Madhur. *World of the East Vegetarian Cooking.* New York: Knopf, 1981.

Johnny's Selected Seeds. Available online at www.johnnyseedsonlinecatalog.com.

Kennedy, Diana. *The Essential Cuisines of Mexico.* New York: Clarkson N. Potter, 2000.

———. *My Mexico: A Culinary Odyssey with More Than 300 Recipes.* New York: Clarkson N. Potter, 1998.

Kew Plant Cultures. Available online at http:// www.kew.org/plant-cultures/index.html.

Kew Royal Botanic Gardens. "Electronic Plant Information Centre." Available online at http:// epic.kew.org/index.htm.

Landing, James E. *American Essence: A History of the Peppermint and Spearmint Industry in the United States.* Kalamazoo, MI: Kalamazoo Public Museum, 1969.

Leith, Prue, and Caroline Waldegrave. *Leith's Cookery Bible.* 3rd ed. London, England: Bloomsbury Publishing, 2003.

Loewenfeld, Claire, and Phillipa Back. *The Complete Book of Herbs and Spices.* Sydney, Australia: A.H. and A.W. Reed, 1976.

Macoboy, Sterling. *What Tree Is That?* Sydney, Australia: Ure Smith, 1979.

Mallos, Tess. *The Complete Middle East Cookbook.* Sydney, Australia: Lansdowne, 1995.

Miers, Tomasina. *Mexican Food Made Simple.* Great Britain: Hodder & Stoughton, 2010.

Milan, Lyndey, and Hemphill, Ian. *Just Add Spice.* Sydney, Australia: Penguin Books, 2010.

Miller, Mark. *The Great Chile Book.* Berkeley, CA: Ten Speed Press, 1991.

Morris, Sallie, and Lesley Mackley. *The Spice Ingredients Cookbook.* London, England: Lorenz Books, 1997.

Nguyen, Pauline. *Secrets of the Red Lantern.* Australia: Murdoch Books, 2007.

Our Italian Family Recipes. Blog. "Torcetti: Little Twists." Available online at http://www.ouritalianfamilyrecipes.com/recipes/desserts/cookies/torcetti-little-twists.

Ottolenghi, Yotam, and Tamimi, Sami. *Ottolenghi: The Cookbook.* Great Britain: Ebury Press, 2008.

Perikos, John. *The Chios Gum Mastic.* Chios, Greece: John Perikos, 1993.

Plants for a Future Database. Available online at http://www.pfaf.org/user/plantsearch.aspx.

Pruthi, J.S., ed. *Spices and Condiments: Chemistry, Microbiology, Technology.* London, England: Academic Press, 1980.

Purseglove, J.W., E.G. Brown, C.L. Green, and S.R.J. Robbins, *Spices.* Vol. 1 and 2. Tropical Agriculture Series. London, England: Longman Group, 1981.

Raghavan Uhl, Susheela. *Handbook of Spices, Seasonings, and Flavorings.* Lancaster, PA: Technomic Publishing, 2000.

Ridley, H.N. *Spices.* London, England: McMillan and Co., 1912.

Robins, Juleigh. *Wild Lime: Cooking from the Bush Garden.* St. Leonards, NSW, Australia: Allen & Unwin, 1998.

Rogers, J. *What Food Is That? And How Healthy Is It?* Willoughby, NSW, Australia: Weldon Publishing, 1990.

Rosengarten, Frederick, Jr. *The Book of Spices.* New York: Jove Publications, 1973.

Rural Industries Research and Development Corporation. "Plant Industries." Available online at http://www.rirdc.gov.au/research-programs/plant-industries.

Smith, Keith, and Irene Smith. *Grow Your Own Bushfoods.* Sydney, Australia: New Holland Publishers, 1999.

Solomon, Charmaine. *The Complete Asian Cookbook.* Revised and Updated. Victoria, Australia: Hardie Grant Books, 2011.

———. *Encyclopedia of Asian Food: The Definitive Guide to Asian Cookery.* Kew, Victoria, Australia: Hamlyn Australia, 1996.

Spices Board India. *Indian Spices: A Catalogue.* Cochin: Ministry of Commerce, Government of India, 1992.

Stobart, Tom. *Herbs, Spices and Flavourings.* London, England: Grub Street, 1998.

Stuart, Malcolm, ed. *The Encyclopedia of Herbs and Herbalism.* Sydney, Australia: Paul Hamlyn, 1979.

Tannahill, Reay. *Food in History.* London, England: Penguin Books, 1988.

Thompson, David. *Thai Food.* Victoria, Australia: Penguin Group, 2002.

The Tiffin Box: Food and Memories. Blog. "Potato and Pea Samosas." Available online at http://www.thetiffinbox.ca/2013/05/indian-classics-traditional-potato-and-peas-samosas-authentic-recipe.html.

Torres Yzabal, Maria Delores, and Shelton Wiseman. *The Mexican Gourmet: Authentic Ingredients and Traditional Recipes from the Kitchens of Mexico.* San Diego: Thunder Bay Press, 1995.

Toussaint-Samat, Maguelonne. *History of Food.* Oxford, England: Blackwell Publishing, 1998.

Turner, Jack. *Spice: The History of a Temptation.* New York: Knopf, 2004.

United States Department of Agriculture Plant Database. Available online at https://plants.usda.gov.

Von Welanetz, Diana, and Paul Von Welanetz. *The Von Welanetz Guide to Ethnic Ingredients.* Los Angeles: J.P. Tarcher, 1982.

Wikipedia. "List of Plants by Common Name." Available online at http://en.wikipedia.org/wiki/List_of_plants_by_common_name.

Wilson, Sally. *Some Plants Are Poisonous.* Kew, Victoria, Australia: Reed Books Australia, 1997.

Yanuq: Cooking in Peru. Blog. "Ocapa." Available online at http://www.yanuq.com/english/recipe.asp?idreceta=75.

Photography Credits

Library and Archives Canada Cataloguing in Publication

Hemphill, Ian, author
   The spice & herb bible / Ian Hemphill ; with recipes by Kate Hemphill. — Third edition.

Includes indexes.
ISBN 978-0-7788-0493-2 (pbk.). — ISBN 978-0-7788-0496-3 (bound)

1. Spices. 2. Herbs. 3. Cooking (Spices). 4. Cooking (Herbs). 5. Spices—History. 6. Herbs—History. 7. Cookbooks— I. Hemphill, Kate, author II. Title. III. Title: Spice and herb bible.

TX406.H44 2014   641.3'383   C2014-904342-2

Index